Microsoft® Office 2010

ILLUSTRATED

Fundamentals

Microsoft® Office 2010

ILLUSTRATED

Fundamentals

Marjorie Hunt
Barbara M. Waxer

COURSE TECHNOLOGY
CENGAGE Learning

Australia • Brazil • Japan • Korea • Mexico • Singapore • Spain • United Kingdom • United States

COURSE TECHNOLOGY
CENGAGE Learning™

Microsoft® Office 2010—Illustrated Fundamentals
Marjorie Hunt, Barbara M. Waxer

Vice President, Publisher: Nicole Jones Pinard

Executive Editor: Marjorie Hunt

Associate Acquisitions Editor: Brandi Shailer

Senior Product Manager: Christina Kling Garrett

Associate Product Manager: Michelle Camisa

Editorial Assistant: Kim Klasner

Director of Marketing: Cheryl Costantini

Senior Marketing Manager: Ryan DeGrote

Marketing Coordinator: Kristen Panciocco

Contributing Authors: Barbara Clemens, Carol Cram

Developmental Editors: Jennifer T. Campbell, Pamela Conrad

Content Project Manager: Danielle Chouhan

Copy Editor: John Bosco

Proofreader: Brandy Lilly

Indexer: BIM Indexing and Proofreading Services

QA Manuscript Reviewers: John Frietas, GreenPen testers, Susan Pedicini, Jeff Schwartz, Susan Whalen

Print Buyer: Fola Orekoya

Cover Designer: GEX Publishing Services

Cover Artist: Mark Hunt

Composition: GEX Publishing Services

For product information and technology assistance, contact us at
Cengage Learning Customer & Sales Support, 1-800-354-9706
For permission to use material from this text or product, submit all requests online at **www.cengage.com/permissions**
Further permissions questions can be emailed to
permissionrequest@cengage.com

Library of Congress Control Number: 2010931345

ISBN-13: 978-0-538-74944-2

ISBN-10: 0-538-74944-X

Course Technology
20 Channel Center Street
Boston, MA 02210
USA

Cengage Learning is a leading provider of customized learning solutions with office locations around the globe, including Singapore, the United Kingdom, Australia, Mexico, Brazil, and Japan. Locate your local office at:
international.cengage.com/region

Cengage Learning products are represented in Canada by Nelson Education, Ltd.

To learn more about Course Technology, visit **www.cengage.com/coursetechnology**

To learn more about Cengage Learning, visit **www.cengage.com.**

Purchase any of our products at your local college store or at our preferred online store **www.cengagebrain.com**

Credits:

Unit N: Bird video: Fabricio Zuardi http://fabricio.org

Photos from Units M, N, and O are used under the terms of licenses from MorgueFile (www.morguefile.com) and stock.XCHNG® (http://sxc.hu).

Printed in the United States of America
2 3 4 5 6 7 8 9 18 17 16 15 14 13 12 11

Brief Contents

Contents

Office 2010

Word 2010

Access 2010

Preface

Welcome to *Microsoft Office 2010—Illustrated Fundamentals*. If this is your first experience with the Illustrated series, you'll see that this book has a unique design: each skill is presented on two facing pages, with steps on the left and screens on the right. The layout makes it easy to learn a skill without having to read a lot of text and flip pages to see an illustration.

This book is an ideal learning tool for a wide range of learners—the "rookies" will find the clean design easy to follow and focused with only essential information presented, and the "hotshots" will appreciate being able to move quickly through the lessons to find the information they need without reading a lot of text. The design also makes this a great reference after the course is over!

About This Edition

- **Streamlined Approach.** This book is the Illustrated Series' shortest book on Microsoft Office 2010. It covers a wide range of skills at a high level, so that you can cover a lot of ground in a short amount of time. Note that we changed the title of this new edition; we replaced the level name "Brief" with "Fundamentals," to convey more clearly that this book's content is unique and not derived from any other Illustrated Series product. (For a more detailed and comprehensive approach to Microsoft Office 2010, see the Introductory level book by Beskeen et. al.)

- **What's New.** All units are updated to reflect the changes in Microsoft Office 2010. Content enhancements include new lessons on using absolute cell references in Excel and formatting a research paper in Word. New Appendix provides information on using Microsoft Office Web Apps.

Each two-page spread focuses on a single skill.

Introduction briefly explains why the lesson skill is important.

A case scenario motivate the the steps and puts learning in context.

UNIT H Excel 2010

Using Date and Time Functions

There are many categories of functions in Excel. See Table H-2 for a list of common ones. The Excel date and time functions let you display the current date and/or time in your worksheet and can help you calculate the time between events. Some date and time functions produce recognizable text values that you can display as is in your worksheets. Other date and time functions produce values that require special formatting. Serena wants the Western Region Sales worksheet to calculate the date that commission checks are scheduled to be issued. To accomplish this, you decide to use the TODAY function to enter the current date in the worksheet, and enter a formula that uses this information to calculate the check issue date, which is 30 days from today.

STEPS

1. **Click cell B3**
   This cell is to the right of the label Today's Date. You want to enter a function in this cell that returns today's date.

2. **Click the Date & Time button in the Function Library group**
   The list of date and time functions opens. You can point to any item to view a ScreenTip that describes the purpose of that function.

3. **Point to TODAY in the list of functions, as shown in Figure H-8, then click it**
   The Function Arguments dialog box opens, as shown in Figure H-9. The description in the dialog box explains that the TODAY function returns the current date. It also explains that the TODAY function requires no arguments, so you will not need to add values between the parentheses in the formula.

   QUICK TIP
   The TODAY function uses your computer's internal clock to return current date information, and recalculates this result as needed.

4. **Click OK**
   The result of this function, the current date, appears in cell B3.

5. **Click cell B18**
   You want to enter a formula in this cell that returns the date that is 30 days from the date in cell B17, which was the closing date for February.

6. **Type =, press [↑] to select cell B17, then type +30**
   The formula you entered, =B17+30, calculates the day when commission checks are issued, which is 30 days after the date in cell B17 (2/28/2013).

7. **Click the Enter button ✓ on the formula bar, then save your changes**
   The commission due date (3/30/2013) appears in cell B18, as shown in Figure H-10.

TABLE H-2: Categories of common worksheet functions

category	used for	includes
Financial	Loan payments, appreciation, and depreciation	PMT, FV, DB, SLN
Logical	Calculations that display a value if a condition is met	IF, AND, NOT
Text	Comparing, converting, and reformatting text strings in cells	FIND, REPLACE
Date & Time	Calculations involving dates and times	NOW, TODAY, WEEKDAY
Lookup & Reference	Finding values in lists or tables or finding cell references	ADDRESS, ROW, COLUMN
Math & Trig	Simple and complex mathematical calculations	ABS, ASIN, COS

Excel 178   Using Complex Formulas, Functions, and Tables

Tips and troubleshooting advice, right where you need it—next to the step itself.

Tables provide helpful summaries of key terms, buttons, or keyboard shortcuts.

Large screen shots keep students on track as they complete steps

Brightly colored tabs indicate which section of the book you are in.

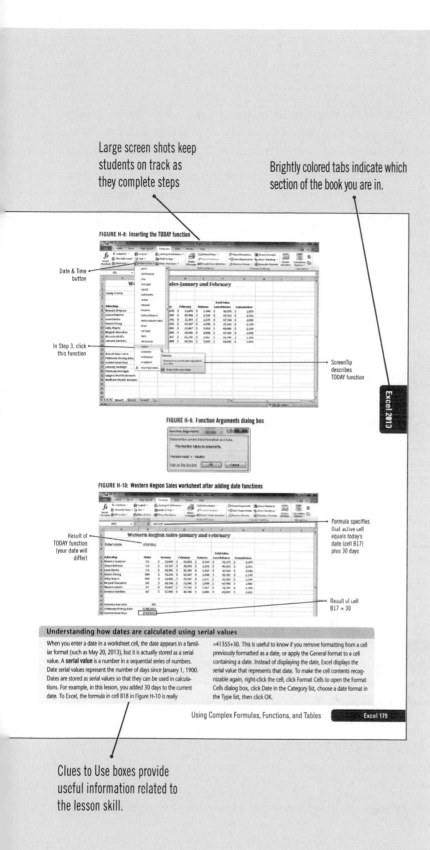

FIGURE H-8: Inserting the TODAY function

Date & Time button

In Step 3, click this function

ScreenTip describes TODAY function

Excel 2010

FIGURE H-9: Function Arguments dialog box

FIGURE H-10: Western Region Sales worksheet after adding date functions

Result of TODAY function (your date will differ)

Formula specifies that active cell equals today's date (cell B17) plus 30 days

Result of cell B17 + 30

Understanding how dates are calculated using serial values

When you enter a date in a worksheet cell, the date appears in a familiar format (such as May 20, 2013), but it is actually stored as a serial value. A **serial value** is a number in a sequential series of numbers. Date serial values represent the number of days since January 1, 1900. Dates are stored as serial values so that they can be used in calculations. For example, in this lesson you added 30 days to the current date. To Excel, the formula in cell B18 in Figure H-10 is really

=41355+30. This is useful to know if you remove formatting from a cell previously formatted as a date, or apply the General format to a cell containing a date. Instead of displaying the date, Excel displays the serial value that represents that date. To make the cell contents recognizable again, right-click the cell, click Format Cells to open the Format Cells dialog box, click Date in the Category list, choose a date format in the Type list, then click OK.

Using Complex Formulas, Functions, and Tables

Excel 179

Clues to Use boxes provide useful information related to the lesson skill.

• **Maps to SAM 2010.** This book is designed to work with SAM (Skills Assessment Manager) 2010. **SAM Assessment** contains performance-based, hands-on SAM exams for each unit of this book, and **SAM Training** provides hands-on training for skills covered in the book. (SAM sold separately.) See page xii for more information on SAM.

Assignments

The lessons feature Outdoor Designs, a fictional company that produces outdoor recreational products, as the case study. The assignments on the light yellow pages at the end of each unit provide a wide range of reinforcement exercises featuring different fictional companies and scenarios. Assignments include:

• **Concepts Review** consist of multiple choice, matching, and screen identification questions.

• **Skills Reviews** are guided, step-by-step exercises that review the skills covered in each lesson in the unit.

• **Independent Challenges** are case projects requiring critical thinking and application of the unit skills. The Independent Challenges increase in difficulty, with the first one in each unit being the easiest. Independent Challenges 2 and 3 become increasingly open-ended, requiring more independent problem solving.

• **Real Life Independent Challenges** are practical exercises in which students create documents to help them with their every day lives.

• **Advanced Challenge Exercises** set within the Independent Challenges provide optional steps for more advanced students.

• **Visual Workshops** are capstone exercises that require students to look at a picture of a completed project, and then create that project using skills covered in the unit.

About SAM

SAM is the premier proficiency-based assessment and training environment for Microsoft Office. Web-based software along with an inviting user interface provide maximum teaching and learning flexibility. SAM builds students' skills and confidence with a variety of real-life simulations, and SAM Projects' assignments prepare students for today's workplace.

The SAM system includes Training, Assessment, and Projects. **SAM Assessment** and **Training** map to the units and pages in this book. Instructors can assign **SAM Training** for each unit to provide animations and hands-on guided activities to reinforce skills covered in that unit. After completing a unit, instructors can assign a **SAM exam** that lets students perform skills covered in that unit in a simulated environment that looks just like Microsoft Office. SAM reports provide exam results and feedback for both students and instructors, as well as page references that specify where each SAM task is covered. **SAM exams** can also include objective questions based on content in the unit. **SAM Projects** is auto-grading software that lets students create projects live in an Office application and receive detailed feedback on their finished project. (*Note*: There are currently no SAM Projects that are based on content in this book. However, there are SAM Projects that require skills covered in this book. Ask your sales representative for a SAM Projects mapping reference for this book.)

SAM Assessment

- Content for these hands-on, performance-based tasks includes Word, Excel, Access, PowerPoint, Internet Explorer, Outlook, and Windows. Includes tens of thousands of objective-based questions from many Course Technology texts.

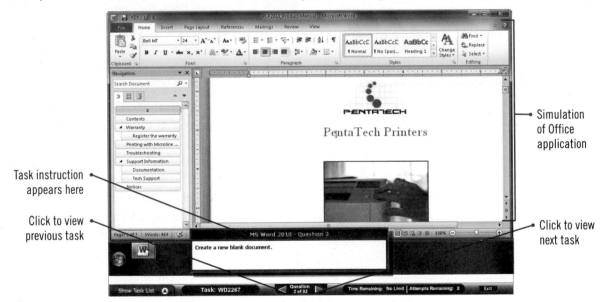

Task instruction appears here

Click to view previous task

Simulation of Office application

Click to view next task

SAM Training

- Observe mode allows the student to watch and listen to a task as it is being completed.
- Practice mode allows the student to follow guided arrows and hear audio prompts to help visual learners know how to complete a task.
- Apply mode allows the student to prove what they've learned by completing a task using helpful instructions.

SAM Projects

- Live-in-the-application auto-grading software that lets students create projects in Word, Excel, Access, and PowerPoint and get immediate feedback on their completed projects.

Note: There are currently no SAM Projects that are based on content in this book. However, there are SAM Projects that require skills covered in this book. Ask your sales representative for a SAM Projects mapping reference for this book.

Instructor Resources

The Instructor Resources CD is Course Technology's way of putting the resources and information needed to teach and learn effectively into your hands. With an integrated array of teaching and learning tools that offer you and your students a broad range of technology-based instructional options, we believe this CD represents the highest quality and most cutting edge resources available to instructors today. The resources available with this book are:

- **Instructor's Manual**—Available as an electronic file, the Instructor's Manual includes detailed lecture topics with teaching tips for each unit.

- **Sample Syllabus**—Prepare and customize your course easily using this sample course outline.

- **PowerPoint Presentations**—Each unit has a corresponding PowerPoint presentation that you can use in lecture, distribute to your students, or customize to suit your course.

- **Figure Files**—The figures in the text are provided on the Instructor Resources CD to help you illustrate key topics or concepts. You can create traditional overhead transparencies by printing the figure files. Or you can create electronic slide shows by using the figures in a presentation program such as PowerPoint.

- **Solutions to Exercises**—Solutions to Exercises contains every file students are asked to create or modify in the lessons and end-of-unit material. Also provided in this section, there is a document outlining the solutions for the end-of-unit Concepts Review, Skills Review, and Independent Challenges. An Annotated Solution File and Grading Rubric accompany each file and can be used together for quick and easy grading.

- **Data Files for Students**—To complete most of the units in this book, your students will need Data Files. You can post the Data Files on a file server for students to copy. The Data Files are available on the Instructor Resources CD-ROM, the Review Pack, and can also be downloaded from cengagebrain.com. For more information on how to download the Data Files, see the inside back cover.

Instruct students to use the Data Files List included on the Review Pack and the Instructor Resources CD. This list gives instructions on copying and organizing files.

- **ExamView**—ExamView is a powerful testing software package that allows you to create and administer printed, computer (LAN-based), and Internet exams. ExamView includes hundreds of questions that correspond to the topics covered in this text, enabling students to generate detailed study guides that include page references for further review. The computer-based and Internet testing components allow students to take exams at their computers, and also saves you time by grading each exam automatically.

Content for Online Learning.

Course Technology has partnered with the leading distance learning solution providers and class-management platforms today. To access this material, visit www.cengage.com/webtutor and search for your title. Instructor resources include the following: additional case projects, sample syllabi, PowerPoint presentations, and more. For additional information, please contact your sales representative. For students to access this material, they must have purchased a WebTutor PIN-code specific to this title and your campus platform. The resources for students might include (based on instructor preferences): topic reviews, review questions, practice tests, and more.

Acknowledgements

Instructor Advisory Board

We thank the members of our Advisory Board, who provided feedback and insights to help shape this new edition:

Paulette Comet, Community College of Baltimore County

Margaret Cooksey, Tallahassee Community College

Sheila Shea, Salem State College

Cynthia Walley, Morton College

Author Acknowledgements

Marjorie Hunt Thank you to all the many wonderful people who worked hard to produce this new edition! Thanks to co-author Barbara Waxer, who expertly updated and reworked the PowerPoint and Integration units with style, infusing just the right mix of instruction and fun into each lesson, example, and exercise. Thank you to our sharp developmental editor Jennifer Campbell, who provided excellent edits and great suggestions on every unit and worked quickly to ensure that we stayed on track. Many thanks, too, to Danielle Chouhan our Content Project Manager, for all her great work in keeping the production of the book on track these many months. I extend a big shout out and thank you to Christina Kling-Garrett, Senior Product Manager, who kept her eye on the development of this book while also managing multiple other high-priority titles with accelerated schedules. Huge thanks, also, to Michelle Camisa, who managed all the instructor resources for this book (and dozens of others). Hats off and thanks to our eagle-eye QA testers Susan Whalen, Susan Pedicini and John Freitas for catching mistakes (that we fixed!) and ensuring the usability and quality of the lessons and exercises. Thanks to all the professionals at GEX, Inc. for their excellent design enhancements and composition. Barbara Waxer and I also thank Fabricio C. Zuardi, who permitted us to use his wonderful video clip of the bird in Unit N. (To see more of Mr. Zuardi's work, go to http://fabricio.org.)

I am deeply grateful to Nicole Pinard, Vice President and Publisher at Cengage Learning, for giving me the opportunity to write several editions of this book over the past ten years—thank you, Nicole. I also give heartfelt thanks to the members of the Illustrated Series team who are amazing at their jobs and creative, smart, and fantastic people: Christina Kling-Garret, Brandi Shailer, Michelle Camisa, Kimberly Klasner, Ryan DeGrote, Kristen Panciocco, Jeff Schwartz, and Fola Orekoya.

I dedicate this book to my family—Cecil, CJ, and Stephen. Thanks, guys, for your endless support and for dreaming up some of the characters and businesses in many of the examples.

Barbara Waxer My thanks to Marjorie Hunt for inviting me to work on this wonderful project. I know this book is near and dear, and I am honored by her trust. Our product manager Christina King-Garrett is always an unwavering ally and support. Thanks to Jennifer Campbell for being the consummate professional and pure joy to work with. Thanks always to my partner, Lindy for putting up with it all.

Read This Before You Begin

Frequently Asked Questions

What are Data Files?

A Data File is a partially completed Word document, Excel workbook, Access database, PowerPoint presentation, or another type of file that you use to complete the steps in the units and exercises to create the final document that you submit to your instructor. Each unit opener page lists the Data Files that you need for that unit.

Where are the Data Files?

Your instructor will provide the Data Files to you or direct you to a location on a network drive from which you can download them. For information on how to download the Data Files from cengagebrain.com, see the inside back cover.

What software was used to write and test this book?

This book was written and tested using a typical installation of Microsoft Office 2010 Professional Plus on a computer with a typical installation of Microsoft Windows 7 Home Premium Edition.

The browser used for any Web-dependent steps is Internet Explorer 8.

Do I need to be connected to the Internet to complete the steps and exercises in this book?

Some of the exercises in this book require that your computer be connected to the Internet. If you are not connected to the Internet, see your instructor for information on how to complete the exercises.

What do I do if my screen is different from the figures shown in this book?

This book was written and tested on computers with monitors set at a resolution of 1024 × 768. If your screen shows more or less information than the figures in the book, your monitor is probably set at a higher or lower resolution. If you don't see something on your screen, you might have to scroll down or up to see the object identified in the figures.

The Ribbon—the blue area at the top of the screen—in Microsoft Office 2010 adapts to different resolutions. If your monitor is set at a lower resolution than 1024 × 768, you might not see all of the buttons shown in the figures. The groups of buttons will always appear, but the entire group might be condensed into a single button that you need to click to access the buttons described in the instructions.

COURSECASTS Learning on the Go. Always Available...Always Relevant.

Our fast-paced world is driven by technology. You know because you are an active participant—always on the go, always keeping up with technological trends, and always learning new ways to embrace technology to power your life. Let CourseCasts, hosted by Ken Baldauf of Florida State University, be your guide into weekly updates in this ever-changing space. These timely, relevant podcasts are produced weekly and are available for download at http://coursecasts.course.com or directly from iTunes (search by CourseCasts). CourseCasts are a perfect solution to getting students (and even instructors) to learn on the go!

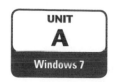
Getting Started with Windows 7

The Windows 7 operating system lets you use your computer. Windows 7 shares many features with other Windows programs, so once you learn how to work with Windows 7, you will find it easier to use the programs that run on your computer. In this unit, you learn to start Windows 7 and work with windows and other screen objects. You work with icons that represent programs and files, and you move and resize windows. As you use your computer, you will often have more than one window on your screen, so it's important that you learn how to manage them. As you complete this unit, you create a simple drawing in a program called Paint to help you learn how to use buttons, menus, and dialog boxes. After finding assistance in the Windows 7 Help and Support system, you end your Windows 7 session.  As a new Oceania tour manager for Quest Specialty Travel (QST), you need to develop basic Windows skills to keep track of tour bookings.

OBJECTIVES

Start Windows 7

Learn the Windows 7 desktop

Point and click

Start a Windows 7 program

Work with windows

Work with multiple windows

Use command buttons, menus, and dialog boxes

Get help

Exit Windows 7

Starting Windows 7

Windows 7 is an **operating system**, which is a program that lets you run your computer. A **program** is a set of instructions written for a computer. When you turn on your computer, the Windows 7 operating system starts automatically. If your computer did not have an operating system, you wouldn't see anything on the screen when you turn it on. For each user, the operating system can reserve a special area called a **user account** where each user can keep his or her own files. If your computer is set up for more than one user, you might need to **log in**, or select your user account name when the computer starts. If you are the only user on your computer, you won't have to select an account. You might also need to enter a **password**, a special sequence of numbers and letters each user can create. A password allows you to enter and use the files in your user account area. Users cannot see each others' account areas without their passwords, so passwords help keep your computer information secure. After you log in, you see a welcome message, and then the Windows 7 desktop. You will learn about the desktop in the next lesson. 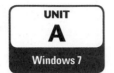 Your supervisor, Evelyn Swazey, asks you to start learning about the Windows 7 operating system.

STEPS

1. **Push your computer's power button, which might look like ⊙ or [⏻], then if the monitor is not turned on, press its power button to turn it on**

   On a desktop computer, the power button is probably on the front panel. On a laptop computer it's most likely at the top of the keys on your keyboard. After a few moments, a Starting Windows message appears. Then you might see a screen that lets you choose a user account, as shown in Figure A-1.

   > **TROUBLE**
   > If you do not see a screen that lets you choose a user account, go to Step 3.

2. **Click a user name if necessary**

   The name you click represents your user account that lets you use the computer. The user account may have your name assigned to it, or it might have a general name, like Student, or Lab User. A password screen may appear. If necessary, ask your instructor or technical support person which user account and password you should use.

   > **TROUBLE**
   > If you clicked the wrong user in Step 2, change to the correct user by clicking the Switch user button on the password screen.

3. **Type your password if necessary, using uppercase and lowercase letters as necessary, as shown in Figure A-2**

   Passwords are **case sensitive**, which means that if you type any letter using capital letters when lowercase letters are needed, Windows will not allow you to access your account. For example, if your password is "book", typing "Book" or "BOOK" will not let you enter your account. As you type your password, its characters appear as a series of dots on the screen. This makes it more difficult for anyone watching you to see your password, giving you additional security.

   > **TROUBLE**
   > If you type your password incorrectly, you see "The user name or password is incorrect." Click OK to try again. To help you remember, Windows shows the Password Hint that you entered when you created your password.

4. **Click the Go button ➡**

   You see a welcome message, and then the Windows 7 desktop, shown in Figure A-3.

Getting Started with Windows 7

FIGURE A-1: Selecting a user name

Name and
picture
represent
each user's
account on
this computer

You might have
a different
version of
Windows 7

Ease of access
button shows
accessibility
options

FIGURE A-2: Password screen

Password
appears as
dots for security

Go button

FIGURE A-3: Windows 7 desktop

Getting Started with Windows 7

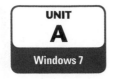
Learning the Windows 7 Desktop

After Windows 7 starts up, you see the Windows 7 desktop. The **desktop** consists of a shaded or picture background with small graphics called icons. **Icons** are small images that represent items such as the Recycle Bin on your computer. You can rearrange, add, and delete desktop icons. Like an actual desktop, the Windows 7 desktop acts as your work area. You can use the desktop to manage the files and folders on your computer. A **file** is a collection of stored information, such as a letter, video, or program. A **folder** is a container that helps you organize your files, just like a cardboard folder on your desk. If you're using a new installation of Windows, the desktop might show only a Recycle Bin icon in the upper-left corner and the **taskbar**, the horizontal bar at the bottom of your screen. 🖐️🖐️🖐️ Evelyn asks you to explore the Windows 7 desktop to begin learning how to communicate with your computer.

DETAILS

Windows 7 computers show these desktop elements. Refer to Figure A-4.

- **Start button**

  The **Start button** is your launching point when you want to communicate with your computer. You can use the Start button to start programs, to open windows that show you the contents of your computer, and to end your Windows session and turn off your computer.

QUICK TIP

If your taskbar is a different color than the one in Figure A-4, your computer might have different settings. This won't affect your work in this chapter.

- **Taskbar**

  The **taskbar** is the horizontal bar at the bottom of the desktop. The taskbar contains the Start button as well as other buttons representing programs, folders, and files. You can use these buttons to immediately open programs or view files and programs that are on your computer.

- **Notification area**

  The **notification area** at the right side of the taskbar contains icons that represent informational messages and programs you might find useful. It also contains information about the current date and time. Some programs automatically place icons here so they are easily available to you. The notification area also displays pop-up messages when something on your computer needs your attention.

- **Recycle Bin**

  Like the wastepaper basket in your office, the **Recycle Bin** is where you place the files and folders that you don't need anymore and want to delete. All objects you place in the Recycle Bin stay there until you empty it. If you put an object there by mistake, you can easily retrieve it, as long as you haven't emptied the bin.

- **Desktop background**

  The **desktop background** is the shaded area behind your desktop objects. You can change the desktop background to show different colors or even pictures.

You might see the following on your desktop:

- **Icons and shortcuts**

  On the desktop background, you can place icons called **shortcuts**, which you can double-click to access programs, files, folders, and devices that you use frequently. That way, they are immediately available to you.

- **Gadgets**

  Gadgets are optional programs that present helpful or entertaining information on your desktop. They include items such as clocks, current news headlines, calendars, picture albums, and weather reports. Some gadgets come with Windows 7 and you can easily place them on your desktop. You can download additional gadgets from the Internet. Figure A-5 shows a desktop that has a desktop background picture and shortcuts to programs, folders, and devices, as well as four gadgets.

FIGURE A-4: Windows 7 desktop after a new Windows installation

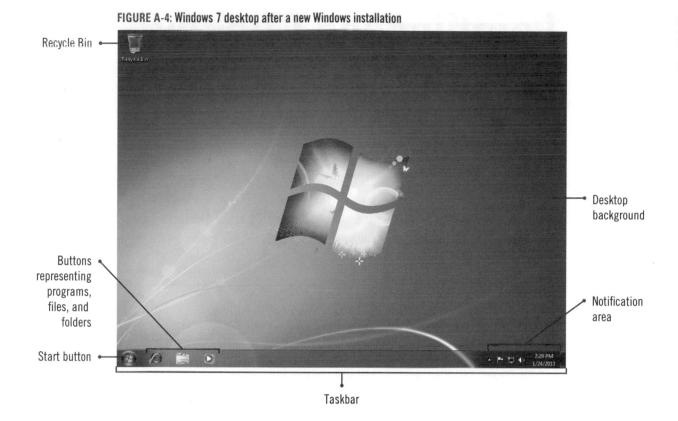

Recycle Bin

Desktop
background

Buttons
representing
programs,
files, and
folders

Notification
area

Start button

Taskbar

FIGURE A-5: Windows 7 desktop with shortcuts, gadgets, and a picture background

Shortcuts
to devices

Shortcuts
to folders

Gadgets for
time, weather,
currency rates,
and news
headlines

Shortcuts
to programs

Taskbar
icons

Desktop
background
picture

What if my desktop looks different from these figures?

If you are using a computer that has been used by others, a different version of Windows 7, or a computer in a school lab, your desktop might be a different color, it might have a different design on it, or it might have different shortcuts and gadgets. Your Recycle Bin might be in a different desktop location. Don't be concerned with these differences. They will not interfere with your work in these units.

Pointing and Clicking

After you start Windows 7 and see the desktop, you can communicate with Windows using a pointing device. A **pointing device** controls the movement of the mouse pointer on your computer screen. The **mouse pointer** is a small arrow or other symbol that moves on the screen. The mouse pointer's shape changes depending on where you point and on the options available to you when you point. Your pointing device could be a mouse, trackball, touchpad, pointing stick, on-screen touch pointer, or a tablet. Figure A-6 shows some common pointing devices. A pointing device might be attached to your computer with a wire, connect wirelessly using an electronic signal, or it might be built into your computer. There are five basic **pointing device actions** you use to communicate with your computer: pointing, clicking, double-clicking, dragging, and right-clicking. Table A-1 describes each action. 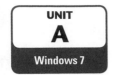 As you prepare to work on your tour schedule, you communicate with your computer using the basic pointing device actions.

STEPS

1. **Locate the mouse pointer on the desktop, then move your pointing device left, right, up, and down**

   The mouse pointer moves in the same direction as your pointing device.

2. **Move your pointing device so the mouse pointer is over the Recycle Bin**

   You are pointing to the Recycle Bin. The pointer shape is the **Select pointer** � . The Recycle Bin icon becomes **highlighted,** looking as though it is framed in a box with a lighter color background and a border.

   > **QUICK TIP**
   > Use the tip of the pointer when pointing to an object.

3. **While pointing to the Recycle Bin, press and quickly release the left mouse button once, then move the pointer away from the Recycle Bin**

   Click a desktop icon once to **select** it, and then the interior of the border around it changes color. When you select an icon, you signal Windows 7 that you want to perform an action. You can also use pointing to identify screen items.

4. **Point to (but do not click) the Internet Explorer button 🄮 on the taskbar**

   The button border appears and an informational message called a **ScreenTip** identifies the program the button represents.

5. **Move the mouse pointer over the time and date in the notification area in the lower-right corner of the screen, read the ScreenTip, then click once**

   A pop-up window appears, containing a calendar and a clock displaying the current date and time.

   > **TROUBLE**
   > You need to double-click quickly, with a fast click-click, without moving the mouse. If a window didn't open, try again with a faster click-click.

6. **Place the tip of the mouse pointer over the Recycle Bin, then quickly click twice**

   You **double-clicked** the Recycle Bin. A window opens, showing the contents of the Recycle Bin, shown in Figure A-7. The area near the top of the screen is the **Address bar**, which shows the name of the item you have opened. If your Recycle Bin contains any discarded items, they appear in the white area below the Address bar. You can use single clicking to close a window.

7. **Place the tip of the mouse pointer over the Close button ▣✕▤ in the upper-right corner of the Recycle Bin window, notice the Close ScreenTip, then click once**

   The Recycle Bin window closes. You can use dragging to move icons on the desktop.

   > **QUICK TIP**
   > You'll use dragging in other Windows 7 programs to move folders, files, and other objects to new locations.

8. **Point to the Recycle Bin icon, press and hold down the left mouse button, move the pointing device (or drag your finger over the touchpad) so the object moves right about an inch, as shown in Figure A-8, then release the mouse button**

   You dragged the Recycle Bin icon to a new location.

9. **Repeat Step 8 to drag the Recycle Bin back to its original location**

FIGURE A-6: Pointing devices

Mouse

Trackball

Touchpad

Pointing stick

FIGURE A-7: Recycle Bin window

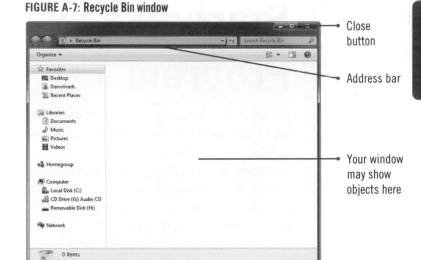

Close button

Address bar

Your window may show objects here

FIGURE A-8: Dragging the Recycle Bin icon

Releasing mouse button moves object to this location

TABLE A-1: Five pointing device actions

action	how to	use for
Pointing	Move the pointing device to position the tip of the pointer over an object, option, or item	Highlighting objects or options, or displaying informational boxes called ScreenTips
Clicking	Quickly press and release the left mouse button once	Selecting objects or commands, opening menus or items on the taskbar
Double-clicking	Quickly press and release the left mouse button twice	Opening programs, folders, or files represented by desktop icons
Dragging	Point to an object, press and hold down the left mouse button, move the object to a new location, then release the mouse button	Moving objects, such as icons on the desktop
Right-clicking	Point to an object, then press and release the right mouse button	Displaying a shortcut menu containing options specific to the object

Using right-clicking

For some actions, you click items using the right mouse button, known as right-clicking. You can **right-click** almost any icon on your desktop to open a shortcut menu. A **shortcut menu** lists common commands for an object. A **command** is an instruction to perform a task, such as emptying the Recycle Bin. The shortcut menu commands depend on the object you right-click. Figure A-9 shows the shortcut menu that appears if you right-click the Recycle Bin. Then you click (with the left mouse button) a shortcut menu command to issue that command.

FIGURE A-9: Right-click to show shortcut menu

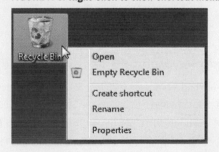

Starting a Windows 7 Program

The Windows 7 operating system lets you operate your computer and see the programs and files it contains. But to do your work, you'll need application programs. **Application programs** let you create letters, financial summaries, and other useful documents as well as view Web pages on the Internet and send and receive e-mail. Some application programs, called **accessories**, come with Windows 7. (See Table A-2 for some examples of accessories that come with Windows 7.) To use an application program, you must start (or open) it so you can see and use its tools. With Windows 7 you start application programs using the Start menu. A **menu** is a list of related commands. You use the Start menu to open the All Programs menu, which contains all the application programs on your computer. You can see some programs on the All Programs menu; some are in folders you have to click first. To start a program, you click its name on the All Programs menu. 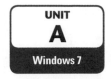 Evelyn asks you to explore the Paint accessory program for creating brochure graphics.

STEPS

1. **Click the Start button 🔵 on the taskbar in the lower-left corner of screen**

    The Start menu opens, showing frequently used programs on the left side. The gray area on the right contains links to folders and other locations you are likely to use frequently. It also lets you get help and shut down your computer. See Figure A-10. Not all the programs available on your computer are shown.

2. **Point to All Programs**

    This menu shows programs installed on your computer. Your program list will differ, depending on what you (or your lab) have installed on your machine. Some program names are immediately available, and others are inside folders.

3. **Click the Accessories folder**

    A list of Windows accessory programs appears, as shown in Figure A-11. The program names are indented to the right from the Accessories folder, meaning that they are inside that folder.

4. **Move the 👆 pointer over Paint and click once**

    The Paint program window opens on your screen, as shown in Figure A-12. When Windows opens an application program, it starts the program from your computer's hard disk, where it's permanently stored. Then it places the program in your computer's memory so you can use it.

5. **If your Paint window fills the screen completely, click the Restore Down button 🔲 in the upper-right corner of the window**

    If your Paint window doesn't look like Figure A-12, point to the lower-right corner of the window until the pointer becomes ⬂, then drag until it matches the figure.

Searching for programs and files using the Start menu

If you need to find a program, folder, or file on your computer quickly, the Search programs and files box on the Start menu can help. Click the Start button, then type the name of the item you want to find in the Search programs and files box. As you type, Windows 7 lists all programs, documents, e-mail messages, and files that contain the text you typed in a box above the Search box. The items appear as links, which means you only have to click the hand pointer 👆 on the item you want, and Windows 7 opens it.

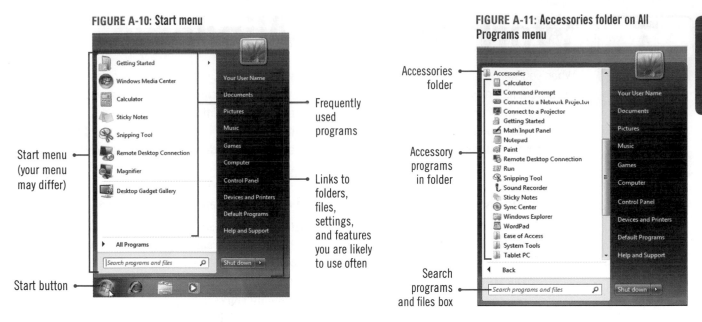

FIGURE A-10: Start menu

Start menu
(your menu
may differ)

Start button

Frequently
used
programs

Links to
folders,
files,
settings,
and features
you are likely
to use often

**FIGURE A-11: Accessories folder on All
Programs menu**

Accessories
folder

Accessory
programs
in folder

Search
programs
and files box

FIGURE A-12: Paint program window

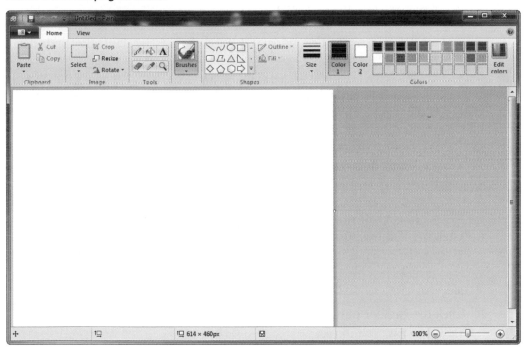

TABLE A-2: Some Windows 7 Accessory programs

accessory program name	use to
Math Input Panel	Interpret math expressions handwritten on a tablet and create a formula suitable for printing or inserting in another program
Notepad	Create text files with basic text formatting
Paint	Create and edit drawings using lines, shapes, and colors
Snipping Tool	Capture an image of any screen area that you can save to use in a document
Sticky Notes	Create short text notes that you can use to set reminders or create to-do lists for yourself
Windows Explorer	View and organize the files and folders on your computer
WordPad	Type letters or other text documents with formatting

Getting Started with Windows 7

Working with Windows

When you start an application program, its **program window** opens, showing you the tools you need to use the program. A new, blank file also opens. In the Paint program, you create a drawing that you can save as a file and print. All windows in the Windows 7 operating system have similar window elements. Once you can use a window in one program, you can then work with windows in many other programs. 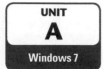 As you develop your tour marketing plans, you work with the open Paint window using Windows 7 elements.

DETAILS

Many windows have the following common elements. Refer to Figure A-13:

- At the top of every open window, you see a **title bar**, a transparent or solid-colored strip that contains the name of the program and document you opened. This document has not been saved, so it has the temporary name "Untitled." On the right side of the title bar, you see three icons.

  The **Minimize button** ⬜ temporarily hides the window, making it a button on the taskbar. The program is still running, but its window is hidden until you click its taskbar button to display it again. The **Maximize button** 🔲 enlarges the window to fill the entire computer screen. If a window is already maximized, the Maximize button changes to the **Restore Down button** 🗗. Restoring a window reduces it to the last nonmaximized size. The **Close button** ❌ closes the program. To use it later, you need to start it again.

- Many windows have a **scroll bar** on the right side and/or on the bottom of the window. You click the scroll bar elements to show parts of your document that are hidden below the bottom edge or off to the right side of the screen. See Table A-3 to learn the parts of a scroll bar.
- Just below the title bar, at the top of the Paint window, is the **Ribbon**, a strip that contains tabs. **Tabs** are pages that contain buttons that you click to perform actions. The Paint window has two tabs, the Home tab and the View tab. Tabs are divided into **groups** of command buttons. The Home tab has five groups: Clipboard, Image, Tools, Shapes, and Colors. Some programs have **menus**, words you click to show lists of commands, and **toolbars**, containing program buttons.
- The **Quick Access toolbar**, in the upper-left corner of the window, lets you quickly perform common actions such as saving a file.

STEPS

1. **Click the Paint window Minimize button** ⬜

   The program is now represented only by its button on the taskbar. See Figure A-14. The taskbar button for the Paint program now has a gradient background with blue and white shading 🖌. Taskbar buttons for closed programs have a solid blue background 🖌.

2. **Click the taskbar button representing the Paint program** 🖌

   The program window reappears.

3. **Drag the Paint scroll box down, notice the lower edge of the Paint canvas that appears, then click the Paint Up scroll arrow** 🔼 **until you see the top edge of the canvas**

   In the Ribbon, the Home tab is in front of the View tab.

4. **Point to the View tab with the tip of the mouse pointer, then click the View tab once**

   The View tab moves in front of the Home tab and shows commands for viewing your drawings. The View tab has three groups: Zoom, Show or hide, and Display.

5. **Click the Home tab**

6. **Click the Paint window Maximize button** 🔲

   The window fills the screen and the Maximize button becomes the Restore Down button 🗗.

7. **Click the Paint window's Restore Down button** 🗗

   The Paint window returns to its previous size on the screen.

FIGURE A-13: Paint program window elements

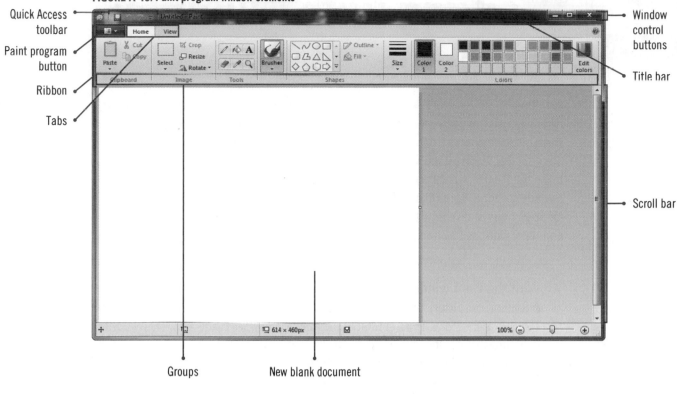

Quick Access toolbar

Paint program button

Ribbon

Tabs

Groups

New blank document

Window control buttons

Title bar

Scroll bar

FIGURE A-14: Taskbar showing Paint program button

Paint program button with gradient background indicates program is open

TABLE A-3: Parts of a scroll bar

name	looks like	use for
Scroll box	▤ (Size may vary)	Drag to scroll quickly through a long document
Scroll arrows	▲ ▼	Click to scroll up or down in small amounts
Shaded area	(Above and below scroll box)	Click to move up or down by one screen

Using the Quick Access toolbar

On the left side of the title bar, the Quick Access toolbar lets you perform common tasks with just one click. The Save button 🖫 saves the changes you have made to a document. The Undo button 🔙 lets you reverse (undo) the last action you performed. The Redo button 🔜 reinstates the change you just undid. Use the Customize Quick Access Toolbar button ⯆ to add other frequently used buttons to the toolbar, move the toolbar below the Ribbon, or hide the Ribbon.

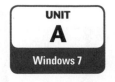

Working with Multiple Windows

Windows 7 lets you work with more than one program at a time. If you open two or more programs, a window opens for each one. You can work with each open program window, going back and forth between them. The window in front is called the **active window**. Any other open window behind the active window is called an **inactive window**. For ease in working with multiple windows, you can move, arrange, make them smaller or larger, minimize, or restore them so they're not in the way. To resize a window, drag a window's edge, called its **border**. You can also use the taskbar to switch between windows. See Table A-4 for a summary of taskbar actions. Keeping the Paint program open, you open the WordPad program and work with the Paint and WordPad program windows.

STEPS

1. **With the Paint window open, click the Start button ⊕, point to All Programs, click the Accessories folder, then click WordPad**

   The WordPad window opens in front of the Paint window. See Figure A-15. The WordPad window is in front, indicating that it is the active window. The Paint window is the inactive window. On the taskbar, the gradient backgrounds on the WordPad and Paint program buttons on the taskbar tell you that both programs are open. You want to move the WordPad window out of the way so you can see both windows at once.

   > **QUICK TIP**
   > To click an inactive window to make it active, click its title bar, window edge, or a blank area. To move a window, you must drag its title bar.

2. **Point to a blank part of the WordPad window title bar, then drag the WordPad window so you can see more of the Paint window**

3. **Click once on the Paint window's title bar**

   The Paint window is now the active window and appears in front of the WordPad window. You can make any window active by clicking it. You can use the taskbar to do the same thing. You can also move among open program windows by pressing and holding down the [Alt] key on your keyboard and pressing the [Tab] key. A small window opens in the middle of the screen, showing miniature versions of each open program window. Each time you press [Tab], you select the next open program window. When you release [Tab] and [Alt], the selected program window becomes active.

   > **QUICK TIP**
   > To instantly minimize all inactive windows, point to the active window's title bar, and quickly "shake" the window back and forth. This feature is called Aero Shake.

4. **On the taskbar, click the WordPad window button 🖼**

   The WordPad window is now active. When you open multiple windows on the desktop, you may need to resize windows so they don't get in the way of other open windows. You can use dragging to resize a window.

   > **TROUBLE**
   > Point to any edge of a window until you see the ⬌ or ⬍ pointer and drag to make it larger or smaller in one direction only.

5. **Point to the lower-right corner of the WordPad window until the pointer becomes ⬂, then drag up and to the left about an inch to make the window smaller**

   Windows 7 has a special feature that lets you automatically resize a window so it fills half the screen.

6. **Point to the WordPad window title bar, drag the window to the left side of the screen until the mouse pointer reaches the screen edge and the left half of the screen turns a transparent blue color, then release the mouse button**

   The WordPad window "snaps" to fill the left side of the screen.

7. **Point to the Paint window title bar, then drag the window to the right side of the screen until it snaps to fill the right half of the screen**

   The Paint window fills the right side of the screen. The Snap feature makes it easy to arrange windows side by side to view the contents of both at the same time.

8. **Click the WordPad window Close button ⊠ then click the Maximize button ⬜ in the Paint window's title bar**

   The WordPad program closes, so you can no longer use its tools unless you open it again. The Paint program window remains open and fills the screen.

FIGURE A-15: WordPad window in front of Paint window

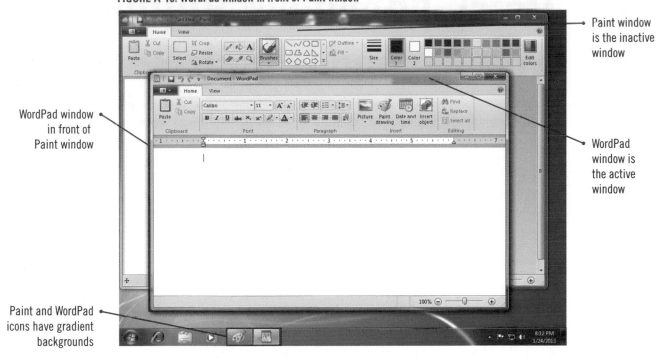

Paint window is the inactive window

WordPad window in front of Paint window

WordPad window is the active window

Paint and WordPad icons have gradient backgrounds

TABLE A-4: Using the Windows taskbar

to	do this
Add buttons to taskbar	Drag a program name from the Start menu over the taskbar, until a ScreenTip reads Pin to Taskbar
Change order of taskbar buttons	Drag any icon to a new taskbar location
See a list of recent documents opened in a taskbar program	Right-click taskbar program button
Close a document using the taskbar	Point to taskbar button, point to document name in jump list, then click Close button
Minimize all open windows	Click Show desktop button to the right of taskbar date and time
Redisplay all minimized windows	Click Show desktop button to the right of taskbar date and time
Make all windows transparent (Aero only)	Point to Show desktop button to the right of taskbar date and time
See preview of documents in taskbar (Aero only)	Point to taskbar button for open program

Switching windows with Windows Aero

Windows Aero is a set of special effects for Windows 7. If your windows have transparent "glass" backgrounds like those shown in the figures in this book, your Aero feature is turned on. Your windows show subtle animations when you minimize, maximize, and move windows. When you arrange windows using Aero, your windows can appear in a three-dimensional stack that you can quickly view without having to click the taskbar. To achieve this effect, called **Aero Flip 3D**, press and hold [Ctrl][⊞], then press [Tab]. Press [Tab] repeatedly to move through the stack, then press [Enter] to enlarge the document in the front of the stack. In addition, when you point to a taskbar button, Aero shows you small previews of the document, photo, or video—a feature called **Aero Peek**. Aero is turned on automatically when you start Windows, if you have an appropriate video card and enough computer memory to run Aero. If it is not on, to turn on the Aero feature, right-click the desktop, left-click Personalize, then select one of the Aero Themes.

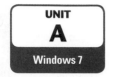
Using Command Buttons, Menus, and Dialog Boxes

When you work in an open program window, you communicate with the program using command buttons, menus, and dialog boxes. **Command buttons** let you issue instructions to modify program objects. Command buttons are sometimes organized on a Ribbon into tabs, and then into groups like those in the Paint window. Some command buttons have text on them, and others only have icons that represent what they do. Other command buttons reveal **menus**, lists of commands you can choose. And some command buttons open up a **dialog box**, a window with controls that lets you tell Windows what you want. Table A-5 lists the common types of controls you find in dialog boxes. You use command buttons, menus, and dialog boxes to communicate with the Paint program.

STEPS

> **QUICK TIP**
> If you need to move the oval, use the keyboard arrow keys to move it left, right, up, or down.

1. **In the Shapes group on the Home tab, click the Rectangle button □**

2. **In the Colors group, click the Gold button ▢, move the pointer over the white drawing area, called the canvas, then drag to draw a rectangle a similar size to the one in Figure A-16**

3. **In the Shapes group, click the Oval button ○, click the Green color button ▉ in the Colors group, then drag a small oval above the rectangle, using Figure A-16 as a guide**

> **TROUBLE**
> Don't be concerned if your object isn't exactly like the one in the figure.

4. **Click the Fill with color icon ◈ in the Tools group, click the Light turquoise color button in the Colors group, click ◈ inside the oval, click the Purple color button, then click inside the rectangle, and compare your drawing to Figure A-16**

5. **In the Image group, click the Select list arrow, then click Select all, as shown in Figure A-17**
   The Select menu has several menu commands. The Select all command selects the entire drawing, as indicated by the dotted line surrounding the white drawing area.

6. **In the Image group, click the Rotate or flip button, then click Rotate right 90°**

7. **Click the Paint menu button ▣▾ just below the title bar, then click Print**
   The Print dialog box opens, as shown in Figure A-18. This dialog box lets you choose a printer, specify which part of your document or drawing you want to print, and choose how many copies you want to print. The **default**, or automatically selected, number of copies is 1, which is what you want.

> **TROUBLE**
> If you prefer not to print your document, click Cancel.

8. **Click Print**
   The drawing prints on your printer. You decide to close the program without saving your drawing.

9. **Click ▣▾, click Exit, then click Don't Save**

TABLE A-5: Common dialog box controls

element	example	description
Text box	132	A box in which you type text or numbers
Spin box	1 ▲▼	A box with up and down arrows; click arrows or type to increase or decrease value
Option button	○ ●	A small circle you click to select the option
Check box	☑	Turns an option on when checked or off when unchecked
List box	Select Printer / Add Printer / Dell Laser Printer 3000cn PCL6 / Fax	A box that lets you select an option from a list of options
Command button	Save	A button that completes or cancels the selected settings

FIGURE A-16: Rectangle and oval shapes with fill

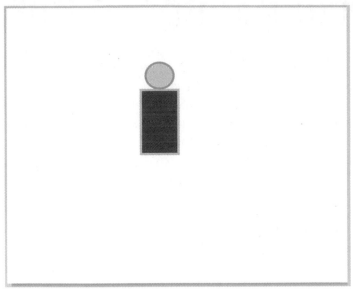

FIGURE A-17: Select list arrow

Select list arrow

Select all command

Select menu

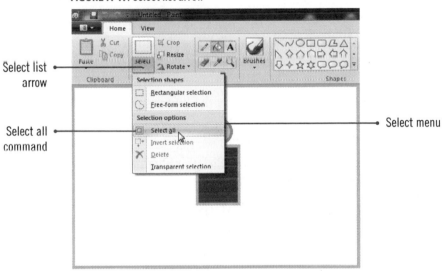

FIGURE A-18: Print dialog box

Your printer name may differ

One copy is the default

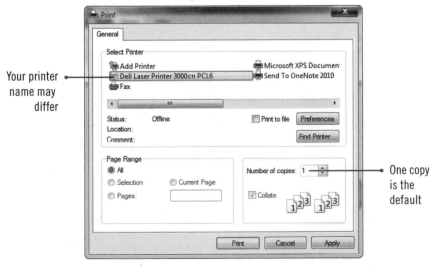

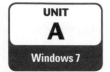

Getting Help

As you use Windows 7, you might feel ready to learn more about it, or you might have a problem and need some advice. You can open the Windows 7 Help and Support to find information you need. You can browse Help and Support topics by clicking a category, such as "Learn about Windows Basics." Within this category, you see more specific categories. Each category has topics in blue or purple text called **links** that you can click to learn more. You can also search Help and Support by typing one or more descriptive words called **keywords**, such as "taskbar," to ask Windows to find topics related to your keywords. The Help toolbar contains icons that give you more Help options. Table A-6 describes the Help toolbar icons. You use Windows 7 help to learn more about Windows and the WordPad accessory.

STEPS

TROUBLE
If your computer is not connected to the Internet, you will see an alert at the top of the Help window. You can continue with the steps in this lesson.

1. **Click the Start button ⊛, then on the right side of the Start menu, click Help and Support**
The Windows Help and Support window opens, as shown in Figure A-19. A search box appears near the top of the window. Three topics appear as blue or purple text, meaning that they are links. Below them, you see descriptive text and a link to a Web site that contains more information about Windows.

2. **Under Not sure where to start?, position the hand pointer ⟨ᑦ⟩ over Learn about Windows Basics, then click once**
Several categories of Windows Basics topics appear, with links under each one.

QUICK TIP
If you are using a mouse with a scroll wheel, you can use the scroll wheel to scroll up and down. If you are using a touchpad, the right side of your touchpad might let you scroll.

3. **Under Desktop fundamentals, click The desktop (overview)**
Help and Support information about the desktop appears, divided into several categories. Some of the text appears as a blue or purple link.

4. **Drag the scroll box down to view the information, then drag the scroll box back to the top of the scroll bar**
You decide to learn more about the taskbar.

5. **Under The desktop (overview), click the blue or purple text The taskbar (overview), then scroll down and read the information about the taskbar**

QUICK TIP
Search text is not case sensitive. Typing wordpad, Wordpad, or WordPad finds the same results.

6. **Click in the Search Help text box, type wordpad, then click the Search Help button 🔎**
A list of links related to the WordPad accessory program appears. See Figure A-20.

7. **Click Using WordPad, scroll down if necessary, then click Create, open, and save documents**

8. **Scroll down and view the information, clicking any other links that interest you**

9. **Click the Close button [✕] in the upper-right corner of the Windows Help and Support window**
The Windows Help and Support window closes.

TABLE A-6: Help toolbar icons

help toolbar icon	name	action
🔘	Help and Support home	Displays the Help and Support Home page
🖨	Print	Prints the currently-displayed help topic
📖	Browse Help	Displays a list of Help topics organized by subject
Ask	Ask	Describes other ways to get help
Options ▾	Options	Lets you print, browse, search, set Help text size, and adjust settings

FIGURE A-19: Windows Help and Support window

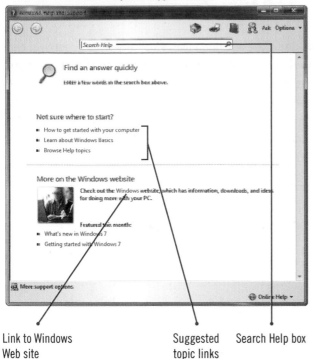

Link to Windows
Web site

Suggested
topic links

Search Help box

FIGURE A-20: Results of a search on WordPad

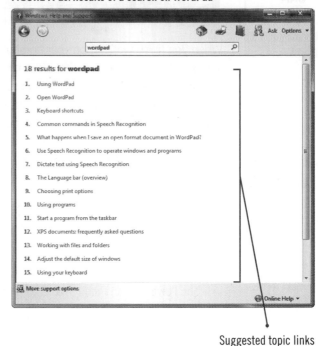

18 results for **wordpad**

1. Using WordPad
2. Open WordPad
3. Keyboard shortcuts
4. Common commands in Speech Recognition
5. What happens when I save an open format document in WordPad?
6. Use Speech Recognition to operate windows and programs
7. Dictate text using Speech Recognition
8. The Language bar (overview)
9. Choosing print options
10. Using programs
11. Start a program from the taskbar
12. XPS documents: frequently asked questions
13. Working with files and folders
14. Adjust the default size of windows
15. Using your keyboard

Suggested topic links
(your links may differ)

Finding other ways to get help

As you use Windows 7, you might want more help than you can find by clicking links or searching. You will find many other methods in the Windows Help and Support Home window. Click the Windows website link to locate blogs (Web logs, which are personal commentaries), downloads, Windows 7 video tours, and other current Windows 7 resources. Click the Ask button in the Help and Support window toolbar to learn about **Windows Remote Assistance**, which lets you connect with another computer, perhaps that of a trusted friend or instructor, so they can operate your computer using an Internet connection. The same window lets you open Microsoft Answers. **Microsoft Answers** is a website the lets you search **forums** (electronic gathering places where anyone can add questions and answers on computer issues), Microsoft help files, and even on-screen video demonstrations about selected topics.

Exiting Windows 7

When you finish working on your computer, save and close any open files, close any open programs, close any open windows, and exit (or **shut down**) Windows 7. Table A-7 shows several options for ending your Windows 7 sessions. Whichever option you choose, it's important to shut down your computer in an orderly way. If you turn off or unplug the computer while Windows 7 is running, you could lose data or damage Windows 7 and your computer. If you are working in a computer lab, follow your instructor's directions and your lab's policies for ending your Windows 7 session. ▓▓▓▓ You have examined the basic ways you can use Windows 7, so you are ready to end your Windows 7 session.

STEPS

1. **Click the Start button ⊙ on the taskbar**
   The lower-right corner of the Start menu lets you shut down your computer. It also displays a menu with other options for ending a Windows 7 session.

2. **Point to the Power button list arrow ▷, as shown in Figure A-21**
   The Power button menu lists other shutdown options.

3. **If you are working in a computer lab, follow the instructions provided by your instructor or technical support person for ending your Windows 7 session. If you are working on your own computer, click Shut down or the option you prefer for ending your Windows 7 session**

4. **After you shut down your computer, you may also need to turn off your monitor and other hardware devices, such as a printer, to conserve energy**

Installing updates when you exit Windows

Sometimes, after you shut down your machine, you might find that your machine does not shut down immediately. Instead, Windows might install software updates. If your power button shows this yellow icon 🔳, that means that Windows will install updates on your next shutdown. If you see a window indicating that updates are being installed, do not unplug or press the power switch to turn off your machine. Allow the updates to install completely. After the updates are installed, your computer will shut down, as you originally requested.

FIGURE A-21: Shutting down your computer

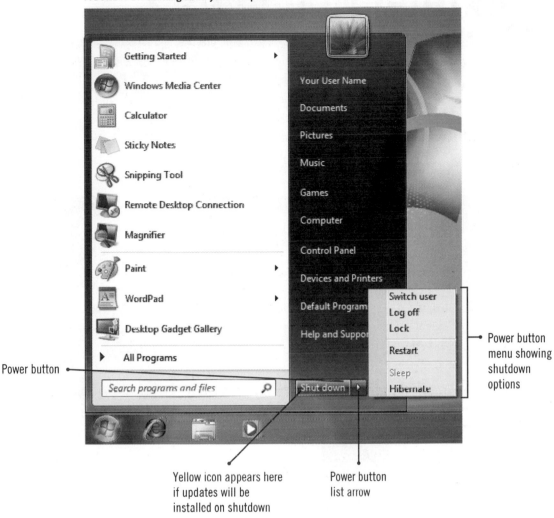

Power button

Power button menu showing shutdown options

Yellow icon appears here if updates will be installed on shutdown

Power button list arrow

TABLE A-7: Options for ending a Windows 7 session

option	description	click
Shut down	Completely turns off your computer	Start button, Shut down
Switch user	Locks your user account and displays the Welcome screen so another user can log on	Start button, Power button list arrow, Switch user
Log off	Closes all windows, programs, and documents, then displays the Log in screen	Start button, Power button list arrow, Log off
Lock	Locks computer so only current user (or administrator) can use it	Start button, Power button list arrow, Lock
Restart	Shuts down your computer, then restarts it	Start button, Power button list arrow, Restart
Sleep	Puts computer in a low-power state while preserving your session in the computer's memory	Start button, Power button list arrow, Sleep
Hibernate	Turns off computer drives and screens but saves image of your work; when you turn machine on, it starts where you left off	Start button, Power button list arrow, Hibernate

Practice

Concepts Review

For current SAM information, including versions and content details, visit SAM Central (http://www.cengage.com/samcentral). If you have a SAM user profile, you may have access to hands-on instruction, practice, and assessment of the skills covered in this unit. Since various versions of SAM are supported throughout the life of this text, check with your instructor for the correct instructions and URL/Web site for accessing assignments.

Label the elements of the Windows 7 window shown in Figure A-22.

FIGURE A-22

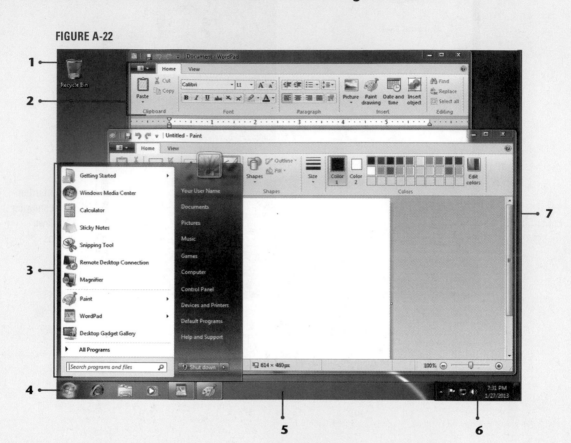

Match each term with the statement that best describes it.

8. Accessory
9. Keyword
10. Trackball
11. Active window
12. Password
13. Operating system
14. Taskbar

a. A sequence of numbers and letters users create to keep information secure
b. The window in front of other windows
c. Horizontal strip at bottom of screen that contains buttons
d. A pointing device
e. Application program that comes with Windows 7
f. Descriptive word you use to search Windows Help and Support
g. A program necessary to run your computer

Select the best answer from the list of choices.

15. What part of a window shows the name of the program you opened?
    a. Title bar
    b. Scroll bar
    c. Ribbon
    d. Quick Access toolbar

16. **You use the Maximize button to:**
    a. Restore a window to a previous size.
    b. Expand a window to fill the entire screen.
    c. Temporarily hide a window.
    d. Scroll down a window.

17. **Which of the following is not an accessory program?**
    a. Snipping Tool
    b. Paint
    c. WordPad
    d. Windows 7

18. **Which button do you click to reduce an open window to a button on the taskbar?**
    a. Maximize button
    b. Restore Down button
    c. Minimize button
    d. Close button

19. **Right-clicking is an action that:**
    a. Starts a program.
    b. Requires a password.
    c. Displays a shortcut menu.
    d. Opens the taskbar.

20. **The Windows 7 feature that shows windows with transparent "glass" backgrounds is:**
    a. Paint.
    b. Aero.
    c. Taskbar.
    d. Sticky Notes.

21. **Windows 7 is a(n):**
    a. Accessory program.
    b. Application program.
    c. Operating system.
    d. Gadget.

Skills Review

1. **Start Windows 7.**
   a. If your computer and monitor are not running, press your computer's and your monitor's power buttons.
   b. If necessary, click the user name that represents your user account.
   c. Enter a password if necessary, using correct uppercase and lowercase letters.

2. **Learn the Windows 7 desktop.**
   a. Examine the Windows 7 desktop to identify the Start button, the taskbar, the notification area, the Recycle Bin, the desktop background, desktop icons, and gadgets, if any.

3. **Point and click.**
   a. On the Windows desktop, select the Recycle Bin.
   b. Open the Start menu, then close it.
   c. Open the clock and calendar on the right side of the taskbar.
   d. Click the desktop to close the calendar.
   e. Open the Recycle Bin window, then close it.

4. **Start a Windows 7 program.**
   a. Use the Start button to open the Start menu.
   b. Open the All Programs menu.
   c. On the All Programs menu, open the Accessories folder.
   d. Open the WordPad accessory.

5. **Work with Windows.**
   a. Minimize the WordPad window.
   b. Redisplay it using a taskbar button.
   c. In the WordPad window, click the WordPad button in the Ribbon, then click the About WordPad command. (*Hint*: The WordPad button is next to the Home tab.)
   d. Close the About WordPad window.
   e. Maximize the WordPad window, then restore it down.
   f. Display the View tab in the WordPad window.

Skills Review (continued)

6. **Work with multiple windows.**

   a. Leaving WordPad open, open Paint.

   b. Make the WordPad window the active window.

   c. Make the Paint window the active window.

   d. Minimize the Paint window.

   e. Drag the WordPad window so it automatically fills the left side of the screen.

   f. Redisplay the Paint window.

   g. Drag the Paint window so it automatically fills the right side of the screen.

   h. Close the WordPad window, maximize the Paint window, then restore down the Paint window.

7. **Use command buttons, menus, and dialog boxes.**

   a. In the Paint window, draw a red triangle, similar to Figure A-23.

   b. Use the Fill with color button to fill the triangle with a gold color.

   c. Draw a green rectangle just below the triangle.

   d. Use the Fill with color button to fill the green triangle with a light turquoise color.

   e. Fill the drawing background with purple and compare your drawing with Figure A-23.

   f. Use the Select list arrow and menu to select the entire drawing, then use the Rotate or flip command to rotate the drawing left 90°.

   g. Close the Paint program without saving the drawing.

FIGURE A-23

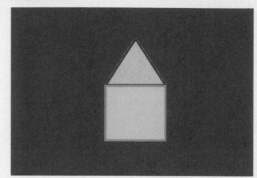

8. **Get help.**

   a. Open the Windows Help and Support window.

   b. Open the "How to get started with your computer" topic.

   c. Open the "First week tasks" topic, click a link called "Create a user account", then read the topic information.

   d. In the Search Help text box, search for help about user accounts.

   e. Find the link that describes what a user account is and click it.

   f. Read the topic, then close the Windows Help and Support window.

9. **Exit Windows 7.**

   a. Shut down your computer using the Shut down command or the command for your work or school setting.

   b. Turn off your monitor.

Independent Challenge 1

You work for Will's Percussion, an Oregon manufacturer of drums and drumsticks. The company ships percussion instruments and supplies to music stores and musicians in the United States and Canada. The owner, Will, gives seminars at drummer conventions on how to avoid repetitive stress injuries to the hands and arms. He knows this can also be a big problem for computer users as well, so he asks you to research the topic and write some guidelines for the company's employees.

   a. Start your computer, log on to Windows 7 if necessary, then open Windows Help and Support.

   b. Click the Learn about Windows Basics link.

   c. In the Learn about your computer section, read the topic about using your mouse.

   d. At the bottom of the topic, read the Tips for using your mouse safely.

   e. Using pencil and paper, write a short memo to Will listing, in your own words, the most important tips for avoiding soreness or injury when using a mouse. Close the Windows Help and Support window, then exit Windows.

Independent Challenge 2

You are the new manager for Katharine Anne's Designs, a business that supplies floral arrangements to New York businesses. The company maintains four delivery vans that supply flowers to various locations. Katharine asks you to investigate how the Windows 7 Calculator accessory can help her company be a responsible energy consumer.

Independent Challenge 2 (continued)

a. Start your computer, log on to Windows 7 if necessary, then open the Windows 7 accessory called Calculator.

b. Drag the Calculator window to place it in the lower-left corner of the desktop just above the taskbar.

FIGURE A-24

c. Minimize the Calculator window, then redisplay it.

d. Click to enter the number 87 on the Calculator.

e. Click the division sign (/) button.

f. Click the number 2.

g. Click the equals sign button (=), and write the result shown in the Calculator window on a piece of paper. See Figure A-24.

h. Click the Help menu in the Calculator window, then click View Help. In the Using Calculator window, determine the three ways of entering calculations in the Calculator. Write the three methods on your handwritten list.

i. Close the Help window.

Advanced Challenge Exercise

- Open the View menu on the Calculator window, and click Date calculation.
- Click the list arrow under Select the date calculation you want, then click Calculate the difference between two dates.
- Write how Katharine's business might use this to calculate the length of time it takes a customer to pay an invoice.
- Click the View menu, point to Worksheets, then click Fuel economy (mpg).
- Click in the Distance (miles) text box and enter 100; click in the Fuel used (gallons) text box and type 5, then use the Calculate button to calculate the mileage.
- Write a short paragraph on how Katharine can use this feature to help calculate her van mileage.
- Click the View menu and return to the Basic view.
- Try to click the Calculator window's Maximize button. Note the result and add this fact to your document.

j. Close the Calculator, then exit Windows.

Independent Challenge 3

You are the office manager for Peter's Pet Shipping, a service business in Vancouver, BC that specializes in air shipping of cats and dogs to Canada and the northern United States. It's important to know the temperature in the destination city, so that the animals won't be in danger from extreme temperatures when they are unloaded from the aircraft. Peter has asked you to find a way to easily monitor temperatures in destination cities. You decide to use a Windows gadget so you can see current temperatures in Celsius on your desktop.

To complete this Independent Challenge, you need an Internet connection. You also need permission to add gadgets to the Windows Desktop. If you are working in a computer lab, check with your instructor or technical support person.

a. Start your computer, log on to Windows 7 if necessary, then click the Start button, open the All Programs menu, then click Desktop Gadget Gallery.

b. Double-click the Weather gadget, then close the Gallery window.

c. Move the pointer over the Weather gadget on the desktop, then notice the small buttons that appear on its right side.

d. Click the Larger size button (the middle button).

e. Click the Options button (the third button down) to open the weather options window.

f. In the Select current location text box, type Juneau, Alaska, then click the Search button.

g. Verify that the window shows the current location as "Juneau, Alaska."

h. Click the Celsius option button, then click OK.

i. To close the gadget, point to the gadget, then click the Close button (the top button).

j. Write Peter a memo outlining how you can use the Windows Weather gadget to help keep pets safe, then exit Windows.

Real Life Independent Challenge

As a professional photographer, you often evaluate pictures. You decide to explore a Windows Desktop gadget that will let you display a slide show on your desktop using photos you choose.

To complete this Independent Challenge, you need an Internet connection. You also need permission to add gadgets to the Windows Desktop. If you are working in a computer lab, check with your instructor or technical support person.

a. Start your computer, log on to Windows 7 if necessary, click the Start button, open the All Programs menu, then click Desktop Gadget Gallery.

b. Double-click the Slide Show gadget, then close the Gallery window.

c. Move the pointer over the Slide Show gadget on the desktop, then notice the small buttons that appear on its right side.

d. Click the Larger size button (the second button down).

e. Click the Options button (the third button down) to open the Slide Show options window.

f. Click the Folder list arrow and click the My Pictures folder. If you do not have pictures on your computer, click the Sample Pictures folder.

g. Click the Show each picture list arrow and select a duration.

h. Click the Transition between pictures list arrow and select a transition.

i. If you want the pictures to be in random order, click the Shuffle pictures check box.

j. Click OK.

Advanced Challenge Exercise

■ Place the mouse pointer over the Slide Show window, then right-click.

■ Point to Opacity and left-click an opacity level, then move the mouse pointer over the desktop. Adjust the opacity to the level you prefer.

■ Drag the gadget to the desktop location you choose.

k. View your slide show, click the Slide Show window's Close button, then exit Windows.

Visual Workshop

As owner of Icons Plus, an icon design business, you decide to customize your desktop and resize your Help window to better suit your needs as you work with Paint. Organize your screen as shown in Figure A-25. Note the position of the Recycle Bin, the location of the Paint window, and the size and location of the Help and Support window. Write a paragraph summarizing how you used clicking and dragging to make your screen look like Figure A-25. Then exit Windows.

FIGURE A-25

Understanding File Management

Files You Will Need:

No files needed.

To work with the folders and files on your computer, you need to understand how your computer stores them. You should also know how to organize them so you can always find the information you need. These skills are called **file management** skills. When you create a document and save it as a file, it is important that you save the file in a place where you can find it later. To keep your computer files organized, you will need to copy, move, and rename them. When you have files you don't need any more, it's a good idea to move or delete them so your computer has only current files.  Your supervisor, Evelyn Swazey, asks you to learn how to manage your computer files so you can begin creating and organizing documents for the upcoming Oceania tours.

OBJECTIVES

Understand folders and files

Create and save a file

Explore the files and folders on your computer

Change file and folder views

Open, edit, and save files

Copy files

Move and rename files

Search for files, folders, and programs

Delete and restore files

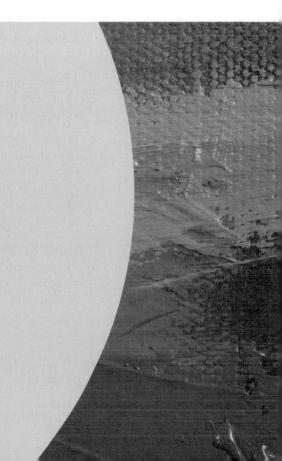

Understanding Folders and Files

As you work with your computer programs, you create and save files, such as letters, drawings, or budgets. When you save files, you usually save them inside folders, which are storage areas on your computer. You use folders to group related files, as with paper folders in a file cabinet. The files and folders on your computer are organized in a **file hierarchy**, a system that arranges files and folders in different levels, like the branches of a tree. Figure B-1 shows a sample file hierarchy. ⬛⬛ Evelyn asks you to look at some important facts about files and folders to help you store your Oceania tour files.

DETAILS

Use the following guidelines as you organize files using your computer's file hierarchy:

- **Use folders and subfolders to organize files**

  As you work with your computer, you can add folders to your hierarchy and rename them to help you organize your work. You should give folders unique names that help you easily identify them. You can also create **subfolders**, which are folders that are inside of other folders. Windows comes with several existing folders, such as My Documents, My Music, and My Pictures, that you can use as a starting point.

QUICK TIP

You can also start Windows Explorer by clicking the Windows Explorer button on the taskbar.

- **View files in windows**

  You view your computer contents by opening a **window**, like the one in Figure B-2. A window is divided into sections. The **Navigation pane** on the left side of the window shows the folder structure on your computer. When you click a folder in the Navigation pane, you see its contents in the **File list** on the right side. The **Details pane** at the bottom of the window provides information about selected files in the File list. A window actually opens in an accessory program called **Windows Explorer**, although the program name does not appear on the window. You can open this program from the Start menu, or just double-click a folder to open its window and view its contents.

- **Understand file addresses**

  A window also contains an **Address bar**, an area just below the title bar that shows the location, or address, of the files that appear in the File list. An **address** is a sequence of folder names separated by the ▶ symbol that describes a file's location in the file hierarchy. An address shows the folder with the highest hierarchy level on the left and steps through each hierarchy level toward the right, sometimes called a **path**. For example, the My Documents folder might contain a subfolder named Notes. In this case, the Address bar would show My Documents ▶ Notes. Each location between the ▶ symbols represents a level in the file hierarchy.

QUICK TIP

Remember that you single-click a folder or subfolder in the Address bar to show its contents. But in the File list, you double-click a subfolder to open it.

- **Navigate upward and downward using the Address bar and File list**

  You can use the Address bar and the File list to move up or down in the hierarchy one or more levels at a time. To **navigate upward** in your computer's hierarchy, you can click a folder or subfolder name in the Address bar. For example, in Figure B-2, you would move up in the hierarchy by clicking once on Users in the Address bar. Then the File list would show the subfolders and files inside the Users folder. To **navigate downward** in the hierarchy, double-click a subfolder in the File list. The path in the Address bar then shows the path to that subfolder.

- **Navigate upward and downward using the Navigation pane**

  You can also use the Navigation pane to navigate among folders. Move the mouse pointer over the Navigation pane, then click the small triangles or to the left of a folder name to show ▷ or hide ◢ the folder's contents under the folder name. Subfolders appear indented under the folders that contain them, showing that they are inside that folder. Figure B-2 shows a folder named Users in the Navigation pane. The subfolders Katharine, Public, and Your User Name are inside the Users folder.

Understanding File Management

FIGURE B-1: Sample folder and file hierarchy

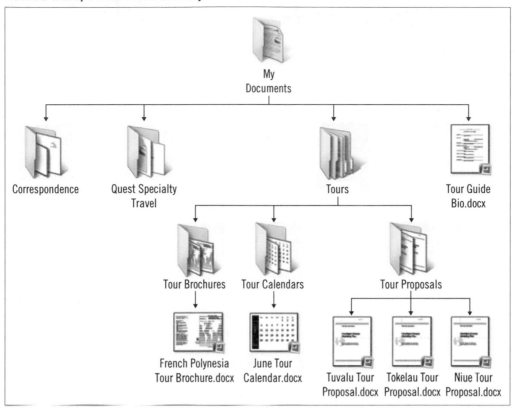

FIGURE B-2: Windows Explorer window

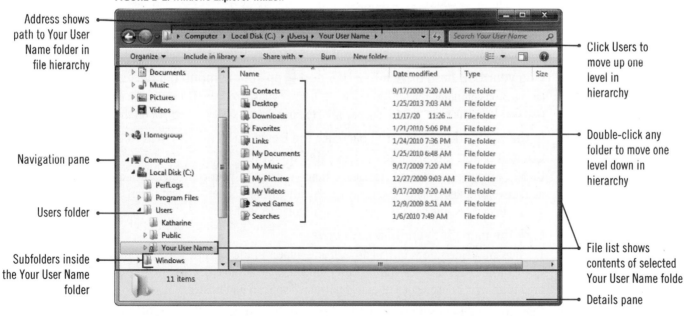

Address shows path to Your User Name folder in file hierarchy

Navigation pane

Users folder

Subfolders inside the Your User Name folder

Click Users to move up one level in hierarchy

Double-click any folder to move one level down in hierarchy

File list shows contents of selected Your User Name folde

Details pane

Plan your file organization

As you manage your files, you should plan how you want to organize them. First, identify the types of files you work with, such as images, music, and reports. Think about the content, such as personal, business, clients, or projects. Then think of a folder organization that will help you find them later. For example, use subfolders in the My Pictures folder to separate family photos from business photos or to group them by year. In the My Documents folder, you might group personal files in one subfolder and business files in another subfolder. Then create additional subfolders to further separate sets of files. You can always move files among folders and rename folders. You should periodically reevaluate your folder structure to make sure that it continues to meet your needs.

Understanding File Management

Creating and Saving a File

After you start a program and create a new file, the file exists only in your computer's **random access memory (RAM)**, which is a temporary storage location. RAM only contains information when your computer is on. When you turn off your computer, it automatically clears the contents of RAM. So you need to save a new file onto a storage device that permanently stores the file so that you can open, change, and use it later. One important storage device is your computer's hard disk built into your computer. Another popular option is a **USB flash drive**, a small, portable storage device. ░░░░░ Evelyn asks you to use the WordPad accessory program to create a short summary of an Oceania tour planning meeting and save it.

STEPS

1. **Start Windows if necessary, click the** Start button 🔵 **on the taskbar, point to** All Programs, **click** Accessories, **then click** WordPad

   The WordPad program opens. Near the top of the screen you see the Ribbon containing command buttons, similar to those you used in Paint in Unit A. The Home tab appears in front. A new, blank document appears in the document window. The blinking insertion point shows you where the next character you type will appear.

2. **Type** Meeting Notes, October 11, **then press [Enter]**

   WordPad inserts a new blank line and places the insertion point at the beginning of the next line.

TROUBLE
If you make a typing mistake, press [Backspace] to delete the character to the left of the insertion point.

3. **Type** The 2013 tour will visit:, **press [Enter], type** Australia, **press [Enter], type** Micronesia, **press [Enter], type** New Zealand, **press [Enter], then type your name; see Figure B-3**

4. **Click the** WordPad button 🔳 **on the upper-left side of the window below the title bar, then click** Save **on the WordPad menu**

   The first time you save a file using the Save button, the Save As dialog box opens. Use this dialog box to name the document file and choose a storage location for it. The Save As dialog box has many of the same elements as a Windows Explorer window, including an Address bar, a Navigation pane, and a File list. Below the Address bar, the **toolbar** contains command buttons you can click to perform actions. In the Address bar, you can see that WordPad chose the Documents library (which includes the My Documents folder) as the storage location.

TROUBLE
If you don't have a USB flash drive, save the document in the My Documents folder instead.

5. **Plug your USB flash drive into a USB port 🔲 on your computer, if necessary**

   On a laptop computer, the USB port is on the left or right side of your computer. On a desktop computer, the USB port is on the front panel (you may need to open a small door to see it), or on the back panel.

6. **In the Navigation pane scroll bar, click the** Down scroll arrow 🔽 **as needed to see** Computer **and any storage devices listed under it**

   Under Computer, you see the storage locations available on your computer, such as Local Disk (C:) (your hard drive) and Removable Disk (H:) (your USB drive name and letter might differ). These storage locations act like folders because you can open them and store files in them.

TROUBLE
If your Save As dialog box or title bar does not show the .rtf file extension, open any Windows Explorer window, click Organize in the toolbar, click Folder and search options, click the View tab, then under Files and Folders, click to remove the check mark from Hide extensions for known file types.

7. **Click the name for your USB flash drive**

   The files and folders on your USB drive, if any, appear in the File list. The Address bar shows the location where the file will be saved, which is now Computer > Removable Disk (H:) (or the name of your drive). You need to give your document a meaningful name so you can find it later.

8. **Click in the** Filename text box **to select the default name Document, type** Oceania Meeting, **compare your screen to Figure B-4, then click** Save

   The document is saved as a file on your USB flash drive. The filename Oceania Meeting.rtf appears in the title bar at the top of the window. The ".rtf" at the end of the filename is the file extension. A **file extension** is a three- or four-letter sequence, preceded by a period, that identifies the file as a particular type of document, in this case Rich Text Format, to your computer. The WordPad program creates files using the RTF format. Windows adds the .rtf file extension automatically after you click Save.

9. **Click the** Close button 🔳 **on the WordPad window**

   The WordPad program closes. Your meeting minutes are now saved on your USB flash drive.

FIGURE B-3: Saving a document

WordPad button

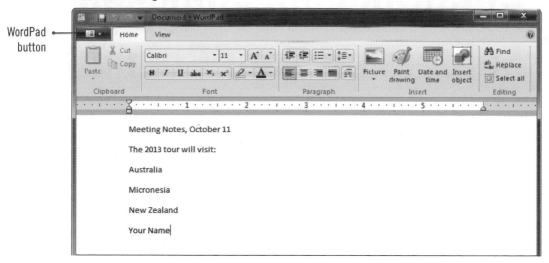

Meeting Notes, October 11

The 2013 tour will visit:

Australia

Micronesia

New Zealand

Your Name

FIGURE B-4: Save As dialog box

After you click Save, your Oceania Meeting.rtf file will be saved at this address

Toolbar

Folders on USB flash drive (your folders will differ)

Storage devices on your computer (yours will differ)

New filename

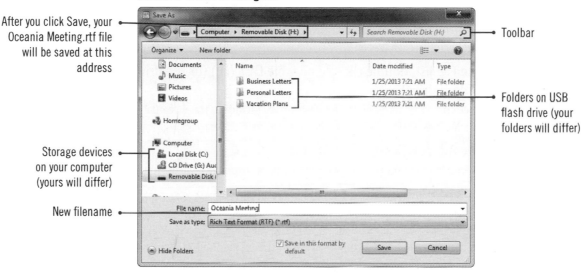

Using Windows 7 libraries

The Navigation pane contains not only files and folders, but also Libraries. A **library** gathers files and folders from different locations on your computer and displays them in one location. For example, you might have pictures in several different folders on your storage devices. You can add these folder locations to your Pictures library. Then when you want to see all your pictures, you open your Pictures library, instead of several different folders. The picture files stay in their original locations, but their names appear in the Pictures library. A library is not a folder that stores files, but rather a way of viewing similar types of documents that you have stored in multiple locations on your computer. Figure B-5 shows the four libraries that come with Windows 7: Documents, Music, Pictures, and Videos. To help you distinguish between library locations and actual folder locations, library names differ from actual folder names. For example, the My Documents folder is on your hard drive, but the library name is Documents. To add a location to a library, click the blue locations link (at the top of the File list) in the library you want to add to, click the Add button, navigate to the folder location you want to add,

then click Include folder. If you delete a file or folder from a library, you delete them from their source locations. If you delete a library, you do not delete the files in it. The Documents Library that comes with Windows already has the My Documents folder listed as a save location. So if you save a document to the Documents library, it is automatically saved to your My Documents folder.

FIGURE B-5: Libraries

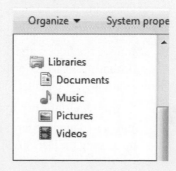

Exploring the Files and Folders on Your Computer

In the last lesson, you navigated to your USB flash drive as you worked in the Save As dialog box. But even if you're not saving a document, you will want to examine your computer and its existing folder and file structure. That way, you'll know where to save files as you work with Windows application programs. In a Windows Explorer window, you can navigate through your computer contents using the File list, the Address bar, and the Navigation pane. ░░░░ As you prepare for the Oceania tours, you look at the files and folders on your computer.

STEPS

TROUBLE
If you don't see the colored bar, click the More Options list arrow ▤▾ on the menu bar, then click Tiles.

1. **Click the Start button ⊕ on the taskbar, then click Computer**

   Your computer's storage devices appear in a window, as shown in Figure B-6, including hard drives; devices with removable storage, such as CD and DVD drives or USB flash drives; and portable devices such as personal digital assistants (PDAs). Table B-1 lists examples of different drive types. A colored bar shows you how much space has been taken up on your hard drive. You decide to move down a level in your computer's hierarchy and see what is on your USB flash drive.

TROUBLE
If you do not have a USB flash drive, click the Documents library in the Navigation pane instead.

2. **In the File list, double-click Removable Disk (H:) (or the drive name and letter for your USB flash drive)**

   You see the contents of your USB flash drive, including the Oceania Meeting.rtf file you saved in the last lesson. You decide to navigate one level up in the file hierarchy.

3. **In the Address bar, click Computer**

   You return to the Computer window showing your storage devices. You decide to look at the contents of your hard drive.

4. **In the Navigation pane, click Local Disk (C:)**

   The contents of your hard drive appear in the File list. The Users folder contains a subfolder for each user who has a user account on this computer. Recall that you double-click items in the File list to open them. In the Address bar and in the Navigation pane, you only need to single-click.

5. **In the File list, double-click the Users folder**

   You see folders for each user registered on your computer. You might see a folder with your user account name on it. Each user's folder contains that person's documents. User folder names are the log-in names that were entered when your computer was set up. When a user logs in, the computer allows that user access to the folder with the same user name. If you are using a computer with more than one user, you might not have permission to view other users' folders. There is also a Public folder that any user can open.

QUICK TIP
Click the Back button, to the left of the Address bar, to return to the window you last viewed. In the Address bar, click ▶ to the right of a folder name to see a list of the subfolders. If the folder is open, its name appears in bold.

6. **Double-click the folder with your user name on it**

   Depending on how your computer is set up, this folder might be labeled with your name; however, if you are using a computer in a lab or a public location, your folder might be called Student or Computer User or something similar. You see a list of folders, such as My Documents, My Music, and others. See Figure B-7.

7. **Double-click My Documents**

   You see the folders and documents you can open and work with. In the Address bar, the path to the My Documents folder is Computer ▶ Local Disk (C:) ▶ Users ▶ Your User Name ▶ My Documents. You decide to return to the Computer window.

8. **In the Navigation pane, click Computer**

   You moved up three levels in your hierarchy. You can also move one level up at a time in your file hierarchy by pressing the [Backspace] key on your keyboard. You once again see your computer's storage devices.

FIGURE B-6: Computer window showing storage devices

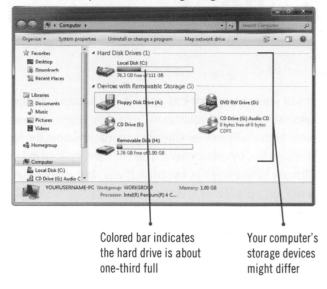

Colored bar indicates the hard drive is about one-third full

Your computer's storage devices might differ

FIGURE B-7: Your User Name folder

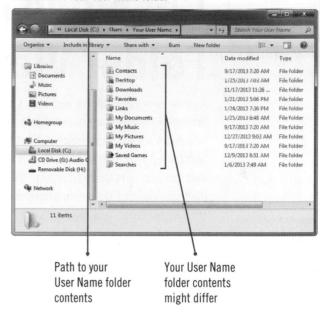

Path to your User Name folder contents

Your User Name folder contents might differ

TABLE B-1: Drive names and icons

drive type	drive icon	drive name
hard drive		C:
CD drive		Next available drive letter, such as D:
DVD drive		Next available drive letter, such as E:
USB flash drive		Next available drive letter, such as F, G:, or H:

Sharing information with homegroups and libraries

Windows 7 lets you create a **homegroup**, a named set of computers that can share information. If your computer is in a homegroup with other Windows 7 computers, you can share libraries and printers with those computers. Click Start, then click Control Panel. Under Network and Internet, click Choose homegroup and sharing options. Click to place a check mark next to the libraries and printers you want to share, then click Save changes. To share libraries that you have created on your computer with others in your homegroup, click Start, click your user name, then in the Navigation pane, click the library you want to share, click Share with on the toolbar, then click the sharing option you want, as shown in Figure B-8.

FIGURE B-8: Sharing a library

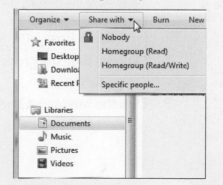

Understanding File Management

Changing File and Folder Views

As you view your folders and files, you might want to see as many items as possible in a window. At other times, you might want to see details about each item. Windows 7 lets you choose from eight different **views**, which are appearance choices for your folder contents. Each view provides different information about the files and folders in different ways. You can list your folders and files by using several different-sized icons or in lists. You can also **sort** them to change the order in which the folders and files are listed. If you want to see what a file looks like, but don't want to open the file, you can see a preview of it in the window. As you plan the Oceania tour, you review picture files in various views.

STEPS

1. **In the Navigation pane, under Libraries, click** Pictures, **then in the File list, double-click the** Sample Pictures folder

   You opened the Sample Pictures folder, which is inside your Pictures library.

2. **In the toolbar, click the** More options list arrow **next to the Change your view icon** 🖼 ▾

   The list of available views appears in a shortcut menu. See Figure B-9.

QUICK TIP

You can also click the Change your view button (not its list arrow) repeatedly to cycle through five of the eight views.

3. **Click** Large Icons

   In this view, the pictures appear as large-sized icons in the File list, as shown in Figure B-10. For image files, this view is very helpful. You can click any view name or you can drag a slider control to move through each of the available views.

4. **Click the** Change your view More options list arrow 🖼 ▾ **again, point to the slider** 🔳, **then drag it so it's next to** Details

   As you drag, Live Preview shows you how each view looks in your folder. In Details view, you can see filenames, the date that files were created or modified, and other information. In Details view, you can also control the order in which the folders and files appear. In the Name column heading, you see a small triangle

   | Name ᵃ |. This indicates that the sample pictures are in alphabetical order (A, B, C,...).

QUICK TIP

Click a column heading a second time to reverse the order.

5. **Click the** Name column heading

   The items now appear in descending (Z, Y, X,...) order. The icon in the column header changes to

   | Name ˅ |.

6. **Click the** Show the preview pane button ▯ **in the toolbar**

   The Preview pane opens on the right side of the screen. The **Preview pane** is an area on the right side of a window that shows you what a selected file looks like without opening it. It is especially useful for document files so you can see the first few paragraphs of a large document.

QUICK TIP

The Navigation pane also contains Favorites, which are links to folders you use frequently. To add a folder to your Favorites list, open the folder in the File list. Right-click the Favorites link in the Navigation pane, then left-click Add current location to Favorites.

7. **Click the name of your USB flash drive in the Navigation pane, then click the** Oceania Meeting.rtf **filename in the File list**

   A preview of the Oceania Meeting file you created earlier in this unit appears in the Preview pane. The Word-Pad file is not open, but you can still see its contents. The Details pane gives you information about the selected file. See Figure B-11.

8. **Click the** Hide the preview pane button ▯

   The Preview pane closes.

9. **Click the window's** Close button ✕

FIGURE B-9: More options shortcut menu showing views

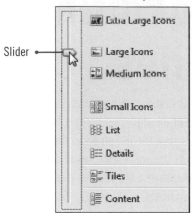

Slider

Extra Large Icons
Large Icons
Medium Icons
Small Icons
List
Details
Tiles
Content

FIGURE B-10: Sample pictures library as large icons

Your pictures might differ

FIGURE B-11: Preview of selected Oceania Meeting.rtf file

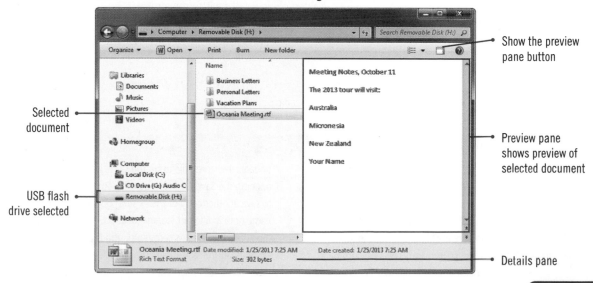

Show the preview pane button

Selected document

USB flash drive selected

Preview pane shows preview of selected document

Details pane

Understanding File Management

Opening, Editing, and Saving Files

Once you have created a file and saved it with a name in a folder on a storage device, you can easily open it and **edit** (make changes to) it. For example, you might want to add or delete text to a document, or change the color in a drawing. Then you save the file again so that it contains your latest changes. Usually you save a file with the same filename and in the same location as the original, which replaces the existing file with the latest, updated version. When you save a file you have changed, you use the Save command. ▨▨▨ Evelyn asks you to complete the meeting notes.

STEPS

1. **Click the Start button ⊕ on the taskbar, point to All Programs, click the Accessories folder, then click WordPad**

   If you use WordPad frequently, it's name might appear on the left side of the Start menu. If it does, you can click it there to open it.

2. **Click the WordPad button 📄▾, then click Open**

   The Open dialog box opens. It has the same sections as the Save As dialog box and the Windows Explorer windows you used earlier in this unit. You decide to navigate to the location where you saved your Oceania Meeting.rtf file so you can open it.

> **TROUBLE**
> If you are not using a USB flash drive, click an appropriate storage location in the Navigation pane.

3. **Scroll down in the Navigation pane if necessary until you see Computer, then click Removable Disk (H:) (or the drive name and letter for your USB flash drive)**

   The contents of your USB flash drive appear in the File list, as shown in Figure B-12.

> **QUICK TIP**
> You can also double-click the filename in the File list to open the file.

4. **Click Oceania Meeting.rtf in the File list, then click Open**

   The document you created earlier opens.

5. **Click to the right of the "d" in New Zealand, press [Enter], then type Evelyn Swazey closed the meeting.**

   The edited document includes the text you just typed. See Figure B-13.

> **QUICK TIP**
> Instead of using the WordPad menu and Save command to save a document, you can also click the Save button. 💾 in the Quick Access toolbar at the top of the WordPad window.

6. **Click the WordPad button 📄▾, then click Save, as shown in Figure B-14**

   WordPad saves the document with your most recent changes, using the filename and location you specified when you saved it for the first time. When you save an existing file, the Save As dialog box does not open.

7. **Click 📄▾, then click Exit**

Comparing Save and Save As

The WordPad menu has two save command options—Save and Save As. When you first save a file, the Save As dialog box opens (whether you choose Save or Save As). Here you can select the drive and folder where you want to save the file and enter its filename. If you edit a previously saved file, you can save the file to the same location with the same filename using the Save command. The Save command updates the stored file using the same location and filename without opening the Save As dialog box. In some situations, you might want to save another copy of the existing document using a different filename or in a different storage location. To do this, open the document, use the Save As command, and then navigate to a different location, and/or edit the name of the file.

FIGURE B-12: Navigating in the Open dialog box

The folders on your drive will differ

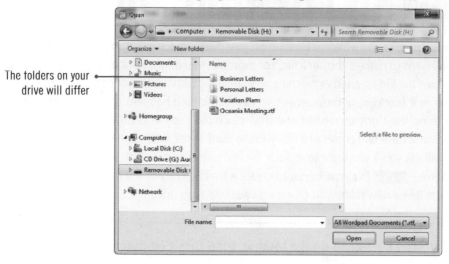

FIGURE B-13: Edited document

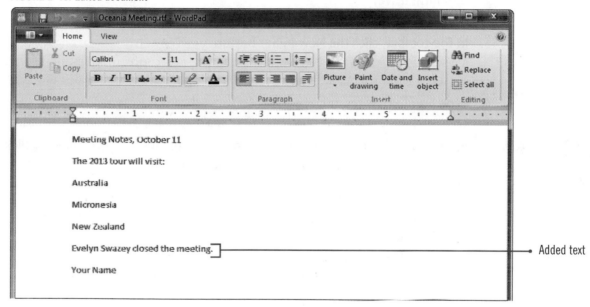

Meeting Notes, October 11

The 2013 tour will visit:

Australia

Micronesia

New Zealand

Evelyn Swazey closed the meeting.

Your Name

Added text

FIGURE B-14: Saving a revised document

Copying Files

As you have learned, saving a file in a location on your hard drive stores it so you can open it later. But sometimes you will want to make a copy of a file. For example, you might want to put a copy on a USB flash drive so you can open the file on another machine or share a file with a friend or colleague. Or you might want to create a copy as a **backup**, or replacement, in case something happens to your original file. You copy files and folders using the Copy command and then place the copy in another location using the Paste command. You cannot have two copies of a file with the same name in the same folder. If you attempt to do this, Windows 7 will ask you if you want to replace the first one then gives you a chance to give the second copy a different name. ▓▓▓▓ Evelyn asks you to create a backup copy of the meeting notes document you created and paste it in a new folder you create on your USB flash drive.

STEPS

1. **Click the Start button ⊛ on the taskbar, then click Computer**

2. **In the File list, double-click Removable Disk (H:) (or the drive name and letter for your USB flash drive)**

   First you create the new folder Evelyn needs.

3. **In the toolbar, click the New folder button**

   A new folder appears in the File list, with its name, New folder, selected. Because the folder name is selected, any text you type replaces the selected text as the folder name.

4. **Type Meeting Notes, then press [Enter]**

   You named the new folder Meeting Notes. Next, you copy your original Oceania Meeting.rtf file.

> **QUICK TIP**
>
> You can also copy a file by right-clicking the file in the File list and then clicking Copy. To use the keyboard, press and hold [Ctrl] and press [C], then release both keys.

5. **In the File list, click the Oceania Meeting.rtf document you saved earlier, click the Organize button on the toolbar, then click Copy, as shown in Figure B-15**

   When you use the Copy command, Windows 7 places a duplicate copy of the file in an area of your computer's random access memory called the **clipboard**, ready to paste, or place, in a new location. Copying and pasting a file leaves the file in its original location. The copied file remains on the clipboard until you copy something else or end your Windows 7 session.

6. **In the File list, double-click the Meeting Notes folder**

   The folder opens.

> **QUICK TIP**
>
> To paste using the keyboard, press and hold [Ctrl] and press [V], then release both keys.

7. **Click the Organize button on the toolbar, then click Paste**

   A copy of your Oceania Meeting.rtf file is pasted into your new Meeting Notes folder. See Figure B-16. You now have two copies of the Oceania Meeting.rtf file: one on your USB flash drive in the main folder, and a copy of the file in a folder called Meeting Notes on your USB flash drive. The file remains on the clipboard so you can paste it again to other locations if you like.

Understanding File Management

FIGURE B-15: Copying a file

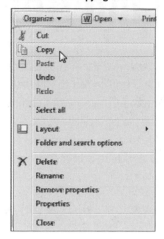

FIGURE B-16: Duplicate file pasted into Meeting Notes folder

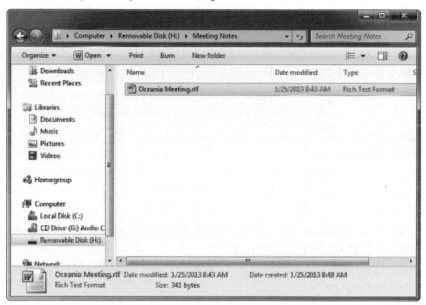

Copying files using Send to

You can also copy and paste a file to an external storage device using the Send to command. In a window, right-click the file you want to copy, point to Send to, then in the shortcut menu, click the name of the device where you want to send a copy of the file. This leaves the original file on your hard drive and creates a copy on the external device, all with just one command. See Table B-2 for a short summary of other shortcut menu commands.

TABLE B-2: Selected Send to menu commands

menu option	use to	menu option	use to
Compressed (zipped) folder	Create a new compressed (smaller) file with a .zip file extension	Documents	Copy the file to the Documents library
Desktop (create shortcut)	Create a shortcut (link) for the file on the desktop	DVD RW Drive (D:)	Copy the file to your computer's DVD drive
Mail recipient	Create an e-mail with the file attached to it (only if you have an e-mail program on your computer)	Removable Disk (H:)	Copy the file to your removable disk (H:)

Moving and Renaming Files

As you work with files, you might need to move files or folders to another location. You can move one or more files or folders. You might move them to a different folder on the same drive or a different drive. When you **move** a file, the file is transferred to the new location and no longer exists in its original location. You can move a file using the Cut and Paste commands. After you create a file, you might find that the original name you gave the file isn't clear anymore, so you can rename it to make it more descriptive or accurate. ▰▰▰ You decide to move your original Oceania Meeting.rtf document to your Documents library. After you move it, you decide to edit the filename so it better describes the file contents.

STEPS

QUICK TIP

You can also cut a file by right-clicking the file in the File list and then clicking Cut. To use the keyboard, press and hold [Ctrl] and press [X], then release both keys.

QUICK TIP

You can also paste a file by right-clicking an empty area in the File list and then clicking Paste. To use the keyboard, press and hold [Ctrl] and press [V], then release both keys.

1. **In the Address bar, click Removable Disk (H:) (or the drive name and letter for your USB flash drive)**

2. **Click the Oceania Meeting.rtf document to select it**

3. **Click the Organize button on the toolbar, then click Cut**

   The icon representing the cut file becomes lighter in color, indicating you have cut it, as shown in Figure B-17. You navigate to your Documents library, in preparation for pasting the cut document there.

4. **In the Navigation Pane, under Libraries, click Documents**

5. **Click the Organize button on the toolbar, then click Paste**

   The Oceania Meeting.rtf document appears in your Documents library. See Figure B-18. The filename could be clearer, to help you remember that it contains notes from your meeting.

6. **With the Oceania Meeting.rtf file selected, click the Organize button on the toolbar, then click Rename**

   The filename is highlighted. In a window, the file extension cannot change because it identifies the file to WordPad. If you delete the file extension, the file cannot be opened. You could type a new name to replace the old one, but you decide to add the word "Notes" to the end of the filename instead.

7. **Click the I after the "g" in "Meeting", press [Spacebar], then type Notes, as shown in Figure B-19, then press [Enter]**

   You changed the name of the document copy in the Documents library. The filename now reads Oceania Meeting Notes.rtf.

8. **Close the window**

FIGURE B-17: Cutting a file

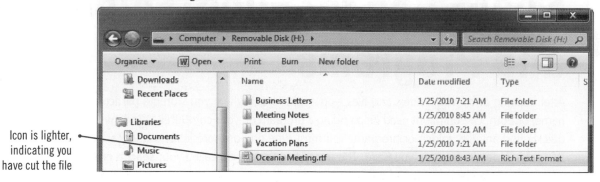

Icon is lighter, indicating you have cut the file

FIGURE B-18: Pasted file in Documents library

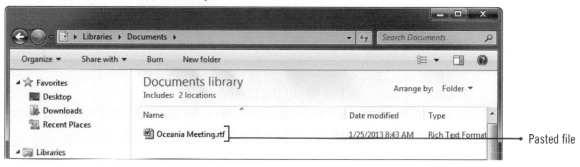

Pasted file

FIGURE B-19: Renaming a file

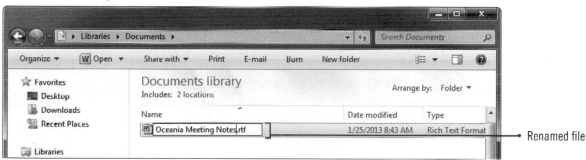

Renamed file

Using drag and drop to copy or move files to new locations

You can also use the mouse to copy a file and place the copy in a new location. **Drag and drop** is a technique in which you use your pointing device to drag a file or folder into a different folder and then drop it, or let go of the mouse button, to place it in that folder. Using drag and drop does not copy your file to the clipboard. If you drag and drop a file to a folder on another drive, Windows *copies* the file. See Figure B-20. However, if you drag and drop a file to a folder on the same drive, Windows 7 *moves* the file into that folder instead. If you want to move a file to another drive, hold down [Shift] while you drag and drop. If you want to copy a file to another folder on the same drive, hold down [Ctrl] while you drag and drop.

FIGURE B-20: Copying a file using drag and drop

Understanding File Management

Searching for Files, Folders, and Programs

After copying or moving folders and files, you might forget where you stored a particular folder or file, its name, or both. Or you might need help finding a program on your computer. **Windows Search** helps you quickly find any file, folder, or program. You must type one or more letter sequences or words that help Windows 7 identify the item you want. The search text you type is called your **search criteria**. Your search criteria can be a filename, part of a filename, or any other characters you choose. Windows 7 will find files with that information in its name or with that information inside the file. For example, if you type "word," Windows 7 will find the program Microsoft Word, any documents with "word" in its title, or any document with "word" inside the file. To search your entire computer, including its attached drives, you can use the Search box on the Start menu. To search within a particular folder, you can use the Search box in a Windows Explorer window. ▰▰▰▰ You want to locate the copy of the Oceania Meeting Notes.rtf document so you can print it for a colleague.

STEPS

1. **Click the Start button ⊕ on the taskbar**

   The Search programs and files box at the bottom of the Start menu already contains the insertion point, ready for you to type search criteria. You begin your search by typing a part of a word that is in the filename.

2. **Type me**

   Even before you finish typing the word "meeting", the Start menu lists all programs, files, and Control Panel items that have the letters "me" in their title or somewhere inside the file or the file properties. See Figure B-21. Your search results will differ, depending on the programs and files on your computer. **File properties** are details that Windows stores about a file. Windows arranges the search results into categories.

QUICK TIP

Search text is not case sensitive. Typing lowercase "mee", you will still find items that start with "Mee" or "mee".

3. **Type e**

   The search results narrow to only the files that contain "mee". The search results become more specific every time you add more text to your criteria finding the two versions of your meeting notes file. See Figure B-22.

4. **Point to the Oceania Meeting.rtf filename under Files**

   The ScreenTip shows the file location. This Oceania Meeting.rtf file is on the USB flash drive. The filenames are links to the document. You only need to single-click a file to open it.

TROUBLE

Your file might open in another program on your computer that reads RTF files. You can continue with the lesson.

5. **Under Documents, click Oceania Meeting Notes.rtf**

   The file opens in WordPad.

6. **Click the Close button ⊠ in the program window's title bar**

   You can search in a folder or on a drive using the search box in any Windows Explorer window.

TROUBLE

If you do not have a USB flash drive, click another storage location in the Navigation pane.

7. **Click ⊕, click Computer, in the Navigation pane click Removable Disk (H:) (or the drive name and letter for your USB flash drive)**

8. **Click the Search Removable Disk (H:) text box, to the right of the Address bar**

9. **Type mee to list all files and folders on your USB flash drive that contain "mee"**

   The search criterion, mee, is highlighted in the filenames. The results include the folder called Meeting Notes and the file named Oceania Meeting.rtf. Because you navigated to your USB flash drive, Windows only lists the document version that is on that drive. See Figure B-23.

10. **Double-click Oceania Meeting.rtf in the File list to open the document file in WordPad, view the file, close WordPad, then close the Windows Explorer window**

FIGURE B-21: Searching on criterion "me"

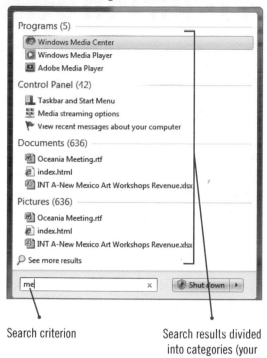

Search criterion

Search results divided
into categories (your
search results will differ)

FIGURE B-22: Searching on criterion "mee"

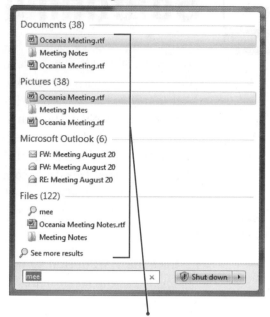

Search results narrow down
to fewer documents (your
search results will differ)

FIGURE B-23: Searching using the Search Computer text box in folder window

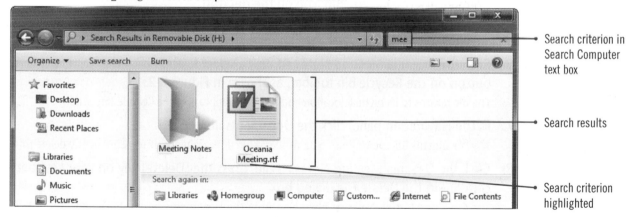

Search criterion in
Search Computer
text box

Search results

Search criterion
highlighted

Performing more advanced searches

To locate all files that have the same file extension (such as .rtf), type the file extension as your search criterion. If you want to locate files created by a certain person, use the first name, last name, or first and last name as your search criteria. If you want to locate files created on a certain date, type the date (for example, 7/9/2012) as your search criterion. If you remember the title in a document, type the title as your search criterion. If you have created e-mail contacts in your Contacts folder, you can type the person's name to find his or her e-mail address.

Deleting and Restoring Files

If you no longer need a folder or file, you can delete (or remove) it from the storage device. By regularly deleting files and folders you no longer need and emptying the Recycle Bin, you free up valuable storage space on your computer. This also keeps your computer uncluttered. Windows 7 places folders and files you delete from your hard drive in the Recycle Bin. If you delete a folder, Windows 7 removes the folder as well as all files and subfolders stored in it. If you later discover that you need a deleted file or folder, you can restore it to its original location, but only if you have not yet emptied the Recycle Bin. Emptying the Recycle Bin permanently removes the deleted folders and files from your computer. However, files and folders you delete from a removable drive, such as a USB flash drive, do not go to the Recycle Bin. They are immediately and permanently deleted and cannot be restored. ▇▇▇▇ You delete the meeting notes copy saved in the Documents library and then restore it.

STEPS

1. **Click the Start button ☻ on the taskbar, then click Documents**

   Your Documents library opens.

2. **Click Oceania Meeting Notes.rtf to select it, click the Organize button on the toolbar, then click Delete**

   The Delete File dialog box opens so you can confirm the deletion, as shown in Figure B-24.

3. **Click Yes**

   You deleted the file from the Documents library. Windows moved it into the Recycle Bin.

> **QUICK TIP**
> If the Recycle Bin icon does not contain crumpled paper, then it is empty.

4. **Click the Minimize button ▭ on the window's title bar and examine the Recycle Bin icon**

   The Recycle Bin icon appears to contain crumpled paper. This tells you that the Recycle Bin contains deleted folders and files.

5. **Double-click the Recycle Bin icon on the desktop**

   The Recycle Bin window opens and displays any previously deleted folders and files, including the Oceania Meeting Notes.rtf file.

> **QUICK TIP**
> To delete a file completely in one action, click the file to select it, press and hold [Shift], then press [Delete]. A message will ask if you want to permanently delete the file. If you click Yes, Windows deletes the file without sending it to the Recycle Bin. Use caution, however, because you cannot restore the file.

6. **Click the Oceania Meeting Notes.rtf file to select it, then click the Restore this item button on the Recycle Bin toolbar, as shown in Figure B-25**

   The file returns to its original location and no longer appears in the Recycle Bin window.

7. **In the Navigation pane, click the Documents library**

   The Documents library window contains the restored file. You decide to permanently delete this file.

8. **Click the Oceania Meeting Notes.rtf file, press the [Delete] key on your keyboard, then click Yes in the Delete File dialog box**

   The Oceania Meeting Notes.rtf file moves from the Documents library to the Recycle Bin. You decide to permanently delete all documents in the Recycle Bin.

   NOTE: If you are using a computer that belongs to someone else, or that is in a computer lab, make sure you have permission to empty the Recycle Bin before proceeding with the next step.

9. **Minimize the window, double-click the Recycle Bin, click the Empty the Recycle Bin button on the toolbar, click Yes in the dialog box, then close all open windows**

FIGURE B-24: Delete File dialog box

FIGURE B-25: Restoring a file from the Recycle Bin

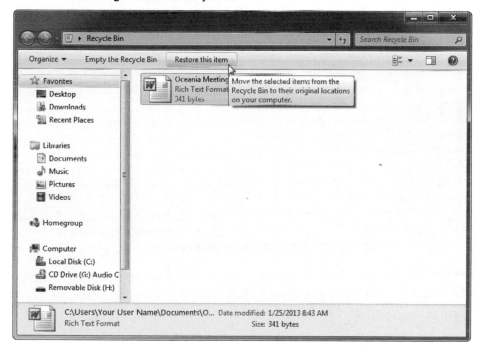

Selecting more than one file

You might want to select a group of files or folders in order to cut, copy, or delete them all at once. To select a group of items that are next to each other in a window, click the first item in the group, press and hold [Shift], then click the last item in the group. Both items you click and all the items between them become selected. To select files that are not next to each other, click the first file, press and hold [Ctrl], then click the other items you want to select as a group. Then you can copy, cut, or delete the group of files or folders you selected.

Practice

Concepts Review

For current SAM information, including versions and content details, visit SAM Central (http://www.cengage.com/samcentral). If you have a SAM user profile, you may have access to hands-on instruction, practice, and assessment of the skills covered in this unit. Since various versions of SAM are supported throughout the life of this text, check with your instructor for the correct instructions and URL/Web site for accessing assignments.

Label the elements of the Windows 7 window shown in Figure B-26.

FIGURE B-26

Match each term with the statement that best describes it.

8. File management
9. File extension
10. Address bar
11. Path
12. Library
13. Toolbar
14. File hierarchy

a. Shows file's path
b. Structure of files and folders organized in different levels
c. Describes a file's location in the file hierarchy
d. Skills that help you organize your files and folders
e. Contains buttons in a Windows Explorer window
f. A three- or four-letter sequence, preceded by a period, that identifies the type of file
g. Gathers files and folders from different computer locations

Select the best answer from the list of choices.

15. **The way your files appear in the Details window is determined by the:**
    a. Path.
    b. View.
    c. Subfolder.
    d. Criterion.

16. **When you move a file:**
    a. It remains in its original location.
    b. It is no longer in its original location.
    c. It is copied to another location.
    d. It is no longer in your file hierarchy.

17. **The text you type in the Search programs and files box on the Start menu is called:**
    a. Search criteria.
    b. RAM.
    c. Sorting.
    d. Clipboard.

18. **Which of the following is not a window section?**

   a. Address bar

   b. File list

   c. Navigation pane

   d. Clipboard

19. **Which part of a window lets you see a file's contents without opening the file?**

   a. File list

   b. Preview pane

   c. Navigation pane

   d. Address bar

20. **In a file hierarchy, a folder inside another folder is called a:**

   a. Subfolder.

   b. Internal hard disk.

   c. Clipboard.

   d. Path.

21. **After you delete a file from your hard disk, it is automatically placed in the:**

   a. USB flash drive.

   b. Clipboard.

   c. Recycle bin.

   d. Search box.

22. **When you copy a file, it is automatically placed on the:**

   a. Preview pane.

   b. My Documents folder.

   c. Hierarchy.

   d. Clipboard.

Skills Review

1. **Understand folders and files.**

   a. Assume that you sell books as a home business. How would you organize your folders and files using a file hierarchy? How would you use folders and subfolders? Draw a diagram and write a short paragraph explaining your answer.

2. **Create and save a file.**

   a. Connect your USB flash drive to a USB port on your computer, then open WordPad from the All Programs menu.

   b. Type **Marketing Plan: Oceania Tours** as the title, then start a new line.

   c. Type your name, then press [Enter] twice.

   d. Create the following list:

   Brochures

   Direct e-mail

   Web ads

   Travel conventions

   e. Save the WordPad file with the filename **Oceania Marketing Plan.rtf** on your USB flash drive.

   f. View the filename in the WordPad title bar, then close WordPad.

3. **Explore the files and folders on your computer.**

   a. Open a Windows Explorer window that shows the contents of your computer.

   b. Use the File list to navigate to your USB flash drive. (If you do not have a USB flash drive, navigate to your Documents library using the Navigation pane.)

   c. Use the Address bar to navigate to Computer again.

   d. Use the Navigation pane to navigate to your hard drive.

   e. Use the File list to open the Users folder, and then open the folder that represents your user name.

   f. Open the My Documents folder. (*Hint*: The path is Local Disk (C:) ▸ Users ▸ [Your User Name] ▸ My Documents.)

   g. Use the Navigation pane to navigate back to your computer contents.

4. **Change file and folder views.**

   a. Navigate to your USB flash drive using the method of your choice.

   b. View its contents as large icons.

   c. Use the View slider to view the drive contents in all the other seven views.

   d. Use the Change your view button to cycle through the five available views.

   e. Open the Preview pane, then click a file and view its preview. Repeat with two more files.

   f. Close the Preview pane.

Skills Review (continued)

5. Open, edit, and save files.

   a. Open WordPad.

   b. Use the Open dialog box to open the Oceania Marketing Plan.rtf document you created.

   c. After the text "Travel conventions," add a line with the text **Canadian magazines**.

   d. Save the document and close WordPad.

6. Copy files.

   a. In the Windows Explorer window, navigate to your USB flash drive if necessary.

   b. Copy the Oceania Marketing Plan.rtf document.

   c. Create a new folder named **Marketing** on your USB flash drive, then open the folder. (If you don't have a USB flash drive, create the folder in your Documents library.)

   d. Paste the document copy in the new folder.

7. Move and rename files.

   a. Navigate to your USB flash drive.

   b. Select the original Oceania Marketing Plan.rtf document, then cut it.

   c. Navigate to your Documents library and paste the file there.

   d. Rename the file **Oceania Marketing Plan - Backup.rtf**.

8. Search for files, folders, and programs.

   a. Use the Search programs and files box on the Start menu to enter the search criterion **ma**.

   b. Change your search criterion so it reads **mar**.

   c. Open the backup copy of your Oceania Marketing Plan document from the Start menu, then close WordPad.

   d. In Windows Explorer, navigate to your Documents library, then use the criterion **mar** in the Search Documents box.

   e. Open the backup copy of the Oceania Marketing Plan document from the File list, then close WordPad.

9. Delete and restore files.

   a. Navigate to your Documents library if necessary.

   b. Delete the Oceania Marketing Plan - Backup.rtf file.

   c. Open the Recycle Bin, and restore the document to its original location, navigate to your Documents library, then move the Oceania Marketing Plan - Backup file to your USB flash drive.

Independent Challenge 1

To meet the needs of pet owners in your town, you have opened a pet-sitting business named PetCare. Customers hire you to care for their pets in their own homes when the pet owners go on vacation. To promote your new business, you want to develop a newspaper ad and a flyer.

   a. Connect your USB flash drive to your computer, if necessary.

   b. Create a new folder named **PetCare** on your USB flash drive.

   c. In the PetCare folder, create two subfolders named **Advertising** and **Flyers**.

   d. Use WordPad to create a short ad for your local newspaper that describes your business:

     • Use the name of the business as the title for your document.

     • Write a short paragraph about the business. Include a fictitious location, street address, and phone number.

     • After the paragraph, type your name.

   e. Save the WordPad document with the filename **Newspaper Ad** in the Advertising folder, then close the document and exit WordPad.

   f. Open a Windows Explorer window, and navigate to the Advertising folder.

   g. View the contents in at least three different views, then choose the view option that you prefer.

   h. Copy the Newspaper Ad.rtf file, and paste a copy in the Flyers folder.

   i. Rename the copy **Newspaper Ad Backup.rtf**.

   j. Close the folder.

Independent Challenge 2

As a freelance editor for several national publishers, you depend on your computer to meet critical deadlines. Whenever you encounter a computer problem, you contact a computer consultant who helps you resolve the problem. This consultant asked you to document, or keep records of, your computer's current settings.

a. Connect your USB flash drive to your computer, if necessary.
b. Open the Computer window so that you can view information on your drives and other installed hardware.
c. View the window contents using three different views, then choose the one you prefer.
d. Open WordPad and create a document with the title **My Hardware Documentation** and your name on separate lines.
e. List the names of the hard drive (or drives), devices with removable storage, and any other hardware devices, installed on the computer you are using. Also include the total size and amount of free space on your hard drive(s) and removable storage drive(s). (*Hint*: If you need to check the Computer window for this information, use the taskbar button for the Computer window to view your drives, then use the WordPad taskbar button to return to WordPad.)

Advanced Challenge Exercise

■ Navigate your computer's file hierarchy, and determine its various levels.
■ On paper, draw a diagram showing your file hierarchy, starting with Computer at the top, and going down at least four levels if available.

f. Save the WordPad document with the filename **My Hardware Documentation** on your USB flash drive.
g. Preview your document, print your WordPad document, then close WordPad.

Independent Challenge 3

You are an attorney at Lopez, Rickland, and Willgor, a large law firm. You participate in your firm's community outreach program by speaking at career days in area high schools. You teach students about career opportunities available in the field of law. You want to create a folder structure on your USB flash drive to store the files for each session.

a. Connect your USB flash drive to your computer, then open the window for your USB flash drive.
b. Create a folder named **Career Days**.
c. In the Career Days folder, create a subfolder named **Mather High**.

Advanced Challenge Exercise

■ In the Mather High folder, create subfolders named **Class Outline** and **Visual Aids**.
■ Rename the Visual Aids folder **Class Handouts**.
■ Create a new folder named **Interactive Presentations** in the Class Handouts subfolder.

d. Close the Mather High window.
e. Use WordPad to create a document with the title **Career Areas** and your name on separate lines, and the following list of items:
Current Opportunities:
Attorney
Corrections Officer
Forensic Scientist
Paralegal
Judge
f. Save the WordPad document with the filename **Careers Listing.rtf** in the Mather High folder. (*Hint:* After you switch to your USB flash drive in the Save As dialog box, open the Career Days folder, then open the Mather High folder before saving the file.)
g. Close WordPad.

Independent Challenge 3 (continued)

h. Open WordPad and the Careers Listing document again, then add **Court Reporter** to the bottom of the list, then save the file and close WordPad.

i. Using pencil and paper, draw a diagram of your new folder structure.

j. Use the Start menu to search your computer using the search criterion **car**. Locate the Careers Listing.rtf document in the list, and use the link to open the file.

k. Close the file.

Real Life Independent Challenge

Think of a hobby or volunteer activity that you do now, or one that you would like to do. You will use your computer to help you manage your plans or ideas for this activity.

a. Using paper and a pencil, sketch a folder structure using at least two subfolders that you could create on your USB flash drive to contain your documents for this activity.

b. Connect your USB flash drive to your computer, then open the window for your USB flash drive.

c. Create the folder structure for your activity, using your sketch as a reference.

d. Think of at least three tasks that you can do to further your work in your chosen activity.

e. Open WordPad and create a document with the title **Next Steps** at the top of the page and your name on the next line.

f. List the three tasks, then save the file in one of the folders you created on your USB flash drive, using the title **To Do.rtf**.

g. Close WordPad, then open a Windows Explorer window for the folder where you stored the document.

h. Create a copy of the file, give the copy a new name, then place a copy of the document in your Documents library.

i. Delete the document copy from your Documents library.

j. Open the Recycle Bin window, and restore the document to the Documents library.

Visual Workshop

You are a technical support specialist at Emergency Services. The company supplies medical staff members to hospital emergency rooms in Los Angeles. You need to respond to your company's employee questions quickly and thoroughly. You decide that it is time to evaluate and reorganize the folder structure on your computer. That way, you'll be able to respond more quickly to staff requests. Create the folder structure shown in Figure B-27 on your USB flash drive. As you work, use WordPad to prepare a simple outline of the steps you follow to create the folder structure. Add your name to the document, and store it in an appropriate location.

FIGURE B-27

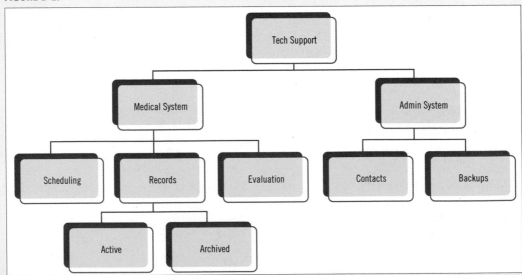

Understanding File Management

Getting Started with Microsoft Office 2010

Microsoft Office 2010, often referred to as Office, is a collection (or **suite**) of programs that you can use to produce a wide variety of documents, including letters, budgets, mailing lists, presentations, Web pages, and reports that combine data, text, graphics, and more. Microsoft Office 2010 Professional includes Word, Excel, Access, PowerPoint, Outlook, Publisher, and OneNote. One of the biggest new benefits of Microsoft Office 2010 is that it lets you work collaboratively with others, whether they are in your office or on the other side of the world. You have just joined the marketing team at Outdoor Designs, a company that sells outdoor recreational products. You need to familiarize yourself with Microsoft Office 2010 and create a simple to do list for your first week on the job.

OBJECTIVES

Understand Office 2010 Professional

Start an Office program

Use the Ribbon and Zoom controls

Use the Quick Access toolbar

Save a file using Backstage view

Get Help

Exit an Office program

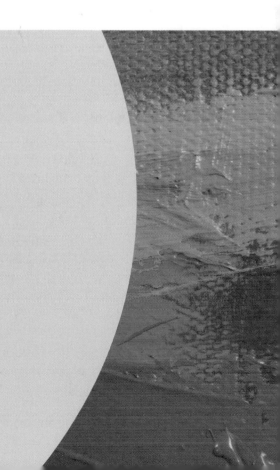

Understanding Office 2010 Professional

Microsoft Office 2010 Professional Edition comes with a variety of **programs** and tools you can use to create documents, analyze data, and complete almost any business task. In this book, you will learn how to use Word, Excel, Access, and PowerPoint. One of the most powerful new benefits of Microsoft Office 2010 is **Microsoft Office Web Apps**, which is a set of scaled-down versions of Microsoft Office applications that run over the Internet. Using Microsoft Office Web Apps, you and your colleagues can work collaboratively on a single document even if you are in different locations, as long as your computer is connected to the Internet. ▓▓▓▓ Karen Rivera, marketing director at Outdoor Designs, suggests that you familiarize yourself with the programs in Office 2010 Professional.

DETAILS

Microsoft Office 2010 Professional contains the following programs:

- **Microsoft Word** is a **word-processing program** you can use to create text documents, such as letters, memos, newsletters, and reports. You can also use Word to add pictures, drawings, tables, and other graphical elements to your documents. At Outdoor Designs, you will use Word to create memos, letters, flyers, and reports to communicate with staff, customers, and distributors. Figure C-1 shows an Outdoor Designs' quarterly report created using Word.

- **Microsoft Excel** is a **spreadsheet program** you can use to manipulate, analyze, and chart quantitative data. Excel is often used to calculate financial information. In your work at Outdoor Designs, you will use Excel to create sales results worksheets, invoices, sales reports, and charts like the one shown in Figure C-2, which presents quarterly sales results.

- **Microsoft Access** is a **database management program** you can use to store, organize, and keep track of information, such as customer names and addresses, product inventories, and employee information. At Outdoor Designs, you will use Access to create customer and product databases, data entry forms that others can use to input additional data, and reports that staff can use to spot important trends in the data. Figure C-3 shows a form used to input data about Outdoor Designs' distributors.

- **Microsoft PowerPoint** is a **presentation graphics program** you can use to develop materials for presentations, including slide shows, computer-based presentations, speaker's notes, and audience handouts. The staff at Outdoor Designs is preparing for the spring selling season, so you will use PowerPoint to create a presentation for the sales reps that describes the new spring products. Figure C-4 shows one of the slides from this presentation.

In addition to the four programs you learn about in this book, Microsoft Office Professional also includes the following programs:

- **Microsoft Outlook** is an e-mail and information manager used to send and receive e-mail; schedule appointments; maintain to do lists; and store names, addresses, and other contact information.

- **Microsoft Publisher** is a **desktop publishing program** used to create printed documents that combine text and graphics, such as newsletters, brochures, letterheads, and business cards.

- **Microsoft OneNote** is a software program you can use to capture and store information, such as Web site addresses, graphics, notes written by you or others, or text pulled from a report. Think of it as an electronic three-ring binder, where you can gather information pulled from various places and keep it neatly organized.

FIGURE C-1: Report created in Microsoft Word

OUTDOOR
DESIGNS

Winter 2013   Quarterly Report and The Road Ahead

This quarterly report to shareholders presents a summary of
profitability and revenue results for the quarter ending December
31, 2012. This report also summarizes the status and progress of
key business initiatives designed to fuel further growth in products
and services for the next twenty-four months. The road ahead
promises continued growth and profitability.

FIGURE C-2: Worksheet and chart created in Microsoft Excel

OUTDOOR DESIGNS
Quarterly Sales by Region

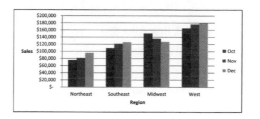

	Oct	Nov	Dec	Total
Northeast	$ 75,209	$ 80,967	$ 95,376	$ 251,552
Southeast	$ 108,789	$ 120,987	$ 125,698	$ 355,474
Midwest	$ 150,119	$ 135,333	$ 126,543	$ 411,995
West	$ 164,567	$ 176,009	$ 178,998	$ 519,574
Total	$ 498,684	$ 513,296	$ 526,615	$ 1,538,595

FIGURE C-3: Database form created in Microsoft Access

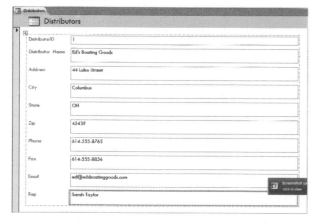

FIGURE C-4: Presentation slide created in Microsoft PowerPoint

Spring
Products

OUTDOOR DESIGNS
Karen Rivera
Marketing Director

Starting an Office Program

To get started using Microsoft Office, you need to start, or **launch**, the Office program you want to use. There are several ways you can start an Office program, including the Start menu on the taskbar. You decide to familiarize yourself with Office by starting Microsoft Word and getting acquainted with the user interface. A **user interface** is the collection of buttons and tools you use to interact with a software program.

1. **Click the Start button 🎯 on the taskbar**

   The Start menu opens.

2. **Click All Programs, then click Microsoft Office**

   Your screen should look similar to Figure C-5.

3. **Click Microsoft Word 2010**

   Microsoft Word starts and the Word program window opens, displaying a blank document on the screen. (Your screen might look a little different, depending on your settings.) Refer to Figure C-6 to identify the elements of the program window described below:

   - The **title bar** is at the top of the program window. It contains the name of the document (currently the temporary name Document1) and the name of the program (currently Microsoft Word).

   - The **Ribbon** is the band directly below the title bar. It contains commands in the form of buttons, icons, lists, galleries, and text boxes. A **command** is an instruction you give to a computer to complete a task, such as printing a document, inserting a picture, or saving your changes.

   - Across the top of the Ribbon are several **tabs**, each of which contains a different set of commands for completing a particular type of task. At the moment, the **Home tab** is active, so it appears in front of the other tabs. The Home tab contains commands for performing the most frequently used commands for creating a document. Clicking a different tab displays a different group of commands related to performing a different type of task. For instance, clicking the **Page Layout tab** displays commands to help you lay out and format paragraphs in a document.

   - Unlike other tabs that help you work with the content in a document, the **File tab** contains commands and tools that let you work with the whole document. For instance, you use the File tab to open, save, print, and close documents. The File tab is present in all Office programs.

   - Each tab is organized into **groups** of related commands, such as the Clipboard group, the Font group, and the Paragraph group. You can see these group names at the bottom of each tab. To the right of many groups is a small arrow called a **dialog box launcher**, or **launcher**. Clicking a launcher opens a dialog box—a pane where you can enter additional information to complete a task.

   - On the left end of the title bar is the **Quick Access toolbar**, containing buttons for saving a file, undoing an action, and redoing an action. The Quick Access toolbar is easy to customize with commands of your choice, and is always available no matter what tab is active, making it easy to access favorite commands whenever you need them. The Quick Access toolbar is available in all Office programs.

   - The **document window** is the work area within the Word program window. This is where you type text into your document and format it to look the way you want. The work area looks different in each Office program based on the type of document you are creating. The **insertion point** is a flashing vertical line in the document window that indicates where text will be inserted when you type. The **status bar** at the bottom of the screen displays key information, such as the current page and the number of total words in the document. At the far right of the status bar are the **View buttons**, which you use to change your view of the document. In Word, you can choose among five View buttons. You can use the **Zoom slider**, located to the right of the View buttons, to set the magnification level of your document. If your vision is less than perfect, you can use the Zoom slider to get a close-up view of your document.

FIGURE C-5: Start menu

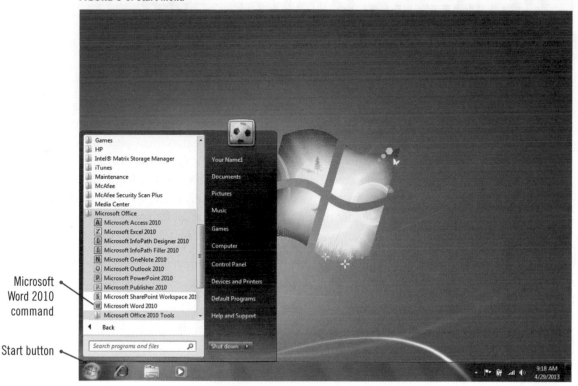

Microsoft
Word 2010
command

Start button

FIGURE C-6: Word program window

Quick Access
toolbar

File tab

Home tab

Launcher

Insertion
point

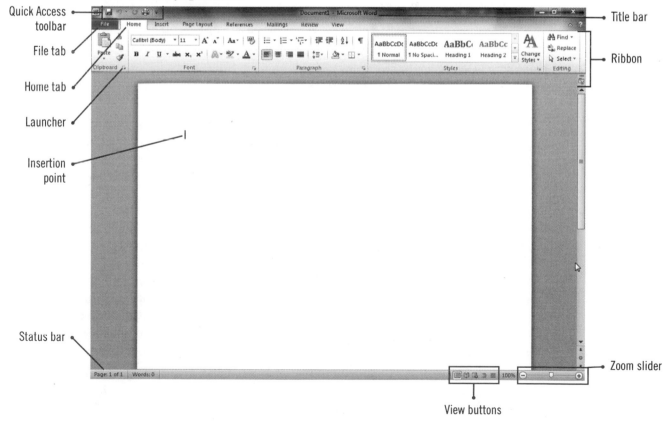

Title bar

Ribbon

Status bar

Zoom slider

View buttons

Using the Ribbon and Zoom Controls

In all Office programs, you use the Ribbon to initiate commands. Some commands on the Ribbon are the same across all Office programs, while others vary according to the application. For instance, all Office programs have similar commands on the View tab for changing the document view. You can use the View commands to switch to a different predefined view, such as Draft or Web Layout, or to adjust the magnification level so that your document appears larger or smaller in size. Many Office programs also contain a Zoom slider on the status bar for changing the magnification level and View shortcut buttons for switching among views. ▰▰▰▰▰ You decide to create a simple to do list for your first week on the job, and then practice viewing it in different ways using the buttons on the View tab and the Zoom slider.

TROUBLE

If the insertion point is not at the top of the document window, press [Ctrl][Home].

1. **With the insertion point at the top of the document, type** To Do List, **then press** [Enter]

   The text you typed appears in the first line of the document, and the insertion point moves down.

2. **Type** Order business cards, **press** [Enter], **type** Get photo ID, **press** [Enter], **then type** Sign up for orientation class

3. **Click the** View tab **on the Ribbon**

   The View tab is now active. This tab contains commands for changing your view of the document window, as shown in Figure C-7. Changing your view does not change the document itself; it just lets you see a document differently in order to focus on different stages of the project, such as entering text, formatting, or reading. You are currently working in Print Layout view, which shows you exactly how a document will look when it is printed.

QUICK TIP

You can also switch to Full Screen Reading view by clicking the Full Screen Reading button 🔲 on the status bar.

4. **Click the** Full Screen Reading button 🔲 **in the Document Views group**

   Your to do list now appears in a view better for reading on a computer screen, as shown in Figure C-8. The Ribbon is no longer visible, leaving more room for the document. Buttons along the top left of the screen are for common tasks such as saving and printing, controls in the middle are for navigating through a long document, and buttons on the right are for customizing the options in this view.

5. **Click the** Close button **on the far right end of the title bar**

   Your to do list now appears in the default view—Print Layout—and the View tab on the Ribbon is visible again.

QUICK TIP

You can also click the Minimize the Ribbon 🔼 and Expand the Ribbon buttons 🔽 at the right end of the Ribbon to minimize and maximize the Ribbon.

6. **Double-click the** View tab **on the Ribbon, observe the change, then double-click the** View tab **again**

   Double-clicking any Ribbon tab minimizes the Ribbon so that only the tab names appear, giving you more room on the screen. Double-clicking any tab restores the Ribbon to its full size.

7. **Click the** Zoom button **in the Zoom group**

   The Zoom dialog box opens, as shown in Figure C-9. It contains options for changing the magnification level of the screen. Zooming affects only your view of the content in a file, not the file itself. You can zoom in, to get a closer view of certain content, or zoom out, to get a wider view and see more content at a reduced size. You can click an option button to choose a predefined view, such as 200%, or enter a specific percentage (up to 500%) by typing or clicking the arrows in the Percent field. Options such as Page width and Text width change the magnification automatically to fit your screen. A Preview area helps you decide which option will work best.

QUICK TIP

To increase the magnification level by 10% at a time, click the Zoom In button ⊕ on the Zoom slider; to decrease the magnification level by 10% at a time, click the Zoom Out button ⊖ on the Zoom slider.

8. **Click the** 200% option button, **then click** OK

   Now the text in your to do list appears double its actual size, as shown in Figure C-10. Note that the actual text size in your document has not changed; only the magnification level has.

9. **Drag the** Zoom slider **to the middle of the bar, until the magnification level reads** 100%

   Your list appears again at 100%, the actual size of the document as it would look printed.

FIGURE C-7: Document in Print Layout view with the View tab active

Full Screen
Reading button

Print Layout
button is active

View tab

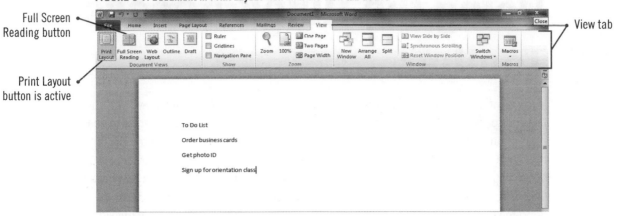

FIGURE C-8: Viewing a document in Full Screen Reading view

Click to save
the document

Click to print
the document

Click to return to
Print Layout view

Click to modify
view options

Navigation tool

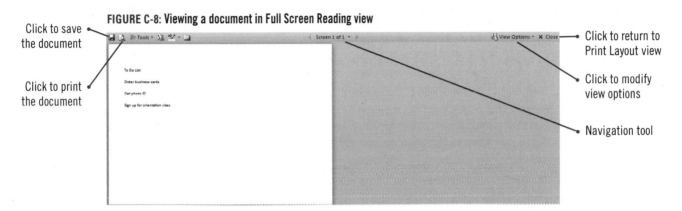

FIGURE C-9: Zoom dialog box

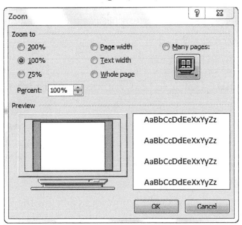

FIGURE C-10: Document with zoom set to 200%

Magnification level

Zoom Out button

Zoom In button

Zoom slider

Using the Quick Access Toolbar

If you want to click a particular button in an Office program to perform a task, you first need to make sure the tab that contains that button is in front. However, the buttons on the Quick Access toolbar, located just above the Ribbon on the left side of the screen, are available anytime, except when the File tab is active. By default, the Quick Access toolbar contains buttons that let you save a file, undo your last action, and redo the last action you undid. These buttons are also available on other tabs in the Ribbon; having them available on the Quick Access toolbar lets you work faster. You can add buttons you frequently use to the Quick Access toolbar using the Customize Quick Access Toolbar menu, or move its location to below the Ribbon. You continue working on your to do list while exploring the buttons on the Quick Access toolbar.

STEPS

1. **Press [Ctrl][End] to place the insertion point at the end of the document if necessary, then press [Enter]**

   The insertion point is now below the third item in your to do list.

2. **Type Read employee manual, then press [Enter]**

   Your list now contains four items, and the insertion point is below the last item.

3. **Click the Undo button on the Quick Access toolbar**

   The last words you typed, "Read employee manual," are deleted, and the insertion point moves back up to the end of the fourth line. The Undo button reverses your last action. You can click the Redo button to restore your document to the state it was in before you clicked the Undo button.

4. **Click the Redo button on the Quick Access toolbar**

   The text "Read employee manual" is now back as the fourth item in your to do list.

5. **Type your name**

   Compare your screen to Figure C-11.

6. **Click the Customize Quick Access Toolbar button on the right side of the Quick Access toolbar**

   A menu opens and displays a list of common commands, as shown in Figure C-12. Notice that Save, Undo, and Redo all have checkmarks next to them, indicating that these commands are already on the Quick Access toolbar.

7. **Click Show Below the Ribbon**

   The Quick Access toolbar moves, and is now located below the Ribbon, as shown in Figure C-13.

8. **Click the Customize Quick Access Toolbar button, then click Show Above the Ribbon**

   The Quick Access toolbar moves back to its default location above the Ribbon.

Customizing the Quick Access toolbar

You can add any button that you use frequently to the Quick Access toolbar. To do this, click the Customize Quick Access Toolbar button, then click More Commands to open the Quick Access Toolbar tab of the Word Options dialog box. Click any command listed in the Popular Commands list, click Add, then click OK. Another way to add a button to the Quick Access toolbar is to right-click the button you want to add on the Ribbon, then click Add to Quick Access Toolbar on the shortcut menu. To remove any button from the Quick Access toolbar, right-click the button, then click Remove from Quick Access Toolbar on the shortcut menu.

Getting Started with Microsoft Office 2010

FIGURE C-11: Completed To Do List

File tab

Undo button

Redo button

Quick Access toolbar

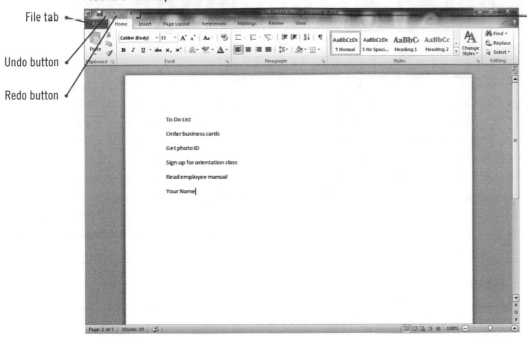

FIGURE C-12: Customize Quick Access Toolbar menu

Checkmarks indicate buttons on the Quick Access toolbar

Click to move Quick Access toolbar below the Ribbon

Customize Quick Access Toolbar button

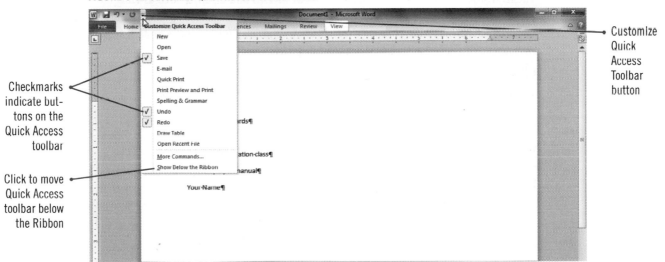

FIGURE C-13: Moving the Quick Access toolbar

Quick Access toolbar is now below the Ribbon

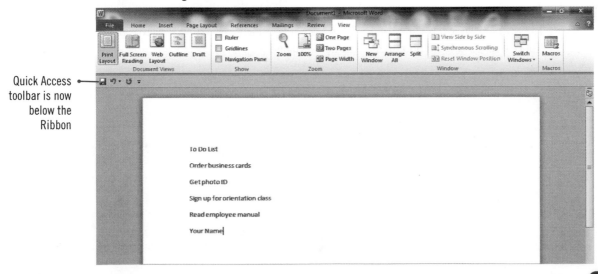

Office 2010

Saving a File Using Backstage view

In order to keep a document permanently so that you can access it later, you must save it to a specific place, such as in a folder on your computer's hard drive, on a removable flash drive, or on a drive located on a network or on the Internet. You also must assign your document a **filename**, which is a unique name for a file, so that you can identify and access it later. You use the Save As command to save a file for the first time. You access the Save As command in **Backstage view**, which provides commands and tools to help you work with your files. In addition to saving files, you can use Backstage view to view and set properties for your document, open and print files, quickly access recent documents, and more. To open Backstage view, you click the File tab on the Ribbon. █████ You have finished your to do list for now, so you decide to save it.

STEPS

1. **Click the File tab on the Ribbon**

   A large window opens and completely hides your document. You are now in Backstage view, which provides commands that let you work with files, as shown in Figure C-14.

2. **Notice the navigation bar on the left side of your screen**

   > **QUICK TIP**
   > Items on the navigation bar that are preceded by icons are commands; items that have no icons are tabs.

   The navigation bar contains commands (such as Save As and Open) as well as tabs that contain other commands. The Info tab is selected. You use the tools on the Info tab to specify various settings for the open document. The Properties pane on the right shows information about the to do list document, including its size, number of pages, author, and last-modified date.

3. **Click Save As on the navigation bar**

   The Save As dialog box opens, showing the list of folders and files in the current folder. The File name text box displays the text "To Do List" because this is the first line of text in the document; Word always suggests a filename based on the first few words in the unsaved open document.

4. **Verify that To Do List.docx appears in the File name text box**

   The ".docx" at the end of the filename is the default file extension for this document. When you save a file, the program automatically assigns it a **file extension** to identify the program that created it. Documents created in Word 2010 have the file extension ".docx". Your computer may not be set to display file extensions, in which case you will not see this information in the File name text box or in the title bar of the program; this is not a problem, as the information is still saved with the file.

5. **Navigate to the drive and folder where you store your Data Files**

   Compare your screen to Figure C-15.

   > **QUICK TIP**
   > If you click the Save command before you save a file for the first time, the Save As dialog box opens, so that you can assign the file a name and folder location.

6. **Click Save**

   The Save As dialog box closes, and your To Do List document is saved in the drive and folder you specified. Notice that the title bar now displays the new filename.

FIGURE C-14: Backstage view with Info tab selected

File tab

Save As command

Info tab

Navigation bar

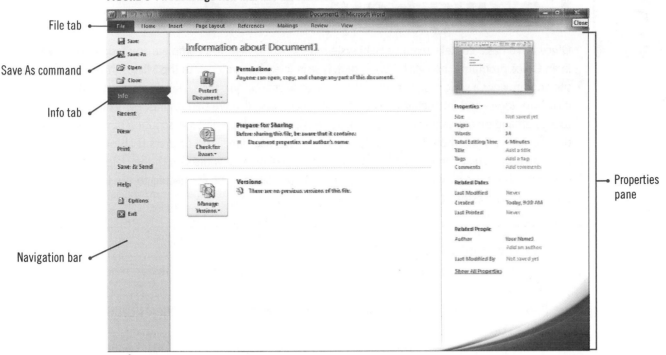

Properties pane

FIGURE C-15: Save As dialog box

The folder where you save your Data Files may differ

File name text box

Save as type list box

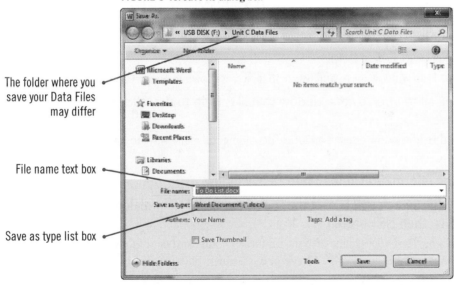

Windows Live and Microsoft Office Web Apps

All Office programs include the capability to incorporate feedback—called online collaboration—across the Internet or a company network. Using cloud computing (work done in a virtual environment), you can take advantage of Web programs called Microsoft Office Web Apps, which are simplified versions of the programs found in the Microsoft Office 2010 suite. Because these programs are online, they take up no computer disk space and are accessed using Windows Live

SkyDrive, a free service from Microsoft. Using Windows Live SkyDrive, you and your colleagues can create and store documents in a "cloud" and make the documents available to whomever you grant access. To use Windows Live SkyDrive, you need a free Windows Live ID, which you obtain at the Windows Live Web site. You can find more information in the Working with Windows Live and Microsoft Office Web Apps appendix.

Getting Help

Office 2010 has a context-sensitive Help system designed to help you complete any task or use any feature in an Office program. The Office Help system is seamlessly integrated with the Microsoft Office Online Web site and provides a wide range of content to help answer your questions. Help is **context-sensitive** in that it displays topics and instructions geared to the specific task you are performing. For example, if you point to a command on any tab on the Ribbon, a ScreenTip opens, displaying a description of what the command does as well as its keyboard shortcut. Many ScreenTips also direct you to press [F1] for more information about that particular command.  You decide to familiarize yourself with the Help system by finding out more about the new features of Word 2010. *Note*: You must be connected to the Internet to perform the steps in this lesson.

STEPS

1. **Click the Insert tab on the Ribbon**

   The Insert tab is now active and displays commands that help you insert shapes, pages, illustrations, and other elements.

   QUICK TIP
   You can also open the Help window in any Office application by clicking the Microsoft Office Help button ? at the right end of the Ribbon or by pressing [F1].

2. **Position the mouse pointer over the Cover Page button in the Pages group until the ScreenTip appears**

   As shown in Figure C-16, the ScreenTip displays the command name (Cover Page) and describes its purpose (Insert a fully formatted cover page). It also displays a graphic of a cover page to give you a visual image of this command.

3. **Click the File tab, then click Help**

   Your screen displays Backstage view with the Help tab open, as shown in Figure C-17. This tab provides links you can use to access support resources for using Microsoft Office. The links below "Support" let you access the Help system, get training, and contact Microsoft.

4. **Click Microsoft Office Help**

   The Word Help window opens and lists help topics, as shown in Figure C-18.

5. **Click see all to open a new window that lists Help topics, click Saving and printing, then click Save a file**

   The Word Help window displays an article describing the many ways to save documents in Word, as shown in Figure C-19.

6. **Read the information in the Word Help window**

7. **Click in the Search text box at the top of the Word Help dialog box, type keyboard shortcuts, then click Search**

   Word searches the Office Online Web site for the keywords "keyboard shortcuts," then lists Help articles from the site that contain those words. A **keyword** is a searchable word that is contained in the Help database.

8. **Click Keyboard shortcuts for Microsoft Word in the results list, read the topic, then click the Close button ⊠ in the Word Help window**

   The Help window closes, but your To Do List document remains open.

Cover Page button

Insert tab

ScreenTip

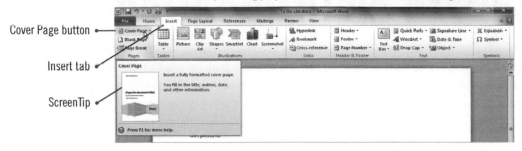

FIGURE C-17: Help tab in Backstage view

Help button

Click to open
Word Help window

Help tab

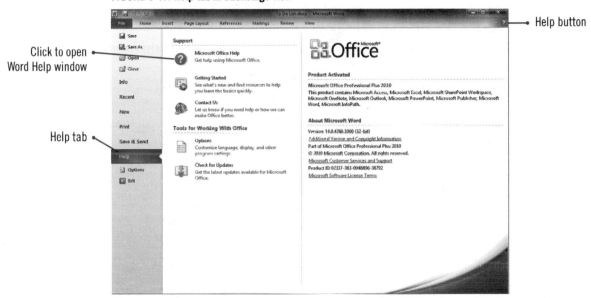

FIGURE C-18: Word Help window

Click to
view
articles on
these topics

Click to
view list of
common
Help topics

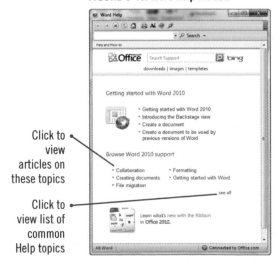

FIGURE C-19: Word Help window displaying an article
about saving documents in Word

Search
text box

Getting Started with Microsoft Office 2010

Exiting an Office Program

When you complete all the work you want to accomplish in an Office program session, you can use Backstage view to close your document. Later, when you want to work on the document again, you can quickly locate it and open it using the Recent tab in Backstage view. The Recent tab, which opens by default in Backstage view when no documents are open, displays a list of the documents you most recently opened. Click a document name to open it. When you are finished working in an Office program, you use the File tab to exit the program. ▨▨▨▨▨ You decide to practice using Backstage view to close a document, open it again using the Recent tab, and then exit Word.

STEPS

1. **Click the Home tab, then click the Save button ▨ on the Quick Access toolbar**

   Clicking the Save button on the Quick Access toolbar is a fast way to save any recent changes you have made to your document. It is a good idea to click the Save button frequently as you work to make sure you do not lose any data if you lose power or your computer crashes.

2. **Click the File tab, then click Close**

   The To Do List document closes but Word remains open. The Home tab is now active. You can quickly locate and open the To Do List document by using Backstage view.

3. **Click the File tab**

   Backstage view opens, and the Recent tab is active, as shown in Figure C-20. The Recent Documents list displays the names of documents opened recently. To Do List.docx is at the top of the list because it was the most recently opened document. You might see other document names listed below To Do List.

4. **Click To Do List.docx below Recent Documents**

   The To Do List document opens. You are now ready to close the document and end your Word session.

5. **Click the File tab, then click Exit**

   Both the To Do List document and the Word program close.

FIGURE C-20: The Recent Documents tab in Backstage view

Click to open
To Do List document

Recent tab

Exit command

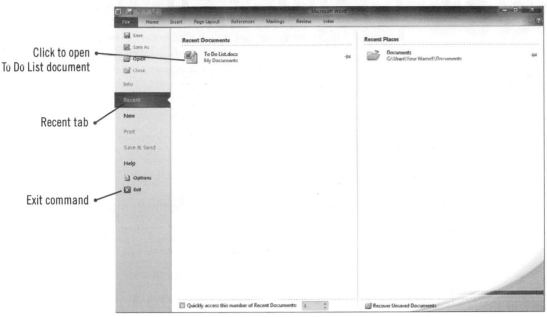

E-mailing your saved documents

As you work through this book, you will create many documents that you will need to submit to your instructor. To conserve paper, your instructor might ask you to submit your completed documents via e-mail rather than print them. You can e-mail your saved documents easily from within Office using the Save & Send page in Backstage view. To do this, click the File tab to open Backstage view, then click Save & Send. On the Save & Send page, click the Send Using E-mail button to attach the document to an e-mail message. If your file is already saved in a shared location, such as on Windows Live or a network drive, you can click the Send a Link button to create an e-mail containing a link to where the recipient can download the document. The Save & Send page also lets you fax a document or e-mail a copy of a document in PDF or XPS formats. These formats preserve the content and formatting in the document, but make the content difficult for others to change or edit.

Practice

Concepts Review

Label each of the elements shown in Figure C-21.

FIGURE C-21

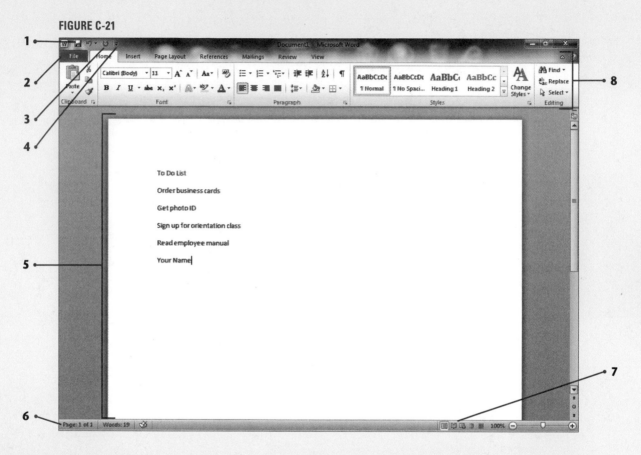

Match each of the following tasks with the most appropriate program for completing it.

9. Create a budget
10. Create a report containing graphics
11. Organize your inventory of products
12. Store contact information and send e-mail
13. Create slides for a company-meeting presentation

a. Microsoft Access
b. Microsoft Excel
c. Microsoft Word
d. Microsoft PowerPoint
e. Microsoft Outlook

Creating a Document

Files You Will Need:

D-1.docx
D-2.docx
D-3.docx
D-4.docx
D-5.docx

You can create professional-looking documents using Microsoft Word 2010. In this unit, you will learn some basic skills to help you create, edit, and print a document. You will also learn how to copy and move text, find and replace text, enhance the appearance of text, check spelling and grammar, and preview a document before printing. Karen Rivera, the marketing director for Outdoor Designs, asks you to finish creating a letter to the winner of the annual Outdoor Designs birdhouse competition. The letter congratulates the winner and provides information on his prizes and benefits. Karen has already created a document that contains part of the letter. You will open Karen's letter; add, edit, and rearrange text in it; proof it for spelling errors; then print it.

OBJECTIVES

Create a new document from an existing file

Enter text in a document

Select and edit text

Copy text

Move text

Find and replace text

Format text using the Mini toolbar

Check spelling and grammar

Preview and print a document

Creating a New Document from an Existing File

Sometimes it is useful to create a new document that uses content from an existing document. For instance, suppose you need to write a memo that will use content from a memo you already wrote. You use the Open dialog box to open the existing memo. Then, before making any changes to the opened memo, you can use the Save As command to save a copy of it with a new name. This keeps the original file intact in case you want to use it again, while saving you the trouble of creating the new memo from scratch. 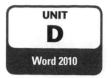 You need to complete Karen's letter to the winner of the birdhouse competition. You need to open Karen's document and save it with a different name, to keep Karen's original letter intact.

STEPS

1. **Click the** Start button **on the taskbar, click** All Programs, **click** Microsoft Office, **then click** Microsoft Word 2010

   The Word program window opens with a new untitled document in the document window.

QUICK TIP

To create a new, blank document, click the File tab, click New to open the New tab of Backstage view, then click Create.

2. **Click the** File tab, **then click** Open

   The Open dialog box opens and displays the folders and files in the current folder.

3. **Navigate to where you store your Data Files**

   See Figure D-1.

4. **Click** D-1.docx, **then click** Open

   Karen's partially completed document opens in the document window.

QUICK TIP

If your computer is not set up for displaying file extensions, then the filenames in the Save As dialog box will not contain the extension .docx.

5. **Click the** File tab, **then click** Save As

   The Save As dialog box opens, as shown in Figure D-2. You use the Save As dialog box to create a copy of the document with a new name. Notice that the name in the File name text box is **selected**, or highlighted because the text is selected, any words you type replace the selected text in the File name text box.

6. **Type** D-Birdhouse Winner Letter

   The File name text box now contains the new title you typed. Because the filename begins with "D-", you will be able to identify it as a file you created for Unit D of this book.

7. **Navigate to where you store your Data Files, then click** Save

   Word saves the D-Birdhouse Winner Letter file in the drive and folder you specified. The title bar changes to reflect the new name, as shown in Figure D-3. The file D-1 closes and remains intact.

Creating a new document from a template

If you need to create a certain type of document, you might want to start from a template. A template is a file that contains predesigned formatting and text for common business documents such as letters, business cards, or reports. To create a document from a template, click the File tab, then click New to open the New page in Backstage view. To use a template that is available on your computer, click Sample templates in the Available Templates section, click the template you want, then click Create. A new document based on the template opens on your screen, ready for you to customize and save. To download a template from the Office.com site, click a template category under Office.com Templates on the New tab, click a template you like, then click download.

FIGURE D-1: Open dialog box

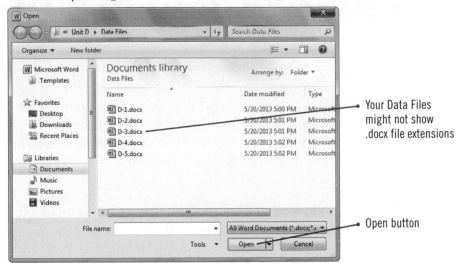

Your Data Files might not show .docx file extensions

Open button

FIGURE D-2: Save As dialog box

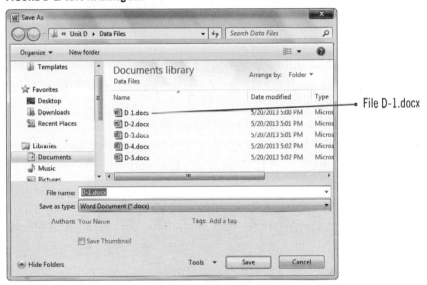

File D-1.docx

FIGURE D-3: Word program window with D-Birdhouse Winner Letter file open

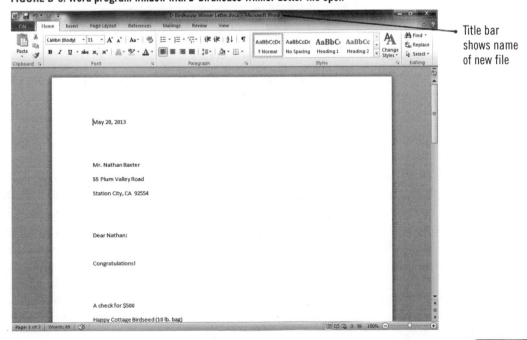

Title bar shows name of new file

Creating a Document

Entering Text in a Document

To add text to a document, you first need to click to position the insertion point where you want to insert text, and then start typing. Typing text is also called **entering** text. Before you start typing, you should check that you are viewing the document in a way that is suitable for entering and editing text. **Draft** view is best for entering and editing text. In Draft view, several of the page elements are hidden so that you can focus on writing and editing. It is also a good idea to turn on formatting marks when you enter text in a document so that you can see blank spaces and paragraph marks. ■■■■ Karen's letter contains some text. You need to add a paragraph informing the recipient that he won the contest.

STEPS

1. **Click the Show/Hide ¶ button ¶ in the Paragraph group on the Home tab**

   Your screen now displays formatting marks. Dots between words represent spaces, and a ¶ (paragraph mark) represents a paragraph return that Word inserts when you press [Enter]. Showing formatting marks when you write and edit makes it easier to see extra spaces, paragraph returns, and other punctuation errors.

2. **Click the Draft button ▤ on the right end of the status bar**

   The document now appears in Draft view, which is a better view for focusing on entering and editing text. Notice that you can see more of the document text in Draft view.

3. **Click to the right of the word Congratulations! in the sixth line of text**

   Clicking in this location sets the **insertion point**, the blinking vertical line on the screen that controls where text will be inserted when you type.

4. **Press ↓ (the down arrow key) two times**

   The insertion point is now next to the second paragraph mark below "Congratulations!"

5. **Type I am pleased to inform you that you won the Outdoor Designs annual birdhouse competition!**

   The insertion point moved to the right as you typed each word.

6. **Press [Spacebar], then type the following text, but do not press [Enter] when you reach the right edge of your screen: Your Chickadee Cottage birdhouse received the highest scores from our judges.**

   At some point, the words you typed moved down, or **wrapped**, to the next line. This is known as **word wrap**, a feature that automatically pushes text to the next line when the insertion point meets the right margin.

7. **Press [Spacebar], type teh, then press [Spacebar]**

   Notice that even though you typed "teh", Word assumed that you meant to type "The" and automatically corrected it. This feature is called **AutoCorrect**.

8. **Type the following text exactly as shown (including errors): follong prizes will be shipped shipped to you separately:**

   You should see red wavy lines under the word "follong" and the second instance of "shipped." These red lines indicate that the spelling checker automatically identified these as either misspelled or duplicate words. Green wavy lines indicate possible grammatical errors.

9. **Press [Enter], then click the Save button ▤ on the Quick Access toolbar**

   Compare your screen to Figure D-4. Pressing [Enter] inserted a blank line and moved the insertion point down two lines to the left margin. Although you pressed [Enter] only once, an extra blank line was inserted because the default style in this document specifies to insert a blank line after you press [Enter] to start a new paragraph. **Styles** are settings that control how text and paragraphs are formatted. Each document has its own set of styles, which you can easily change. You will work with styles in a future unit.

FIGURE D-4: Letter with new text entered

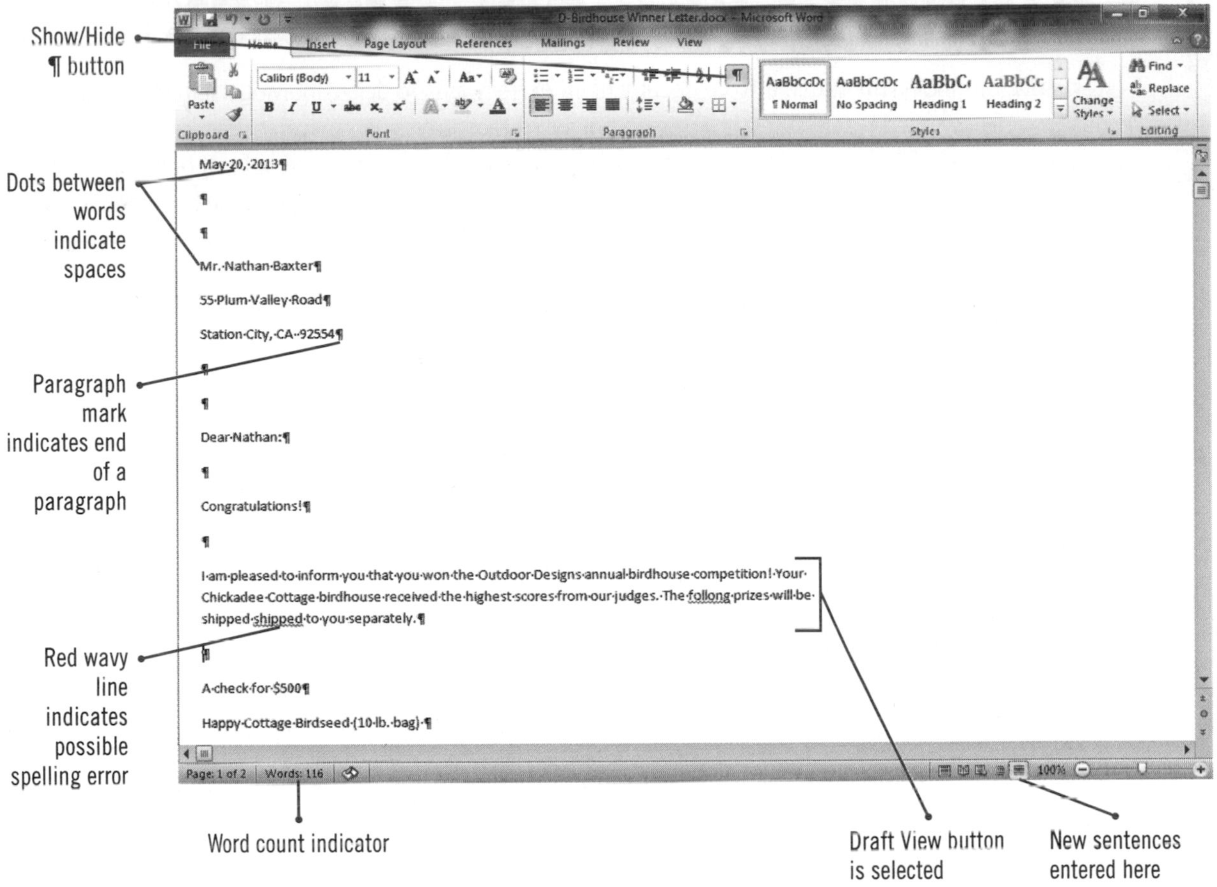
Show/Hide ¶ button
Dots between words indicate spaces
Paragraph mark indicates end of a paragraph
Red wavy line indicates possible spelling error
Word count indicator
Draft View button is selected
New sentences entered here
May 20, 2013
Mr. Nathan Baxter
55 Plum Valley Road
Station City, CA 92554
Dear Nathan:
Congratulations!
I am pleased to inform you that you won the Outdoor Designs annual birdhouse competition! Your Chickadee Cottage birdhouse received the highest scores from our judges. The follong prizes will be shipped shipped to you separately.
A check for $500
Happy Cottage Birdseed (10 lb. bag)
Page: 1 of 2
Words: 116

Using AutoCorrect

The AutoCorrect feature works automatically to catch and correct incorrect spellings of common words as you type them. For example, if you type "comapny" instead of "company," as soon as you press [Spacebar], Word corrects the misspelling. After Word makes the correction, you can point to the word to make a small blue bar appear under the corrected text. If you place the pointer over this bar, the AutoCorrect Options button appears. Click the AutoCorrect Options button to display a list of options, as shown in Figure D-5; then click an option.

You can change AutoCorrect settings in the AutoCorrect dialog box. To open this dialog box, click Control AutoCorrect Options on the AutoCorrect menu, or right-click any word underlined with a red wavy line, point to AutoCorrect, then click AutoCorrect Options. To open this dialog box at any time, click the File tab, click Help, click Options, click Proofing in the Word Options dialog box, then click AutoCorrect Options.

FIGURE D-5: AutoCorrect Options menu

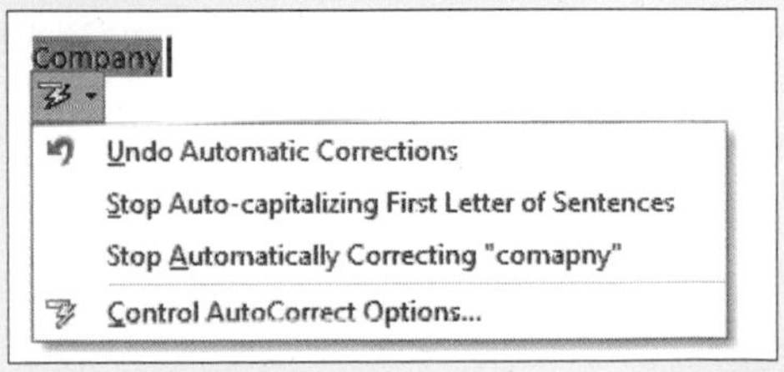
Company
Undo Automatic Corrections
Stop Auto-capitalizing First Letter of Sentences
Stop Automatically Correcting "comapny"
Control AutoCorrect Options...

Selecting and Editing Text

You can **edit**, or modify, the text in a Word document in several ways. To delete individual letters, first click to the right of the unwanted letters to set the insertion point and then press [Backspace], or click to the left of the letters and then press [Delete]. To delete several words or paragraphs, you must first **select**, or highlight, the unwanted text, then press [Delete]. To select text, drag the I-beam mouse pointer across the text, then release the mouse button. To edit text, you need to move the insertion point around the document. You can do this by pointing and clicking or by using the keyboard. Table D-1 describes other useful methods for selecting text. Table D-2 describes keys you can use to move the insertion point around the document. 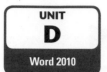 You need to make some changes to the letter to correct errors and improve wording. You also decide to change the spacing of the document to single spaced, so it is properly formatted for a letter.

STEPS

1. **Click to the right of $500 in the line of text below the paragraph you typed**

   The insertion point is just after the second 0 in 500.

2. **Press [Backspace] three times**

   You deleted "500". Each time you pressed [Backspace], you deleted the character to the left of the insertion point.

3. **Type 250**

   The amount of the prize money now reads $250, the correct amount.

4. **Double-click the second instance of shipped in the third line of the new paragraph you typed**

   The word "shipped" is now selected. Double-clicking a word selects the entire word.

5. **Press [Delete]**

   The second instance of the word "shipped" is removed from the document. You could have deleted either instance of the duplicated word to remove the red wavy line and correct the error. The text after the deleted word wraps back to fill the empty space.

6. **Scroll to the end of the document, place the mouse pointer to the left of Karen Rivera (the last line of the document) until the pointer changes to ⚗, then click**

   See Figure D-6. The entire line of text (Karen Rivera) is selected, including the ¶ at the end of the line. The area to the left of the left margin is the **selection bar**, which you use to select entire lines. When you place the mouse pointer in the selection bar, it changes to ⚗.

7. **Type your name**

   Your name replaces Karen's name in the letter. Notice that the line spacing of the letter is double-spaced after each paragraph mark (¶). So that the letter is properly formatted, you want to change the line spacing to be single-spaced. To do this, you first need to select all the text in the document.

8. **Press [Ctrl][A] to select the entire document, then click the No Spacing button in the Styles group**

   The document is now single-spaced.

9. **Press [Ctrl][Home] to move the insertion point to the top of the document and deselect the text, then click 🖫**

   Compare your screen to Figure D-7.

Creating a Document

FIGURE D-6: Selecting an entire line of text

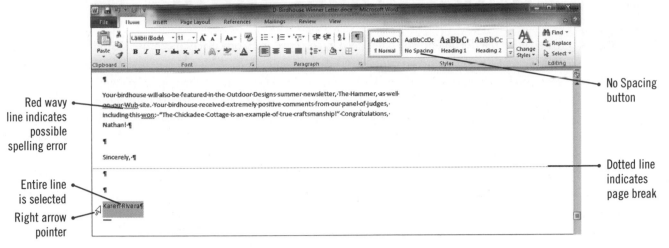

Red wavy line indicates possible spelling error

Entire line is selected

Right arrow pointer

No Spacing button

Dotted line indicates page break

FIGURE D-7: Document after applying No Spacing style

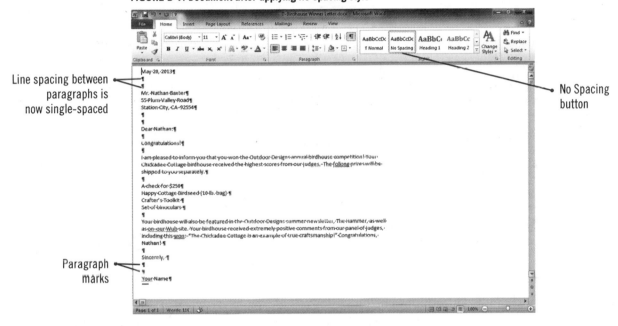

Line spacing between paragraphs is now single-spaced

No Spacing button

Paragraph marks

TABLE D-1: Methods for selecting text

text to select	selection method
One word	Double-click the word
A paragraph	Triple-click in the paragraph
An entire document	Press [Ctrl][A]
A line of text	Position ⌐ to the left of the line, then click

TABLE D-2: Useful keyboard shortcuts for moving the insertion point

keyboard method	moves insertion point
[up arrow][down arrow]	Up or down one line
[left arrow][right arrow]	To the left or right
[Ctrl][right arrow] or [Ctrl][left arrow]	One word to the left or right
[Home] or [End]	To the beginning or end of the line
[Ctrl][Home] or [Ctrl][End]	To the beginning or end of the document

Copying Text

When editing a document, you often need to copy text from one place to another. **Copying** leaves the text in its original location, and **pasting** moves a duplicate of it to the location you specify. To copy and paste text, you first need to select the text you want to copy. Next, you use the Copy command to place a copy of the selected text on the **Windows Clipboard**, a temporary storage area in your computer's memory for copied or cut items. Finally, you use the Paste command to insert the copied text to a new location. If you need to copy multiple items, you can use the **Office Clipboard**, which works like the Windows Clipboard but stores up to 24 items at a time and is available only in Office programs. To use the Office Clipboard, you need to open the Clipboard task pane. You can also duplicate text using a technique called **drag and drop**, in which you select the text you want to copy, press and hold [Ctrl], and then use the mouse to drag a copy of the selected text to a new location. Items you copy using drag and drop do not get placed on the Windows or Office Clipboard.  You decide to make further edits to the letter by copying and pasting text.

STEPS

QUICK TIP
If your Clipboard is not empty, click Clear All on the task pane.

1. **Click the launcher 🔲 in the Clipboard group on the Home tab**

   The Clipboard task pane opens to the left of the document window. You use the Clipboard task pane to gather multiple cut and copied items. The task pane is empty because you have not copied or cut any text.

2. **Click to the left of the first C in Chickadee in the second line of the second paragraph to set the insertion point, press and hold the left mouse button, drag the mouse pointer to the end of the word Cottage and the space after it, then release the mouse button**

   The words "Chickadee Cottage" and the space after it are now selected.

QUICK TIP
To copy selected text using the keyboard, press [Ctrl] [C]; to paste text, press [Ctrl][V].

3. **Click the Copy button 📋 in the Clipboard group**

   The selected text is copied to the Office Clipboard and appears in the Clipboard task pane, as shown in Figure D-8.

QUICK TIP
You can also paste an item by clicking it on the Office Clipboard task pane.

4. **Click to the left of birdhouse in the first line of the last paragraph, then click the Paste button 📋 in the Clipboard group**

   The copied text is pasted into the document and also remains on the Office Clipboard, from which you can paste it as many more times as you like, as shown in Figure D-9. The Paste Options button appears under the pasted text.

5. **Click the Paste Options button 📋 (Ctrl)▾**

   The Paste Options menu opens and displays buttons for applying formatting to the pasted text. By default, the pasted text maintains its original formatting, which in this situation is fine, since it matches the text.

6. **Press [Esc] to close the Paste Options menu**

7. **Select Outdoor Designs in the first line of the second paragraph**

QUICK TIP
Pressing [Delete] or [Backspace] does not place the text on the Clipboard.

8. **Press and hold [Ctrl], drag the selected text to the left of Crafter's Toolkit three lines below the paragraph, release the mouse button, and then release [Ctrl]**

   As you drag, the pointer changes to 📋 and an indicator line shows where the text will be inserted. This instance of "Outdoor Designs" does not get copied to the Clipboard, as shown in Figure D-10.

9. **Click the Save button 🖫 on the Quick Access toolbar**

Creating a Document

FIGURE D-8: Selected text copied to the Office Clipboard

Paste button

Copy button

Clipboard launcher

Clipboard task pane

Selected Chickadee Cottage text copied to Office Clipboard

Selected Chickadee Cottage text

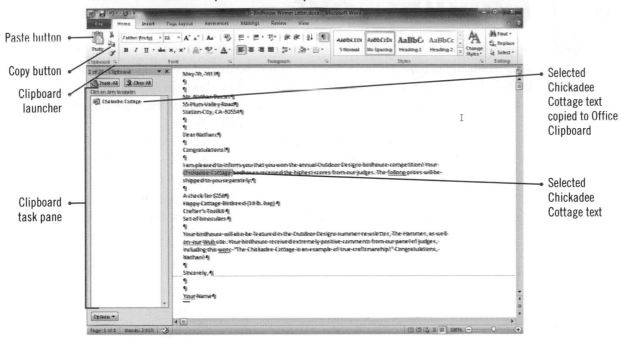

FIGURE D-9: Text pasted from the Office Clipboard

Paste button

Pasted text remains on Office Clipboard and can be pasted again

Pasted text from Office Clipboard

Paste Options button

Your text might wrap differently, depending on your settings

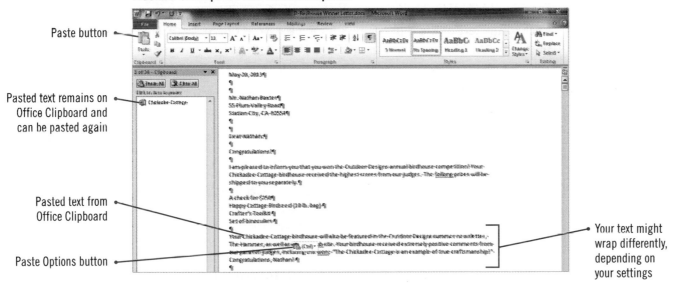

FIGURE D-10: Dragged and copied text

Dragged text is not copied to Office Clipboard

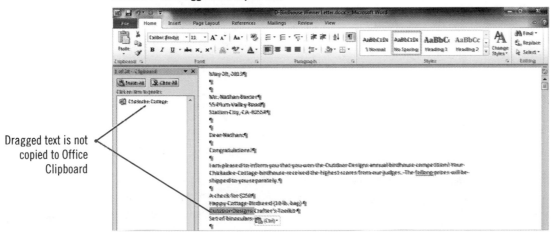

Creating a Document

Moving Text

While editing a document, you may decide that certain text works better in a different location. Perhaps you want to switch the order of two paragraphs, or two words in a sentence. Instead of deleting and retyping the text, you can move it. **Moving** text removes it from its original location and places it in a new location that you specify. You can move text to a new location using the Cut and Paste commands. Using the **Cut** command removes selected text from your document and places it on the Windows Clipboard as well as the Office Clipboard if activated. To place the cut text in another location, you can either click the Paste button on the Home tab of the Ribbon or click the item in the Clipboard task pane. You can also move text by selecting it and then dragging it to a new location. Items that you move using the drag-and-drop method do not get copied to the Windows or Office Clipboard. ■■■ While checking your letter, you decide that you want to rearrange the list of prizes so that they appear in a more logical order.

STEPS

1. **Position the mouse pointer to the left of Outdoor Designs Crafter's Toolkit until it changes to ⬩, then click**

   The entire line, including the paragraph mark, is selected, as shown in Figure D-11.

QUICK TIP
To cut selected text using the keyboard, press [Ctrl][X].

2. **Click the Cut button ✄ in the Clipboard group on the Home tab**

   The text is cut from the document and is now the first item in the Clipboard task pane. The last item you cut or copy becomes the first item in the task pane. If you cut or copy more than 24 items without clearing the task pane, the oldest item is deleted to make room for the new one.

3. **Click to the left of the H in Happy Cottage Birdseed (10 lb. bag), then click the Paste button in the Clipboard group on the Ribbon**

   The text from the Clipboard is pasted to the new location, on the line below "A check for $250".

QUICK TIP
You can copy and move text with the Clipboard task pane closed, but only the last item you cut or copied is available for pasting.

4. **Place the mouse pointer in the selection bar to the left of Set of binoculars until it changes to ⬩, then click to select the entire line**

5. **Move the pointer over the selected text, drag it up to the left of Happy, then release the mouse button**

   As you drag, the pointer changes to ⬩, and an indicator line shows you where the text will be placed. Notice that the dragged text does not appear as an item on the Clipboard. Now the prizes are listed in a more logical order, with the best prizes listed first, as shown in Figure D-12.

QUICK TIP
You can also copy or move text from one document to another using the Office Clipboard.

6. **Click the Clipboard task pane Close button ☒**

   The task pane closes.

7. **Click the Save button 🖫 on the Quick Access toolbar**

Activating the Office Clipboard

The Office Clipboard stores multiple items only if it is active. Opening the Clipboard task pane automatically makes it active. If you want to activate the Office Clipboard without showing the task pane, click Options on the Clipboard task pane, then click Collect Without Showing Office Clipboard. If the Office Clipboard is not active, you can only copy one item at a time using the Windows Clipboard.

FIGURE D-11: Selecting a line of text of text to the Clipboard

Cut button

Paste button

Selection bar

Right arrow pointer

Entire line is selected

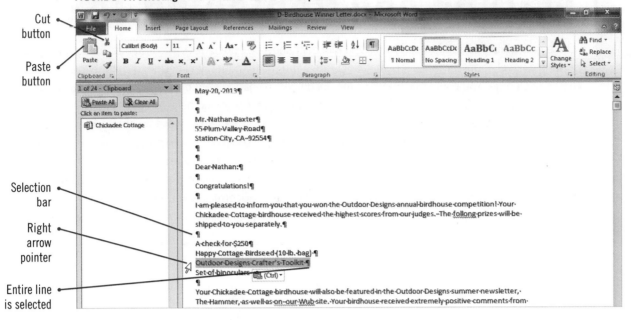

FIGURE D-12: Moving text by dragging it

Clipboard task pane Close button

Text that was cut appears as first item in Clipboard

Dragged text is not copied to Office Clipboard

Text dragged to new location

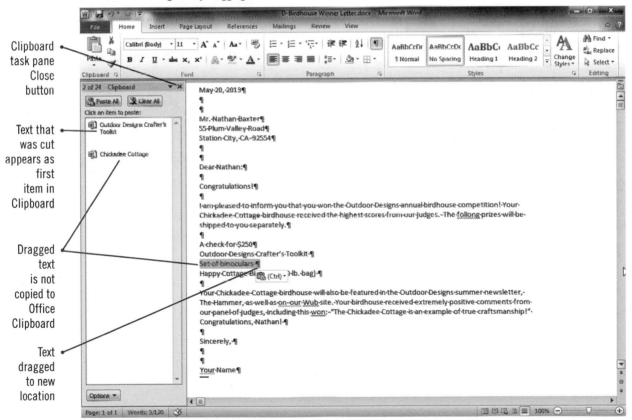

Finding and Replacing Text

Once in a while you might need to make a global change in a document. For instance, let us say you are writing a novel about a character named Bob. After writing fifty pages, you decide to change the character's name to George. You could manually edit the document to change each occurrence of "Bob" to "George", but there is an easier, more automated method. The **Replace** command helps you quickly and easily substitute a new word or phrase for one or more occurrences of a particular word or phrase in a document. Choosing the Replace command opens the Find and Replace dialog box, which you use to specify the text you want to find and the text with which you want to replace it. You can replace every occurrence of the text in one action, or you can review each occurrence and choose to replace or keep the text. 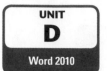 Karen just told you that the winning birdhouse name in the letter is incorrect. You need to replace all instances of the incorrect name with the correct name. You decide to use the Replace command to make these changes.

STEPS

1. **Press [Ctrl][Home]**

   Pressing [Ctrl][Home] moves the insertion point to the beginning of the document and deselects any text. This ensures that Word starts searching for occurrences of your specified text at the beginning of the document and checks the entire document, not just within a selection of text.

2. **Click Replace in the Editing group on the Home tab**

   The Find and Replace dialog box opens, with the Replace tab in front.

3. **Type Cottage in the Find what text box, press [Tab], then type Cabana in the Replace with text box**

   Compare your screen to Figure D-13.

4. **Click Find Next**

   Word searches the document from the insertion point and highlights the first instance of "Cottage", as shown in Figure D-14.

   QUICK TIP

   Clicking More in the Find and Replace dialog box expands the dialog box to display additional options, such as matching the case or format of a word or phrase.

5. **Click Replace**

   Word replaces the first instance of "Cottage" with "Cabana", then moves to the next instance of "Cottage", which is the brand name of the birdseed prize. You do not want to replace this instance.

6. **Click Find Next**

   Word locates the next instance of "Cottage".

7. **Click Replace two more times**

   An alert box opens, indicating that Word has finished searching the document.

8. **Click OK**

   The alert box closes.

9. **Click Close in the Find and Replace dialog box, then click the Save button 🖫 on the Quick Access toolbar**

   Your changes are saved.

Using the Navigation pane to find text

You can use the Navigation pane to quickly locate and highlight all instances of specified text. Click Find in the Editing group on the Home tab to open the Navigation pane. Type the text you want to find in the Search box. All instances of the text are highlighted in yellow in the document, and the Navigation pane displays excerpts containing the text. Click an excerpt in the Navigation pane to jump to the location of that instance of the text in the document.

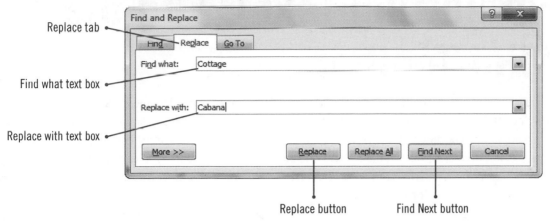

FIGURE D-13: Find and Replace dialog box

Replace tab

Find what text box

Replace with text box

Replace button   Find Next button

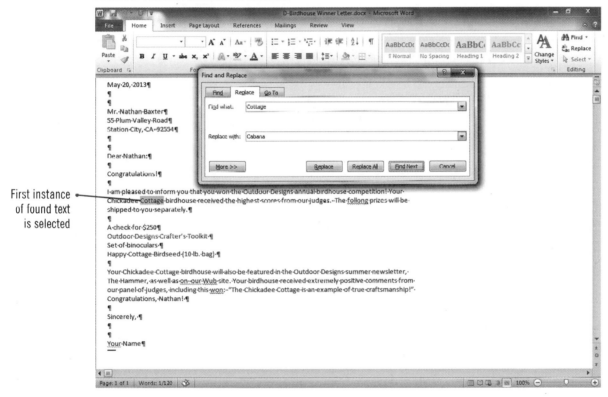

FIGURE D-14: First occurrence of found text

First instance
of found text
is selected

Using the Research task pane

As you create documents in Word or presentations in PowerPoint, you might want to look up words and other information on the Internet. Before you go to a search engine or dictionary Web site, you should know that you have a powerful research tool at your fingertips in Office 2010 called the Research task pane. The Research task pane lets you look up information from several data sources provided by Microsoft and a growing number of partners. For instance, if you want to look up the definition of a word, press [Alt] and click the word. The Research task pane opens on the right side of your screen and provides the definition from Wikipedia, as well as additional information. You can also tap into many other data sources in the Research task pane, including a thesaurus, Bing, and several business and financial sites. To open the Research task pane manually, click the Review tab on the Ribbon, then click Research in the Proofing group.

Formatting Text Using the Mini Toolbar

As you work in Word 2010, you will discover many tools for enhancing a document's appearance and readability by applying formatting. Perhaps the simplest of these is the Mini toolbar, which appears near your mouse pointer whenever you select text. The Mini toolbar contains only the most common formatting commands, so it is perfect for making quick, basic changes to text. For instance, you can use the Mini toolbar to change the font of selected text. A **font** is the design of a set of characters, such as **Arial** or Times New Roman. You can also use it to change the **font style** by applying bold, underline, or italic formatting, or to change the **font size** of selected text so that it is larger or smaller. You can also format selected paragraphs as a bulleted list using the shortcut menu, which opens just above or below the Mini toolbar when you right-click selected text. All of the Mini toolbar buttons are also available on the Home tab of the Ribbon, in the Font and Paragraph groups. You will format text using the Ribbon in a future unit. You decide to enhance the appearance of the letter by formatting the word "Congratulations!" in a larger font size, formatting the prizes as a bulleted list, and applying italic font style to the newsletter title.

STEPS

1. **Click the Print Layout button 🔲 on the status bar**

   Now that you are going to make formatting changes to your document, it is a good idea to change the view to Print Layout so that you can see a more accurate picture of how the changes will look on the page.

2. **Position the mouse pointer 🔏 to the left of Congratulations! in the first paragraph, then click**

   The Word "Congratulations" and the exclamation point and ¶ that follow it are selected. The Mini toolbar appears as a ghosted image near the selected text.

3. **Move the mouse pointer toward the Mini toolbar until it appears in a solid form, then click the Bold button B on the Mini toolbar**

   The selected text "Congratulations!" now appears in a darker and thicker font, to set it apart from the other text in the letter.

4. **Click the Grow Font button A˙ on the Mini toolbar three times**

   The selected text grows in size from 11 to 16, as shown in Figure D-15. The new font size appears in the Font Size box on the Mini toolbar. You measure font size using points. A **point** is 1/72", so a font size of 12 is 1/6".

5. **Select the four lines of text containing the prizes, starting with A check for $250 and ending with Happy Cottage Birdseed (10 lb. bag)**

   The four prizes are now selected. You can now apply formatting to the selected text. You decide to make the prizes look more ordered by formatting them as a bulleted list.

6. **Right-click the selected text**

   The Mini toolbar opens, and a shortcut menu opens above or below the Mini toolbar. The shortcut menu contains a list of commands and tools that can be used to work with selected text, as shown in Figure D-16.

7. **Click the Bullets button ⬚ on the shortcut menu, then click outside the selected text**

   Each prize is indented and preceded by a small round dot, or **bullet**. The listed prizes now stand out much better from the body of the letter and help create a more organized appearance.

8. **Select the text The Hammer in the paragraph below the bulleted list, then click the Italic button I on the Mini toolbar**

   The title of the Outdoor Designs newsletter, *The Hammer*, now appears in italic. Compare your screen to Figure D-17.

Creating a Document

FIGURE D-15: Using the Mini toolbar to format text

Font Size box

Bold button

Grow Font button

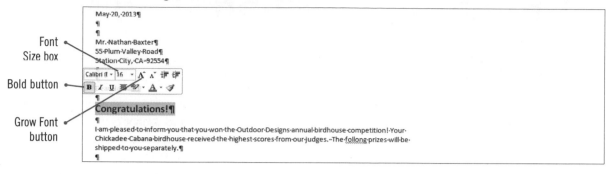

FIGURE D-16: Using the shortcut menu to create a bulleted list

Bullets button

Shortcut menu

Selected paragraphs

Italic button

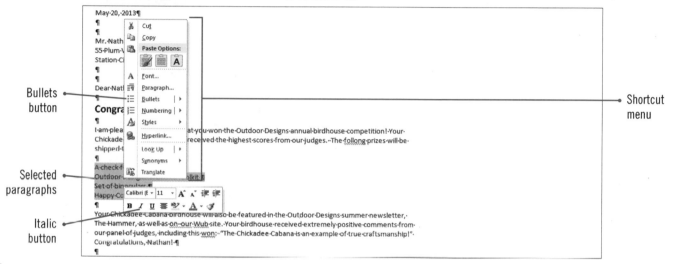

FIGURE D-17: Letter with formatted text and bulleted list

Prizes formatted as bulleted list

Italic formatting

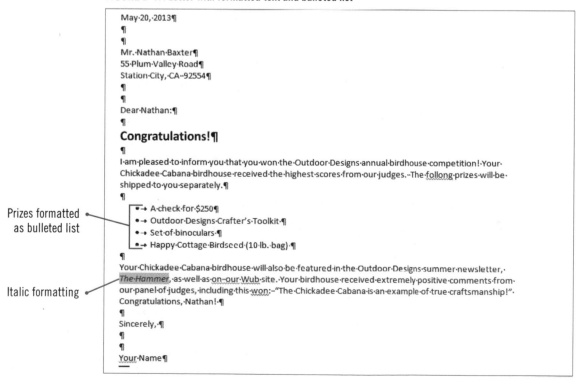

Checking Spelling and Grammar

Word provides tools to help you make sure that your documents are free of spelling and grammatical errors. Word's AutoCorrect feature corrects your errors as you type them, but Word cannot correct all mistakes in this way. The program identifies possible misspelled words by comparing each word to its built-in dictionary, then underlines any words that are not in its dictionary with red wavy lines. Word identifies possible grammatical errors such as passive voice by underlining them with green wavy lines. If you right-click the flagged misspelled words or grammatical errors, a shortcut menu opens, displaying a list of correctly spelled or phrased alternatives. You can also open the Spelling and Grammar dialog box to check a document for misspelled words and grammatical errors. 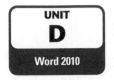 You decide to use Word's spelling and grammar checking tools to ensure that your letter is free of errors.

STEPS

1. **Right-click the word Wub in the second line of the last paragraph in the letter**

   A shortcut menu opens, displaying a list of alternatives to the misspelled word, as shown in Figure D-18. Other options you can choose in this menu include Ignore All (if you want Word to stop alerting you to the possible misspelling of this word in the document), Add to Dictionary (if you want Word to add this word as spelled to its built-in dictionary), and AutoCorrect (if you want Word to automatically correct this spelling in the future).

2. **Click Web from the list at the top of the shortcut menu**

   The shortcut menu closes, and the word "Web" replaces the misspelled word.

3. **Click the Review tab on the Ribbon**

   QUICK TIP
   If the correct spelling of the word does not appear in the list, you can edit the text in the top section of the dialog box, then click Change.

4. **Press [Ctrl][Home] to move the insertion point to the top of the letter, then click the Spelling & Grammar button 🗹 in the Proofing group**

   The Spelling and Grammar dialog box opens, as shown in Figure D-19. The top text box displays text in red that is flagged as a problem, and the bottom text box displays suggestions for fixing it. The dialog box also contains an Ignore Once button, which you can click if you do not want Word to make a change. Word identifies the word "follong" as a possible misspelled word. It suggests changing the spelling to "following," which is correct

5. **Verify that the Check grammar check box is selected, then click Change**

   Word changes "follong" to "following" and moves to the next possible error, an extra space between "on" and "our" in the last paragraph.

6. **Click Change**

   The next error that is identified is a grammatical error. Even though "won" is not an incorrectly spelled word, Word is able to tell that it is used incorrectly in this context. The correct word should be "one".

   TROUBLE
   If your first or last name is flagged as a possible misspelled word, click Ignore Once.

7. **Click Change**

   An alert box opens, indicating that the spelling and grammar check is complete.

8. **Click OK, then click 🖫 to save your changes**

Creating a Document

FIGURE D-18: Spelling shortcut menu with possible alternatives

Click to change "Wub" to "Web"

Shortcut menu opens when you right-click misspelled word

Red wavy line indicates misspelled word

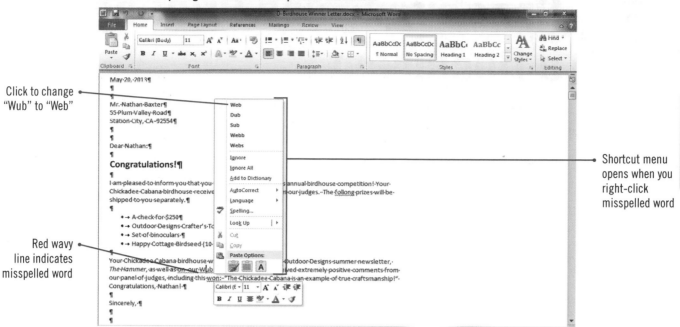

FIGURE D-19: Spelling and Grammar: English (U.S.) dialog box with spelling error

Possible misspelled word is flagged in red

Click when you want to skip suggested change and keep text as is

When a misspelled word is flagged, possible alternatives appear here

Click to change word to highlighted suggestion

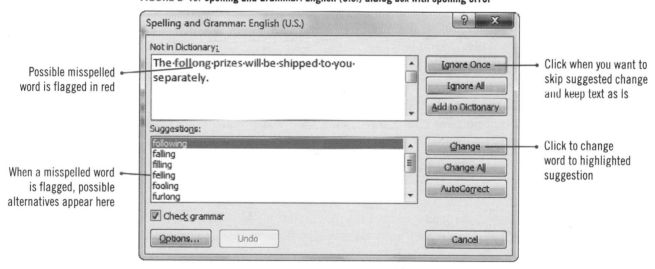

Translating words or documents into other languages

Word 2010 has the ability to translate any word in your document, or even an entire document, into more than 20 different languages. The Mini Translator displays a screen tip of any word you point to in a specified language. To use the Mini Translator, you first need to specify the language. To do this, click the Review tab, click the Translate button in the Language group, then click Choose Translation Language to open the Translation Language Options dialog box. In the Choose Mini Translator language section, click the Translate to arrow, click the language you want to translate to, then click OK. To activate the Mini Translator, click the Review tab, click Translate in the Language group, then click Mini Translator. To translate an entire document from one language to another, click the Translate button in the Languages group on the Review tab, click Choose Translation Language in the Choose document translation languages section, specify the Translate from and Translate to languages, then click OK. Once you have specified your language, click Translate in the Language group, then click Translate Document. An alert box opens, telling you that the document will be sent over the Internet in unencrypted HTML format. Click Send to send the document, and seconds later your document appears in your browser window fully translated. Use the Views buttons in the Translator window to view the translated text in a separate pane above or beside the original text. To create a new document for the translation, select all of the translated content, copy it to the Clipboard, then paste it into a new Word document.

Previewing and Printing a Document

When you finish creating and editing a document, you can print it using the Print tab in Backstage view. The tools on the Print tab let you specify various print settings, including the printer you want to use, how many copies to print, and the specific pages of the document you want to print. The Print tab also displays a preview of your document so that you can see exactly how it will look when printed. Seeing the preview of the document before printing it is useful and can save paper. There are many other ways to view a document in Word. See Table D-3 for a description of these views. ▰▰▰▰▰ You are ready to preview and print the letter now. (*Note*: Many schools limit printing in order to conserve paper. If your school restricts printing, skip Step 7.)

QUICK TIP
You can also close Backstage view by pressing [Esc].

1. **Click the File tab, then click Print**

   The Print tab opens in Backstage view, as shown in Figure D-20. The Preview pane on the right shows how the document will look when printed. Notice that the text of the letter is positioned at the top of the paper. You need to move it down to make room for the company letterhead, which is preprinted on your company paper. To move the text down, return to the document by clicking any tab on the Ribbon except the File tab.

2. **Click the Home tab on the Ribbon**

   The Home tab opens, and the document window displays the letter.

3. **Press [Ctrl][Home] to move the insertion point to the beginning of the document, then press [Enter] seven times**

   You inserted seven blank lines at the top of the document. The text is now positioned further down the page. You can preview how this looks using the Print tab.

QUICK TIP
If you want to change any of the print settings, click the print setting button you want to change, then click a different option.

4. **Click the File tab, then click Print**

   The Print tab opens again, and you can see that the document text looks more centered in the Preview area, as shown in Figure D-21.

5. **Notice the buttons to the left of the Preview section**

   These buttons let you specify your print settings. The button below Printer shows the default printer. The buttons below Settings let you specify which pages you want to print (if you do not want to print the entire document), the number of copies you want to print, the orientation of the document, the size of the paper on which the document will print, and more. The default settings are appropriate for the letter.

TROUBLE
If the correct printer name is not showing on the button below Printer, click the button, then click the printer you want to use.

6. **Verify that the button below Printer displays the name of the printer you want to use**

7. **If your school allows printing, click the Print button; otherwise, skip to Step 8**

   The document prints, the Print tab closes, and your screen displays your document with the Home tab open.

QUICK TIP
If you do not print your document, submit it in the format specified by your instructor.

8. **Save your changes, click the File tab, then click Exit**

   The letter is saved, and the document and Word both close.

Creating a Document

FIGURE D-20: Print tab showing a preview of the letter

File tab ●

Print tab ●

● Preview of printed document

Zoom slider

FIGURE D-21: Previewing the final letter

Your printer appears here ●

Specify the pages you want to print here ●

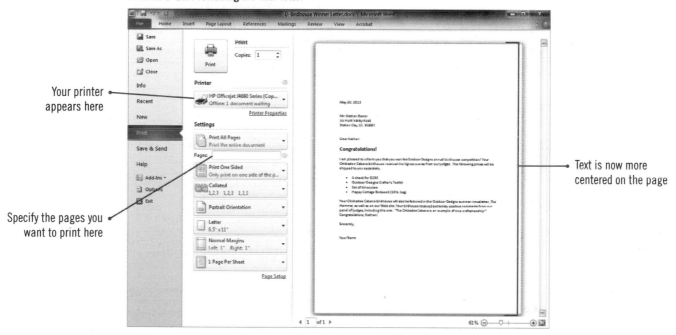

● Text is now more centered on the page

TABLE D-3: Available views in Word

view	button	how it displays a document	use for
Print Layout		Shows all elements of the printed page	Previewing the layout of printed page
Full Screen Reading		Optimized for onscreen reading	Reading documents on a computer screen
Web Layout		As it would appear as a Web page	Creating a Web page
Outline		Shows only the headings in a document	Reviewing the structure of a document
Draft		Does not show all page elements	Typing, editing, and simple formatting

Practice

Concepts Review

For current SAM information, including versions and content details, visit SAM Central (http://www.cengage.com/samcentral). If you have a SAM user profile, you may have access to hands-on instruction, practice, and assessment of the skills covered in this unit. Since various versions of SAM are supported throughout the life of this text, check with your instructor for the correct instructions and URL/Web site for accessing assignments.

Label the Word window elements shown in Figure D-22.

FIGURE D-22

Match each of the items with its function.

11. Launcher
12. Shortcut menu
13. Mini toolbar
14. File tab
15. Clipboard task pane

a. Opens Backstage view
b. Appears when text is selected, and contains buttons used for formatting
c. Stores cut and copied items that can be pasted
d. Appears after right-clicking in the document window, and displays a list of commands
e. Opens a dialog box or task pane

Select the best answer from the list of choices.

16. **Which of the following tasks can you perform in Backstage view?**
    a. Printing a document
    b. Copying text to the Clipboard
    c. Formatting paragraphs as a bulleted list
    d. Checking the spelling of your document

17. **Which of the following tasks should you perform before moving text from one location to another?**
    a. Opening the Mini toolbar
    b. Clicking the View tab
    c. Selecting the text
    d. Clicking the File tab

18. **Which of the following tasks can you complete using the Mini toolbar?**
    a. Changing the document view
    b. Saving a document
    c. Formatting text
    d. Editing text

19. **Which of the following keyboard shortcuts moves the insertion point to the beginning of the document?**
    a. [Ctrl][A]
    b. [Ctrl][End]
    c. [Ctrl][Home]
    d. [Ctrl][right arrow]

20. **Which tab should you click to locate the Spelling & Grammar button?**
    a. Home
    b. Review
    c. View
    d. File

Skills Review

1. **Create a new document from an existing file.**
   a. Start Word, then open the Open dialog box.
   b. Use the Browse button to navigate to where you store your Data Files, then open the file D-2.docx.
   c. Save the file as **D-Restaurant Info Sheet** where you save your Data Files.

2. **Enter text in a document.**
   a. Make sure formatting marks are displayed in the document.
   b. Switch to Draft view.
   c. Move the insertion point to the right of -2100 (the end of the fax number at the end of line four), then press [Enter] twice.
   d. Type the following text: **About the Company**. Press [Enter].
   e. Type the following text: **The company was created to serve working parents who want to feed their families nutritious meals with the freshest ingredients.**
   f. Move the insertion point to the end of the paragraph below the heading About Our Chef, press [Spacebar], then type **Chef Nancy is also the author of the best-selling cookbook Dinner in a Flash.**
   g. Save your changes.

3. **Select and edit text.**
   a. In the paragraph under the heading About Our Kitchen, replace the text 2500 with **3500**.
   b. In the paragraph above, delete **New York's** in the second line and replace it with **Boston's**.
   c. Scroll down if necessary so that you can see the paragraph under the heading Our Menus, then use the [Backspace] key to delete the words **Monday through Friday** at the end of that paragraph.
   d. Type **five days a week** so that the last sentence of that paragraph reads "Here are just a few of our best-selling meals, available five days a week:"
   e. Select the entire document, then click the No Spacing button.
   f. Save your changes.

4. **Copy text.**
   a. Open the Clipboard task pane. If there are entries on it, clear them.
   b. Select the text **The Last Minute Chef** in the first line of the document, then copy this text to the Clipboard. (*Note*: Be careful not to select the paragraph mark after the word Chef.)
   c. Delete the words **the Company** in the heading About the Company. (*Note*: Be careful not to delete the paragraph mark at the end of the line.)

Skills Review (continued)

    d. Paste the copied text where the deleted text used to be. (*Note*: If a blank line was inserted between the heading and paragraph, delete it before proceeding to Step e.)

    e. Select the text **Last Minute Chef** in the heading About The Last Minute Chef.

    f. Drag a copy of the selected text to the line just below it and to the left of the word company while holding [Ctrl].

    g. Edit the **c** in company that follows the dragged text so that it is capitalized.

    h. Save your changes.

5. Move text.

    a. In the paragraph below the heading Our Hours, select the text **Stop by or call tonight!** and the space following it, then use the Cut command to move this text to the Clipboard.

    b. Paste the text you cut after the sentence **Or go straight home and call us: we deliver!** at the end of the paragraph.

    c. Scroll down if necessary so that the bottom of the document is visible on your screen.

    d. Select the heading **Our Hours**, the paragraph below it, and the paragraph mark below the paragraph, then drag the entire selection down to the end of the document.

    e. Close the Clipboard task pane, then save your changes.

6. Find and replace text.

    a. Move the insertion point to the beginning of the document.

    b. Use the Replace command to replace all instances of **Green Beans** with **Asparagus**.

    c. Close the Find and Replace dialog box.

    d. Save your changes.

7. Format text using the Mini toolbar.

    a. Change the view to Print Layout view.

    b. Select **The Last Minute Chef** in the first line of the document, then use the Mini toolbar to apply bold formatting to this text.

    c. With the first line of text still selected, use a button on the Mini toolbar to increase the font size of **The Last Minute Chef** to 20.

    d. Use the Mini toolbar to apply bold formatting to each of the following headings in the document: **About The Last Minute Chef**, **About Our Chef**, **About Our Kitchen**, **Our Menus**, and **Our Hours**.

    e. At the end of the paragraph below the heading About Our Chef, use the Mini toolbar to apply italic formatting to the book title **Dinner in a Flash**.

    f. Scroll down if necessary so that all the text under the heading Our Menus is visible, then select the list of meals starting with **Pot Roast with Garlic Mashed Potatoes and Peas** and ending with **Beef Teriyaki with Fried Rice**.

    g. Use the shortcut menu to format the selected text as a bulleted list.

    h. Save your changes.

8. Check spelling and grammar.

    a. In the paragraph below About Our Kitchen, correct the spelling of the misspelled word **kitchn** by right-clicking and choosing the correct spelling from the shortcut menu.

    b. Move the insertion point to the beginning of the document.

    c. Click the tab on the Ribbon that contains the Spelling & Grammar button.

    d. Open the Spelling and Grammar dialog box.

    e. Review each spelling and grammatical error that Word identifies, and correct or ignore it depending on what seems appropriate for this document.

    f. Save your changes.

9. Preview and print a document.

    a. Preview the document using the Print tab.

    b. Return to the Home tab and insert two line spaces above the first line of the document.

    c. Move the insertion point to the end of the document, then type your name.

    d. Preview the document again using the Print tab.

e. Save your changes, then submit your finished document to your instructor. Your final document should look like Figure D-23.

f. Close the document, then exit Word.

FIGURE D-23

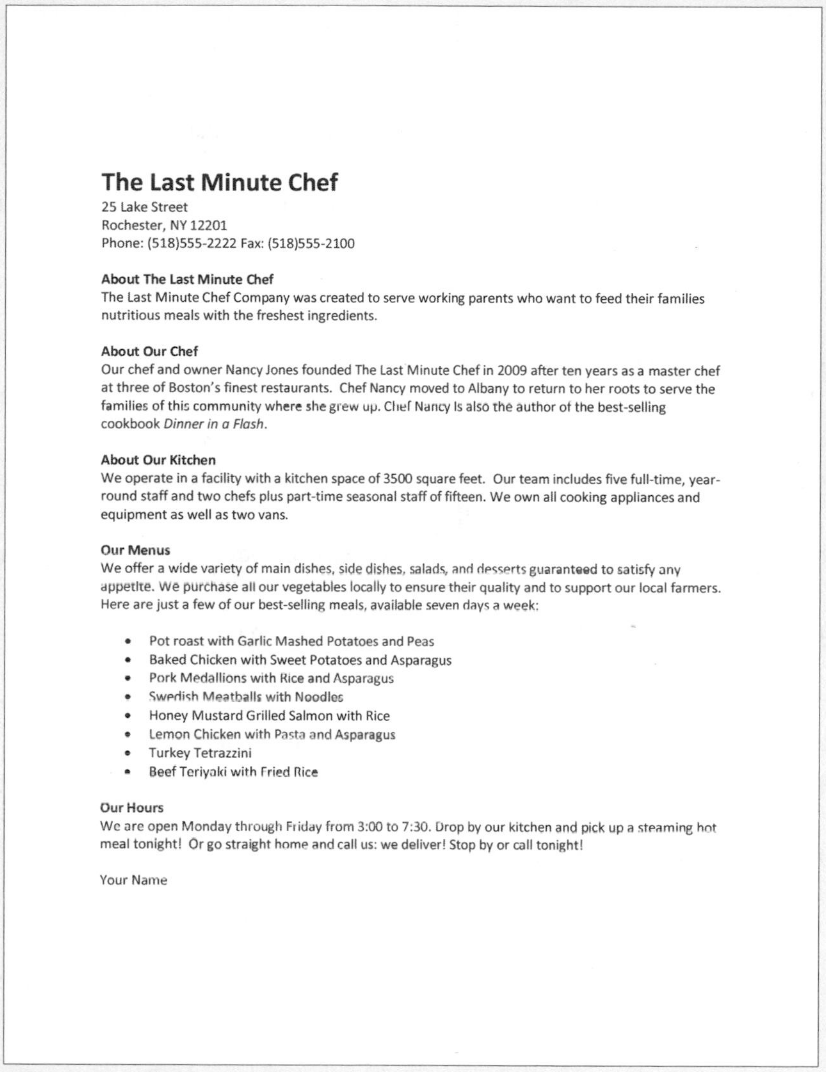

The Last Minute Chef

25 Lake Street
Rochester, NY 12201
Phone: (518)555-2222 Fax: (518)555-2100

About The Last Minute Chef
The Last Minute Chef Company was created to serve working parents who want to feed their families nutritious meals with the freshest ingredients.

About Our Chef
Our chef and owner Nancy Jones founded The Last Minute Chef in 2009 after ten years as a master chef at three of Boston's finest restaurants. Chef Nancy moved to Albany to return to her roots to serve the families of this community where she grew up. Chef Nancy Is also the author of the best-selling cookbook *Dinner in a Flash*.

About Our Kitchen
We operate in a facility with a kitchen space of 3500 square feet. Our team includes five full-time, year-round staff and two chefs plus part-time seasonal staff of fifteen. We own all cooking appliances and equipment as well as two vans.

Our Menus
We offer a wide variety of main dishes, side dishes, salads, and desserts guaranteed to satisfy any appetite. We purchase all our vegetables locally to ensure their quality and to support our local farmers. Here are just a few of our best-selling meals, available seven days a week:

- Pot roast with Garlic Mashed Potatoes and Peas
- Baked Chicken with Sweet Potatoes and Asparagus
- Pork Medallions with Rice and Asparagus
- Swedish Meatballs with Noodles
- Honey Mustard Grilled Salmon with Rice
- Lemon Chicken with Pasta and Asparagus
- Turkey Tetrazzini
- Beef Teriyaki with Fried Rice

Our Hours
We are open Monday through Friday from 3:00 to 7:30. Drop by our kitchen and pick up a steaming hot meal tonight! Or go straight home and call us: we deliver! Stop by or call tonight!

Your Name

Independent Challenge 1

As the human resources director for Recycling Enterprises, Inc., you are in charge of organizing the company's summer executive retreat. You need to prepare a memo inviting the executive team to the retreat. You have already created a partially completed version of this memo, so now you need to make final edits to finish it.

a. Start Word, open the file D-3.docx from where you store your Data Files, then save it as **D-Executive Retreat Memo**.

b. Select the entire document, then apply the No Spacing style to the whole document.

c. In the fourth line of text, replace the text **Your Name** with your name.

d. In the sixth line of text (which begins "Our Summer Sales Offsite Meeting"), change the words **Offsite Meeting** to **Retreat**.

e. In the first line below the heading Dates and Location, delete **meeting**, then replace it with **Executive Retreat**.

f. At the end of the paragraph under Dates and Location, type the following text: **Please book your flight home anytime after 5:00 on June 17**.

Independent Challenge 1 (continued)

g. In the first line of text under the heading Trip Planning, move the text **I look forward to seeing you there!** to the end of the paragraph.

h. Increase the font size of **Memo** in the first line of the document to 20, then apply bold formatting to it.

i. Apply bold formatting to the following headings in the memo: **Dates and Location**, **About the Hotel and Conference Center**, **Meeting Information**, **Planned Activities**, and **Trip Planning**.

j. Under the Planned Activities heading, format the lines that start with **June 15**, **June 16**, and **June 17** as a bulleted list.

k. You suddenly learn that the Orange Tree Hotel will not be able to accommodate the meeting. Fortunately, you are able to make a reservation at the Palm Grove Golf Resort, also in San Diego. Replace all instances of **Orange Tree Hotel** with **Palm Grove Golf Resort**.

l. After you enter all the text, check the spelling and grammar, and correct any errors as needed. Ignore any proper names that are flagged as misspelled words.

m. Save your changes, then preview the memo.

Advanced Challenge Exercise

(*Note*: **These steps require an Internet connection.**)

- Click the Review tab, click Translate in the Language group, then click Choose Translation Language to open the Translation Language Options dialog box.

- In the Choose document translation languages section, click the Translate from list arrow, click English (U.S.), click the Translate to list arrow, click Danish, then click OK.

- Click Translate in the Language group, then click Translate Document [English (U.S.) to Danish], then click Send in the Translate Whole Document dialog box.

- In the Translator window, click the Side by side button next to Views to see the translated text in a pane next to the original text, if necessary.

- Click anywhere in the right pane containing the Danish text, then press [Ctrl][A] to select all of the text. Press [Ctrl] [C] to copy the text to the Clipboard, then click the Word program button on the taskbar to return to Word. Press [Ctrl][N] to open a new document, then press [Ctrl][V] to paste the translated text from the Clipboard into the new document.

- Save the file as **D-Executive Retreat Memo ACE**.

n. Close all documents, then exit Word. Submit your completed documents to your instructor.

Creating a Document

Independent Challenge 2

You own and operate an ice cream company based in Portland, Oregon. Business is booming, so you would like to expand your product line and offer new types of products. You would also like to have a better understanding of what your customers like about your ice cream products. You decide to create a simple customer survey that your customers can fill out in the store for a chance to win a prize. You have already started the survey document but need to edit it and improve its appearance before it is ready for distribution.

a. Start Word, open the file D-4.docx from where you store your Data Files, then save it as **D-Ice Cream Survey**.

b. Replace all instances of the name **Aunt Tilly** in the survey document with your first name. In the last line of the document, replace the text **Your Name** with your full name.

c. Select all the text in the document, then apply the No Spacing style to all the selected text.

d. In the third line of text in the document, delete **weekly ice cream** and replace it with **a pint of ice cream each week**.

e. Type **Question 1:** before the first question in the document, press [Spacebar], then apply bold formatting to **Question 1:**.

f. Insert **Question 2:**, **Question 3:**, and **Question 4:** to the left of the remaining three questions in the survey, insert a space, and apply bold formatting to the new text.

g. Below each of the four questions, format the list of answers as a bulleted list.

h. Reorder the bulleted items under Question 4 so that they are in alphabetical order.

i. Increase the font size of the text in the first line of the document to 20, then apply bold and italic formatting to it.

j. Check the spelling and grammar and correct all spelling and grammar errors. Ignore flagged words that are spelled correctly.

k. Save your changes to the document. Use Print Preview to see how the printed survey will look.

Advanced Challenge Exercise

■ Save a copy of the survey document with the name **D-Ice Cream Survey ACE**.

■ Replace the first line of the document with the text **Definitions.**

■ Delete all other text in the document except **Butter**, **Cookie**, **Pralines**, and your name. Remove the bulleted list formatting, but keep each word on a separate line.

■ Type a colon after each word, then press [Spacebar] after each colon.

■ Press [Alt] and click **"Butter"** to open the Research task pane to view definitions of cookie.

■ Copy the first sentence of the Wikipedia definition of "Butter," then paste the copied definition to the right of **Butter:** in the document.

■ Use the Research task pane to look up and copy the definitions of "cookie" and "pralines," then paste them to the right of **Cookie:** and **Pralines:** in the document.

■ Format **Butter**, **Cookie**, and **Pralines** in bold formatting. Format the definitions in italic.

■ Close the Research task pane, then save your changes. Preview the document, then close it.

l. Submit your work to your instructor.

Independent Challenge 3

You are the director of marketing for a sports and fitness equipment company. You have contracted with A Plus Recruiters, an executive search firm in Chicago, to find candidates to fill the position of marketing manager, reporting to you. The recruiter you hired to locate candidates for the job has requested that you create the document shown in Figure D-24 that describes the position and the qualifications that candidates must have.

a. Start Word, open the file D-5.docx from where you store your Data Files, then save it as **D-Marketing Manager Job Description**.

b. Place the insertion point at the end of the document, type **Reporting Structure**, press [Enter], type **This position reports to the Vice President of Marketing**, then press [Enter].

c. Delete the words **Vice President** in the line that you typed in Step b, then type **Director** in its place.

d. In the second line of the document, delete **Essential Duties and** as well as the space after it, so that only the word **Responsibilities** remains in this line.

e. In the third line of the document, move the first sentence that begins **Requires travel to key customer accounts** so that it is the last sentence in that paragraph.

f. Use the Mini toolbar to apply bold formatting to the first line of text in the document, then increase the font size of this text to 24.

g. Use the Mini toolbar to apply bold formatting to each of the following headings in the document: **Responsibilities**, **Required Skills**, **Work Environment**, **Education and Work Experience**, and **Reporting Structure**.

h. Move the heading **Education and Work Experience** and the paragraph below it so that it is located below the Reporting Structure paragraph.

i. Check the spelling and grammar in the document, and make all appropriate changes. Ignore any occurrences of sentence fragments that Word identifies. Type your name below the last line of the document.

j. Preview the document, compare your screen to Figure D-24, then save and close the document.

k. Submit the document to your instructor, then exit Word.

FIGURE D-24

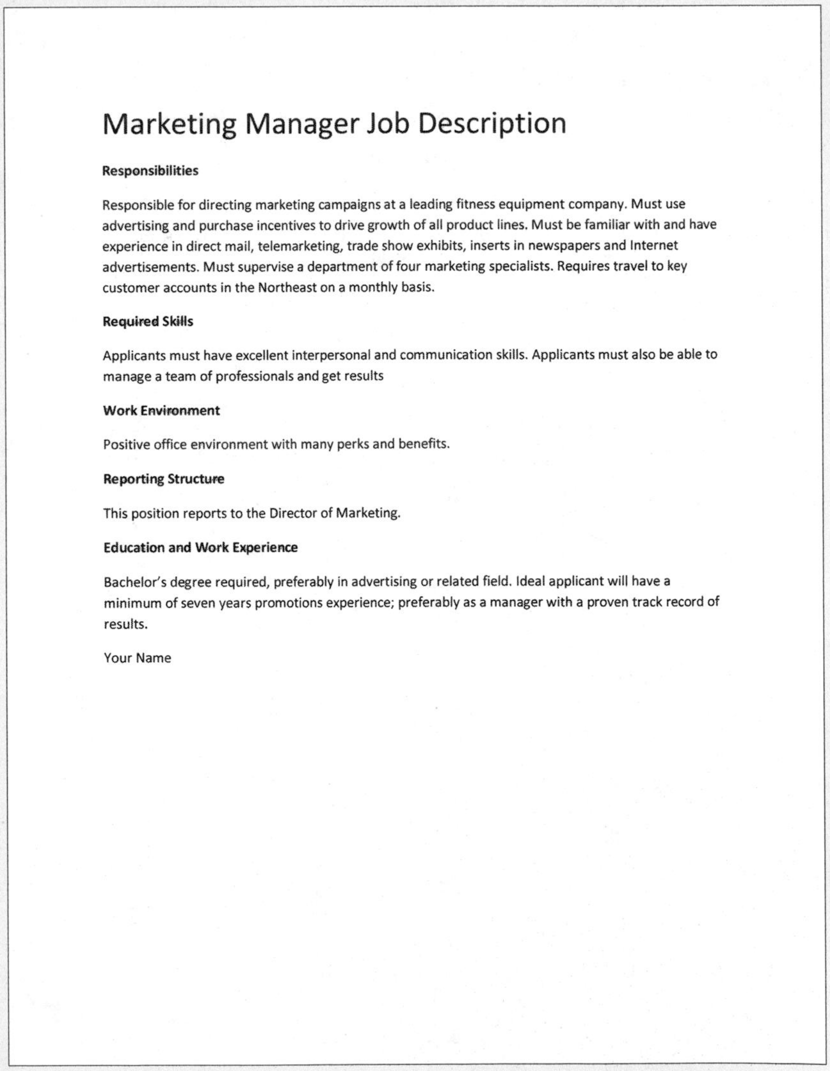

Marketing Manager Job Description

Responsibilities

Responsible for directing marketing campaigns at a leading fitness equipment company. Must use advertising and purchase incentives to drive growth of all product lines. Must be familiar with and have experience in direct mail, telemarketing, trade show exhibits, inserts in newspapers and Internet advertisements. Must supervise a department of four marketing specialists. Requires travel to key customer accounts in the Northeast on a monthly basis.

Required Skills

Applicants must have excellent interpersonal and communication skills. Applicants must also be able to manage a team of professionals and get results

Work Environment

Positive office environment with many perks and benefits.

Reporting Structure

This position reports to the Director of Marketing.

Education and Work Experience

Bachelor's degree required, preferably in advertising or related field. Ideal applicant will have a minimum of seven years promotions experience; preferably as a manager with a proven track record of results.

Your Name

Real Life Independent Challenge

When you apply for a job, it is important to make a case for why you would be ideally suited for the position for which you are applying. In this Real Life Independent Challenge, you are interested in applying for your dream job at a company for which you would love to work. The job and the company can be in any field you want—it is your choice! You have already submitted your résumé to the human resources director at this company, and she has requested that you now write a letter that states the reasons why you are ideally suited for the job.

a. Start Word, then save the blank document as **D-Dream Job Letter**.

b. Before you begin typing, apply the No Spacing style to the document. (*Hint*: Click the No Spacing button on the Home tab.)

c. Type today's date in the first line of the document, press [Enter] three times, then type **Marianne Johnson**, the fictional name of the human resources director at your dream company. Below Marianne's name, type the name and address of the company. (Make up this information.) Press [Enter] twice after typing the address.

d. Write a letter that contains three paragraphs and a closing. Make sure to insert a blank line between paragraphs. Use the guidelines in the table below to write your letter.

part of the letter	directions for what to write
First paragraph	Thank Marianne for the opportunity to apply for the specific job at your dream company. (Be sure to name a specific job and a specific company name—the company can be made up or real.)
Second paragraph	Write three or four sentences (or more) stating why you are the ideal candidate for the job.
Third paragraph	Thank Marianne for her consideration.

e. Type **Sincerely**, two lines below the third paragraph.

f. Three lines below **Sincerely**, type your name. Save your changes. Preview the letter to make sure it looks good on paper. If necessary, insert blank lines at the top of the letter so that the text is balanced on the page. Save and close the document. Submit your letter to your instructor.

Visual Workshop

Use the skills you have learned in this unit to create the document shown in Figure D-25. Start Word, use the Blank document command to create a new untitled document, then type and format the text as shown. (*Hint*: Click the File tab, click New, click Blank document in the Available Templates section, then click Create in the Preview pane.) Set the font size of the heading text to 24, and set the font size of the body text to 14. Save the document as **D-Apartment Ad** in the location where you store your Data Files. Type your name below the last line of the document. Check the spelling and grammar in the entire document, then save and print it. When you are finished, close the document, then exit Word. Submit your completed document to your instructor.

FIGURE D-25

Apartment for Rent

Description:

LUXURY LIVING AT AN AFFORDABLE PRICE! Live in style without paying a fortune in this 2-bedroom apartment near the lake! Walk to parks and shopping. Enjoy water views from two windows.

- Modern building near the lake
- Convenient location—close to shopping, train, lake, and parks
- Great views of the water
- 2 bedrooms
- 1 full bath
- Modern appliances
- Washer/dryer in unit
- Granite countertops
- Built-in shelves
- Utilities included

Rent: $1250 per month

For more information or to schedule an appointment, call Frank at 773-555-9090

Your Name

Enhancing a Document

Microsoft Word provides a variety of tools you can use to enhance the appearance of your documents. In this unit, you will learn to change the formatting of characters and paragraphs using tools on the Ribbon and Mini toolbar. You will also learn how to take advantage of Quick Styles, a feature in Microsoft Word that helps you create great-looking documents efficiently. Karen Rivera, marketing director for Outdoor Designs, gives you a product fact sheet for a new canoe product. Karen asks you to format the information in the sheet so that it is attractive and easy to read.

OBJECTIVES

Change font and font size

Change font color, style, and effects

Change alignment and line spacing

Change margin settings

Set tabs

Set indents

Add bulleted and numbered lists

Apply Quick Styles

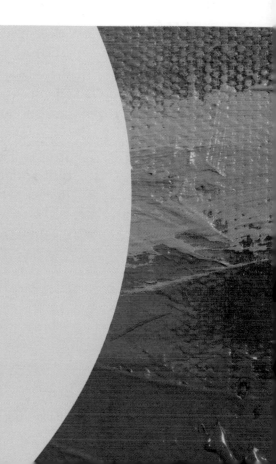

Changing Font and Font Size

Choosing an appropriate font is an important part of formatting a document. The fonts you use help communicate the tone you want to set. For instance, if you are creating a report that discusses the harmful effects of global warming, you should choose a conservative, traditional font, such as Times New Roman. On the other hand, if you are creating a formal wedding invitation, you should choose a font that conveys a sense of elegance and celebration, such as French Script. Table E-1 shows some examples of fonts available in Word. You can use either the Home tab or the Mini toolbar to change font and font size. You can change font and font size before you begin typing, or you can select existing text and apply changes to it. ▰▰▰ All the text in the canoe fact sheet is the same font (Calibri) and size (11 point). You decide to change the font and font size of the first two lines so that they stand out from the rest of the text in the document. First, you will open the document and save it with a new name to keep Karen's original document intact.

1. **Start Word, open the file E-1.docx from where you store your Data Files, then save it as E-Canoe Fact Sheet**

   The E-Canoe Fact Sheet document is now open in Print Layout view.

2. **Place the pointer in the selection bar to the left of Outdoor Designs in the first line until it changes to ⇗, then click to select the entire line**

   To format existing text, you must first select it.

3. **Click the Font Size list arrow in the Font group, then point to 20, as shown in Figure E-1**

   Just by pointing to 20, the font size of the selected text increases in size on the page. You might have noticed that pointing to any other font size option instantly caused the selected text to change in size to reflect that point size. This feature is called **Live Preview**, and makes it possible to preview how a formatting option will look on the page before actually choosing that option. Live Preview is available in many formatting lists and galleries.

4. **Click 20**

   The Font Size list closes, and the selected text changes to 20 point. The first line of text is now much larger than the rest of the text in the document.

5. **Select Build-Your-Own Canoe Kit in the second line of the document, click the Font Size list arrow, then click 22**

   The second line of text increases in size to 22 point and is now larger than the first line.

6. **Click the Font list arrow in the Font group on the Home tab, then point to any font to preview it in the document, but do not click**

   Notice that anytime you point to a font in the Font list, the selected text changes to that font.

7. **Scroll in the Font list until you see Cambria, click Cambria as shown in Figure E-2, then click outside the selected text to deselect it**

   The selected text changes to the Cambria font. "Cambria" appears in the Font list box and will be displayed as long as the insertion point remains in any text with the Cambria font applied.

8. **Click the Save button 💾 on the Quick Access toolbar to save your changes**

Enhancing a Document

FIGURE E-1: Changing the font size of selected text using the Font Size list

Font size of selected text is set at 11; it will not change until you click a new size

Font group

Font Size list

Font Size list arrow

Using Live Preview, font increases to 20 when pointer is placed on 20 in the Font Size list

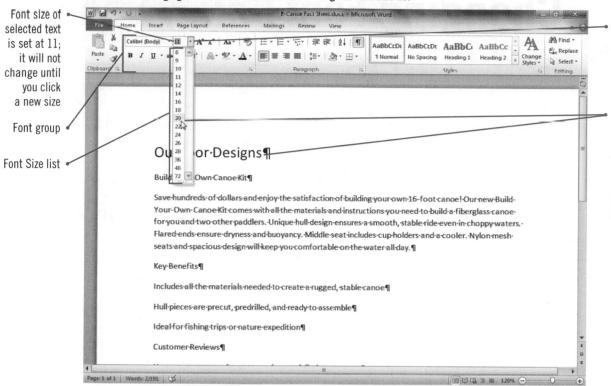

FIGURE E-2: Changing the font type of selected text using the Font list

Font list arrow

Font list

Live Preview feature shows preview of Cambria font

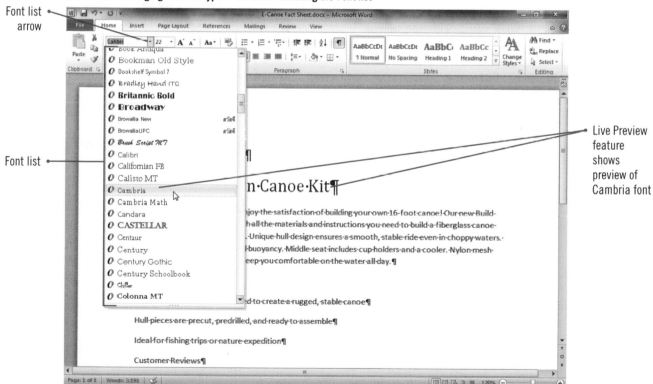

TABLE E-1: Samples of fonts and font sizes

font formats	samples
Font	Times New Roman, *French Script*, **Impact**, ALGERIAN, **Broadway**, Chiller
Size	eight point, twelve point, fourteen point, eighteen point

Changing Font Color, Style, and Effects

Sometimes you want to emphasize certain words, phrases, or lines of text. To do this, you can use font styles, which are font attributes such as **bold** (darker type), *italic* (slanted type), and underline. You can also make certain words stand out by changing their color, or you can apply font effects to selected text. **Font effects** are special enhancements—such as shadow (shadow looks like this) or strikethrough (~~strikethrough looks like this~~)—that you can apply to selected text. You can use the buttons in the Font group of the Home tab to apply font effects and formatting to selected text. To save time, you can use the Format Painter button to copy the formatting of selected text to other text. You continue to format the canoe kit fact sheet by applying font styles, colors, and effects to certain words.

STEPS

QUICK TIP

The Gradient option on the color palette lets you add lighter and darker tones.

1. **Select the second line of text, Build-Your-Own Canoe Kit, then click the Font Color list arrow**

   In the color palette that opens, you can choose from Theme Colors, Standard Colors, and More Colors, as shown in Figure E-3. A **theme** is a predesigned set of formatting elements, including colors, which you can use to achieve a coordinated overall look in your document. **Standard colors** are the basic hues red, orange, and so on. If you want a color you do not see in the palette, you can click More Colors to specify a particular shade.

QUICK TIP

To remove formatting from selected text, click the Clear Formatting button in the Font group.

2. **Click the red color in the top row of Theme Colors (ScreenTip reads "Red, Accent 2")**

   The second line of the document is now red. The Font Color button now displays a dark red stripe, indicating that this is the current color. Clicking the Font Color button (not the list arrow) applies the current color to selected text.

3. **Select Outdoor Designs (the first line of text), then click the Text Effects button [A] in the Font group on the Home tab**

   The Text Effects gallery opens.

4. **Click the fourth option in the top row (Fill - White, Outline - Accent 1), as shown in Figure E-4**

QUICK TIP

To underline text, click the Underline button [U] in the Font group.

5. **Scroll down until you see the line that begins Stable ride:, select Stable ride:, click the Bold button [B] in the Font group, then click the Italic button [I] in the Font group**

   "Stable ride:" is now formatted in bold and italic, and is still selected.

6. **Click the Format Painter button [✑] in the Clipboard group on the Home tab**

   Notice that the pointer shape changes to [✑I] when you place it on the document, indicating that you can apply the formatting of the selected text to any text you click or select next.

QUICK TIP

Double-clicking the Format Painter button [✑] lets you apply the selected formatting multiple times.

7. **Select Easy to build: three lines below Stable ride:**

   The bold and italic formatting is applied to Easy to build:.

8. **Click outside the selected text, then save your changes**

   See Figure E-5.

FIGURE E-3: Font Color list with red color selected

Italic button

Bold button

Underline button

Font Color list arrow

Click this shade of red

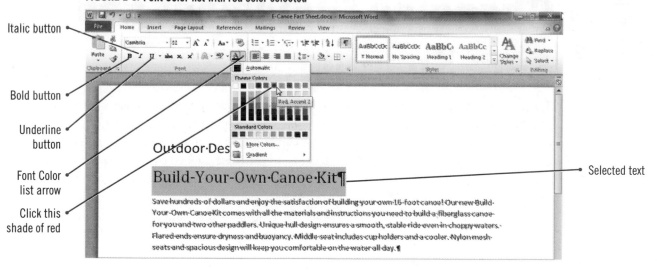

Selected text

FIGURE E-4: Applying a text effect

Text Effects button

Live Preview shows text with text effect applied

In Step 4, click this option

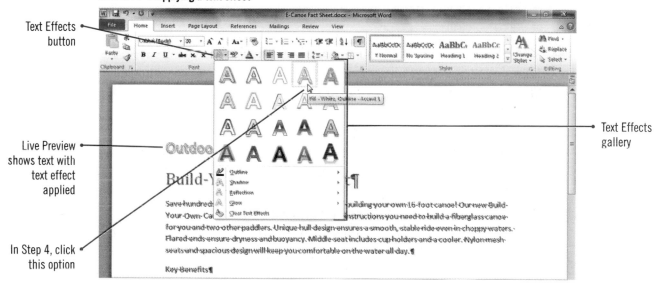

Text Effects gallery

FIGURE E-5: Bold and italic formatting applied to text

Format Painter button

Bold button

Italic button

Text formatted in bold italic using Format Painter button

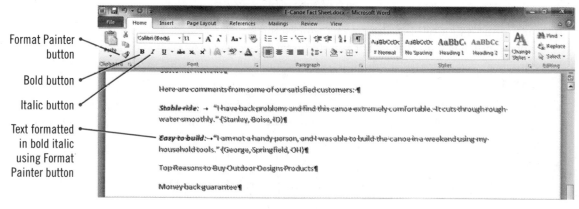

Enhancing a Document

Changing Alignment and Line Spacing

The amount of space between the edge of the page and your document text is called the **margin**. You can change the **alignment**, or position of text within a document's margins, using the alignment buttons in the Paragraph group on the Home tab, or the Center button on the Mini toolbar. For example, titles are often centered, headings left-aligned, and paragraphs **justified** (aligned equally between the left and right margins). You can also adjust the spacing between lines using the Line Spacing button in the Paragraph group on the Home tab.  All of the text in the canoe fact sheet is aligned along the left margin. You decide to center the first two lines and justify the descriptive paragraph. You also want to decrease the amount of spacing between the lines in the paragraph so that it is single spaced, and increase the amount of space both above and below the paragraph.

1. **Press [Ctrl][Home] to move the insertion point to the beginning of the document**
   Although you need to select text to change character formats such as font size or font style, you can change most paragraph formatting, such as alignment, just by positioning the insertion point anywhere in the paragraph. In Word, a **paragraph** is any text that ends with a hard return, so it can be as short as a one-word title or as long as you like.

2. **Click the Center button ≡ in the Paragraph group on the Home tab**
   The text is centered between the two margins.

3. **Click anywhere in the second line of text (Build-Your-Own Canoe Kit), then click the Center button ≡**
   See Figure E-6.

4. **Click anywhere in the paragraph text below Build-Your-Own Canoe Kit**
   The insertion point is now set in the paragraph. Any paragraph formatting you specify will affect the formatting of the entire paragraph.

5. **Click the Justify button ≡ in the Paragraph group**
   The paragraph's alignment changes to justified. When you select justified alignment, Word adds or reduces the space between each word so that the text is aligned along both the right and left margins. This is different from **center-aligning** text, which does not adjust spacing but merely places the text equally between the margins.

6. **Click the Line and Paragraph Spacing button ≡▾ in the Paragraph group on the Home tab, then click 1.0, as shown in Figure E-7**
   The paragraph is now both justified and single spaced, making it more compact and set off from the other text on the page.

7. **Click the launcher ◳ in the Paragraph group**
   The Paragraph dialog box opens with the Indents and Spacing tab in front. Alignment is set to Justified and Line spacing is set to Single, reflecting your settings. This dialog box offers another way to change paragraph settings, including some that are not available in the Paragraph group, such as customizing the amount of space above and below a paragraph. The Preview section shows you what the paragraph will look like with the selected settings.

8. **In the Spacing section, click the Before up arrow twice to set spacing above the paragraph to 12 pt, then click the After up arrow once to set spacing below the paragraph to 12 pt**
   See Figure E-8.

9. **Click OK, then save your changes**
   Notice that the spacing above and below the paragraph text increases to 12 point.

FIGURE E-6: Center-aligned text

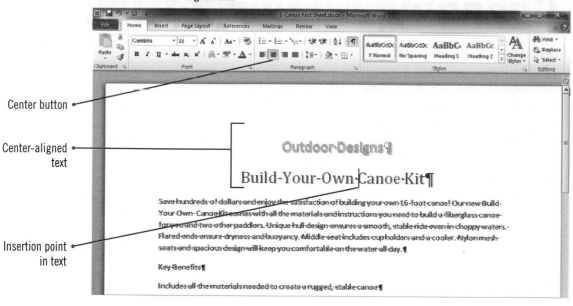

Center button

Center-aligned text

Insertion point in text

FIGURE E-7: Paragraph with justified alignment and line spacing set to 1.0

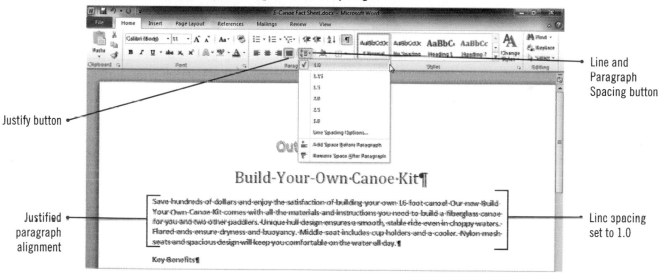

Justify button

Justified paragraph alignment

Line and Paragraph Spacing button

Line spacing set to 1.0

FIGURE E-8: Indents and Spacing tab of Paragraph dialog box

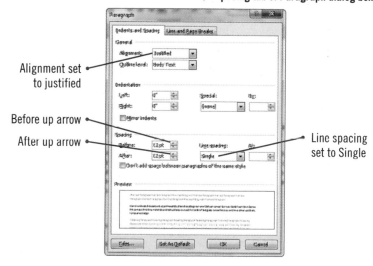

Alignment set to justified

Before up arrow

After up arrow

Line spacing set to Single

Enhancing a Document

Changing Margin Settings

By default, Word sets page margins at one inch from the top, bottom, left, and right sides of the page. Word also provides a number of additional preset margin settings that you can easily view and choose by clicking the Margins button on the Page Layout tab, or the Print tab in Backstage view. If you do not like any of the preset margin settings, you can specify custom settings by using the Margins tab of the Page Setup dialog box. When you change the margins, Word automatically adjusts line wrapping and **repaginates** (renumbers the pages of) your document. To evaluate what margin settings to use in a specific document, you should set the zoom level to One Page so you can see and work with the actual margins as they will appear on the page. ▓▓▓▓ The canoe fact sheet is currently formatted with the default margins. You decide to explore other margin settings to see whether a different setting would make the document look better.

STEPS

QUICK TIP
You can also display the rulers by clicking the View Ruler button 🔳 at the top of the vertical scroll bar.

1. **Click the View tab, then click the Ruler check box to display the rulers, if necessary**

    The View tab is in front, and the vertical and horizontal rulers appear along the top and left edge of the document window.

2. **Click the One Page button 🔳 in the Zoom group**

    You can now see your whole document in the document window, making it possible to see the margin settings at the top, bottom, left, and right of the page. Using the rulers, you can see that the left and right margins are 1". To change the default margin settings, you need to use the Page Layout tab.

3. **Click the Page Layout tab, then click the Margins button 🔳 in the Page Setup group**

    The Margins list opens and displays ready-made options for margin settings. Currently, the Normal option is selected, which specifies a one-inch margin at the top, bottom, left, and right of the page, as shown in Figure E-9.

4. **Click Narrow in the Margins list**

    The Margins list closes, and the Narrow margins setting is applied to the document, as shown in Figure E-10. You can see that there is only a ½" margin at the top, bottom, left, and right. This margin setting is too narrow and makes the text placement look unbalanced; all the text is stretched out at the top of the document, and there is a large blank space at the bottom.

QUICK TIP
The Margins button also appears in the Print tab in Backstage view

5. **Click the Margins button, then click Wide**

    The Wide margins setting is applied to the document.

6. **Click the Margins button, then click Custom Margins**

    The Page Setup dialog box opens with the Margins tab active, as shown in Figure E-11. You use this dialog box to set specific margin settings. The Margins tab contains Margins text boxes, a Preview section, and a Default button (to restore **default settings**, or the settings that are automatically set when you first install Word). The first margin text box, Top, is currently selected.

7. **Press [Tab] twice**

    The Left text box is selected. Pressing [Tab] moves the insertion point from one text box to the next.

QUICK TIP
Most printers require at least a ¼" margin around the page.

8. **Type 1.1 in the Left text box, then press [Tab]**

    The Left text box shows 1.1, and the Right text box is selected. The Preview box shows the new left margin.

9. **Type 1.1 in the Right text box, click OK, then save your changes**

    The left and right margins in the product information sheet change to 1.1".

FIGURE E-9: Margins list

Your Last Custom Setting option may differ or not appear

Current setting

Narrow setting

Wide setting

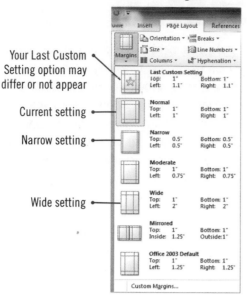

FIGURE E-10: Canoe fact sheet with Narrow margins setting applied

Ruler

Margin is distance between page edge and edge of document text

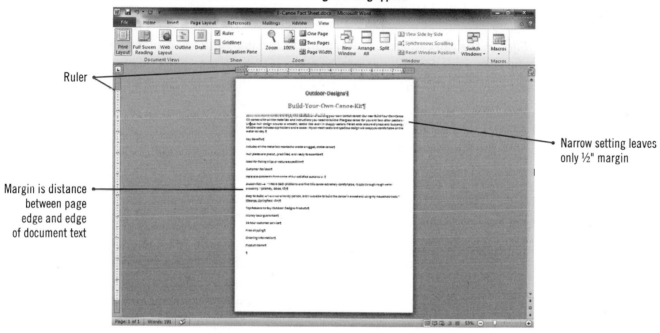

Narrow setting leaves only ½" margin

FIGURE E-11: Margins tab of Page Setup dialog box

Margins tab

Left margin setting for Wide preset margin setting

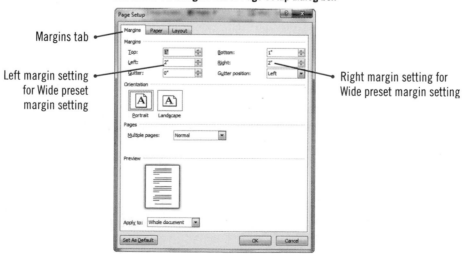

Right margin setting for Wide preset margin setting

Enhancing a Document

Setting Tabs

You can improve the appearance of a document by using tabs to align text within a line at specific positions on the page. A **tab** is a set position where text following a tab character aligns. (When you press [Tab], Word inserts a tab character—a right-facing arrow—to indicate the presence of a tab.) The ruler makes it easy to set **tab stops** (locations the insertion point moves to when you press [Tab]) and to see immediately how they affect your document. By default, Word sets left-aligned tab stops every ½". The default tab stops are marked as small black slashes in the thin gray bar below the ruler. Any tab stop that you add to the ruler will appear as a tab icon on the ruler and will override the default tab stop settings to the left of it. By default, new tab stops that you set on the ruler are left-aligned tab stops and appear as a ⌊L⌋ on the ruler. You can use the **tab indicator** on the ruler to align text differently, such as to the right or center of a tab stop. When you set tabs, they apply only to text you selected or, if no text is selected, to the paragraph containing the insertion point. You need to enter ordering information for the canoe products at the end of the document. You will use tabs to align the information in columns.

STEPS

1. **Click the View tab, click 100% in the Zoom group, then scroll down so that the bottom of the document is visible**

   You need to type the heading row for the product ordering information.

2. **Click to the right of Product Name in the last line of the document, press [Tab], type Item Number, press [Tab], type Price, then press [Enter]**

   You can see that the word Item, which follows the first tab, is left-aligned at the default 1" tab stop. The word Price is aligned at the 2" mark, also a default tab stop. Notice that the tab appears as a right-arrow in the text. Now you need to enter the product information below each heading.

3. **Type Canoe Kit, press [Tab], type OD-555, press [Tab], type $795, then press [Enter]**

   You typed the first row of data. Notice that OD-555 is aligned with the word Item at the default 1" tab stop. Notice that $795 is not aligned with the Price heading above. Instead, it is aligned at the 1 ½" default tab stop.

4. **Type Canoe Paddles, press [Tab], type OD-556, press [Tab], then type $99**

   You entered all the product data; now you need to select the lines of text you just typed so that you can set the tab stops for all three.

5. **Click to the left of Product Name, press and hold [Shift], then press [down arrow] three times**

   The three lines of text are selected, from the line beginning with Product through the line beginning with Canoe Paddles, as shown in Figure E-12. Any tab stop changes you make will now apply to all three selected lines of text.

6. **Notice the tab indicator at the top of the vertical ruler**

   The tab indicator currently displays an image of a left tab stop ⌊L⌋. This means that clicking the ruler will add a left tab stop, which is what you want.

7. **Click the 2 ½" mark on the ruler**

   The left-aligned tab stop appears on the ruler at the 2 ½" mark, and the Item Number heading and the two item numbers below it are now all left-aligned at the 2 ½" mark. Notice that the default tab stops in the thin bar below the ruler no longer appear to the left of the new tab stop.

8. **Click the tab indicator at the top of the vertical ruler twice so that the Right Tab icon ⌉ appears, then click the 5" mark on the ruler**

   The Price heading and the two prices below it are right-aligned. When you arrange numbers in a column, it is a good idea to right-align them.

9. **Select the line of text beginning with Product (the column headings), click the Bold button B on the Mini toolbar, click the document to deselect the text, then save your changes**

   Compare your screen to Figure E-13.

Enhancing a Document

FIGURE E-12: Selected text with tabs inserted

Tab indicator with left tab stop displayed

Default tab stops every .5 inch on the ruler

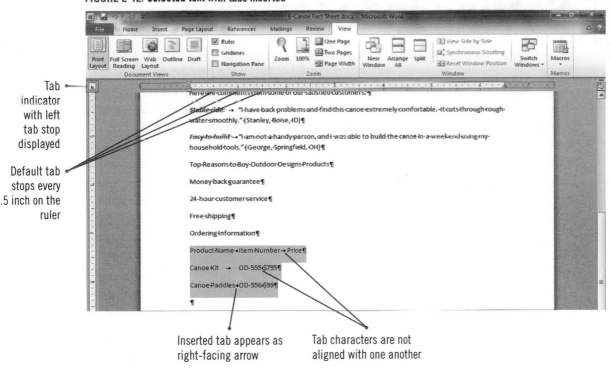

Inserted tab appears as right-facing arrow

Tab characters are not aligned with one another

FIGURE E-13: Text arranged in columns with left and right tabs set

Tab indicator with right tab stop displayed

Default tab stops to the left of the 5" mark are gone

Bolded heading row

Text left-aligned at 2.5" tab stop

Right tab stop at 5" mark on the ruler

View Ruler button

Default tab stops to the right of 5" mark still appear

Text right-aligned at 5" tab stop

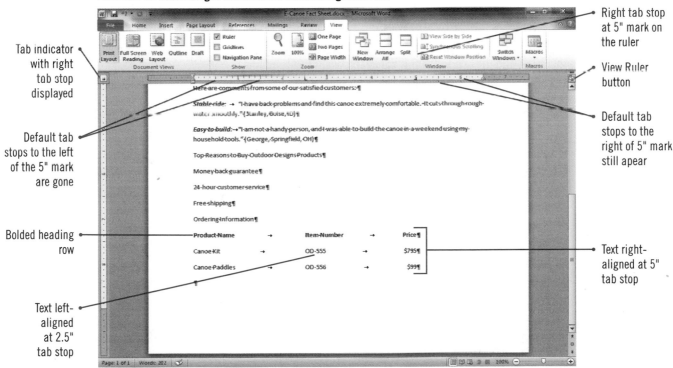

Setting Indents

You can improve the appearance of text on a page by setting indents. An **indent** is a set amount of space between the edge of a paragraph and the right or left margin. Different types of indents are appropriate for different situations. A **first line indent** indents the first line of text in a paragraph. A **left indent** indents the left edge of an entire paragraph; a **right indent** indents the right edge of an entire paragraph. A **hanging indent** aligns the text below the first line of paragraph text. You can set indents using the sliding markers on the ruler. Table E-2 describes these markers. You can set left and right indents at ½" increments using the Increase Indent and Decrease Indent buttons on the Mini toolbar or the Home tab. � ▰▰▰▰ The text containing the customer quotes would look neater if it was aligned under the first word after the tab. You want to set a hanging indent to improve the appearance of this text. You also decide to set a left indent for the paragraph text that describes the product.

STEPS

1. **Select the four lines of text beginning with** Stable ride: **and ending with** George, Springfield, OH)

2. **Click the** Home tab, **then click the** Increase Indent button **in the Paragraph group**

QUICK TIP

Make sure the ScreenTip identifies the marker as Hanging Indent and not First Line Indent or Left Indent.

3. **Position the pointer over the** Hanging Indent marker ⌂ **on the ruler so that the Hanging Indent ScreenTip appears, then click and hold so that a vertical dotted line appears on the screen**

   This dotted vertical line helps you position the marker in the desired location on the ruler.

4. **Drag** ⌂ **to the 1 ½" mark on the ruler**

   The first line in each of the selected paragraphs remains flush left, and the text below the first line of each paragraph is now aligned at the 1 ½" mark on the ruler, where you dragged the Hanging Indent marker, as shown in Figure E-14.

QUICK TIP

When you drag an indent marker, make sure the tip of the pointer—and not the body of the pointer—is positioned over the marker; otherwise, you might have difficulty dragging it.

5. **Drag the** Right Indent marker ⌂ **to the 5 ½" mark on the ruler**

   The text indents on the right side of the selected paragraphs at the 5 ½" mark. The paragraphs are narrower now, and the text in the first paragraph wraps to a third line.

6. **Select the last three lines of text in the document**

7. **Position the pointer over the** Left Indent marker ▭ **on the ruler until the Left Indent ScreenTip appears, then drag** ▭ **to the ½" mark on the ruler**

   The product information columns are now indented by ½", as shown in Figure E-15.

8. **Save your changes**

TABLE E-2: Ruler markers used for setting indents

ruler marker name	ruler marker	indents
First Line Indent marker	▽	The first line of a paragraph
Hanging Indent marker	⌂	The lines below the first line of text in a paragraph
Left Indent marker	▭	The left edge of an entire paragraph
Right Indent marker	△	The right edge of an entire paragraph

FIGURE E-14: Setting a hanging indent

First line indent marker at ½" mark

Hanging Indent marker

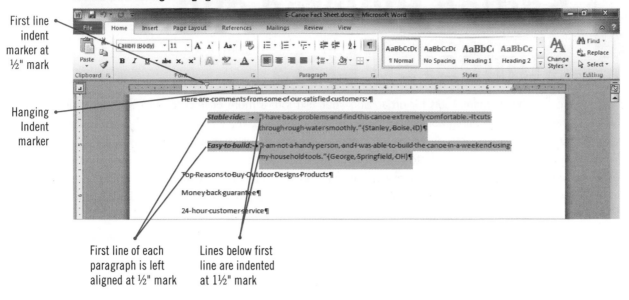

First line of each paragraph is left aligned at ½" mark

Lines below first line are indented at 1½" mark

FIGURE E-15: Paragraphs formatted with left indent

Left Indent marker is positioned at ½" mark

Paragraphs indented at ½" mark

Right indent marker

Right indent set at 5 ½" for these paragraphs

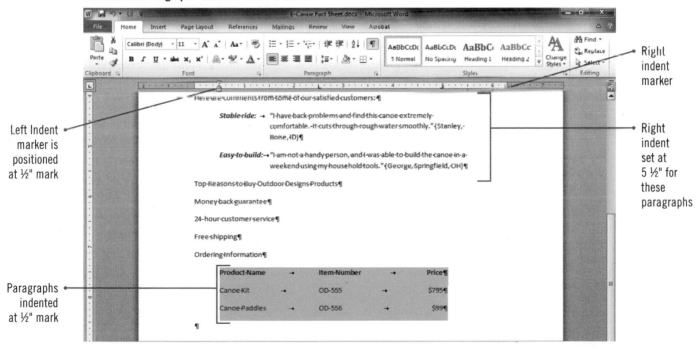

Adding Bulleted and Numbered Lists

Word provides many tools for organizing your text into a more orderly format. You can easily organize groups of related paragraphs into bulleted or numbered lists. You already learned how to create a bulleted list using the Bullets button on the Mini toolbar. The Bullets button is also available on the Home tab. When you apply the bullet format to a paragraph, Word sets off the paragraph with a bullet and automatically formats the text with a hanging indent. Use a numbered (ordered) list when you want to present items in a particular sequence, and use a bulleted (unordered) list when the items are of equal importance. There are many bullet and numbering styles to choose from when using the Bullets list and Numbering list on the Home tab, or you can create a custom style. ▨▨▨▨ You decide to add bulleted and numbered lists to the canoe kit fact sheet to make it easier to reference.

STEPS

1. **Scroll to the top of the document, then select the three lines of text under the heading Key Benefits**

QUICK TIP

With Live Preview, you can point to any format in the Bullet Library to see how the format will look if you apply it to the selected text.

2. **Click the Bullets list arrow** ▤ ▾ **in the Paragraph group on the Home tab**

   The Bullets list opens and displays bullet formatting options in the Bullet Library, as shown in Figure E-16. The Define New Bullet dialog box provides you with even more bullet options.

3. **Click Define New Bullet**

   The Define New Bullet dialog box opens. You use this dialog box to create a custom bullet.

QUICK TIP

To create a picture bullet using your own graphic, click Import in the Picture Bullet dialog box, navigate to the location of the image file you want to use, then click Add. The picture is added to the Picture Bullet dialog box.

4. **Click Picture to open the Picture Bullet dialog box, scroll down until you see the blue triangle as shown in Figure E-17, click the blue triangle, click OK twice, then click outside the selected text**

   The text you selected now appears as a bulleted list. Word has automatically indented each bullet in the list and placed a tab after each triangle. You can see by the ruler that a hanging indent has been automatically set. If any text in the bulleted list wrapped to a second line, it would align with the first line of text, not the bullet.

5. **Click to the right of the third item in the list (after expedition), then press [Enter]**

   A fourth triangle bullet appears automatically in the new row.

6. **Type Building it yourself saves hundreds of dollars**

   The text you typed is now formatted as a fourth item in the bulleted list.

7. **Scroll down until you can see the bottom of the page**

8. **Select the three lines of text under the heading Top Reasons to Buy Outdoor Designs Products, then click the Numbering list arrow in the Paragraph group**

   The Numbering list opens and displays the Numbering Library, containing different formatting options for a numbered list.

9. **Click the option shown in Figure E-18 (the one with the parenthesis after each number), then save your changes**

   The selected text is now formatted as a numbered list.

FIGURE E-16: Bullet library

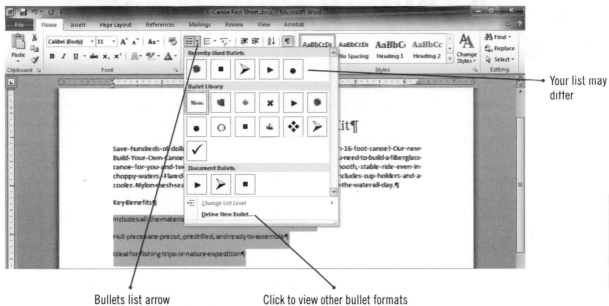

Bullets list arrow

Click to view other bullet formats

Your list may differ

FIGURE E-17: Picture Bullet dialog box

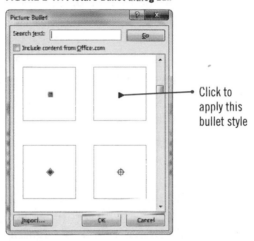

Click to apply this bullet style

FIGURE E-18: Canoe fact sheet with bulleted and numbered lists

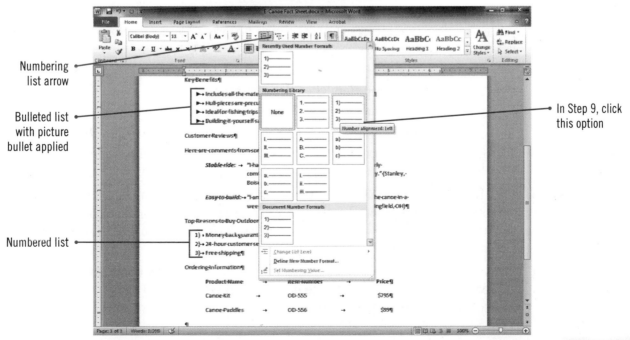

Numbering list arrow

Bulleted list with picture bullet applied

Numbered list

In Step 9, click this option

Applying Quick Styles

You can save a lot of formatting time and ensure that your document looks professional by applying styles and Quick Styles to your document. A **style** is a set of predefined formatting attributes. For instance, the Normal Paragraph style (which is applied to any text you type in a new document) includes the Calibri 11-point font with 1.15 line spacing. Besides paragraph styles, you can also apply built-in styles for other types of text elements in your document, including headings, titles, and captions. To apply a style, you can choose from **Quick Styles**, which are available in the Quick Styles gallery in the Styles group on the Home tab, or other styles available in the Style pane, which opens when you click the launcher in the Styles group. Once you apply styles to your document, you can then change the look of the entire document in one click by applying a new Quick Style set. A **Quick Style set** is a group of professionally coordinated styles that look great together; changing a Quick Style set changes all the Quick Styles in the document to a different overall look. ▆▆▆▆ You decide to use styles to complete the formatting of the canoe fact sheet.

STEPS

1. **Scroll up, then click anywhere in Key Benefits in the line below the long paragraph**
   To apply a Quick Style to a paragraph, you first click in the paragraph to which you want to apply the style.

2. **In the Styles group on the Home tab, click the Heading 1 style in the Quick Styles gallery**
   See Figure E-19. The Key Benefits paragraph now has the Heading 1 style applied to it and is formatted in Cambria 14-point blue.

3. **Using the process you followed in Steps 1 and 2, apply the Heading 1 style to the following lines: Customer Reviews, Top Reasons to Buy Outdoor Designs Products, and Ordering Information**
   All of the headings in the document now have the Heading 1 style applied.

4. **Scroll up if necessary to view the text below Customer Reviews, select the customer quote that begins with "I have back problems, then click the More button on the Quick Styles gallery**
   When you want to apply a style to only part of a paragraph, you need to first select the desired text before applying the style; otherwise, the style will be applied to the entire paragraph. The Quick Styles gallery opens and displays all the Quick Styles you can apply to paragraphs or characters, as shown in Figure E-20.

5. **Click the Quote style in the Quick Styles gallery**
   The selected text is now formatted in italic, the preset formatting specifications for the Quote style. Because you selected text instead of clicking in the paragraph, the style was applied only to the characters you selected rather than to the whole paragraph.

6. **Select the customer quote that begins with "I am not a handy person, click the Quote style in the Quick Styles gallery, then deselect the text**
   Next, you decide to change the Style set to change the overall look of the document.

7. **Click the Change Styles button in the Styles group, point to Style Set, then click Modern**
   The Modern style set is applied to the document. This style set specifies that the Heading 1 style includes white type against a blue background, all capital letters, and Calibri 10-point body text.

8. **Click the Change Styles button in the Styles group, point to Colors, then click Grid**
   The color of the Heading 1 background is now red, and the title of the document is now maroon. In addition to changing the Quick Style set, you can apply a different color scheme so that the style colors change but remain coordinated for a polished final document.

9. **Press [Ctrl][End], type your name, save your changes, preview the document and compare it to Figure E-21, close the document, then exit Word**
   Submit your document to your instructor.

QUICK TIP
You can add additional Quick Style sets, so you may see additional options on your Style Set list

QUICK TIP
To change the font in a Quick Style set for a document, click the Change Styles button in the Styles group, point to Fonts to open the Font Scheme list, then choose a Font Scheme.

Enhancing a Document

FIGURE E-19: Heading 1 style applied to a paragraph

Quick Styles gallery

Heading 1 style

Paragraph with Heading 1 style applied

FIGURE E-20: Quick Styles gallery

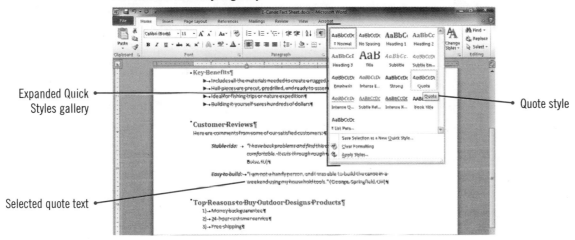

Expanded Quick Styles gallery

Quote style

Selected quote text

FIGURE E-21: Completed E-Canoe Fact Sheet

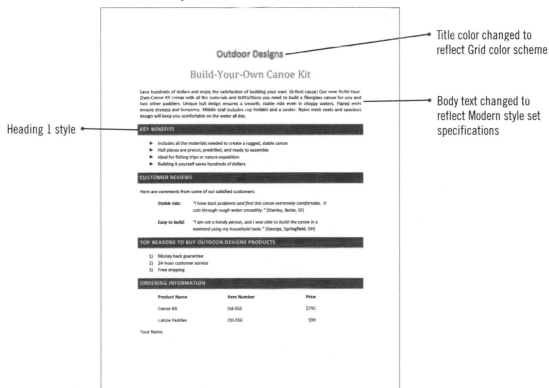

Title color changed to reflect Grid color scheme

Heading 1 style

Body text changed to reflect Modern style set specifications

For current SAM information, including versions and content details, visit SAM Central (http://www.cengage.com/samcentral). If you have a SAM user profile, you may have access to hands-on instruction, practice, and assessment of the skills covered in this unit. Since various versions of SAM are supported throughout the life of this text, check with your instructor for the correct instructions and URL/Web site for accessing assignments.

Label the Word window elements shown in Figure E-22.

FIGURE E-22

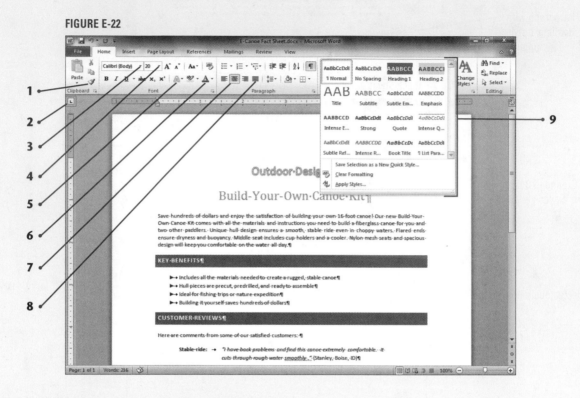

Match each button or icon with its function.

10. ▤

11. ⌐

12. ⋹

13. ⌐

14. ⌂

a. Mark on the ruler indicating a right-aligned tab stop

b. Increases the indent by ½"

c. Mark on the ruler indicating a left-aligned tab stop

d. Center-aligns the current paragraph between the right and left margins

e. Indents text following the first line in a paragraph at a specified mark on the ruler

Select the best answer from the list of choices.

15. Which of the following tabs on the Ribbon contains tools for letting you preview a whole page of a document?
    - **a.** View
    - **b.** Home
    - **c.** Page Layout
    - **d.** Review

16. Which of the following tabs on the Ribbon do you use to change margin settings?
    - **a.** Home
    - **b.** Page Layout
    - **c.** View
    - **d.** Insert

17. Tabs are useful when you want to:
    - **a.** Set line spacing for a paragraph.
    - **b.** Organize information into columns.
    - **c.** Set paragraph alignment.
    - **d.** Format characters.

18. A set of predefined formatting attributes is a:
    - **a.** Font.
    - **b.** Font effect.
    - **c.** Style.
    - **d.** Tab stop.

19. Which of the following methods describes how to set a hanging indent 2" from the left edge of the paper?
    - **a.** Drag ▢ to the 2" mark on the ruler.
    - **b.** Use the Paragraphs dialog box to specify a 2" left margin.
    - **c.** Click at the 2" mark on the ruler.
    - **d.** Drag ⌂ to the 2" mark on the ruler.

Skills Review

1. **Change font and font size.**
   - **a.** Start Word, use the Open command in Backstage view to open the file E-2.docx from where you store your Data Files, then save it as **E-Photo Exhibit Info**.
   - **b.** Select the entire first line of the document.
   - **c.** Change the font size to 26.
   - **d.** Change the font to Franklin Gothic Book.
   - **e.** Select the entire second line of the document. Change the font size to 18.
   - **f.** Save your changes.

2. **Change font color, style, and effects.**
   - **a.** Select the first line of the document, then change the font color to dark blue (the fourth color in the first row under Theme Colors).
   - **b.** Format the selected blue text in bold.
   - **c.** Select the second line of the document, open the Text Effects gallery, then apply the solid orange option (second option in fourth row)
   - **d.** Select the text **Deer Park Arts Commission** in the third line of the document, then apply bold formatting to the selection. Change the font color to dark blue.
   - **e.** Use the Format Painter to apply the formatting from Deer Park Arts Commission to the other instance of Deer Park Arts Commission in the document.
   - **f.** Apply bold formatting to **Pete Miller** (in the thirteenth line of text) and **Rita Jones** (in the fifteenth line of text).
   - **g.** Save your changes.

3. **Change alignment and line spacing.**
   - **a.** Change the alignment of the paragraph located below New England Photography Exhibition to justified.
   - **b.** Change the line spacing to 1.15 for the justified paragraph.
   - **c.** Use the Paragraph dialog box to specify to add 6 point spacing before and after the paragraph.
   - **d.** Center-align the first two lines of the document.
   - **e.** Save your changes.

Skills Review (continued)

4. **Change margin settings.**

   a. Use a command on the View tab to adjust the view so that you can see the whole page on the screen.

   b. Verify that the ruler is visible in the document window. (If it is not visible, adjust your settings so that it is visible.)

   c. Apply the preset Narrow margins setting to the document.

   d. Apply the preset Wide margins setting to the document.

   e. Open the Page Setup dialog box with the Margins tab displayed, and set the left margin to 1.2 and the right margin to 1.2.

   f. Change the zoom level back to 100%.

   g. Save your changes.

5. **Set tabs.**

   a. Scroll down until you see the line of text that begins with **Item**.

   b. Select this line and the three lines below it (through the line that begins with **Exhibition**).

   c. Set a left tab stop at the 2 ½" mark on the ruler for the four selected lines.

   d. Set a right tab stop at the 4 ½" mark on the ruler for the four selected lines.

   e. Apply bold formatting to the line that contains **Item Description Date**.

   f. Save your changes.

6. **Set indents.**

   a. Select the four lines of text below Important Dates, then set the left indent to ¼".

   b. Locate the line of text that starts with Pete Miller (the thirteenth line of text in the document).

   c. Select the line of text that begins with Pete Miller and the three lines below it (ending with "photojournalist").

   d. Set a hanging indent at the 1" mark on the ruler for the selected lines of text.

   e. Save your changes.

7. **Add bulleted and numbered lists.**

   a. Format lines eight through ten (**Nature** through **New Englanders at Work**) as a bulleted list using the checkmark bullet.

   b. Format the last three lines in the document as a numbered list, choosing the style 1) 2) 3) (a number followed by a parenthesis).

   c. Save your changes.

8. **Apply Quick Styles.**

   a. Apply the Heading 1 Quick Style to the text **Submissions** (line 6 in the document).

   b. Apply the Heading 1 style to the following headings: **Judges**, **Submission Guidelines**, **Important Dates**, and **Awards**.

   c. Use the Change Styles button to apply the Thatch style set to the document.

   d. Use the Change Styles button to change the color scheme to Foundry.

   e. Type your name in the last line of the document. (*Note*: Make sure your name is not formatted as a numbered list. If you need to remove the numbered list format from any text in the document, click in the paragraph from which you want to remove it, then click the Numbering button.)

   f. Save your changes.

   g. Preview the document, compare your document with Figure E-23, then exit Word. Submit your completed document to your instructor.

FIGURE E-23

Call for Entries

New England Photography Exhibition

The Deer Park Arts Commission is seeking submissions for the first annual Exhibition of New England Photography and Photographers. The exhibition will open March 2, 2013, and will feature photographs of New England's people, places, and landscapes.

Submissions

We are seeking photograph submissions of New England subjects in the following areas:
- Nature
- Landscapes
- New Englanders at Work

Judges

Two renowned photographers from New England will select the winning submissions.

Pete Miller: Pete is a widely exhibited photographer and an instructor of photography at the Burlington Fine Arts Academy.

Rita Jones: Rita is a staff photographer at the Vermont Chronicle. Before settling in Vermont, Rita travelled to more than 30 countries as a photojournalist.

Submission Guidelines

Color photographs must be your own original work. Digital images on a CD should be mailed to:
Deer Park Arts Commission
P.O. Box 1023
Stowe, VT 12887

Important Dates

Item	Description	Date
Photographs	on CD	1/3/13
Notice of Acceptance:	by email	2/1/13
Exhibition	at Stowe Arts Center	3/1/13

Awards

The judges will choose the winners in each category for the following awards:
1) Best of Show
2) Best of Category
3) Runner Up

Your Name

Enhancing a Document

Independent Challenge 1

You work in the marketing department for the Bay City Community Center. Rhonda Johnson, the marketing manager, needs to create a one-page document that describes the programs and classes offered in October. Rhonda has already created a draft with all the necessary information; however, she is not happy with its appearance. She has provided you with her unformatted draft and has asked you to format it so that all the information is presented effectively and looks attractive and professional.

a. Start Word, open the file E-3.docx from where your Data Files are stored, then save it as **E-October Calendar**.

b. Center-align the first four lines of the document.

c. Change the font of **October Calendar** to Century Gothic, and increase the font size to 24.

d. Change the font color of **October Calendar** to dark orange (ScreenTip reads "Orange Accent 6"), then apply bold formatting to it.

e. Increase the font size of **Bay City Community Center** and the two lines below it to 14 points.

f. In the paragraph under What's New (lines 6–9), align the paragraph so that it is justified, then set the line spacing to 1.5. Increase the space before and after this paragraph to 6 points.

g. Apply the Heading 1 style to the following lines of text: **What's New, New Resident Orientation Classes, Cooking Classes,** and **Adult Fitness Class**.

h. In the four lines of text that contain tabs below the heading New Resident Orientation Classes, set two left tab stops—the first at 2" and the second at 4".

i. In the four lines of text that contain tabs below the heading Cooking Classes, set a left tab stop at 2", a second left tab stop at 3 ½", and one right tab stop at 5 ½".

j. Format the last three lines in the document as a bulleted list. Choose the Picture bullet style that looks like a red X.

k. Apply the Manuscript style set to the document, then compare the document to Figure E-24.

l. Type your name at the end of the document, then right-align it.

FIGURE E-24

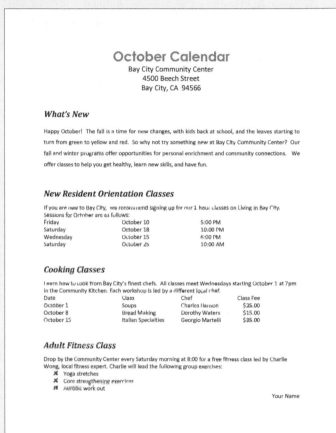

Advanced Challenge Exercise

- Use the Change Styles button to change the Font scheme to the Urban scheme.
- Change the color of the **What's New** heading to dark orange (ScreenTip reads "Orange, Accent 6").
- Select the **What's New** heading, right-click, point to Styles in the shortcut menu, then click Save Selection as a New Quick Style. In the Create New Style from Formatting dialog box, type **Calendar Heading 1** in the Name text box, then click OK.
- Apply the Calendar Heading 1 style to the other headings in the document.

m. Save your changes, then preview the document, close it, and exit Word. Submit the completed document to your instructor.

Independent Challenge 2

You provide administrative help to the owner of Walking Adventures, a small tour company that offers walking tours in the United States, Canada, and Brazil. Raven Smith, the marketing director, has given you an unformatted document that provides information about the tours the company will offer in the summer. Raven has asked you to format the sheet so that the information is attractive and easy to understand.

a. Open the file E-4.docx from where you store your Data Files, then save it as **E-Walking Adventures Fact Sheet**.

b. Center-align the first five lines of text in the document, which include the company name and contact information.

c. Format the Walking Adventures company name in line 1 of the document using any font, font style, or effects you like to make it look attractive and appropriate for an adventure tour company.

d. Apply the Heading 1 style to the following lines of text: **About Walking Adventures**, **Summer 2013 Walking Tours**, and **All Adventures Include**.

e. Use the Change Styles button to apply the Simple style set to the document.

f. Justify the paragraph of text below the About Walking Adventures heading, then set line spacing for this paragraph at 1.15.

g. Select the last four paragraphs below the heading Summer 2013 Walking Tours, beginning with **Grand Canyon** and ending with **($2295)**. Set a left tab stop for these four selected paragraphs to the 2" mark on the ruler.

h. For the same four paragraphs, apply a hanging indent at the 2" mark on the ruler, so that the paragraph text wraps at the 2" mark (the same position of the tab stop that you set in Step g).

i. Apply the Strong style to the text **Grand Canyon:**, **Alaska:**, **British Columbia:**, and **Amazon Adventure:**.

j. Format the last four lines of text in the document as a bulleted list, choosing a Picture bullet style that looks appropriate for this document.

k. Add your name in the last line of the information sheet, then center-align it.

l. Save your changes, preview, and print the information sheet.

m. Close the document, then exit Word.

Independent Challenge 3

You work for Stephen Wood, the marketing director of Happy Land—a family resort in Tallahassee, Florida. Stephen has asked you to create a Premium One-Day Pass for the park. The pass will be given to groups of 20 or more who buy passes to the resort. Stephen typed the information for the pass in Word and has given the document to you to format.

a. Open the file E-5.docx from where you store your Data Files, then save it as **E-One Day Pass**.

b. Using the skills you learned in this unit, format the pass using fonts, sizes, styles, and effects that you think are appropriate. Use your creativity to produce an attractive document.

c. Format some of the text on the pass as a bulleted list, choosing whatever style you like.

d. Change the paper orientation to Landscape, and adjust the margins to different settings. (*Hint*: To specify to print the document in landscape orientation, click the Page Layout tab, click the Orientation button in the Page Setup group, then click Landscape.)

e. Type your name somewhere on the pass.

Advanced Challenge Exercise

- Type an asterisk (*) to the right of the word **Pass** in the first line of the document. Format the asterisk with the superscript effect in the Font dialog box.
- Move to the end of the document, type an asterisk (*) on a new line, then type **Must be at least 15 years old or accompanied by an adult to use this pass.**. Format this text and the asterisk you inserted in the previous step so that they are a different color than the rest of the text in the document.

f. Save your changes, print the pass, then close the document and exit Word.

Real Life Independent Challenge

You are planning a party to celebrate a special occasion. The party can be for any type of event—a birthday celebration, a pizza party, or whatever you want. You need to create a flyer to hand out to your friends or invitees that announces the party, gives information about the reason for the celebration, and provides directions for how to get there.

a. Start Word, then save a new, blank document as **E-Party Flyer.docx**.

b. Type the name of the party in the first line. Format the text using a large font size, then apply a font style that is appropriate for this type of party. Center-align the party name.

c. Below the name of the party, type one line that extends an invitation to this party and one line that explains the reason for celebrating.

d. Below the description you typed in Step c, type the date and time of the party on two separate lines.

e. In the line below the time, type the location and address of the party.

f. Center-align all the text you typed in Steps b through e.

g. Below the location and address of the party, add three highlights of the party, and format the three highlights as a bulleted list, using a Picture bullet style of your choice that is appropriate for the party's theme. Left-align the bulleted list at the 2" mark on the ruler.

h. Below the bulleted list, type **Directions:**. Left-align **Directions:** at the 2" mark on the ruler.

i. Below **Directions:**, type three lines of text that provide directions on how to get to the party from a specific location (such as from the center of town or from a main road). Format the directions as a numbered list. Left-align the numbered list at the 2" mark on the ruler.

j. Type your name on the last line of the flyer. Right-align it.

k. Format all the text in the flyer using fonts, font sizes, and formatting effects that are appropriate for the theme. Preview, save, and close the document, then submit the file to your instructor.

l. Exit Word.

Visual Workshop

Open the file E-6.docx from where your Data Files are stored, then save it as E-Diner Menu. Format the document so that it appears as shown in Figure E-25. (*Hint*: A different style set has been applied to the document, and the color scheme was changed, so you may need to experiment with different combinations of Quick Styles, style sets, and color schemes until you find the right mix. If you do not have or cannot find the font used in the title, apply the closest match you can find.) Add your name at the bottom of the document, then preview the document. Close the document, then exit Word. Submit the document to your instructor.

FIGURE E-25

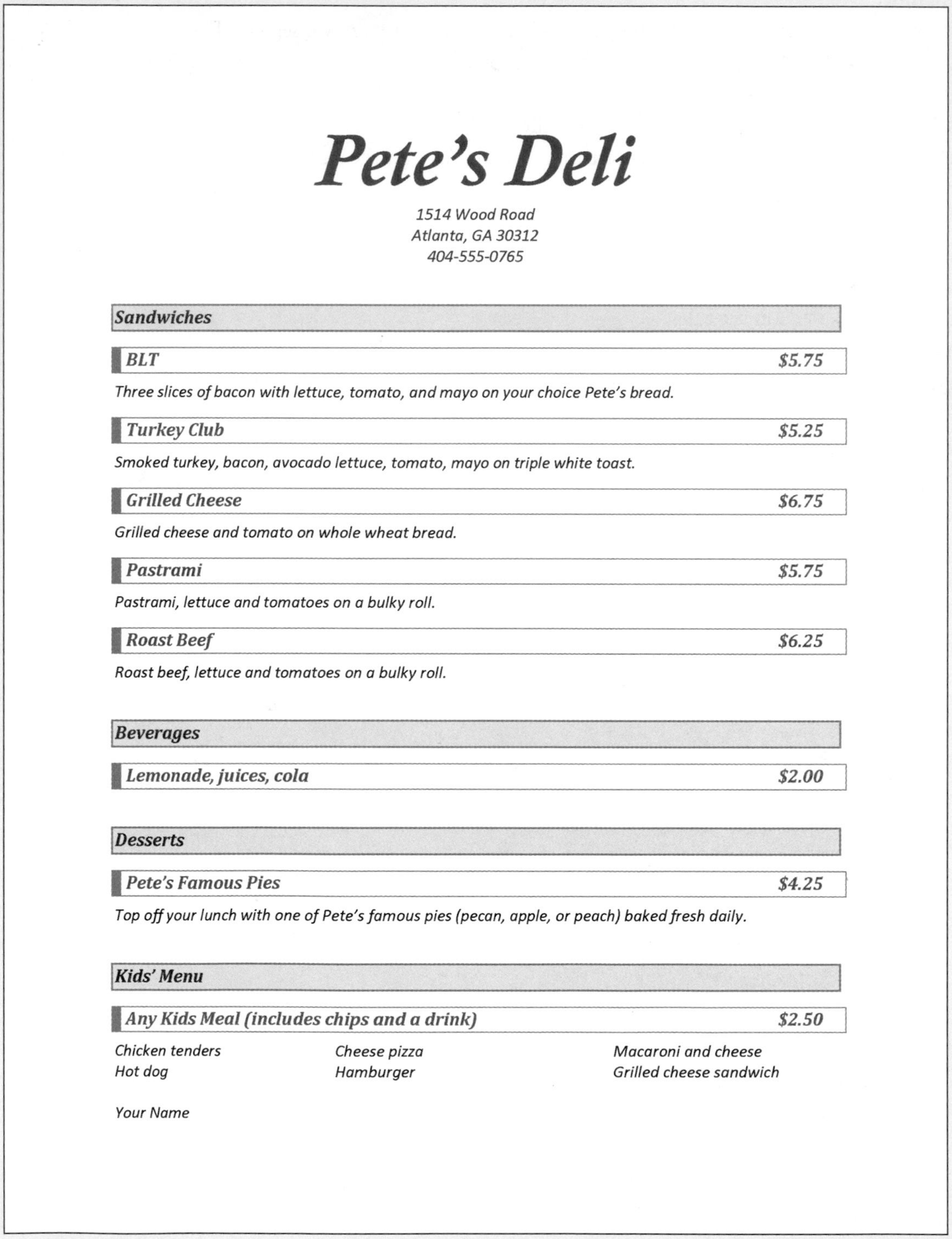

Pete's Deli

1514 Wood Road
Atlanta, GA 30312
404-555-0765

Sandwiches

BLT	*$5.75*

Three slices of bacon with lettuce, tomato, and mayo on your choice Pete's bread.

Turkey Club	*$5.25*

Smoked turkey, bacon, avocado lettuce, tomato, mayo on triple white toast.

Grilled Cheese	*$6.75*

Grilled cheese and tomato on whole wheat bread.

Pastrami	*$5.75*

Pastrami, lettuce and tomatoes on a bulky roll.

Roast Beef	*$6.25*

Roast beef, lettuce and tomatoes on a bulky roll.

Beverages

Lemonade, juices, cola	*$2.00*

Desserts

Pete's Famous Pies	*$4.25*

Top off your lunch with one of Pete's famous pies (pecan, apple, or peach) baked fresh daily.

Kids' Menu

Any Kids Meal (includes chips and a drink)	*$2.50*

Chicken tenders	*Cheese pizza*	*Macaroni and cheese*
Hot dog	*Hamburger*	*Grilled cheese sandwich*

Your Name

Enhancing a Document

UNIT
F
Word 2010

Adding Special Elements to a Document

Files You Will Need:

F-1.docx
F-2.docx
F-3.docx
F-4.docx
F-5.docx
F-6.docx
F-7.docx

Word provides many tools to help you create professional documents, such as reports that incorporate graphics and other special elements. For instance, you can insert a table to present detailed information in a row-and-column format. To add visual interest to your document, Word provides a wide variety of **clip art**, which are ready-made art objects you can insert in documents. If your document contains multiple pages, it is a good idea to insert headers and footers at the top and bottom of each page, containing the page number and other information you want to appear on every page of your document. Word also makes it easy to insert footnotes and citations. You can easily change the entire look of your document by applying a theme. Karen Rivera, marketing director for Outdoor Designs, has asked you to finish a report that both summarizes global corporate efforts to adopt green business practices to preserve the environment and recommends a plan for launching green initiatives at Outdoor Designs.

OBJECTIVES

Create a table

Insert and delete table columns and rows

Format a table

Add clip art

Add footnotes and citations

Insert a header or footer

Add borders and shading

Work with themes

Format a research paper

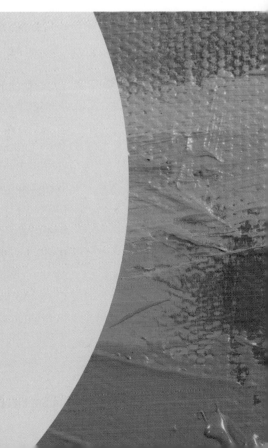

Creating a Table

It can be effective to present information within a table. A **table** is a grid of rows and columns. The intersection of a row and column is called a **cell**. Cells can contain either text or graphics. You can insert a table using the Table button on the Insert tab. When you create a table, you specify the number of rows and columns; you can also add and delete rows and columns as you modify a table. You can use tabs to organize text into rows and columns, but working with tables is often easier. Another benefit to using tables is that Word provides a wide range of professionally designed table styles that you can apply to your table.  Karen gives you a file containing the content for the recommendation report. You begin by inserting a table on the last page to present the information about a new task-force organization.

STEPS

1. **Start Word, open the file** F-1.docx **from where you store your Data Files, then save it as** F-Going Green Report

   The report opens in Print Layout view. The status bar indicates that there are four pages. You need to insert the table on page 4. You can use the Navigation Pane to help you move to any page quickly.

2. **Click the** Find button **in the Editing group on the Home tab**

   The Navigation Pane opens on the left of your screen. There is a Search Document text box at the top, where you can enter keywords you want to find. Below the Search Document text box are three view tabs.

3. **Click the** middle tab **in the Navigation Pane, scroll down in the Navigation Pane until you see the page 4 thumbnail, then click the** page 4 thumbnail

   The top of the fourth page is now open on your screen, as shown in Figure F-1. You want to insert the table in the blank line above the heading "Outdoor Designs Vision".

4. **Click to the left of the** paragraph mark ¶ **in the blank line above** Outdoor Designs Vision

5. **Click the** Navigation Pane Close button ☒, **click the** Insert tab, **then click the** Table button ▦ **in the Tables group**

   The Table menu opens and displays a grid for choosing the number of rows and columns for your table.

6. **Point to the** third square **in the third row of the grid, as shown in Figure F-2, then click**

   A table with three rows and three columns appears below the paragraph, and the insertion point is in the first cell. Notice that two additional tabs now appear on the Ribbon: the Table Tools Design tab and the Table Tools Layout tab. These are **contextual tabs**, meaning that they appear only when a particular type of object is selected and are not otherwise available.

7. **Type** Task Force, **then press [Tab]**

   Pressing [Tab] moves the insertion point to the next cell. The symbol in each cell is an **end-of-cell mark**. The marks to the right of each row are **end-of-row marks**.

8. **Type** Leader, **press [Tab], type** Department, **then press [Tab]**

   Pressing [Tab] in the last cell of a row moves the insertion point to the first cell in the next row.

9. **Type the text shown below in the rest of the table, pressing [Tab] after each entry to move to the next cell, but do not press [Tab] after the last entry**

Recycling	Stefanie Lin	Finance
Reducing Waste	George Fitzgerald	Operations

   All the cells in the table have data in them. Compare your screen to Figure F-3.

10. **Click the** Save button 🖫 **on the Quick Access Toolbar**

    Notice that when you move the mouse pointer over the table, the Table move handle ✛ appears above the upper-left corner of the table. Clicking this icon selects the entire table.

Adding Special Elements to a Document

FIGURE F-1: Using the Navigation Pane to move to page 4

Insertion point at top of page 4

Navigation Pane

In Step 3, click middle tab

Page 4 thumbnail

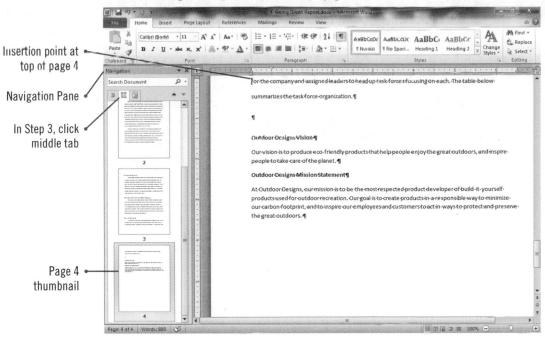

FIGURE F-2: Inserting a 3 x 3 table

Insert tab

Table button

In Step 6, click this square

Table is inserted at location of insertion point

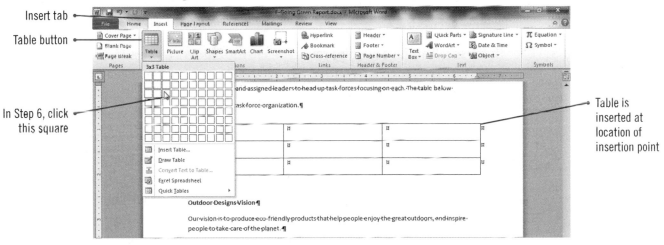

FIGURE F-3: Table with all information entered

Table Tools Design tab

Column

End-of-cell mark

Row

End-of-row mark

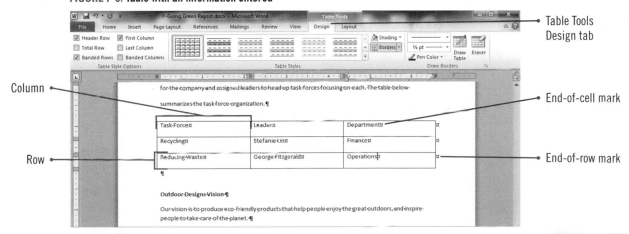

Adding Special Elements to a Document

Inserting and Deleting Table Columns and Rows

After you create a table, you might need to add more information or delete existing information. To accommodate the new information, you can add rows to the top, bottom, or middle of a table. You can add columns anywhere in a table, too. You can use commands on the Table Tools Layout tab to add or delete columns and rows.  You need to add a new row in the middle of the table to add information about another task force. You also need to add a column to the table that indicates each leader's job title. Finally, you need to delete one of the rows.

STEPS

1. **Click Operations in the last cell of the table if necessary, then press [Tab]**

   Pressing [Tab] in the last cell of a table inserts a new row at the bottom of the table. The table now has four rows, and the insertion point is in the first cell of the new row.

2. **Type Green Product Packaging, press [Tab], type Marco Lopez, press [Tab], then type Manufacturing**

3. **Click any cell in the second row of the table, then click the Table Tools Layout tab**

   The Table Tools Layout tab displays tools and commands for adjusting settings in a table. Because the Table Tools Layout tab is a contextual tab, it appears only when you click in a table or select a table.

QUICK TIP

To insert a row or column using the shortcut menu, right-click a cell in the table, point to Insert, then click an option to insert a row above or below, or a column to the left or right of the current position.

4. **Click the Insert Below button in the Rows & Columns group on the Layout tab**

   A new empty row appears below the second row.

5. **Click the first cell of the new third row, type Energy Efficiency, press [Tab], type Rhonda Wyman, press [Tab], then type Office Management**

6. **Click the Insert Left button in the Rows & Columns group on the Layout tab**

   A new empty column appears between the Leader and Department columns. Compare your screen to Figure F-4. Notice that Word automatically narrowed the existing columns to accommodate the new column.

7. **Click the top cell of the new column, type Position, then press [↓]**

   The insertion point moves down to the second row in the third column.

8. **Type Director, press [↓], type Senior Manager, press [↓], type Director, press [↓], then type Vice President**

   You have just learned that the Recycling and Reducing Waste task forces will be combined into one. You need to delete the Reducing Waste task force row.

9. **Click any cell in the row that begins with Reducing Waste, click the Delete button in the Rows & Columns group, click Delete Rows, then save your changes**

   The entire row is deleted, and the other rows move up to close up the space. Compare your screen to Figure F-5.

FIGURE F-4: Table with new column and rows added

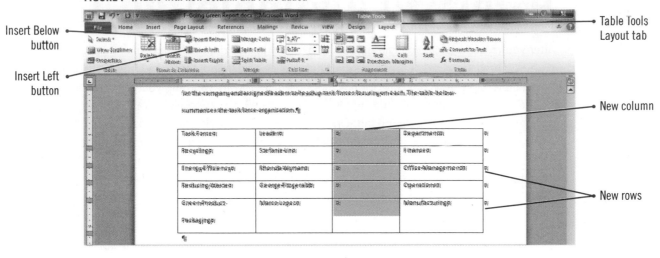

Insert Below button

Insert Left button

Table Tools Layout tab

New column

New rows

FIGURE F-5: Table after deleting row

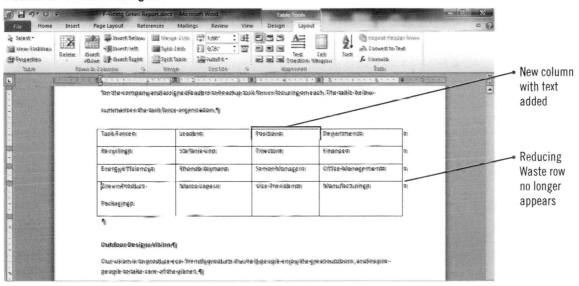

New column with text added

Reducing Waste row no longer appears

Creating a table with the Draw Table button

You can also create a table by drawing using the Draw Table command. To do so, click the Insert tab, click the Table button, then click Draw Table. This command is also available for drawing new rows and columns in an existing table in the Draw Borders group on the Table Tools Design tab. The pointer changes to $\mathscr{O}$, which you can drag in a diagonal motion to create the outside border of the table. To create or add columns, drag vertically from the top border down. To create or add rows, drag horizontally from the right border to the left border. When you are finished drawing the table, press [Esc] to turn off the Draw Table feature. You can use commands in the Draw Borders group on the Table Tools Design tab to change the pen color or line width and style, or to delete column or row lines. Drawing a table or cells onto an existing table gives you more freedom to create tables with unequal columns, unequal rows, or merged cells.

Word 2010

Formatting a Table

After you create a table, you can quickly format it by applying one of many built-in table styles. A **table style** is a predefined set of formatting attributes, such as shading, fonts, and border color, which specify how a table looks. You could also format your table manually by choosing your own settings, but applying a table style makes your table look professionally designed. You choose a table style using the Table Styles gallery on the Table Tools Design tab. Once you apply a table style that you like, you can further enhance and customize your table's appearance using the Shading and Borders tools in the Table Styles group. You can also improve the appearance and readability of a table by adjusting column widths. ▟▟▟ Now that the information in the task force table is complete, you decide to apply a table style to it and adjust the width of the first column so that all task-force names fit on one line.

STEPS

1. **Click anywhere in the table if necessary, then click the Table Tools Design tab**

   The Design tab is now active and displays tools and buttons for formatting a table. The Table Styles group displays thumbnails of preset styles that you can apply to your table.

2. **Point to each Table Style visible in the Table Styles group, and observe the change in your document**

   With Live Preview, the table in the report changes to display a preview of each style as you move the mouse from one style to the next. You can view all available table styles by clicking the More button ▾ at the right end of the Table Styles group.

3. **Click the More button ▾ in the Table Styles group, then click the first style in the second row (Light List), as shown in Figure F-6**

   The table is now formatted with a black top row. Notice that "Green Product Packaging" in the first column wraps to two lines. You want this task-force name to fit on one line.

4. **Position the mouse pointer just above Task Force until it changes to ↓, then click**

   The first column is now selected, making it easy to see the right edge of the first column.

5. **Position the mouse pointer on the right edge of the selected column until the pointer changes to +‖+, drag the pointer to the right about ¼", then release the mouse button**

   The width of the first column increases, and now the text in each first column cell fits on one line instead of two. The second column is now narrower.

6. **Point to the upper-left corner of the table until the ✛ pointer appears, then click**

   The entire table is selected. Any formatting settings you choose at this point will be applied to all the cells in the table. You decide that you want to add column gridlines to the table.

7. **Click the Borders list arrow in the Table Styles group, then click the All Borders option**

   Black gridlines now outline all of the cells in the table, as shown in Figure F-7.

8. **Save your changes**

Adding Special Elements to a Document

FIGURE F-6: Applying a table style

In Step 3, click this table style

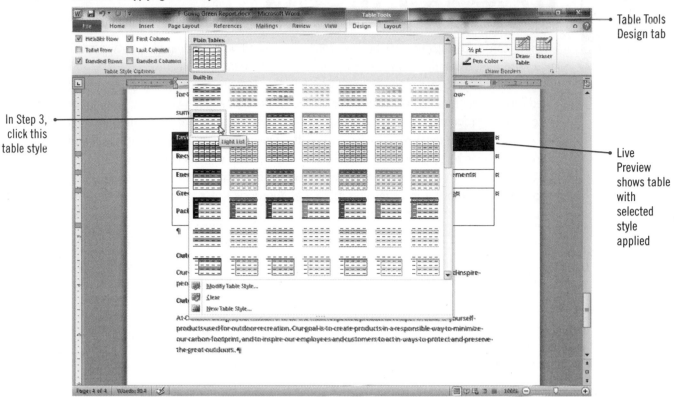

Table Tools Design tab

Live Preview shows table with selected style applied

FIGURE F-7: Formatted table with table style and borders added

Table Tools Design tab

Borders list arrow

Vertical borders applied

Wider column allows all text to fit on one line

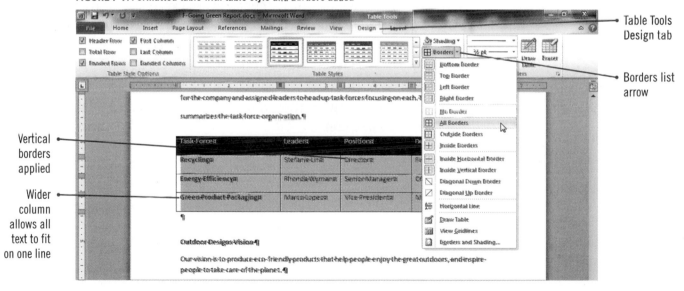

Adding SmartArt

Microsoft Office 2010 offers many tools for adding graphics to your documents to enhance their visual appeal and better communicate your message. **SmartArt** is a feature that lets you easily create professional-looking business diagrams, such as organizational charts, process diagrams, and time lines. To create a SmartArt graphic, click the SmartArt button in the Illustrations group on the Insert tab. The Choose a SmartArt Graphic dialog box opens. In the left pane, click the category of graphic that you want to insert, then click the SmartArt thumbnail you want to create. A preview of the SmartArt graphic appears in the right pane, along with a description of what it is used for. Click OK, then edit the placeholder text to suit your needs.

Adding Special Elements to a Document

Adding Clip Art

Graphics can help illustrate a point or enhance the overall visual appeal of a document. You can insert images from files stored on disk or downloaded from the Web, add SmartArt graphics, and draw images using tools on the Shapes menu on the Insert tab. You can also access hundreds of ready-made images, called clip art, via the **Clip Art task pane**. The Clip Art task pane lets you search for clip art, animations, videos, and photographs, all of which are called **clips**. Word searches the clip art folders on your hard drive and also searches the database of clips on the Office Online Web site if your computer is connected to the Internet. The search results appear as small pictures called **thumbnails** in the task pane. Once you select a clip and insert it into a document, you can enhance it by applying picture styles, changing the way text wraps around it, moving it, or resizing it. You decide to add a picture of the earth next to the Outdoor Designs Mission Statement heading and paragraph.

STEPS

1. **Click to the left of Outdoor Designs Mission Statement (five lines below the table), click the Insert tab, then click the Clip Art button in the Illustrations group**
   The Clip Art task pane opens.

> **TROUBLE**
> Make sure the Include Office.com content check box is selected.

2. **Click in the Search for text box in the task pane, select any existing text if necessary, type earth, select it, then click Go**
   The task pane displays thumbnail previews of all available images that are associated with the word "earth." These images are either fed from the Office.com Web site or stored on your computer.

> **TROUBLE**
> Your selection of clip art might differ. If the image shown in the figure does not appear in your task pane, click a different image.

3. **Click the image of the earth, as shown in Figure F-8, then click the Clip Art task pane Close button X**
   The image is inserted in the report. Round **sizing handles** in the corners and square sizing handles on the sides of the image indicate that the image is selected. Notice that the Picture Tools Format tab is active. It contains many tools to enhance the appearance of graphics, including tools to change the color of the image.

4. **Click the Color button in the Adjust group, then click the fourth option in the third row (Olive Green, Accent color 3 Light), as shown in Figure F-9**
   The image is now all green. You can change the look of the image by applying a Picture Style.

5. **Click the More button ⊞ in the Picture Styles group to open the Picture Styles gallery, then click the Soft Edge Oval option**
   The image now has soft edges. The image looks awkward because its bottom edge is aligned with the last line of paragraph text. This is known as an **inline graphic**. To fix this so that the text flows next to the image, you need to change its wrapping style, or the settings for how text flows in relation to a graphic.

6. **Click the Wrap Text button 🖼 in the Arrange group tab, then click Square**
   The image's left edge should be left-aligned with the paragraph text. Because you set the wrapping style to square, the image is now a **floating image**, which means you can drag it anywhere on the page. The anchor icon next to it indicates it is now a floating image. You need to move the image down a little.

> **QUICK TIP**
> You can move a selected image in small increments by using the arrow keys.

7. **Point to the image so that the pointer changes to ✛, then drag the image down so that its bottom edge is aligned with the last line of text in the paragraph**
   Notice that the text automatically rewrapped itself around the image as you moved it down.

> **QUICK TIP**
> To see an image's exact measurements, right-click the image and look at the Height and Width settings.

8. **Drag the upper-right sizing handle up and to the right diagonally about ¼", then save your changes**
   Compare your screen to Figure F-10. You made the graphic larger, so its top edge is aligned with the mission statement heading and the bottom edge is aligned with the last line of text.

FIGURE F-8: Clip Art task pane with "earth" search results

Search for text box

Clip Art task pane

Image is inserted at insertion point

In Step 3, click this image

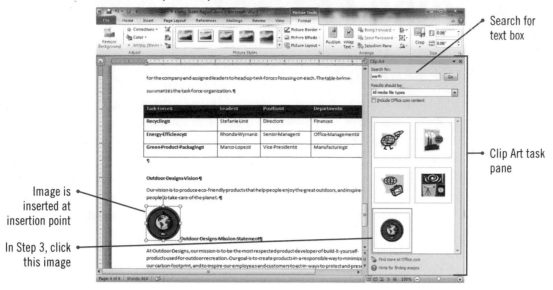

FIGURE F-9: Applying a new color to an image using the Color Styles gallery

Color button

Color Styles gallery

Click this style (Olive Green, Accent color 3 Light)

Live Preview shows image with olive green style applied

FIGURE F-10: Resized earth image with color and picture style applied

Wrap Text button

Soft Edge Oval Picture Style

Round sizing handles and anchor icon signify floating image

Upper-right sizing handle

Text flows to the right of image in a square

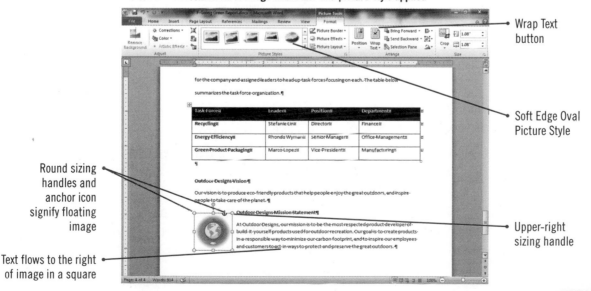

Adding Special Elements to a Document

Adding Footnotes and Citations

If your document includes quotes or paraphrased material from another source, you need to credit that source by inserting a citation. A **citation** is a reference to a source that usually includes the author's name and page number of the referenced material. There are different styles for using citations; MLA style is often used for research papers. Citations that follow MLA guidelines appear in parentheses after a quote or paraphrase. If a document contains citations, it must also include a **bibliography**, which is a listing of detailed source information for citations in the document. The References tab in Word contains tools to manage sources, insert citations, and add a bibliography. You can also use the References tab to add footnotes. A **footnote** is a comment that appears at the bottom of a document page; it consists of two linked parts: the reference mark in the body of the document and the corresponding note text.  You need to add a footnote to the report that comments on recent energy savings. You also need to add a new source and citation, and insert a bibliography.

STEPS

1. **Click the Home tab, click the Find button in the Editing group, then click the first tab in the Navigation Pane**

   You can click a heading in the Navigation Pane to jump to that heading in the document.

QUICK TIP

You can reorganize a document by reordering the headings in the Navigation Pane. To move a heading, drag it to where you want it. All the text in that heading's section will move accordingly.

2. **Click the Recommended Initiatives heading in the Navigation Pane to move to page 3, then click to the right of footprint in the first line of the paragraph**

3. **Click the References tab, then click the Insert Footnote button in the Footnotes group**

   The insertion point moves to the footnote area. A superscript "1" appears after the word "footprint."

4. **Type Efforts to date resulted in a 10% reduction in energy costs at our Seattle office from the prior year, as shown in Figure F-11**

   Now you need to add a citation to the quote at the end of the Customer Perception paragraph.

5. **Click the Customer Perception heading in the Navigation Pane, then click after materials." at the end of the paragraph**

QUICK TIP

The default style for citations in new documents is APA. To choose a different style, click the Style list arrow in the Citations & Bibliography group, then click the style you want.

6. **Click the Insert Citation button in the Citations & Bibliography group, then click Add New Source**

   The Create Source dialog box opens, where you can specify information about the source.

7. **Click the Type of Source list arrow, click Article in a Periodical, enter the information shown below, compare your screen to Figure F-12, then click OK**

   Author: Jake Allen   **Month:** October

   Title: Eco-Friendly Packaging   **Day:** [leave blank]

   Periodical Title: Build-It Monthly   **Pages:** 7-8

   Year: 2012

   The Create Source dialog box closes. A reference to the source you added is inserted as "(Allen)".

QUICK TIP

To insert a page break using the Ribbon, click the Insert tab, then click the Page Break button.

8. **Press [Ctrl][End] to move to the end of the document, then press [Ctrl][Enter]**

   Pressing [Ctrl][Enter] inserted a hard page break, which is a page break inserted by a user. Now the insertion point is set at the top of a new page.

9. **Click the Bibliography button in the Citations & Bibliography group, click Works Cited, click the Works Cited heading in the Navigation Pane, then save your changes**

   See Figure F-13. Word inserts the bibliographic information for all the sources cited in the report.

FIGURE F-11: Footnote added to document

Insert Footnote button

In Step 1, click this tab to view headings

Recommended Initiatives heading

Reference mark

Footnote

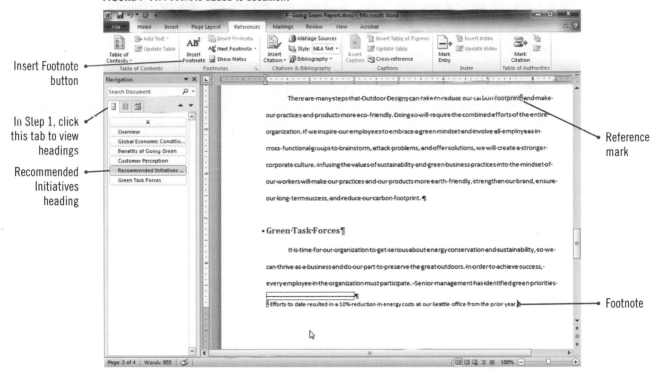

FIGURE F-12: Create Source dialog box with source information added

Year text box with publication year

Leave Day text box blank

Pages text box

Type of Source list arrow

Title of article in Title text box

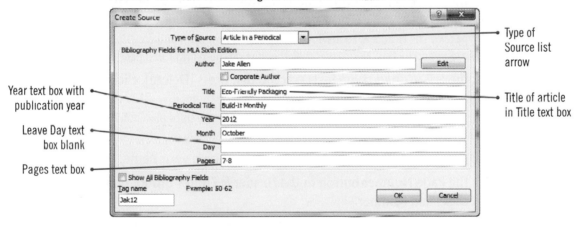

FIGURE F-13: Report with bibliography added

Insert Citation button

Bibliography button

Style list with MLA style selected

New source appears at top of list

Bibliography inserted in MLA style; includes all sources cited in this report

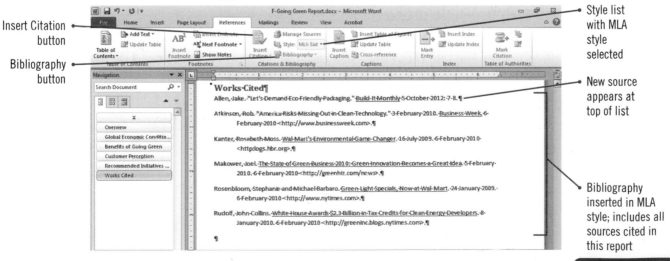

Word 2010

Inserting a Header or Footer

When you create a document that contains several pages, you might want to add page numbers and other information to the top or bottom of every page. You can do this easily by adding headers or footers. A **header** is text that appears in the top margin of a page, and a **footer** is text that appears in the bottom margin of a page. Headers and footers usually repeat from page to page. In addition to page numbers, headers and footers often contain such information as the date, the document author's name, or the filename. You add headers and footers using the Header and Footer buttons on the Insert tab. You can format header and footer text in the same way you format regular text, and you can even add graphics. You decide to add a header and footer to the report.

STEPS

1. **Click the Navigation Pane Close button ☒ ,click the Insert tab, click the Footer button in the Header & Footer group, then click Blank**

   The footer area is now active. The [Type text] placeholder is selected. You want to replace the text placeholder with the current date.

2. **Click the Date & Time button in the Insert group**

   The Date and Time dialog box opens, displaying several preset date formats. The first option in the list is selected, as shown in Figure F-14, and is the one that is most appropriate for the report.

3. **Click OK, then save your changes**

   The current date now appears left-aligned in the footer.

> **QUICK TIP**
> You can open the header or footer by double-clicking in the header or footer area in a document in Print Layout view.

4. **Click the Insert tab, click the Header button, then click Blank (Three Columns)**

   The insertion point moves to the header area, which contains three placeholders into which you can click and type text. The Header & Footer Tools Design tab is now open and contains buttons and tools for working with headers and footers. Notice that the other text on the Works Cited page is dimmed.

5. **Click the left-aligned [Type text] placeholder, press [Delete], click the center-aligned [Type text] placeholder, then press [Delete]**

   You deleted two of the three placeholders. You can replace the third placeholder with your name and the page number.

6. **Click the right-aligned [Type text] placeholder, type your name, then press [Spacebar]**

> **QUICK TIP**
> When working in a header or footer, the text of the main document appears dimmed, indicating that you cannot edit it.

7. **Click the Page Number button in the Header & Footer group, point to Current Position, then click Plain Number**

   The header now contains your name and the page number, as shown in Figure F-15. This header will appear at the top of every page in the report. You do not want it to appear on the first page.

8. **Click the Different First Page check box in the Options group on the Header & Footer Tools Design tab to select it**

   This option applies the header and footer to all pages in the document except the first page.

> **QUICK TIP**
> You can see headers and footers only in Print Layout view and in Print Preview; you cannot see headers and footers in Draft view.

9. **Click the File tab, click Print, then click the Previous Page button ◀ at the bottom of the Print Preview pane four times to view each page of the report**

   Notice that the header and footer appear on all pages except page 1. Figure F-16 shows page 3.

Adding Special Elements to a Document

FIGURE F-14: Date and Time dialog box

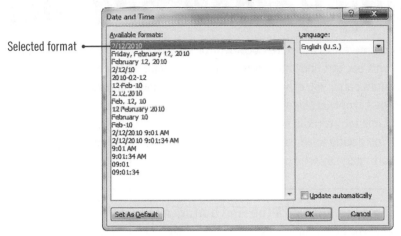

Selected format

FIGURE F-15: Header with name and page number

Click to remove header and footer from page 1

Header button

Footer button

Date & Time button

Header & Footer Tools Design tab

Header contains your name and page number

FIGURE F-16: Report in Print Preview showing header and footer on third page

Next Page button

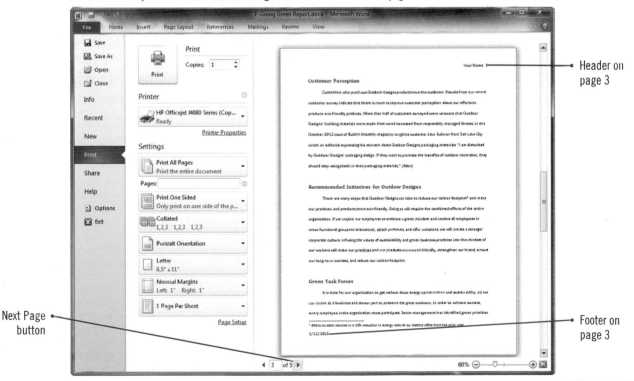

Header on page 3

Footer on page 3

Adding Borders and Shading

You can add visual interest to an entire document or set a block of text apart from the rest of the page by adding borders and background shading to words, paragraphs, graphics, or entire pages. To add these elements to an entire page, you can use the Page Color and Page Borders buttons in the Page Background group on the Page Layout tab; to add them to selected text, it is easiest to use the Shading and Borders buttons on the Home tab. You can add borders at the top, bottom, left, or right edges of text, or around a graphic.  You decide to add a border and shading to the "Outdoor Designs Vision" paragraph at the bottom of the fourth page to set it off from the rest of the report's text.

STEPS

1. **Click the Home tab, then click the Find button in the Editing group**

   The Navigation Pane opens. Entering keywords in the Search Document text box in the Navigation Pane is a fast way to locate specific text.

2. **Click in the Search Document text box in the Navigation Pane, then type Outdoor Designs**

   The Find command temporarily highlights all instances of "Outdoor Designs" in yellow. You can see there are several occurrences on page 1. The Navigation Pane displays a list of links to all the occurrences in the report; you can click a link to move to that occurrence. You want to locate the text "Outdoor Designs Vision."

3. **Press [Spacebar], then type Vision in the Search Document text box**

   The document window now shows the first and only occurrence of "Outdoor Designs Vision", which is on page 4 of the report.

4. **Select Outdoor Designs Vision and the two lines of text below it**

5. **Click the Shading list arrow 🖌▾ in the Paragraph group, then click the green color in the second row of Theme colors (ScreenTip reads "Olive Green, Accent 3, Lighter 80%"), as shown in Figure F-17**

   The selected text now has green shading applied to it. Notice that the Shading button displays the olive green shade you applied. If you wanted to apply this shade of green somewhere else, you could simply select the text and click the Shading button.

   > **QUICK TIP**
   > To apply a border around specific edges of a selected text block, click the Borders list arrow in the Paragraph group, then click the border option you want.

6. **Click the Navigation Pane Close button ✖, click the Borders list arrow ▦▾ in the Paragraph group, then click Borders and Shading**

   The Borders and Shading dialog box opens, with the Borders tab in front. The Borders tab lets you specify a border color and a style of border.

7. **Click the Box setting, click the Color list arrow, then click the darkest shade of green in the Theme colors (seventh shade in the sixth row)**

   Compare your screen to Figure F-18.

   > **QUICK TIP**
   > To apply a border around the edge of an entire page, click the Page Border tab in the Borders and Shading dialog box, choose the page border settings you want, then click OK.

8. **Click OK, click anywhere in the document to deselect the text, then save your changes**

   The Outdoor Designs Vision heading and paragraph are now shaded in a green box with a green border. Compare your screen to Figure F-19.

Adding Special Elements to a Document

FIGURE F-17: Live Preview of paragraphs with light green shading applied

Search text box in Navigation Pane

Click this link to move to this occurrence of Outdoor Designs Vision

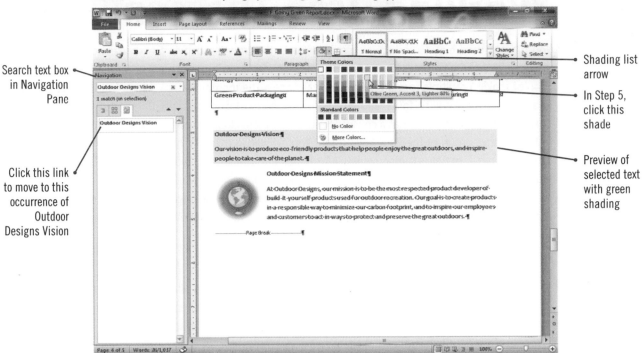

Shading list arrow

In Step 5, click this shade

Preview of selected text with green shading

Word 2010

FIGURE F-18: Borders tab of Borders and Shading dialog box

Borders tab

Box setting

Darkest shade of green selected

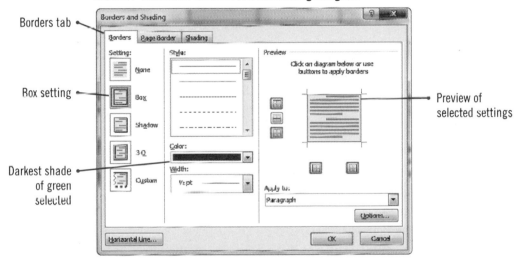

Preview of selected settings

FIGURE F-19: Paragraph with a box border and shading applied

Borders button

Green shading applied

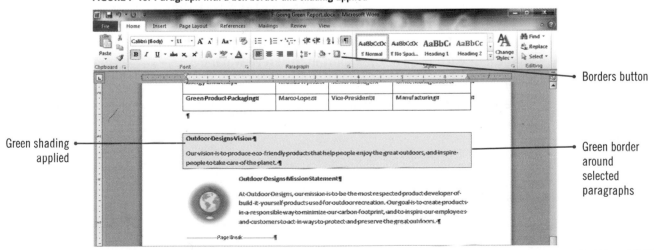

Green border around selected paragraphs

Adding Special Elements to a Document

Working with Themes

You have learned how to format individual document elements, such as a text selection or an object, and also how to use Quick Styles to change multiple formatting attributes in a selection. An even more powerful tool for making multiple formatting changes at once is the themes feature. Changing the **theme** applies a coordinated set of colors, fonts, and effects to your entire document, updating any styles applied. Themes ensure that your document has a consistent and professional look. To apply a theme, use the Themes button in the Themes group of the Page Layout tab. You can vary a theme's fonts and colors by applying different sets of theme fonts and theme colors. All themes are available in Word, Excel, Access, PowerPoint, and Outlook, which means that a company can produce many different documents and ensure that they all have a consistent, branded look. ███████ You decide to change the overall look of the report by applying a theme to it. You want to use the Essential theme, but you want to keep the Office theme colors, to preserve the green shading you added.

STEPS

1. **Click the Zoom Out button ⊖ seven times on the Zoom slider until the zoom level is set at 30%**

   With the zoom set at 30%, all five pages of the report are visible on-screen, so you can see at a glance how your changes will affect the whole document.

2. **Click the Page Layout tab, then click the Themes button in the Themes group**

   The Themes gallery opens and displays thumbnails of available themes, as well as other options, such as resetting your document to the original theme and accessing more themes from the Office Online Web site or your computer.

> **QUICK TIP**
>
> Every template has a theme applied to it by default. If you apply a theme to a document but then decide you want to go back to the original template theme, click the Themes button, then click Reset to Theme from Template.

3. **Point to each theme in the gallery and observe the change in the document window**

   With Live Preview, you can see how the colors and fonts in each theme would affect the document if applied. Notice the change in colors, including the background color in the image, and how the text wraps differently depending on the theme. Figure F-20 shows a preview of the Aspect theme, which is less compact and forces the report to six pages. The Essential theme keeps the report to five pages.

4. **Click the Essential theme**

   The Themes gallery closes, and the Essential theme is applied to the report.

5. **Click the Theme Colors button ▣▾ in the Themes group**

   The Theme Colors gallery opens and displays a list of all the sets of theme colors. You want to apply the Office theme colors to the report to preserve the green shading you added.

> **QUICK TIP**
>
> You can create your own customized themes. To do this, change the formatting of any element you want (such as the font used in headings), click the Themes button, click Save Current Theme, type a name for the theme, then click Save. The new theme will appear at the top of the Themes gallery under Custom.

6. **Point to each set of Theme Colors to preview the effect in the report, then click Office, as shown in Figure F-21**

   By applying a different theme and customizing it with different theme colors, you have completely transformed the look of the report in just a few clicks.

7. **Click the File tab, click Print on the navigation bar, then click the Previous Page button ◀ to preview each page of the report in the Preview pane**

   Compare your report to Figure F-22.

8. **Save your changes, close the document, exit Word, then submit your completed report to your instructor**

Adding Special Elements to a Document

FIGURE F-20: Themes gallery and document showing Live Preview of Aspect theme

Themes button

Aspect theme

Live Preview shows effects of Aspect theme

Aspect theme adds a page to the report

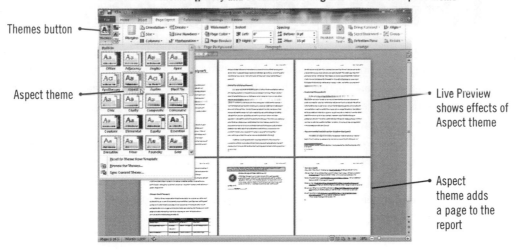

FIGURE F-21: Theme Colors gallery with Essential theme and Office theme colors applied

In Step 6, click Office theme colors set

Essential theme is applied

Live Preview shows effects of Office theme colors

Green shading from Office theme colors

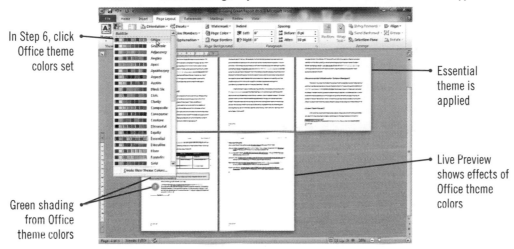

FIGURE F-22: Finished report with Essential theme and Office theme colors applied

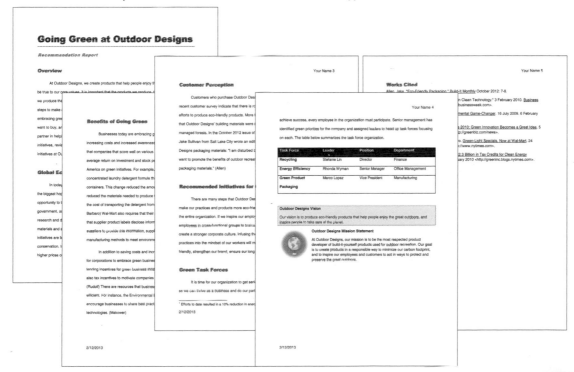

Formatting a Research Paper

Now that you have completed all the units on Word, you have learned skills to help you create many kinds of documents, including research papers. If you need to write research papers for a class, then you should be aware that there are guidelines that you need to follow to format them correctly. Modern Language Association (MLA) style is a popular standard for formatting academic research papers, which many schools require. This lesson provides some basic guidelines for formatting a research paper using MLA style. Use Table F-1 and Figure F-23 to learn the guidelines for formatting the first page of a research paper using MLA style. Use Table F-2 and Figure F-24 to learn the guidelines for formatting the whole paper. The guidelines provided here will just get you started; for detailed information on MLA guidelines, search online or ask your school librarian for help. (*Note*: You can format the research paper shown in this lesson by completing the Real Life Independent Challenge for this unit.)

TABLE F-1: Formatting guidelines for the first page of a research paper

required first page element	MLA guideline
Header	Your last name followed by the page number (on all pages including page 1), right-aligned
Your Name	Left-aligned, 1" from top of page
Professor's Name	Two lines below your name, left-aligned
Course Number	Two lines below professor's name, left-aligned
Title	Two lines below course number, center-aligned
Beginning of body text	First paragraph is double-spaced below title; first line is indented ½"

TABLE F-2: Formatting guidelines for a whole research paper

setting	MLA guideline	Word quick reference
Line spacing	Double-space all text in the document	Press **[Ctrl][A]** to select all the text in the document, click the **Line and Paragraph Spacing list arrow** on the Home tab, then click **2.0**
Margins	All margins set to 1"	Click the **Page Layout tab**, click the **Margins button**, then click **Normal**
Paragraph formatting	Indent first line of each paragraph ½"	Press **[Tab]** at the start of a new paragraph or press **[Ctrl][A]** to select all the text in the document, then drag the First Line Indent marker ▽ to the ½" mark on the ruler
Font	Times New Roman	Click the **Font list arrow** on the Home tab, then click **Times New Roman**
Font size	12 point	Click the **Font Size list arrow** on the Home tab, then click **12**
Header	Right-aligned; your last name followed by the page number (on all pages including page 1)	Click the **Insert tab**, click the **Header button**, click the **Blank style**, delete the placeholder, press **[Tab]** twice, type your last name, press **[Spacebar]**, click **Page Number** in the Header & Footer group, point to **Current Position**, then click **Plain Number**
Citations	Insert author's name and page number in parentheses after quote or reference to work	Click the **References tab**, click the **Insert Citation button**, then click the source name or **Add New Source** to add source information
Bibliography	Include Works Cited page with sources that you reference in the paper	Insert a page break at the end of the document, click the **References tab**, click the **Bibliography button**, then click **Works Cited**

Adding Special Elements to a Document

FIGURE F-23: First page of research paper formatted according to MLA style

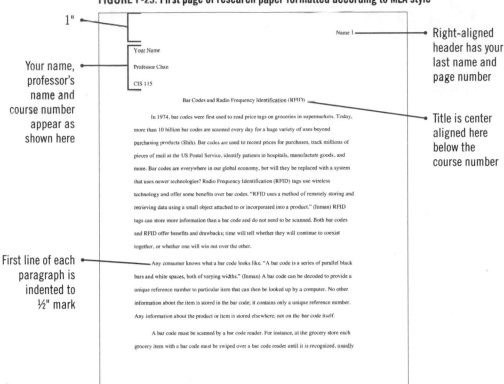

1"

Your name, professor's name and course number appear as shown here

Right-aligned header has your last name and page number

Title is center aligned here below the course number

First line of each paragraph is indented to ½" mark

FIGURE F-24: Page 2 of research paper and Works Cited page

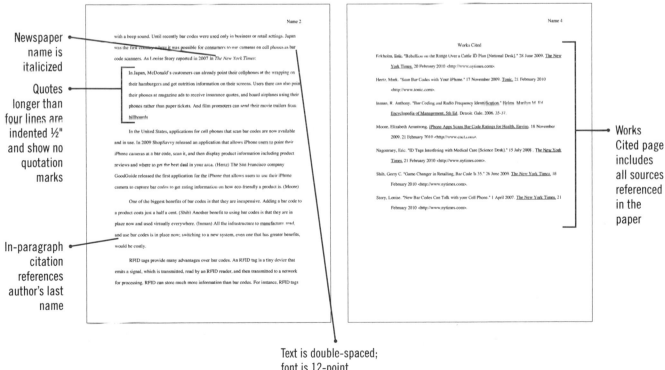

Newspaper name is italicized

Quotes longer than four lines are indented ½" and show no quotation marks

In-paragraph citation references author's last name

Works Cited page includes all sources referenced in the paper

Text is double-spaced; font is 12-point Times New Roman

Adding Special Elements to a Document

Practice

For current SAM information, including versions and content details, visit SAM Central (http://www.cengage.com/samcentral). If you have a SAM user profile, you may have access to hands-on instruction, practice, and assessment of the skills covered in this unit. Since various versions of SAM are supported throughout the life of this text, check with your instructor for the correct instructions and URL/Web site for accessing assignments.

Concepts Review

Label the Word window elements shown in Figure F-25.

FIGURE F-25

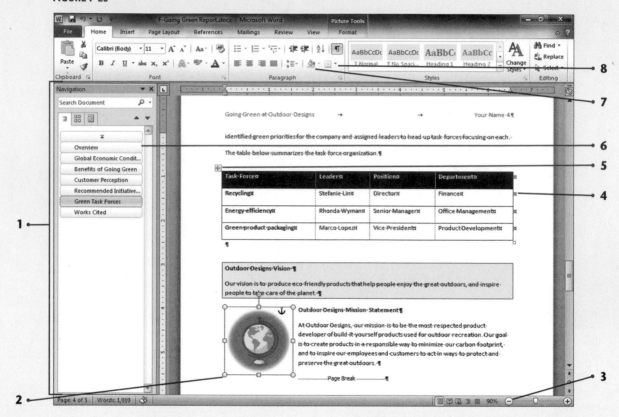

Adding Special Elements to a Document

Select the best answer from the list of choices.

9. **Which tab do you use to create a table?**
   a. Home
   b. Table Tools Design
   c. Page Layout
   d. Insert

10. **Which tab is an example of a contextual tab?**
    a. Picture Tools Format
    b. Home
    c. View
    d. Page Layout

11. **Which tab do you use to change the margin settings?**
    a. Home
    b. Page Layout
    c. View
    d. Insert

12. **A predefined set of formatting attributes for a table, such as shading, borders, and colors, is called a**
    _____.
    a. SmartArt
    b. Table Design tab
    c. Table style
    d. Table gallery

13. **Which of the following actions moves the insertion point to the next cell in a table?**
    a. Pressing [Tab]
    b. Pressing [Ctrl][Enter]
    c. Pressing [Ctrl][Home]
    d. Pressing [Alt] and clicking

14. **The way that text flows around a graphic is called** _____.
    a. text blocking
    b. text wrapping
    c. word wrapping
    d. text formatting

Skills Review

1. **Create a table.**
   a. Start Microsoft Word, open the file F-2.docx from where you store your Data Files, then save the new document as **F-Nova Scotia Report.docx**.
   b. Open the Navigation Pane and display the thumbnails of each page in the document. Use the Navigation Pane to move to page 2. Set the insertion point in the blank line above Classic Walking Adventures at the bottom of page 2. Close the Navigation Pane.
   c. Insert a table that is four columns wide and three rows high.
   d. Enter the information shown in the table below into the table you created.

Tour Name	Start Date	End Date	Price
Senior Weekender	June 14	June 16	$1,295
Thrill Seeker	June 21	June 28	$2,195

   e. Save your changes to the document.

2. **Insert and delete table columns and rows.**
   a. Insert a new row as the last row in the table.
   b. Enter the following information into the cells in the new row:

Family Fun	July 5	July 12	$1,995

   c. Insert a new row below the row that contains the column headings, then enter the following information into the new cells:

Family Fun	June 7	June 9	$1,095

   d. Delete the row that contains the July 5 Family Fun tour.
   e. Insert a new column to the right of the Tour Name column.

f. Enter the information from the table below into the new column.

Tour Type
Walking
Walking
Hiking and Kayaking

g. Save your changes.

3. Format a table.

    a. Format the table by applying the Medium Shading 1 – Accent 6 table style.

    b. Increase the width of the second column so that Hiking and Kayaking fits on one line.

    c. Apply black borders to all the cells in the table.

    d. Save your changes.

4. Add clip art.

    a. Use the Navigation Pane to move to page 1. Close the Navigation Pane. Set the insertion point before the word Nova in the first line of paragraph text below the heading About Nova Scotia.

    b. Open the Clip Art task pane, then search for an image of a lighthouse. (*Hint*: Make sure to click the Include Office.com content check box to select it.)

    c. Insert the image shown in Figure F-26, or a similar one.

FIGURE F-26

    d. Close the Clip Art task pane, then reduce the size of the image so that it is approximately 1½" wide. (*Hint*: Use the ruler as a guide to help you size it. You can also right-click the image, then set the Shape Width to 1.5".)

    e. Set the wrapping style of the image to Square.

    f. Drag the image as necessary so that its bottom edge is aligned with the last line of the paragraph and its left edge is aligned with the left edge of paragraph text.

    g. Recolor the image with the Orange, Accent color 6 Light.

    h. Apply the Soft Edge, Rectangle Picture Style to the image.

    i. Save your changes.

5. Insert footnotes and citations.

    a. Use the Headings tab of the Navigation Pane to navigate to the heading Reasons to Offer Tours in Nova Scotia.

    b. Set the insertion point to the right of the word **survey** in the line below the Reasons to Offer Tours in Nova Scotia heading.

    c. Insert a footnote.

    d. Type the following text as footnote text: **Survey was conducted in June 2012 and completed by 124 customers.**

    e. Use the middle tab of the Navigation Pane to move to page 2, so that the paragraph above the heading Reasons to Offer Tours in Nova Scotia is visible.

    f. Set the insertion point after the closing quotation mark that follows the word **spectacular** at the end of the paragraph, then use the Insert Citation button to add a new source.

    g. Enter the following information in the Create Source dialog box:

        Type of Source: Article in a Periodical

        Author: Lindsay Sheridan

        Title: Nova Scotia by Foot

        Periodical Title: The Walking Stick News

        Year: 2012

        Month: June

        Day: 26

        Pages: 10-11

Skills Review (continued)

h. Close the Create Source dialog box, use the Navigation Pane to move to the heading Recommended Tour Dates, then set the insertion point in the blank line below the table.

i. Insert a page break, then insert a bibliography using the Works Cited style. Use the Navigation Pane to move to the Works Cited heading.

j. Save your changes.

6. Insert a header or footer.

a. Insert a footer using the Blank option.

b. Replace the [Type text] placeholder with the current date, specifying the format that looks like January 1, 2013.

c. Insert a header using the Blank (Three Columns) option.

d. Delete the left-aligned and the center-aligned [Type text] placeholders. Replace the right-aligned [Type text] placeholder with your name. Insert a space after your name, then insert the page number after the space, choosing the Plain Number style.

e. Specify that the header and footer be different on the first page.

f. Close the header area, then save your changes.

7. Add borders and shading.

a. Use the Navigation Pane to move to the Works Cited heading. Select the last five lines of text in the document, then apply Orange, Accent 6, Lighter 80% shading to the selection.

b. Use the Borders tab of the Borders and Shading dialog box to apply a box border around the selection that is Orange, Accent 6, Darker 50%.

c. Save your changes.

8. Work with themes.

a. Set the zoom level of the document to 30% so that you can see all three pages of the report.

b. Apply the Composite theme to the document.

c. Apply the Equity theme colors to the document.

d. Move the clip art on page 1, if necessary, so that its bottom edge is aligned with the last line of the paragraph.

e. Compare your screen with Figure F-27, then close the document and exit Word.

FIGURE F-27

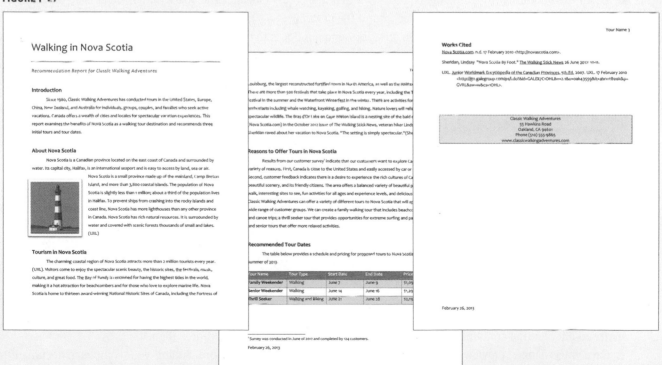

Independent Challenge 1

You are the new marketing manager at Broad Strokes Art Studio, a small art studio in Indiana that offers art classes to the community. You need to create a one-page information sheet for prospective students. You have a partially completed document that you need to finish. You will add a table containing the class schedule and a bibliography that lists titles of books that key instructors have written.

a. Open the file F-3.docx from where you store your Data Files, then save it as **F-Art Classes Info Sheet**.

b. Insert a new line below the heading Summer Classes, then insert a 4 x 6 table.

c. Enter the information from the table below into the new table.

Class Name	Start Date	Time	Sessions
Figure Drawing	June 3	7:00-9:00	8
Studio Drawing	June 4	7:00-9:00	6
Basic Watercolor	June 5	7:00-8:30	4
Advanced Oil Painting	June 6	4:00-6:00	8
Basic Calligraphy	June 6	7:00-9:00	6

d. Add a new row below the Studio Drawing row that contains the following information:

Basic Oil Painting   June 5   6:00-7:30   8

e. Add a column to the right of the Start Date column, then enter the information from the table below into it.

Day
Monday
Tuesday
Wednesday
Wednesday
Thursday
Thursday

f. Apply the Light List – Accent 1 table style to the table. Make sure that the First Column check box and the Header Row check box in the Table Style Options group are both selected.

g. Adjust the column width of the first column so that each class name fits on one line.

h. Open the Borders and Shading dialog box, click the Page Border tab, click the Box style border, choose the Blue Accent 1 color, then click OK to insert a border around the page.

i. Insert a clip art image appropriate for an art studio, and position it to the right of the two paragraphs about the instructors. Apply the Square text wrapping style to it. Resize it so that it fits well and looks good in the space next to the paragraphs.

j. Insert a footer containing your name, left-aligned, and today's date, center-aligned.

k. Add a new citation source in MLA style about the book that Rachelle Koh wrote. Click the Type of Source list arrow, click Book, then enter the following information:

Author:	**Rachelle Koh**
Title:	**Painting for Fun**
Year:	**2008**
City:	**Detroit**
Publisher:	**Paint Brush Press**

l. Insert a citation after Painting for Fun in the last line of text in the document for the source you just added.

m. In the last line of the document, insert the bibliography for the source you entered. (*Hint*: Click the Bibliography button in the Citations & Bibliography group on the References tab, then click Bibliography.)

n. Replace the heading Bibliography with **Information on Rachelle Koh's Book**

o. Apply the Trek theme to the document.

p. Apply the Foundry theme colors to the document.

q. Insert a footer that contains your name, left-aligned, and the current date, center aligned.

r. Save your changes, preview the document, close the document and exit Word. Submit your completed document to your instructor.

Adding Special Elements to a Document

Independent Challenge 2

You are the human resources manager at Taco Now, a Mexican fast-food chain with headquarters in Chicago. A new employee, Brenda Ingersoll, starts her first day tomorrow as an associate brand manager. You need to create a schedule for Brenda that shows the times and locations of her meetings and appointments as well as the contact people with whom she will meet.

a. Open the file F-4.docx from where you store your Data Files, then save it as **F-Schedule.docx.**

b. Set the insertion point in the blank line two lines above To: Brenda Ingersoll.

c. Insert today's date using the Insert Date and Time dialog box. (*Hint*: Click the Date & Time button on the Insert tab.) Choose any date format that you like.

d. In the line below To: Brenda Ingersoll, type your name to the right of From:.

e. Two lines below the first long paragraph, insert a table containing the information shown in the table below.

Time	Location	Contact Person	Description
9:00	Reception	Lee Allen	Benefits review
9:30	Taco Room	Juan Herrera	Orientation training
11:00	Queso Room	Sandy Landon	Team meeting
12:00	Cafeteria	Leslie Rust	Team lunch
1:30	Burrito Room	Jose Ortiz	Product overview

f. Apply a table style of your choosing to the table.

g. Insert a row in the table between the 9:30 and 11:00 time slot. Enter the information shown in the following table into the new row.

10:30	Supply Room	Julie Rosen	Get office supplies

h. Add a border around the Taco Now Philosophy heading and the paragraph below it at the bottom of the page, and add shading to this text. Format the text in this box using fonts, formatting, alignment, and font styles to make it look attractive.

i. Insert a footnote to the right of Leslie Rust's name in the table. The footnote text should read **Leslie will meet you and the rest of the team in the cafeteria.** Format this footnote text so that it looks different from the main text in the document.

j. Insert a footer that contains your name, right-aligned.

k. Apply a theme to the document that you think looks good and is appropriate for this type of document.

l. Preview the document, then save your changes.

Advanced Challenge Exercise

- Click anywhere in the table, then click the Table Tools Design tab.
- Click the Draw Table button in the Draw Borders group, then use the pen pointer to draw a new row below the 1:30 row. (*Hint*: Drag a line from the middle of the left edge of the 1:30 cell all the way to the right edge of the cell containing Product overview.) Use the pen pointer to draw vertical lines for the cell borders in the new row. Then format the new row so that it looks like the other rows in the table. When you are finished, click the Draw Table button again to turn off the pen pointer.
- Enter the following information in the new row:

4:00	Burrito Room	Karen Fogg	Get company ID card

- Adjust the border formatting if necessary so that the borders in your new row match the rest of the table.

m. Save, preview, and close the document. Submit the document to your instructor.

Independent Challenge 3

Serena Dunbar in the Human Resources Department at Haskin Paper Products has asked you to create a one-page flyer for the annual company picnic. The picnic will take place at Bradley Park from 9:00 a.m. until 3:00 p.m. Attendees can swim, compete in a volleyball tournament, play basketball, and participate in a relay race. A barbecue lunch will be served.

a. Open the file F-5.docx from where you store your Data Files, then save it as **F-Company Picnic Flyer**.docx.

b. Format the text in the document so that it reflects the casual, festive nature of the event. Choose fonts, font sizes, and formatting attributes that make the key information stand out.

c. Apply shading to the first line of the document (Haskin Paper Products) using a fill color and font that look good together.

d. Insert a table containing the information shown in the table below.

Activity	Time	Location
Buses Depart	9:00	Lobby
Relay Race	10:00	Field A
Volleyball Tournament	10:30	Beach
Basketball Game	11:00	Basketball Courts
BBQ Lunch	12:00	Pavilion
Buses Return	3:00	Parking Lot

e. Format the table using a table style of your choosing.

f. Insert an appropriate piece of clip art for the occasion.

g. Insert a footer that contains your name, center-aligned.

h. Save your changes, preview the flyer, then close the document. Figure F-28 shows one possible solution; yours will vary depending on the formatting choices you made. Submit your flyer to your instructor.

FIGURE F-28

Haskin Paper Products

Company

Picnic!

July 15
9:00-3:00
Bradley Park

Don't miss the annual **Company Picnic** at **Bradley Park** on Friday **July 15!** Work up a sweat playing volleyball or competing in the Relay Race. Play basketball, go for a swim or simply relax on the beach. Enjoy great food with your colleagues at the barbecue lunch! See below for the schedule. See you there!

Activity	Time	Location
Buses Depart	9:00	Lobby
Relay Race	10:00	Field A
Volleyball Tournament	10:30	Beach
Basketball Game	11:00	Basketball Courts
BBQ Lunch	12:00	Pavilion
Buses Return	3:00	Parking Lot

Your Name

Adding Special Elements to a Document

Real Life Independent Challenge

Research papers are frequently assigned for history and English classes in college. Knowing how to format a research paper according to standards is extremely important. A common standard used for writing and formatting research papers is MLA. Another popular standard is APA. If your professor assigns a research paper, he or she will probably specify that you write and format your paper according to MLA or APA standards. In this Real Life Independent Challenge, you will create a research paper and format it according to MLA guidelines. So that you do not have to actually research and write the paper, you will use text from an existing file for the paper. Before completing the steps below, review the lesson Formatting a Research Paper located just before the end-of-unit exercises.

a. Open the file F-6.docx from where you store your Data Files, then save it as **F-Research Paper.docx**.

b. With the insertion point set before the first line of text in the document, type your name.

c. Press [Enter], type **Professor Chan**, then press [Enter].

d. Type **CIS 115**, then press [Enter].

e. Center-align the title of the paper, Bar Codes and Radio Frequency Identification (RFID).

f. Find "The New York Times" on pages 1 and 2 in the text. Format both of these occurrences in italic.

g. Immediately below *The New York Times*: on page 1, select the four-line quote that begins "In Japan, McDonald's customers..." Set the left indent at the ½" mark on the ruler for this paragraph.

h. Press [Ctrl][A] to select all the text in the document. Set the line spacing to double-spaced (2.0).

i. Change the font for all the selected text to Times New Roman, then change the font size to 12 point.

j. Indent the beginning of each paragraph of body text in the paper to the ½" mark on the ruler. Do not further indent the quote that you indented in Step g. (*Hint*: You can either press [Tab] before the first character in the paragraph or create a first line indent by dragging the First Line Indent marker ▽ to the ½" mark on the ruler.)

k. Create a header that contains your last name followed by the page number. Right-align the header. Change the font in the header to 12-point Times New Roman if necessary.

l. Insert a citation to author R. Anthony Inman after the quote in the first paragraph of body text (which ends "... incorporated into a product"). (*Note*: To choose this source, click Insert Citation, then click Inman, R. Anthony.)

m. Move the insertion point to the end of the document. Insert a page break. Insert a bibliography using the Works Cited option. Format all the text in the Works Cited section in 12-point Times New Roman. Center-align the Works Cited heading.

n. Save your changes. Compare your research paper to the one shown in Figures F-23 and F-24.

Advanced Challenge Exercise

- Save the document with the name **F-Research Paper ACE**.
- Click the Insert tab, click Cover page button in the Pages group, then click the Conservative style.
- Delete the placeholder at the top of the cover page.
- Type **Bar Codes and Radio Frequency Identification (RFID)** in the Title placeholder.
- Delete the document subtitle placeholder. If your name is not displayed on the title page as the author, replace the author name that is there with your name. Use the Pick the Date placeholder to enter today's date.
- Replace the text at the bottom of the cover page with a short summary that describes what the paper is about. (You will need to read the paper to write this.)
- Save the document, preview each page of the document, then close the file.

Visual Workshop

Open the file F-7.docx from where you store your Data Files, then save it as **F-Beach Cottage Ad.docx**. Use the skills you learned in this unit to create the flyer shown in Figure F-29. (*Hints:* Use TW Cen MT Condensed Extra Bold for the headings and Californian FB for the body text and table text. Select a different clip-art image if the one shown in the figure is not available to you. Set the wrapping style to tight for the top image. Insert the table and apply the style shown in the figure. Apply a Box style blue border around the whole page using the Page Border tab of the Borders and Shading dialog box.) Type your name somewhere on the flyer, save your changes, preview the flyer, then submit it to your instructor.

FIGURE F-29

Beach Cottage for Rent

Relax and enjoy spectacular views of the Pacific Ocean on Maui's south shore. The white sandy beach is just steps away! Located on five acres of landscaped grounds, with swaying palm trees and fragrant flowering plants, this cozy 2-bedroom cottage features updated appliances, and is fully stocked to ensure you have everything you need while on vacation. Enjoy breathtaking sunsets year round. Prepare meals outside on the propane grill and dine on the lanai. Enjoy swimming, snorkeling, tennis, and windsurfing. Watch humpback whales before they migrate north. World-class restaurants are minutes away!

Property Details

Feature	Description
Location	Maui, HI
Weekly rate	$2,700
Bedrooms	2
Bathrooms	2
Outdoor grill	Yes
Lanai	Yes
Beach access	Yes
Hot tub	Yes
Air conditioning	Yes
Phone	Unlimited free local calls
Internet	Free high speed Internet access

For more details, contact:

Mindy Lee
4455 Palm Drive
Kihei, HI 96753
Phone: (800) 555-2090

Your Name

Adding Special Elements to a Document

Creating a Worksheet

Files You Will Need:

No files needed.

In this unit, you learn how to create and work with an Excel worksheet. A **worksheet** is an electronic grid in which you can perform numeric calculations. You can use a worksheet for many purposes, such as analyzing sales data, calculating a loan payment, organizing inventory, and displaying data in a chart. An Excel file, called a **workbook**, can contain one or more worksheets. People sometimes refer to a worksheet or a workbook as a **spreadsheet**.  Karen Rivera, the marketing director for Outdoor Designs, asks you to help her create a worksheet that provides a sales forecast for the kite product line. You will create the worksheet, enter values and labels into it, create formulas to make calculations, format it, and print it.

OBJECTIVES

Navigate a workbook

Enter labels and values

Work with columns and rows

Use formulas

Use AutoSum

Change alignment and number format

Enhance a worksheet

Preview and print a worksheet

Navigating a Workbook

Every new Excel workbook contains three worksheets. You can use only one worksheet and leave the other sheets blank, or you can use more than one worksheet to help organize your information. You can also add more worksheets if you need more than three. An Excel worksheet consists of a grid of rows and columns. Similar to a Word table, the intersection of a row and column is called a **cell**. ▰▰▰▰▰ Before working on the sales forecast worksheet, you need to start Excel, familiarize yourself with the workbook window, and save a blank workbook.

STEPS

1. **Click the Start button ⊛ on the taskbar, click All Programs, click Microsoft Office, then click Microsoft Excel 2010**

   Excel starts and a blank workbook opens, as shown in Figure G-1. Excel contains elements that are in every Office program, including the Ribbon, the File tab, the Quick Access toolbar, a document window, scroll bars, a status bar, View buttons, and window sizing buttons.

   QUICK TIP
   You can quickly move the cell pointer to cell A1 by pressing [Ctrl][Home].

2. **View the worksheet window**

   The cell with the dark border in the upper-left corner of the worksheet is called the **active cell**. The dark border surrounding the active cell is the **cell pointer**. You must click a cell to make it active before entering data. Every cell in a worksheet has a unique **cell address**, which is a specific location of a cell in a worksheet where a column and row intersect. A cell address consists of a column letter followed by a row number (such as B33). When you first start Excel, the active cell in the new workbook (Book1) is cell A1, where column A and row 1 intersect.

   QUICK TIP
   To navigate quickly to a specific cell, press [Ctrl][G] to open the Go To dialog box, type the cell address you want to navigate to in the Reference text box, then click OK.

3. **Click cell C1**

   Cell C1 becomes the active cell. Clicking a cell selects it and makes it active. Table G-1 lists several methods for selecting cells with the mouse or keyboard. Notice that the column and row headings of the active cell (column C and row 1) appear in a contrasting color. The **name box** shows the address of the selected cell, and the **formula bar**, located just above the column headings, shows the contents of the selected cell (it is currently empty). The mouse pointer changes to ⊕ when you move it over any cells in the workbook.

4. **Press [→], press [↓], then press [Tab]**

   Cell E2 is now the active cell. You can move to and select a cell by clicking it, by using the arrow keys, or by pressing [Tab] (to move one cell to the right), [Shift][Tab] (to move one cell to the left), or [Enter] (to move one cell down).

5. **Click the Sheet2 sheet tab**

   Sheet2 becomes the active sheet, and cell A1 is the active cell. To work with different sheets in a workbook, you click the sheet tab of the sheet you want to see.

6. **Drag the ⊕ pointer from cell A1 to cell C5**

   Cells A1 through C5 are selected, a total of fifteen cells, as shown in Figure G-2. A group of cells that share boundaries and are selected is called a **cell range**. To reference a cell range, use the cell address of the first cell in the range followed by a colon and the cell address of the last cell in the range. The cell range you selected is A1:C5.

   QUICK TIP
   To add a new worksheet, click the Insert Worksheet button 🗐 next to the Sheet3 sheet tab.

7. **Select the cell range D8:D14**

   Cells D8 through D14 (a total of seven cells) are selected.

8. **Click the Sheet1 sheet tab, then press [Ctrl][Home]**

   Clicking the sheet tab returns you to Sheet1, and the keyboard shortcut returns the cell pointer to cell A1.

9. **Click the Save button 🖫 on the Quick Access toolbar, navigate to where you store your Data Files, then save the file as G-Kite Sales Forecast**

FIGURE G-1: Excel program window

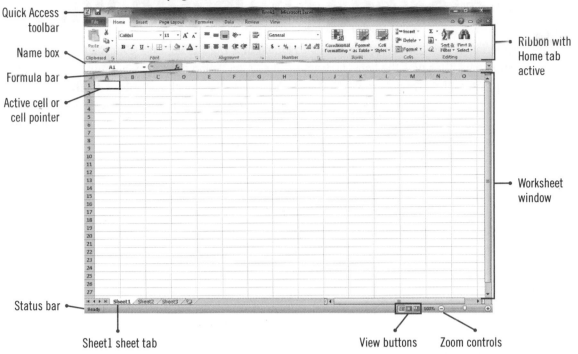

Quick Access toolbar

Name box

Formula bar

Active cell or cell pointer

Ribbon with Home tab active

Worksheet window

Status bar

Sheet1 sheet tab

View buttons

Zoom controls

FIGURE G-2: Selecting a range of cells in Sheet2

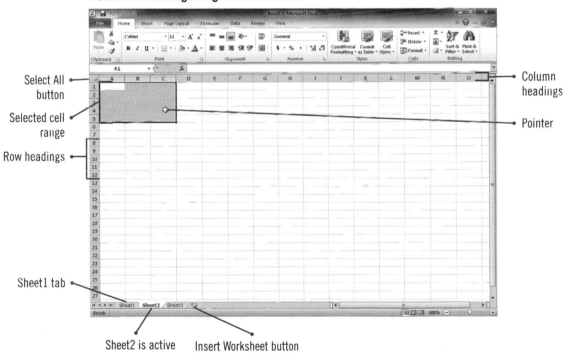

Select All button

Selected cell range

Row headings

Sheet1 tab

Column headings

Pointer

Sheet2 is active

Insert Worksheet button

TABLE G-1: Methods for selecting worksheet cells

to select	with the mouse	with the keyboard
A cell	Click the cell	Use arrow keys
A row	Click the row heading	Select a cell in the row, then press [Shift][Spacebar]
A column	Click the column heading	Select a cell in the column, then press [Ctrl][Spacebar]
A cell range	Drag across the cells	Press [Shift], then press the arrow keys
A worksheet	Click the Select All button to the left of column heading A	Press [Ctrl][A]

Creating a Worksheet

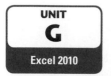
Entering Labels and Values

Entering data in a worksheet is similar to typing in a Word table. First, click the cell in which you want to enter data, then type the data you want to enter. After typing the data, you must accept the entry by pressing [Enter], [Tab], or an arrow key. Most worksheets contain labels and values. A **label** is text that describes data in a worksheet. **Values** are numeric data that can be used in calculations. You can edit a cell entry by double-clicking the cell to put the cell in Edit mode. In Edit mode, select the part of the cell entry you do not want, then type your corrections. ▰▰▰▰ This worksheet needs to provide the names of the kite products, net prices, estimated first year units, and estimated first year sales for each kite. To begin your work on the sales forecast worksheet, you decide to enter the labels and values.

STEPS

1. **In cell A1, type Product**

   As you type, the text appears in cell A1 and in the formula bar, as shown in Figure G-3. The text you typed is a label that describes the first column of data in the worksheet.

   > **QUICK TIP**
   > Pressing [Tab] has the same effect as pressing [→].

2. **Press [Tab]**

   Pressing [Tab] accepts your entry and activates the next cell in the row, cell B1. The name box shows B1 as the active cell. You need to type two more labels.

3. **Type Net Price, press [Tab], then type Year 1 Units**

   Year 1 Units is too long to fit in cell C1; although it extends into cell D1, it is actually contained only in cell C1. If cell D1 contained any data, then only the part of the label that fits in C1 would appear.

4. **Press [Enter]**

   Cell A2 is now the active cell. You need to type a kite product name in this cell.

5. **Type Apache Delta, then press [↓]**

   Cell A3 is now the active cell. Pressing [↓] accepted the cell entry and moved the cell pointer to the cell below.

6. **Type Volcano Blaster, press [Enter], type Tornado Twirler, press [Enter], type Whirling Delta, press [Enter], type Rocket Stuntman, press [Enter], type Soaring Eagle, then press [Enter]**

   You have typed all the product names. Cell A8 is the active cell. You need to make an edit to one of the names.

7. **Double-click cell A4**

   Double-clicking the cell put cell A4 in Edit mode. Notice that the insertion point is flashing in cell A4. You can now select part of the cell entry to edit it, just like in Word.

8. **Double-click Twirler, type Trickster, then press [Enter]**

   Cell A4 now contains the label Tornado Trickster.

   > **QUICK TIP**
   > Pressing [Ctrl][Enter] has the same effect as clicking the Enter button.

9. **Click cell B2, type 15.75, then press the Enter button ☑ on the formula bar**

   Unlike pressing [Enter] on the keyboard, clicking the Enter button keeps the cell active. Notice that some of Apache Delta is cut off in cell A2 because cell B2 now contains data.

10. **Press [→], type 7500, then press ☑**

    You entered the value for Year 1 Units for the Apache Delta kite in cell C2.

11. **Enter the values shown in Figure G-4 for the range B3:C7, then save your changes**

FIGURE G-3: Worksheet text in active cell and formula bar

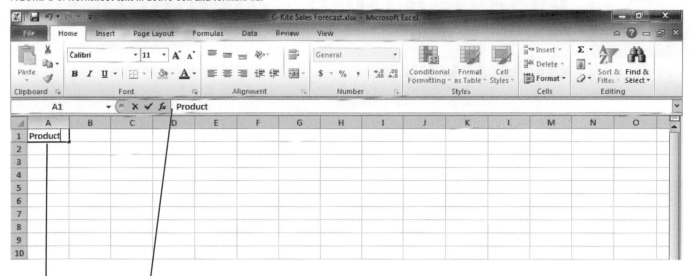

Cell A1 displays
text you typed

Formula bar displays
contents of active cell

FIGURE G-4: Worksheet after entering labels and values

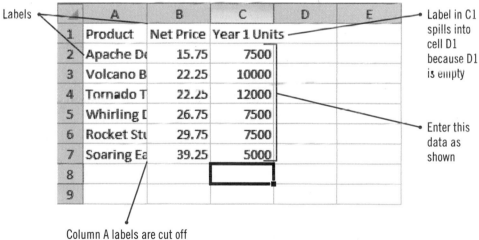

Labels

	A	B	C	D	E
1	Product	Net Price	Year 1 Units		
2	Apache De	15.75	7500		
3	Volcano B	22.25	10000		
4	Tornado T	22.25	12000		
5	Whirling [	26.75	7500		
6	Rocket Stu	29.75	7500		
7	Soaring Ea	39.25	5000		
8					
9					

Label in C1
spills into
cell D1
because D1
is empty

Enter this
data as
shown

Column A labels are cut off
on right side because
adjacent cells contain data

Working with Columns and Rows

You can adjust the width of a column or the height of a row using the mouse, Ribbon, or shortcut menu. Using the mouse is a quick and easy method when you do not need an exact width or height. You can also insert or delete columns and rows using the Insert and Delete buttons in the Cells group on the Home tab.  You need to insert two rows above the labels and enter a worksheet title in the new top row. You also need to adjust the column widths so that the labels will be visible.

1. **Position the mouse pointer on the** column boundary **between column heading A and column heading B so that the pointer changes to ↔, as shown in Figure G-5**

   The boxes containing the letters A and B are **column headings**, and the boxes containing numbers in front of each row are **row headings**.

QUICK TIP

To AutoFit more than one column at a time, drag to select all the column headings of the columns you want to widen, then double-click any column boundary in the selection.

2. **Double-click ↔ between column headings A and B**

   Double-clicking a column boundary automatically widens or narrows it to fit the longest entry in the column using a feature called **AutoFit**. The kite names in cells A2:A7 are now fully visible.

3. **Point to the** column boundary **between columns C and D, then drag ↔ to the right of the** s **in "Units" in row 1**

   Column C is now wider, so that the entire label Year 1 Units now fits in cell C1. When you drag a boundary, a dotted line appears to help you position it right where you want it.

4. **Click the** row 1 **row heading**

   Row 1 is now selected. Clicking a row heading selects the entire row. You want to insert two rows above row 1.

QUICK TIP

To insert a column, click the column heading to the right of where you want the new one, then click Insert in the Cells group.

5. **Click the** Insert button **in the Cells group twice**

   Two new rows are inserted above the labels row. The cell addresses for the cells containing the labels and values you entered have all changed to reflect their new locations.

6. **Click cell A1, type** Year 1 Kite Product Sales Forecast**, then press [Enter]**

   The worksheet title now appears in cell A1.

7. **Point to the boundary between the row 2 and 3 row headings, then drag ↕ down until the ScreenTip reads** Height: 24.00 (32 pixels)**, as shown in Figure G-6**

   The height of row 2 changes from 12 to 24 points (32 pixels). The extra space creates a visual separation between the worksheet title and the labels. You can also use the Format button in the Cells group to adjust column width or row height if you know the precise measurement you want.

8. **Click cell A2, click the** Format button **in the Cells group on the Home tab, then click** Row Height

   The Row Height dialog box opens, as shown in Figure G-7. The Row height text box displays the selected value 24, the height you specified in Step 7.

9. **Type** 30**, click** OK**, then save your changes**

   The height of row 2 increases to 30 points (40 pixels) to reflect the change you made.

FIGURE G-5: Changing column width in the worksheet

In Step 1, position the pointer here

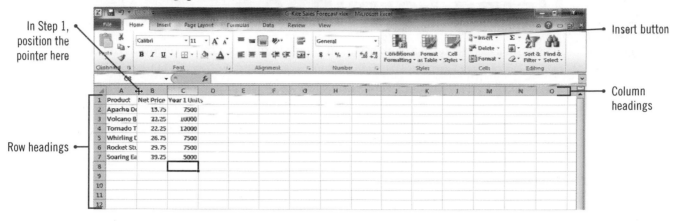

Insert button

Column headings

Row headings

FIGURE G-6: Changing row height in the worksheet

ScreenTip shows row height

In Step 7, drag Resize pointer down

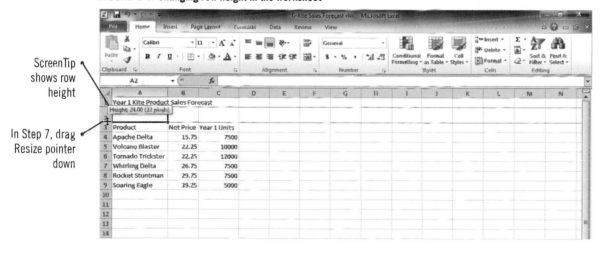

FIGURE G-7: Row Height dialog box

Using Formulas

To perform a calculation in a worksheet, you enter a formula in a cell. A **formula** is an equation that performs a calculation. Formulas start with an equal sign (=) and can contain numbers, mathematical operators, and cell references. A **cell reference** is a cell address, such as E44, that identifies the location of a value used in a calculation. Table G-1 lists some mathematical operators and sample formulas. If more than one operator is used in a formula, Excel performs the calculations in the order listed in Table G-2, which is a standard order used in math called the **order of precedence**. You can copy and move formulas just like other data in a worksheet. When you copy a formula to a new cell, Excel automatically replaces the original cell references with cell references that are in the *same relative position* as those in the original formula. This is called **relative cell referencing**. In the kite sales forecast worksheet, you need to create a formula that calculates the year 1 forecast for each product, which is the net price multiplied by the year 1 units. You first create a formula that calculates the year 1 sales for the first product, then copy the formula to other cells.

STEPS

1. **Click cell D3, type Year 1 Sales, then press [Enter]**

   Year 1 Sales is now a label in cell D3, and the active cell is now D4.

2. **Type =**

   The equal sign (=) indicates that you are about to enter a formula in cell D4. Everything you enter in a cell after the equal sign, including any numbers, mathematical operators, cell references, or functions, is included in the formula.

3. **Click cell B4**

   A dotted border appears around cell B4, and B4 now appears in both the formula bar and cell D4.

4. **Type * (an asterisk), then click cell C4**

   See Figure G-8. In Excel, the asterisk symbol is the operator for multiplication. When Excel calculates the formula, it will multiply the value in cell B4 by the value in cell C4. Using cell references ensures that the formula will automatically update if the values in B4 and C4 change.

QUICK TIP
You can also enter cell references in a formula by typing them, using either uppercase or lowercase letters.

5. **Click the Enter button ✓ on the formula bar**

   The result of the formula (118125) appears in cell D4. Notice that although the formula's result appears in cell D4, the formula =B4*C4 appears in the formula bar. To save time, you can copy the formula in D4 to cells D5:D9.

QUICK TIP
You can also double-click the fill handle to Auto Fill a formula to the adjacent cells below. The formula will be copied down to the last cell that is next to a cell containing data.

6. **Point to the small black square in the lower-right corner of cell D5, then when the pointer changes to ✛, drag ✛ down to cell D9**

   Excel copies the amount formula in cell D4 into cells D5 through D9. Notice that cells D5:D9 display the results of the copied formulas, as shown in Figure G-9. The small black square that you dragged is called the **fill handle**. The icon that appears after you release the mouse button is the Auto Fill Options button, which you can click to choose additional options when copying cells.

QUICK TIP
If you want your worksheet to display formulas instead of their results in cells, click the Formulas tab, then click Show Formulas in the Formula Auditing group.

7. **Click cell D6, then save your changes**

   The formula bar shows the formula =B6*C6. Notice that the copied formula uses different cell references than those used in the original formula. When Excel copied the formula to cell D6, it adjusted the original cell references relative to the new formula location.

FIGURE G-8: Entering a formula

Enter button

Formula bar displays formula of active cell

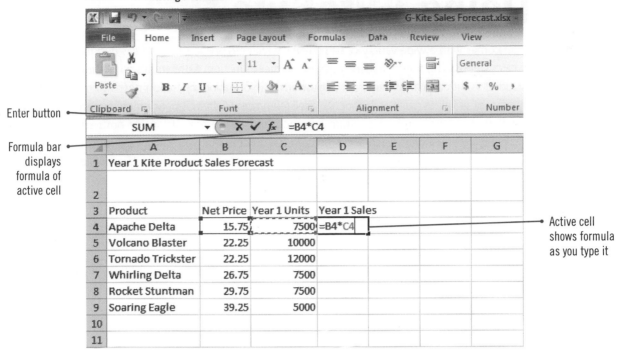

Active cell shows formula as you type it

FIGURE G-9: Worksheet after using fill handle to copy formulas to cells D5:D9

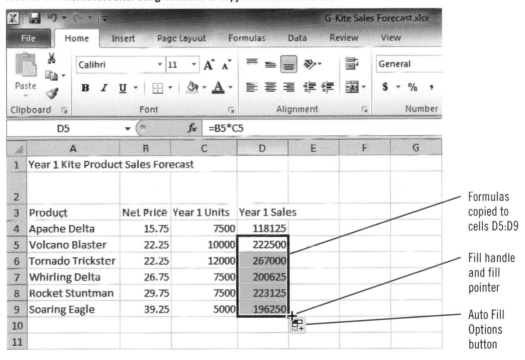

Formulas copied to cells D5:D9

Fill handle and fill pointer

Auto Fill Options button

TABLE G-2: Useful mathematical operators and sample formulas listed in order of precedence

operator	description	sample formula	result	sample worksheet (used in sample formulas)		
					A	B	C
( )	Parentheses	=(A2*B2)*3	$1500	1	Price	Quantity	
^	Exponent	=B2^2	10,000	2	$ 5.00	100	
*	Multiplication	=B2*2	200	3			
/	Division	=B2/2	50	4			
+	Addition	=B2+10	110				
–	Subtraction	=B2–20	80				

Creating a Worksheet

Using AutoSum

Excel comes with a wide variety of **functions**, which are prewritten formulas designed for particular types of calculations. The most frequently used worksheet function, **SUM**, totals all numbers and cell references included as function arguments. An **argument** is information a function needs to make a calculation, and can consist of values (such as 100 or .02), cell references (such as B3), or range references (such as A9:G16). Functions save time and help ensure accuracy, and they are available for both simple calculations and extremely complex ones. Each Excel function has a name that you usually see in all capital letters, such as AVERAGE or DATE. Because the SUM function is so commonly used, it has its own button on the Home tab also known as, the AutoSum button.  You are now ready to add up the Year 1 Units and Year 1 Sales columns. You decide to use the AutoSum button.

STEPS

1. **Click cell C10**

   Cell C10 is now the active cell. You want C10 to display the total year 1 units for all of the kite products, which is the sum of the range C4:C9.

   QUICK TIP

   You can view the sum and average of a selected range on the status bar, as well as the number of cells in the range (indicated by the Count: value).

2. **Click the AutoSum button Σ in the Editing group on the Home tab**

   A flashing dotted border appears around the cells in the range C4:C9, as shown in Figure G-10, indicating that these are the cells that Excel assumes you want to add together. The function =SUM(C4:C9) appears in cell C10 and in the formula bar, ready for you to edit or accept. When you use a function, Excel suggests a cell or range to add. With AutoSum, it is usually the group of cells directly above or to the left of the cell containing the function.

3. **Click the Enter button ☑ on the formula bar**

   Excel accepts the formula and the result, 49500, appears in cell C10.

4. **Click cell D10, click the AutoSum button, then click ☑**

   When you clicked the AutoSum button, Excel guessed (correctly) that you wanted to calculate the sum of cells D4:D9, the cells directly above cell D10. See Figure G-11.

5. **Click cell B4, type 22.25, then click ☑**

   Changing cell B4 automatically changed the formula results in cell D4 (for the Apache Delta Year 1 Sales) and also for the total sales in cell D10, as shown in Figure G-12, because these formulas use the value in cell B4. You can see what a valuable tool Excel is; changing one value in a cell changes the results in any cell that contains a cell reference to that cell.

6. **Save your changes**

FIGURE G-10: Using the AutoSum button

SUM function in formula bar with selected range as argument

Excel "guesses" the range you want to sum

AutoSum button

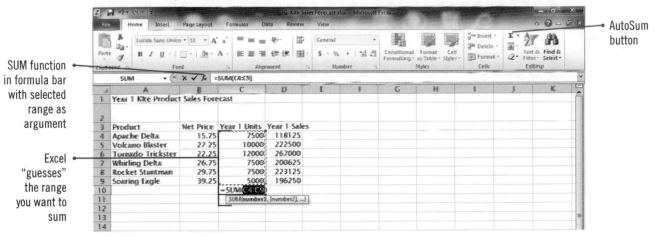

FIGURE G-11: Worksheet with totals calculated using SUM function

Formula bar displays formula of active cell (D10)

Cell D10 displays result of formula

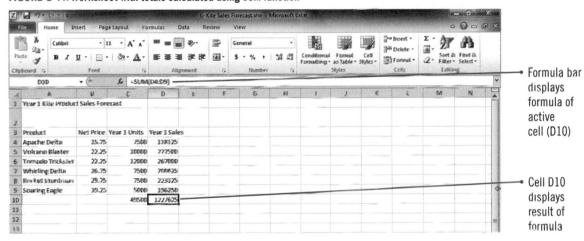

FIGURE G-12: Worksheet after changing the net price in cell B4

B4 with new price

Value in cell D4 automatically updated

Value in cell D10 automatically updated

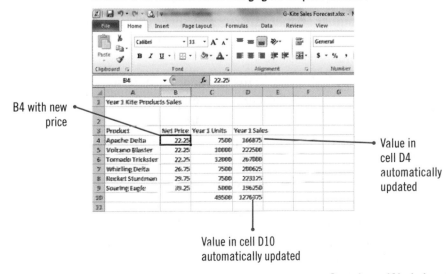

Creating a Worksheet

Changing Alignment and Number Format

When you enter data in a cell, Excel automatically left-aligns text and right-aligns values. You can change the alignment to left-, right-, or center-align cell contents using the buttons in the Alignment group on the Home tab. You can also use the Merge and Center button to merge several cells into one cell and center the text in the merged cell. Using the Merge and Center button is helpful for formatting a worksheet title so that it is centered above the worksheet data. You can also change the format of numbers to make your worksheet easier to read using the buttons in the Numbers group. For instance, you can quickly format a value or range as currency or as a date, or format numbers so that they contain commas, decimals, or both. You can also insert rows and columns in your worksheet; when you do so, any cell references are updated to reflect the change. ░░░░ You decide to apply number formats and adjust alignments to improve the worksheet's appearance. You also need to add a new column that includes the release date for each kite, format the column labels in bold, and merge and center the worksheet title.

STEPS

1. **Select the range C4:C10, then click the Comma Style button** ⑨ **in the Number group**

   The numbers in column C are now formatted with a comma and include two decimal places. The decimal places are not necessary for the unit estimates, since all the values are whole numbers.

QUICK TIP
To increase the number of digits following a decimal point, click the Increase Decimal button in the Number group.

2. **Click the Decrease Decimal button** ⬚ **in the Number group twice**

   The numbers in column C now appear without decimals.

3. **Select the range B4:B9, press and hold [Ctrl], select the range D4:D10, then click the Accounting Number Format button** $ **in the Number group**

   Pressing and holding [Ctrl] when you select cells lets you select nonadjacent cell ranges. The Net Price values in column B and Year 1 Sales values in column D are now formatted as currency, as shown in Figure G-13.

4. **Click the column C heading, then click the Insert button in the Cells group**

   A new column is inserted to the left of the Year 1 Units column. You need to enter a label in cell C3.

5. **Click cell C3, type Release Date, click the Enter button** ✔ **on the formula bar, then click the Wrap Text button** 🗐 **in the Alignment group**

   Clicking the Wrap Text button wrapped the Release Date text to two lines. Now the entire label is visible in cell C3.

6. **Click cell C4, type March 1, 2013, then click** ✔

   Excel recognized that you typed a date in cell C4 and changed the format to 1-Mar-13. You can use the Number Format list in the Number group to change the date format.

7. **Click the Number Format list arrow, as shown in Figure G-14, then click Short Date**

   The format of the date in cell C4 is now 3/1/2013. You can copy this date to the other cells in column C using the Copy and Paste commands.

QUICK TIP
The Alignment group also has buttons to align text at the top, middle, or bottom of a cell.

8. **Click the Copy button** 🖺 **in the Clipboard group, select the range C5:C9, click the Paste button** 🖺 **in the Clipboard group, then press [Esc]**

   Now all cells in the range C5:C9 display the date 3/1/2013.

9. **Click the row 3 heading, click the Center button** ≣ **in the Alignment group, then click the Bold button** **B** **in the Font group**

   Each label in row 3 is now center-aligned and bold, and stands out from the data in the worksheet.

QUICK TIP
The Orientation button in the Alignment group lets you align cell contents at any angle you specify.

10. **Select the range A1:E1, click the Merge and Center button in the Alignment group, then save your changes**

    As shown in Figure G-15, the worksheet title is centered across the five selected cells, which have merged into one cell. Note that the cell address for this cell is still A1.

Creating a Worksheet

FIGURE G-13: Worksheet after using the Accounting, Comma, and Decrease Decimal buttons

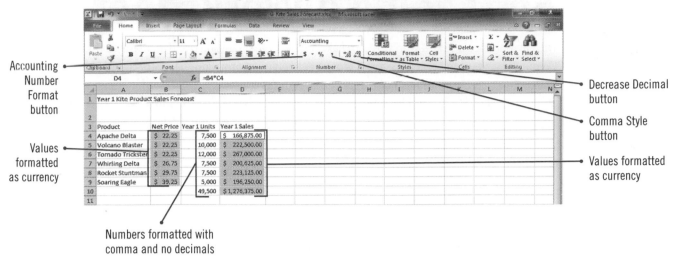

Accounting Number Format button

Values formatted as currency

Numbers formatted with comma and no decimals

Decrease Decimal button

Comma Style button

Values formatted as currency

FIGURE G-14: Applying a date format using the Number Format list

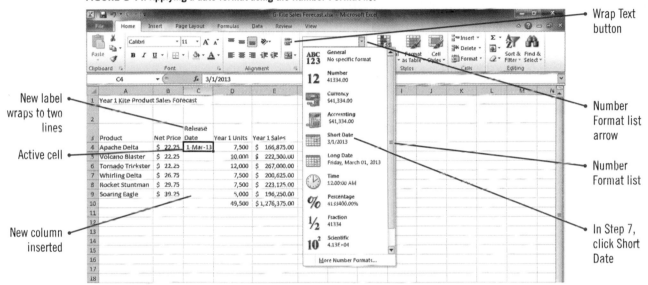

New label wraps to two lines

Active cell

New column inserted

Wrap Text button

Number Format list arrow

Number Format list

In Step 7, click Short Date

FIGURE G-15: Worksheet after changing alignment and number formats

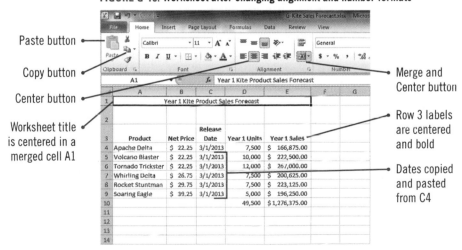

Paste button

Copy button

Center button

Worksheet title is centered in a merged cell A1

Merge and Center button

Row 3 labels are centered and bold

Dates copied and pasted from C4

Creating a Worksheet

Enhancing a Worksheet

You can enhance an Excel worksheet to make it look more professional and increase its visual appeal. In Page Layout view, you can add headers and footers containing information that you want to include at the top or bottom of each page. You can also apply a theme, and add shading and borders to set apart titles, labels, and values. ▇▇▇▇▇ You decide to add a header that contains your name, and a footer that contains the date and file name. You also decide to apply a theme and add borders and shading.

STEPS

1. **Click the Page Layout button 🔲 on the status bar, then click the Click to add header placeholder in the header area**

   The worksheet is now in Page Layout view, and the insertion point is above the worksheet title in the middle of the header's three sections.

2. **Click the right section of the header area, then type your name**

   Your name appears in the right section of the header, right-aligned, as shown in Figure G-16. The Header & Footer Tools Design tab is now available on the Ribbon.

3. **Click the Header & Footer Tools Design tab if necessary, then click the Go to Footer button 🔳 in the Navigation group**

4. **Click the left section of the footer area, then click the Current Date button in the Header & Footer Elements group**

   Excel inserts the code "& [Date]" into the left section of the footer area. When you click outside of this section, the actual date will appear here.

5. **Click the right section of the footer area, click the File Name button in the Header & Footer Elements group, then click any cell in the worksheet**

   The filename appears in the right side, and the date is in the left side of the footer area, as shown in Figure G-17.

6. **Click the Normal view button ▦ on the status bar, then press [Ctrl][Home]**

   Cell A1 is now active, and the worksheet appears in Normal view. The vertical dotted line to the right of column H indicates the page break line. This line is helpful to see if your worksheet contains many columns and you need to fit all columns on one page.

7. **Click the Page Layout tab, click the Themes button in the Themes group, then click the Concourse theme**

   The Concourse theme is applied to the worksheet.

8. **Click the Home tab, select the range A1:E10, click the Borders list arrow 🔲 ▾ in the Font group, then click All Borders**

   Cells A1:E10 now have borders applied to them.

9. **Select the range A3:E3, click the Fill Color list arrow 🎨 ▾ in the Font group, click Light Turquoise, Background 2 (third square in top row), click cell A1, then save your changes**

   The column labels are now shaded in light blue. Compare your screen to Figure G-18.

FIGURE G-16: Header with text added

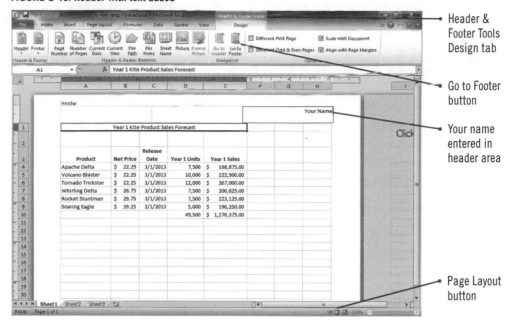

Header &
Footer Tools
Design tab

Go to Footer
button

Your name
entered in
header area

Page Layout
button

FIGURE G-17: Footer with current date and file name added

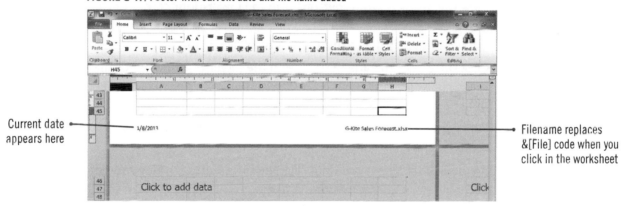

Current date
appears here

Filename replaces
&[File] code when you
click in the worksheet

FIGURE G-18: Worksheet with Concourse theme, borders, and shading applied

In Step 7, click the
Page Layout tab,
then apply the
Concourse theme

Lucida Sans Unico
font from
Concourse theme

Cell range
A1:E10 now
has borders

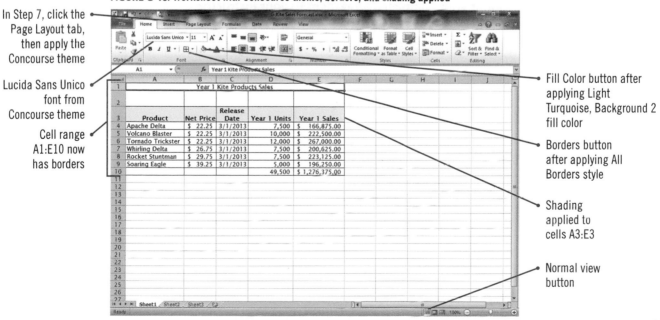

Fill Color button after
applying Light
Turquoise, Background 2
fill color

Borders button
after applying All
Borders style

Shading
applied to
cells A3:E3

Normal view
button

Creating a Worksheet

Previewing and Printing a Worksheet

When you finish working with a worksheet and have saved your work, you are ready to print it. Just like in Word, you can use the Print tab in Backstage view to preview the printed worksheet and specify settings. You can change the orientation, adjust margins, specify the printer, specify the paper size, and more. ▰▰▰▰ You have finished working with the worksheet, and are ready to preview and print it. (*Note*: Many schools limit printing in order to conserve paper. If your school restricts printing, skip Step 6.)

STEPS

1. **Click the File tab, then click Print**

   The Print tab opens in Backstage view, and the sales forecast worksheet appears in the Print Preview area, as shown in Figure G-19. Notice that the header and footer text appear at the top and bottom of the page. The worksheet is set to print in **portrait orientation** (where the page is taller than it is wide); you can change this to **landscape orientation** (where the page is wider than it is tall).

2. **Click Portrait Orientation in the Settings area, then click Landscape Orientation**

   The Print Preview area shows the worksheet in landscape orientation, as shown in Figure G-20.

3. **Click the Show Margins button 🔲 in the lower-right corner of the Print Preview area**

   Lines appear on the worksheet indicating the location of the margins at the Normal setting. The margins look fine at the Normal setting, so there is no need to change this setting.

4. **Click the Zoom to Page button 🔲 in the lower-right corner of the Print Preview area**

   The worksheet appears up close in the Print Preview area, giving you a magnified view of the worksheet data, as shown in Figure G-21.

5. **Verify that your printer is on and connected to your computer, and that the correct printer appears in the Name text box**

6. **If your school allows printing, click the Print button, otherwise skip to Step 7**

   The document prints, and the Home tab opens.

7. **Save your changes, click the File tab, then click Exit**

   The worksheet is saved, and the worksheet and Excel both close.

8. **Submit your completed worksheet to your instructor**

FIGURE G-19: Worksheet in Print Preview in Backstage view, portrait orientation

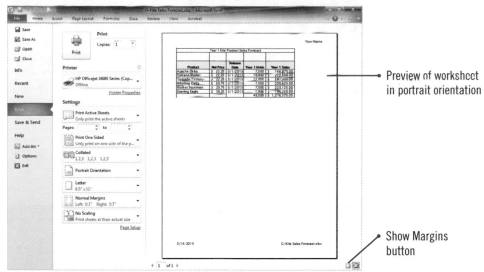

Preview of worksheet
in portrait orientation

Show Margins
button

FIGURE G-20: Worksheet in Print Preview in Backstage view, landscape orientation

File tab

Print tab

Setting shows
Landscape
Orientation

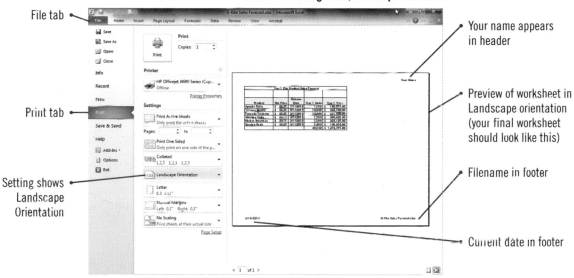

Your name appears
in header

Preview of worksheet in
Landscape orientation
(your final worksheet
should look like this)

Filename in footer

Current date in footer

FIGURE G-21: Zooming in on the worksheet in Print Preview

Print button

Selected printer
(yours will differ)

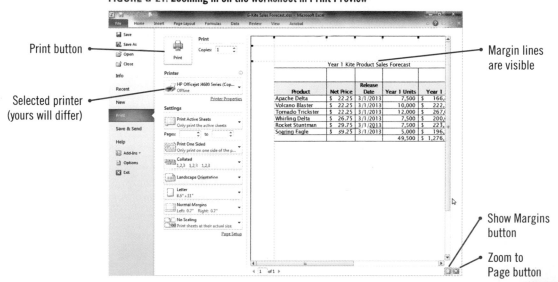

Margin lines
are visible

Show Margins
button

Zoom to
Page button

Creating a Worksheet

Practice

Concepts Review

For current SAM information, including versions and content details, visit SAM Central (http://www.cengage.com/samcentral). If you have a SAM user profile, you may have access to hands-on instruction, practice, and assessment of the skills covered in this unit. Since various versions of SAM are supported throughout the life of this text, check with your instructor for the correct instructions and URL/Web site for accessing assignments.

Label each worksheet element shown in Figure G-22.

FIGURE G-22

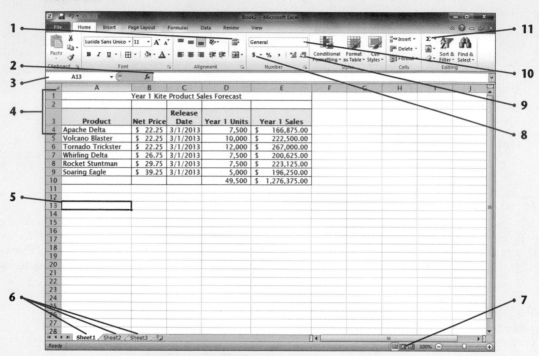

Match each icon with its appropriate use.

12.
13.
14.
15.
16.
17.

a. Pointer shape when it is positioned over a Fill handle

b. Pointer shape when it is placed over a worksheet cell

c. Button used to merge and center a cell across a range of cells

d. Button used to accept the contents of a cell

e. Button used to view the header in a worksheet

f. Pointer shape used to resize a row

Select the best answer from the list of choices.

18. The name of the cell located in column F and row 223 is:
    a. 223F
    b. F223
    c. F222
    d. 22F3

19. Which of the following formulas is NOT correctly written?
    a. B7+A5=
    b. =A5*B/
    c. =7+B55
    d. =B22*7

20. Cell E7 contains the formula =C7+D7. If you copy the formula in E7 to cell E8, which of the following formulas will E8 contain?
    a. =C6+D6
    b. =D7+D8
    c. =C8+D8
    d. =C7+C8

21. Which of the following actions does NOT accept a formula after you type it?
    a. Pressing [Tab]
    b. Pressing [Enter]
    c. Clicking ✔
    d. Pressing [Ctrl][P]

22. For which of the following tasks would you NOT use the fill handle?
    a. Copying a formula from cell A5 to cell F10
    b. Copying a formula from cell A2 to the range A3:A7
    c. Copying a label from cell A2 to A3
    d. Copying a formula from cell F22 to the range F23:F25

Skills Review

1. **Navigate a workbook.**
   a. Start Microsoft Excel.
   b. Identify the program window elements without referring to the lesson material.
   c. Click cell H22, then click cell B25.
   d. Switch to Sheet2, select the range H2:K22.
   e. Switch to Sheet1, then use the keyboard to place the cell pointer in cell A1.
   f. Save the workbook as **G-Weekly Sales** in the drive and folder where you store your Data Files.

2. **Enter values and labels.**
   a. Starting in cell A1, type the following labels in the range A1:D1:
      Bread Type   Quantity Sold   Unit Price   Total Sales
   b. Enter the following labels for Bread Type in the range A2 through A8: **White**, **Whole Wheat**, **Rye**, **Pumpernickel**, **Bagels**, **Muffins**, **Specialty Breads**.
   c. Use the table below as a guide to enter the values for Quantity Sold (in the range B2:B8) and the values for Unit Price (in the range C2:C8):

Quantity Sold	Unit Price
1217	2.25
1457	2.95
122	2.95
87	2.95
1356	.75
1785	.95
102	5.95

3. **Work with Columns and Rows.**
   a. Increase the size of column A by dragging the appropriate column boundary so that the column is wide enough to fit all the labels in the range A1:A8.
   b. Increase the width of column B by double-clicking the appropriate column boundary.
   c. Insert two rows above row 1.

Skills Review (continued)

d. Enter the label **Uncle Bob's Bread Shop Weekly Sales** in cell A1. Apply bold formatting to cell A1.

e. Increase the height of row 2 to 33 pixels using the dragging method. Open the Row Height dialog box to verify that the row height is 33.

f. Save your changes.

4. Use formulas.

a. Type a formula in cell D4 that multiplies the value of cell B4 and the value of cell C4, then use a button on the formula bar to accept the entry. When you create the formula, add the cell references to the formula by clicking the cells.

b. Type a formula in cell D5 that multiplies the value of cell B5 and the value of cell C5, then use a keyboard command to accept the entry.

c. Use the fill handle to copy the formula you entered in cell D5 to the range D6:D10.

d. Save your changes.

5. Use AutoSum.

a. Use the AutoSum button to enter a formula in B11 that adds the values in the cell range B4:B10.

b. Use the AutoSum button to enter a formula in C11 that adds the values in the cell range C4:C10.

c. Use the AutoSum button to enter a formula in D11 that adds the values in the cell range D4:D10.

d. Change the Quantity Sold value for Pumpernickel to 99, then view the changes in cells D7 and D11.

e. Save your changes.

6. Change alignment and number format.

a. Apply the Comma Style number format to the cell range B4:B11. Use a button to remove the decimals for the selected range.

b. Apply the Accounting number format to the cell range C4:D11.

c. Insert a column to the left of column D. Enter the label **Close Date** in cell D3. Format this cell so that the label wraps to two lines in the cell.

d. Enter the date **May 4, 2013** in cell D4. Use the Number Format list to apply the Short Date format to this cell. Use the fill handle to copy cell D4 to the range D5:D10. Widen column D, if necessary, so that all the dates are visible.

e. Center the labels in the cell range A3:E3. Apply bold formatting to cells A3:E3.

f. Merge and center cells A1:E1.

g. Save your changes.

7. Enhance a worksheet.

a. Change to Page Layout view.

b. Type your name in the right section of the header.

c. Switch to the footer, then insert the current date in the left section of the footer. Insert a code for the filename in the right section of the footer.

d. Move the cell pointer to cell A1, then change the view to Normal view.

e. Apply the Angles theme to the worksheet.

f. Apply the fill color Orange, Accent 2, Lighter 80% to the labels in row 3 (range A3:E3).

g. Apply the All Border border style to the range A1:E11.

h. Save your changes.

8. Preview and print a worksheet.

a. Preview the worksheet using the Print tab in Backstage view.

b. Change the orientation to Landscape.

c. Change the orientation back to Portrait.

d. Use a button to view the margin rules on the worksheet.

e. Use a button to zoom in on the worksheet.

FIGURE G-23

f. If your school permits printing, verify that the printer settings are correct, then print the worksheet. Compare your completed worksheet to Figure G-23.

g. Save your changes, close the workbook, exit Excel, then submit your completed workbook to your instructor.

Uncle Bob's Bread Shop Weekly Sales				
Bread Type	Quantity Sold	Unit Price	Close Date	Total
White	1,217	$ 2.25	5/4/2013	$ 2,738.26
Whole Wheat	1,467	$ 2.95	5/4/2013	$ 4,298.15
Rye	122	$ 2.95	5/4/2013	$ 359.90
Pumpernickel	99	$ 2.95	5/4/2013	$ 292.05
Bagels	1,356	$ 0.75	5/4/2013	$ 1,017.00
Muffins	1,785	$ 0.95	5/4/2013	$ 1,695.75
Specialty Breads	102	$ 5.95	5/4/2013	$ 606.90
	6,138	$ 18.75		$ 11,008.00

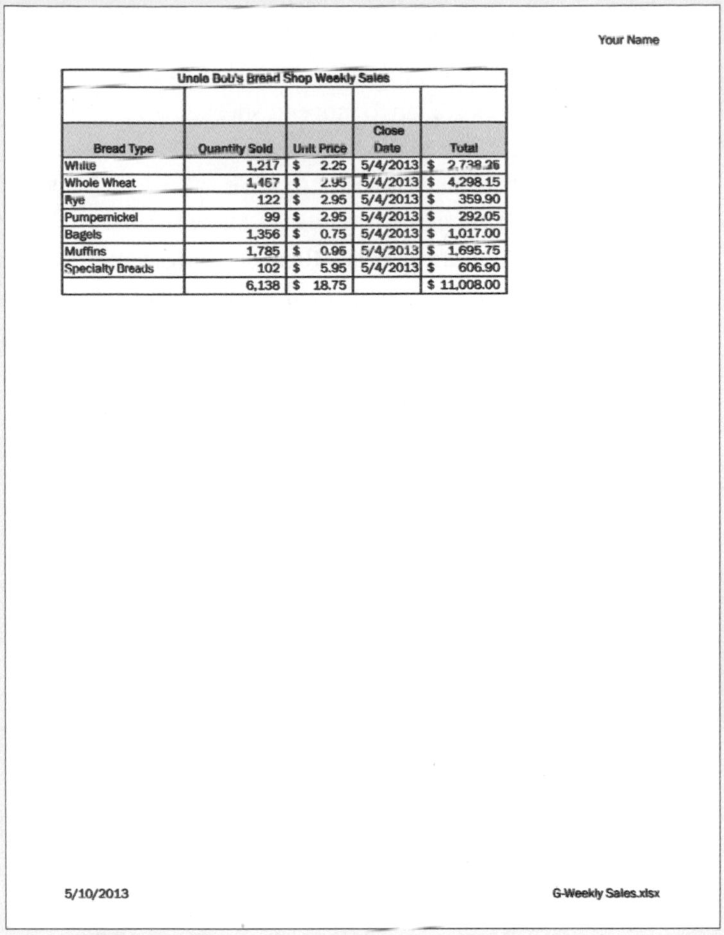

5/10/2013   G-Weekly Sales.xlsx

Independent Challenge 1

You are a sales representative at Green Earth Stationery, Inc., a small environmentally friendly paper products company based in Chicago. Your manager, Anne Badders, has asked you to provide her with a worksheet that shows the top five orders in your region for the month of April. The summary needs to include the order number, account name, order date, order total, and payments received. The worksheet also needs to show the monthly sales total and the outstanding balance due.

a. Open a new workbook, then save it as **G-Top Five Orders** in the drive and folder where you store your Data Files.

b. Enter the title **Top Five Orders for April, Midwest Region** in cell A1.

c. Enter the information shown in the table below, starting in cell A3.

Order Number	Account Name	Date	Total	Paid
4596	Card Giant, Inc.	April 10, 2013	15946	7865
4597	Office Hub	April 17, 2013	7247	0
4987	Stationery, Etc.	April 19, 2013	6534	5024
5094	Paper Mega Store	April 22, 2013	12259	8540
5895	Office Champ	April 30, 2013	4095	4095

d. Widen or narrow each column as necessary so that all the labels and data in the range A3:E8 are visible.

e. Add the label **Balance Due** in cell F3. Apply bold formatting to the range A3:F3. Widen the column if necessary.

f. Enter a formula in cell F4 that subtracts cell E4 from cell D4, then use the fill handle to copy the formula to cells F5:F8.

g. Use the AutoSum button to enter a formula in cell D9 that adds the values in the range D4:D8. Then change the amount in cell D6 to 9544.

h. Use the fill handle to copy the formula in cell D9 to cells E9 and F9.

i. Center-align the order numbers in cells A4:A8, then center-align the labels in row 3.

j. Apply the Accounting number format to cells D4:F9.

k. Merge and center cells A1:F1. Apply bold formatting to the merged cell. Increase the font size of the title in cell A1 to 14 point. (*Hint*: Select cell A1, click the Font Size list arrow, then click 14.)

l. Change the date format in the range C4:C8 to the Short Date format.

m. Apply bold formatting to the totals in row 9.

n. Add your name in the right section of the header. Add the filename to the right section of the footer.

o. Apply the Solstice theme to the workbook.

p. Apply All Borders to the range A3:F9, then apply a Thick Box Border around the range A3:F8.

q. Apply a fill color to the range A9:F9, choosing the lightest shade of green (Green, Accent 4, Lighter 80%). Apply this same shading to the range A3:F3.

Independent Challenge 1 (continued)

Advanced Challenge Exercise

- Select cells A1:F9, then click the Copy button.
- Click the Sheet2 tab to move to Sheet 2.
- Click the Paste list arrow, then click the Keep Source Formatting option on the Paste Options button to copy the cells with formatting intact from Sheet1.
- Click the Formulas tab, then click Show Formulas in the Formula Auditing group. Adjust column widths so that all of the cells fit in the screen without scrolling. Notice that all the formulas are showing in the cells that contain formulas.
- Double-click the Sheet2 tab, then type **Show Formulas**. Preview the Show Formulas worksheet in Backstage view, change the orientation to Landscape for this worksheet, then save your changes.

r. Save the workbook, then preview it using Backstage view.

s. Close the workbook, exit Excel, then submit the workbook to your instructor.

Independent Challenge 2

You are the national franchise manager for Relax Now Day Spa, which has five spas in California and the Pacific Northwest. You need to create a worksheet that analyzes second quarter sales by franchise. Your worksheet needs to compare second quarter sales for the current year (2013) to those of the previous year (2012). You also want to show how second quarter actual sales compare to the forecast. Each franchise was forecast to meet a sales increase of 10% over the prior year.

a. Create a new workbook, then save it as **G-Q2 Sales Analysis** in the drive and folder where you store your Data Files.

b. Enter the company name **Relax Now Day Spa** in cell A1, then enter **Q2 2013 Sales Analysis** in cell A2.

c. Enter the information shown in the table below in the worksheet, starting with the **Franchise** label in cell A4. First type the values, then apply the proper number formatting and adjust decimal places so that your data matches the table.

Franchise	Q2 2013	Q2 2012
Los Angeles	$25,500	$20,675
Portland	$12,750	$15,645
San Diego	$17,010	$14,563
San Francisco	$21,663	$23,087
Seattle	$21,876	$19,843

d. Enter **Increase** in cell D4, then enter a formula in cell D5 that calculates the increase in sales in Q2 2013 over Q2 2012 for the Los Angeles franchise. (*Hint*: The formula should subtract cell C5 from cell B5.)

e. Copy the formula in cell D5 to cells D6 through D9. Apply the Accounting number format to D5:D9. Remove the decimal places in D5:D9.

f. Enter **Forecast** in cell E4, then enter a formula in cell E5 that multiplies the Q2 2012 sales by 1.10. (*Hint*: The formula should use the * operator to multiply cell C5 by 1.10.) Copy this formula to cells E6 through E9. Apply the Accounting number format to E5:E9. Remove the decimal places in E5:E9.

g. Enter the label **Actual vs. Forecast** in cell F4. Format the label so that it wraps to two lines. Enter a formula in cell F5 that subtracts the amount in cell E5 from the amount in cell B5. Copy this formula to cells F6 through F9. Apply the Accounting number format to F5:F9. Remove the decimal places in F5:F9.

h. Enter **Totals** in cell A10, then use the AutoSum button to enter a formula in cell B10 that calculates the total of cells B5 through B9. Copy this formula to the range C10:F10.

i. Increase the row height of row 3 to 33 pixels. Center-align the labels in row 4.

Independent Challenge 2 (continued)

j. Merge and center cells A1:F1, so that the worksheet title is centered in the merged cell A1. Then merge and center cells A2:F2, so that the worksheet subtitle is centered in the merged cell A2.

k. Apply bold formatting to the worksheet title, the labels in row 4, the city labels in A5:A9, and the Totals label and values in row 10.

l. Apply a theme of your choosing to the workbook. Enhance the worksheet further by applying fill colors and borders where appropriate to make the worksheet visually appealing. Increase column widths as necessary so that all labels and values are visible in each cell.

m. Insert your name in the left section of the header.

n. Preview the worksheet in Backstage view. Save your changes, close the workbook, and exit Excel. Submit your completed workbook to your instructor.

Independent Challenge 3

You own a used car business called Joe's Car Shop. You buy preowned vehicles, pay contractors to fix them up, and then resell them for a profit. You decide to create a spreadsheet to track your profits for cars you have sold in the first quarter.

a. Create a new workbook and save it as **G-Q1 Profits** in the drive and folder where you store your Data Files.

b. Enter the company name **Joe's Used Autos** in cell A1. Enter **Q1 Profits** in cell A2.

c. Enter the labels and data shown in the table below, starting in cell A4. Use Accounting number formatting for the cells that contain dollar amounts.

Vehicle	Purchase Price	Cost to Fix	Sale Price	Date Sold
Toyota Corolla	$750	$350	$1,750	January 15, 2013
Nissan Sentra	$2,025	$764	$7,995	February 1, 2013
Ford Taurus	$2,250	$578	$5,995	February 8, 2013
Honda Civic	$2,015	$1,095	$7,775	March 1, 2013
Mazda Protege	$1,725	$775	$7,995	April 1, 2013

d. Adjust the width of the columns as necessary, so that all the data in each cell in the data area is visible.

e. Insert a new column to the left of Sale Price. Enter the label **Total Investment** in cell D4. Format the label and adjust the column width so that the label is on one line in the cell.

f. Enter a formula in cell D5 that sums cells B5 and C5.

g. Copy the formula in cell D5 to cells D6:D9.

h. Type the label **Profit** in cell G4. Enter a formula in cell G5 that calculates the total profit for the Toyota Corolla. (*Hint:* The formula needs to subtract the value in the Total Investment cell from the Sale Price cell.)

i. Copy the formula in cell G5 to cells G6:G9.

j. Add the label **Total** to cell A10. Enter a formula in cell B10 that sums cells B5:B9. Use the Copy and Paste commands to copy this formula to cells C10:E10 and to cell G10.

k. Center-align the labels in row 4, then apply bold formatting to these cells. Apply bold formatting to row 10.

l. Change the number format of the Date Sold values to the Short Date format.

m. Format the worksheet by applying a theme, adding borders, and adding fill colors to enhance its appearance. Format the worksheet title in cell A1 so that the font size is larger than that in the rest of the worksheet.

Independent Challenge 3 (continued)

n. Add your name to the center section of the header. Add the filename to the right section of the header. Save your changes.

o. Preview the worksheet in Backstage view. Change the orientation to Landscape. Save your changes. Figure G-24 shows the completed worksheet with possible formatting options applied.

FIGURE G-24

Your Name   G-Q1 Profits.xlsx

Joe's Used Autos
Q1 Profits

Vehicle	Purchase Price	Cost to Fix	Total Investment	Sale Price	Date Sold	Profit
Toyota Corolla	$ 750.00	$ 350.00	$ 1,100.00	$ 1,750.00	1/15/2013	$ 650.00
Nissan Sentra	$ 2,025.00	$ 764.00	$ 2,789.00	$ 7,995.00	2/1/2013	$ 5,206.00
Ford Taurus	$ 2,250.00	$ 578.00	$ 2,828.00	$ 5,995.00	2/8/2013	$ 3,167.00
Honda Civic	$ 2,015.00	$ 1,095.00	$ 3,110.00	$ 7,775.00	3/1/2013	$ 4,665.00
Mazda Protégé	$ 1,725.00	$ 775.00	$ 2,500.00	$ 7,995.00	4/1/2013	$ 5,495.00
Total	$ 8,765.00	$ 3,562.00	$ 12,327.00	$ 31,510.00		$ 19,183.00

Advanced Challenge Exercise

- Enter the label **Profit as %** in cell H4. Use the Format Painter button to copy the formatting of cell G4 to H4. Widen column H if necessary so that the entire label fits in cell H4.
- Enter a formula in cell H5 that calculates the percent of the profit made. (*Hint:* Divide cell G5 by cell D5.)
- Copy the formula in cell H4 to cells H5:H10.
- Select cells H4:H10, then click the Percent style button in the Number group on the Home tab.
- Apply the same border style and fill colors that are applied to cells G5:G10 to the cells in range H5:H10. Save your changes.

p. Close the workbook, exit Excel, then submit your completed workbook to your instructor.

Real Life Independent Challenge

You just got a new job that pays more than your current position. You have decided to move into a better apartment, without roommates, and you have found a new apartment that looks perfect. However, you are concerned that the new apartment will hurt your ability to save for a house. Not only will the new apartment cost more to rent, but you will need to pay additional money for other living expenses that will be necessary in this new situation. For instance, you currently walk to work, but the new job will require you to lease a car and pay for gas and insurance. You will also have to pay more for utilities and cable TV, since you will not be sharing these expenses anymore. You decide to create a budget spreadsheet that compares your current living expenses to your expected new expenses in the new apartment, and determine what impact this will have on your monthly savings.

a. Start Excel, then save a new workbook as **G-Budget Comparison** in the drive and folder where you store your Data Files.

b. Enter the title **Budget Comparison** in cell A1.

c. Enter the following labels in cells A3:A5:
   New Monthly Salary
   Current Monthly Salary
   Salary Increase

Real Life Independent Challenge (continued)

d. Adjust the width of column A so that all labels fit.

e. Enter a formula in cell B3 that calculates your new weekly net salary (which is $725) multiplied by 4.

f. Enter a formula in cell B4 that calculates your current weekly salary (which is $550) multiplied by 4.

g. Enter a formula in cell B5 that calculates the difference between your new monthly salary and your current salary.

h. Enter the following labels and values in cells A7 through C17:

Expense	Current Cost	New Cost
Rent	$675	$1,200
Food	$400	$400
Utilities	$50	$100
Car Payment	$0	$225
Car Insurance	$0	$100
Gas/Parking	$0	$90
Student Loan	$100	$100
Cable	$50	$100
Phone	$95	$95
Entertainment	$140	$140

i. Format all the cells in B8:B17 with the Accounting number format. Display decimals in the formatting.

j. Enter the label **Change** in cell D7, then enter a formula in cell D8 that calculates the difference between the current cost for rent and the new cost for rent. Copy this formula to cells D9:D17. Format cells D9:D17 with the Accounting number format. Keep decimal formatting.

k. Add the label **Total Expenses** to cell A18. Enter a formula in cell B18 that calculates the total expenses in the Current Cost column. Copy this formula to cells C18 and D18.

l. Enter the label **Available for Savings** in cell A21. Apply bold formatting to this label.

m. Type the label **Current** in cell A22. Type the label **New** in cell A23.

n. In cell B22, type a formula that subtracts B18 from B4.

o. In cell B23, type a formula that subtracts C18 from B3.

p. Apply a theme of your choosing to the worksheet. Then, format the worksheet using fonts, borders, shading, and alignment so that it is visually appealing and easy to read. Make sure to use formatting to emphasize the key cells in the worksheet, such as the title, labels, and totals.

q. Insert a header that contains your name centered and the current date left-aligned.

r. Save the worksheet, print it, then exit Excel.

Visual Workshop

Create the worksheet shown in Figure G-25 using the commands, formulas, and formatting skills you learned in this unit. Use formulas in cells D5:D12 to calculate the June total revenue for each cottage. Use formulas in G5:G12 to calculate the July total revenue for each cottage. Use the AutoSum button for the totals shown in row 13. Enter a formula in cell B15 that sums the June and July weeks. Use a formula in cell B17 that sums the total revenue for June and July. Apply the Apothecary theme, and apply the borders and shading shown. Save the workbook as **G-Summer Rental Revenue** in the drive and folder where you store your Data Files, with your name in the center section of the footer. Save and preview the worksheet, then submit it to your instructor.

FIGURE G-25

Castaway Cottage Rentals
June and July Rental Revenue

Cottage Name	June Weekly Rate	June Weeks Rented	June Total Revenue	July Weekly Rate	July Weeks Rented	July Total Revenue
Bird's Nest	$ 695	2	$ 1,390	$ 995	4	$ 3,980
Cozy Cabana	$ 795	3	$ 2,385	$ 1,095	3	$ 3,285
Bear Cave	$ 645	4	$ 2,580	$ 945	4	$ 3,780
Sunset Hideaway	$ 1,095	2	$ 2,190	$ 1,395	3	$ 4,185
Sunshine Cabin	$ 1,125	1	$ 1,125	$ 1,495	4	$ 5,980
Blossom Cottage	$ 725	2	$ 1,450	$ 1,025	4	$ 4,100
Munchkin Castle	$ 695	3	$ 2,085	$ 995	3	$ 2,985
Captain's Nook	$ 895	3	$ 2,685	$ 1,195	4	$ 4,780
Totals		20	$ 15,890		29	$ 33,075

Total Weeks	49

Total Revenue:	$48,965

Using Complex Formulas, Functions, and Tables

In addition to the simple, single-operator formulas you learned about in the previous unit, Excel includes powerful data analysis tools. These tools include **complex formulas**, which perform more than one calculation at a time, and functions. **Functions** are prewritten formulas, many containing multiple operators, which you can use instead of typing all the formula parts. Excel **tables** let you quickly analyze rows of data that have the same kind of information, such as customer or transaction lists. To analyze table data, you can automatically **sort** the information to change its order and **filter** it to display only the type of data you specify. You can also make certain data stand out in your worksheets by applying conditional formatting.  Serena Henning, director of sales for Outdoor Designs, has given you a worksheet that shows sales for the company's western region for January and February. She has asked you to perform some calculations on the data, organize it so that it is easier to read, and highlight important information.

OBJECTIVES

Create complex formulas

Use absolute cell references

Understand functions

Use date and time functions

Use statistical functions

Apply conditional formatting

Sort rows in a table

Filter table data

Creating Complex Formulas

When you create worksheets that contain many calculations, you often need to create formulas that contain more than one mathematical operator. For instance, to calculate profits for a particular product, a formula would first need to calculate product sales (product price multiplied by number of products sold) and then subtract costs from that result. Formulas that contain more than one operator are called **complex formulas**. When a formula contains multiple operators, Excel uses standard algebraic rules to determine which calculation to perform first. Calculations in parentheses are always evaluated first. Next, exponential calculations are performed, then multiplication and division calculations, and finally addition and subtraction calculations. If there are multiple calculations within the parentheses, they are performed according to this same order. Table H-1 lists the common mathematical operators and the order in which Excel evaluates them in a formula. Serena provides you with a worksheet showing January and February sales for the western region and year-to-date returns. She asks you to add a new column that calculates the adjusted sales total for both months.

STEPS

1. **Start Excel, open the file H-1.xlsx from where you store your Data Files, then save it as H-Western Region Sales**

   A copy of Serena's partially completed worksheet is open and saved with a new name.

2. **Click cell F6**

   You need to enter a formula in this cell that calculates Brenda Simpson's total sales for January (cell C6) and February (cell D6), then subtracts Brenda's returns (cell E6).

3. **Type =, click cell C6, press [+], click cell D6, press [-], click cell E6, then click the Enter button ✔**

   See Figure H-1. The formula bar displays the formula =C6+D6-E6, and cell F6 displays the formula result, $33,575. This formula added the value in cell C6 (Brenda's January sales) to the value in cell D6 (Brenda's February sales), then subtracted the value in cell E6 (the returns). In effect, Excel calculated $22,045+$13,876-$2,346. Now you need to copy the formula to the range F7:F13, to calculate the total sales less returns for the other sales reps.

   > **QUICK TIP**
   > You can also double-click the fill handle to copy the formula to the range F7:F13.

4. **Drag the cell F6 fill handle pointer ✚ down through cell F13 to copy the formula to the range F7:F13**

   The results of the copied formula appear in cells F7 through F13, as shown in Figure H-2.

5. **Click the Save button ▣ on the Quick Access Toolbar**

   Excel saves your changes to the workbook.

TABLE H-1: Review of order of operations

order of operations	operators
1. Calculate items in parentheses	( )
2. Calculate exponents	^
3. Multiply or divide (from left to right)	* or /
4. Add or subtract (from left to right)	+ or -

FIGURE H-1: Complex formula and its returned value

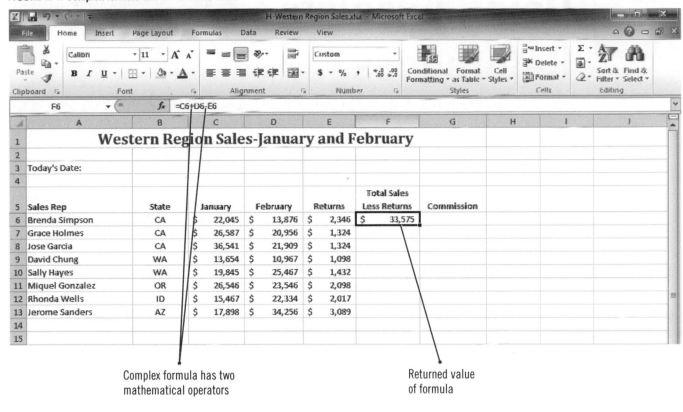

Complex formula has two
mathematical operators

Returned value
of formula

FIGURE H-2: Copying a formula to a range of cells

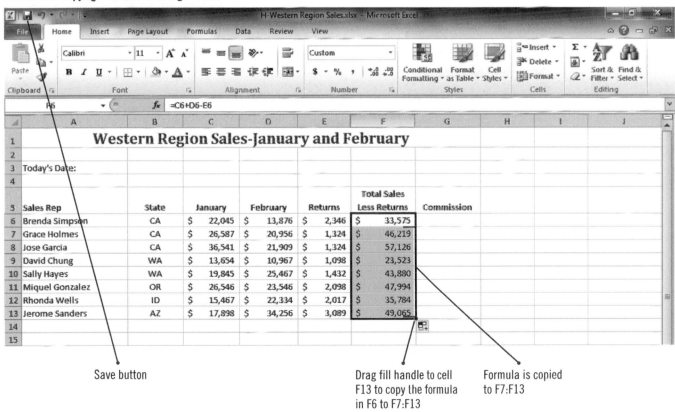

Save button

Drag fill handle to cell
F13 to copy the formula
in F6 to F7:F13

Formula is copied
to F7:F13

Excel 2010

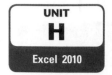
Using Absolute Cell References

When you copy a formula from one cell to another, Excel automatically adjusts the cell references in the copied formula to reflect the new formula location. For example, a formula in cell D5 that reads "=B5*C5" changes to "=B6*C6" when you copy the formula to cell D6. As you learned in Unit G, a relative cell reference changes when you move it, to reflect its relative location to the new cell. There may be times when you want a cell reference in a formula to refer to a specific cell, even when you copy the formula to a different cell. In this case, you use an absolute cell reference in the formula. An **absolute cell reference** is a cell reference that always stays the same, even when you copy a formula that contains it to a new location. An absolute cell reference contains a $ symbol before the column letter and row number (such as $A$1). To insert an absolute cell reference in a formula, click the cell you want to use as an absolute reference, then press [F4]. You need to create a formula for the cells in the Commission column that multiplies the commission rate (5%) in cell B16 by the Total Sales Less Returns value in column F. You use the absolute cell reference $B$16 for the commission rate in the formula.

STEPS

1. **Click cell G6**

   You need to enter a formula in this cell that calculates Brenda Simpson's commission. The formula needs to multiply the commission rate contained in cell B16 (5%) by the Total Sales Less Returns value in cell F6. You begin the formula by entering the absolute cell reference $B$16.

QUICK TIP

The [F4] key is a toggle key—press it to change a relative cell reference to an absolute cell reference; press it again to change an absolute cell reference to a relative cell reference.

2. **Type =, click cell B16, then press [F4]**

   The formula bar and cell G6 display =$B$16. Pressing [F4] automatically added two $ symbols to the B16 cell reference to format it as an absolute cell reference. Now you need to complete the formula.

3. **Type *, then click cell F6**

   The formula bar and cell G6 display the formula =$B$16*F6, as shown in Figure H-3. Cells B16 and F6 are highlighted because they are referenced in the formula.

4. **Click the Enter button ✔**

   Cell G6 shows the formula result of 1678.75, the commission amount for Brenda Simpson. You need to apply the Accounting number format to the cell and round to the nearest whole number.

5. **Click the Accounting Number Format button $ in the Number group, then click the Decrease Decimal button in the Number group twice**

   The value in cell G6 is now formatted as currency with no decimal places. You need to copy the formula to the range G7:G13, to calculate the commission amounts for the other sales reps.

6. **Double-click the cell G6 fill handle ✛ to copy the formula to G7:G13**

   Double-clicking the fill handle automatically filled cells G7:G13. Double-clicking a fill handle automatically fills adjacent cells down a column or across a row; this method can be faster and more efficient than dragging the fill handle. Now cells G6:G13 display the commission amounts for all the sales reps.

7. **Click cell G7, then save your changes**

   As shown in Figure H-4, the formula bar displays =$B$16*F7, which is the formula for cell G7. Notice that the formula contains the absolute cell reference $B$16; it was copied exactly from cell G6. The other cell reference in the formula, F7, is a relative cell reference, which changed when the formula was copied to cell G7. Cell G7 displays the value $2,311, the commission for Grace Holmes.

FIGURE H-3: Using an absolute cell reference in a formula

Absolute cell reference for commission rate in cell B16

Cell B16 contains commission rate and is used for absolute cell reference

Formula

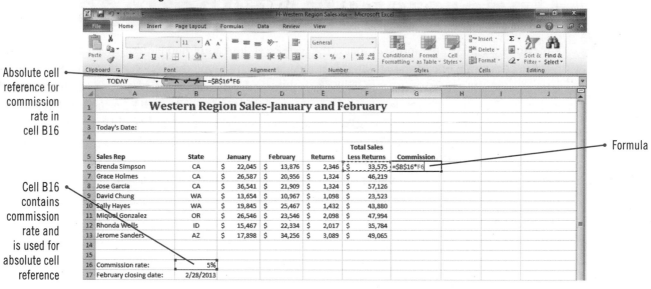

FIGURE H-4: Viewing an absolute cell reference in a copied formula

Absolute cell reference stays the same when copied to the range G7:G13

Formula is copied to these cells

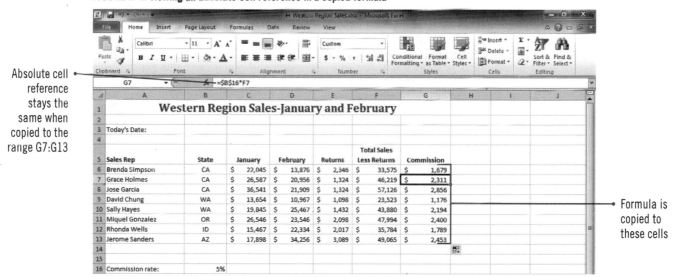

Understanding Functions

Functions are prewritten formulas that come with Excel. Instead of figuring out which calculations you need to achieve a particular result—and what order in which to type them so that the final result is accurate—you can use a function to compose the formula for you. Functions save time and help ensure accuracy, and are available for both simple calculations and extremely complex ones. Each Excel function has a name, usually written in capital letters. The SUM function, for example, adds values; the AVERAGE function calculates the average value of a specified range of cells or values and so on. There are four parts to every function: an equal sign, the function name, a set of parentheses, and arguments separated by commas and enclosed in parentheses. **Arguments** are all the information a function needs to perform a task, and can be values (such as 100 or .02), cell references (such as B3), or range references (such as A9:G16). You want to familiarize yourself with functions so that you can use them in the Western Region Sales worksheet, so you decide to practice this new skill in a blank worksheet.

1. **Click the Sheet2 worksheet tab**

   The Sheet2 worksheet opens. This sheet contains no data; it is blank and is therefore a perfect place to practice using functions.

   > **QUICK TIP**
   > When using Formula AutoComplete to enter a function, you can type either capital or lowercase letters; the feature is not case sensitive.

2. **Click cell A5, type =, then type s**

   See Figure H-5. A list of functions beginning with the letter S appears below cell A5. Anytime you type an equal sign followed by a letter, a list of valid functions and names beginning with that letter appears. This feature is called **Formula AutoComplete**. Notice that the first function in the AutoComplete list, Search, is selected, and that a description of it appears in a ScreenTip to help guide you.

   > **QUICK TIP**
   > You can also insert a function from the list by first selecting the function you want, then pressing [Tab].

3. **Type U**

   Typing the letter U shortens the list, so that only the functions beginning with SU are listed. The SUM function is one of the most commonly used functions.

4. **Double-click SUM in the list of functions**

   Now SUM is entered into cell A5 along with an open parenthesis. A ScreenTip appears below cell A5 showing the proper structure for the SUM function. The placeholders, number1 and number2, indicate arguments, which should be separated by commas; you can insert values, cell references, or ranges. The ellipsis (...) indicates that you can include as many arguments as you wish.

5. **Type 1,2,3 then click the Enter button ☑ on the formula bar**

   The formula bar displays the function =SUM(1,2,3), and cell A5 displays the value 6, which is the result of the function. Notice that Excel automatically added a closing parenthesis for the formula, as shown in Figure H-6.

6. **Click the Formulas tab**

   The Formulas tab contains commands for adding and working with formulas and functions. The Function Library group lets you choose a function by category or by using the Insert Function command.

7. **Click cell A7, then click the Insert Function button in the Function Library group**

   The Insert Function dialog box offers several ways to choose a function. You can click a function in the Select a function list, you can use the Search for a function box, or you can click the Or select a category list arrow to view a list of categories of functions. The Search box is great if you have forgotten the name of a function or are not sure which one to use. You can type a function name, business problem, or related word; if Excel recognizes part of the phrase you entered, it lists the related functions in the Select a function list.

8. **Type calculate loan payments in the Search for a function box, then click Go**

   Excel displays a list of functions related to calculating a loan payment. The first function in the list, PMT, is listed, and a description of what it does appears below the list, as shown in Figure H-7.

9. **Click Cancel, click the Sheet1 tab, then save your changes**

   The Sheet1 worksheet containing the western region YTD sales information is open on your screen.

FIGURE H-5: Entering a formula using Formula AutoComplete

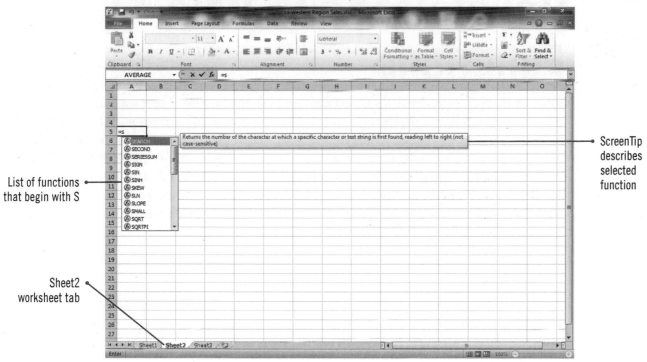

List of functions
that begin with S

ScreenTip
describes
selected
function

Sheet2
worksheet tab

FIGURE H-6: Completed formula containing the SUM function

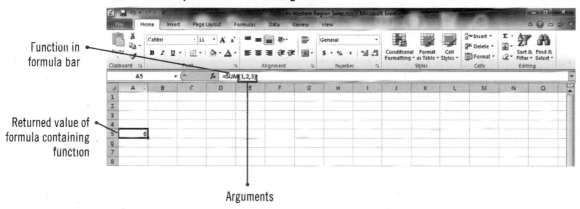

Function in
formula bar

Returned value of
formula containing
function

Arguments

FIGURE H-7: Insert Function dialog box

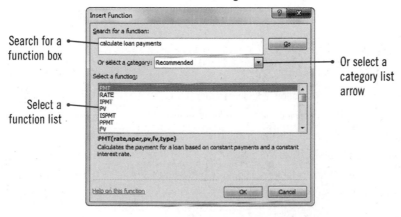

Search for a
function box

Or select a
category list
arrow

Select a
function list

Using Complex Formulas, Functions, and Tables

Using Date and Time Functions

There are many categories of functions in Excel. See Table H-2 for a list of common ones. The Excel date and time functions let you display the current date and/or time in your worksheet and can help you calculate the time between events. Some date and time functions produce recognizable text values that you can display as is in your worksheets. Other date and time functions produce values that require special formatting.  Serena wants the Western Region Sales worksheet to calculate the date that commission checks are scheduled to be issued. To accomplish this, you decide to use the TODAY function to enter the current date in the worksheet, and enter a formula that uses this information to calculate the check issue date, which is 30 days from today.

STEPS

1. **Click cell B3**

   This cell is to the right of the label Today's Date. You want to enter a function in this cell that returns today's date.

2. **Click the Date & Time button in the Function Library group**

   The list of date and time functions opens. You can point to any item to view a ScreenTip that describes the purpose of that function.

3. **Point to TODAY in the list of functions, as shown in Figure H-8, then click it**

   The Function Arguments dialog box opens, as shown in Figure H-9. The description in the dialog box explains that the TODAY function returns the current date. It also explains that the TODAY function requires no arguments, so you will not need to add values between the parentheses in the formula.

4. **Click OK**

   The result of this function, the current date, appears in cell B3.

5. **Click cell B18**

   You want to enter a formula in this cell that returns the date that is 30 days from the date in cell B17, which was the closing date for February.

6. **Type =, press [↑] to select cell B17, then type +30**

   The formula you entered, =B17+30, calculates the day when commission checks are issued, which is 30 days after the date in cell B17 (2/28/2013).

7. **Click the Enter button ✓ on the formula bar, then save your changes**

   The commission due date (3/30/2013) appears in cell B18, as shown in Figure H-10.

TABLE H-2: **Categories of common worksheet functions**

category	used for	includes
Financial	Loan payments, appreciation, and depreciation	PMT, FV, DB, SLN
Logical	Calculations that display a value if a condition is met	IF, AND, NOT
Text	Comparing, converting, and reformatting text strings in cells	FIND, REPLACE
Date & Time	Calculations involving dates and times	NOW, TODAY, WEEKDAY
Lookup & Reference	Finding values in lists or tables or finding cell references	ADDRESS, ROW, COLUMN
Math & Trig	Simple and complex mathematical calculations	ABS, ASIN, COS

Using Complex Formulas, Functions, and Tables

FIGURE H-8: Inserting the TODAY function

Date & Time button

In Step 3, click this function

ScreenTip describes TODAY function

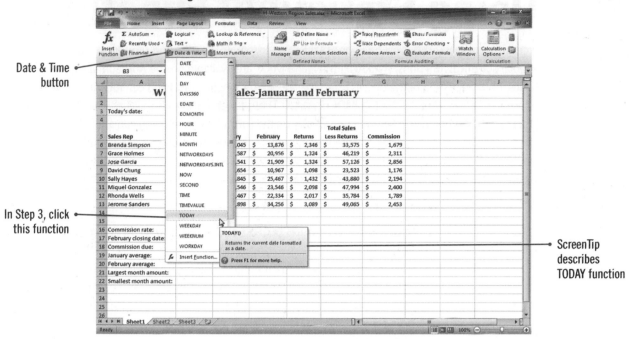

FIGURE H-9: Function Arguments dialog box

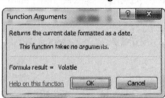

FIGURE H-10: Western Region Sales worksheet after adding date functions

Result of TODAY function (your date will differ)

Formula specifies that active cell equals today's date (cell B17) plus 30 days

Result of cell B17 + 30

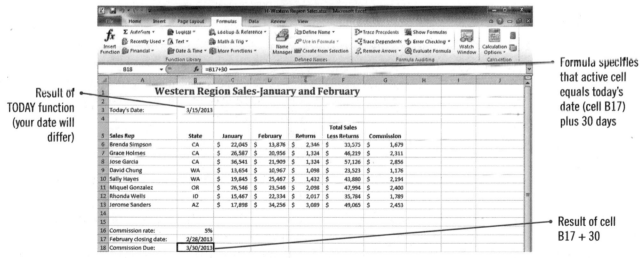

Understanding how dates are calculated using serial values

When you enter a date in a worksheet cell, the date appears in a familiar format (such as May 20, 2013), but it is actually stored as a serial value. A **serial value** is a number in a sequential series of numbers. Date serial values represent the number of days since January 1, 1900. Dates are stored as serial values so that they can be used in calculations. For example, in this lesson, you added 30 days to the current date. To Excel, the formula in cell B18 in Figure H-10 is really

=41355+30. This is useful to know if you remove formatting from a cell previously formatted as a date, or apply the General format to a cell containing a date. Instead of displaying the date, Excel displays the serial value that represents that date. To make the cell contents recognizable again, right-click the cell, click Format Cells to open the Format Cells dialog box, click Date in the Category list, choose a date format in the Type list, then click OK.

Using Statistical Functions

Excel includes many statistical functions that let you assemble, classify, and tabulate numeric data. The most popular statistical functions, AVERAGE, MIN, and MAX, are available on the AutoSum list arrow. You can calculate the average of a range of cells using the **AVERAGE** function, and you can identify the smallest or largest value in a range of cells using **MIN** or **MAX**. These functions are also available under Statistical in the More Functions category of the Function Library on the Formulas tab, and you can also access them using the Insert Function dialog box. ░░░░ Serena wants you to include the average sales amounts for each month in the Western Region Sales worksheet. She also wants you to indicate the largest and smallest order amounts for the whole region. You decide to use functions to add the necessary calculations to the worksheet.

STEPS

1. **Click cell B19, click the More Functions button in the Function Library group, point to Statistical, then click Average**

   The Function Arguments dialog box opens. You use this dialog box to specify the arguments you want to include in the function. In this case, you need to specify the range of cells C6:C13 for January sales.

2. **Select the range C6:C13, as shown in Figure H-11; then click OK in the Function Arguments dialog box**

   The formula =AVERAGE(C6:C13) is entered in the formula bar. The active cell (B19) displays the result of the formula ($22,323). This is the average sales amount among the sales reps for January. Next you need to enter a formula in B20 that calculates the average for February sales.

3. **Click cell B20, click the AutoSum list arrow in the Function Library group, then click Average**

   Notice that Excel automatically highlights cell B19. Excel is guessing that you want to calculate the average of the cells containing numbers directly above the active cell. This is not what you want to do; you want to calculate the average February sales amounts in the range D6:D13.

> **QUICK TIP**
> You can also use the MAX function by clicking More Functions in the Function Library group, pointing to Statistical, clicking MAX, selecting the range you want in the Function Arguments dialog box, then clicking OK.

4. **Select the range D6:D13, then click the Enter button ☑ on the formula bar**

   The average sales amount for February ($21,664) now appears in cell B20. The formula =AVERAGE(D6:D13) appears in the formula bar. Now you need to enter a formula in cell B21 that returns the highest sales amount in both months.

5. **Click cell B21, click the AutoSum list arrow in the Function Library group, then click Max**

   Notice that Excel automatically highlights cells B19 and B20. Excel is guessing that you want to calculate the average of the cells containing numbers directly above the active cell (B19 and B20). This is not what you want to do; you want to find the highest sales amounts in the range C6:D13.

> **QUICK TIP**
> You can include one function as an argument in another function if its result is compatible. For example, the formula =SUM(C25, AVERAGE(C6:C13)) adds cell C25 to the average of the cell range C7:C25.

6. **Select the range C6:D13, then click ☑**

   The formula =MAX(C6:D13) appears in the formula bar, as shown in Figure H-12. The active cell B21 displays the formula's result ($36,541), which is the largest sales amount. This amount, found in cell C8, is the January sales for Jose Garcia.

7. **Click cell B22, click the AutoSum list arrow in the Function Library group, click Min, select the range C6:D13, click ☑, then save your changes to the workbook**

   The formula =MIN(C6:D13) appears in the formula bar, as shown in Figure H-13. This formula returns the smallest value contained in the cell range C6:D13. The active cell B22 displays the formula's result ($10,967), which is the smallest sales amount. This amount, found in cell D9, is the February sales for David Chung.

Using the status bar to view average and sum data

The status bar provides information on average and sum on any selected range. When a range of cells containing values is selected, the status bar displays data for the average of the selected cells and the sum of selected cells. The status bar also displays a value for **Count**, which represents the number of cells selected.

FIGURE H-11: Selecting a range using the Function Arguments dialog box

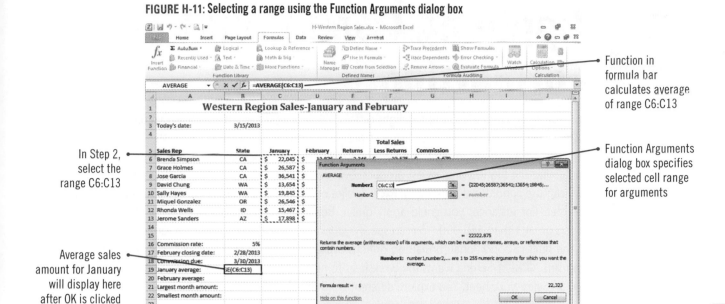

In Step 2, select the range C6:C13

Average sales amount for January will display here after OK is clicked

Function in formula bar calculates average of range C6:C13

Function Arguments dialog box specifies selected cell range for arguments

FIGURE H-12: Using the MAX function

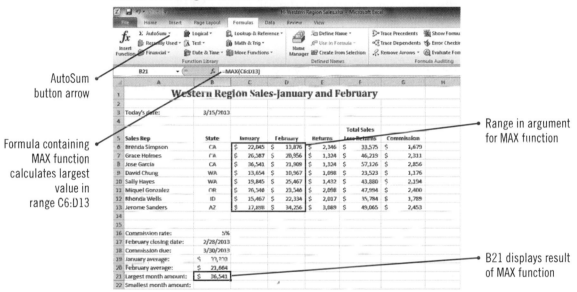

AutoSum button arrow

Formula containing MAX function calculates largest value in range C6:D13

Range in argument for MAX function

B21 displays result of MAX function

FIGURE H-13: Using the MIN function

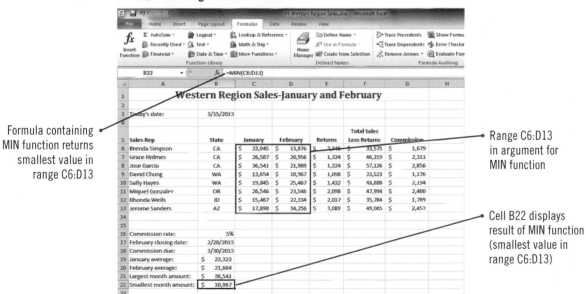

Formula containing MIN function returns smallest value in range C6:D13

Range C6:D13 in argument for MIN function

Cell B22 displays result of MIN function (smallest value in range C6:D13)

Using Complex Formulas, Functions, and Tables

Applying Conditional Formatting

Sometimes you might want to highlight certain cells in a worksheet that contain significant data points. For instance, if your worksheet lists customer orders, you might want to highlight the cells containing orders that exceed a certain amount. If your worksheet shows product sales, you might want to highlight cells containing the highest and lowest product revenues. Instead of manually formatting each highlighted cell, you can use conditional formatting. Excel applies **conditional formatting** to cells when specified criteria are met. For instance, you could apply green, bold formatted text as conditional formatting to all sales orders greater than $50,000. You can specify your own customized conditional formats, or you can use one of the built-in conditional formatting options available in Excel 2010, such as data bars, color scales, and icon sets. 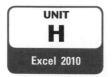 Serena wants the worksheet to highlight the high and low total amounts in the Western Region Sales worksheet. You explore different conditional formatting options to find the right effect.

STEPS

1. **Click the Home tab, then select the cell range F6:F13**

   You selected the cells in the Total Sales Less Returns column. These cells display the total sales amounts for each rep (minus returns).

2. **Click the Conditional Formatting button in the Styles group, point to Color Scales, then click the Green - Yellow - Red Color Scale option (first option, top row), as shown in Figure H-14**

   Color scales are shading patterns that use two or three colors to show the relative values of a range of cells. The selected cells now contain shading gradations of three different colors. The green shades highlight the cells containing the higher values; the yellow shades highlight the values in the middle, and the red shades highlight the lower values. You decide to remove this shading so that you can explore other conditional formats.

3. **Click the Conditional Formatting button in the Styles group, point to Clear Rules, then click Clear Rules from Selected Cells**

   With all the conditional formatting rules cleared, the color scales no longer appear in the selected cells.

4. **Click the Conditional Formatting button, point to Data Bars, then click the Green Data Bar option in the Gradient Fill section, as shown in Figure H-15**

   The cells in the selected range now contain green shading. The cells with the highest values have the most shading, and the cells with the lowest values have the least. **Data bars** make it easy to quickly identify the large and small values in a range of cells and also highlight the relative value of cells to one another.

5. **Select cells C6:D13, click the Conditional Formatting button, point to Highlight Cells Rules, then click Less Than**

   The Less Than dialog box opens. You decide to apply shaded red highlighting to cells containing values less than $15,000.

6. **Type 15000 in the Format cells that are LESS THAN text box, compare your screen to Figure H-16, then click OK**

   The cells containing values less than $15,000 in cells C6:D13 are now shaded in red, making it easy to pick out the lowest sales amounts. It is now easy to see that David Chung's sales for January and February and Brenda Simpson's sales for February are less than $15,000.

7. **Save your changes to the worksheet**

QUICK TIP

You can apply red, yellow, and green icons as conditional formats to indicate high, medium, and low values in a selected range. Click the Conditional Formatting button, point to Icon Sets, then click the icon set you want.

QUICK TIP

To specify your own custom formatting choices in the Less Than dialog box, click Custom Format in the drop-down list, choose the options you want in the Format Cells dialog box, then click OK.

Using Complex Formulas, Functions, and Tables

FIGURE H-14: Selected cells with color scales applied

Conditional Formatting button

Color scales highlight high values in green, mid-range values in yellow, and low values in red

Green - Yellow - Red Color Scale option

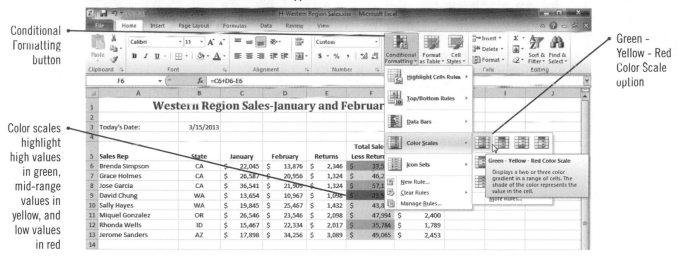

FIGURE H-15: Applying data bars to selected cells

Green data bars show relative value of cells in range

Green Data Bar option

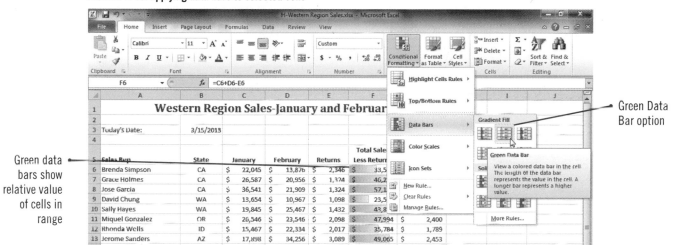

FIGURE H-16: Less Than dialog box with conditional format rules specified

Cells with values less than $15,000 have red fill

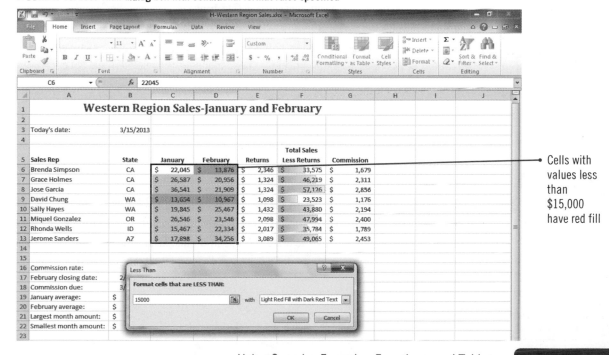

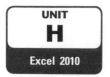
Sorting Rows in a Table

Excel lets you analyze a separate range of worksheet data called a **table**, or rows and columns of data with a similar structure. When you designate a cell range as a table, you can manage and analyze its data separately from other parts of the worksheet. For instance, you can **sort**, or change the order of the table rows, by specifying that the rows be arranged by a particular column in the table. An Excel table is similar to a table in a **database** because you can sort data in much the same way. As in database tables, Excel table columns are often called **fields** (such as a Last Name field), and rows of data are called **records** (such as a record for each customer). You use the Format as Table button in the Styles group to specify the cell range for the table and an appropriate table style. Serena wants the data sorted by state—alphabetically—and then within each state by total sales amount from largest to smallest. You format the data as a table in order to sort it.

1. **Click cell A5, click the** Format as Table button **in the Styles group, then click** Table Style Light 9 (second style in the second row), **as shown in Figure H-17**

   Notice that a dotted border surrounds the range A5:G13; this is the range that Excel assumes you want to format as table. The Format As Table dialog box is also open, with the range A5:G13 specified. The 'My table has headers' check box is selected. In a table, the **header row** is the row at the top that contains column headings.

2. **Click OK, then click any cell in the table**

   The Tables dialog box closes, and the range you selected is now defined as a table. Notice that each cell in the header row contains a list arrow ▾ on its right edge. On the Table Tools Design tab in the Table Style Options group, notice that the Total Row check box is deselected. A **total row** is an extra row at the bottom of a table that Excel adds. You want to add a Total row to the table.

3. **Click the** Total Row check box **in the Table Style Options group**

   Row 14 now contains a Total label (in cell A14). By default, the last cell in the Total row contains the SUBTOTAL function, which calculates the sum total of the table's last column of data. Cell G14 now shows the subtotal of the Commissions (for the range G6:G13).

4. **Click cell G14, position the pointer over the fill handle in the lower right corner of cell G14 until it changes to ✛, then drag ✛ to cell C14**

   You copied the formula that summed cells G6:G13 from cell G14 to cells C14:F14. Now cells C14:G14 display the sum totals for the data in columns C through G.

5. **Click the** State list arrow ▾ **in cell B5, then click** Sort A to Z, **as shown in Figure H-18**

   The items in the table are now sorted by state in alphabetical order, with the Arizona reps at the top and the Washington reps at the bottom. Notice that there is now a small Up arrow to the right of the list arrow in cell B5, indicating that this column is sorted in ascending order (or smallest to largest). Serena also wants the list to be sorted by totals within each state, from largest to smallest.

6. **Click the Home tab, click the** Sort & Filter button **in the Editing group, then click** Custom Sort

   The Sort dialog box opens. Because you already performed one sort on this data, your sort criteria is listed in the dialog box. You can use this dialog box to sort on up to three levels.

7. **Click** Add Level, **click the** Then by list arrow, **click** Total Sales Less Returns, **click the** Order list arrow, **click** Largest to Smallest, **compare your screen to Figure H-19, then click** OK

   The list is now sorted first by the State column in alphabetical order. Within each State listing, the cells containing the highest value in the Total Sales Less Returns column are listed first, as shown in Figure H-20.

8. **Save your changes**

Using Complex Formulas, Functions, and Tables

FIGURE H-17: Choosing a table style and defining a table range

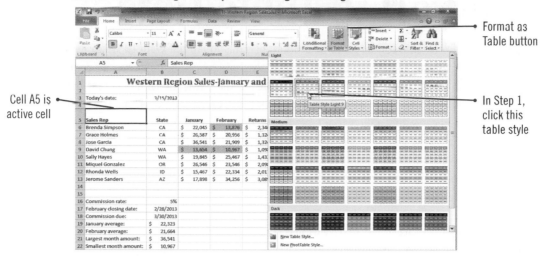

Cell A5 is active cell

Format as Table button

In Step 1, click this table style

FIGURE H-18: Sorting a list from A to Z

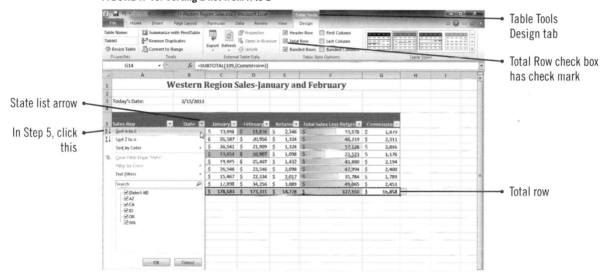

State list arrow

In Step 5, click this

Table Tools Design tab

Total Row check box has check mark

Total row

FIGURE H-19: Sort dialog box

FIGURE H-20: Table sorted by two sort criteria

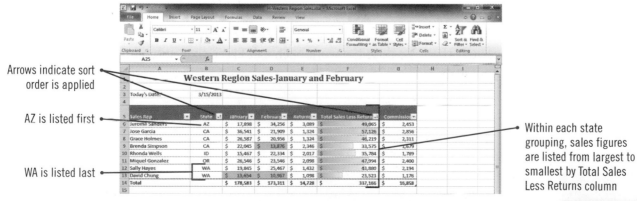

Arrows indicate sort order is applied

AZ is listed first

WA is listed last

Within each state grouping, sales figures are listed from largest to smallest by Total Sales Less Returns column

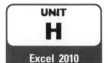
Filtering Table Data

If your Excel table contains a large amount of data, you might want to **filter** it to display only the data you need. Applying a filter tells Excel to show only those rows that meet specific requirements, such as customers with a particular zip code, or orders that exceed a certain dollar amount. When you tell Excel which rows in a table you want to see, you are specifying the **criteria** for your filter. Just as when you sort data in a table, you can apply a filter to a table by using the filter list arrows that appear to the right of each column heading. Unlike a sort, a filter does not change the order of the items in your table; instead, it temporarily hides the rows that do not meet your criteria. ▨▨▨▨ Serena wants you to filter the table data so that it shows only the sales reps for California and Washington State whose sales amounts are less than $50,000.

1. **Click the State list arrow in cell B5**

   The filter drop-down list opens and displays the list of available filters for this column. Excel creates filters for each of the values in the column, plus filters to automatically select all values, custom values, specified text, or numeric values. You can even filter a table by cell color.

2. **Click the (Select All) check box**

   The check marks are now removed from all the check boxes. You want to check the CA and WA check boxes, to specify that rows containing CA or WA in the States column display.

   > **QUICK TIP**
   > To remove an applied filter, click the Sort & Filter button in the Editing group, then click Filter.

3. **Click the CA check box, click the WA check box, compare your screen to Figure H-21, then click OK**

   You have applied a filter that shows only the rows that contain the values CA and WA in the State column (five rows). You can tell that the table is filtered because the arrow in the column header contains a filter icon ▼🔽, and the row numbers have breaks in their numeric sequence.

4. **Click the Total Sales Less Returns list arrow in cell F5, point to Number Filters, then click Less Than**

   The Custom AutoFilter dialog box opens. You use this dialog box to specify one or more criteria for a filter. The list box below Total Sales Less Returns displays "is less than," and the insertion point is in the box where you need to specify an amount.

   > **QUICK TIP**
   > To change a table back to a normal range, right-click anywhere in the table, point to Table, click Convert to Range, then click Yes.

5. **Type 50000, compare your screen to Figure H-22, then click OK**

   The table is filtered to show sales reps whose Total Sales Less Returns amounts are less than $50,000, as shown in Figure H-23. Now the table displays only four rows. By using the filter drop-down arrows in succession like this, you can apply more than one criterion to the same data in your table.

6. **Type your name in cell A25**

   > **QUICK TIP**
   > You can also adjust how pages break in Page Break view. Click the Page Break View button 🔲 on the status bar, then drag the blue page break lines to where you want the breaks to occur.

7. **Click the File tab, then click Print**

   The Print tab is now open and the worksheet appears in the Preview pane You can see that the last two columns in the worksheet (Total Sales Less Returns and Commission) do not fit on the page. You can fix this by changing the Scaling settings in the Settings area.

8. **Click the No Scaling button in the Settings area, then click Fit Sheet on One Page**

   The worksheet shrinks down just enough so that all the columns fit on the page, as shown in Figure H-24.

9. **Save your changes, close the worksheet, exit Excel, then submit the completed worksheet to your instructor**

FIGURE H-21: Applying filters to the State column

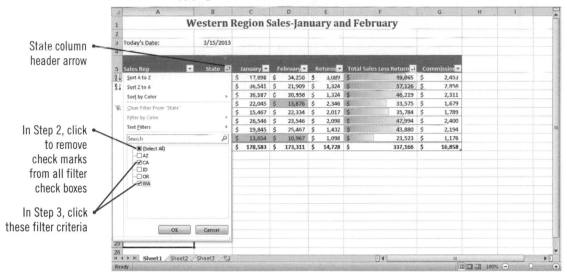

State column header arrow

In Step 2, click to remove check marks from all filter check boxes

In Step 3, click these filter criteria

FIGURE H-22: Custom AutoFilter dialog box

Filter criterion

FIGURE H-23: Worksheet with two filters applied

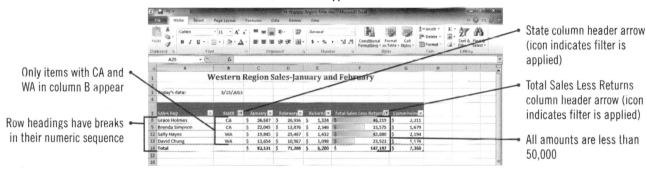

Only items with CA and WA in column B appear

Row headings have breaks in their numeric sequence

State column header arrow (icon indicates filter is applied)

Total Sales Less Returns column header arrow (icon indicates filter is applied)

All amounts are less than 50,000

FIGURE H-24: Worksheet in Print Preview

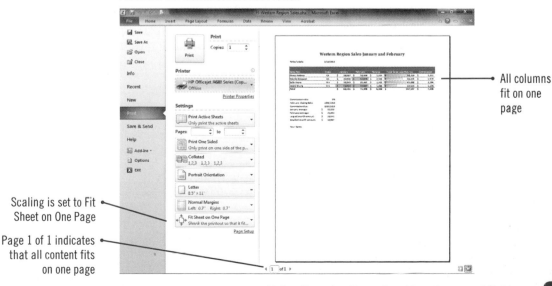

All columns fit on one page

Scaling is set to Fit Sheet on One Page

Page 1 of 1 indicates that all content fits on one page

Practice

For current SAM information, including versions and content details, visit SAM Central (http://www.cengage.com/samcentral). If you have a SAM user profile, you may have access to hands-on instruction, practice, and assessment of the skills covered in this unit. Since various versions of SAM are supported throughout the life of this text, check with your instructor for the correct instructions and URL/Web site for accessing assignments.

Concepts Review

Label each of the elements of the Excel worksheet window shown in Figure H-25.

FIGURE H-25

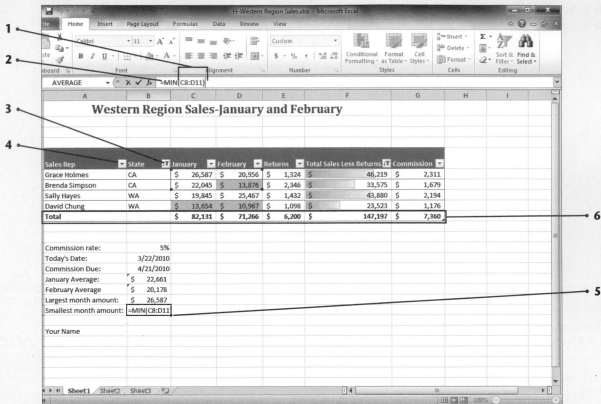

Match components of the formula =MIN(D2:H7,J2:L7) with their descriptions.

7. J2:L7   a. Second argument in the function
8. MIN   b. Symbol that separates arguments in functions
9. D2:H7   c. Symbol that indicates that the subsequent text is a formula
10. =   d. First argument in the function
11. ,   e. Function name

Using Complex Formulas, Functions, and Tables

Select the best answer from the list of choices.

12. **Which of the following is a complex formula?**
    a. =SUM(A2:A10)
    b. =(E2+E3)*.20
    c. =F2+1400
    d. =MIN(A7:24)

13. **In a complex formula, which of the following is evaluated first?**
    a. - Subtraction
    b. + Addition
    c. * Multiplication
    d. () Items in parentheses

14. **Which of the following functions is correctly structured and calculates the sum of 77 plus the values in cells A7, A8, and A9?**
    a. =SUM(77,A7,A8)
    b. =SUM(77:A7-A9)
    c. =SUM(77,A7,A9)
    d. =SUM(77,A7:A9)

15. **In the formula =MIN(D5:D6, E8:F10), which of the following are the arguments?**
    a. D5, D6, E8, and F10
    b. D5 and E8
    c. D5:D6 and E8:F10
    d. E8:F10, D5

16. **Which of the following functions returns the value 2013?**
    a. =MAX(4,10,2013, 2103)
    b. =AVERAGE(4,10,2013)
    c. =MIN(2013, 2011)
    d. =SUM((1000*2)+13)

17. **What value would Excel return in calculating the formula =SUM(5,MIN(1,5,7))?**
    a. 6
    b. 18
    c. 12
    d. 10

18. **What value would Excel return in calculating the formula =MAX(8,(2*3),100,(90+12),50)?**
    a. 150
    b. 100
    c. 50
    d. 102

19. **If you want an Excel table to display only rows containing values less than 50 in the Revenue column, which of the following actions should you take?**
    a. Choose the 50 filter on the Revenue column filter list.
    b. Sort the rows from smallest to largest in the Revenue column filter list.
    c. Sort the rows from smallest to largest in the Revenue column filter list.
    d. Use the Custom AutoFilter dialog box to specify to show only rows in which the Revenue field is less than 50.

Skills Review

1. **Create complex formulas.**
   a. Start Excel, open the file H-2.xlsx from where your Data Files are stored, then save it as **H-May Orders**.
   b. Enter a complex formula in cell G6 that calculates the sum of cells D6 and E6 minus the value in cell F6.
   c. Copy the formula from cell G6 to the range G7:G14.
   d. Save your changes to the workbook.

2. **Use absolute cell references.**
   a. In cell H6, enter a formula that multiplies the value in cell D6 by the value in B17, using an absolute cell reference for B17.
   b. Use the fill handle to copy the formula in cell H6 to cells H7:H14.
   c. Save your changes to the workbook.

3. **Use date and time functions.**
   a. Use the TODAY function to enter today's date in cell B22.
   b. Enter a formula in cell J6 that calculates the date that is 30 days later than the Order Date for Harold's Tea Shop.
   c. Use the fill handle to copy the formula in cell J6 to cells J7:J14.
   d. Save your changes to the workbook.

Skills Review (continued)

4. Use statistical functions.

   a. Enter a formula in cell B18 that uses the AVERAGE function to determine the average May order amount for the range D6:D14.

   b. Enter a function in cell B19 that determines the smallest May order amount for the range D6:D14.

   c. Enter a function in cell B20 that determines the largest May order amount for the range D6:D14.

   d. Save your changes to the workbook.

5. Apply conditional formatting.

   a. Select the range D6:D14.

   b. Apply a Color Scales conditional formatting to the selected range, choosing any style you like.

   c. Clear the conditional formatting rules you applied in Step 5b.

   d. Apply Gradient Fill Blue Data Bars conditional formatting to the range D6:D14.

   e. Select the range G6:G14, then apply conditional formatting to the cells in this range, specifying that all cells containing values that are greater than 1000 be formatted in Light Red Fill with Dark Red Text.

   f. Save your changes to the worksheet.

6. Sort rows in a table.

   a. Format the cell range A5:J14 as a table, applying Table Style Light 11 (fourth style in second row of Table Styles gallery).

   b. Specify to add a Total row to the table. Delete the value in cell J15 of the Total row (because it is a date). Click the cell D15 down arrow, then click Sum.

   c. Drag the cell D15 fill handle to cell H15.

   d. Sort the table in alphabetical order by Town.

   e. Use the Sort dialog box to sort the list data first by Town in alphabetical order, then by May Order Amount in largest to smallest order.

   f. Save your changes to the workbook.

7. Filter table data.

   a. Apply a filter so that only the rows containing Bay City and Gulfwood appear.

   b. Apply a custom filter to the filtered table that displays only those items whose Balance Due amount is greater than $500.

   c. Enter your name in cell A25 of the worksheet.

   d. View the worksheet in Print Preview, change the orientation to landscape, then adjust the scaling so that all columns fit on one sheet.

   e. Save your changes, close the worksheet, then exit Excel. Submit your completed worksheet to your instructor. Compare your completed worksheet to Figure H-26.

FIGURE H-26

Queen of Hearts Pastries
May Orders and Balances--Week 1

Customer	Customer Number	Town	May Order Amount	Previous Balance	Credits	Balance Due	May Delivery Fee	Order Date	Payment Due Date
County Hospital	2254	Bay City	$ 1,378.00	$ 548.00	$ 548.00	$ 1,378.00	$ 110.24	5/2/2013	6/1/2013
The Bay Hotel	4456	Bay City	$ 1,066.00	$ 655.00	$ 568.00	$ 1,153.00	$ 85.28	5/1/2013	5/31/2013
Kennedy Elementary School	1543	Gulfwood	$ 1,855.00	$ 755.00	$ 500.00	$ 2,110.00	$ 148.40	5/4/2013	6/3/2013
Total			$ 4,299.00	$ 1,958.00	$ 1,616.00	$ 4,641.00	$ 343.92		

Delivery Fee:	8%	
Average Order Amount:	$	629.67
Smallest Order Amount:	$	143.00
Largest Order Amount:	$	1,855.00
Today's Date:	5/15/2013	
Your Name		

Independent Challenge 1

You are the sales manager for the Midwest region at Plushkin Fine Linens and Towels, Inc. You need to create a worksheet that analyzes sales results for each state in your region. In addition, you need to highlight the total sales, the average sales, and the best and worst performing sales regions. You also need to calculate the bonuses for each sales rep. A sales rep is eligible for a bonus only if his or her average sales increase for each state exceeds 10%. If a sales rep is eligible for a bonus, his or her bonus is calculated by multiplying total sales by 3%.

a. Start Excel, open the file H-3.xlsx from where you store your Data Files, then save it as **H-Midwest Q1 Sales**.

b. In cell E5, enter a formula that subtracts the value in D5 (Q1 Sales Prior Year) from the value in cell C5 (Q1 Sales). Use the fill handle to copy the formula to cells E6:E16.

c. Enter a formula in cell F5 that calculates the percentage that Q1 Sales increased over Q1 Sales in the prior year. (*Hint*: Your formula needs to divide the value in cell E5 by the value in cell D5.) Use the fill handle to copy the formula to cells F6:F16.

d. In cell B18, use the AVERAGE function to compute the average sales total for all states. (*Hint*: Specify the range C5:C16.)

e. In cell B19, use the MAX function to calculate the maximum (or highest) quarterly sales total for the states.

f. In cell B20, use the MIN function to compute the minimum (or lowest) quarterly sales total for the states.

g. Define the range A4:F16 as a table, and apply a table style that you like. Include a Total row. Delete the value in cell F17. Click cell E17, click the down arrow in cell E17, then click Sum. Drag the E17 fill handle to cells D17:C17.

h. Sort the data in the table by the Sales Rep column (column B) in order from A to Z. Using the Custom Sort dialog box, apply a second sort level that sorts by Q1 Sales vs. Prior Year Q1 ($) from largest to smallest.

i. In cell B23, use the AVERAGE function to compute the average Q1 increase (as a percentage) for Jonathan Stephens' states. (Use the range F5:F9.)

j. In cell B24, use the AVERAGE function to compute the average Q1 increase (as a percentage) for Patricia Morley's states. (Use the range F10:F13.)

k. In cell B25, use the AVERAGE function to compute the average Q1 increase (as a percentage) for Ricardo Juarez's states. (Use the range F14:F16.)

l. Apply Data Bars conditional formatting to the range E5: E16. Choose any Data Bars style you like; make sure that the color you choose contrasts well with the colors in the table style you chose.

m. If Jonathan Stephens' average Q1 increase (shown in cell B23) exceeds 10%, then enter a formula in cell F23 that calculates his bonus amount. (*Hint*: The formula needs to multiply cell F20 by the sum of cells C5:C9.)

n. If Patricia Morley's average Q1 increase (shown in cell B24) exceeds 10%, then enter a formula in cell F24 that calculates her bonus amount. (*Hint*: The formula needs to multiply cell F20 by the sum of cells C10:C13.)

o. If Ricardo Juarez's average Q1 increase (shown in cell B25) exceeds 10%, then enter a formula in cell F25 that calculates his bonus amount. (*Hint*: The formula needs to multiply cell F20 by the sum of cells C14:C16.)

p. Preview the worksheet in Backstage view. Change the orientation to landscape, then adjust the scaling so that all columns fit on one sheet. Save your changes.

Advanced Challenge Exercise

- Select the range C5:C16.
- Click the Conditional Formatting button, then click the Star icon set under the Ratings section.
- Save your changes.

q. Save your changes, close the workbook, then exit Excel. Submit your completed worksheet to your instructor.

Independent Challenge 2

The sales director at Wexler Organics, Inc., has just received the raw sales data for the month of August. She has asked you to finish creating a worksheet that she started. She wants you to highlight key information on this worksheet, including the highest individual sale, the overall sales total, and the number of sales reps who logged individual sales transactions greater than $5,000 for the month.

a. Open the file H-4.xlsx from where you store your Data Files, then save it as **H-August Sales Rep Report**.

b. Enter a formula in cell E7 that calculates the commission owed to the rep. (*Hint*: Multiply cell D7 by the absolute reference B4.) Use the fill handle to copy the formula to cells E8:E39.

c. Create a formula in cell F7 that subtracts the rep's commission in cell E7 from the Sales amount in cell D7.

d. Copy the formula in cell F7 to the range F8:F39.

e. Create a table from the range A6:F39. Apply a table design style that you like to the table. Include a Total row. Use the fill handle to copy the formula in cell F40 to cells E40:D40.

f. Sort the table data by sales in order from largest to smallest. Look at the sorted list, then enter the name of the rep that has the largest sales amount in cell B42.

g. Select cell B43, then enter a formula that uses the MAX function to identify the highest individual sale in the month. Apply the Accounting number format to cell B43 with no decimal places.

h. Enter a formula in cell B44 that calculates the average for all sales in cells D7:D39. Apply the Accounting Number format, and remove all decimals.

i. Apply Data Bars conditional formatting to the range D7:D39, choosing any data bar color you like.

j. Enter your name in cell A3.

k. Preview the worksheet in Backstage view. Adjust the scaling so that all columns fit on one sheet in portrait orientation. Save your changes.

l. Save your changes, close the workbook, then exit Excel. Submit your completed worksheet to your instructor.

Independent Challenge 3

You own and operate The Last Minute Chef, a restaurant and caterer that serves busy families in Rochester, New York. You are building an Excel spreadsheet to calculate your profits for the previous year. You have entered sales and most of the expense data in the worksheet. Now you need to enter the necessary formulas to calculate the delivery costs and the profits for each month.

a. Open the file H-5.xlsx from where you store your Data Files, then save it as **H-Restaurant Profits**. Enter your name in cell A26.

b. The Last Minute Chef pays for food deliveries through a delivery service, which charges a $7.00 flat fee per delivery. The delivery fee is in cell B20. Enter a formula in cell I5 that calculates the cost of deliveries for the month of January. (*Hint*: The formula needs to multiply cell H5—the cell that contains the number of deliveries for January—by cell B20, with B20 as an absolute cell reference.)

c. Enter a complex formula in cell J5 that calculates profits for January. The formula should subtract the sum total of cells C5:G5 and cell I5 from B5 (Sales for January). (*Hint*: Start the formula with B5 followed by the - mathematical operator, followed by the SUM function to add C5:G5 and cell I5. You will need to use two sets of parentheses—one set around the arguments, and the other around the whole SUM function part of the formula.)

d. Select cells I5 and J5, then use the fill handle to copy the formulas down the columns.

e. Enter a formula in cell B21 that identifies the highest profit amount.

f. Enter a formula in cell B22 that identifies the smallest profit amount.

g. Enter a formula in cell B23 that calculates the average monthly profit for the entire year.

h. Apply conditional formatting to the cells J5:J16 to format any cells containing values greater than 55000 with green fill and dark green text.

i. Format the range A4:I16 as a table, choosing any table style you like. Add a Total row. Use the fill handle to copy the formula in cell J17 to cells I17:B17.

Using Complex Formulas, Functions, and Tables

Independent Challenge 3 (continued)

j. Sort the table in the Profits column by Largest to Smallest.

k. Preview the worksheet in Backstage view. Change the orientation to landscape, then adjust the scaling so that all columns fit on one sheet.

Advanced Challenge Exercise

■ Click cell A17 (the Total label) then type Average.

■ Click cell B17, click the down arrow that appears in the right side of the cell, then click Average.

■ Copy the new formula in cell B17 to cells C17:J17 by dragging the fill handle. Save your changes.

l. Save your changes, close the workbook, then exit Excel. Submit your completed worksheet to your instructor.

Real Life Independent Challenge

You can take advantage of dozens of prebuilt Excel worksheets that are available as templates in the New dialog box from Microsoft Office Online. These templates provide a wide range of tools for helping you with school, work, and life tasks. For instance, you can find templates for creating invoices, memos, calendars, and time sheets. You can even find templates for helping you plan a party or clean your house. In this Real Life Independent Challenge, you use a loan calculator to calculate monthly payments for a car loan.

a. Click the File tab, then click New.

b. Click More templates in the Office.com Templates section, then click Calculators.

c. Double-click Loan calculator with extra payments, then click Download.

d. Save the workbook as **H-Loan Calculator** where you save your Data Files.

e. In cell D4, enter 10000 as the loan amount.

f. In cell D5, enter 5 as the annual interest rate amount.

g. In cell D6 enter the number of years you want to pay off your loan.

h. In cell D7, enter a formula that returns a date that is 30 days from today. Leave cell D8 blank.

i. Enter your name in cell F7.

j. Save your changes, then preview the worksheet in Backstage view. Close the workbook, exit Excel, then submit the workbook to your instructor.

Visual Workshop

Open the file H-6.xlsx and save it as **H-Spring Classes Profits** where you store your Data Files. Modify the worksheet so that it contains all the formulas, functions, and formatting shown in Figure H-27. The Total Student Fees cells need to include formulas that multiply the number of students by the student fee by the number of classes. The Instructor Cost cells need to include formulas that multiply the number of classes by the instructor fee ($75.00) in cell B19. (Use an absolute cell reference.) The Profit cells need to subtract the Instructor Cost from the Total Student Fees. Convert the range A4:H16 to a table, then resize column widths to match the figure. Sort the table as shown. Enter appropriate formulas and labels in the range E19:E20. Change alignments to match the figure. Add your name to cell A21. Adjust the print settings to landscape orientation. Save and close the workbook, exit Excel, then submit your finished workbook to your instructor.

FIGURE H-27

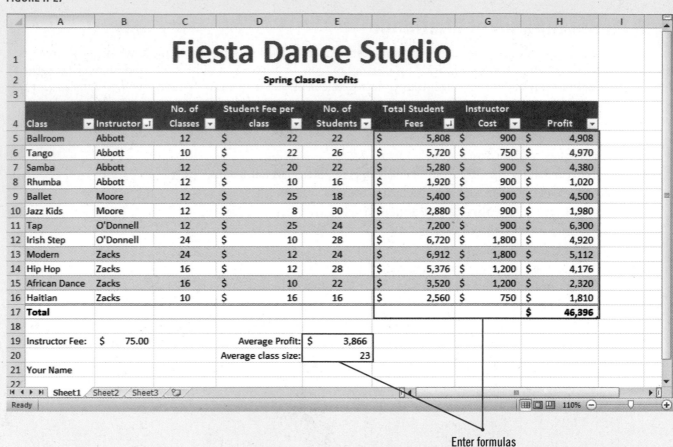

Enter formulas
in these cells

Using Complex Formulas, Functions, and Tables

Working with Charts

A worksheet is great for presenting and summarizing data, but interpreting numbers in rows and columns takes time and effort. A much more effective way to communicate worksheet data to an audience is to present the data as a chart. A **chart** is a visual representation of worksheet data. For example, a chart can illustrate the growth in sales from one year to the next in a format that makes it easy to see the increase. Excel provides many tools for creating charts to help you communicate key trends and facts about your worksheet data. In this unit, you learn how to create and work with charts. Serena Henning, director of sales for Outdoor Designs, has asked you to create a chart from worksheet data that shows first-quarter sales of the Canoe Kit by region. You will create and customize two different types of charts for Serena. You will also add sparklines, which are miniature charts, to help illustrate the sales trends for each region in the worksheet.

OBJECTIVES

Understand and plan a chart

Create a chart

Move and resize a chart and chart objects

Apply chart layouts and styles

Customize chart objects

Enhance a chart

Create a pie chart

Create sparklines

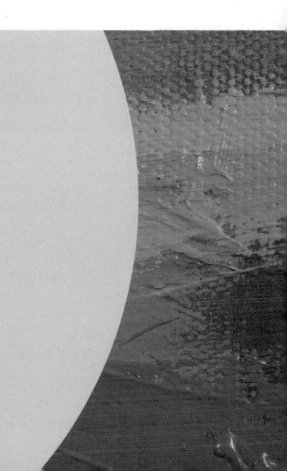

Understanding and Planning a Chart

Before you create a chart, you need to understand some basic concepts about charts. You also need to determine what data you want your chart to show and what chart type you want to use. <!-- --> Before you create the chart that Serena has requested, you decide to review your data and think about which chart type best represents the information you want to convey.

DETAILS

In planning and creating a chart, it is important to:

- **Understand the different parts of a chart**

    The chart in Figure I-1 shows sales of the Canoe Kit by region for January, February, and March. This chart is based on the range A3:D7 in the worksheet. Like many charts, the one shown here is two-dimensional, meaning it has a horizontal axis and a vertical axis. The **horizontal axis** (also called the **x-axis**) is the horizontal line at the base of the chart that shows categories. The **vertical axis** (also called the **y-axis**) is the vertical line at the left edge of the chart that provides values. The vertical axis is sometimes called the **value axis**. In Figure I-1, the vertical axis provides values for sales, and the horizontal axis shows months. The **axis titles** identify the values on each axis. The blue, red, green, and orange bars each represent a data series. A **data series** is a sequence of related numbers that shows a trend. For example, the blue data series shown in Figure I-1 represents Canoe Kit sales for the West region. A **data marker** is a single chart symbol that represents one value in a data series. For example, the orange data marker on the far right of the chart represents the Canoe Kit sales in March for the Northeast region. A chart **legend** identifies what each data series represents. The **gridlines** in the chart are vertical and horizontal lines that help identify the value for each data series. The **plot area** is the part of the chart contained within the horizontal and vertical axes; in the figure, the plot area is yellow. The **chart area** is the entire chart and all the chart elements.

    > **QUICK TIP**
    > Some charts also contain a **z-axis**, called the **depth axis**, for comparing data equally across categories and series.

- **Identify the purpose of the data and choose an appropriate chart type**

    You can use Excel to create many different kinds of charts; each chart type is appropriate for showing particular types of data. Before you create a chart, decide what aspect of your data you want to emphasize, such as making a comparison between two categories, so that you can choose the appropriate chart type. Table I-1 provides descriptions of common Excel chart types and examples of what each type looks like. As the chart in Figure I-1 demonstrates, column charts are good for comparing values. This chart shows that all regions except the Midwest had sales increases in March. It also shows that the Northeast region (represented by the orange bars) had the highest overall sales for February and March, and that the West region (represented by the blue bars) had the highest sales for January.

- **Design the worksheet so that Excel creates the chart you want**

    Once you have decided on the chart type that best conveys your meaning, you might want to arrange your rows and columns so that the chart data illustrates the points you want to make. In the figure, notice that the region with the highest revenues in March (Northeast) appears on the right. Serena arranged the data series in this order in the underlying worksheet, so that the chart would show the Northeast's revenues in the far right column.

FIGURE I-1: Example of a column chart

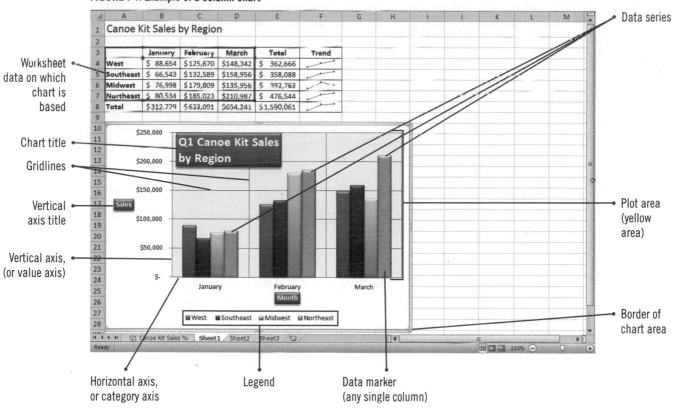

Worksheet data on which chart is based

Chart title

Gridlines

Vertical axis title

Vertical axis, (or value axis)

Horizontal axis, or category axis

Legend

Data marker (any single column)

Data series

Plot area (yellow area)

Border of chart area

TABLE I-1: Common chart types in Excel

chart type	description	example
Area	Shows relative importance of values over a period of time	
Bar	Compares values across categories, with minimal emphasis on time	
Column	Compares values across categories over time	
Line	Shows trends by category over time	
Pie	Describes the relationship of parts to the whole	
Scatter	Shows the relationship between two kinds of related data	

Creating a Chart

You can create Excel charts from your worksheet data automatically. In a worksheet, you select the cells that contain the data you want to chart, then use commands in the Charts group on the Insert tab to specify the chart type you want to add. Any changes you make to the worksheet data are automatically reflected in the chart. You can change the chart type to explore different options until you find the type that best illustrates your data.  First-quarter sales results for the Canoe Kit just became available at Outdoor Designs. Serena has provided you with a worksheet that shows sales for each month by region. You need to create a chart based on the worksheet data.

STEPS

1. **Start Excel, open the file I-1.xlsx from where you store your Data Files, then save it as I-Canoe Kit Sales by Region**

2. **Select the range A4:D8**

   The range A4:D8 contains the data you want to chart. Notice that you selected the row and column labels but not the column totals. For most charts, you should avoid including totals when selecting worksheet cells.

3. **Click the Insert tab**

   The Charts group on the Insert tab contains buttons for inserting common types of charts, including Column, Line, Pie, Bar, Area, and Scatter. The Line chart type is good for showing trends in data over time.

   TROUBLE
   There are two Line buttons on the Insert tab; be sure to click the one in the Charts group.

4. **Click the Line button in the Charts group**

   The Line chart menu opens and displays two subcategories, 2-D Line and 3-D Line. The thumbnails provide a visual guide for what each chart subtype looks like.

   QUICK TIP
   Depending on your screen resolution, your vertical (value) axis might show different values or number intervals.

5. **Click the Line option (first thumbnail under 2-D Line), as shown in Figure I-2**

   A line chart is inserted into the current worksheet, as shown in Figure I-3. The region names from the worksheet are on the chart's horizontal axis, and sales amounts are on the chart's vertical axis. Colored lines representing the sales data for January, February, and March appear in the chart. The double-line border and sizing handles around the chart indicate that the chart is selected. Notice that the Chart Tools Design, Layout, and Format tabs are all available on the Ribbon; these contextual tabs become available when a chart is selected.

6. **Click the Change Chart Type button in the Type group on the Chart Tools Design tab**

   The Change Chart Type dialog box opens. This dialog box lets you apply dozens of different chart types to a selected chart. The left pane displays each chart category. The Line category is currently selected because the selected chart is a line chart.

7. **Click the Column category in the left pane, click the Clustered Column option, as shown in Figure I-4, then click OK**

   The chart in the worksheet changes to a clustered column chart, with three data series (blue, red, green) representing January, February, and March sales for each region. See Figure I-5.

8. **Click the Save button 🖫 on the Quick Access toolbar**

   The chart is saved as part of the workbook file.

FIGURE I-2: Choosing a line chart type

Insert tab •

In Step 5, click • the Line option

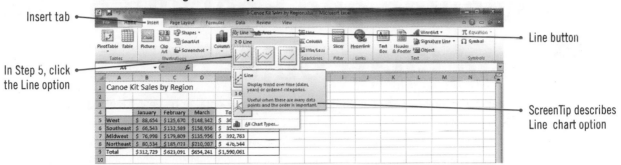

• Line button

• ScreenTip describes Line chart option

FIGURE I-3: Line chart in the worksheet

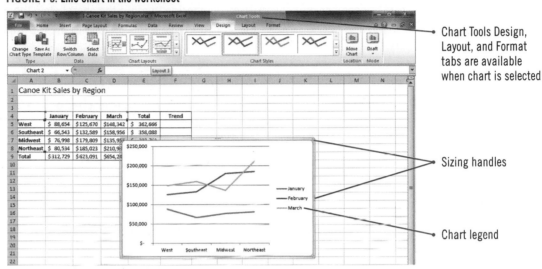

• Chart Tools Design, Layout, and Format tabs are available when chart is selected

• Sizing handles

• Chart legend

FIGURE I-4: Change Chart Type dialog box

Column category •

Clustered • Column option

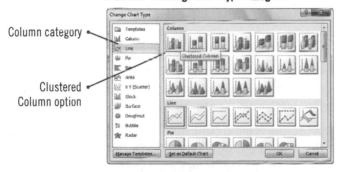

FIGURE I-5: Column chart inserted into worksheet

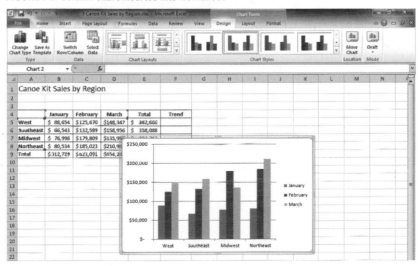

Working with Charts

Moving and Resizing a Chart and Chart Objects

You can easily move a chart if it obscures your worksheet data, or resize it if it is too large or too small. You can also move or resize many of the individual components of a chart—sometimes called **chart objects**—such as the chart background or the legend. To move a chart object, select it and drag it to a new location. To resize a chart object, drag one of its sizing handles. Note that some chart objects (such as the chart axis) cannot be moved and that others (such as the chart title) cannot be resized by dragging. ▓▓▓▓▓ To improve the overall appearance of the worksheet, you decide to move the chart below the worksheet data and make it bigger. You also decide to move the legend so that it is aligned with the top edge of the chart.

STEPS

1. **If the chart is not selected, click the chart border to select it**

2. **Point to the top edge of the chart so that the pointer changes to ⌖, drag the chart so that its upper-left corner is aligned with the upper-left corner of cell A11, then release the mouse button**

   The chart is now directly below the worksheet data. As you dragged the chart, a dimmed image of the chart moved with the pointer.

   > **QUICK TIP**
   > To move a chart, point to an edge but not to a sizing handle; pointing to a sizing handle allows you to resize the chart rather than move it.

3. **Scroll down until you can see row 29**

4. **Position the pointer over the chart's lower-right sizing handle so that the pointer changes to ⤡, drag the sizing handle down so that the chart's lower-right corner is aligned with the lower-right corner of cell H29, as shown in Figure I-6, then release the mouse button**

   The chart enlarges to the new dimensions. If you drag a corner sizing handle, you increase or decrease a chart's height and width simultaneously. To increase or decrease only the height or width of a chart, drag a side, top, or bottom sizing handle.

   > **QUICK TIP**
   > If you make a mistake when moving or resizing a chart, click the Undo button on the Quick Access toolbar, then try again.

5. **Click the chart legend**

   Sizing handles appear around the edge of the legend, indicating that it is selected. Note that the sizing handles on the legend—and on all chart objects—are circular at the legend corners and square on the border midpoints. This is different from the sizing handles on the chart itself, where they are groups of dots.

6. **Point to any border of the legend (but not to a sizing handle) until the pointer changes to ⌖, then drag the legend up to the position shown in Figure I-7**

   The legend is now positioned to the right of the upper-right corner of the chart.

   > **QUICK TIP**
   > To delete a chart or chart object, select it, then press [Delete].

7. **Save your changes to the worksheet**

FIGURE I-6: Resizing a chart

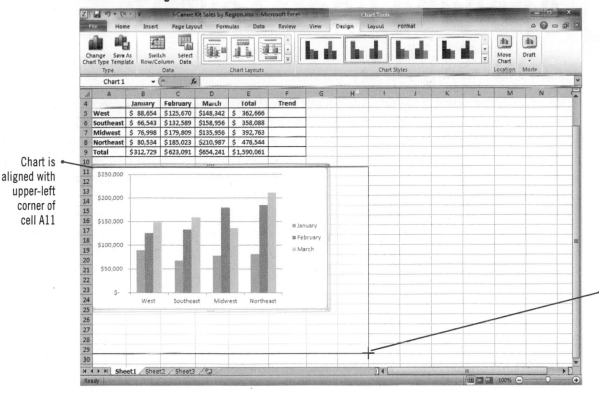

Chart is aligned with upper-left corner of cell A11

Drag right corner resizing handle to here (lower-right corner of H29)

FIGURE I-7: Moving the legend

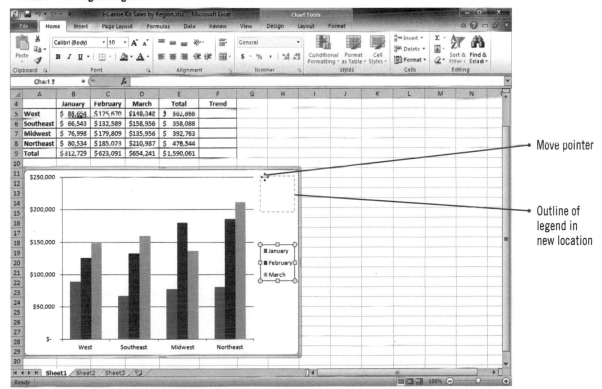

Move pointer

Outline of legend in new location

Applying Chart Layouts and Styles

When you create a chart, it has default layout and style settings for the chart type applied. A **chart layout** is a predefined arrangement of chart elements, such as the legend and chart title. A **chart style** is a predefined set of chart colors and fills. Instead of modifying individual chart elements, such as moving the legend or changing the color of a data series, you can instantly change the way chart elements are positioned and whether certain elements are displayed or hidden by choosing a different layout. Chart layouts are available from the Chart Layouts gallery on the Chart Tools Design tab. You can change fill colors and textures by choosing a chart style from the Chart Styles group on the Chart Tools Design tab. You can also get a different view of your data by reversing the rows and columns.  You decide to experiment by switching the rows and columns of the chart to see the effect. You also want to improve the appearance of your chart by applying a different chart layout and style.

STEPS

QUICK TIP

The Chart Tools Design tab is a contextual tab; it is available only when a chart is selected.

1. **Click the Chart Tools Design tab, if necessary**
   The Chart Tools Design tab displays commands for changing the appearance of a chart.

2. **Click the Switch Row/Column button in the Data group**
   See Figure I-8. The chart now shows only three clusters of data series (instead of the original four), one for each month. Each data series now represents the revenue for each region (instead of each month), so there are four data points for each cluster instead of three. The horizontal axis labels now list the three months of the first quarter (instead of the regions). This view of the data shows more clearly the overall growth trend for each month.

3. **Click the More button 🔽 in the Chart Layouts group**
   The Chart Layout gallery displays an assortment of thumbnails of different layouts. Some have gridlines, some have data labels, and a few have chart and axis titles. You want a layout that has a chart title and axis titles.

4. **Click Layout 9 (third layout in third row)**
   Your chart now has placeholder text for a chart title, a vertical axis title, and a horizontal axis title. You need to replace the placeholder text for these titles with appropriate text for your chart.

TROUBLE

When you click the Chart Title placeholder and type text for your chart title, notice that the text you type appears only in the formula bar (not in the Chart Title placeholder). This can be confusing, but don't be alarmed—the chart title text will appear when you press [Enter].

5. **Click Chart Title, then type Q1 Canoe Kit Sales by Region, then press [Enter]**
   The title "Q1 Canoe Kit Sales by Region" appears above the chart. You can also edit chart titles and axis titles using the formula bar.

6. **Click Axis Title in the vertical axis, type Sales, then press [Enter]**
   The vertical axis label now reads "Sales," clarifying that each data series represents sales figures.

7. **Click Axis Title in the horizontal axis, type Month, then press [Enter]**
   The horizontal axis label changes to "Month." The chart and axis titles make it easier to interpret the meaning of the chart. Compare your screen to Figure I-9.

8. **Click 🔽 in the Chart Styles group, click Style 26 (second style in fourth row), then save your changes**
   The new style is applied to the chart, as shown in Figure I-10. This style has a three-dimensional appearance and makes your chart more visually appealing.

FIGURE I-8: Chart with rows and columns switched

Chart Tools
Design tab

Switch Row/
Column button

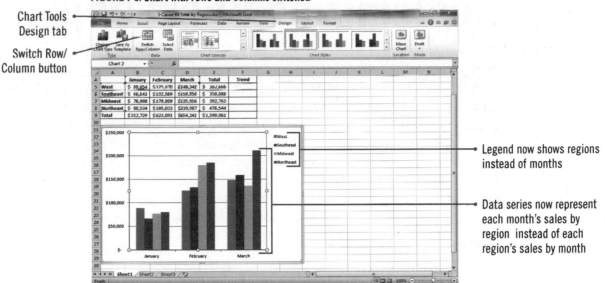

Legend now shows regions
instead of months

Data series now represent
each month's sales by
region instead of each
region's sales by month

FIGURE I-9: Chart with layout applied and customized chart axis titles

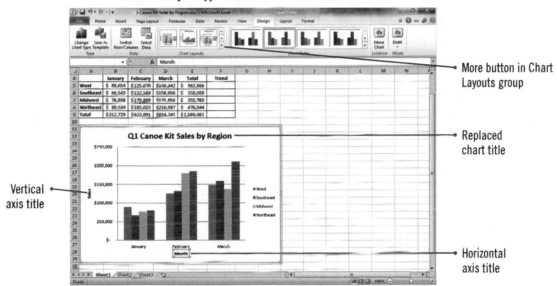

More button in Chart
Layouts group

Replaced
chart title

Vertical
axis title

Horizontal
axis title

FIGURE I-10: Applying a chart style using the Chart Style gallery

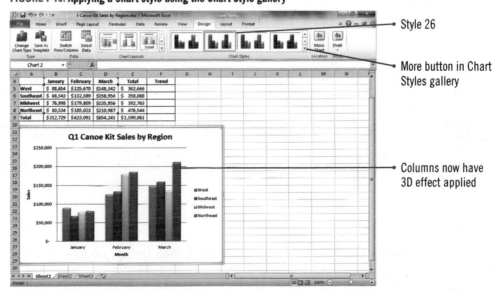

Style 26

More button in Chart
Styles gallery

Columns now have
3D effect applied

Working with Charts

Customizing Chart Objects

When you create a chart, each chart object has default layout settings applied. For instance, the clustered column chart with the chart layout you applied positions the chart title above the chart and positions the legend to the right of the chart. You can easily change the positioning and attributes of individual chart objects by choosing from additional preset options on the Chart Tools Layout tab, or by making custom choices in the Format dialog box. Chart elements that can be modified include the chart title, axis titles, legend, data labels, axes, gridlines, plot area, and data table. A **data table** in a chart is a grid containing the chart's underlying worksheet data, which is added below the x-axis in certain types of charts. You decide to position the chart title so that it is inside the plot area. You also want to position the legend at the bottom of the chart to make more room for the data series, and change the orientation of the vertical-axis title so that it is easier to read. You also decide to explore other options to improve the chart's appearance.

1. **Click the Chart Tools Layout tab**

   The Chart Tools Layout tab contains buttons and commands for changing the layout of a selected chart. You use this tab to work with individual chart elements.

2. **Click the Chart Title button in the Labels group, then click Centered Overlay Title**

   The chart title is now positioned in the chart just above the largest data series. This arrangement increases the size of the plot area without requiring you to enlarge the chart.

3. **Click Axis Titles in the Labels group, point to Primary Vertical Axis Title, then click Horizontal Title**

   See Figure I-11. The vertical axis title changes from a vertical to a horizontal position.

4. **Right-click the legend, click Format Legend, click the Bottom option button in the Format Legend dialog box, as shown in Figure I-12, then click Close**

   The legend now appears below the chart, and the chart expands to fill the empty space on the right.

5. **Click the Data Labels button in the Labels group, then click Outside End**

   Labels for each worksheet value in cells B5 through D8 now appear above each data marker. Unfortunately, the values are too big to fit in the chart and the labels overlap, making them look cluttered and difficult to read.

6. **Click the Data Labels button in the Labels group, then click None**

   The data labels are removed.

7. **Click the Gridlines button in the Axes group, point to Primary Vertical Gridlines, then click Major Gridlines**

   Vertical gridlines now appear in the chart, enclosing the monthly sales for each region. This effect helps to visually separate each region's monthly sales.

8. **Click the Data Table button in the Labels group, then click Show Data Table with Legend Keys**

   See Figure I-13. A data table is inserted, with a legend in the first column that identifies the data series in each row. Data tables are helpful when you want to show both the chart and the underlying worksheet data. Because this worksheet already contains the data for the chart, you don't need the data table here; it makes the worksheet look cluttered.

9. **Click the Data Table button in the Labels group, click None, then save your changes**

FIGURE I-11: Chart with repositioned vertical axis title and chart title

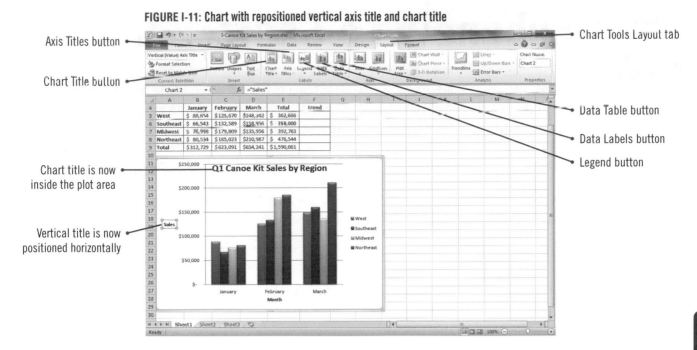

Axis Titles button

Chart Title button

Chart title is now inside the plot area

Vertical title is now positioned horizontally

Chart Tools Layout tab

Data Table button

Data Labels button

Legend button

FIGURE I-12: Format Legend dialog box

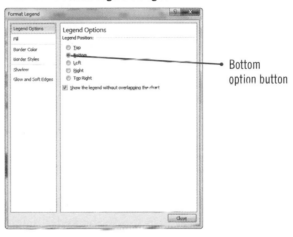

Bottom option button

FIGURE I-13: Data table in chart with legend added

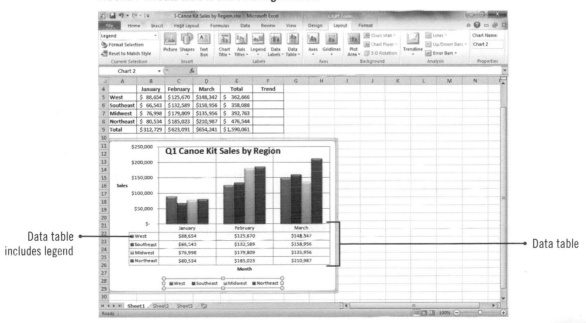

Data table includes legend

Data table

Enhancing a Chart

You can choose from a large variety of styles and effects to improve the appearance of a chart and increase its visual appeal and effectiveness. In addition to using the Format dialog box to modify any selected chart object, you can choose from a variety of commands and galleries on the Chart Tools Format tab to make further enhancements and adjustments. For instance, you can apply a shape style to a chart title or axis title and then adjust the fill, outline, and shape effect to your liking. You can apply WordArt styles to any text to make it stand out. You can also align and reposition multiple objects. To format an object, you first must select it. You can select an object by clicking it or by using the Chart Elements list arrow on the Chart Tools Format tab. ▓▓▓▓ Serena asks you to change the color of the Northeast data series and to add visual effects to the chart and axis titles to make the chart more visually appealing.

STEPS

1. **Click the Chart Tools Format tab**

   The Chart Tools Format tab is active. You can apply special styles and effects to selected chart objects using the Format dialog box or the Chart Tools Format tab.

   > **QUICK TIP**
   > To select a single data marker, double-click the data marker.

2. **Click any one of the purple Northeast data markers in the chart**

   Sizing handles and a border surround all the data markers in the Northeast data series. Clicking a single data marker selects all the data markers in that series. You decide to change the selected data series color to orange.

   > **QUICK TIP**
   > You can open the Format dialog box for any chart object from either the Layout tab or the Format tab.

3. **Click the Format Selection button in the Current Selection group on the Chart Tools Format tab**

   The Format Data Series dialog box opens, providing options you can select to enhance and change the appearance of the selected data marker. You need to adjust the Fill setting.

4. **Click Fill in the left pane under Series Options, click the Solid fill option button; click the Color list arrow, click the Orange, Accent 6 color, as shown in Figure I-14, then click Close**

   The Format Data Series dialog box closes, and the Northeast data series color is now orange.

   > **TROUBLE**
   > If you have trouble locating the Chart Elements list, look directly above the Format Selection button in the Current Selection group; the text Series "Northeast" should be displayed in the Chart Elements box.

5. **Click the Chart Elements list arrow in the Current Selection group, click Chart Title, then click the More button ▾ in the Shape Styles gallery**

   The Shape Styles gallery displays several shape styles that you can apply to the selected chart title.

6. **Click the Intense Effect - Blue, Accent 1 style, as shown in Figure I-15**

   The chart title is now formatted with a three-dimensional blue background and white font. You decide to add a shadow special effect so that the title matches the style of the data series.

   > **QUICK TIP**
   > To remove formatting that you have applied to a chart object, select the object, then click the Reset to Match Style button in the Current Selection group on the Chart Tools Format tab.

7. **Click the Shape Effects button in the Shape Styles group, point to Shadow, then click the Offset Bottom style in the Outer category**

   The chart title now has a shadow along its bottom edge, enhancing the impression that it is three dimensional.

8. **Click the vertical axis title (Sales), then click the Intense Effect - Blue, Accent 1 style in the Shape Styles gallery**

9. **Click the horizontal axis title (Month), click the Intense Effect - Blue, Accent 1 style in the Shape Styles gallery, then save the worksheet**

   Compare your screen to Figure I-16.

Working with Charts

FIGURE I-14: Format Data Series dialog box

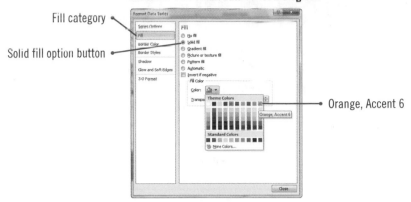

Fill category

Solid fill option button

Orange, Accent 6

FIGURE I-15: Applying a shape style to a chart object

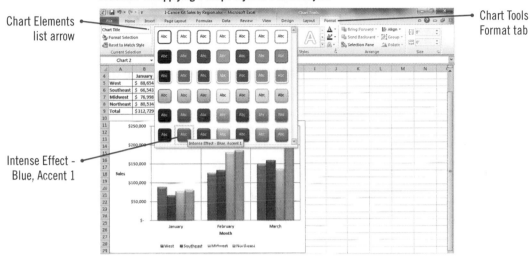

Chart Elements
list arrow

Chart Tools
Format tab

Intense Effect -
Blue, Accent 1

FIGURE I-16: Completed chart with formatting enhancements

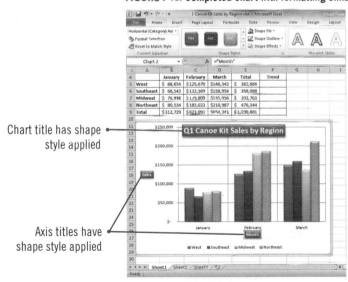

Chart title has shape
style applied

Axis titles have
shape style applied

Printing charts with or without worksheet data

If your worksheet contains both a chart and worksheet data, you can preview or print only the chart by itself by selecting the chart before printing it. To do this, click the chart to select it, click the File tab, then click Print. The Preview pane will display a preview of the chart by itself. Then, if you click Print, only the chart will print. If you want to preview or print both the chart and the worksheet data, make sure the chart is not selected when you preview or print the worksheet. If any cell (outside of the chart) is active when you preview the chart, both the worksheet data and the chart will appear in the Preview pane.

Creating a Pie Chart

Column charts are great for comparing values across categories, but they are not very useful for comparing percentages or parts to a whole. For instance, the column chart does not convey the West region's percentage of total first-quarter sales. A pie chart is an effective tool for comparing the relative values of parts to a whole. Just like any other type of chart, you can add it to a worksheet, or you can add it on a separate chart sheet. A **chart sheet** is a sheet in a workbook that contains only a chart; it contains no worksheet cells. ▰▰▰▰ Serena wants you to create a pie chart on a separate chart sheet that compares total first-quarter revenues of the Canoe Kit by region.

1. **Select the** range A5:A8, **press and hold [Ctrl], then select the** range E5:E8

   You selected two nonadjacent ranges (the region names and total first-quarter sales for each region); this is the only worksheet data you want reflected in the pie chart. You want to create a pie chart that shows each region's percentage of total sales.

2. **Click the** Insert tab, **click the** Pie button **in the Charts group on the Insert tab, then click the** Pie in 3-D option

   See Figure I-17. A 3D-style pie chart now appears in the worksheet and covers part of the column chart. The pie chart shows that the purple pie wedge (representing the Northeast region) is slightly bigger than the others, and the blue pie wedge (representing the West region) is the smallest. You decide to move the pie chart to a new chart sheet in the workbook, so that it can be viewed separately from the column chart.

3. **Click the** Move Chart button **in the Location group on the Chart Tools Design tab**

   The Move Chart dialog box opens.

4. **Click the** New sheet option button, **type** Q1 Canoe Kit Sales % **in the New sheet text box as shown in Figure I-18, then click** OK

   The pie chart moves to a new chart sheet called "Q1 Canoe Kit Sales %".

5. **Click the** More button ▾ **in the Chart Layouts group, then click** Layout 1

   Each pie slice in the chart now contains a label for the region and for the region's percentage of total sales. A chart title placeholder is displayed above the chart.

6. **Click the** Chart Title placeholder, **type** Q1 Canoe Kit Sales by Region, **then press [Enter]**

7. **Click** Northeast **on the purple pie slice, notice that the labels on all the slices are now selected, then right-click the pie slice**

   The Mini toolbar and a shortcut menu open. You can use the Mini toolbar to apply formatting to selected text or objects.

8. **Click the** Increase Font Size button A⁺ **on the Mini toolbar seven times to increase the font size to 20, click the** File tab, **then click** Print

   A preview of the chart sheet is displayed in the preview area in Backstage view. Notice that the orientation is set to Landscape, the default setting for chart sheets. Compare your screen to Figure I-19.

9. **Click the** Home tab, **then save your changes**

FIGURE I-17: Creating a pie chart

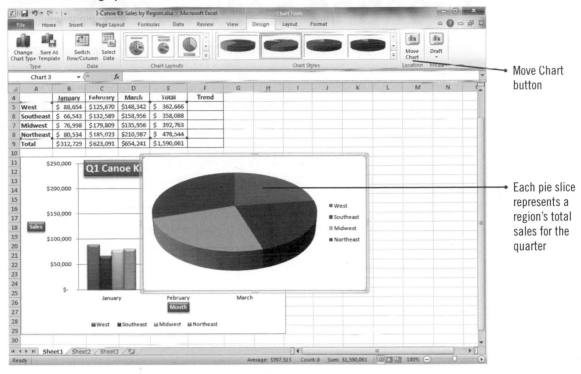

Move Chart button

Each pie slice represents a region's total sales for the quarter

FIGURE I-18: Move Chart dialog box

New sheet option button

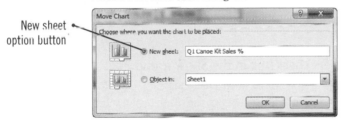

FIGURE I-19: Preview of completed pie chart in Backstage view

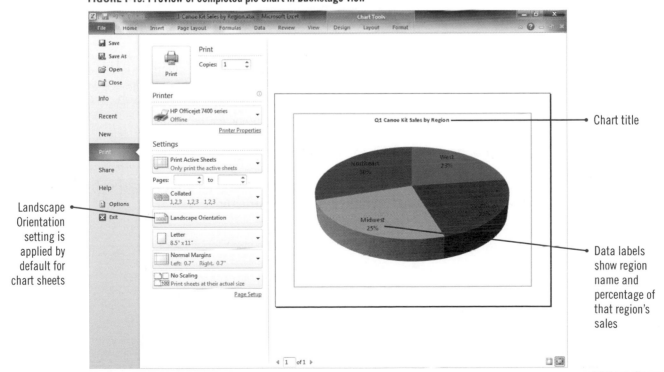

Chart title

Landscape Orientation setting is applied by default for chart sheets

Data labels show region name and percentage of that region's sales

Creating Sparklines

In addition to charts, you can also add sparklines to a worksheet to communicate patterns or trends visually. **Sparklines** are tiny charts that fit in one cell and illustrate trends in selected cells. There are three types of sparklines you can add to a worksheet. A **line sparkline** is a miniature line chart that is ideal for showing a trend over a period of time. A **column sparkline** is a tiny column chart that includes a bar for each cell in a selected range. A **win/loss sparkline** shows only two types of bars: one for gains and one for losses. Table I-2 provides descriptions and example of sparkline types. You should place sparklines close to the cells containing the data they illustrate.  You decide to create sparklines next to your worksheet data to illustrate sales trends in the quarter for each of the regions.

STEPS

1. **Click the Sheet1 sheet tab, click the Insert tab, then click cell F5**

   This is where you need to insert a sparkline for the range B5:D5, the data series for the West region sales from January to March.

2. **Click the Line button in the Sparklines group**

   The Create Sparklines dialog box opens. You need to select the cells for which you want to create a sparkline: the range B5:D5.

3. ▶ **Select the range B5:D5, compare your screen to Figure I-20, then click OK**

   Cell F5 now contains a sparkline that starts in the bottom left of the cell and slants upward to the upper right corner, indicating an increase from cell B5 to C5 to D5. At a glance, the sparkline communicates that sales increased steadily from January to March. You can add markers on the line to indicate values for each cell in the selected range.

4. **Click the Markers check box in the Show group**

   The sparkline now displays three small square markers. The left marker represents the West region's January sales (B5), the middle marker represents the West region's February sales (C5), and the far-right marker represents the West region's March sales (E5). You want to change the sparkline to a different color.

5. ▶ **Click the More button ⊟ in the Style group, then click Style 12 (last style in second row)**

   The sparkline color is now red, and the sparkline markers are black.

6. ▶ **Drag the cell F5 fill handle to cell F9**

   Cells F6:F9 now contain red sparklines with black markers that show sales trends for the other regions, as well as the total sales, as shown in Figure I-21. Notice that the sparkline in cell F7 shows a downward trend from the second to third marker. All other sparklines show an upward direction. You can see how sparklines make it easy to see at a glance the sales performance of each region for the quarter.

7. **Enter your name in cell A2, then save your changes**

8. ▶ **Click the File tab, click Print, preview the worksheet, close the worksheet, exit Excel, then submit your completed worksheet to your instructor**

FIGURE I-20: Create Sparklines dialog box

In Step 3, select range B5:D5

Line button

Range you select appears here

FIGURE I-21: Completed worksheet with sparklines added

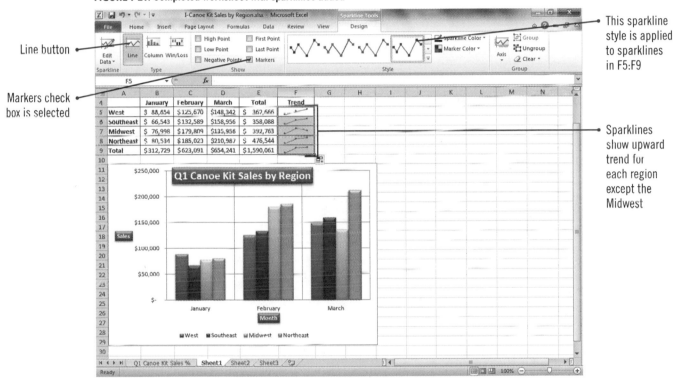

Line button

Markers check box is selected

This sparkline style is applied to sparklines in F5:F9

Sparklines show upward trend for each region except the Midwest

TABLE I-2: Sparkline types and their uses

sparkline type	used for	example
Line	Showing trends over time	
Column	Comparing values over time	
Win/Loss	Showing gains and/or losses over time	

Working with Charts

Practice

Concepts Review

Label each chart element shown in Figure I-22.

FIGURE I-22

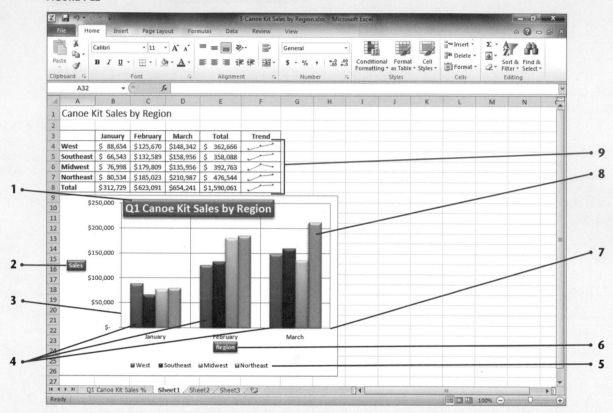

Match each chart type with its description.

10. **Line chart**	**a.** Shows trends by category over time
11. **Pie chart**	**b.** Compares values across categories over time
12. **Area chart**	**c.** Shows relative importance of values over a period of time
13. **Column chart**	**d.** Describes the relationship of parts to a whole

Select the best answer from the list of choices.

14. **Which of the following axis titles would most likely be shown on a vertical axis in a chart?**
    a. Years
    c. Months
    b. Costs
    d. Countries

15. **In a chart, a sequence of related numbers that shows a trend is called a(n) _____.**
    a. legend
    c. axis
    b. data marker
    d. data series

16. **You just finished a 10-week math class, in which you had a quiz every week. You want to create a chart that shows each quiz score for each week. Which of the following charts would NOT be a good choice for your chart?**
    a. Pie chart
    c. Column chart
    b. Bar chart
    d. Line chart

17. **Which of the following tabs on the Ribbon do you use to add a chart title?**
    a. Chart Tools Design tab
    c. Chart Tools Format tab
    b. Chart Tools Layout tab
    d. Insert tab

18. **Where should you place a sparkline in a worksheet?**
    a. In a chart below its underlying data
    b. In a separate chart sheet, away from its underlying data
    c. In a single cell adjacent to the cells containing its underlying data
    d. In a group of cells below its underlying data

Skills Review

1. **Understand and plan a chart.**
   a. Open the file I-2.xlsx from where you store your Data Files, then save it as **I-Recycling Revenue**.
   b. Examine the worksheet data, then consider what Excel chart types would best present this type of information.
   c. Is the worksheet designed in such a way that it will be easy to create a chart? Why or why not?

2. **Create a chart.**
   a. Select the range A4:D9.
   b. Display the tab on the Ribbon that contains commands for inserting charts.
   c. Insert a 3-D Clustered Column chart.
   d. Save your changes to the workbook.

3. **Move and resize a chart and chart objects.**
   a. Drag the chart so that the upper-left corner of the chart is aligned with the upper-left corner of cell A12.
   b. Use the lower-right corner sizing handle to align the lower-right corner of the chart with the lower-right corner of cell G28.
   c. Move the legend so that its top edge aligns with the top of the tallest data marker in the chart.
   d. Save your changes.

4. **Apply chart layouts and styles.**
   a. Open the Chart Tools Design tab, if necessary.
   b. Use a button on the Design tab to reverse the columns and rows and get a different view of the data. Examine the chart and identify what new meaning this new structure conveys.
   c. Apply the Layout 3 chart layout to the chart.
   d. Replace the placeholder chart title with **Recycling Revenue, 2011-2013**.
   e. Apply Style 26 chart style to the chart.
   f. Save your changes.

5. **Customize chart objects.**
   a. Display the Chart Tools Layout tab.
   b. Add a horizontal-axis title to the chart. Replace the placeholder axis title with **Years**.
   c. Add a vertical-axis title that is rotated. Replace the placeholder axis title with **Revenue**.

Skills Review (continued)

   d. Add major gridlines for the vertical axis.

   e. Save your changes.

6. **Enhance a chart.**

   a. Display the Chart Tools Format tab.

   b. Select one of the West data markers in the chart.

   c. Open the Format Data Series dialog box.

   d. In the Format Data Series dialog box, select the Fill category, specify a solid fill, choose Orange, Accent 6 from the Color palette, then close the dialog box.

   e. Use the Chart Elements list arrow to select the chart title, then apply the Moderate Effect – Orange, Accent 6 shape style.

   f. Apply the Offset Top Shadow shape effect to the title.

   g. Apply the Moderate Effect – Orange, Accent 6 shape style to the vertical-axis title and the horizontal-axis title.

   h. Save your changes.

7. **Create a pie chart.**

   a. Select cells A5:A9, then press and hold [Ctrl] while selecting cells E5:E9.

   b. Insert a pie chart, choosing the Exploded pie in 3-D option.

   c. Move the pie chart to a new sheet in the workbook. Name the sheet **Revenue by Region**.

   d. Apply the Layout 6 chart layout to the chart.

   e. Increase the font size of the percentage amounts on the pie slices to 24.

   f. Click the chart title placeholder, type **Recycling Revenue by Region, 2011-2013**, then press [Enter].

   g. Save your changes.

8. **Create sparklines.**

   a. Click the Sheet1 sheet tab to return to the worksheet.

   b. Add a line sparkline to cell F5 that is based on the data range B5:D5.

   c. Specify to add data markers to the sparkline.

   d. Apply Style 31 to the sparkline.

   e. Use the fill handle to copy the sparkline in cell F5 to the range F6:F10.

   f. Enter your name in cell A30. Save your changes.

   g. Preview the worksheet in Print Preview. Change the scaling settings to Fit Sheet on One Page, then save your changes. View the chart sheet in Print Preview. Close the workbook, exit Excel, then submit your completed workbook to your instructor. Compare your completed worksheet and chart sheet to Figures I-23 and I-24.

FIGURE I-23

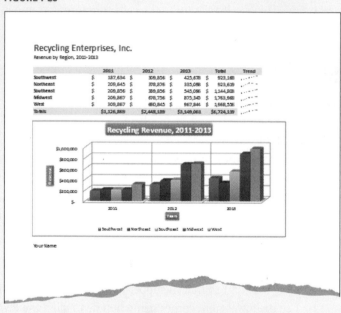

FIGURE I-24

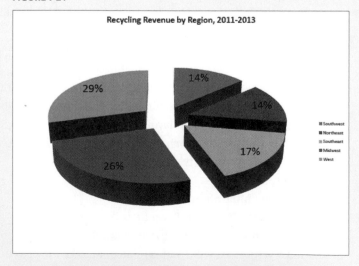

Independent Challenge 1

You work for a landscaping services company called Landscapes for Good Living, located in the midwest. The company offers landscaping services, including brick paving, landscape design, sodding and seeding, landscape lighting, and irrigation. Frank Langdon, the general manager, has created a worksheet that contains revenue data for the five categories of services that the company offers. He has asked you to create a chart using the worksheet data to show the results for each quarter.

a. Open the file I-3.xlsx from where you store your Data Files, then save it as **I-Landscape Revenue**.

b. Create a stacked area chart based on the data in the range A4:E9.

c. Move the chart so that it is positioned directly below the worksheet data, then enlarge it so that the bottom-right corner of the chart is aligned with cell G30.

d. Switch the rows and columns, so that May, June, July, and August are on the x-axis.

e. Apply the Layout 3 chart layout to the chart, then apply a chart style that you like.

f. Replace the placeholder chart title with **Revenue, May-August**.

g. Add a rotated vertical-axis title **Revenue**. Add a horizontal-axis title with the text **Months**. Apply a shape style that you like to the vertical and horizontal axis titles.

h. Apply a shape style that you like to the chart title.

i. Add line sparklines to the range G5:G10. Include markers in the sparklines. Apply a sparkline style of your choosing to the sparklines.

j. Create a 2-D Exploded pie chart by selecting the noncontiguous ranges A5:A9 and F5:F9. Move the pie chart to a separate chart sheet named **Revenue by Service Type**. Apply the Layout 2 chart layout to the pie chart. Change the chart title to **Revenue by Service Type**. Increase the font size of the percentage amount labels on each pie slice to 20.

k. Open Sheet1, then type your name in cell A32. Format the worksheet data and worksheet title using fonts, font sizes, borders, alignments, and shading to make the worksheet look professional and easy to understand. Choose formatting options that are complementary to the colors and style of the chart.

l. Preview the Sheet1 worksheet in Print Preview. Change the scaling settings to Fit Sheet on One Page, then save your changes. Figure I-25 shows one possible solution for the worksheet and chart.

Advanced Challenge Exercise

- Open the Revenue by Service Type chart sheet.
- Click one of the data labels on the pie chart (such as 10%) to select all the data labels.
- Click the Chart Tools Format tab, click the More button ▾ in the WordArt Styles group, then click the Fill - White, Drop Shadow style.
- Right-click the legend, then click the Increase Font Size button on the Mini toolbar four times to increase the legend font to 14.
- Click the Chart Tools Layout tab, click the Text Box button, click in the lower right corner of the chart sheet, then type your name.

m. View the chart sheet in Print Preview. Close the workbook, exit Excel, then submit your completed workbook to your instructor.

FIGURE I-25

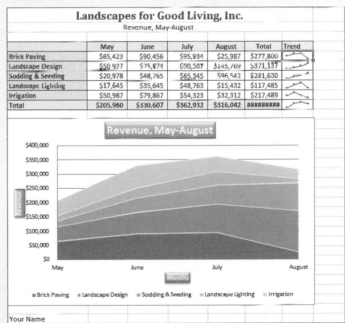

Independent Challenge 2

You work for Thelma Watson, the general manager of an online bakery retailer. Thelma has created an Excel worksheet showing product sales for June and the revenue generated by each product category. She has asked you to create a chart in the worksheet that shows the percentage of total sales each category represents.

a. Open the file I-4.xlsx from where your Data Files are located, then save it as **I-June Product Sales**.

b. Create a pie chart using the data in the range A4:B9. Choose the Pie in 3-D style.

c. Move the chart below the worksheet data.

d. Resize the chart so that its lower-right corner is aligned with the lower-right corner of cell G29.

e. Change the value in cell B9 (the number of pies sold) to **5,275**. Observe the change in the chart.

f. Apply the Layout 1 chart layout to the chart. Apply a chart style that you like.

g. Display the Chart Tools Layout tab, then use the Chart Elements list box to select the Chart Area. Click the Format Selection button in the Current Selection group to open the Format Chart Area dialog box. Select Fill, then specify to add a solid fill, choosing settings in the dialog box that you think will look good. Experiment by choosing different settings, then close the dialog box to view the settings. Repeat this process until you are satisfied with how the chart area looks.

h. Increase the size of the labels and percentage amounts in each pie slice to 12.

i. Format the worksheet data and worksheet title using fonts, font sizes, borders, alignments, and shading to make the worksheet look professional, visually pleasing, and easy to understand. Choose formatting options that are complementary to the colors and style of the chart. Make any other formatting enhancements to the chart and to the worksheet data to make it attractive and more professional looking. Enter your name in cell A31 in the worksheet.

j. Preview the worksheet and chart in Print Preview. Close the workbook, exit Excel, then submit your completed workbook to your instructor.

Independent Challenge 3

You work for Stephen Briggs, the manager of an art gallery. In September, the gallery opened an exhibit of paintings from a private collector that included never-before-seen masterpieces by several famous artists. Museum attendance increased dramatically in that month due to the high public interest in the exhibit and a strong marketing campaign. Stephen is preparing to meet with the museum's board of directors to discuss the increased attendance. He has asked you to create a chart that shows the number of people who visited the museum from May through September. He also needs the chart to show a breakdown of children, adults, and seniors who attended. The data you need to create the chart has already been put into a worksheet.

a. Open the file I-5.xlsx from where you store your Data Files, then save it as **I-Gallery Visitors**. Enter your name in cell A9.

b. Create a 2D line chart of all three customer categories during the months May through September. Choose the 2-D Line with Markers chart type. Choose a chart style that you like.

c. Move the chart to a new chart sheet in the workbook. Name the chart sheet **Gallery Visitors May-Sept**.

d. Apply the Layout 9 chart layout to the chart. Change the chart title to **Gallery Visitors, May–Sept**.

e. Add minor vertical gridlines to the chart. Add an appropriate vertical-axis title that is rotated, then add an appropriate horizontal-axis title.

f. Apply a solid color fill to the plot area, choosing a color you think looks good. (*Hint*: To select the plot area, open the Layout or Format tab, click the Chart Elements list arrow in the Current Selection group, and click Plot Area. Then open the Format Plot Area dialog box and specify a fill color.)

Independent Challenge 3 (continued)

g. Apply a shape style of your choosing to the chart title and axis titles. Figure I-26 shows one possible example of the completed chart.

FIGURE I-26

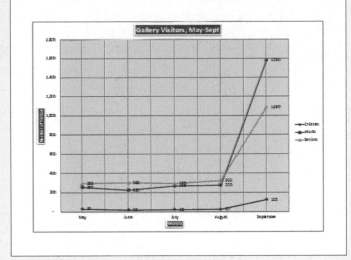

Advanced Challenge Exercise

- Switch to the Sheet1 worksheet that contains the chart data. Enter **Trend** in cell H3. Notice that the label you entered is formatted like the label in cell G3.
- Click cell H4, click the Insert tab, click the Column button in the Sparklines group, select the range B4:F4, then click OK. Notice the column sparkline that appears in H4.
- Use the fill handle in cell H4 to copy the column sparkline in H4 to the range H5:h7.

h. Save your changes, preview the worksheet and chart sheet, close the workbook, then exit Excel. Submit your completed workbook to your instructor.

Real Life Independent Challenge

Creating a personal budget is a great way to keep your finances in order. In this Real Life Independent Challenge, you will create a personal budget for monthly expenses. For the purposes of this exercise, imagine that you earn $2,500 per month. Your budget needs to include categories of expenses and the amounts for each expense. The total expenses in the worksheet must add up to $2,500. Once you enter all your monthly expenses in the worksheet, you will then create a pie chart that shows the percentage of each individual expense.

a. Start a blank Excel workbook, and save it as **I-My Budget** where you store your Data Files.
b. Enter **My Budget** in cell A1. Format the title so that it stands out. Enter your name in cell A2.
c. Enter the label **Expense** in cell A3, and enter the label **Amount** in cell B3.
d. Enter the following labels for the expenses in cells A4:A12: **Housing**, **Utilities**, **Car Payment**, **Insurance**, **Student Loans**, **Food**, **Entertainment**, **Gas**, **Savings**.
e. Enter appropriate amounts for each expense in cells B4:B12.
f. When you have entered all your expenses in the worksheet, enter the label **Total** in cell A13. Enter a formula in cell B13 that totals all the expense amounts in cells B4:B12. If the returning value in the formula cell does not add up to $2,500, then adjust the numbers in your budget so that the total adds up to $2,500.
g. Insert a pie chart based on the data in your chart. (*Hint*: Remember not to include the Total row when you select the data; select only the heading row, the labels, and expense amounts.) Choose any pie chart option that you like. Move the chart so that it is located below the worksheet data.
h. Apply a chart layout and chart style that you like. If the chart layout that you choose does not include a chart title, add one to the chart using the appropriate options on the Chart Layout tab. Replace the chart title placeholder with the title **My Monthly Expenses**.
i. Save your changes, preview the worksheet with the chart, close the file, then exit Excel. Submit your completed workbook to your instructor.

Visual Workshop

Open the Data File I-6.xlsx, then save it as **I-Charity Challenge Results** where you store your Data Files. Make formatting changes to the worksheet so that it looks like Figure I-27, then add the two charts so that they match the figure, using the commands and techniques you learned in this unit and previous units. You will need to make formatting changes to both charts so that they match the figure. Enter your name in cell A3 as shown. (*Hint*: You will need to merge and center the ranges A1:G1, A2:G2, and A3:G3 so that the company name, worksheet title, and your name match the figure.) Save your changes, preview the worksheet and charts, close the file, then exit Excel. Submit your completed workbook to your instructor.

FIGURE I-27

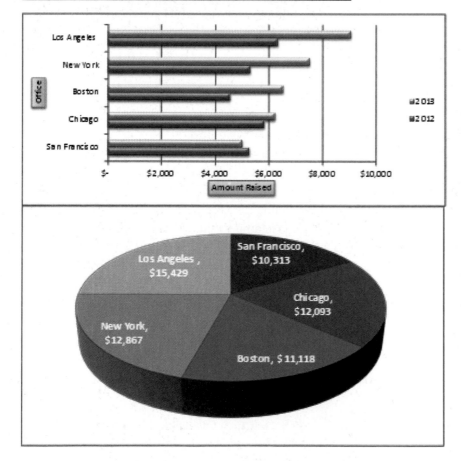

Creating a Database

Files You Will Need:

No files needed.

You can use Access to create a database to help you manage and track a large collection of related data. A **database** is an organized collection of related information. A database can contain information of any kind, such as sales and financial records for a business, products in a warehouse, or employee information.  In this unit, you learn about and use Microsoft Access, the database program in Microsoft Office. Karen Rivera, marketing director for Outdoor Designs, has asked you to create a database that helps Outdoor Designs keep track of sales reps and sales managers.

OBJECTIVES
Understand databases
Create a database
Create a table in Datasheet view
Create a table in Design view
Modify a table and set properties
Enter data in a table
Edit data in Datasheet view
Create and use a form

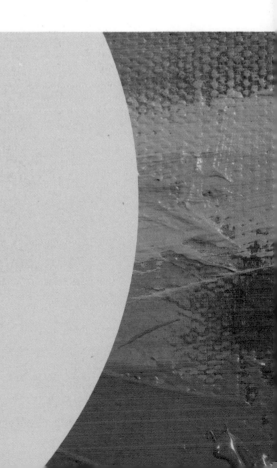

Understanding Databases

Access is a **database management system (DBMS)**, a powerful tool for storing, organizing, and retrieving information. Before you start using Access, you need to know some basic concepts about databases and database management systems.

Databases can help you:

- **Store information**

    A database stores data in one or more spreadsheet-like lists called **tables**. For instance, one table in a database might store all data about a company's products, another table might store data about the company's customers, and another might store data about the company's orders. A database containing just one table is called a **simple database**, while one that contains two or more tables of related information is called a **relational database**. Figure J-1 shows the Sales Reps table you will create in this unit, which will be used to keep track of sales rep information. Each row in the table is called a **record**. Records consist of **fields**, which contain information about one aspect of a record, such as the rep's last name or the sales goal. The column headings in the table are called **field names**. Because entering data in the rows and columns format of a table is tedious, you can create a form to make data entry easier. A **form** is a user-friendly window that contains text boxes and labels that let users easily input data, usually one record at a time. Each text box in a form corresponds with a field from a table. Figure J-2 shows the form you will create in this unit that is based on the Sales Reps table.

- **Retrieve information**

    Once you add data to a database, you can use Access queries or reports to retrieve or display all or part of the information in meaningful ways. A **query** extracts data from one or more database tables according to criteria that you set. For instance, at Outdoor Designs, you could create a query that displays all the customers in California. You can also create reports that print selected information from the database. A **report** is a summary of information pulled from the database, specifically designed for printing. Tables, forms, queries, and reports are program components called **objects**. Table J-1 provides a summary of common database objects.

- **Connect information**

    As a relational database management system, Access is particularly powerful because you can enter data once and then retrieve information from all or several tables as you need it. For example, Figure J-3 shows a report that contains fields from two related tables, Sales Reps and Sales Managers. Each table has mostly unique information, but they share Manager ID as a common field. Because the Manager ID field is shared by both tables, the tables can be linked, allowing you to pull information from both at once. Also, if you make changes to the data in a particular field in a table, any other object (such as a report or a query) that contains that field will automatically update to reflect the new value. For instance, in the example shown in Figure J-3, let's imagine that sales rep Linda Davis changed her name to Linda Brown. If you delete Davis from the Last Name field in the Sales Reps table and replace it with Brown, the report at the top of the figure would automatically update to show the last rep's name as Linda Brown. Likewise, if you replaced Davis with Brown in the Last Name field in the report, the field value in the table would automatically change from Davis to Brown.

TABLE J-1: Common database objects in Access

objects	description
Table	A list of data organized in rows (records) and columns (fields)
Query	A set of criteria you specify to retrieve data from a database
Form	A window that lets you view, enter, and edit data in a database one record at a time
Report	A summary of database information designed specifically for distributing or printing

Creating a Database

FIGURE J-1: Sales Reps table

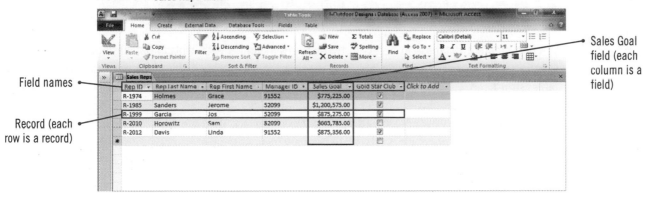

Field names

Record (each row is a record)

Sales Goal field (each column is a field)

FIGURE J-2: Sales Reps form

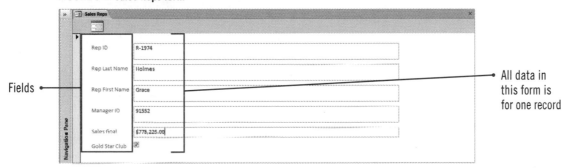

Fields

All data in this form is for one record

FIGURE J-3: Report in a relational database containing fields from two related tables

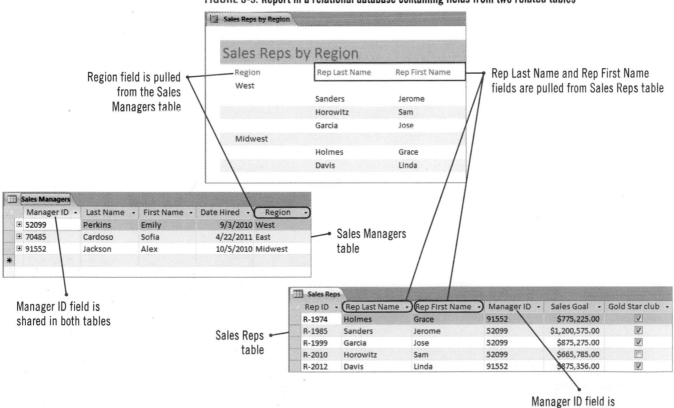

Region field is pulled from the Sales Managers table

Rep Last Name and Rep First Name fields are pulled from Sales Reps table

Sales Managers table

Manager ID field is shared in both tables

Sales Reps table

Manager ID field is shared in both tables

Creating a Database

Creating a Database

You can create a database in Access in two ways: by starting with a blank database or from a template. Creating a database from a template can save time, as it contains ready-made database objects, such as tables structured with field names appropriate to a particular type of database. By using a template, you can focus on entering data instead of designing appropriate database objects. When you first start Access, the File tab in Backstage view opens, with the New tab displayed. The New tab provides options for creating a new blank database or creating a database from a variety of templates. ▰▰▰▰ To begin your work on the Outdoor Designs database, you need to start Access, specify a name and location for the database file, and then create the database.

STEPS

1. **Click the Start button 🟦 on the taskbar, click All Programs, click Microsoft Office, then click Microsoft Access 2010**

   Access starts. Notice that both the File tab and the New tab on the navigation bar are active. The New tab lets you create a new database using a blank database or a template. The Blank database icon is selected. In the right pane, the File Name text box displays the temporary filename Database1.accdb. You need to change this temporary name to a name that is appropriate for the Outdoor Designs database.

2. **Click in the File Name text box, then type J-Outdoor Designs**

   You specified a name for the database, now you need to specify a folder location for where the database will be stored.

3. **Click the Browse for a location button 🗁 to the right of the File Name text box**

   The File New Database dialog box opens. Like the Save As dialog box in Excel and Word, you use this dialog box to specify the folder and drive where you want to save the database file.

4. **Navigate to where you store your Data Files, then click OK**

   The dialog box closes. Notice that the path to the database under the File Name text box now shows the drive and folder location you specified, as shown in Figure J-4.

5. **Click Create**

   The Access program window opens in Datasheet view with the Table Tools Fields tab in front, as shown in Figure J-5. Below the Ribbon are two panes. In the right pane, a blank table datasheet with the temporary name Table1 is open. The left pane is called the **Navigation Pane**; this is where all database objects for the open database are listed. Table1 is the only object listed.

Understanding Access File formats

By default, Access 2010 saves new databases with the file extension .accdb, which is the file format established for Access 2007. This explains why the Access program window title bar displays (Access 2007) in the title bar after you open a database. The Access 2007 file format allows for features that are not supported by previous versions of Access, such as Access 2003. If you need to share your database with users of Access 2003 or earlier, you can create a copy of it in the .mdb format, the file format used in Access 2003. To do this, click the File tab, click Save & Publish, click Access 2002-2003 under Save Database As, click Save As, specify the folder where you want to save the copy of the database, then click Save. A copy of the database in .mdb format opens.

FIGURE J-4: New page of File tab in Access with name and file location specified

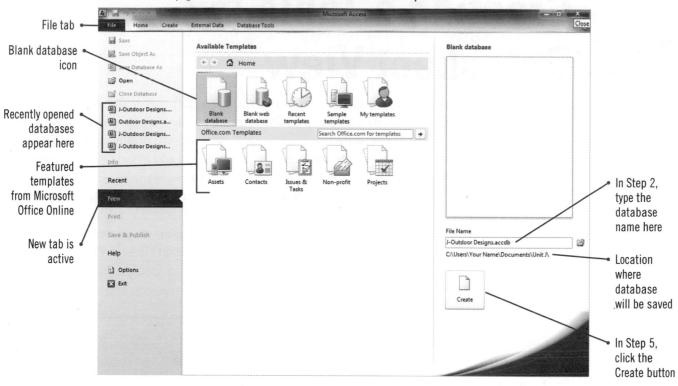

File tab

Blank database icon

Recently opened databases appear here

Featured templates from Microsoft Office Online

New tab is active

Available Templates

Blank database

Blank web database

Recent templates

Sample templates

My templates

Office.com Templates

Search Office.com for templates

Assets

Contacts

Issues & Tasks

Non-profit

Projects

Blank database

File Name
J-Outdoor Designs.accdb

C:\Users\Your Name\Documents\Unit J\

Create

In Step 2, type the database name here

Location where database will be saved

In Step 5, click the Create button

Access 2010

FIGURE J-5: Blank table datasheet

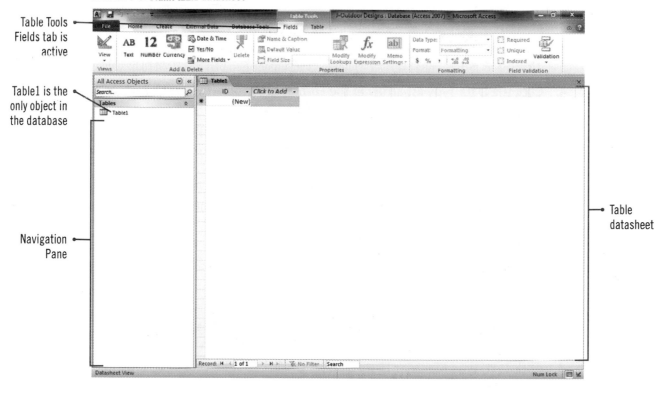

Table Tools Fields tab is active

Table1 is the only object in the database

Navigation Pane

Table datasheet

Creating a Table in Datasheet View

When you start working in a new database, a blank table opens in Datasheet view. In **Datasheet view**, you can add fields to a table and view any data that the table contains. Before you begin adding fields to the table, it is a good idea to save the table with an appropriate name. Although you already saved the database, you also need to save each object you create within it, including tables. To add a field to a table, you need to specify its data type (such as Text or Currency) and then specify a name. See Table J-2 for a description of field data types you can use. Every table in a database must contain one field that is designated as the **primary key field**, which uniquely identifies each record among all other records in a database. By default, every blank new table in Access includes a blank ID field, which is automatically designated the primary key field. ▓▓▓ You need to save the blank table with the name Sales Managers. Then, before you add new fields, you need to change the ID field data type to Text. Finally, you need to specify names and data types for new fields in the table.

STEPS

1. **Click the Save button 🖫 on the Quick Access toolbar**
   The Save As dialog box opens. You need to specify a name for the new table.

QUICK TIP

Objects are saved within and are only available from the database file, not as separate files.

2. **Type Sales Managers in the Table Name text box, then click OK**
   The Sales Managers table is saved to the Outdoor Designs database. The name Sales Managers now appears under the Tables heading in the Navigation Pane and in the tab above the datasheet. Notice the ID field. In this table, the ID field name can be used to store each manager's ID number.

QUICK TIP

The AutoNumber data type guarantees that each record is uniquely identified, even if some fields contain identical information (for instance, two customers with the same last name). AutoNumber fields cannot be modified.

3. **Click ID in the table**
   The ID field is selected. Notice that the Data Type text box in the Formatting group indicates that the field has the AutoNumber data type applied to it. The **AutoNumber** data type assigns a unique number for each record in the table, starting with 1 and increasing sequentially by 1 for each record. You need to change the data type to Text, because Manager ID numbers are unique numbers that need to be entered individually.

4. **Click the Data Type list arrow in the Formatting group, then click Text, as shown in Figure J-6**
   The ID field now has the Text data type applied to it. The Text data type is appropriate here because it lets you enter text (such as names), numbers that do not require calculations (such as phone numbers), or combinations of text and numbers (such as street addresses).

5. **Click Click to Add in the second field in the table**
   A menu of available field types opens, as shown in Figure J-7. You want to apply the Text data type to this field because it will be used for manager last names.

6. **Click Text**
   The Text data type is now applied to the second field, and the temporary field name Field1 is selected. You can now type the name for this field.

QUICK TIP

To rename a field, double-click the field name, then type the new name.

7. **Type Manager Last Name, then press [Tab]**
   The second field in the table now displays the name Manager Last Name. The Data Type list is now open for the third field in the table, which you need to use for manager first names.

QUICK TIP

To access a variety of named fields with data types applied, click More Fields in the Add & Delete group, then click a field.

8. **Click Text, type Manager First Name, click Click to Add, click Text, type Region, then save your changes**
   You entered the Manager First Name field name and the Region field name and applied the Text data type for each. The table now contains four text fields, as shown in Figure J-8.

FIGURE J-6: Applying the Text data type to the ID field

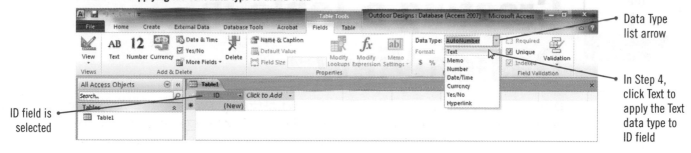

- Data Type list arrow
- In Step 4, click Text to apply the Text data type to ID field
- ID field is selected

FIGURE J-7: Specifying a data type for a new field

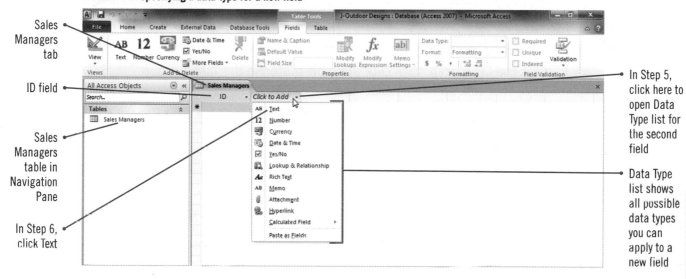

- Sales Managers tab
- ID field
- Sales Managers table in Navigation Pane
- In Step 6, click Text
- In Step 5, click here to open Data Type list for the second field
- Data Type list shows all possible data types you can apply to a new field

FIGURE J-8: Sales Managers table with four fields

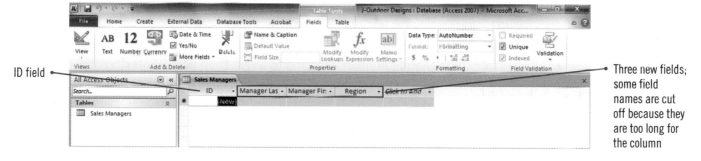

- ID field
- Three new fields; some field names are cut off because they are too long for the column

TABLE J-2: Common field data types

data type	description
Text	A word or string of words, numbers that do not require calculations, or a combination of text and numbers
AutoNumber	Unique sequential numbers that Access assigns to each new record, which cannot be edited
Date/Time	Date and time values
Number	Numeric data to be used in calculations
Currency	Currency values and numeric data used in calculations
Yes/No	Values that can be only Yes or No; used to identify the presence or absence of specific criteria
Memo	Lengthy text (which can also contain numbers that do not require calculations)
Calculated	Displays a value that is the result of a formula that includes field values

Creating a Database

Creating a Table in Design View

Databases usually contain many tables. To add a new table to a database, click the Table button in the Tables group on the Create tab. Although you can add fields to a new or an existing table using Datasheet view, it is often easier to use Design view. In Design view, you use a grid to enter fields and specify field data types. You can also add field descriptions to fields in Design view. A **field description** identifies the purpose of a field and helps users of the database understand the information that the field is meant to contain. You can also use Design view to view and change the primary key field in a table. ▟▟▟ You need to create a new table that contains information about the Sales Reps. You decide to create this table using Design view.

STEPS

1. **Click the Create tab, then click the Table button in the Tables group**

   A new blank table with the temporary name Table1 opens in Datasheet view.

2. **Click the Save button 🖫 on the Quick Access toolbar, type Sales Reps in the Save As dialog box, then click OK**

   The Sales Reps table is saved to the Outdoor Designs database. The name Sales Reps now appears under the Tables heading in the Navigation Pane and in the tab above the datasheet, next to the Sales Managers tab.

> **QUICK TIP**
> You can also change to a different view by clicking the view buttons on the right end of the status bar.

3. **Click the View list arrow in the Views group, then click Design view**

   The main window now displays a grid with the headings Field Name, Data Type, and Description. The ID field is listed as the first field; the key icon to the left of ID indicates that this is the primary key field. You want to change the name of the ID field to Rep ID.

4. **Type Rep ID, then press [Tab]**

   The ID field name is changed to Rep ID. This field currently has the AutoNumber data type applied to it. You want to change the data type to Text because each rep is assigned a unique Rep ID.

5. **Click the AutoNumber arrow in the Data Type column as shown in Figure J-9, then click Text**

   The Rep ID field now has the Text data type. You need to enter a description for this field, which will appear in the status bar and help users understand what type of data should be entered for this field.

6. **Press [Tab], type Unique number assigned to a rep, then press [Enter]**

   Pressing [Tab] or [Enter] moves the pointer to the next cell in the grid. The blank field below Rep ID is now active and ready for you to type a new field name in it.

7. **Type Rep Last Name, press [Enter] three times, type Rep First Name, press [Enter] three times, type Manager ID, then press [Enter] three times**

   You entered three new fields and specified the data types for each as Text. If you specify no particular data type, the Text data field is automatically applied.

> **QUICK TIP**
> To show the description message in the status bar wherever the Gold Star Club field is used, click the Property Update Options button 🖅 below the Description you typed, then click Update Status Bar Text everywhere the Gold Star Club is used.

8. **Type Sales Goal, press [Enter], click the Data Type list arrow, click Currency, then press [Enter] twice**

   You applied the Currency data type to the Sales Goal field. The Currency data type is appropriate because this field will contain the dollar amount of a rep's sales goal for the year. Any numbers entered in this field will automatically be formatted as currency.

9. **Type Gold Star Club, press [Enter], type Y, press [Enter], type Yes if rep met sales goal in prior year, press [Enter], then save your changes**

   Typing the letter Y in the Data Type column applied the Yes/No data type for the Gold Star Club field. In Datasheet view, any field with a Yes/No data type will contain a check box; a check mark in a field check box indicates a Yes value for the field. The description you typed in the Description column will let users know to mark this field as Yes if the rep achieved his or her sales goal in the prior year. Compare your screen to Figure J-10.

Creating a Database

FIGURE J-9: Specifying a data type for the Rep ID field in Design view

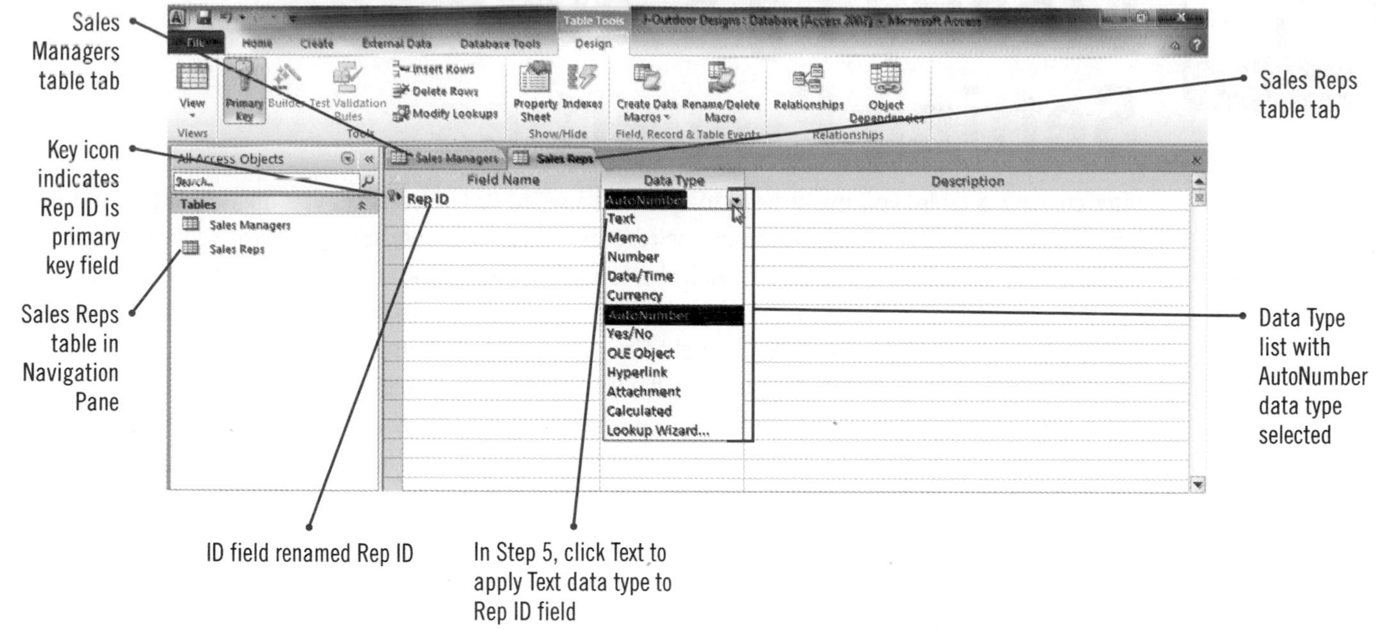

Sales Managers table tab
Key icon indicates Rep ID is primary key field
Sales Reps table in Navigation Pane
Sales Reps table tab
Data Type list with AutoNumber data type selected
ID field renamed Rep ID
In Step 5, click Text to apply Text data type to Rep ID field
Field Name
Data Type
Description
Rep ID
AutoNumber
Text
Memo
Number
Date/Time
Currency
AutoNumber
Yes/No
OLE Object
Hyperlink
Attachment
Calculated
Lookup Wizard...
All Access Objects
Tables
Sales Managers
Sales Reps

FIGURE J-10: Sales Reps table with six fields in Design view

View list arrow
Table now includes six fields
Descriptions help users understand what data to enter in the field
Data types for each field
Property Update Options button
Field Name
Data Type
Description
Rep ID
Text
Unique number asssigned to a rep
Rep Last Name
Text
Rep First Name
Text
Manager ID
Text
Sales Goal
Currency
Gold Star Club
Yes/No
Yes if rep met sales goal in prior year
All Access Objects
Tables
Sales Managers
Sales Reps

Access 2010

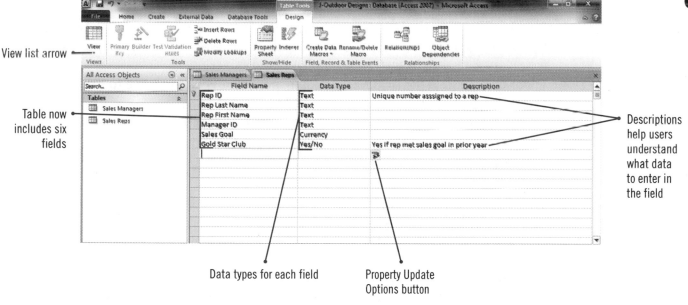

Modifying a Table and Setting Properties

After creating a table, you might need to make changes to it. For instance, you might want to add field descriptions, or insert, delete, rearrange, or rename fields. Although you can make some table design changes in Datasheet view, Design view is the best view for modifying a table's structure. In Design view, you can set field properties. **Field properties** are data characteristics that dictate how Access stores, handles, and displays field data. For instance, the Field Size property for the Text data type specifies the number of characters that a user can enter for that field. If a field name is long, is technical, or uses abbreviations, you might want to change its Caption property. The **Caption property** is a label that appears in a form or in Datasheet view in place of the field name to clarify the field's contents for data entry or interpretation. You use the Field Properties pane to view and change properties for a selected field. ▓▓▓▓ You need to make changes to the Sales Managers table. You need to change the name of the ID field, limit its field size to 5, and add a field description for it. You also need to add captions to two fields and insert a new Date Hired field.

STEPS

1. **Click the Sales Managers table tab, click the View list arrow in the Views group, then click Design view**

   The Sales Managers table opens in Design view. The Field Name column shows the four fields this table contains. The middle Data Type column shows that each field has the Text data type applied. You want to change the name of the ID field to Manager ID. The ID field is selected, so you are ready to type the new name.

QUICK TIP

To rename a field in Datasheet view, double-click the field name to select it, then type the new name.

2. **Type Manager ID**

   The field name is changed to Manager ID. The Field Properties pane at the bottom of the screen displays the field properties for the Manager ID field. The settings reflect the default settings for the Text data type. By default, text fields have a limit of 255 characters.

QUICK TIP

The Field Properties pane changes depending on which field is currently selected. Different data types have different field property options.

3. **Double-click 255 in the Field Size text box in the Field Properties pane, then type 5**

   Users will not be able to enter more than five characters for this field, as shown in Figure J-11. This will help prevent data entry errors because the manager ID is a five-digit number.

4. **Click Manager ID in the Field Name column, press [Tab] twice to move to the Description text box, type Unique ID number assigned to manager**

   This description will appear in the status bar in Datasheet view or Form view when this field is active.

5. **Click Region in the fourth row of the Field Name column, then click the Insert Rows button in the Tools group**

   A new, blank row is inserted between Manager First Name and Region.

6. **Type Date Hired, press [Enter], click the Data Type arrow, then click Date/Time**

   You added a new Date Hired field and specified its data type as Date/Time.

7. **Click Manager Last Name, click in the Caption text box in the Field Properties pane, type Last Name, then press [Enter]**

   The caption for the Manager Last Name field is now Last Name. This means that only Last Name will be displayed as the field name for this field in Datasheet view and in any form that includes this field.

8. **Click Manager First Name, click in the Caption text box in the Field Properties pane, type First Name, then press [Enter]**

   You specified the caption for the Manager First Name field as First Name, as shown in Figure J-12.

QUICK TIP

You must save changes to an object before switching views.

9. **Save your changes, then click the View button in the Views group**

   The view changes to Datasheet view, as shown in Figure J-13. Notice that the Manager Last Name and Manager First Name fields now appear as Last Name and First Name, reflecting the changes you made to the Caption property for these fields.

FIGURE J-11: Changing the Field Size property for the Manager ID field in Design view

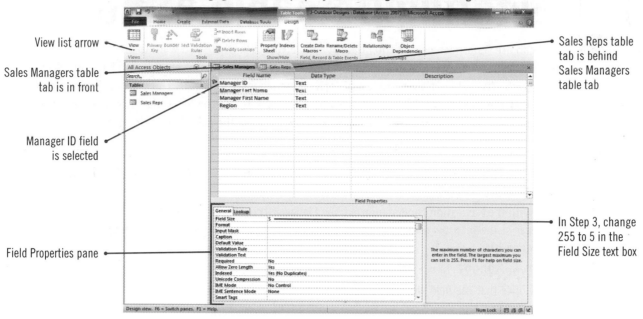

View list arrow

Sales Managers table tab is in front

Manager ID field is selected

Field Properties pane

Sales Reps table tab is behind Sales Managers table tab

In Step 3, change 255 to 5 in the Field Size text box

FIGURE J-12: Sales Managers table in Design view after adding a field and changing properties

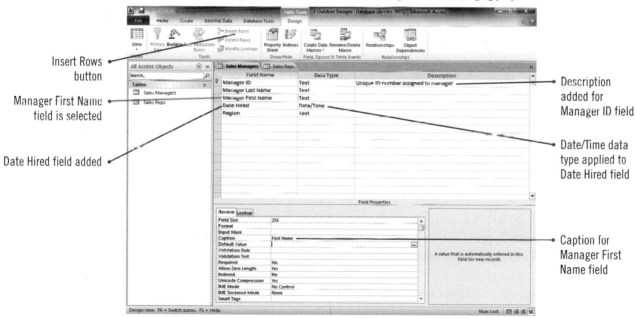

Insert Rows button

Manager First Name field is selected

Date Hired field added

Description added for Manager ID field

Date/Time data type applied to Date Hired field

Caption for Manager First Name field

FIGURE J-13: Sales Managers table in Datasheet view after changes

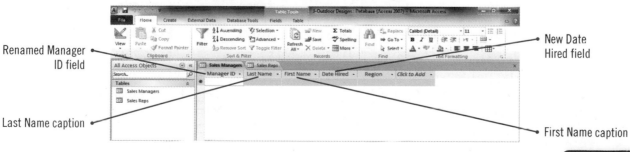

Renamed Manager ID field

Last Name caption

New Date Hired field

First Name caption

Creating a Database

Entering Data in a Table

You can use Datasheet view to enter data in a table; just click where you want to enter a value and start typing. Each row of the table is one record. A **row selector** to the left of each record lets you select a record or records. The field names at the top of each column identify the fields. The data you enter in each field is called a **field value**. ▰▰▰ You are ready to enter records into the Sales Managers and Sales Reps tables. You decide to enter all three Sales Manager records, but only the Sales Reps records for the West region.

STEPS

QUICK TIP
You can also press [F11] to open or close the Navigation Pane.

1. **Click the Shutter Bar Close button ⟪ on the Navigation Pane, then click in the Manager ID field**

   With the Navigation Pane minimized, the Manager ID field name is highlighted, indicating it is selected. A star in the first row selector indicates it is a new record. The Manager ID field description appears in the status bar.

QUICK TIP
A pencil icon appears in the row selector for the first record, indicating that this record is being edited.

2. **Type 520997**

   Notice that the field will not accept the sixth digit (7) because you set the Field Size property to five. The manager ID for this record is actually 52099, so you can move on to the next field.

3. **Press [Enter]**

   Pressing [Enter] or [Tab] accepts your entry and moves the insertion point to the next field.

QUICK TIP
You can also enter a date by clicking the calendar icon that appears when you click in a field formatted as a date, then using the calendar window to complete the entry.

4. **Type Perkins, press [Enter], type Emily, press [Enter], type 9/3/10, press [Enter], type West, then press [Enter]**

   Access changed the date to the date format 9/3/2010. The Manager ID in the second record is now active.

5. **Use the table below to add two more records to the Sales Managers table, press [Enter], then compare your screen to Figure J-14**

Manager ID	Last Name	First Name	Date Hired	Region
91552	Jackson	Alex	10/5/2010	Midwest
70485	Cardoso	Sofia	4/22/2011	East

6. **Click the Sales Reps table tab, then click the Datasheet View button ▥ on the status bar**

   In Datasheet view, the six fields you added in Design view appear as column headings, and the Rep ID field is active. You need to enter the records for the reps who report to Emily Perkins. Emily's Manager ID is 52099.

QUICK TIP
To indicate No in a Yes/No field, no action is required; just press [Enter] or [Tab] to skip to the next field. If you inadvertently add a check mark, click it again to remove the check mark.

7. **Type R-1985, press [Enter], type Sanders, press [Enter], type Jerome, press [Enter], type 52099, press [Enter], type 1200575, press [Enter], click the check box in the Gold Star Club field, then press [Enter]**

   The value you entered for the Sales Goal field (1200575) is formatted as currency. The check box in the Gold Star Club field indicates a Yes value.

QUICK TIP
To delete a record, click the row selector for the record, then press [Delete].

8. **Use the table below to add three more records to the Sales Reps table, save your changes, then compare your screen to Figure J-15**

Rep ID	Rep Last Name	Rep First Name	Manager ID	Sales Goal	Gold Star Club
R-1999	Garcia	Jose	52099	$875,275	Yes
R-1974	Holmes	Grace	52099	$775,865	Yes
R-1981	Chung	David	52099	$665,785	No

Creating a Database

FIGURE J-14: Field values entered in Sales Managers table in Datasheet view

Sales
Managers
table tab

Shutter Bar
Open/Close
button

Row
selectors
for first
three
records

Star icon
indicates
next new
blank
record

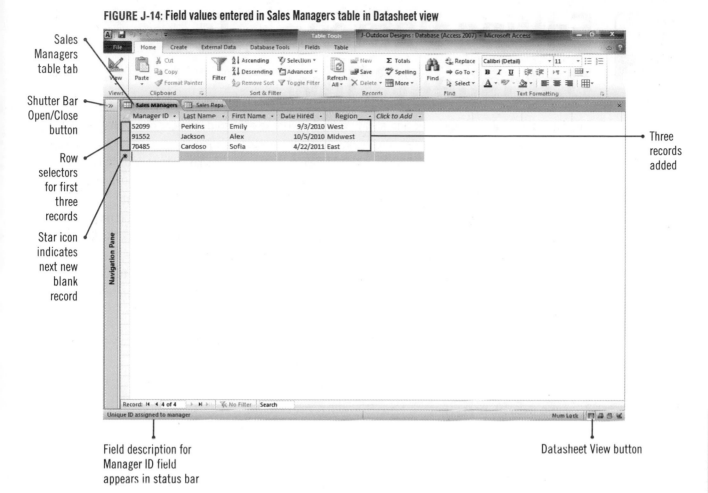

Three
records
added

Field description for
Manager ID field
appears in status bar

Datasheet View button

FIGURE J-15: Field values entered in Sales Reps table in Datasheet view

Sales Reps
table tab

Four
records
added

Creating a Database

Editing Data in Datasheet View

The data in a database is dynamic and always changing. Unlike a Word document or an Excel workbook, a database is never "finished"; the data it contains constantly needs updating to reflect changes. To keep the data in a database current, you need to add and delete records and make edits to individual fields on a regular basis. You can edit the data in a table in Datasheet view using the editing skills you learned for Word and Excel. To edit a field value, you need to select either the entire field value or the part of it you want to edit, then type the replacement data. As you make edits in a datasheet, you might find it helpful to resize columns to make the data easier to see. To resize a column to fit its contents, double-click the line between the column headings. To resize a column to a specific width, drag the line between the column headings to the desired width.  You just learned that sales rep Grace Holmes moved to Ohio and now reports to the Midwest sales manager, and that a new rep has taken over David Chung's territory. You need to edit these records in the Sales Reps table.

STEPS

1. **In the Sales Reps table, click R-1981 in the fourth row, then press [F2]**

   Pressing [F2] selects the entire field value R-1981, the Rep ID for David Chung.

   > **QUICK TIP**
   > If you start editing a field and realize you want to keep the original entry, press [Esc] to undo the edit.

2. **Type R-2010, press [Enter], type Horowitz, press [Enter], type Sam, then press [Enter]**

   The text you typed replaced the original field values for the Rep ID, Rep Last Name, and Rep First Name fields for the fourth record. No other changes are needed for this record.

3. **In the Sales Goal field for the Grace Holmes record, click to the right of $775,865.00, press [Backspace] six times, type 225, then press [Enter]**

   The field value in the Sales Goal field for the third record now reads $775,225.00, the new sales goal for Grace Holmes. Using the [Backspace] key is another useful method for editing field values in a datasheet. You can also edit text by selecting it and then typing new text.

   > **QUICK TIP**
   > To move to the previous field in a datasheet, press [Shift][Tab].

4. **In the Manager ID field for Grace Holmes, double-click 52099, type 91552, then press [Enter]**

   The Manager ID field value for the third record now reads 91552, which is the Manager ID for the Midwest sales manager (Alex Jackson).

   > **QUICK TIP**
   > You can also resize columns by dragging the column separator to the width you want.

5. **Point to the border between the Rep Last Name field and the Rep First Name field names until the pointer changes to ↔, as shown in Figure J-16, then double-click**

   The Rep Last Name column widened just enough to fit the entire field name. The border between the field names that you clicked is called the **column separator**. Double-clicking the column separator automatically resizes a column to make it larger or smaller to fit the widest field name or field contents.

6. **Double-click the column separator ↔ between each of the field names in the field name row**

   Each column is now resized, as shown in figure J-17.

   > **QUICK TIP**
   > You can also save or close a table by right-clicking its tab, then clicking Save or Close.

7. **Save your changes to the Sales Reps table, then click the Close 'Sales Reps' button ✕**

   The Sales Reps table closes.

8. **Save your changes to the Sales Managers table, then click ✕**

   The Sales Manager table closes.

Creating a Database

FIGURE J-16: Resizing a column in Datasheet view

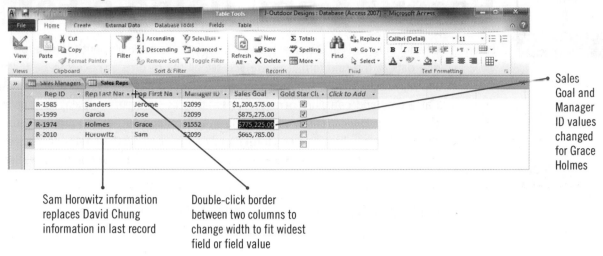

Sam Horowitz information replaces David Chung information in last record

Double-click border between two columns to change width to fit widest field or field value

Sales Goal and Manager ID values changed for Grace Holmes

FIGURE J-17: Edited records in Sales Reps Table in Datasheet view

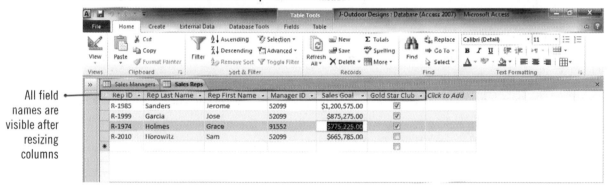

All field names are visible after resizing columns

Printing objects in Access

If you want to print information from a database, you would usually create a report that includes selected fields, then print it. However, there might be times when you want to print a datasheet or form. To print any object in Access, select the object in the Navigation Pane, click the File tab, then click Print. The Print page opens in Backstage view and displays three print options. Click Quick Print to print the object using default print settings. Click Print to open the Print dialog box, which lets you adjust print settings. Click Print Preview to preview the object with its default settings. In Print Preview, you can use the tools on the Print Preview tab to adjust settings, then click the Print button when you are ready to print.

Creating and Using a Form

Entering and editing records in Datasheet view is easy, but it is more efficient to use a form. In Datasheet view, entering data in the grid format where you see all the records at once can be tedious and cause eyestrain, and may risk introducing errors by entering data into the wrong record. A form usually displays one record at a time and contains **form controls**—devices for inputting data, such as text boxes, list arrows, or check boxes. You can create a form using a variety of approaches; the simplest is to click the Form button on the Create tab, which creates a form based on the open database table or the currently selected object in the Navigation Pane. Karen asks you to create a form based on the Sales Reps table.

STEPS

1. **Click the Shutter Bar Open button ⏩ in the Navigation Pane, then click the Create tab**
   The Navigation Pane is now open and lists the Sales Managers table and the Sales Reps table. The Create tab allows you to add new objects to your database.

   > **QUICK TIP**
   > To apply a theme to a form, click the Theme button in the Themes group on the Form Layout Tools Design tab, then click the theme you want.

2. **Click the Sales Reps table in the Navigation Pane, then click the Form button in the Forms group**
   A new form based on the Sales Reps table opens in Layout view, as shown in Figure J-18. You use Layout view to change the structure of the form. The data for the first record (Grace Holmes) is shown in the form. In Layout view, you can view records but cannot add, delete, or edit records. To view different records, you use the buttons on the **navigation bar**.

3. **Click the Next record button ▶ twice on the navigation bar**
   The record for Jose Garcia (record 3 of 4) is now open.

4. **Click the Previous record button ◀ on the navigation bar**
   The record for Jerome Sanders (record 2 of 4) is now open.

   > **QUICK TIP**
   > You can also create a new record by pressing [Tab] or [Enter] after the last field in a record.

5. **Click the New (blank) record button ▶✳ on the navigation bar**
   A blank form for a new record opens. In order to enter data in a form, you must switch to Form view.

6. **Click the View list arrow in the Views group, then click Form view**
   The form is now displayed in Form view, which you use to add, edit, and delete records.

7. **Use the table below to enter the field values for the new record, pressing [Tab] or [Enter] to move to the next field, then compare your screen to Figure J-19**

Rep ID	Rep Last Name	Rep First Name	Manager ID	Sales Goal	Gold Star Club
R-2012	Davis	Linda	91552	$875,356	Yes

   > **QUICK TIP**
   > A **split form** is a form that displays the data entry form above the underlying datasheet. To create a split form, click the Create tab, click More forms in the Forms group, then click Split Form.

8. **Click the Save button 🖫 on the Quick Access toolbar, click OK in the Save As dialog box, then click the Close 'Sales Reps' button ✖**
   The Sales Reps form closes. You are now ready to close the J-Outdoor Designs database and exit Access.

9. **Click the File tab as shown in Figure J-20, click Close Database, then click Exit**

FIGURE J-18: New form in Layout view

View button arrow

Form displays fields and field values for first record

Record navigation bar

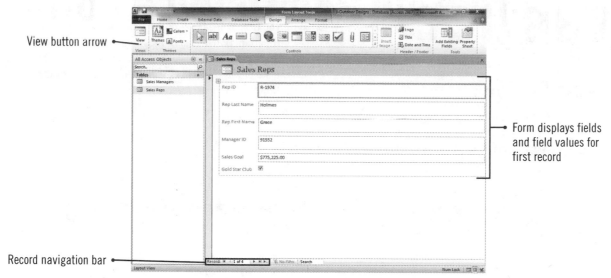

FIGURE J-19: New record added to Sales Reps form in Form view

Saved Sales Reps form appears in Navigation Pane

New record in Form view

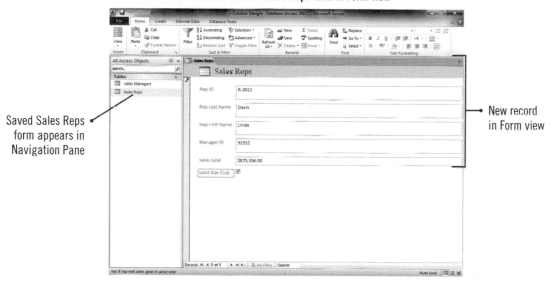

FIGURE J-20: Closing the database and exiting Access

Click to close J-Outdoor Designs database

Click to exit Access

Practice

For current SAM information, including versions and content details, visit SAM Central (http://www.cengage.com/samcentral). If you have a SAM user profile, you may have access to hands-on instruction, practice, and assessment of the skills covered in this unit. Since various versions of SAM are supported throughout the life of this text, check with your instructor for the correct instructions and URL/Web site for accessing assignments.

Concepts Review

Label the elements of the Access window shown in Figure J-21.

FIGURE J-21

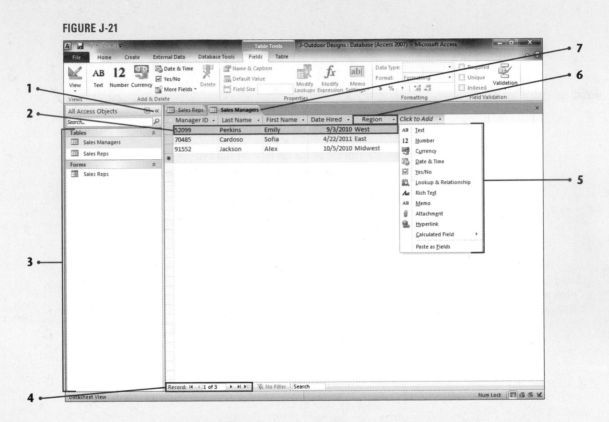

Match each term with the statement that best describes it.

8. **Form**
9. **Table**
10. **Object**
11. **Field**
12. **Database**

a. Information about one item in a particular record in a database
b. A collection of information organized in columns and rows and stored electronically in a file
c. A program component, such as a table or form, that is saved in a database
d. Window containing text boxes and labels into which you enter data in a database
e. A program component in a database that is used to view, enter, and edit data in a gridlike format

Select the best answer from the list of choices.

13. In Datasheet view, each row in a table is a(n) _____.
    a. Field
    b. Object
    c. Field value
    d. Record

14. Form view is the best view for:
    a. Viewing all records at once.
    b. Entering data for a single record at a time.
    c. Adding a field to a table.
    d. Applying a style to a form.

15. Which of the following activities is *not* possible to do in Datasheet view?
    a. View multiple records at once.
    b. Edit a field name.
    c. Enter a field value.
    d. Specify the Field Size property.

16. Which of the following is a database object?
    a. Form
    b. Field
    c. Caption
    d. Field value

17. Which of the following activities is possible to do in Form Layout view?
    a. Edit a record.
    b. Add a record.
    c. Change a field value.
    d. View a specific record in a table.

18. Where does a field description appear in Datasheet view?
    a. In the status bar
    b. In the Field Properties pane
    c. In the Navigation Pane
    d. On the Create tab

19. Which of the following data types should you use if you want each record to be numbered sequentially starting with 1?
    a. Number
    b. AutoNumber
    c. Calculated
    d. Currency

Skills Review

1. **Create a database.**
   a. Start Access.
   b. Create a new, blank database with the name **J-Seaside Boat Rentals**, then save it where you store your Data Files.

2. **Create a table in Datasheet view.**
   a. Save the blank table that is open in Datasheet view with the name **Boats**.
   b. Use a button on the Ribbon to change the data type of the ID field to Text.
   c. Use the table below to add fields to the table.

Field Name	Data Type
Boat Type	Text
Rental Rate	Currency
GPS System	Yes/No
Data Entered By	Text

   d. Save your changes to the table.

Skills Review (continued)

3. Create a table in Design view.

  a. Create a new table and save it as **Rental Orders**.

  b. View the Rental Orders table in Design view, then change the name of the ID field name to **Rental ID**. Change the data type for the Rental ID field to Text.

  c. Use the table below to add fields to the Rental Orders table.

Field Name	Data Type
Rental Date	Date/Time
Customer Last Name	Text
Customer First Name	Text
Boat ID	Text
Hours Rented	Number
Data Entered By	Text

  d. Save your changes to the table.

4. Modify a table and set properties.

  a. Open the Boats table in Design view, then change the ID field name to **Boat ID**.

  b. Change the Field Size property for the Boat ID field to **6**.

  c. Add a new field between Boat Type and Rental Rate. Rename the new field **Date Purchased** and apply the Date/Time data type to it.

  d. Add the following description to the Rental Rate field: **Rental rate is for one hour of use**.

  e. Change the Caption property for the Rental Rate field to **Rate**.

  f. Add the following description to the GPS System field: **Specify yes if boat includes GPS system**.

  g. Save your changes to the table.

5. Enter data in Datasheet view.

  a. View the Boats table in Datasheet view.

  b. Using the table below, enter the three records shown into the Boats table in Datasheet view, then save the Boats table.

Boat ID	Boat Type	Date Purchased	Rate	GPS System	Data Entered By
765234	Jetski	4/1/2013	$55.00	no	Your Name
787544	Jet Boat Twin	3/1/2009	$60.00	no	Your Name
876345	Cape Ann Cruiser	2/1/2012	$75.00	yes	Your Name

  c. View the Rental Orders table in Datasheet view.

  d. Using the table below, enter the three records shown into the Rental Orders table in Datasheet view.

Rental ID	Rental Date	Customer Last Name	Customer First Name	Boat ID	Hours Rented	Data Entered By
B-2277	6/16/13	Rigby	Charles	765234	2	Your Name
B-2278	6/17/13	Marsh	Peter	876345	4	Your Name
B-2279	6/19/13	Brown	Jamal	787544	5	Your Name

  e. Save your changes to the Rental Orders table.

Skills Review (continued)

6. Edit data in Datasheet view.

    a. In the Boats table, change the Rate field value for the Jet Boat Twin to **$80.00**.

    b. In the Boats table, change the Boat Type field value for the Jet Boat Twin to **Ultra Light Jet Boat Twin**.

    c. Adjust all the column widths in the Boats table datasheet for best fit.

    d. In the Rental Orders table, in the third record, change the Hours Rented field value to **4**.

    e. Adjust all the column widths in the Rental Orders table datasheet for best fit.

    f. Save your changes to the Boats table. Compare the Boats table to Figure J-22. Save your changes to the Rental Orders table. Compare the Rental Orders table to Figure J-23.

FIGURE J-22

Boat ID ▾	Boat Type ▾	Date Purchased ▾	Rate ▾	GPS System ▾	Data Entered By ▾	Click to Add ▾
765234	Jetski	4/1/2013	$55.00	☐	Your Name	
787544	Ultra Light Jet Boat Twin	3/1/2009	$80.00	☐	Your Name	
876345	Cape Ann Cruiser	2/1/2012	$75.00	☑	Your Name	
*				☐		

FIGURE J-23

Rental ID ▾	Rental Date ▾	Customer Last Name ▾	Customer First Name ▾	Boat ID ▾	Hours Rented ▾	Data Entered By ▾	Click to Add ▾
B-2277	6/16/2013	Rigby	Charles	765234	2	Your Name	
B-2278	6/17/2013	Marsh	Peter	876345	4	Your Name	
B-2279	6/19/2013	Brown	Jamal	787544	5	Your Name	
*							

7. Create and use a form.

    a. Create a new form based on the Rental Orders table.

    b. In Layout view, view each record one by one using the Record Navigation buttons.

    c. Switch to Form view, then add a new record using the information in the table below:

Rental ID	Rental Date	Customer Last Name	Customer First Name	Boat ID	Hours Rented	Data Entered By
B-2280	6/20/13	Hoover	Maggie	765234	2	Your Name

    d. Save the form as **Rental Orders Form**, then compare your screen to Figure J-24.

    e. Close the database, then exit Access.

    f. Submit your completed database to your instructor.

FIGURE J-24

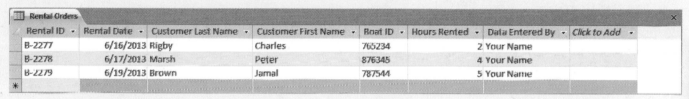

Rental Orders

Rental ID	B-2280
Rental Date	6/20/2013
Customer Last Name	Hoover
Customer First Name	Maggie
Boat ID	765234
Hours Rented	2
Data Entered By	Your Name

Independent Challenge 1

As human resources manager for Haskell-Barnes Insurance, you are responsible for hiring people to fill positions and tracking employee information. You decide to create a database to keep track of this information. Your database needs to contain a table for positions and a table for employees.

a. Create a new, blank database named **J-Haskell-Barnes** where you store your Data Files.

b. Save the blank table that appears in Datasheet view as **Positions**.

c. View the table in Design view. Change the ID field name to **Position ID** and change its data type to Text. Use the table below to enter the field names and their data types for the table.

Field	Data Type
Position Name	Text
Dept	Text
Starting Salary	Currency
Data Entered By	Text

d. Save your changes. Create a new table, save it as **Employees**, then enter the following fields into it in Design view.

Field Name	Data Type
Employee ID	AutoNumber
First Name	Text
Last Name	Text
Position ID	Text
Hire Date	Date/Time
Full Time?	Yes/No
Data Entered By	Text

e. Add the following field description to the Full Time? field: **Yes if the employee works more than 35 hours per week**.

f. View the Positions table in Design view. Specify the Caption field property as **Department** for the Dept field. Save your changes.

g. View the Positions table in Datasheet view, then enter the records shown below into it.

Position ID	Position Name	Dept	Starting Salary	Data Entered By
44599	Customer Service Rep	Customer Service	$26,500	Your Name
48976	Marketing Coordinator	Marketing	$27,500	Your Name
50987	Receptionist	Office Administration	$24,500	Your Name

h. Resize the column widths in the datasheet for best fit. Save your changes, then close the table.

i. View the Employees table in Datasheet view, then enter the records shown below into it. (*Hint*: Press [Tab] to accept the AutoNumber in the Employee ID field.)

First Name	Last Name	Position ID	Hire Date	Full Time?	Data Entered By
Ellen	Tsao	48976	4/1/2012	No	Your Name
Cheryl	Winters	50987	1/9/2013	Yes	Your Name
Luis	Posada	44599	2/19/2012	Yes	Your Name

j. Adjust the column widths in the datasheet for best fit, then save the table.

k. Create a form based on the Employees table, then save the form as **Employees**.

l. Switch to Form view, than add the following record:

First Name	Last Name	Position ID	Hire Date	Full Time?	Data Entered By
Matthew	Marshall	44599	3/1/12	Yes	Your Name

m. Save and close the form.

Independent Challenge 1 (continued)

Advanced Challenge Exercise

- Select the Employees table in the Navigation Pane, then display the Create tab on the Ribbon.
- Click the More Forms button in the Forms group, then click Split Form. A new form appears and is divided into two parts, with the entry form on top and the datasheet on the bottom. Save the form as **Employees Split Form**.
- Click the Next Record button in the navigation bar a few times and observe what happens on the screen.
- Change to Form view, click the New (blank) record button on the navigation bar, then add a new record in the form part of the split form, using the following information:
- First Name: **Edward**; Last Name: **Chalmers**; Position ID: **44599**; Hire Date: **2/15/13**; Full Time?: **Yes**; Data Entered By: **Your Name**
- Save your changes.

n. Close the database, then exit Access. Submit your completed database to your instructor.

Independent Challenge 2

You own an online souvenir store called Knick Knack Nation that sells souvenirs relating to popular cities. You decide to create a database to keep track of your products.

a. Create a new, blank database with the name **J-Knick Knack Nation** and save it where you store your Data Files.

b. Save the blank new table as **Products**. Switch to Design view, then rename the ID field **Product ID**. Keep the data type AutoNumber for the Product ID field. Then, enter the fields and data types shown in the table on the right.

Field Name	Data Type
Product Name	Text
Theme	Text
Net Price	Currency
List Price	Currency
On Hand	Number
Data Entered By	Text

c. Add the following description to the Theme field: **City or place the product represents**.

d. Save your changes to the Products table.

e. Create a form based on the Products table using the Form tool.

f. Save the form as **Products**, then switch to Form view.

g. Add the following records to the form:

Product Name	Theme	Net Price	List Price	On Hand	Data By Entered
Golden Gate Bridge Clock	San Francisco	$20.00	$39.95	10	Your Name
Empire State Building Lamp	New York	$40.00	$79.95	10	Your Name
White House Platter	Washington, D.C.	$15.00	$29.95	30	Your Name
Space Needle Watch	Seattle	$20.00	$39.95	15	Your Name

h. Save and close the form.

Independent Challenge 2 (continued)

Advanced Challenge Exercise

- Open the Products form, then apply the NewsPrint theme.
- Click the File tab, click Save Object As, type **Products ACE** in the Save As dialog box, then click OK.
- Click the Home tab, then close the Products ACE form and table.

i. Close the database, then exit Access. Submit your completed database to your instructor.

Independent Challenge 3

As part of a long-term marketing strategy at Fiesta Dance Studios, you decide to create a database that contains names, addresses, and other information about people who have participated in your programs. You will use the database to promote future classes.

a. Create a new, blank database named **J-Fiesta Dance Studios** and save it where you store your Data Files.

b. Save the blank open table as **Students**, then switch to Design view.

c. Use Design view to design your table. Keep the ID field name and data type the same, and keep it as the primary key field.

d. Add at least seven fields that seem appropriate for this type of database. Of those fields, you must include **First Name** and **Last Name**. Include at least one field with each of the following data types: **Date/Time** and **Yes/No**.

e. Add a field called **Data Entered By** that has the Text data type.

f. Add at least one description for one of the fields.

g. Save the table.

h. Use the Form tool to create a form based on the Students table. In Layout view, apply a theme that you like, then save the form with the name **Students**.

i. Switch to Form view, then add three fictional records. Enter your name in the Data Entered By field. Save and close the form and table.

j. Close the database, then exit Access. Submit your completed database to your instructor.

Creating a Database

Real Life Independent Challenge

You can use Access to keep track of information in your life. As a student, you might be enrolled in several classes at your school. In this Real Life Independent Challenge, you create a database to keep track of your classes.

a. Start Access.

b. Create a new, blank database named **J-My Classes** and save it where you store your Data Files.

c. Save the blank open table as **Classes**, then switch to Design view.

d. Use Design view to design your table. Change the ID field name to **Class ID**, and change its data type to Text. Keep it as the primary key field.

e. Add the following fields to the table: **Class Name**, **Days**, **Classroom**, **Building**, **Instructor Last Name**, and **Start Time**.

f. Add a description to the Days field: **Days when class meets (M T W Th F)**.

g. Add a **Data Entered By** field that has the Text data type.

h. Change the Caption property for the Instructor Last Name field to **Instructor**.

i. Save the Classes table.

j. Create a form based on the Classes table. Enter all your information about your classes into the form.

k. Save the form as **Classes**.

l. Close the Classes form. View the Classes table in Datasheet view, then resize the columns for best fit.

m. Close the table. Close the database and exit Access. Submit your completed database to your instructor.

Visual Workshop

Create the database form shown in Figure J-25. (*Hint*: First create a new, blank database called **J-Cottage Rentals** where you store your Data Files, then create a table called **Cottages** that contains the fields shown in the form.) Set the Field Size property to **4** for the Year Built field. Add the description shown in the status bar in the figure for the Summer Rate field. Create a form based on the table and save it as **Cottages**. In Layout view, apply the Essential theme. Enter the data shown in the figure into the form. Save and close the table and the form, close the database, then exit Access. Submit your completed database to your instructor.

FIGURE J-25

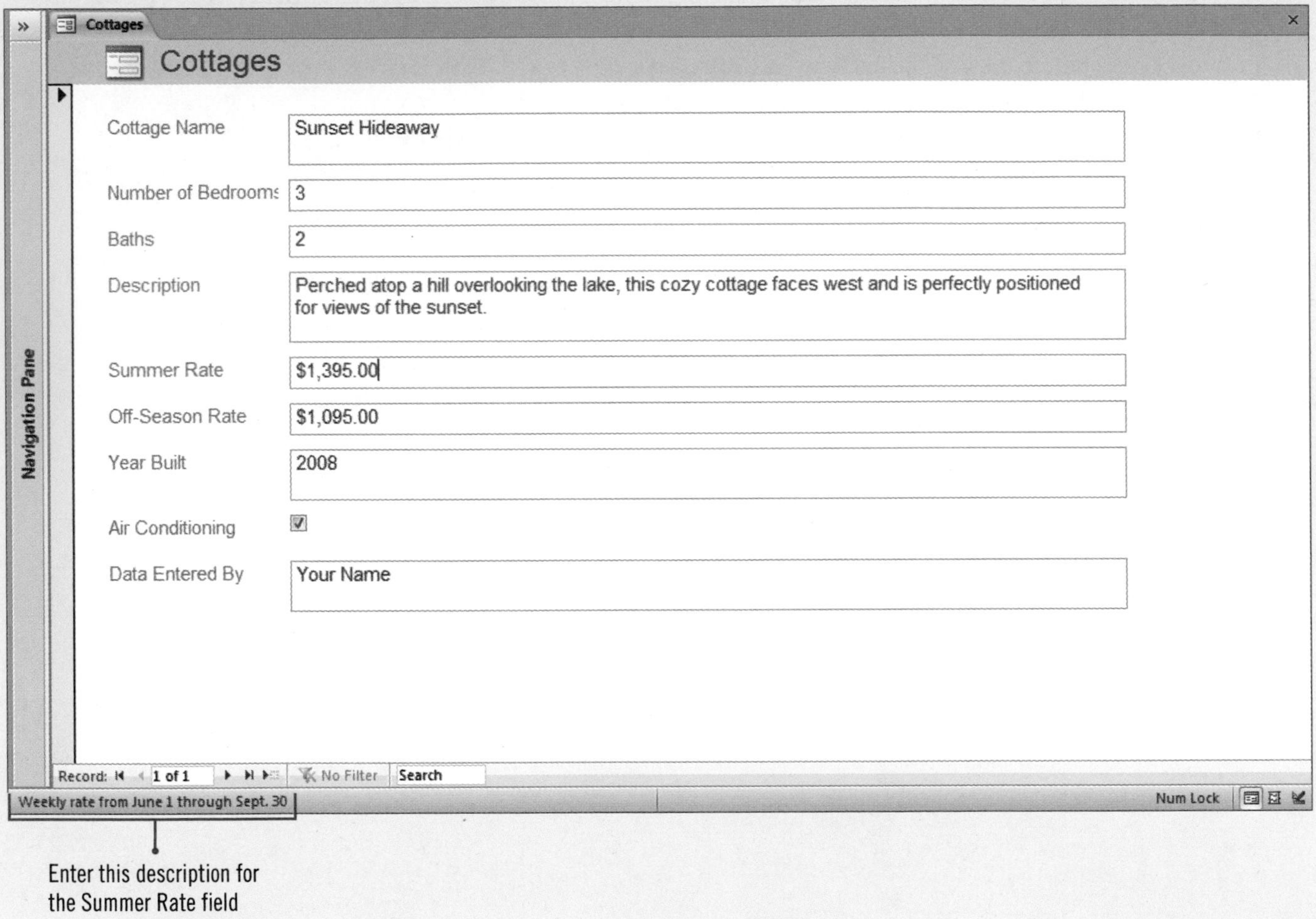

Enter this description for the Summer Rate field

Working with Data

Once you have entered data into a database, you can pull out the information you need by filtering and querying the data and by sorting it in useful ways. In this unit, you learn how to open an existing database and work with the data by sorting, using filters, creating queries, and using calculated fields, which are fields that show the result of a mathematical expression. You also learn how to set up a relationship between two tables so that you can use the fields from both tables in a query. Serena Henning, sales director at Outdoor Designs, has given you a database that contains two tables. She asks you to sort and filter the data so that it is more useful. She also needs you to retrieve some information from these tables by using queries. Finally, she wants you to add a calculated field to one of the tables.

OBJECTIVES

Open an existing database

Sort records in a table

Filter records in a table

Create a query using the Query Wizard

Modify a query in Design view

Relate two tables

Create a query using two tables

Add a calculated field to a table

Opening an Existing Database

Opening an existing Access database is similar to opening a Word or an Excel file. You click the Open command on the File tab in Backstage view to open the Open dialog box. You can also open a recently used database file by clicking its file name on the File tab, or by clicking Recent on the File tab, then clicking the file name. One difference between opening an Access database and opening a file in Word or Excel is that you can only open one Access database file at a time. If you want two databases open at once, you need to start an additional session of Access, then open the additional database in that second session.  To get started on your project for Serena, you decide to open the database and then save it with a new name, so that the original database will remain intact. Then, you decide to view the tables it contains in Datasheet view.

STEPS

1. **Start Access, then click Open on the File tab**
   The Open dialog box opens and displays the files and folders in your Documents folder.

2. **Navigate to the drive and folder where you store your Data Files, click K-1.accdb, then click Open**
   The database opens, as shown in Figure K-1. Notice the Security Warning in the yellow bar below the Ribbon, which says, "Some active content has been disabled. Click for more details." Unless you change the standard default settings in Access, this security warning appears any time you open an existing database. This warning is Microsoft's way of protecting your computer from potentially harmful files. Because you can trust that this file is safe, you can enable the content for this file and for all data files for this book.

3. **Click Enable Content in the Security Warning bar**

4. **Click the File tab, then click Save Database As**
   The Save As dialog box opens.

5. **Type K-Outdoor Designs in the File Name text box, navigate to the folder where you save your Data Files, then click Save**
   The copy of the database opens with the new name K-Outdoor Designs.accdb. The Security Warning appears below the Ribbon again, as Access recognizes this is a database file you have not opened before.

   > **TROUBLE**
   > If your Navigation Pane is closed, click the pane's Shutter Bar Open button >> to open it.

6. **Click Enable Content, then double-click Customers: Table in the Navigation Pane**
   The Customers table opens in Datasheet view, as shown in Figure K-2. You can see in the navigation bar at the bottom of the screen that this table contains 73 records.

7. **Double-click Sales Reps: Table in the Navigation Pane**
   A new tab opens in the database window and displays the Sales Reps table, as shown in Figure K-3. This table has only ten records (one for each sales rep) and contains only four fields (Rep ID, Region, Rep Last Name, and Rep First Name). Note that the Rep ID is the primary key field. You will use this table later in the unit, but you do not need it now.

8. **Click the Sales Reps Table Close button ⊠ in the database window**

Working with Data

FIGURE K-1: Database open with Security Warning

Security Warning appears when you open an existing database

This database contains two tables

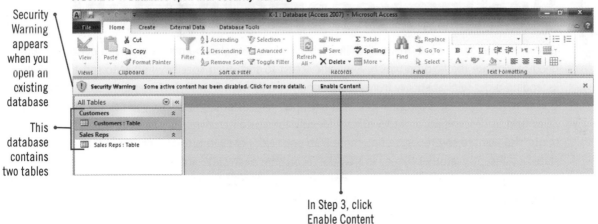

In Step 3, click Enable Content

FIGURE K-2: Customers table in Datasheet view

Customers table

Sales Reps table

Customers table contains 73 records

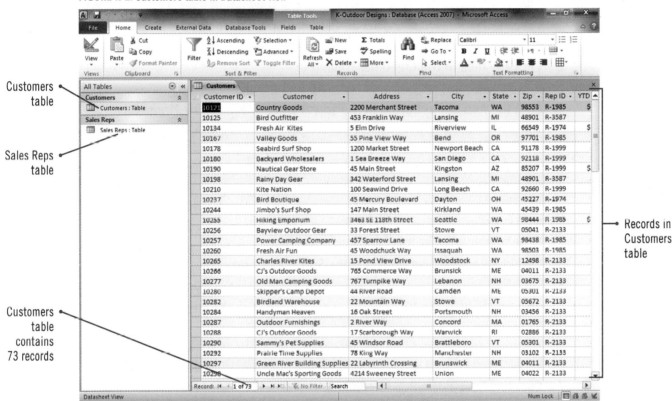

Records in Customers table

FIGURE K-3: Sales Reps table in Datasheet view

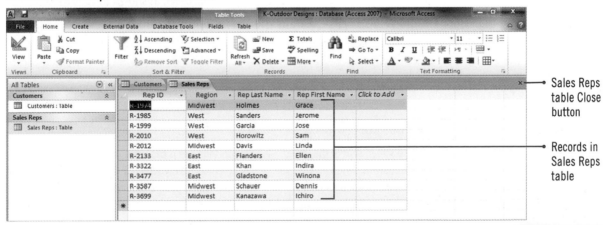

Sales Reps table Close button

Records in Sales Reps table

Sorting Records in a Table

You can rearrange, or **sort**, the records in a table in alphabetical or numerical order. To perform a sort, you need to indicate the field on which you want Access to sort, then specify whether to sort the database in ascending order (alphabetically from A to Z or numerically from 0 to 9) or descending order (alphabetically from Z to A or numerically from 9 to 0). For example, in a customer database, you could sort records by the Sales field in descending order to quickly identify the customers who purchased the most products. You might also want to sort records using more than one field. For example, you might wish to sort primarily by state but also by customer name, so that the records for each state are grouped together, with customers listed in alphabetical order within each state grouping. Serena asks you to create a sorted list that groups the records first by Rep ID and then, within each Rep ID grouping, by YTD Orders in descending order. First, you experiment with sorting in different ways.

STEPS

1. **Click the Shutter Bar Close button** ≪ **in the Navigation Pane**

   The database window now displays the Customers table with all its fields in view. Just to experiment, you decide to sort the table in ascending order by customer name.

2. **Click any field in the Customer column**

   Before performing a sort, you need to select the field by which you want to sort.

3. **Click the Ascending button in the Sort & Filter group on the Home tab**

   The table is now sorted by customer name in alphabetical order, with Al's Sports Hut listed first. Notice that there is a small upward-pointing arrow to the right of the Customer column header, indicating that the table is sorted in ascending order by this field, as shown in Figure K-4.

QUICK TIP

If you select two columns in a table, click either the Ascending or the Descending button—Access will first sort the records in the left column, then sort the records in the right column.

4. **Click the Descending button in the Sort & Filter group on the Home tab**

   The table is now sorted by customer name in descending alphabetical order (Z to A), with Wilderness Outfitter listed first. Notice the downward-pointing arrow in the Customer column heading, indicating that the records in the table are sorted in descending order by this field.

5. **Click the Remove Sort button in the Sort & Filter group**

   The table is now ordered in its original order, with Country Goods listed first in the Customer column.

6. **Click any field in the YTD Orders column, then click the Descending button in the Sort & Filter group**

   The records are now sorted in descending order by year-to-date order amounts. You see that Hiking Emporium has purchased the most this year, with $75,764.00 in the YTD Orders field value text box.

QUICK TIP

To capture a screen shot of your sorted table after Step 7, follow the instructions in the yellow box below.

7. **Click any field in the Rep ID column, then click the Ascending button in the Sort & Filter group**

   The records in the Customers table are now sorted first by Rep ID in ascending order and then, within each Rep ID grouping, by YTD Order amounts in descending order, as shown in Figure K-5.

8. **Click the Remove Sort button in the Sort & Filter group**

   The table reverts to its original order.

Capturing a screen shot of your sorted table

Your instructor might ask you to capture a screen shot of the sorted Customers table and submit it. To do this, start Microsoft Word, click the Insert tab, click the Screenshot button, then click the image of the screenshot in the Available Windows menu. The screen shot of your sorted table is pasted into a new word document. Save this document as Unit K Screen Shots and submit it to your instructor. Click the Access program button on the taskbar to return to Access.

FIGURE K-4: Customers table in alphabetical order by Customer

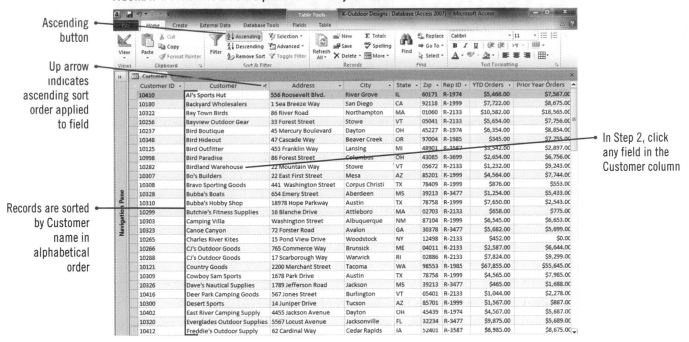

Ascending button

Up arrow indicates ascending sort order applied to field

Records are sorted by Customer name in alphabetical order

In Step 2, click any field in the Customer column

FIGURE K-5: Records sorted by two different fields

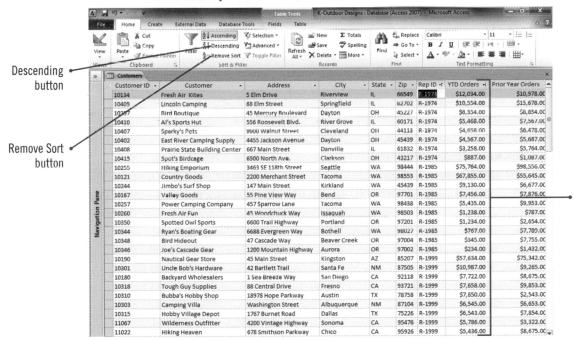

Descending button

Remove Sort button

Records are grouped in ascending order by Rep ID and then descending order by YTD Orders

Sorting on multiple fields

Before you sort records in a table by two different fields, you first need to decide which field you want to be the primary sort field and which field you want to be sorted within the primary field grouping. The field that is the primary sort field is called the outermost sort field, and the field that is the secondary sort field is called the innermost sort field. For example, in Figure K-5, the Rep ID field is the outermost sort field, and the YTD Orders field is the innermost sort

field; the records are first sorted by Rep ID in ascending order, then by YTD Orders in descending order. Ironically, to get the results you want, you need to first sort the records by the innermost field and then sort by the outermost field. This can be confusing because it is counterintuitive; thus, it is important that you understand these rules before you sort on two fields.

Filtering Records in a Table

Just as you can apply a filter to an Excel worksheet to display only the information that you want to see, you can also apply a filter to an Access table to display only those records that meet criteria that you specify. **Criteria** are conditions that must be met for a record to be displayed. For example, you might want to filter a database to see only the records for customers who are located in Florida, or only those for customers who made a purchase within the past three months. The simplest way to filter a table is to select a field that matches your criterion (for instance, a State field containing FL), and then use the Equals command to display those records that match the selection. You can also apply a Number Filter to a selected field to filter records that are greater than, less than, or equal to a specific number, or between two different numbers. You cannot save a filter as a database object, but you can save it as part of the table or form you are working on and reapply it the next time. You can also print the results of a filter.  Serena needs you to print a list of customers whose year-to-date orders are greater than $5000 for sales rep Jose Garcia. You decide to apply filters to display records that meet these criteria.

STEPS

1. Click a field in the Rep ID column containing the value R-1999

This Rep ID number (R-1999) is the ID number for Jose Garcia, a rep in the West region.

2. Click the Selection button in the Sort & Filter group

The Selection menu opens and displays four commands. These commands let you filter records that are equal or not equal to the selected field value, or that do or do not contain the selected value.

3. Click Equals "R-1999"

Seventeen records containing R-1999 in the Rep ID field appear in the datasheet window, as shown in Figure K-6. These records are all Jose Garcia's customers. Notice that a filter icon appears to the right of the Rep ID column heading, indicating that a filter is applied to this field.

4. Click the Toggle Filter button in the Sort & Filter group

The filter is removed, and all the records in the table appear again. Clicking the Toggle Filter button once removes the filter; clicking it again reapplies it.

> **QUICK TIP**
> When a filter is applied to a table, the word "Filtered" appears in the record navigation bar; when you click the Toggle Filter button, the navigation bar displays "Unfiltered". If no filter is applied, the navigation bar displays "No filter".

5. Click the Toggle Filter button

The filter is reapplied, so that only the 17 customer records for rep R-1999 (Jose Garcia) appear.

6. Click any value in the YTD Orders field, then click the Filter button in the Sort & Filter group

The Filter menu opens and displays commands for filtering and sorting records specific to the YTD Orders field. The bottom of the list displays all the specific values for the YTD Orders field, with check boxes next to each. To show only records with one of these specific values, you can click the check box next to that value. You want to display records that are greater than 5000, so you need to use a Number Filter command.

> **QUICK TIP**
> To capture a screen shot of your filtered table after Step 7, follow the steps in the yellow box in the previous lesson.

7. Point to Number Filters in the Filter list, click Greater Than, type 5000 in the Custom Filter dialog box, compare your screen to Figure K-7, then click OK

The filtered list now shows ten records, with two filter criteria applied. All the records contain R-1999 in the Rep ID field, and all the values in the YTD Orders field are greater than 5000, as shown in Figure K-8.

8. Click the Toggle Filter button, then save your changes

The filter is removed, and your changes are saved.

Working with Data

FIGURE K-6: Filtered Customers table with one filter applied

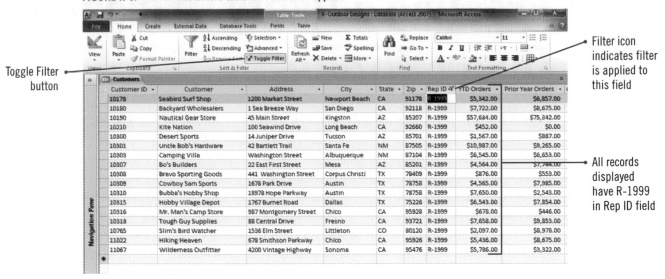

Toggle Filter button

Filter icon indicates filter is applied to this field

All records displayed have R-1999 in Rep ID field

FIGURE K-7: Custom Filter dialog box

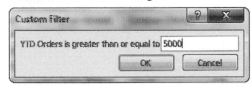

FIGURE K-8: Customers datasheet with two filters applied

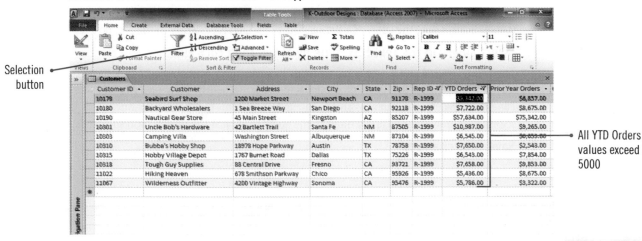

Selection button

All YTD Orders values exceed 5000

Creating a Query Using the Query Wizard

Filtering data in tables is helpful, but it has some limitations. For one thing, you cannot limit or change the order of the fields Access displays when you apply a filter. You also cannot save a filter. For greater flexibility and control, you need to use a query. A **query** is a database object that extracts data from one or more tables in a database according to criteria that you set. A query displays only the fields you specify. For instance, in a database that contains ten fields that store product information, you could create a query that displays only the fields for product names and prices. You can also use a query to pull together information from several tables. Because a query is an object, you can save it for later use. The simplest way to create a query is to use the Query Wizard. ▰▰▰▰ Serena wants to see a view of the data that shows customer names, their state, and Rep ID numbers. To accomplish this, you decide to use the Query Wizard.

STEPS

1. **Click the Customers table Close button ✖ in the database window, then click the Shutter Bar Open button ≫**

   You need to close a table before creating a query that is based on it. The Navigation Pane is now open.

2. **Click the Create tab, then click the Query Wizard button in the Queries group**

   The New Query dialog box opens, as shown in Figure K-9, where you select the type of Query Wizard you want to use. By default, Simple Query Wizard is selected. This wizard creates a **select query**, a query that retrieves or selects data from one or more tables or queries according to your criteria. This is the most commonly used type of query and is the one you want to create.

3. **Click OK**

   The Simple Query Wizard dialog box opens. First you need to specify the table or query from which you want to select fields for your query.

4. **Click the Table/Queries list arrow, then click Table: Customers**

   Notice that all the fields from the Customers table are listed in the Available Fields list. You now need to choose the fields you want from this list.

> **QUICK TIP**
> You can also select a field by double-clicking its name in the Available Fields list.

5. **Click Customer in the Available Fields list, then click the Select Single Field button ▷**

   The Customer field moves to the Selected Fields list. You can move fields back and forth between the Available Fields list and the Selected Fields list using the buttons shown in Table K-1.

6. **Click State, click ▷, click Rep ID, then click ▷**

   Now the Customer, State, and Rep ID fields are listed in the Selected Fields area, as shown in Figure K-10.

7. **Click Next**

   In this dialog box, you specify a name for the query. Unless you specify otherwise, the Query Wizard will automatically name the query "Customers Query", which is currently in the text box.

> **QUICK TIP**
> Records resulting from a query look like a table but are actually a view based on the query.

8. **Select Query in the text box, type by State, then click Finish**

   The Query Wizard closes and the Customers by State query results appear in Datasheet view, showing the Customer, State, and Rep ID fields. Notice that the Customers by State query is now listed in the Navigation Pane below Sales Reps: Table, as shown in Figure K-11. This query contains only fields that Serena needs to see. She can now sort and apply filters to the query to get just the information she needs.

9. **Save your changes**

FIGURE K-9: New Query dialog box

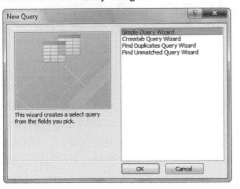

Simple Query Wizard
Crosstab Query Wizard
Find Duplicates Query Wizard
Find Unmatched Query Wizard

This wizard creates a select query from the fields you pick.

OK   Cancel

FIGURE K-10: Specifying a table and fields for a simple query

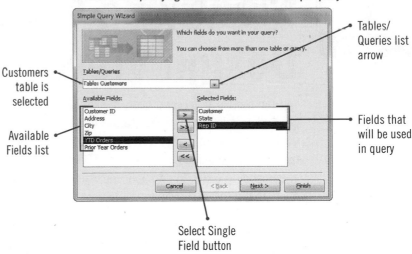

Customers table is selected

Available Fields list

Tables/Queries list arrow

Fields that will be used in query

Select Single Field button

FIGURE K-11: Customers by State query results

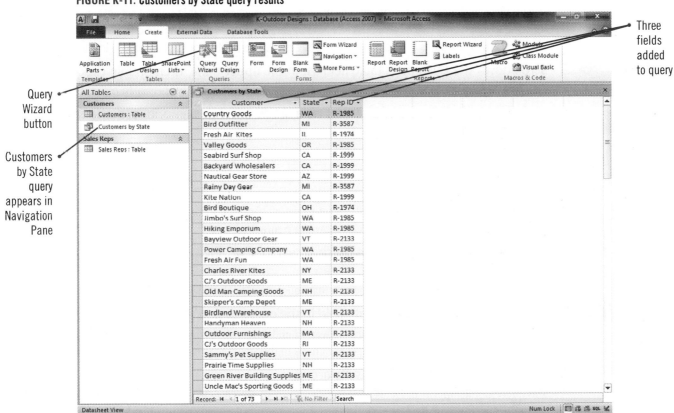

Query Wizard button

Customers by State query appears in Navigation Pane

Three fields added to query

TABLE K-1: Select Field buttons in Query Wizard

button	use to
>	Move a single field to the Selected Fields area
>>	Move all available fields to the Selected Fields area
<	Remove a single field from the Selected Fields area and restore it to the Available Fields list
<<	Remove all fields from the Selected Fields area and restore them to the Available Fields list

Modifying a Query in Design View

You can modify an existing query if you need to make changes to it using Design view. In Design view, you can add or delete fields, specify a sort order for one or more fields, or specify criteria for fields. You can also use Design view instead of Query Wizard to create a query. ▓▓▓▓ Serena asks you to modify the Customers by State query so that it includes the YTD Orders field. She also wants the results to be sorted by YTD Orders in descending order. In addition, she wants you to create another query based on the Customers by State query that displays customers in the state of California. You decide to create this new query in Design view.

STEPS

1. **Click the Home tab, then click the View button in the Views group**

   The database window displays the Customers by State query in Design view, and the Query Tools Design tab is active. In Design view, the database window is divided into two panes. The upper pane displays the Customers table field list. The lower pane is called the query design grid. You use the cells in this grid to specify fields and their criteria for the current query. The query design grid currently contains the three fields in the Customers by State query (Customer, State, and Rep ID). Notice that the check box in the Show cell under each field contains a check mark, indicating that these fields should be displayed in the query.

   QUICK TIP
   You can also add fields to the query design grid by dragging them from the field list.

2. **Scroll down the Customers table field list in the upper pane, then double-click YTD Orders**

   The YTD Orders field is now added to the query design grid and appears in the fourth column.

3. **Click the Sort cell for the YTD Orders field in the query design grid, click the Sort list arrow, then click Descending**

   See Figure K-12.

4. **Click the View button in the Results group**

   The query results appear in Datasheet view, and the records are sorted by the YTD Orders field in descending order. As you modify a query, it is convenient to switch back and forth between Design view and Datasheet view to see the modified query results, as shown in Figure K-13.

5. **Click the Save button 🖫 on the Quick Access toolbar, then click the View button in the Views group**

   The changes you made to the Customers by State query are saved, and the query appears in Design view.

   QUICK TIP
   Criteria that you type are not case sensitive; typing "WA" in the Criteria cell displays records with "WA", "wa", "Wa", or "wA" in the State field.

6. **Click the Criteria cell for the State field in the query design grid, type ca, then press [Enter]**

   After you press [Enter], quotation marks appear around your entry. The criteria "ca" specifies that the query results should only display records that contain CA in the State field.

7. **Click the View button in the Results group**

   The query results appear in Datasheet view, as shown in Figure K-14. The results show seven records that contain CA in the State field. Notice that the records are sorted in descending order by YTD Orders.

8. **Click the File tab, click Save Object As, type California Customers in the Save 'Customers by State' to text box in the Save As dialog box, then click OK**

   The modified query is saved as California Customers and appears in the Navigation Pane below Customers: Table.

9. **Click the Home tab, then click the California Customers query Close button ☒**

   The California Customers query closes.

FIGURE K-12: Adding a field to the Customers by State query in Design view

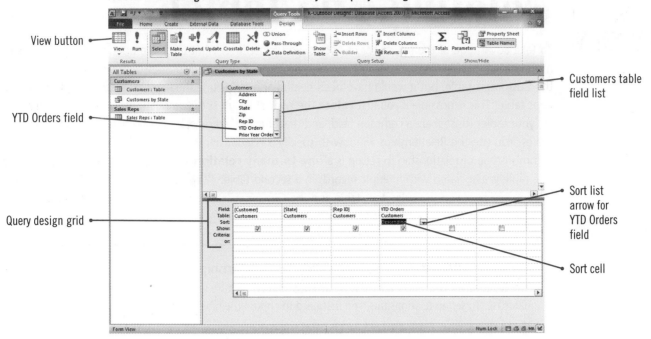

View button

Customers table field list

YTD Orders field

Query design grid

Sort list arrow for YTD Orders field

Sort cell

FIGURE K-13: Modified Customers by State query results in Datasheet view

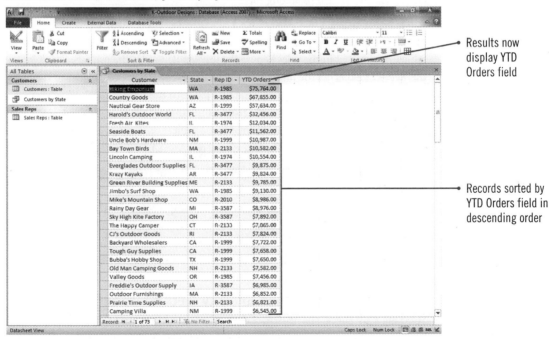

Results now display YTD Orders field

Records sorted by YTD Orders field in descending order

FIGURE K-14: Modified query in Datasheet view

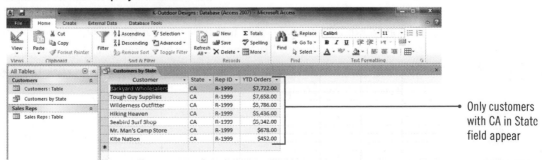

Only customers with CA in State field appear

Working with Data

Relating Two Tables

To take advantage of the full power of Access, you sometimes want to create queries that pull fields from more than one table. For instance, the queries you created in the previous lesson pulled from a single table, the Customers table, but it would have been helpful also to include the Rep Last Name field from the Sales Reps table. This is possible if you first **relate** the two tables, or specify a relationship between them. To do so, your tables must share a common field, and that shared field must be the primary key field in one of the tables. You use the Relationships window to specify a relationship between two or more tables. The most common type of relationship to set up is a **one-to-many relationship**, in which the primary key field in one table is associated with multiple records in a second table. ██████ You need to specify a one-to-many relationship between the Sales Reps table and the Customers table so that you can create queries that pull fields from both tables.

STEPS

1. **Click the Database Tools tab, then click the Relationships button in the Relationships group**

   The Relationships window opens. It is currently empty, because there are no related tables or queries in this database. To set up relationships, you first need to choose the tables you want to relate.

2. **Click the Show Table button in the Relationships group**

   The Show Table dialog box opens, with the Tables tab in front and the Customers table selected, as shown in Figure K-15. You use this dialog box to add specific tables or queries to the Relationships window, so that you can specify relationships among them.

3. **Click Sales Reps, click Add, click Customers, click Add, then click Close**

   The Show Table dialog box closes, and the Relationships window displays the Sales Reps and Customers tables. Notice that in the Sales Reps table, the Rep ID field is the primary key field, but in the Customers table, the Rep ID field is *not* the primary key field. This is appropriate; in order to relate two tables, the shared field must be a primary key field in *only* the first table. In the second table, the common field shared with the first table is called the **foreign key**. To create a one-to-many relationship, you need to drag the primary key from the first table to the foreign key in the second table.

4. **Drag the Rep ID field from the Sales Reps table to the Rep ID field in the Customers table**

   The Edit Relationships dialog box opens. The current settings reflect the relationship you just specified by dragging. The Rep ID field from the Sales Reps table is on the left, and the Rep ID field from the Customers table is on the right. At the bottom, the Relationship Type is listed as One-To-Many. These settings are exactly what you want; one sales rep is associated with multiple customers, but each customer is associated with a single sales rep. Therefore, it makes sense to set up a one-to-many relationship with the Rep ID field in the Sales Reps table on the "one" side of the relationship, and the Rep ID field in the Customers table on the "many" side.

5. **Click the Enforce Referential Integrity check box to add a check mark**

   Selecting this check box tells Access to reject any attempts to enter data that would be inconsistent. For instance, if a user entered "55" as a Rep ID number in the Customers table, Access would reject the entry because that Rep ID number does not exist in the Sales Reps table. See Figure K-16.

6. **Click Create**

   A relationship line now connects the Rep ID field in the Sales Reps table and the Rep ID field in the Customers table, as shown in Figure K-17. Note that there is a 1 at the top of the line and an infinity symbol at the bottom of the line, indicating that these two fields have a one-to-many relationship.

7. **Click the Save button ▣ on the Quick Access toolbar, then click the Close button ▣ in the Relationships group**

FIGURE K-15: Show Table dialog box

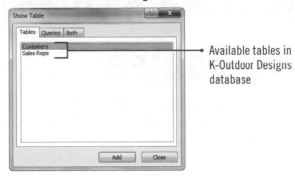

Available tables in K-Outdoor Designs database

FIGURE K-16: Edit Relationships dialog box

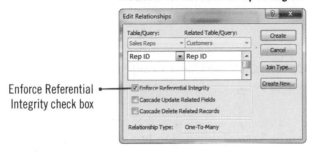

Enforce Referential Integrity check box

FIGURE K-17: Relationships window with a one-to-many relationship established

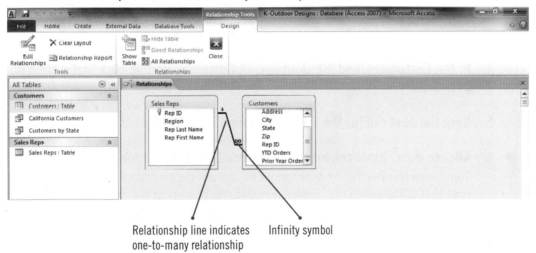

Relationship line indicates one-to-many relationship

Infinity symbol

Understanding good database design

Creating a well-designed database requires careful planning. First, decide on the main goals of the database. What is its purpose? What data will it store? Once you decide this, you need to organize the database into categories of data. For instance, if your database will track information about your sports league, you might have categories called Teams, Players, Coaches, and Games. You can then turn each of these categories into tables in your database. Then, you need to define fields and the data types for each table. Remember that each table must have a primary key field that uniquely identifies each record from any other in the database. Once you have created your tables, you need to decide how each table relates to the others in the database and set up appropriate relationships between them. You might need to add new fields to the tables to create these relationships. Creating a well-designed structure for your database will ensure that your data is easy to access, maintain, and update.

Creating a Query Using Two Tables

Setting up relationships between tables offers many advantages. One is that you can create a query that pulls fields from two or more related tables. Also, if you specify to enforce referential integrity in related tables, any changes you make to fields in one table are instantly reflected in all related tables or queries that contain that field. This is a huge benefit and ensures that the data in your database is consistent. Setting up table relationships also ensures that your data is valid and accurate. Access will prohibit any attempt to enter data in the foreign key field that is not consistent with the data in the primary key field.  Serena would like a view of the data that shows customers whose year-to-date orders exceed $10,000. Because you have set up a one-to-many relationship between the Sales Reps table and the Customers table, you can create a query that contains the information Serena needs.

STEPS

1. **Click the Create tab, then click the Query Design button in the Queries group**

   A new blank query opens in Design view, and the Show Table dialog box opens with the Customers table selected.

TROUBLE

If the Show Table dialog box is covering the field lists, drag its title bar to a new location.

2. **On the Tables tab of the Show Table dialog box, click Sales Reps, click Add, click Customers, click Add compare your screen to Figure K-18, then click Close**

   The field lists for the Sales Reps table and the Customers table appear. Notice that the relationship you created between the Rep ID field in the Sales Reps table and the Rep ID field in the Customers table is shown.

QUICK TIP

To delete a field from a query, click anywhere in the field column in the query design grid, then click the Delete Columns button in the Query Setup group.

3. **In the Sales Reps field list, double-click Rep Last Name, then double-click Region**

   The Rep Last Name and Region fields are added to the query design grid.

4. **In the Customers field list, double-click Customer, double-click State, then double-click YTD Orders**

5. **Click the Sort cell for the YTD Orders field, click the Sort list arrow, then click Descending**

QUICK TIP

To specify multiple criteria for a field, type additional criteria in the Or cell for that field in the query design grid; results will include any records that match either the Criteria cell contents or the Or cell contents.

6. **Click in the Criteria cell for the YTD Orders field, then type >10000**

   This criteria specifies that the query results should only display records whose YTD Sales field value is greater than 10,000. The greater than symbol (>) is one type of operator you can use in the Criteria cell to return the query results that you want. Table K-2 displays useful comparison operators.

7. **Click the Sort cell for the Rep Last Name field, click the Sort list arrow, click Ascending, then compare your screen to Figure K-19**

QUICK TIP

You can also view query results by clicking the Run button in the Results group in Design view.

8. **Click the View button in the Results group**

   The query results appear in Datasheet view, as shown in Figure K-20. You can see that the results are grouped first by Rep Last Name in alphabetical order, then by YTD Orders in descending order.

9. **Click the Save button 🖫 on the Quick Access toolbar, type Top Customers by Rep in the Save As dialog box, click OK, then close the Top Customers by Rep query**

   The query is saved as Top Customers by Rep and appears in the Navigation Pane. It appears in both the Customers grouping and the Sales Reps grouping because it contains fields from both of these tables.

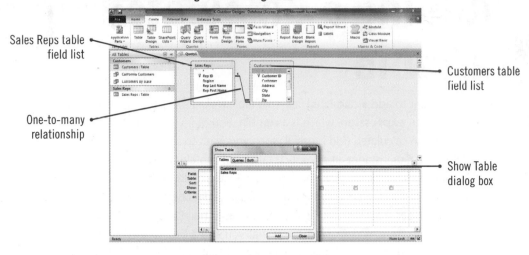

Sales Reps table field list

One-to-many relationship

Customers table field list

Show Table dialog box

FIGURE K-19: Query with specified fields, sorts, and criteria in Design view

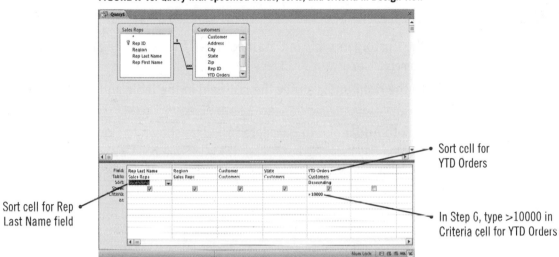

Sort cell for YTD Orders

Sort cell for Rep Last Name field

In Step G, type >10000 in Criteria cell for YTD Orders

Access 2010

FIGURE K-20: Query results in Datasheet view

Records are grouped by Rep Last Name in alphabetical order

Query results contain YTD Orders values that exceed $10,000

TABLE K-2: Comparison operators

operator	description
>	Greater than
<	Less than
=	Equals
<>	Not equal to

Adding a Calculated Field to a Table

You might want to add a calculated field to a table if the table contains values. A **calculated field** is a field that contains an **expression**, which is a combination of fields, values, and mathematical operators (similar to a formula). A calculated field is useful when you want to show the results of calculations based on values in certain fields. For instance, in a products table that contains a field for net price, you could add a calculated field for determining the sales tax; the expression would multiply the Net Price field by .08 (or the appropriate tax percentage). Calculated fields have the Calculated data type. Choosing a Calculated data type opens the Expression Builder dialog box, where you can easily build the expression you want by specifying fields, values, and operators. Serena asks that you add a field to the Customers table that shows the total orders for each customer. You need to create a calculated field that adds the Prior Year Orders field to the YTD Orders field.

STEPS

1. **Open the Customers table in Datasheet view, then click the Shutter Bar Close button** ⟪
   The Customers table opens in Datasheet view.

2. **Scroll to the right until you see the last field in the table and the blank field to the right of it**

3. **Click Click to Add, point to Calculated Field, as shown in Figure K-21, then click Currency**
   The Expression Builder dialog box opens, which lets you build the expression using fields, values, and mathematical operators. You need to build an expression that sums the Prior Year Orders field and the YTD Orders field.

> **QUICK TIP**
> Unlike Excel formulas, expressions do not start with an equal sign (=).

4. **Double-click Prior Year Orders in the Expression Categories section**
   The Prior Year Orders field appears in the top part of the dialog box in brackets. This field is the first part of your expression. Next you need to enter the addition operator.

5. **Type +**
   You typed the plus sign (the addition operator). You can now add the YTD Orders field to complete the expression.

> **QUICK TIP**
> Note that a calculated field in a table can only include field references to fields in that table.

6. **Double-click YTD Orders in the Expression Categories section**
   The top section of the dialog box shows the completed expression, as shown in Figure K-22.

7. **Click OK**
   The new column (next to Prior Year Orders) is now populated with currency values, which are the result of the expression you built (Prior Year Orders + YTD Orders). You need to type a label for this field. The placeholder label is selected, so you can type a new label.

8. **Type Total Orders, then press [Enter]**
   The field name Total Orders now appears as the last field name in the table, as shown in Figure K-23.

9. **Click 🖫, click the File tab, click Close Database, then click Exit**
   The Customers table, the database, and Access all close.

FIGURE K-21: Adding a calculated field to a table

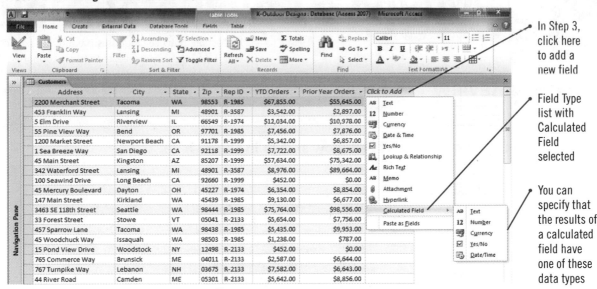

In Step 3, click here to add a new field

Field Type list with Calculated Field selected

You can specify that the results of a calculated field have one of these data types

FIGURE K-22: Building an expression using the Expression Builder dialog box

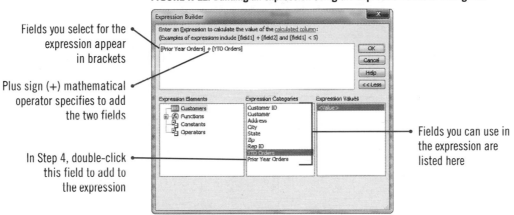

Fields you select for the expression appear in brackets

Plus sign (+) mathematical operator specifies to add the two fields

In Step 4, double-click this field to add to the expression

Fields you can use in the expression are listed here

FIGURE K-23: Customers table with new calculated field added

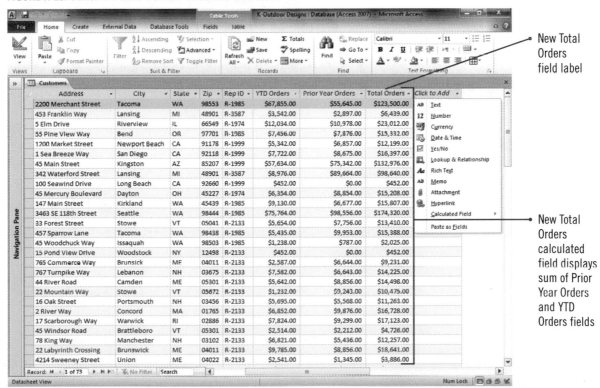

New Total Orders field label

New Total Orders calculated field displays sum of Prior Year Orders and YTD Orders fields

Practice

For current SAM information, including versions and content details, visit SAM Central (http://www.cengage.com/samcentral). If you have a SAM user profile, you may have access to hands-on instruction, practice, and assessment of the skills covered in this unit. Since various versions of SAM are supported throughout the life of this text, check with your instructor for the correct instructions and URL/Web site for accessing assignments.

Concepts Review

Label the elements of the Access window shown in Figure K-24.

FIGURE K-24

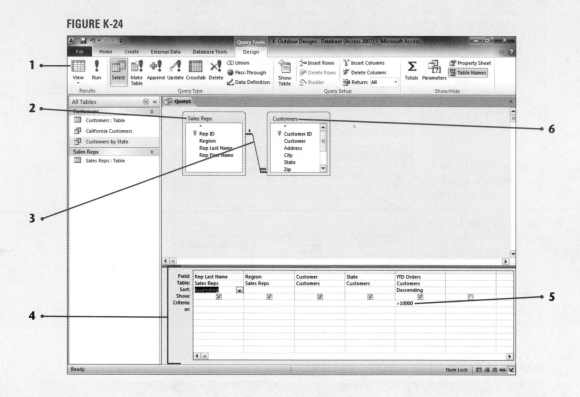

Match each term with the statement that best describes it.

7. Expression
8. Query
9. Filter
10. Criteria
11. Primary key
12. Foreign key

a. A database object that pulls fields from one or more related tables or objects to help answer questions about the data

b. A combination of fields, values, and mathematical operators

c. View of a table that displays only fields that meet specified criteria

d. A field in a table that uniquely identifies a record

e. Conditions that must be met for a particular field in order for a record to appear in query results

f. A field in a table that is the primary key field in a related table

Select the best answer from the list of choices.

13. **Which of the following cannot be saved as an object in Access?**
    a. A query
    b. A table
    c. A form
    d. A filter

14. **Which of the following shows how the Year 1 Sales field would appear in an expression?**
    a. =Year 1 Sales
    b. <Year 1 Sales>
    c. [Year 1 Sales]
    d. (Year 1 Sales)

15. **Which of the following is not possible to do in Query Design view?**
    a. Specify a relationship between two fields in two tables.
    b. Specify criteria for a field in a query.
    c. Specify a sort order for one of the fields in the query.
    d. Add a field to a query.

16. **To apply a filter that displays all the records that display Ohio in the State field, which of the following actions would you take?**
    a. Click the Filter button, then type Ohio.
    b. Click Ohio in the table, click the Selection button, then click Equals Ohio.
    c. Click any field in the table, click the Selection button, then click Equals Ohio.
    d. Click the State field name in the column heading, click the Selection button, then click Equals Ohio.

17. **Which of the following cannot be included in an expression?**
    a. Fields
    b. Mathematical operators
    c. Field descriptions
    d. Values

18. **Table A and Table B are related in a one-to-many relationship. Table A is on the "one" side of the relationship, and Table B is on the "many" side of the relationship. Which of the following statements about these tables is NOT true?**
    a. In Table A, the shared field is the foreign key.
    b. In Table B, the shared field is not the primary key field.
    c. The shared field is the foreign key in Table B.
    d. One record in Table A is related to many records in Table B.

Skills Review

1. **Open an existing database.**
   a. Start Access.
   b. Open the Data File K-2.accdb from the drive and folder where you store your Data Files. Specify to enable the content in the database.
   c. Save the database as a new database with the name **K-Puzzle Universe.accdb**. Enable the content.
   d. Open the Suppliers table in Datasheet view, and review the fields and records it contains. View the Products table in Datasheet view, and review its fields and records.
   e. View each table in Design view. Note the number of fields in each table and the data type assigned to each.
   f. Close the Suppliers table.

2. **Sort records in a table.**
   a. View the Products table in Datasheet view. Close the Navigation Pane.
   b. Sort the table by the Puzzle Name field in ascending order. What is the product ID of the first record in the sorted list? Reverse the sort order so that the records are sorted descending by Puzzle Name. What is the product ID of the first record now?
   c. Clear all sorts, so that the records appear in their original order.
   d. Sort the table by the Units Sold field in descending order. What is the Puzzle Name of the first record? Then sort the table by the Category field in ascending order. Now what is the Puzzle Name for the top record in the sorted list?
   e. Select the first Puzzle ID value (11242), then type your name. Save your changes to the Products table. If your instructor asks you to provide a screen shot of your sort results, follow the instructions in the yellow box on page 248.

Skills Review (continued)

3. Filter records in a table.

a. Apply a filter to the Products table to show only records that contain the field value **Cityscapes** in the Category field. How many records are displayed with the filter applied? What is the Puzzle Name of the first record?

b. Remove the filter using a button on the Home tab.

c. Apply a Number filter to show only records with values greater than 17500 in the Units Sold field. How many records are displayed with the filter applied? What is the Puzzle Name for the last record?

d. Save your changes. If your instructor asks you to provide a screen shot of your sort results, follow the instructions in the yellow box on page 248. Remove the filter, then save your changes.

4. Create a query using the Query Wizard.

a. Close the Products table, then open the Navigation Pane. Create a new query using the Simple Query Wizard.

b. Base the query on the Products table, and include the Puzzle Name, Target Age Group, and Units Sold fields in the query.

c. Name the query **Puzzles by Target Age Group**, then finish the Wizard and view the query results in Datasheet view.

d. Sort the query in ascending order by the Target Age Group field.

e. Save your changes.

5. Modify a query in Design view.

a. View the Puzzles by Target Age Group query in Design view.

b. Add the Category field to the query design grid.

c. Set the sort order to **Descending** for the Units Sold field.

d. Use the query design grid to enter the criteria **Nature** for the Category field.

e. View the query results in Datasheet view. Use the Save Object As command on the File tab to save the modified query as **Nature Units Sold**. Compare your datasheet to Figure K-25.

f. Close the Nature Units Sold query.

6. Relate two tables.

a. Open the Relationships window.

b. Add the Products table to the Relationships window, then add the Suppliers table to the Relationships window. Close the Show Tables dialog box.

c. Drag the Supplier ID field from the Suppliers table to the Supplier ID field in the Products table.

d. Specify to enforce referential integrity, then create the relationship.

e. View the tables in the Relationships window, and make sure there is a one-to-many relationship set between the Supplier ID fields.

f. Save your changes, then close the Relationships window.

FIGURE K-25

Puzzle Name	Target Age Group	Units Sold	Category
Volcano	8 and up	38765	Nature
Tornado	8 and up	26543	Nature
Grand Canyon	8 and up	15436	Nature
Sunset	8 and up	15436	Nature
Palm Trees	8 and up	13453	Nature
Rain Forest	8 and up	12975	Nature
Lake	8 and up	12098	Nature
Beach	8 and up	10234	Nature

7. Create a query using two tables.

a. Create a new query in Query Design view.

b. Use the Show Table dialog box to add the Suppliers table and the Products table to the upper pane of the query design window. Close the Show Table dialog box.

c. Notice the relationship line between the Suppliers table and the Products table.

d. Add the Puzzle Name and Units Sold fields from the Products table to the query design grid.

e. Add the Supplier Name and Contact Email fields from the Suppliers table to the query design grid.

f. In the Criteria cell for the Units Sold field, enter an operator and value that will return records with values greater than 20,000.

Skills Review (continued)

g. Set the Units Sold sort order to Descending.

h. View the query results in Datasheet view. Type your name in the first cell in the Puzzle Name field. Save the query as **Top Puzzles by Supplier**.

i. Compare your datasheet to Figure K-26. Close the query.

8. Add a calculated field to a table.

a. Open the Products table in Datasheet view, then close the Navigation Pane.

b. Add a calculated field to the table with the Currency data type.

c. In the Expression Builder dialog box, enter an expression that multiplies the Net Price field by the Units Sold field. (*Hint*: The multiplication operator is *.) Click OK to close the Expression Builder dialog box.

FIGURE K-26

Puzzle Name	Units Sold	Supplier Name	Contact Email
Your Name	78976	Morales Paper	esme@planktonps.com
Saturn	78654	Choy Paper Products	linyau@choypaperproducts.com
Satellites	76456	Choy Paper Products	linyau@choypaperproducts.com
Truck	54667	Lee Industries	imoi@leeindustries.com
Cow	45876	Lee Industries	imoi@leeindustries.com
Volcano	38765	Lee Industries	imoi@leeindustries.com
Pizza	32765	Lee Industries	imoi@leeindustries.com
Fire Truck	28987	Lee Industries	imoi@leeindustries.com
Mona Lisa	28654	Korea Paper Traders	nancy@kpt.com
Boston	28377	Morales Paper	esme@planktonps.com
Airplane	27876	Lee Industries	imoi@leeindustries.com
Tornado	26543	Lee Industries	imoi@leeindustries.com
London	25654	Morales Paper	esme@planktonps.com
Chocolates	23667	Choy Paper Products	linyau@choypaperproducts.com
The Scream	20988	Korea Paper Traders	nancy@kpt.com

d. Enter the field name Total Revenue for the new field. Increase the width of the column so that the entire field name is visible.

e. Save your changes, close the Products table, then close the database. Exit Access. Submit your completed database to your instructor.

Independent Challenge 1

You work for Jorge Suarez, the director of the Bay Town Sports Camp. He recently hired you to help manage information about his campers and coaches. Applications for camp have just started coming in for the summer session. Jorge has created a database to manage the data about each counselor and camper. He wants you to answer some questions about the campers and counselors so that he can make appropriate plans for the summer session.

a. Start Access, then open the Data File **K-3.accdb** from the drive and folder where you store your Data Files. Enable the content in the database. Save the database as **K-Bay Town Sports Camp**, and enable the content. Open each table in the database, and review the fields and records of each.

b. View the Counselors table in Datasheet view. Replace **Johnson** in the Counselor Last Name field with your last name. Replace **Lamont** in the counselor First Name field with your first name. Save and close the Counselors table.

c. View the Campers table in Datasheet view, then sort the table by the Age field in ascending order. Then sort the Campers table in ascending order by Counselor ID.

d. Apply a filter to the Campers table so that only the campers for Counselor ID CO-110 are displayed. Apply a second filter to show only the campers who are 11 and under. (*Hint*: Use an appropriate number filter.) If your instructor asks you to provide a screen shot of your results, follow the instructions in the yellow box on page 248. Save your changes. Close the Campers table.

e. Create a simple query using the Query Wizard. Base the query on the Campers table, and include the fields Camper First Name, Camper Last Name, and Age. Name the query **Campers Query**. In Datasheet view, sort the query results in ascending order by the Camper Last Name field, and then by Age. Replace the first name of the first camper with your name. Save your changes.

Independent Challenge 1 (continued)

f. Open the Campers Query in Design view. Add the Counselor ID field to the query. Add appropriate criteria to one of the Sort cells in the query design grid specifying to show only the records containing 110 in the Counselor ID field. View the query results in Datasheet view, then save the modified query as **CO-110 Campers**. Close the query.

g. Open the Relationships window, then add the Counselors table and the Campers table to the window.

h. Drag the Counselor ID field from the Counselors table to the Counselors ID field in the Campers table. In the Edit Relationships dialog box, specify to enforce referential integrity, then create the relationship.

i. Save the layout of the relationship, then close the Relationships window.

j. Create a new query in Query Design view. Add the Counselors table and the Campers table to the grid. Use the appropriate tables to add the following fields to the query design grid in this order: Camper First Name, Camper Last Name, Age, Counselor First Name, Counselor Last Name, and Sport.

k. Set the sort order for the Age field to Ascending. Set the criteria for the Sport field to **Soccer**.

l. Save the query as **Soccer Campers**. View the query results in Datasheet view, then close the Soccer Campers query.

Advanced Challenge Exercise

- Create a new table, and save it as **Sports**. Change the ID field name to **Sport**, and apply the Text data type to it. Add a second field named **Cost**, then apply the Currency data type to it.
- Enter five records into the table using the following information:

Sport	Cost
Baseball	$275
Gymnastics	$250
Soccer	$350
Tennis	$300
Volleyball	$250

- Close the table. Open the Relationships window, then set up a one-to-many relationship with the Sport field in the Sports table to the Sport field in the Counselors table. (Hint: Add the Sports table to the Relationships window. Drag the tables in the Relationships window so that the Sports table appears to the left of the Counselors table.) Specify to enforce referential integrity. Save the layout of the relationship, then close the Relationships window.
- Create a new query in Query Design view. Show the Sports, Counselors, and Campers tables (in that order). Add the Sport, Camper First Name, Camper Last Name, and Cost fields to the query design grid.
- Save the query as **Camper Payments Due**. View the query results in Datasheet view, then close the query.

m. Close the database, then exit Access. Submit your completed database to your instructor.

Independent Challenge 2

You manage the Fiesta Dance Studios. You have created an Access database to manage information about your classes and your students. In preparation for upcoming classes, you want to filter and query the data.

a. Start Access, then open the Data File **K-4.accdb** from the drive and folder where you store your Data Files. Enable the content in the database. Save the database as **K-Fiesta Dance Studio**.

b. Open the Students table in Datasheet view, then filter the data to show students who are signed up to take the class with Class Code 2014. Sort the filtered results in alphabetical order by the Last field. Type your name in the Data Entered By field for the first filtered record, then save your changes. If your instructor asks you to provide a screen shot of your results, follow the instructions in the yellow box on page 248. Remove the filter, then close the table.

c. Use the Relationships window to create a one-to-many relationship from the Classes table to the Students table using the Class Code field. Specify to enforce referential integrity in the Edit Relationships dialog box. Save the relationship, then close the Relationships window.

d. Open the Classes table. Add a calculated field to the table that has the Currency data type. Build an expression for this new field that multiplies the Sessions field by the Fee Per Class field. Name the field **Total Cost**.

e. Create a new query in Query Design view. Use the Show Table dialog box to open both the Classes table field list and the Students table field list. Close the Show Table dialog box.

f. Add the following fields to the query design grid: First, Last, Class Name, Start Date, Instructor Last Name, and Total Cost.

g. Set the sort order to Ascending for the Class Name field. Use the Save Object As command on the File tab to save the query with the name **Students Class List**. View the query in Datasheet view.

h. Return to Design view, then set the criteria for the Class Name field as **Tango**. Set the sort order to Ascending for the Last field. Use the Save Object As command to save the modified query as **Tango Class List**. View the query results in Datasheet view.

i. Click the Classes table tab in Datasheet view. Select **Howard** in the Instructor Field for the Tango class, then type your name.

j. Save and close the Classes table. Now look at the Tango Class List query in Datasheet view, and observe the change in the Instructor Last Name field. Close the Tango Class List query.

k. View the Students Class List query in Datasheet view. Observe your name in the Instructor Last Name field for the Tango class. Close the Students Class List query.

l. Close the database, then exit Access.

Independent Challenge 3

You own a small, residential pet-care business called We Love Pets. You employ three people who make service calls to clients and care for their pets. You have created a database to help you manage information about your clients and their pets as well as your pet-care providers. You need to create a schedule for your Friday appointments that combines information from two tables in your database. You also need to create some handouts for your pet-care providers that list schedule information and service notes. You first need to relate the two tables, then you will use queries to create the schedule and handouts you need.

a. Start Access, then open the Data File **K-5.accdb** from the drive and folder where you store your Data Files. Enable the content in the database. Save the database as **K-We Love Pets** and enable the content.

b. Open each table in Design view, and review the fields and field types each contains. Note which fields are the primary key fields. Get a sense of the information that each table contains. Close both tables when you have finished reviewing them.

c. Open the Relationships window, then establish a one-to-many relationship between the Care Provider ID field in the Care Providers table and the Care Provider ID field in the Clients table. Specify to enforce referential integrity. Save the relationship, then close the Relationships window.

d. Open the Care Providers table. Replace Aglio in the Last Name field for the first record with your last name. Replace Julio in the First Name field for the first record with your first name.

e. Add a calculated field in the Care Providers table that has the Currency data type. Build an expression for this field that multiplies the Hours Per Week field by the Hourly Rate field. Name the field **Weekly Pay**. Close the Care Providers table.

f. Create a new query in Query Design view. Use the Show Table dialog box to open the field lists for the Care Providers table and the Clients table, then close the Show Table dialog box. Save the query as **My Friday Schedule**.

g. Add the following fields in the order listed to the query design grid: **Day to Visit**, **First Name**, **Last Name**, **Client Name**, **Street Address**, **Pet Name**, **Animal**, and **Visit Time**.

h. Enter **Friday** as the criteria for the Day to Visit field. Enter your first name as the criteria for the First Name field. Save your changes.

i. View the query results in Datasheet view.

j. Switch back to Query Design view, then save the query as **My Cat Visits**. Delete "Friday" in the Criteria cell for the Day to Visit field. Enter **cat** as the criteria for the Animal field. View the query in Datasheet view, then save and close the query.

k. Create a new query in Design view that pulls from both database tables and contains the following fields: Last Name, Client Name, Pet Name, Service Notes. Set the criteria for the Last Name field to **Slatsky**. Save the query as **Slatsky Weekly Service Notes**. View the query results in Datasheet view.

Advanced Challenge Exercise

- Return to Query Design view.
- In the Or cell for the Last Name field, enter **Grasso**. (*Hint*: This cell is below the Criteria cell.)
- Add the Day to Visit field, enter **Monday** in the Criteria cell, then enter **Tuesday** in the Or cell for the Day to Visit field. Set the sort order to Ascending for this field.
- Save the query as **Mon and Tues Notes for Slatsky and Grasso**. View the query results in Datasheet view, then close the query.

l. Close the database, then exit Access.

Working with Data

Real Life Independent Challenge

You can use relational databases to help you manage information in your own life. For instance, you could create a database to track your personal expenses, your assets, or your music collection. In this Real Life Independent Challenge, you create a database to help you keep track of your classes.

a. Start Access, then open the Data File **K-6.accdb** from the drive and folder where you store your Data Files. Enable the content in the database. Save the database as **K-My Class Information**.

b. Open the Classes, Professors, and Books tables in Datasheet view, review the fields that each contains, and identify the data types for each field.

c. Add appropriate records to all three of the tables using information from your classes, professors, and books. (*Note*: You may need to make up Professor ID numbers. Therefore, it is recommended that you enter your Professors' records first, then enter those made-up Professor IDs in the Classes table.) When you are done, widen columns as necessary to ensure that all field names and field values are visible onscreen. Save your changes, then close all open tables.

d. Open the Relationships window. Show the Professors table, the Classes table, and the Books table (in that order). Create a one-to-many relationship between the Professor ID field in the Professors table and the Professor ID field in the Classes table. Enforce referential integrity. Then create a one-to-many relationship between the Class ID field in the Classes table and the Class ID field in the Books table. Enforce referential integrity. Save your changes, then close the Relationships window.

e. Create a new query in Design view. Display the Professors, Classes, and Books tables (in that order) in the upper pane. Save the query as **MyBook List**.

f. Add the following fields to the query design grid in the order specified: **Book Title**, **Author**, **Class Name**, **Class Schedule**, **Professor Last Name**, **Data Entered By**. View the query results in Datasheet view, then type your name in the first Data Entered By field. Save your changes.

g. Close all open objects, then exit Access. Submit your completed database to your instructor.

Visual Workshop

Open the Data File **K-7.accdb** from the drive and folder where you store your Data Files, enable the content, then save it as **K-Teen Charity Race**. Enable the content. Create the query shown in Figure K-27 using fields from the three related tables in the database. Specify the appropriate sort order for the Biker Last Name field and the appropriate criteria for the Charity Name field. View the query in Datasheet view, then replace the sponsor name for the first record with your name. Save the query as **Red Cross Donations**. Close the database, then exit Access. Submit your completed database to your instructor.

FIGURE K-27

Charity Name	Biker Last Name	Sponsor Name	Amount
Red Cross	Estevez	Your Name	$50.00
Red Cross	Grace	Brown Hardware	$25.00
Red Cross	Homes	Franco's Body Shop	$50.00
Red Cross	Jordan	Peppy's Hot Dogs	$50.00
Red Cross	Jordan	Hogan's Flooring	$100.00
Red Cross	Jordan	Pizza Nation	$50.00
Red Cross	Perlman	Bay City Fitness	$199.00
Red Cross	Rajashekar	Gentle Optometry	$25.00
Red Cross	Turkson	Fred's Bowling Alley	$50.00
Red Cross	Turkson	Flapjack's Pancakes	$25.00
Red Cross	Watson	Waterville Surgery	$100.00
Red Cross	Williams	Simonson Coffee	$100.00
Red Cross	Wilson	Valley View Dental	$100.00
Red Cross	Wyatt	Fairways Dental	$25.00
Red Cross	Wyatt	Crystal Cleaners	$100.00
Red Cross	Wyatt	Pringle Plumbing	$100.00
Red Cross	Wyatt	Garvey's Pest Removal	$50.00

UNIT
L
Access 2010

Creating Database Reports

**Files You
Will Need:**

L-1.accdb
L-2.accdb
L-3.accdb
L-4.accdb
L-5.accdb
L-6.accdb
L-7.accdb

A **report** is a summary of database information designed specifically for printing. A report can include one or more database fields, summary information, clip art, and descriptive labels. You create reports from tables or queries in a database. In this unit, you learn how to create and modify reports that present your information clearly and attractively. Karen Rivera, the marketing director for Outdoor Designs, has asked you to create a series of reports containing information from the customer database.

OBJECTIVES

Create a report using the Report Wizard

View a report

Modify a report

Add a field to a report

Apply conditional formatting to a report

Add summary information to a report

Create mailing labels

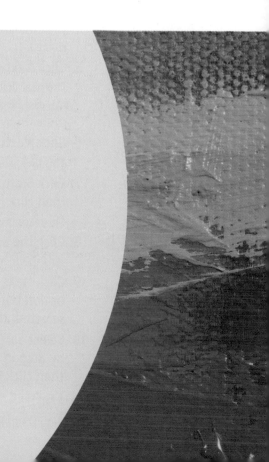

Creating a Report Using the Report Wizard

Spotting statistical trends in a large database can be difficult. For example, if a sales database contains hundreds of records, it's hard to determine average sales or total sales just by looking at the data. You can solve this problem by creating reports based on table or query data. Report data can be from one database object, such as a table, or from multiple database objects. You can create new reports quickly using the **Report Wizard**, which automatically creates a report based on settings that you specify and displays it in Print Preview. You can save reports as objects in a database, so that you can open or print them anytime. All reports are composed of sections, each of which contains specific information.  Karen asks you to create a report that shows customers for each region and year-to-date sales for each customer. You decide to use the Report Wizard to create this report.

STEPS

QUICK TIP

Another way to create a report is to use the Report tool; click the object that is the record source in the Navigation Pane, click the Create tab, then click the Report button in the Reports group.

1. **Start Access, open the Data File L-1.accdb from the drive and folder where you store your Data Files, then save the database as** L-Outdoor Designs

2. **Enable the content, click the** Create tab, **then click the** Report Wizard button **in the Reports group**

   The first dialog box of the Report Wizard opens. You use this dialog box to choose the **record source(s)**, to select the database object(s) from which a report gets its data, and to specify the fields you want to include in the report.

3. **Click the** Tables/Queries list arrow, **click** Table: Sales Reps, **click** Region **in the Available Fields list, then click the** Select Single Field button >

   The Region field now appears in the Selected Fields list.

QUICK TIP

To add a field, you can double-click it instead of clicking >.

4. **Click the** Tables/Queries list arrow, **click** Table: Customers, **double-click** Customer **in the Available Fields list, double-click** Address, **double-click** City, **double-click** State, **then double-click** YTD Orders

   The Customer, Address, City, State, and YTD Orders fields are added to the Selected Fields list, as shown in Figure L-1.

5. **Click** Next

   The next dialog box lets you organize records in the report so they are grouped by a recommended field (in this case, Region) or ungrouped. **Grouping** organizes a report by field or field values. You want to group the customers by Region, which is the current setting.

6. **Click** Next

   This dialog box lets you specify additional grouping levels in the report.

7. **Click** State, **click** >, **notice that State now appears in blue below the Region grouping, then click** Next

   The records will be grouped by State within each Region grouping. The next dialog box sets the sort order.

QUICK TIP

Clicking the Ascending button changes the button name to Descending. Clicking the Descending button changes the name back to Ascending.

8. **Click the** Sort list arrow **for the first field, then click** Customer

   This specifies to sort the records in ascending order by Customer.

9. **Click** Next, **verify that the** Stepped Layout option button **is selected, click the** Landscape option button, **verify that the** Adjust the field width so all fields fit on a page check box **is selected, then click** Next

10. **Select** Sales Reps **in the What title do you want for your report? text box, type** Customers by Region **as the report title, verify that the** Preview the report option button **is selected, then click** Finish

    The Report opens in Print Preview, as shown in Figure L-2.

Creating Database Reports

FIGURE L-1: Report Wizard dialog box

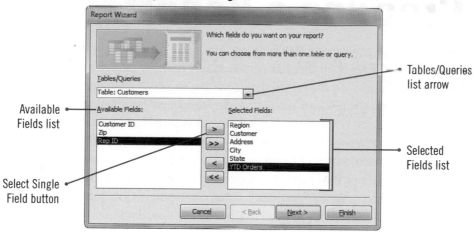

Tables/Queries list arrow

Available Fields list

Selected Fields list

Select Single Field button

FIGURE L-2: Customers by Region report in Print Preview

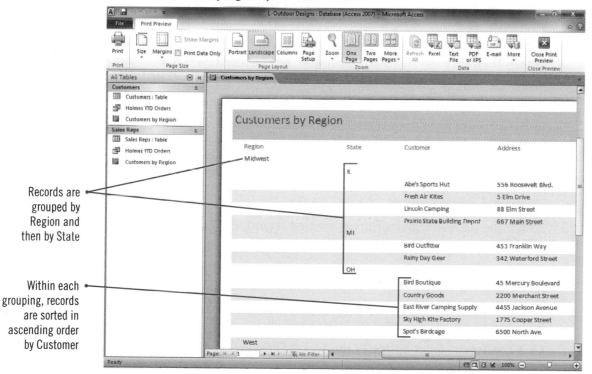

Records are grouped by Region and then by State

Within each grouping, records are sorted in ascending order by Customer

Creating Database Reports

Viewing a Report

Access offers several ways to view a report. After you create a report using the Report Wizard, the report opens in **Print Preview**, which shows you exactly how the printed report will look. In Print Preview, you can use the buttons on the record navigation bar to view each page of the report. **Report view** is the default view when you open a report from the Navigation Pane. Report view looks similar to Print Preview, except that it displays the report in a continuous flow, without page breaks. If you need to make layout changes to your report, you can use either Design view or Layout view. **Design view** includes many powerful tools for modifying a report; however, it can be a difficult view in which to work because it shows only the structure of the report, not the data contained in it. **Layout view** does not include as many modification tools as Design view, but it shows you report data as you work. Table L-1 describes the views that are available for reports. To switch views, click the View buttons on the status bar. 🖳🖳🖳 You decide to view the Customers by Region report.

STEPS

QUICK TIP

Clicking on the report when the Zoom In pointer ⊕ is active will cause the view to zoom in again.

1. **Click the Shutter Bar Close button ⪡ on the Navigation Pane, then click 🔍 anywhere on the report**

   The Zoom Out pointer 🔍 appears when you place the pointer over the report. Clicking the report when the 🔍 is active will let you see the full page. The first page of the report is now fully visible on the screen in Print Preview, as shown in Figure L-3. Notice that the title Customers by Region appears at the top in the **Report Header** section. Below the Report Header, the **Page Header** section contains all the fields you selected in the wizard. Also notice that the report is first grouped by Region and then by State in alphabetical order.

2. **Click the Next Page button ▶ three times on the navigation bar to view each page of the report, then click the First Page button ⏮ on the navigation bar**

   Notice that each page contains a **Page Footer**, which contains the date and the page number.

3. **Click the Close Print Preview button ⊠ in the Close Preview group**

   See Figure L-4. The report appears in **Design view**, which you can use to make formatting and layout changes and to modify the structure of the report. Design view does not display any records; instead, the screen displays all six sections of the report, each of which contains controls you can modify.

4. **Click the Report View button 🖼 on the status bar**

   The report appears in Report view.

5. **Select Abe (in Abe's Sports Hut) in the first record, then attempt to type Joe**

   As you can see, it is not possible to edit data in Report view. You can, however, sort and filter in Report view.

6. **Click IL in the State column, click the Selection button in the Sort & Filter group, then click Equals "IL"**

   See Figure L-5. You just applied a filter to the report specifying to show only records that have "IL" in the State field. You can remove a filter using the Toggle Filter button.

7. **Click the Toggle Filter button in the Sort & Filter group, then save your changes**

   The filter is removed, and all the records reappear.

TABLE L-1: Available report views in Access

button	view	use to
🖳	Print Preview	See exactly how your report will look when printed
🖳	Report view	View records in a report; apply a filter; copy data to the clipboard
🖳	Design view	Add or edit controls; change properties; view the underlying report structure (but not its data)
🖳	Layout view	Add or delete fields; resize, move, or delete columns while also viewing records; add grouping levels; change sort order

Creating Database Reports

FIGURE L-3: Page 1 of Customers by Region report in Print Preview

Shutter Bar Open button

Report Header section

YTD Orders field name and data is too wide to fit in column

Details section contains table data

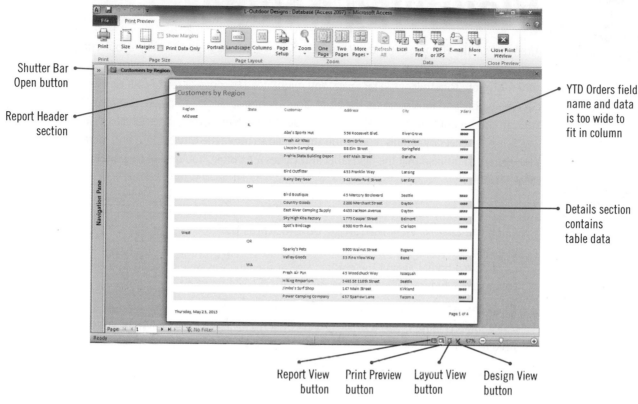

Report View button   Print Preview button   Layout View button   Design View button

FIGURE L-4: Customers by Region report in Design view

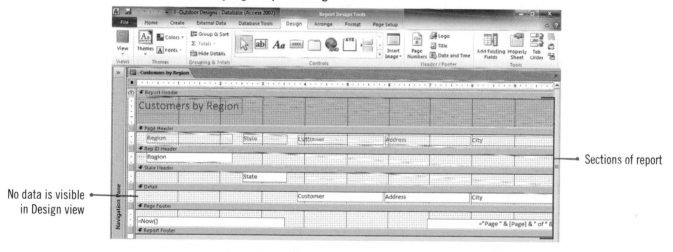

No data is visible in Design view

Sections of report

FIGURE L-5: Filtering a report in Report view

Toggle Filter button

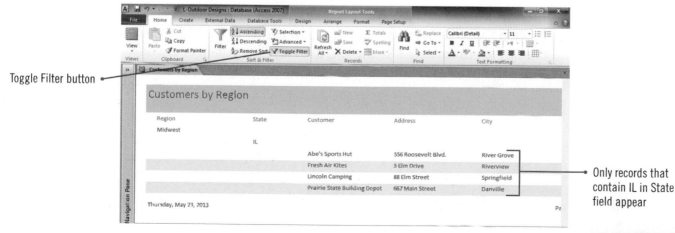

Only records that contain IL in State field appear

Modifying a Report

After you create a report using the Report Wizard, you might need to make layout changes to improve its appearance. For instance, sometimes columns are not wide enough to display field names or values, or either too close together or too far apart. You might need to move or resize columns so that all the fields and data are visible and look good on the page. You might also decide to delete columns that aren't necessary. You can use Layout view to resize, move, and delete columns.  You need to delete the Address field, which is not necessary for this report. You then need to move the City column and increase the width of the YTD Orders column so that the field label and values are visible. You decide to work in Layout view to make these changes.

STEPS

1. **Click the Layout View button ▣ on the status bar**

   The view changes to Layout view, which at first glance looks very much like Report view. However, you can see a dotted border around the outside edge of the report as well as yellow borders around the Customer column cells, indicating that they are selected.

2. **Click the Address column header, then press [Delete]**

   The Address column header is deleted. Notice that the data below the column header is still in the report; you need to select the data in a column separately from the column header.

3. **Click 556 Roosevelt Blvd. (the address in the first record)**

   Clicking the first value in a column selected the entire column of address data, as shown in Figure L-6.

4. **Press [Delete]**

   The Address data column is deleted from the report.

5. **Click the City column header, press and hold [Shift], then click River Grove (the first city below the City heading)**

   The City column header and all the data in the City column are selected. You need to move this entire column over to the left, so that it is closer to the Customer column.

6. **Position the ⬚ pointer over the City column header, drag the column approximately 1" to the left, then scroll to the top of the report if necessary**

   The City column is now 1" closer to the Customer column, as shown in Figure L-7. Next, you need to increase the width of the YTD Orders column so that the column header and all the values are visible.

7. **Scroll to the right edge of the report**

   The YTD Orders column header is only partially visible, and the field values below it appear as #### characters because the column is too narrow. You need to increase the width of the column.

8. **Click the YTD Orders column header, press and hold [Shift], then click the first instance of #### below the YTD Orders column header**

   The entire YTD Orders column is now selected.

TROUBLE
If the YTD Orders column overlaps the dotted vertical line (which represents the edge of the page) drag the YTD Orders column to the left of the dotted line.

9. **Position the ↔ pointer over the left yellow border of the YTD Orders column header, drag ↔ approximately 1" to the left, then save your changes**

   The YTD Orders column header and all the values in the column are now visible, as shown in Figure L-8.

Creating Database Reports

FIGURE L-6: Selecting a field in Layout view

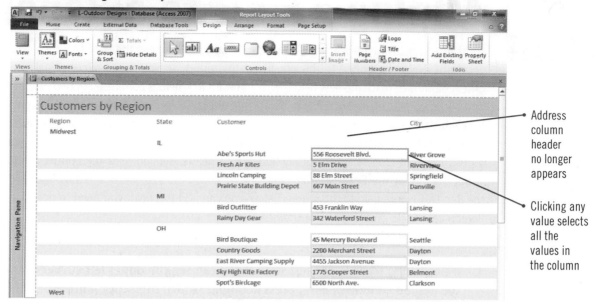

Address
column
header
no longer
appears

Clicking any
value selects
all the
values in
the column

FIGURE L-7: Report in Layout view after moving City column

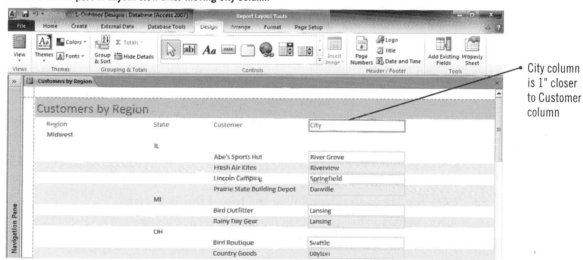

City column
is 1" closer
to Customer
column

FIGURE L-8: Repositioned and resized fields in Layout view

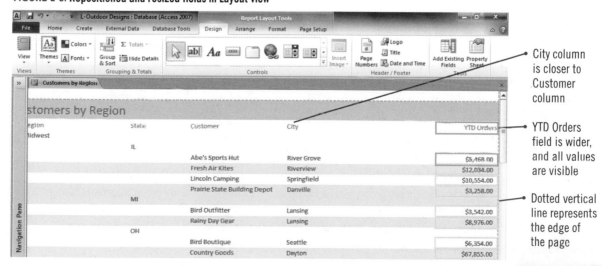

City column
is closer to
Customer
column

YTD Orders
field is wider,
and all values
are visible

Dotted vertical
line represents
the edge of
the page

Creating Database Reports

Adding a Field to a Report

You can add fields to a report in Layout view. To add a field, open the Field List, then double-click the field you want. Fields are added to the left side of the report, so you might need to make adjustments to the other columns to place the new field where you want it. A field is composed of two parts: the field label, and its associated control. A **control** is an object that displays information in a report. Different controls are used for each data type. For instance, a text box control is used to display field values that have the Text data type; a check box control is used for field values that have the Yes/No data type. When you add a field to a report, the field label is automatically added to a header section, and the control is added to either the Group Header or the Detail section. Table L-2 describes the sections of a report.  You need to add the Rep Last Name field to the report. Before you can add this field, you need to decrease the width of the Region column to create space for the new field.

STEPS

1. **If necessary, scroll to the left so that you can see the upper left corner of the report, click the Region column header, press and hold [Shift], then click Midwest**

   You selected both the Region field label and the first text box control for the Region field (which displays "Midwest"). Clicking the first text box control in the column selected all the controls in that column. So, now the Region field label and all the region names below it are selected. You can now resize the column by dragging the left border to the right to make room for the new field.

2. **Place the ↔ pointer on the left side of the Region column header, then drag it to the right about 1"**

   The Region column is now narrower. Because the text in the column is left aligned, the text is now closer to the State column. Resizing the column opened up a space on the left of the report, as shown in Figure L-9. There is now room to fit the Rep Last Name field.

3. **Click the Add Existing Fields button in the Tools group on the Report Layout Tools Design tab**

   The Field List task pane opens and displays the fields that are used in the open report. The Rep Last Name field is not shown because it is in the Sales Reps table.

4. **Click the Show all tables link at the top of the Field List**

   All the fields from the two tables in the database are now displayed in the Field List.

   QUICK TIP
   You can also drag a field from the Field List to the report.

5. **Double-click the Rep Last Name field in the Field List task pane**

   Access automatically places a new field and field control in the far left of the report. The Rep Last Name field is now the first column in the report. See Figure L-10.

6. **Click the Field List Close button ☒, then save your changes**

TABLE L-2: Report section

section	description
Report Header	Contains the report name or company logo and appears only at the top of the first page of the report
Page Header	Contains field labels and appears at the top of every page (but below the Report Header on the first page)
Group Header	Contains the chosen group field name and appears at the beginning of a group of records ("Group" is replaced by the chosen field name)
Detail	Usually contains bound controls and appears once for every record in the underlying datasheet
Group Footer	Contains the chosen group field name and appears at the end of every group of records ("Group" is replaced by the field name)
Page Footer	Usually contains the current date and page number and appears at the bottom of every page
Report Footer	Appears at the end of the last page of the report, just above the page footer

FIGURE L-9: Report after resizing the Region column

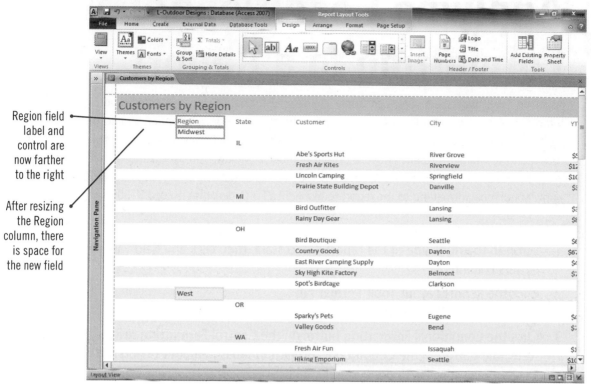

Region field label and control are now farther to the right

After resizing the Region column, there is space for the new field

FIGURE L-10: Adding the Rep Last Name field using the Field List

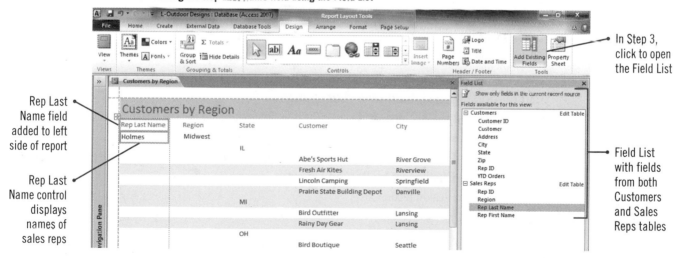

Rep Last Name field added to left side of report

Rep Last Name control displays names of sales reps

In Step 3, click to open the Field List

Field List with fields from both Customers and Sales Reps tables

Applying Conditional Formatting to a Report

As in an Excel worksheet, you can apply conditional formatting in an Access report to highlight key information. Applying conditional formatting is a great way to draw attention to information that meets specific criteria. For instance, in a report that summarizes product sales results, you could use conditional formatting to highlight results above a certain number in yellow. You access the Conditional Formatting Rules Manager dialog box from the Report Layout Tools Format tab in Layout view. ▰▰▰ You want to apply conditional formatting to the report to highlight YTD Orders that exceed $7500.

STEPS

1. **Scroll to the right side of the report if necessary, then click any field value in the YTD Orders column**

2. **Click the Report Layout Tools Format tab**

   The Report Layout Tools Format tab is now active.

3. **Click the Conditional Formatting button in the Control Formatting group, then click the New Rule button in the Conditional Formatting Rules Manager dialog box**

   The New Formatting Rule dialog box opens. It displays options for specifying one condition and setting a format, but you can click the Add button to set additional conditions and formats.

4. **Click the between list arrow, then click greater than**

5. **Press [Tab] to move to the next text box, then type 7500**

   You have set the conditions for which the conditional formatting will take effect. Now you need to specify formatting to apply if these conditions are met.

6. **Click the Bold button B, click the Font Color list arrow A▾, then click the Green square in the top row (Screen tip reads "Green")**

   Compare your screen to Figure L-11.

7. **Click OK twice**

   All values greater than 7500 in the YTD Orders column appear in green bold.

8. **Click Customers by Region in the Report header, press [F2], press [Spacebar], type (your name), press [Enter], then save your changes**

   Pressing [F2] activated Edit Mode and placed the insertion point after the last character in the Report Header. Your name, enclosed in parentheses, now appears in the report title.

QUICK TIP
If the last part of your name is cut off in the Page Header section in Print Preview, return to Layout View, click the report title, then double-click the right border of the report title resize it for best fit.

9. **Click the Print Preview button ▣ on the status bar, compare your screen to Figure L-12, then close the Customers by Region report**

   The Customers by Region report closes.

FIGURE L-11: New Formatting Rule dialog box

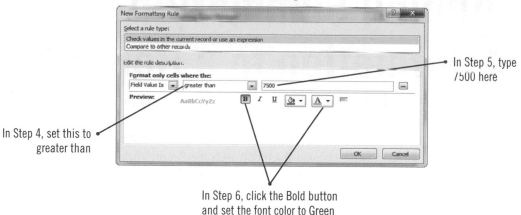

In Step 4, set this to greater than

In Step 5, type 7500 here

In Step 6, click the Bold button and set the font color to Green

FIGURE L-12: Customers by Region report with conditional formatting applied

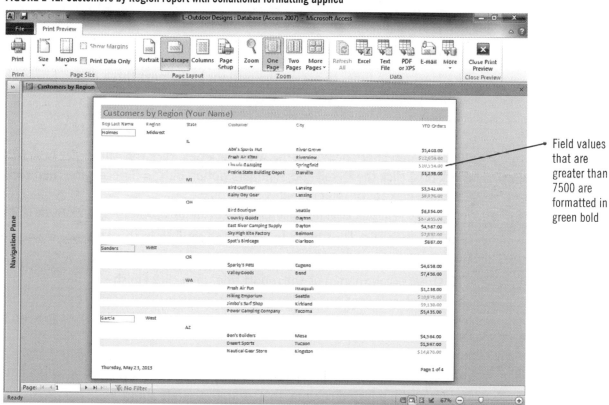

Field values that are greater than 7500 are formatted in green bold

Access 2010

Applying a theme to a report

You can instantly change the appearance of a report by applying a theme to it. To apply a theme to an open report, click the Report Layout Tools Design tab on the Ribbon, click the Themes button in the Themes group, then click the theme you want. Access includes 40 different themes.

Adding Summary Information to a Report

Summary information in a report displays statistics about one or more fields in a database. Summaries can include statistics for the sum, average, minimum, or maximum value in any numeric field. Table L-3 describes the five summary calculations you can use in your database reports. You can add summary information to a report while creating the report with the Report Wizard.  Karen has asked you to create a new report that shows customer YTD orders by state for Grace Holmes, a sales rep for the Midwest region. The record source for this report is a query that Karen created.

1. **Click the** Shutter Bar Open button ⏩ **on the Navigation Pane, click** Holmes YTD Orders **in the Navigation Pane, click the** Create tab, **then click the** Report Wizard button **in the Reports group**

   The Report Wizard dialog box opens. Query: Holmes YTD Orders appears in the Tables/Queries list box because you selected it in the Navigation Pane before starting the Report Wizard.

2. **Click the** Select All Fields button ⏩

   All the fields from the Holmes YTD Orders query now appear in the Selected Fields list in the first Report Wizard dialog box.

3. **Click** Next **three times to accept the settings in the next three dialog boxes, then click** Summary Options

   The Summary Options dialog box opens. Of the fields you selected for this report, summary options are available only for the YTD Orders field because this is the only field containing numeric values.

4. **Click the** Sum check box, **click the** Avg check box, **click the** Min check box, **click the** Max check box, **click the** Detail and Summary option button **if necessary, then click the** Calculate percent of total for sums check box

   You specified to include all of the summary values in the dialog box, as shown in Figure L-13.

5. **Click** OK, **then click** Next **twice to accept the settings in the next two dialog boxes**

6. **Select** Sales Reps **in the What title do you want for your report? text box, type** Holmes YTD Orders (your name) **as the report title, then click** Finish

   The report opens in Print Preview. Notice that #### appears in the YTD Orders column because the column is not wide enough to display the values. To fix this, you need to switch to Layout view and widen the YTD Orders column.

7. **Click the** Layout View button 🖽 **on the status bar, click any cell containing #### below the YTD Orders column header if necessary, place the ↔ pointer over the left yellow border of the selected column, then drag to the left about ½"**

   All of the field values in the YTD Orders column are now visible. Notice the summary information you specified in the Report Wizard at the bottom of the report. The #### characters appear in the column containing the summary values. You need to widen each cell that contains these #### characters.

8. **Click the first cell that contains #### at the bottom of the report, press and hold [Shift], then click each of the remaining cells containing ####**

   All the cells containing the summary values are now selected, so you can resize all the cells at once.

9. **Position the ↔ pointer over the left yellow border of any selected cell, drag approximately 1" to the left, click outside of the selected area to deselect it, compare your screen to Figure L-14, save your changes, then close the report**

FIGURE L-13: Summary Options dialog box

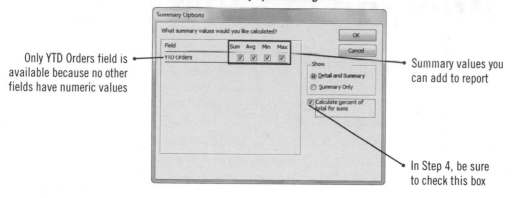

Only YTD Orders field is available because no other fields have numeric values

Summary values you can add to report

In Step 4, be sure to check this box

FIGURE L-14: Report in Layout view after widening columns

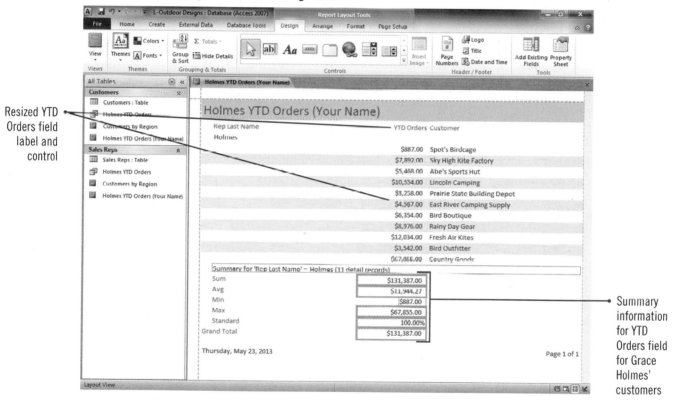

Resized YTD Orders field label and control

Summary information for YTD Orders field for Grace Holmes' customers

TABLE: L-3: Common summary calculations available in database reports

summary	statistic	calculates
SUM	Sum	Total of all values in the field
AVG	Average	Average of all values in the field
COUNT	Count	Number of records in the database
MIN	Minimum	Smallest value in the field
MAX	Maximum	Largest value in the field

Creating Mailing Labels

You don't have to print all reports on sheets of paper. You can use the data in a database to create other forms of printed output, such as labels or envelopes. Access includes a Label Wizard to help you create labels containing data from any fields in a database. As with the reports you have already created, you can create labels based on queries or tables, such as a mailing to all customers in California or all employees in the marketing department. ▃▃▃▃▃ Karen has asked you to create labels for a promotional mailing announcing some new product lines. The mailing will be sent to all Outdoor Designs customers. You decide to use the Label Wizard to create the mailing labels.

STEPS

1. **Click Customers: Table in the Navigation Pane, click the Create tab, then click the Labels button in the Reports group**

   The first dialog box of the Label Wizard opens.

2. **Click the Filter by manufacturer list arrow, click Avery if necessary, then click C2243 in the Product number list**

   This option has four labels that are each 1½" × 1½" aligned across a sheet.

3. **Click Next, click the Font name list arrow, click Arial Narrow, click the Font Size list arrow, click 10, set the Font weight to Normal, verify that the Text color is set to black, then click Next**

   In this dialog box, you choose which fields you want to include on the label and how to arrange them. You select each field from the Available Fields list in the order in which you want them on the label. You need to enter any spaces, punctuation, or hard returns using the keyboard.

4. **Click Customer, click the Select Single Field button > , press [Enter], double-click Address, press [Enter], double-click City, type , (a comma), press [Spacebar], double-click State, press [Spacebar], then double-click Zip**

   Your screen should look similar to Figure L-15.

5. **Click Next**

   In this dialog box, you specify how you want to sort the records when you print them.

QUICK TIP

You will only see the labels arranged in four columns in Print Preview. If you view the labels report in Report view or Layout view, the labels will appear in a single column.

6. **Double-click Customer, click Next, select Labels Customers in the What title do you want for your report? text box, type Customer Labels (your name) as the report name, click Finish, then click the Shutter Bar Close button ≪**

   The labels appear in Print Preview. They are sorted alphabetically by Customer. Notice that the labels are sorted going across the page in rows rather than down the page in columns.

7. **Click the Design View button ▨ on the status bar**

8. **Position the pointer over the bottom of the Page Footer bar until it changes to ✛, drag down ½", click the Label button Aa in the Controls group, click the left side of the Page Footer section, type your name, then press [Enter]**

   See Figure L-16. You added your name as a label to the Page Footer section, which will appear on every page of the report.

9. **Click the Print Preview button ▣ on the status bar, then click the report to zoom out**

   Your name now appears at the bottom of the labels in the Page Footer section. Because it is in the Page Footer section, it will appear on every page. Compare your labels with Figure L-17.

10. **Save your changes, close the L-Outdoor Designs database, then exit Access**

Creating Database Reports

FIGURE L-15: Label Wizard dialog box

FIGURE L-16: Adding a label to Page Footer section in Design view

Label button

Page Footer bar

Label control
added to Page
Footer section

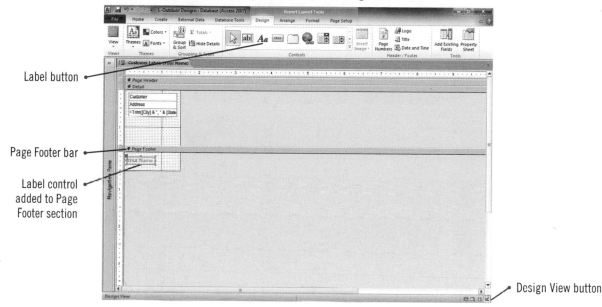

Design View button

FIGURE L-17: Customer Labels report in Print Preview

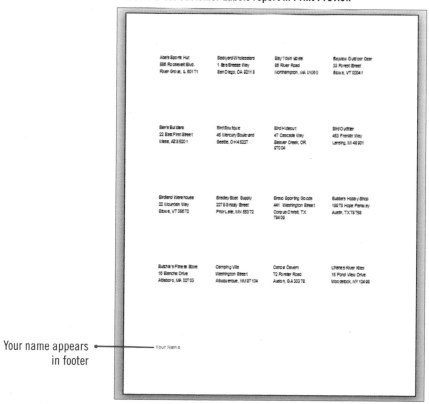

Your name appears
in footer

Creating Database Reports

Practice

Concepts Review

For current SAM information, including versions and content details, visit SAM Central (http://www.cengage.com/samcentral). If you have a SAM user profile, you may have access to hands-on instruction, practice, and assessment of the skills covered in this unit. Since various versions of SAM are supported throughout the life of this text, check with your instructor for the correct instructions and URL/Web site for accessing assignments.

Label the elements of the Access window shown in Figure L-18.

FIGURE L-18

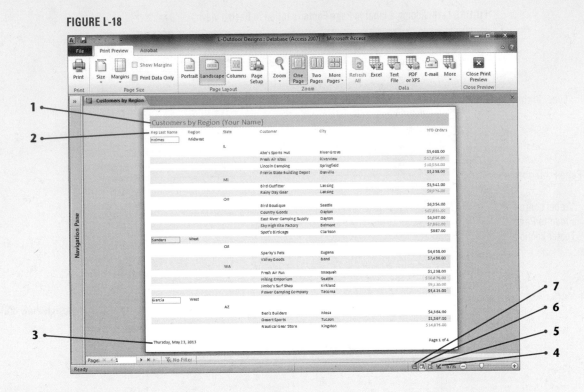

Match each view description with the correct view.

8. **Design view**
9. **Report view**
10. **Print Preview**
11. **Layout view**

a. Displays only the structure of a report and not the data in it
b. Shows records but not individual pages of a report
c. Displays a report with data and lets you make formatting changes
d. Shows the individual pages of a report

Select the best answer from the list of choices.

12. Which of the following tasks is not possible to do in Layout view?
   a. Add a field
   b. Edit a record
   c. Modify a column width
   d. Apply conditional formatting

13. Which section of a report usually contains record data?
   a. Report Header
   b. Detail
   c. Group Header
   d. Report Footer

14. In a report, a field consists of two parts: a field label and a _____.
   a. Record
   b. Control
   c. Summary option
   d. Rule

15. Summary options can be used in a report for a field that has which of the following data types?
   a. Currency
   b. Yes/No
   c. Memo
   d. Text

Skills Review

1. Create a report using the Report Wizard.
   a. Start Access, then open the database **L-2.accdb** from where you store your Data Files. Enable the content. Save the database as a new database with the name **L-Puzzle Universe.accdb**. Enable the content.
   b. Use the Report Wizard to create a new report based on the Suppliers table and the Products table. Include the Supplier Name field from the Suppliers table, and the Puzzle Name, Target Age Group, Category, and Units Sold fields from the Products table.
   c. Specify to view the data by Supplier Name, then specify to group the data by Category. Sort in ascending order by Units Sold. Select the Stepped layout and Landscape orientation.
   d. Type **Products by Suppliers** as the report title.
   e. View the report in Print Preview.

2. View a report.
   a. Close the Navigation Pane, then zoom out in Print Preview to see the full first page.
   b. Close Print Preview to view the report in Design view.
   c. View the report in Report view.
   d. Filter the report to show only records containing **Choy Paper Products** in the Supplier Name field. If your instructor asks you to provide a printout of your filtered results, follow the instructions in the yellow box on page 248. Toggle the filter.

3. Modify a report.
   a. View the report in Layout view.
   b. Increase the width of the Units Sold field so that the entire field name is visible. Delete the Target Age Group field and field values from the report.
   c. Decrease the width of the Puzzle Name column by dragging its right yellow border to the left about 1". (*Hint*: Be sure to select both the field name and a field value in the column so that you resize the entire column.)
   d. Move the Units Sold column to the right of the Puzzle Name column.
   e. Save your changes.

4. Add a field to a report.
   a. Select Supplier Name and Lee Industries so that the entire Supplier Name column and all the field values are selected.
   b. Drag the left border of the selected column to the right about an inch to make room for a new field.
   c. Display the Field List if necessary, and show all tables in the list.
   d. Add the Region field to the report. Close the Field List.
   e. Save your changes.

Skills Review (continued)

5. **Apply conditional formatting to a report.**
   a. Select one of the Units Sold values in the report, then open the Conditional Formatting Rules Manager dialog box, then create a new rule.
   b. Set the conditions as greater than 15000, then specify green bold formatting. Close the Conditional Formatting dialog boxes, then preview the report in Print Preview. Compare your report to Figure L-19.
   c. Save and close the report.

FIGURE L-19

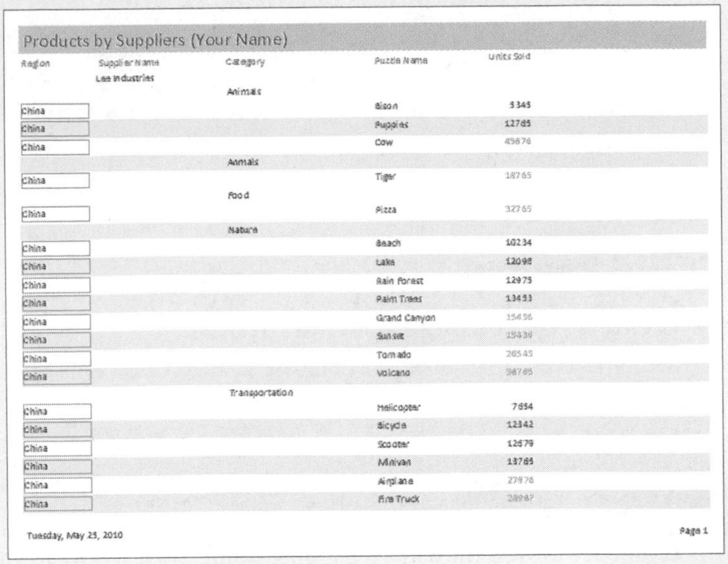

Products by Suppliers (Your Name)

Region	Supplier Name	Category	Puzzle Name	Units Sold
	Lee Industries			
		Animals		
China			Bison	5345
China			Puppies	12765
China			Cow	45876
		Animals		
China			Tiger	18765
		Food		
China			Pizza	32765
		Nature		
China			Beach	10234
China			Lake	12098
China			Rain Forest	12975
China			Palm Trees	13453
China			Grand Canyon	15456
China			Sunset	19436
China			Tornado	26545
China			Volcano	38765
		Transportation		
China			Helicopter	7654
China			Bicycle	12342
China			Scooter	12679
China			Minivan	13765
China			Airplane	27876
China			Fire Truck	28987

Tuesday, May 25, 2010 Page 1

6. **Add summary information to a report.**
   a. Use the Report Wizard to create a new report based on the Preschool Puzzles Units Sold query
   b. Select all the fields, then specify to group by Target Age Group.
   c. Open the Summary Options dialog box, then specify to add the Sum, Avg, Min, and Max summary values for the Units Sold field. Also, specify to calculate percent of total for sums.
   d. Sort in descending order by the Units Sold field, choose the Stepped layout, choose Landscape orientation, and type **Preschool Puzzles Units Sold** as the report title.
   e. Preview the report. If necessary, use Layout view to adjust the column widths of the summary information columns so that all information is visible and the page looks balanced.
   f. Add your name to the Report Header in parentheses, preview and print the report, compare your screen to Figure L-20, then save and close the report.

FIGURE L-20

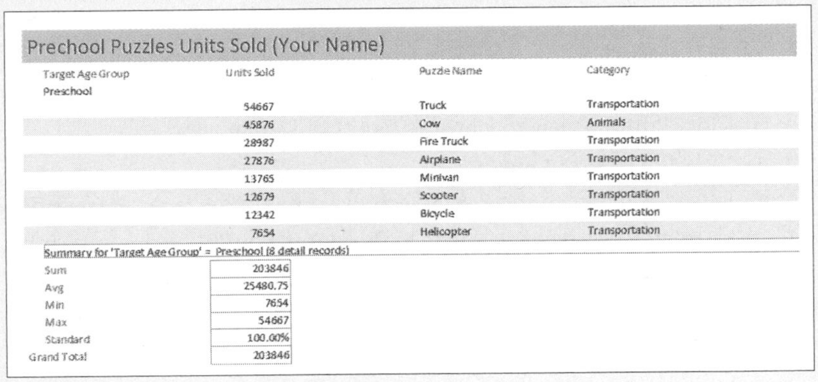

Prechool Puzzles Units Sold (Your Name)

Target Age Group	Units Sold	Puzzle Name	Category
Preschool			
	54667	Truck	Transportation
	45876	Cow	Animals
	28987	Fire Truck	Transportation
	27876	Airplane	Transportation
	13765	Minivan	Transportation
	12679	Scooter	Transportation
	12342	Bicycle	Transportation
	7654	Helicopter	Transportation
Summary for 'Target Age Group' = Preschool (8 detail records)			
Sum	203846		
Avg	25480.75		
Min	7654		
Max	54667		
Standard	100.00%		
Grand Total	203846		

7. **Create mailing labels.**
   a. Create a new report using the Label Wizard, based on the Products table.
   b. Choose Avery in the Filter by manufacturer list, choose the English option button, then choose label C2160.
   c. Choose font settings of black 10-point Arial with Italic formatting.
   d. Set up the label as shown in Figure L-21. Be sure to type the additional text shown in the figure.

FIGURE L-21

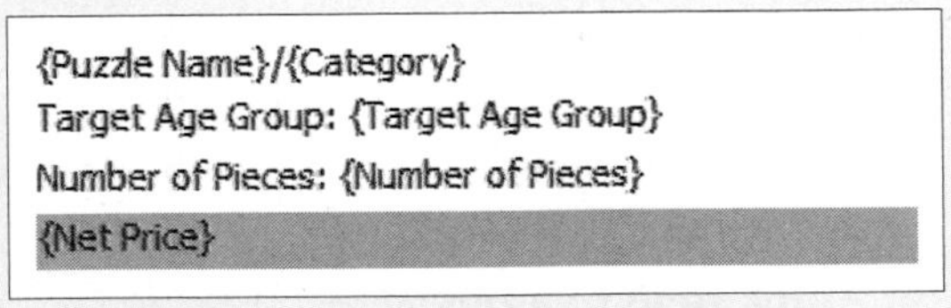

{Puzzle Name}/{Category}
Target Age Group: {Target Age Group}
Number of Pieces: {Number of Pieces}
{Net Price}

   e. Sort the records first by Category and then by Puzzle Name. Title the report **Puzzle Labels**.
   f. Preview the labels, then switch to Design view. Add your name as a label to the Page Footer section, then preview the first page of labels.
   g. Save the labels, close the report, then exit Access. Submit your completed database to your instructor.

Independent Challenge 1

You work for Jorge Suarez, the director of the Bay Town Sports Camp. Jorge wants to distribute information about this summer's campers to the camp staff. He also would like to have name labels to affix to each camper's locker. You need to create reports to provide him with the information he needs.

a. Start Access, then open the file **L-3.accdb** from where you store your Data Files. Save the database as **L-Bay Town Sports.accdb**. Enable the content.

b. Create a report using the Report Wizard based on the Counselors and Campers tables. Include the Sport and Counselor Last Name fields from the Counselors table, then include the Camper First Name, Camper Last Name, Camper ID, Age, and Phone fields from the Campers table.

c. Specify to view the data by Sport and Counselor Last Name, then specify to group the data by Age. Sort the records by Camper Last Name in ascending order. Choose the Block Layout style and Landscape orientation. Title the report **Campers By Sport**.

d. View the report in Layout view. Resize the width of the Age column by about half its original width by dragging its right edge to the left ½". (*Hint*: Select both the Age column header and an Age field value before dragging so that the entire column is resized.)

e. Delete the Camper ID field and field values. Move the Phone field and field values over to the left by 1".

f. Add your name after the report title in parentheses. Save your changes. View the report in Print Preview, then compare your finished report to Figure L-22. Close the report.

g. Create a label for all campers based on the Camper Label query. Use Avery label C2160, and choose Calibri for the font, 10 for the font size, Normal for the font weight, and black for the font color. Place the fields for the label as shown in Figure L-23. Sort the labels first by Sport, then by Camper Last Name. Save the report as **Campers Labels**, then preview it.

h. View the labels in Design view, then add your name as a label to the Page Footer section. Save your changes.

i. Preview the first page of the labels, close the Campers Labels report, then exit Access. Submit your completed database to your instructor.

FIGURE L-22

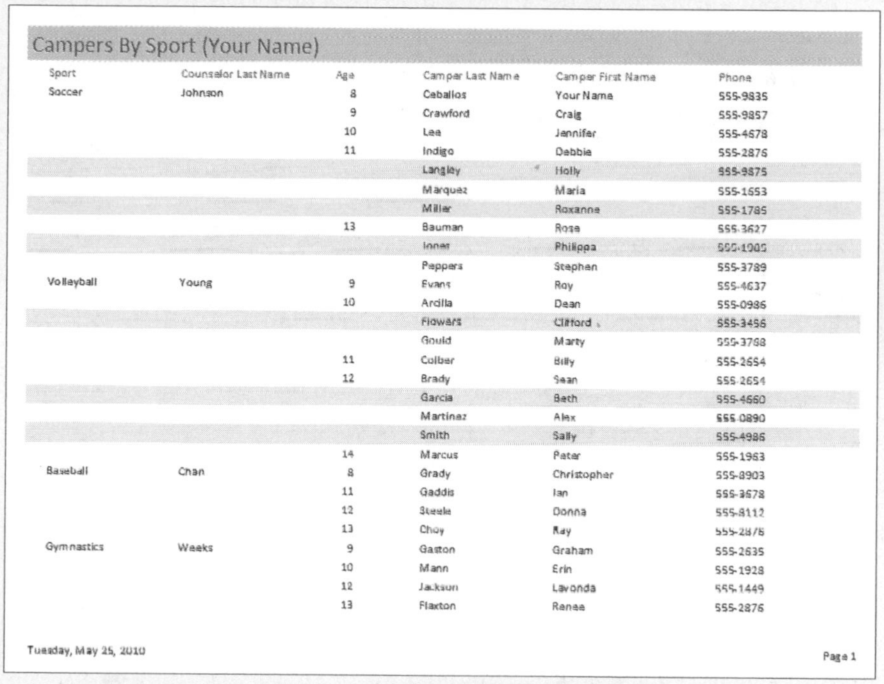

Sport	Counselor Last Name	Age	Camper Last Name	Camper First Name	Phone
Soccer	Johnson	8	Ceballos	Your Name	555-9835
		9	Crawford	Craig	555-9857
		10	Lea	Jennifer	555-4678
		11	Indigo	Debbie	555-2875
			Langley	Holly	555-9875
			Marquez	Maria	555-1653
			Miller	Roxanne	555-1785
		13	Bauman	Rose	555-3627
			Ioner	Philippa	555-1905
			Peppers	Stephen	555-3789
Volleyball	Young	9	Evans	Roy	555-4637
		10	Ardila	Dean	555-0986
			Flowers	Clifford	555-3456
			Gould	Marty	555-3768
		11	Colber	Billy	555-2654
		12	Brady	Sean	555-2654
			Garcia	Beth	555-4660
			Martinez	Alex	555-0890
			Smith	Sally	555-4986
		14	Marcus	Peter	555-1963
Baseball	Chan	8	Grady	Christopher	555-8903
		11	Gaddis	Ian	555-3678
		12	Steele	Donna	555-8112
		13	Choy	Ray	555-2876
Gymnastics	Weeks	9	Gaston	Graham	555-2635
		10	Mann	Erin	555-1928
		12	Jackson	Lavonda	555-1449
		13	Flaxton	Renee	555-2876

Campers By Sport (Your Name)

Tuesday, May 25, 2010   Page 1

FIGURE L-23

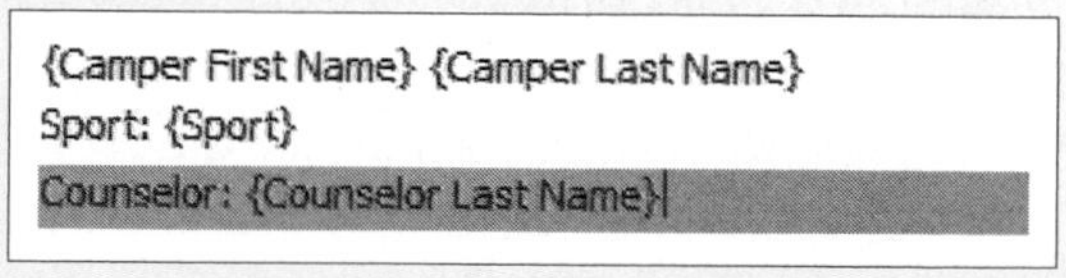

{Camper First Name} {Camper Last Name}
Sport: {Sport}
Counselor: {Counselor Last Name}

Independent Challenge 2

You manage the Fiesta Dance Studios. You recently purchased Access to track information about your students, classes, and instructors. You need to create a report that shows a listing of all your students for the upcoming classes, grouped by class. The report also needs to show the amounts due for each student. You will create this report from existing tables in the database.

a. Start Access, then open the database **L-4.accdb** from where you store your Data Files. Save the database as **L-Fiesta Dance Studio.accdb**.

b. Use the Report Wizard to create a report based on the Classes and Students tables. Include the Class Name, Instructor Last Name, and Fee Per Class fields from the Classes table, and the Last and First fields from the Students table. Specify to view the data by the Classes table, then group the fields by Class Name.

c. Sort the records by the Last field in ascending order, and choose the Stepped layout with Landscape orientation. Type **Students by Class** as the report title.

d. View the report in Layout view. Move the Fee Per Class field to the right of the Class Name field. Resize and move the Instructor Last Name column and the Class Name column as needed so that the field names and field values are all visible and the report looks balanced.

e. Add your name in parentheses to the Report Header after the title, preview the report, then close the report.

f. Create a report using the Report Wizard based on the query Class Fees Due. Include all the fields from the query in the report. Specify to view by Classes and do not specify any additional grouping levels. Sort the records by the Last field in ascending order. Set the orientation to Portrait and choose the Stepped layout. Save the report with the name **Class Fees Due (your name)**.

g. View the report in Layout view, then make column width adjustments so that all information is visible and the columns are balanced. View the report in Print Preview, then close the report.

Advanced Challenge Exercise

- Click the Students table in the Navigation Pane, then open the Create tab.
- Click the Report button in the Reports group to create a new report.
- Click the Themes button in the Themes group. Click the Essential theme to apply it to the report. (Notice that when you change the theme of this report, the theme is automatically applied to the other reports in the database.)
- Add your name in parentheses to the right of the title, save your changes, name the report **Students**, then preview and close the report.

h. Close the database. Submit your completed database to your instructor. Exit Access.

Independent Challenge 3

You own a small, residential pet-care business called We Love Pets. You have decided to initiate a Premium Customer program for any customers who purchase $500 or more of services in a calendar year. To manage this program, you decide to create a report based on the tables in your database to track customer payments, and use conditional formatting in the report to identify all customers whose purchases are equal to or greater than $500.

a. Start Access, then open the file **L-5.accdb** from where you store your Data Files. Save the database as **L-We Love Pets.accdb**. Enable the content.

b. Use the Report Wizard to create a report based on the Client YTD Payments query. Specify to include all the fields from the query in the report. In the first dialog box, after you specify the fields for the report, click Finish.

c. View the report in Layout view. Resize the Pet Name column so that the pet names in the column are aligned with the Pet Name field label.

d. Save the report with the name **Client YTD Payments**.

e. View the report in Layout view. Adjust the Client Name column width so that it is as wide as its longest field entry.

Independent Challenge 3 (continued)

f. Apply conditional formatting to the YTD Payments field. Add a new rule that formats values greater than 500 in green bold. Add a second rule that formats field values that are less than 200 in red. (*Hint*: To add a second condition, click the New Rule button in the Conditional Formatting Rules Manager dialog box, then enter the settings for the new rule.)

g. Type your name in parentheses next to the report title, then save your changes. Preview the report, then close the report.

Advanced Challenge Exercise

■ Create a new report using the Report Wizard based on the Clients table. Include only the Client Name and YTD Payment fields from the Clients table in the report. Specify no grouping levels for the report, and do not specify a sort order. Apply a layout that you like, then save the report as **Client Payments**.

■ View the report in Layout view, then click the Group & Sort button in the Grouping & Totals group on the Report Layout Tools Design tab. Click Add a group, then choose Care Provider ID from the Field List that appears. Observe the change in the report.

■ Click Add a sort in the Group, Sort, and Total pane, click Client Name in the Field List, then observe the change in the report.

■ Click one of the field values in the report, click the Totals button in the Grouping & Totals group, then click Sum. Scroll through the report and observe the sums added at the end of each grouping.

■ Type your name in parentheses in the Report Header section to the right of the Client Payments title, then save, preview, and close the report.

h. Exit Access. Submit your completed report to your instructor.

Real Life Independent Challenge

You can create reports to help you view and understand the information in any personal databases that you create. For instance, if you create a database to track your DVD collection, you could create a report that shows a listing of movies starring a particular actor or directed by a particular director. In this Real Life Independent Challenge, you will create a report that shows your class information. (*Note*: If you completed the Real Life Independent Challenge in Unit K, you can build on your completed solution from that exercise.)

a. Start Access, then open the database **L-6.accdb** from where you store your Data Files. (Or, if you completed the Real Life Independent Challenge in Unit K, you can open your completed solution from that exercise by opening the database **K-My Class Information.accdb**.) Save the database as **L-My Class Information.accdb**. Enable the content.

b. Open the Classes, Professors, and Books tables in Datasheet view. Review the fields contained in each table, and identify the field types for each. If you are using a completed solution file that you created in the Real Life Independent Challenge in Unit K, skip Step c.

c. If you did not complete the Real Life Independent Challenge in Unit K and are working with the file L-My Class Information.accdb, add appropriate records to all three of the tables using information from your classes, professors, and books. (*Note*: You will probably need to make up Instructor ID numbers. Therefore, it is recommended that you enter your Instructor records first, then enter those made-up Instructor IDs in the Classes table.) When you are done, widen columns as necessary to ensure that all field names and field values are visible on the screen. Save your changes.

d. Create a report using the Report Wizard that is based on all three tables. Include the following fields: Class Schedule, Class Name, Class Location, Professor Last Name, and Book Title. Specify to view the report by the Classes table. Specify to group by the Class Schedule field. Do not specify a sort order. Choose a layout that you like. Choose Landscape orientation. Save the report with the name **My Class Schedule (Your Name)**.

e. View the report in Layout view. Rearrange the fields so that they are in the following order: Class Schedule, Class Name, Professor Last Name, Book Title, and Class Location.

f. Adjust the widths of the columns as necessary to ensure that all information is visible and the page looks balanced.

g. Save, print, and close the report. Close all open objects, then exit Access.

Visual Workshop

Open the database **L-7.accdb** from where you store your Data Files, then save it as **L-Teen Charity Race.accdb**. Enable the content. Create the report shown in Figure L-24, based on the Charities, Bikers, and Sponsors tables. (*Hints*: In the Report wizard, choose the fields shown and specify the Stepped layout and Landscape orientation. Save the report as **Donations**. Apply a filter that displays only the records shown. Apply the Grid theme. Adjust the position of the Amount column as shown.) Preview the report in Print Preview, then close the database and exit Access.

FIGURE L-24

Donations (Your Name)

Charity Name	Biker Last Name	Amount	Sponsor Name
Save the Children			
	Hannaford	$75.00	Scooter's Bikes
	Jordan	$100.00	Brown Cow Grocer
	Plummer	$200.00	A & M Insurance
	Turkson	$100.00	Hanson Plumbing
	Watson	$100.00	Strickland Auto Body
	Watson	$100.00	Elm City Paper
	Williams	$100.00	Garden Realtors
	Williams	$50.00	County Hospital

Creating Database Reports

Creating a Presentation

Files You Will Need:

M-1.pptx
M-2.pptx
M-3.pptx

PowerPoint is a **presentation graphics program** that allows you to create dynamic **slides**, which are on-screen pages for use in a slide show. You can select from an array of templates and themes, and add such media as photographs, clip art, sound, and video. PowerPoint also contains features that convert ordinary text into stunning graphics. You can create handouts, notes, and outlines to augment the presentation and ensure its success when delivering it to an audience. Once your presentation is complete, you can show it on a computer or video projector, burn it to a CD, or publish it to a Web page. 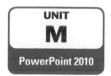 Karen Rivera, marketing director for Outdoor Designs, has asked you to create a presentation to educate the company's sales reps so that they will have strong talking points when they present this year's product line. The presentation will name each product line to better brand it to customers.

OBJECTIVES

View a presentation

Use a theme

Enter text on a slide

Format text

Add a text box

Create SmartArt

Add a header and footer

Print handouts

Viewing a Presentation

PowerPoint includes several different ways to view a presentation. When you start PowerPoint, the workspace opens by default in **Normal view** and is divided into three areas. The largest area, the Slide pane, shows the full layout of a slide. On the left side of the window, the **Slides tab** and **Outline tab** show slide thumbnails and text-only hierarchical versions of the slides, respectively, and are useful for navigating through the presentation. You use the **Notes pane** at the bottom of the window to input text relevant to a specific slide; you can use these notes as part of your audience handout or as reference notes during your presentation. You can also switch to other views. **Slide Sorter view** shows thumbnails of the entire presentation and is very useful for reordering and deleting slides. To preview a presentation, you can switch to **Slide Show view** to view the slide show as your audience will see it, or **Reading view,** to view it full screen but also see the title and status bars. PowerPoint also includes a dedicated Notes Page view, plus three master views for working with recurring elements within a presentation. ▰▰▰ Before you get started using PowerPoint, you view a presentation from an installed template to become familiar with the workspace.

STEPS

1. **Click the Start button ⊛ on the taskbar, click All Programs, click Microsoft Office, then click Microsoft PowerPoint 2010**

   The PowerPoint program window opens in Normal view with a new untitled presentation.

2. **Click the File tab, then click New**

   The templates and themes that are available on your computer or at Office.com appear in the center pane, as shown in Figure M-1. When you select a category, a larger thumbnail of the currently selected template appears in the Preview pane.

   QUICK TIP
   To resize a pane, point to a gray pane border, then when the pointer changes to ↔ or ↕, drag the pane.

3. **Click Sample templates, click Introducing PowerPoint 2010, then click the Create button in the right pane**

   The presentation opens in Normal view and is titled Presentation2, as shown in Figure M-2. **Scroll bars** in each pane allow you to move within the sections of the workspace. The **status bar** includes buttons for switching among the three most commonly used views: Normal view, Slide Sorter view, and Slide Show view.

4. **Click the Next Slide button ⮟ at the bottom of the right scroll bar**

   Slide 2 becomes the active slide. You can move to the next or previous slide by clicking the Next Slide button ⮟ and Previous Slide button ⮝, or by pressing the Up and Down arrow keys or the Page Up and Page Down keys on the keyboard.

5. **Click the Outline tab, then click anywhere in the text for Slide 4**

   The text outline form of the presentation appears in the Outline tab. Viewing a presentation in this tab makes it easy to read and organize text.

   QUICK TIP
   You can also switch views using buttons on the Presentation Views group on the View tab.

6. **Click the Slide Sorter button ▦ on the status bar**

   The view changes to Slide Sorter view, as shown in Figure M-3. The slides are arranged in rows across the window. The currently selected slide, Slide 4, is highlighted in orange. To move a slide, click and hold the pointer on the selected slide, then drag it to its new location. The presentation is divided into sections, which helps organize slides in your presentation.

   QUICK TIP
   Press [Esc] to return to the previous view at any time.

7. **Click Slide 1, then click the Slide Show button ⬚ on the status bar**

   The currently selected slide fills the screen.

8. **Press [Page Down] until you reach the end of the presentation, then click the black screen**

   The slide show advances and ends with a black screen. Clicking the black screen returns you to Slide Sorter view. You can also advance a slide show by clicking the screen, or pressing [Enter], [Spacebar], or the Down arrow key.

9. **Click the File tab, then click Close**

   The Presentation2.pptx file closes.

Creating a Presentation

FIGURE M-1: Templates and themes on the New tab

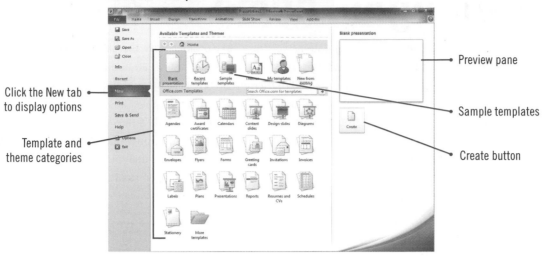

Click the New tab to display options

Template and theme categories

Preview pane

Sample templates

Create button

FIGURE M-2: Presentation open in Normal view

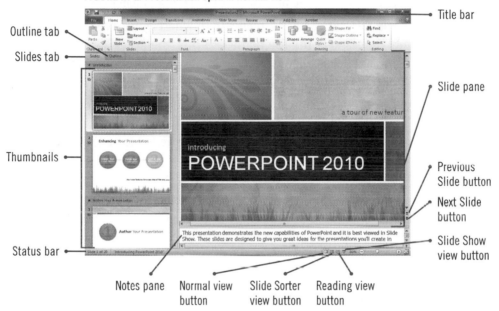

Outline tab

Slides tab

Thumbnails

Status bar

Title bar

Slide pane

Previous Slide button

Next Slide button

Slide Show view button

Notes pane   Normal view button   Slide Sorter view button   Reading view button

FIGURE M-3: Viewing a presentation in Slide Sorter view

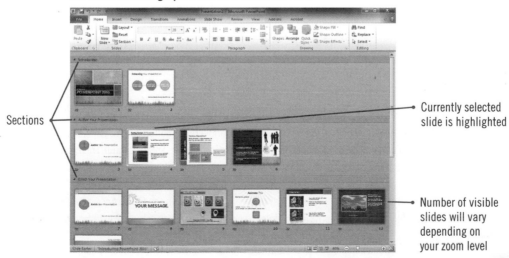

Sections

Currently selected slide is highlighted

Number of visible slides will vary depending on your zoom level

Creating a Presentation

Using a Theme

When you create a new presentation, you need to consider how the slide show will help convey your message. Even the most interesting subject matter can be lost on an audience if the visual presentation is monotonous or overpowering. PowerPoint themes can give a distinctive look to the text, bullets, background colors, and graphics in a presentation. Using a theme is a big time-saver and immediately adds a professional touch to any presentation. You can apply a theme when you create a new presentation, apply it to all slides or just the current slide, and/or change the theme after creating one. It is also easy to customize themes by changing the background, colors, or fonts, giving you a great deal of flexibility while developing your presentation. ▓▓▓▓ You are ready to create the presentation Karen requested, and you begin by selecting a theme and changing its background style.

STEPS

QUICK TIP
You can double-click a theme thumbnail to create a presentation.

1. **Click the File tab, click New, then click Themes**
   Installed themes appear in the center pane.

2. **Scroll down, click the Pushpin theme, then click the Create button**
   The Pushpin theme is applied to the new presentation, as shown in Figure M-4.

QUICK TIP
You can also add commands to the Quick Access toolbar to create, open, or save a presentation, among other commands.

3. **Click the File tab, click Save As, navigate to where you store your Data Files, type M-Product Branding in the File name text box, then click Save**
   The Save As dialog box closes and the presentation is saved to the designated location. Although you like the Pushpin theme, you want a more subtle look for the presentation.

4. **Click the Design tab, then click the More button ⊽ in the Themes group**
   Theme thumbnails appear in the **Themes gallery**, as shown in Figure M-5. Here you can find themes used in the open presentation, any custom themes you have created, and all built-in themes on this computer. At the bottom of the gallery, you can click commands to update your themes from the Microsoft Web site, browse your computer for additional themes, or save a customized theme.

QUICK TIP
Design themes are listed in alphabetical order within each category.

5. **Point to each theme in the Built-In category, then click the Hardcover theme**
   The Hardcover theme is applied to the slides, as shown in Figure M-6. When you point to a theme, its name appears in a ScreenTip, a live preview of the theme appears in the Slide pane, and options for modifying the theme appear on the Ribbon.

6. **Click the Background Styles button in the Background group, point to a few styles and note the change in the slide, click the main slide in the Slide pane, then click the Save button 🖫 on the Quick Access toolbar**
   The Background Styles gallery closes and PowerPoint saves the changes to the presentation.

Using Themes gallery options

Clicking a thumbnail in the Themes gallery applies it to every slide in a presentation. You can choose additional options for applying a theme by right-clicking a thumbnail in the gallery to open a shortcut menu of options. Apply to All Slides applies the theme to every slide in the presentation (the default). Apply to Selected Slides applies the theme to the slides you choose, which allows you to have multiple themes in a presentation. Of course, having too many themes in a single presentation can be visually overwhelming and diminish their effectiveness. Set As Default Theme applies the selected theme to all new presentations and moves the theme to the top of the Themes gallery. Lastly, Add Gallery to Quick Access toolbar creates a link to the gallery on the Quick Access toolbar, eliminating the need to first click the Design tab on the Ribbon or the New tab in Backstage view to access themes.

FIGURE M-4: Pushpin theme applied to presentation

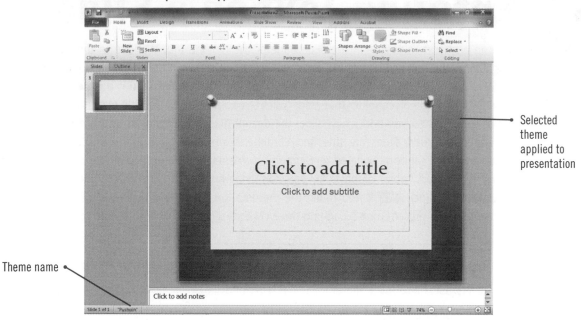

Selected
theme
applied to
presentation

Theme name

FIGURE M-5: Viewing the Themes gallery

Design tab

Your custom
themes might
differ

Additional
theme options

FIGURE M-6: Hardcover theme applied to presentation

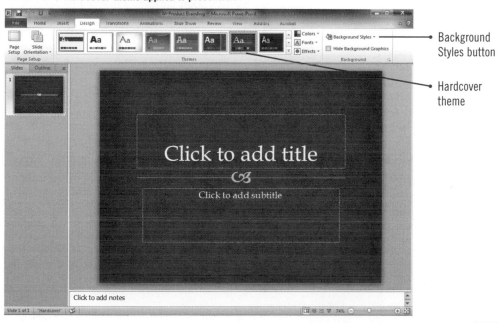

Background
Styles button

Hardcover
theme

PowerPoint 2010

Entering Text on a Slide

You can add text to a slide in the Slide pane or the Outline tab. Working in the Slide pane shows you exactly how the text will look on the slide, while Outline view can be useful when you have a lot of text to edit and rearrange. When you create a new presentation, the first slide is a **title slide**. It contains two placeholders: a title placeholder that reads 'Click to add title' and a subtitle placeholder that reads 'Click to add subtitle.' When you add a new slide, the default placeholders adjust to the new content. By default, subsequently added slides are title and content slides; they have a title placeholder and a content placeholder that supports bulleted text, graphic elements, and other media. Once you fill in a placeholder of any type—text, table, graphics, or any combination thereof—the placeholder becomes an editable **object** in the slide. You begin the presentation by adding text to the title slide. You fill in the substance of the presentation by adding three content slides and adding text to them.

STEPS

1. **Click the Home tab, then position the mouse over the title placeholder in the Slide pane**
   The pointer changes to I, indicating that it is positioned in a text placeholder.

2. **Click the title placeholder**
   A dashed-line **selection box** surrounds the title placeholder, the placeholder text is hidden, and a blinking vertical insertion point indicates where the new text will be entered, as shown in Figure M-7.

3. **Type Sustainable Lifestyle & Fun**
   The title text appears in the title font and style and automatically wraps in the title placeholder.

4. **Click the subtitle placeholder, then type Green, Healthy, and Profitable**
   The subtitle text appears in the subtitle font and style.

TROUBLE
Be sure to click the top of the New Slide button, not the arrow.

5. **Click the New Slide button in the Slides group**
   A new slide with Title and Content layout appears in the Slide pane. A **layout** is an arrangement of placeholders and formatting configured to support a particular type of content.

6. **Click the 'Click to add title' placeholder, type Recyclable Bird Houses, then click the 'Click to add text' placeholder**

QUICK TIP
Press [Tab] to create a second-level bullet indented from a first-level main bullet.

7. **Type Meet the Peeps, press [Enter], type Wings Aloft, press [Enter], then type Sky Condo**
   Each time you press [Enter], the insertion point moves to a new bulleted line, as shown in Figure M-8.

QUICK TIP
You can also press [Ctrl][M] to add a slide.

8. **Click the New Slide button, then enter the text shown below**

Title:	Bullets:
Fitness Paddling	• Dragon Kayak
	• Trident Canoe
	• Loch Ness Hybrid

9. **Click the New Slide button, enter the text shown below, then save your changes**

Title:	Bullets:
Lounge Chairs	• Sustained Relaxation
	• Kick Back
	• Tranquility Base

   Each completed slide thumbnail appears in the Slides tab, as shown in Figure M-9. The presentation has four slides total. To specify the type of slide layout you want to add, click the New Slide list arrow or click the Layout button in the Slides group.

FIGURE M-7: Entering text in a placeholder

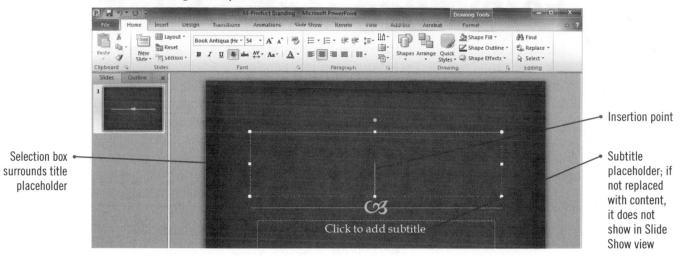

Selection box surrounds title placeholder

Insertion point

Subtitle placeholder; if not replaced with content, it does not show in Slide Show view

Click to add subtitle

FIGURE M-8: Entering bulleted text

New Slide button

Title and Content layout

Press [Enter] to create a new bulleted line

Text entered in the title placeholder

Recyclable Bird Houses

Meet the Peeps
Wings Aloft
Sky Condo

FIGURE M-9: Completed slides

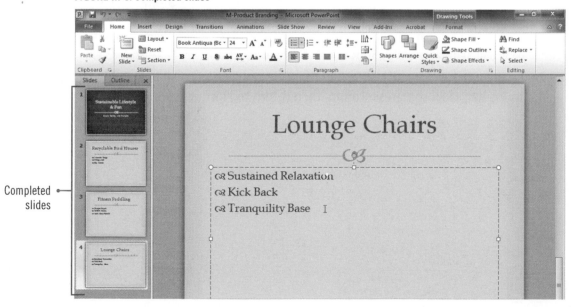

Completed slides

Lounge Chairs

Sustained Relaxation
Kick Back
Tranquility Base

Creating a Presentation

Formatting Text

You can format presentation text to emphasize specific words or phrases, or to improve the way text appears in a slide, such as by adding or deleting a line. For example, in a bulleted list, you might want to enhance one bullet point by changing its color or by increasing its font size. Formatting text in a slide is similar to formatting text in other Microsoft Office applications, particularly Word. You can use commands on the Ribbon to alter font type, size, and color; many formatting options are also available on the Mini toolbar. You can change the fonts in a presentation by using the Fonts button in the Themes group. Karen wants you to make a few changes to the text in the presentation. You will also show her the effect of changing the theme fonts in the presentation.

STEPS

> **QUICK TIP**
> To select a single word, double-click the word.

1. **Click Slide 1 in the Slides tab, then triple-click the text in the subtitle**
   The phrase "Green, Healthy, and Profitable" is selected, and the Mini toolbar is partially visible.

2. **Click the Bold button B in the Font group on the Home tab, then click a blank area of the slide**
   The text is deselected and bolded.

3. **Click just before the word and in the subtitle, then press [Enter]**
   The words "and Profitable" are centered on their own line, as shown in Figure M-10.

4. **Click Slide 2 in the Slides tab, select the letter R in "Recyclable," then click the Increase Font Size button A⁺ on the Mini toolbar twice**
   The text increases in size from 54 pt to 66 pt.

5. **Select the bulleted text, click the Font Color button list arrow A ▾ in the Font group, then click the Dark Red, Accent 1, Darker 50% effect (bottom of the fifth column from the left), as shown in Figure M-11**
   The text color changes to a shade of dark red.

6. **Move to Slide 3, increase the size of the letter F in "Fitness" twice, select the bulleted list, then click the Font Color button A ▾ in the Font group to apply the dark red color used in Step 5**

7. **Move to Slide 4, increase the size of the letter L in "Lounge" twice, select the bulleted list, then click A ▾**

8. **Click the Design tab, click the Fonts button in the Themes group, scroll down, click Urban, click a blank part of the slide, then compare your screen to Figure M-12**
   The title and bulleted fonts change to a different font style. Changing theme fonts changes all the text in a presentation instantaneously, which can be a big time-saver.

9. **Save your changes, click Slide 1 in the Slides tab, click the Slide Show button 🖵 on the status bar, view the presentation, then return to Normal view**

FIGURE M-10: Bolded and formatted subtitle text

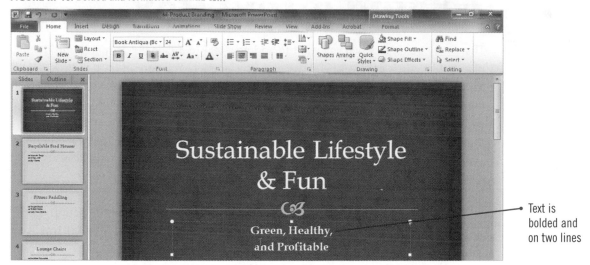

Text is bolded and on two lines

FIGURE M-11: Selecting a theme color

In Step 5, click this color

New font color applied to bulleted text

FIGURE M-12: Different theme fonts applied to presentation

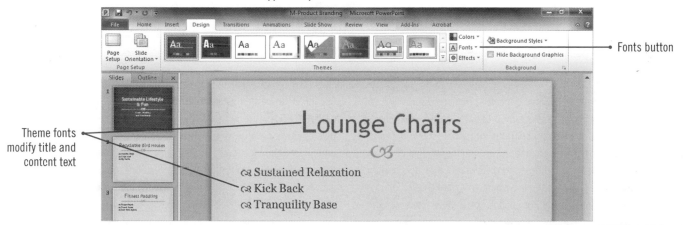

Fonts button

Theme fonts modify title and content text

Adding a Text Box

There may be times when you want to add new text to a slide but format it outside the confines of a text placeholder, such as in a label or as part of a graphic. You can add a text box, apply a style to it, and manually place it anywhere on the slide or align it to other objects on the slide. As with any object, you can modify a text box by moving, resizing, and realigning it. As in Word, PowerPoint includes Quick Styles that you can use to apply multiple formatting attributes at once. ▰▰▰▰ Karen wants you to add a slide about the Outdoor Designs' Community Partner Award and create a colorful text box that reminds sales reps to play up the award with their clients.

STEPS

1. **Click the Home tab, click the New Slide list arrow in the Slides group, click Title Only, click the 'Click to add title' placeholder, click the Decrease Font Size button A˅ in the Font group twice, then type Community Partner Award**
   The new slide has only a title text placeholder at the top.

QUICK TIP
As soon as you click a slide to create a text box, the Home tab becomes active, so you can easily apply Font and Paragraph options.

2. **Click the Insert tab, click the Text Box button in the Text group, then click the approximate center of the slide**
   A blank text box appears on the slide.

3. **Type Prepare media kit, press [Enter], then type Upload video of awards ceremony**
   The text appears in a new text box, as shown in Figure M-13.

TROUBLE
The right side of the text box may extend past the edge of the slide.

4. **Select the text, then click the Center button ≡ in the Paragraph group**
   The text is centered in the text box.

5. **Click the Font Size list arrow in the Font group, then click 28**

QUICK TIP
You can also access Quick Style shapes in the Shape Styles group on the Drawing Tools Format tab.

6. **Click the Quick Styles button in the Drawing group, then click the Colored Fill – Dark Red, Accent 1 effect (second row and second column), as shown in Figure M-14**
   This Quick Style is applied to the text box.

7. **Click the Arrange button in the Drawing group, point to Align, then click Align Center**
   The text box is center-aligned beneath the title object.

QUICK TIP
To align a single object on the slide, verify that Align to Slide has a check mark; to align objects to each other, select Align Selected Objects.

8. **Click the Arrange button, point to Align, click Distribute Vertically, click a blank area in the slide to deselect the text box, then save your changes**
   The object is distributed vertically on the slide, as shown in Figure M-15.

Using sections

Long presentations can become difficult to manage, especially if you need to find a particular slide or group of slides quickly. You can easily organize slides by inserting **sections** into a slide show. You can apply formatting, themes, animations, transitions, and other presentation enhancements to entire sections. To create a section, position the mouse pointer before the slide where you want the section to begin, in either the Slides tab or in Slide Sorter view. Next, click the Section button list arrow in the Slides group on the Home tab, then click Add Section. You can also click the Section button to rename, delete, move, collapse, or expand sections. In both the Slides tab and Slide Sorter view, you can right-click a section name to access these commands. To print only certain sections, click the File tab, click Print, click the Print All Slides list arrow, then select the sections you want to print at the bottom of the menu.

FIGURE M-13: Creating a text box

Text box; your location might differ

FIGURE M-14: Applying a Quick Style to a text box

Quick Styles button

In Step 6, click this color

Live Preview of Quick Style applied to text box

FIGURE M-15: Completed text box

Text box center-aligned and distributed vertically

Creating a custom theme

In addition to applying a predefined theme to a presentation, you can create a truly unique document theme using an existing theme, theme colors, theme fonts, and theme effects. To customize theme colors, click the Colors button in the Themes group of the Design tab, then click Create New Theme Colors. Select colors for the text, background, accent, and hyperlink boxes, then type a Colors Theme name in the Name text box. To customize theme fonts, click the Fonts button, click Create New Theme Fonts, then select a heading and body text font. To change theme effects, click the Effects

button, then click an effect. The unique names you assigned to the theme colors and theme fonts are now visible in their respective galleries. To create an overall custom theme, apply the theme and theme colors, theme fonts, and theme effects as desired. Click the More button in the Themes group, then click Save Current Theme. In the Save Current Theme dialog box, type a unique name in the File name text box, then click Save. The custom theme appears in the Themes gallery.

PowerPoint 2010

Creating SmartArt

Although regular or bulleted text can be effective in capturing a viewer's attention, there may be times when you need a more striking visual. You can convert text or transform photographs to **SmartArt** and instantly create visually rich and professional-looking diagrams. SmartArt includes dozens of layouts from which to choose, organized by category, as listed in Table M-1. For example, you can show proportional or hierarchical relationships, various processes, and directional flows. You can also include photos with the graphics. Once you create a SmartArt graphic, you can modify its style just as you can with any object. ▰▰▰▰ You want to create another slide about the Community Partner Award and decide to use SmartArt to create a diagram for the text. You also want to convert some existing text to SmartArt.

STEPS

TROUBLE
If you select the text inside an object instead of the object itself, the border of the text box will appear as a dotted line; click the border until it becomes a solid line.

1. **Select Slide 5, click the New Slide list arrow in the Slides group, click Duplicate Selected Slides, select the text box on the new slide in the Slide pane, then press [Delete]**

   A duplicate of Slide 5 is inserted, and the text box is deleted. Duplicating a slide is a quick way to reuse content. On the new slide 6, you want to use the title text but not the content placeholder.

2. **Click the Insert tab, then click the SmartArt button in the Illustrations group**

   The Choose a SmartArt Graphic dialog box opens, as shown in Figure M-16. The dialog box consists of three panes. The left pane lists the types of layouts, the middle pane shows thumbnails of each layout, and the right pane shows a preview of the layout and a description of how to use it.

QUICK TIP
To close the text pane, click the Close button; to open it, click the text pane button on the left border of the SmartArt graphic.

3. **Click Process, click each layout to preview its configuration preview and description, click Step Up Process (in the first row), then click OK**

   A blank SmartArt object with the Multidirectional layout appears in the slide, using the current slide Theme Colors, and the SmartArt Tools Design tab is active, as shown in Figure M-17. The SmartArt object also contains a text pane that you can use to enter text for the graphic. Depending on your settings, the text pane might open, or it might be closed and display only the text pane button on the left side of the object.

4. **Click the text placeholder in the selected text box, then type ID Stakeholders**

   The text automatically wraps and resizes to fit the text box. Notice that the text in the other placeholders resize as well.

5. **Click the middle text placeholder, type Spotlight Activities, click the third text placeholder, type Engage Public, then click outside of the SmartArt object to deselect it**

   The SmartArt object is complete.

QUICK TIP
You do not have to first select all the bulleted text you want to convert to SmartArt; you only need to click in the bulleted text object you want to convert.

6. **Click Slide 4, click anywhere in the bulleted text, then click the Convert to SmartArt Graphic button** 🖼️▾ **in the Paragraph group, then click More SmartArt Graphics**

   The Choose a SmartArt Graphic dialog box opens.

7. **Click List, scroll down, click the Target List layout in the third column in the second row from the bottom, then click OK**

   The Target List layout is applied to the bulleted list, and the SmartArt Tools Design tab opens.

8. **Click the More button** ▾ **in the SmartArt Styles group, click the Sunset Scene style in the 3-D section, click outside of the SmartArt object, then save your changes**

   The objects appear three-dimensional with an engraved texture, as shown in Figure M-18.

FIGURE M-16: Choose a SmartArt Graphic dialog box

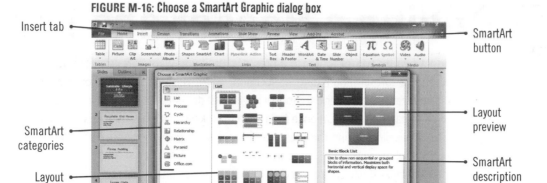

Insert tab

SmartArt button

SmartArt categories

Layout thumbnails

Layout preview

SmartArt description

FIGURE M-17: SmartArt inserted in a slide

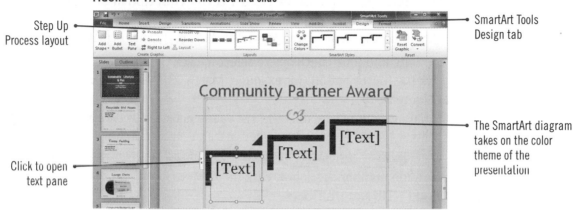

Step Up Process layout

SmartArt Tools Design tab

Click to open text pane

The SmartArt diagram takes on the color theme of the presentation

FIGURE M-18: Style applied to SmartArt

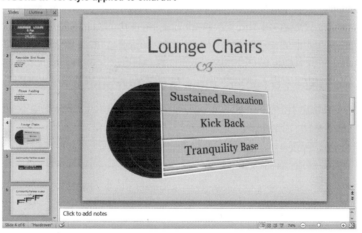

TABLE M-1: SmartArt Categories

type	use	type	use
List	Nonsequential information	Matrix	Complex relationships relating to a whole
Process	Directional flow and connections between parts of a process	Pyramid	Proportional or hierarchical relationship
Cycle	Repeating or circular processes	Picture	Highlight photos with or without text
Hierarchical	Decision tree, chain of command, and organizational chart	Office.com	Layouts downloadable online at Office.com
Relationship	Connections between two or more sets of information		

Adding a Header and Footer

You can add a header and/or footer to a presentation if you want certain information, such as the current slide number; the presentation date or location; a copyright disclaimer; or the presenter's name and company, organization, or college to appear on each slide. Because the text in headers and footers appears on every slide, it can help the audience (and presenter) keep track of and focus on the presentation. Footers appear both in the slide during the presentation and when you print notes, outlines, or handouts. Headers are only visible when you print notes and handouts. 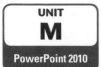 Karen wants everyone to know that this information is not yet finalized. You decide to add a header and footer to the presentation to include this and other useful information.

STEPS

1. **Click the Insert tab, then click the Header & Footer button in the Text group**

   The Header and Footer dialog box opens with the Slide tab in front. You use this tab to specify the information you want visible in the footer. The Preview box shows the location of the footer and header information.

2. **Click the Date and time check box to select it, click the Update automatically list arrow, then click the fourth option (for example, March 23, 2013), then compare your dialog box to Figure M-19**

   The date will appear in a formal date style. The Update automatically selection means that the date on the slide is dynamic and will always update to the date the presentation is opened. To select a date that is static so that it never changes, select the Fixed option and type the date you want shown on the slide.

3. **Click the Slide number check box, click the Footer check box, then in the Footer text box type DRAFT – Do Not Distribute**

4. **Verify that the Don't show on title slide check box is not selected, click Apply to All, compare your screen to Figure M-20, then press [Page Up] three times to move to the title slide**

   The dialog box closes, and the footer information is applied to each slide. Because you did not select the Don't show on title slide check box, the footer information appears on the title slide. Usually, the title slide is not numbered. You decide to customize the footer for the title slide and remove the page number.

5. **Click the Header & Footer button in the Text group**

6. **Click the Slide number check box and the Footer check box to deselect them, click Apply, then save your changes**

   Only the date appears in the title slide. Because you clicked Apply instead of Apply to All, the change affects only the title slide, as shown in Figure M-21.

Editing the slide master

Themes and templates come with default settings. However, there may be times when you want to make a design change to every slide, change the alignment or font size of text, or add a logo or other graphic to every slide. Instead of making the change manually on each slide, you can modify the slide master. Every PowerPoint presentation contains a slide master. The **Slide Master** contains the layouts, design elements, and other formatting attributes for a presentation. After you apply a theme or a template, you can customize the slide master and save it for future use. To modify the slide master, click the View tab, then click the Slide Master button in the Master Views group. On the Slide Master tab, you can select additional slide masters, insert placeholders, apply multiple themes, and change backgrounds and layouts. To create a new slide master, right-click a slide thumbnail, click Duplicate Layout, then customize the slide master as desired. To save it with a unique name, click the Rename button in the Edit Master group, then type a name.

FIGURE M-19: Header and Footer dialog box

Update automatically option button makes date dynamic

Fixed option button makes date static

Slide number check box

Footer check box

Click to exclude header and footer on title slide

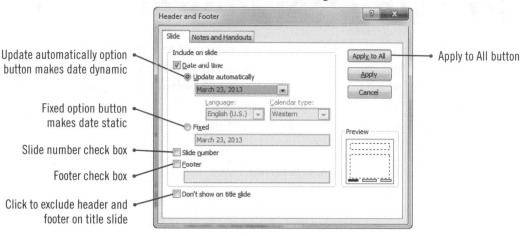

Apply to All button

FIGURE M-20: Footer text and page number applied to slides

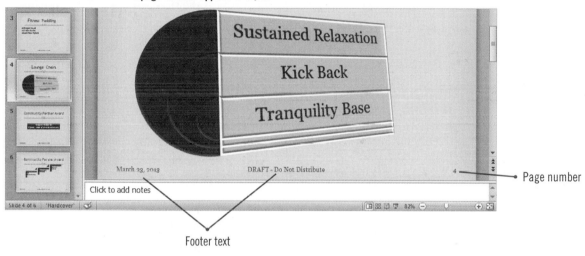

Page number

Footer text

FIGURE M-21: Footer applied to title slide only

Only the date appears in the footer

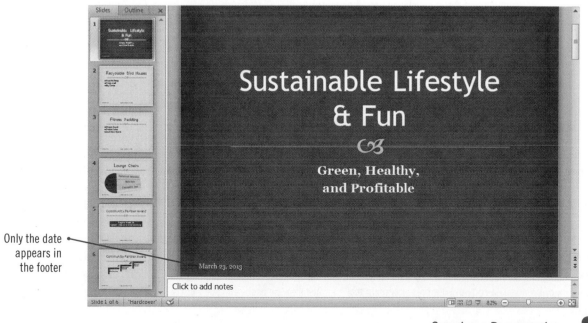

Creating a Presentation

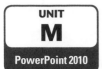
Printing Handouts

When you give a presentation, having a printed copy to which you can refer and on which your audience can take notes is helpful. You can print a few different types of supporting materials. For example, you can print the actual slides, one to a page. You can also print **handouts**, which contain one or more slides per page, and can include blank lines for audience members to use for notes. **Notes pages** contain a thumbnail of each slide plus any speaker notes you added in the Notes pane, as well as any header and footer information. Before printing any document, it is always a good idea to preview it. You have completed the draft of the slide show for Karen. Now, you want to preview the presentation, select a handout layout, add a header, and print out a handout for her to review. *Note*: Many schools limit printing in order to conserve paper. If your school restricts printing, skip Step 7.

STEPS

1. **Click the** View tab, **then click the** Handout Master button **in the Master Views group**

   The view changes to Handout Master view, where you can determine how the handouts will appear on a page and what information to include in the header or footer. The default layout for handouts appears in the window, and the Handout Master tab is active, as shown in Figure M-22. You can quickly change the page orientation, number of slides per page, headers and footers, themes, and styles using this tab. By default, only the page number and date print; header and footer information you entered for slides does not carry over to handouts.

2. **Click the** Header placeholder, **type** Karen's Review, **then click the** Close Master View button **in the Close group**

   The Handout Master layout closes.

3. **Click the** Save button 🖫 **on the Quick Access toolbar, click the** File tab, **then click** Print

4. **Click the** Full Page Slides list arrow **in the Settings section in the middle pane, compare your screen to Figure M-23, then click** 3 Slides

   The Preview pane shows three slides per page with note lines.

   > **QUICK TIP**
   > To select all, current, or a range of slides to print, click Print All Slides, then select the option you want.

5. **Click the** Next Page button ▶ **at the bottom of the Preview pane to view the next handout page, then compare your screen to Figure M-24**

   To see more or less detail in the preview, use the Zoom slider and the Zoom In ⊕ and Zoom Out ⊖ buttons in the lower-right corner of the Preview pane.

   > **QUICK TIP**
   > If you do not have a color printer selected, the preview will display in grayscale.

6. **Click the** Color list arrow **in the Settings section, then click** Grayscale

   The handouts will print shades of white and black.

7. **If your school allows printing, click the** Print button **in the Print section to print the handouts**

   > **QUICK TIP**
   > To select another printer, click the selected printer in the Printer section, then click a printer.

8. **Save your changes to the presentation, close it, then exit PowerPoint**

Sharing a presentation

The ultimate goal of creating a slide show is to have viewers watch it. To examine the many avenues PowerPoint offers for sharing a presentation, click the File tab, then click Save & Send. Here you can attach your presentation to an e-mail as a .pptx, .pdf, or .xps file, or send it as an Internet fax. Before sending an attachment, first click Info, and then optimize or compress media in the presentation to reduce its file size. To reach online users, you can either post your presentation online to Windows SkyDrive, where viewers can access it using the PowerPoint Web App, or broadcast a copy of your presentation in real time, where viewers just need a free Windows Live ID to be able to experience your presentation as you give it—just as if you were in the same room. If you want viewers to be able to watch your presentation at their convenience, record a video of your presentation in Windows Media Video (.wmv) format, playable in the Windows Media Player. Finally, you can package your presentation for a CD, in which case the presentation will play automatically. Packaging also copies the PowerPoint Viewer, so that even if the user does not have PowerPoint installed, he or she can still view the presentation.

FIGURE M-22: Viewing the Handout Master layout

Handout
Master tab

Header
placeholder

The date
prints by
default

Footer
placeholder

The page number
prints by default

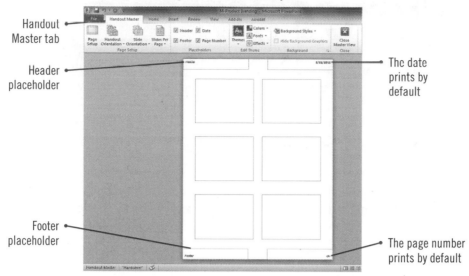

FIGURE M-23: Viewing a handout in Print Preview

Your printer will differ

Print tab

Depending on your
printer setup, your
slides will print and
preview in black and
white or color

Click to select print
layout or handouts

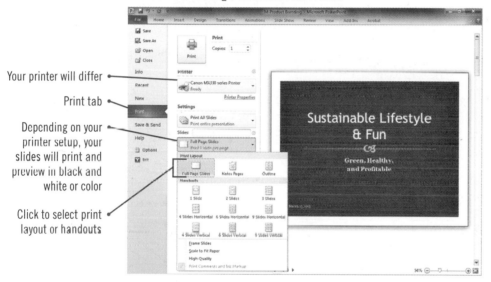

FIGURE M-24: Previewing handouts

Print button

Click to select color,
grayscale, or
black-and-white
printing

Next Page button

3 Slides layout
has note lines for
the audience to
take notes

Use zoom controls
to adjust your view

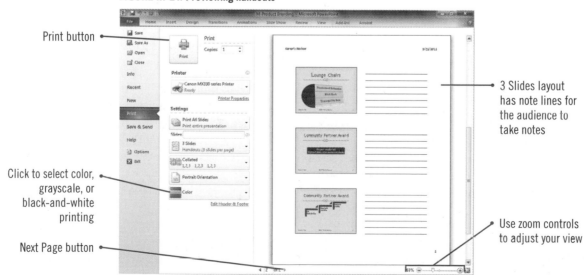

Practice

Concepts Review

Label the PowerPoint window elements shown in Figure M-25.

FIGURE M-25

Match each term with the statement that best describes it.

10. **Slide Sorter view**
11. **Placeholders**
12. **Notes pane**
13. **Themes gallery**
14. **Handout Master**

a. Allows you to choose how slide thumbnail images are displayed on a printed page
b. Contains a collection of predefined colors and styles you can apply to a presentation
c. Displays presentation slides as thumbnails, for easy rearranging of slides
d. Contains text written specifically to the audience or for the speaker's reference
e. Objects in which you can enter text or add graphics

Select the best answer from the list of choices.

15. **Which view allows you to see sections in a presentation?**
    a. Presentation view
    b. Slide Sorter view
    c. Slide Show view
    d. Slide view

16. **Which of the following is not a feature of SmartArt?**
    a. Transforms graphics to bullets
    b. Formats text in rich graphical shapes
    c. Provides diagram layouts
    d. Applies a textured style

17. **Which of the following is not true about Design themes?**
    a. You can change the background style.
    b. You can view theme thumbnails in Backstage view.
    c. You can only apply one theme to a presentation.
    d. You can print handouts that show the theme.

Skills Review

1. **View a presentation.**
   a. Start Microsoft PowerPoint, click the File tab, click New, view sample templates, then create a presentation using the Contemporary Photo Album template. (*Hint*: Search for and download the template from Office.com templates.)
   b. Move to Slide 4 using the Next Slide button.
   c. Make the Outline tab active, then move to Slide 5.
   d. View the presentation in Slide Sorter view, then click Slide 1.
   e. View the presentation in Slide Show view, then view each slide in the presentation.
   f. Return to Normal view.
   g. Close the presentation.

2. **Use a theme.**
   a. Click the File tab, click New, then click Themes.
   b. Create a new presentation using the Aspect theme.
   c. Save the presentation as **M-Telecommunicate** where you save your Data Files.
   d. Make the Design tab active, then apply the Slipstream theme to the presentation. (*Hint*: Click the More button in the Themes group.)
   e. Apply the Style 7 background style to the presentation.
   f. Save your changes.

3. **Enter text on a slide.**
   a. Type **Tech Factoids** in the title placeholder.
   b. Type **Hold the Phone & Pass the Technology** in the subtitle placeholder.
   c. Use a command on the Home tab to add a new slide.
   d. Type **19th Century Tech** in the title placeholder on the new slide.
   e. Type **Telegraph**, **Phonograph**, **Telephone**, and **Radio** on separate lines in the content placeholder.

Skills Review (continued)

f. Add Slides 3 and 4 to the presentation, and enter the following information on the slides:

Slide Title	Bullets
3 20th & 21st Century Tech	Television
	Satellite Communication
	Computer/E-mail
	Text Messaging
	Twitter

Slide Title	Bullets
4 First Messages	Telegraph: What hath God wrought?
	Telephone: Watson, come here. I need you.
	Phonograph: Mary had a little lamb
	E-mail: QWERTYUIOP
	Text message: Merry Christmas
	Tweet: just setting up my twttr

g. Save your changes.

4. **Format text.**

   a. Move to Slide 1, select the title text, then make the text italic.

   b. Move to Slide 3, select the title text, then change the font size to 40.

   c. Move to Slide 4, select the title text, then use a button on the Home tab to change the font Theme Color to the top color in the middle column (ScreenTip reads "Turquoise, Accent 2").

   d. On Slide 4, select the bulleted text, change the font size to 24, then italicize the text following each colon in the bulleted list.

   e. Use a command on the Design tab to apply the Waveform Theme Fonts to the presentation.

   f. View the slide show, return to Normal view, then save your changes.

5. **Add a text box.**

   a. Insert a new blank slide following Slide 4.

   b. Insert a text box in the approximate center of the slide, type **"I think there is a world market**, press [Enter], type **for maybe five computers."**, press [Enter], then type **Thomas Watson, President IBM, 1943**. (*Hint*: Make the "f" lowercase in "for" after you type it.)

   c. Select the first two lines of text, then change the font size to 32.

   d. Select all the text, then make it italic and right-aligned.

   e. Use a command on the Home tab to apply the Quick Style option at the top of the third column (ScreenTip reads "Colored Outline – Turquoise, Accent 2") to the text box.

   f. Use commands on the Home tab to arrange the text box with the Align Middle and Distribute Horizontally settings.

   g. Save your changes.

6. **Create SmartArt.**

   a. Insert a title slide following Slide 5, then delete the title and content placeholders.

   b. Use a command on the Insert tab to open the Choose a SmartArt Graphic dialog box, preview a few Cycle layouts, then insert a Circle Arrow Process SmartArt layout in the slide.

   c. Type **Design** in the first text placeholder, then type the following text in each text box: **Test** and **Implement**. Click the Add Shape button in the Create Graphic group, then type **Modify** in the text box.

   d. Apply the Intense Effect SmartArt style to the SmartArt shape, then increase the height of the SmartArt diagram approximately one inch. (*Hint*: To help you measure, show the ruler by clicking the View tab and then clicking the Ruler check box in the Show group.)

   e. Select Slide 2, select the bulleted text, then convert the text to Vertical Bullet List SmartArt style. (*Hint*: Look near the top of the gallery.)

   f. Select Slide 3, then repeat Step e for the bulleted text.

   g. Save your changes.

Skills Review (continued)

7. Add a header and footer.

a. Use a button in the Text group on the Insert tab to open the Header and Footer dialog box. (*Hint*: Open the Header and Footer dialog box from the Text group on the Insert tab, then make sure each option is deselected.)

b. Select the Date and time check box, then select the top option in the Update automatically date list.

c. Add a checkmark to the Slide number check box and to the Don't show on title slide check box.

d. Add a footer with your name, then click Apply to All.

e. Save your changes.

8. Print handouts.

a. Use a command on the View tab to switch to Handout Master view.

b. Click the header placeholder, then type **Brown Bag Lunch**.

c. Close Master view, click the File tab, click Print, then use a command in the Settings section to select Handouts 2 Slides.

d. Use the Previous Page button to move to the first page, then compare your Preview pane to Figure M-26.

e. Click Color, then select Pure Black and White as the Color option.

f. Print the handouts if your lab allows printing.

g. Save your changes, close the M-Telecommunicate presentation, then exit PowerPoint.

FIGURE M-26

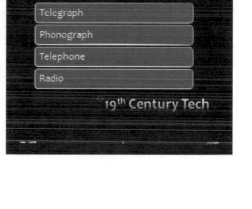

Independent Challenge 1

You are the fitness director for CoreWerks, a trendy health club and spa in the LoDo section of Denver. The club is updating its Web page, and you are responsible for briefing the Web designer and other marketing staff on the fitness classes the club offers. You will be presenting to the entire staff at a company meeting and want to encourage input from the audience.

a. Start PowerPoint, open the file M-1.pptx from the drive and folder where you store your Data Files, then save it as **M-CoreWerks**.

b. Apply the Executive theme to the presentation.

c. On Slide 1, change the subtitle font attributes to Font size 32 and Text Shadow.

d. Change the background style in the presentation to Style 11.

e. Change the font color of the title in Slide 3 to black.

f. Convert the bulleted text in Slide 3 to SmartArt and apply the Horizontal Multi-Level Hierarchy style to it. (*Hint*: Click More SmartArt Graphics in the gallery.)

g. Change the SmartArt style to Metallic Scene. (*Hint*: Click the More button in the SmartArt Styles group.)

Independent Challenge 1 (continued)

h. Insert a new slide at the end of the presentation and enter the following information:

Title	Bullets
Aerobics	Salsa
	Hip Hop
	General Dance

Advanced Challenge Exercise

- On Slide 2, move **Pilates** to the end of the list, then move Slide 6 after Slide 7, so that the Pilates slide is the last slide.
- On Slides 2 and 7, type **& Yoga** after the word **Pilates**.
- On the Indoor Cycling slide, add a new bullet after **Century Training**, press [Tab], then type **Prepare for the Old Santa Fe Trail Trek**.
- Press [Enter], press [Tab], then type **100 miles of great scenery and companionship**.

i. Add a page number to every slide except the title slide.

j. View the presentation in Slide Sorter view, then compare your screen to Figure M-27.

k. Add your name as a header to the handout, then print the presentation as handouts (nine slides per page) if your lab allows printing.

l. Save your changes, close the presentation, then exit PowerPoint.

FIGURE M-27

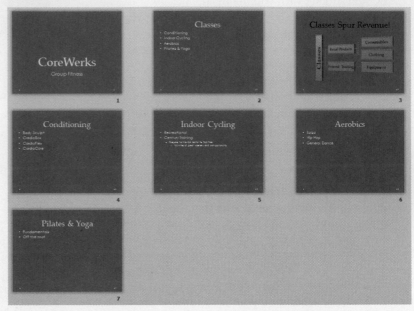

Independent Challenge 2

You are curator of the Sauce and Marinade Museum. Along with cosponsors from the food industry, you are creating a traveling exhibit on vinegars from around the world. The exhibit will also feature classes on making flavored vinegars. The first step is to provide an overview of vinegar to the design and installation staff involved in creating the exhibit. You decide to create a PowerPoint presentation to educate your staff.

a. Start PowerPoint, open the file M-2.pptx from where you store your Data Files, then save it as **M-Vinegar**.

b. Apply the theme of your choice to the presentation. Select a background style if desired.

c. Select fonts and font sizes, and apply formatting attributes to slides as desired, to add a professional touch and enhance the look and feel of the presentation. (*Hint*: Italicize foreign or unfamiliar words.)

d. Use the text in the sub-bullet in Slide 6 to create and format a text box in that slide. (*Hint*: Resize the content placeholder, create a text box, then copy and paste or type the text from the sub-bullet.)

e. Use SmartArt shapes at least twice in the presentation, either by creating from scratch or by converting existing text. (*Hint*: Add slides as desired.)

f. Insert a page number in the header or footer of the presentation, and add your name to the header of the handout.

g. Print handouts using the layout of your choice if your lab allows printing, then save your changes.

h. Close the presentation, then exit PowerPoint.

Independent Challenge 3

You are the new regional marketing director for Belongings, a niche retail chain that specializes in crafts from around the world. The previous year was a bit tumultuous for the company, with individual stores implementing their own sales strategies and policies with varying success. At the upcoming annual meeting, you want to implement company-wide best business practices. You need to create a PowerPoint presentation that centers on this theme.

a. Start PowerPoint, open the file M-3.pptx from where you store your Data Files, then save it as **M-Best Practices**.

b. Apply the Grid theme to the presentation.

c. Apply the Style 6 background style to the presentation.

d. Apply the Couture Color theme to the presentation.

e. Insert a Title Only slide after Slide 1, then type **Mission Statement** in the placeholder. (*Hint*: Click the New Slide list arrow.)

f. Insert a text box with the following text: **Build trade partnerships based on economic justice and sustainable development**.

g. Center-align the text in the text box, change the font to Courier New, then change the font size to 32.

h. Apply the Quick Style of your choice to the text box, then resize and arrange the text box so that it is aligned attractively on the slide.

i. Select Slide 7, then change the font color of the text **green** to Green and make it bold.

j. Select Slide 1, replace the text **Your Name** with your name, then make the title text bold.

k. Insert a page number and a date to each slide except the title slide, preview handouts for 2 slides.

Advanced Challenge Exercise

- Select Slide 1, then arrange the Belongings logo on the slide so that it is left-aligned.
- Select the Belongings logo, then apply a 3-D Rotation Picture Effect style of your choice to the logo. (*Hint*: On the Picture Tools Format tab, click the Picture Effects button in the Picture Styles group.)

l. View the presentation in Slide Show view.

m. Save your changes, print handouts with two slides per page if your lab allows printing, close the presentation, then exit PowerPoint.

Real Life Independent Challenge

You are organizing your upcoming family reunion. You have been collecting facts about your family's history and want to create a PowerPoint presentation that uses this information creatively. You create a presentation about your ancestors using a template that displays information in a quiz format.

a. Start PowerPoint, create a new presentation based on the installed template Quiz Show, then save it as **M-Family Quiz Show** where you store your Data Files.

b. Type your family information in the subtitle placeholder where indicated.

c. Apply a document theme, and change the background style and shape attributes as desired.

d. Modify Theme Colors, Theme Fonts, and Theme Effects in the presentation as needed.

e. Delete the content in Slide 2 and insert a text box with your own content. (*Hint*: Delete the existing placeholders.)

f. Replace the content in Slide 3 with a hierarchical SmartArt graphic.

g. Modify the content in the remaining slides so that it is appropriate for your own family. For Slides 7 and 8, view the slides in Slide Show view so that you know where to put the correct answers.

h. Insert a page number, date, and footer in the presentation.

i. Insert your name in the handout header.

j. Save your changes, then select Outline View as the print layout, and print handouts nine slides per page if your lab allows printing.

k. Save your changes, close the presentation, then exit PowerPoint.

Visual Workshop

Using the skills you learned in this unit, create and format the slide shown in Figure M-28. (*Hint*: Create a new, blank, one-slide slide show. Apply a theme with default settings, and change the background style; for the SmartArt, look in the List layouts and apply a style.) Add your name to the footer, then save the file *as* **M-Condiments We Love** to the drive and folder where you store your Data Files. Print the slide of your presentation if your lab allows printing. Save your changes, close the presentation, then exit PowerPoint.

FIGURE M-28

Condiments We Love

- Chutney
- Salsa
- Pico de gallo
- Relish
- Pickles
- Raita

Your Name

Polishing and Running a Presentation

You can enhance a PowerPoint presentation by adding media—such as shapes, clip art, photographs, sounds, and video—or by customizing the way slides appear on the screen. Adding graphics, such as images and photographs, and video to your slides illustrates your slide content. You can embed sound effects and music clips to narrate or add excitement. 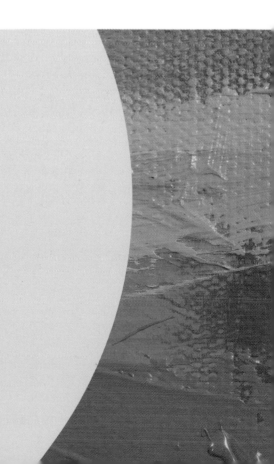 Jihong Chen, assistant sales manager, is preparing detailed background information about each kit. She believes that the sales representatives will have more success if they are familiar with the finer points of each kit. To kick off the training, she asks you to create a distinctive, attention-getting presentation for the sales reps. You begin with the birdhouse kit.

OBJECTIVES

Add a shape

Add clip art

Work with pictures

Add sound and video

Edit a video

Set slide timing and transitions

Animate slide objects

Create speaker notes

Adding a Shape

PowerPoint has dozens of built-in shapes you can use to present, highlight, or connect information, or to simply add visual interest to a slide show. Shapes have the same formatting properties as other Office objects; you can alter various attributes, such as style, fill, and so on. You can also instantly add text to a shape. Among the many ways you can align an object on a slide is to use rulers; the precise measurements allow you to insert a shape in the same location on multiple slides. 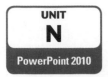 You want to add a shape to a slide in the birdhouse kit presentation to reinforce the impact of the bulleted text. You really want to augment the shape's impact, so you also change its style and fill it with a texture.

STEPS

1. **Start PowerPoint, open the file N-1.pptx from where you store your Data Files, then save it as N-Birdhouse**

2. **Move to Slide 6**

TROUBLE
If rulers are already displayed on your screen, skip Step 3.

3. **Click the View tab, then click the Ruler check box in the Show group**
   The horizontal and vertical rulers appear.

4. **Click the Insert tab, click the Shapes button in the Illustrations group, then click the Bevel shape under Basic Shapes in the Shapes palette, as shown in Figure N-1**
   You can select from a variety of shape styles, including Lines, Rectangles, Basic Shapes, Block Arrows, Equation Shapes, a Flowchart, Stars and Banners, Callouts, and Action Buttons. After you click the shape you want, the palette closes and the pointer changes to $+$ so that you can draw the shape on the slide.

5. **Position $+$ so that it aligns with the 2" mark on the right side of the horizontal ruler and the 1.5" mark at the top of the vertical ruler, then click the mouse**
   The shape is inserted in the slide. Because you clicked to add a shape, the shape is added at a default size. If you click and drag to add a shape, you can make it larger or smaller than the default size.

6. **Click the Home tab, click the Quick Styles button in the Drawing group, then click the Moderate Effect - Gray-50% - Accent 1 effect (second column of the second row from the bottom)**
   The style is applied to the shape.

7. **Click the Shape Fill button in the Drawing group, point to Texture, then click the Walnut texture (bottom of the second column) as shown in Figure N-2**
   The texture is applied to the shape.

8. **Type Build, select the text, then click the Bold button B in the Font group**
   A shape can accept text whenever it is selected in the slide. The text appears centered and bold on the shape.

9. **Click away from the shape, zoom out if necessary, compare your screen to Figure N-3, then click the Save button on the Quick Access toolbar**

Resizing graphics and images

You can modify shapes, clip art, and other images and illustrations using the Picture Tools Format contextual tab, which opens whenever a graphic is selected. To resize an image, you can adjust sizing handles of the graphic in the slide. To resize a graphic proportionally, select the image, then drag a corner sizing handle inward or outward; to resize only the height or width, drag a sizing handle on one side of the image. For additional size and position options, click the launcher in the Size group to open the Format Picture dialog box. Click Size in the category list to adjust size, scale, and crop settings. Click Position in the category list to specify where the image is located on the slide. Click Alt Text in the category list to specify the alternate text, or **Alt text**, which appears as the image loads or if the image is missing when you publish the slide show to the Web.

FIGURE N-1: Selecting a Shape

Shapes button

Ruler

Shapes palette

Shapes in your Recently Used Shapes section will differ

Bevel shape

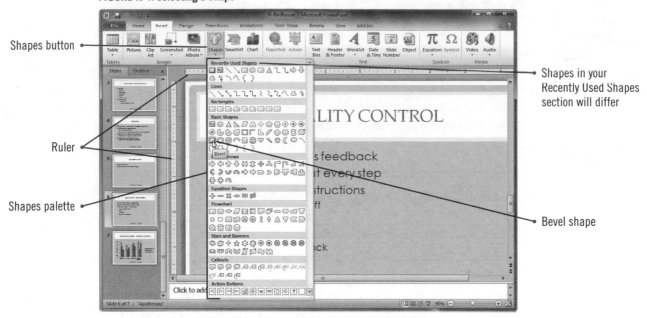

FIGURE N-2: Selecting a Shape Fill texture

In Step 7, click this texture

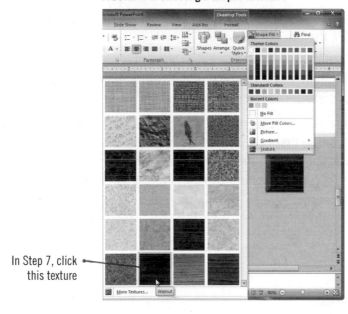

FIGURE N-3: Style, texture, and text added to shape

Shape text is centered by default

Style and texture applied to shape

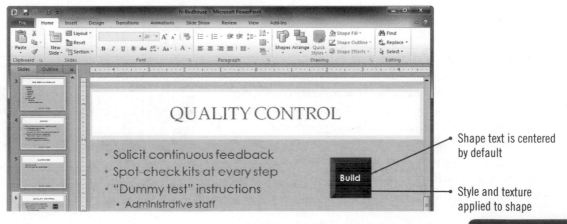

Polishing and Running a Presentation

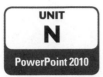
Adding Clip Art

You can insert a clip art illustration—or other media, such as photographs, videos, and audio files—anywhere in a slide using the Clip Art task pane. To open the Clip Art task pane, you can click the Clip Art icon in a content placeholder or click the Clip Art button in the Images group on the Insert tab. You can search for clip art using keywords, select the collections you want to search, and limit the search results to illustrations (clip art) only. You can also apply effects to alter the appearance of clip art. 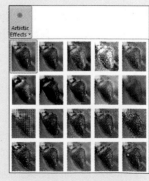 You decide to add clip art to a new slide to tie it in with the birdhouse motif, and then format the clip art to make it stand out.

STEPS

1. **Move to Slide 1, click the New Slide button in the Slides group, click the Click to add title placeholder, then type Avian Construction Crew**

   By default, a new slide includes a content placeholder with icons for inserting media.

2. **Click the Clip Art icon ▥ in the content placeholder, as shown in Figure N-5**

   The Clip Art task pane opens.

3. **Click the Search for text box, type wildlife birds, click the Results should be list arrow, deselect any other check boxes so that only the Illustrations check box is selected, click the Include Office.com content check box if necessary, then click Go**

   Thumbnail previews of bird clip art appear in the Clip Art task pane.

   TROUBLE
   If the clip art image shown in Figure N-6 is not available, click a different image.

4. **Click the Zoom Out button ⊖ on the status bar until the entire slide is visible in the Slide pane, then click the clip art shown in Figure N-6**

   The bird clip art is inserted in the slide.

5. **Click the Shape Height text box in the Size group, type 3.2, then press [Enter]**

   When you adjust the height, the width adjusts automatically to keep the image's proportions the same.

6. **Click the Picture Effects button in the Picture Styles group, point to Shadow, then click the first effect in the first row under Perspective (ScreenTip reads "Perspective Diagonal Upper Left"), as shown in Figure N-7**

   Options for Picture Effects are organized into categories for conveying realistic appearance, angle, and perspective of an image.

7. **Click the Close button on the Clip Art task pane, then save your changes**

Understanding adjustment effects

PowerPoint contains substantial graphics-editing features that give you more creative control over the appearance of your photographs and graphics. First, you must select the image to activate the Picture Tools Format tab. Features in the Adjust group allow you to highlight, contrast, or complement design elements in your presentation, although not all features are available for each file type. You do so by modifying **pixels**, the small squares of color that comprise a digital image. You can isolate an object by removing the background areas around it; sharpen or soften the edges of pixels; adjust their brightness and contrast; change their amount of saturation and hue; and apply artistic effects that emulate painting, sketching, or drawing styles. The Corrections and Artistic Effects galleries are shown in Figure N-4. Here you can view a Live Preview of the effect on the image in a slide before you apply it.

FIGURE N-4: Understanding picture adjustment features

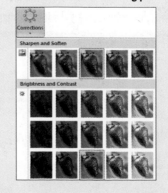

FIGURE N-5: Inserting media using the content placeholder

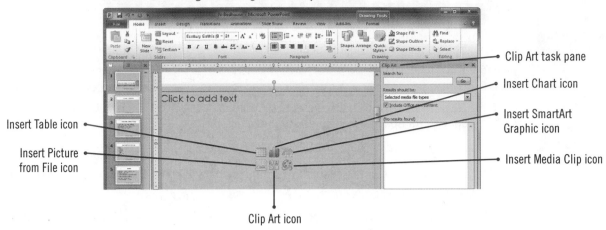

Insert Table icon

Insert Picture from File icon

Clip Art icon

Clip Art task pane

Insert Chart icon

Insert SmartArt Graphic icon

Insert Media Clip icon

FIGURE N-6: Bird clip art inserted in slide

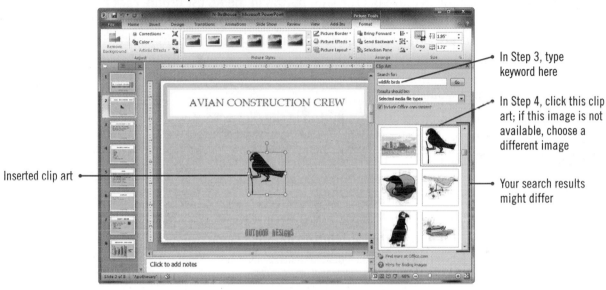

Inserted clip art

In Step 3, type keyword here

In Step 4, click this clip art; if this image is not available, choose a different image

Your search results might differ

FIGURE N-7: Viewing Live Preview effects

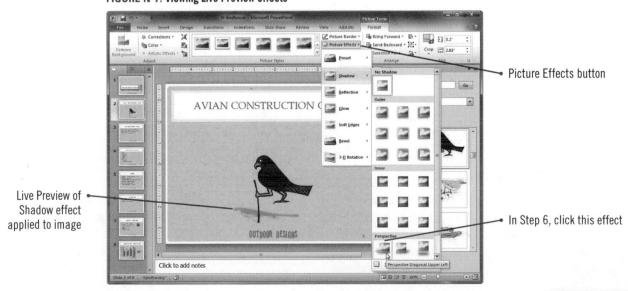

Live Preview of Shadow effect applied to image

Picture Effects button

In Step 6, click this effect

Polishing and Running a Presentation

Working with Pictures

While you may commonly think of "picture" to mean a piece of clip art or a photograph, in PowerPoint a picture can be an image created and saved in any number of file formats. You can use features on the Picture Tools Format tab to adjust the color, add effects and styles to photos, and crop portions of a picture to keep the parts you want. 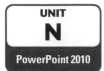 You insert a photograph in a slide and modify it using several drawing features so that it appears transparent in the slide background.

STEPS

1. **Move to** Slide 5, **click the** Insert tab, **then click the** Picture button **in the Images group**
   The Insert Picture dialog box opens.

2. **Navigate to where you store your Data Files, click** birdhouse.jpg, **then click** Insert
   A photograph of a birdhouse is inserted on top of the bulleted text, and the Picture Tools Format tab is active. The photograph obscures a considerable amount of text, so you need to modify it. You begin by deleting the image background

   > **QUICK TIP**
   > To fine-tune areas to remove or keep, use the Mark Areas to Keep, Mark Areas to Remove, or Delete Marks buttons in the Refine group.

3. **Click the** Remove Background button **in the Adjust group, click and drag an** edge **of the selection marquee over the birdhouse, then drag the** sizing handles **on the selection marquee until it surrounds the birdhouse, as shown in Figure N-8**
   The areas that will be removed are highlighted in magenta. The Remove Background feature consists of an adjustable selection marquee and tools that you can use to fine-tune the areas to keep or remove. You are satisfied with the image.

4. **Click the** Keep Changes button **in the Close group**
   The background is removed, and only the birdhouse is visible.

   > **QUICK TIP**
   > To remove parts of an image from top, bottom, or sides, click the Crop button in the Size group, then drag an edge to crop.

5. **On the** Picture Tools Format tab, **click the** Color button **in the Adjust group, then click the** Washout thumbnail **in the Recolor section, as shown in Figure N-9**
   The Washout option adjusts the **opacity**, or the opaqueness or transparency of the image. The washout effect is perfect to use as a background image; now, you move it behind the text.

6. **Click the** Send Backward button **in the Arrange group**
   The photo is in back of the bulleted items, visible but not concealing the text. You balance the slide visually by moving the photo.

   > **QUICK TIP**
   > To further optimize the images in your presentation, click the Compress Pictures button 🖼 in the Adjust group on the Ribbon.

7. **Click the** Align button 📑▾ **in the Arrange group, click** Align Right, **click away from the photo, adjust your zoom, compare your screen to Figure N-10, then save your changes**

Understanding file types

Each file format supports images differently. A **bitmap** graphic displays a picture image as a matrix of pixels on a grid. Most photographs are saved in **Joint Photographic Experts Group (JPEG)** because the format uses and compresses color so well, whereas line art such as clip art is best suited for **Graphics Interchange** **Format (GIF)**. You can insert video in common file formats such as AVI, Windows Media, MOV/QuickTime, MPEG-2, SWF (Macromedia Flash), and MPEG-4 (H.264). Animated clip art and video from Office.com is created in **Windows Metafile Format (WMF)** format.

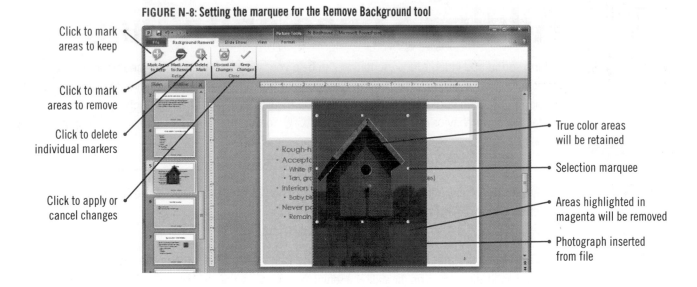

FIGURE N-8: Setting the marquee for the Remove Background tool

Click to mark areas to keep

Click to mark areas to remove

Click to delete individual markers

Click to apply or cancel changes

True color areas will be retained

Selection marquee

Areas highlighted in magenta will be removed

Photograph inserted from file

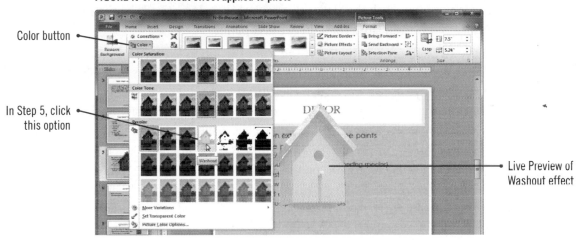

FIGURE N-9: Washout effect applied to photo

Color button

In Step 5, click this option

Live Preview of Washout effect

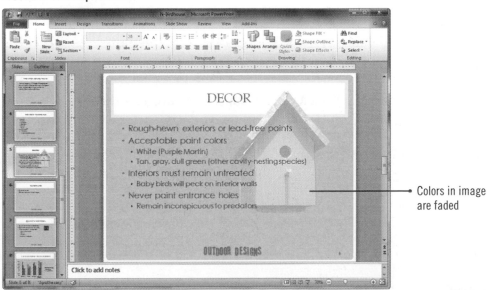

FIGURE N-10: Completed slide

Colors in image are faded

Polishing and Running a Presentation

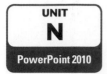
Adding Sound and Video

Adding sound and video to a presentation can help your viewers remember it—and your message. You can insert video and sound from the Clip Art task pane or from any storage device, link to a video on the Web, or record your own audio. You can use features on the Playback tab for Audio Tools or Video Tools to adjust the length and behavior of a sound or video. You decide to add a video and accompanying sound to a slide.

QUICK TIP

You can also click the Insert tab, click the Clip Art button, and then select the Audio check box in the Selected media file types list to search for audio.

1. **Move to Slide 2, click the Insert tab, click the Audio list arrow in the Media group, then click Clip Art Audio**

2. **Click the Search for text box, type parrot, then click Go**

3. **Double-click Parrot Jabber, then click the Play button ▶ on the playback controls**

   The sound clip appears on the slide as a sound icon above a set of playback controls. You can choose to hide or display the sound icon during the slide show. When inserting a sound, you can have it play automatically when the slide show advances to that slide, or have it play only when users click its icon during the slide show.

QUICK TIP

You can also select a sound on a slide and then click the Play button in the Preview group on the Audio Tool Playback tab to listen to a sound.

4. **Click the Audio Tools Playback tab, click the Hide During Show check box in the Audio Options group, click the Start list arrow, click Automatically, compare your screen to Figure N-11, then close the Clip Art task pane**

5. **Move to Slide 6, click the Insert tab, click the Video list arrow in the Media group, click Video from File, navigate to where you store your Data Files in the Insert Video dialog box, click mycloseup.wmv, then click Insert**

   The video is inserted in the slide, as shown in Figure N-12. You can preview the video using the playback controls beneath the image or by using the Play button on the Ribbon.

6. **Click the Play button in the Preview group, watch for a few seconds, press the Pause button, then click the Play button ▶ on the playback controls to watch the rest of the video**

   The video plays and then stops at the last frame. By default, when your audience views the slide show, they will need to click ▶ on the playback controls to watch the video. The size of the video image is a little large for the slide, so you resize it.

7. **Click the Height text box in the Size group, type 3, press [Enter], then drag the video to the location shown in Figure N-13**

   PowerPoint automatically resizes the video proportionately. You preview the slide show as your audience will see it.

QUICK TIP

To start the slide show with the current slide, click the Slide Show button 🖵 on the status bar or press [Shift][F5].

8. **Click the Slide Show tab, click the Slide Show From Beginning button in the Start Slide Show group, then press [Page Down] to view the slide show, making sure you click the Play button ▶ on the playback controls**

   The sound plays in Slide 2, and the movie plays when you click the playback control in Slide 6.

9. **Press [Esc] when you are done, then save your changes**

FIGURE N-11: Inserted sound clip

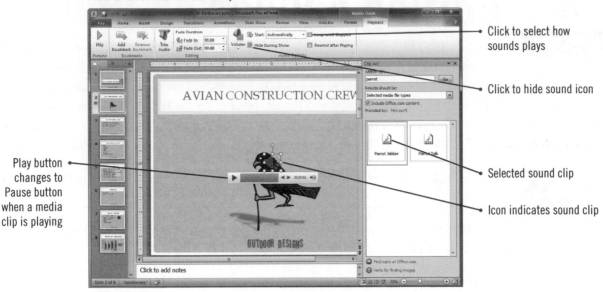

Click to select how sounds plays

Click to hide sound icon

Play button changes to Pause button when a media clip is playing

Selected sound clip

Icon indicates sound clip

FIGURE N-12: Inserting a video in a slide

Play button

Video inserted in slide

Time code

Click to move forward or back .25 seconds

Video courtesy of Fabricio Zuardi, http://fabricio.org

FIGURE N-13: Modified video

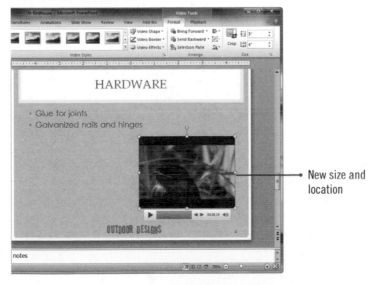

New size and location

PowerPoint 2010

Polishing and Running a Presentation

Editing a Video

You can edit a video from within PowerPoint to create the perfect visual event for your audience. You use features on the Playback tab to edit the length and appearance of an inserted video, such as whether the video fades in or out, how and when it plays or rewinds, and so on. The **Trim** feature lets you determine the video's length and its start and end frames. Features on the Format tab allow you to adjust the video's appearance. For example, you can select a **poster frame**—an image on your computer or an image created from a video frame to serve as the video's "cover," or preview image, on the slide. To have the video best match your theme, you can add styles, shapes, borders, or effects to it.  Jihong asks you to adjust the video to make it shorter and to choose a frame that displays on the slide that she can use in a flyer.

1. **Make sure the video is selected in Slide 6, click the** Video Tools Playback tab, **then click the** Trim Video button **in the Editing group**

   The Trim Video dialog box opens, as shown in Figure N-14, where you can drag the green start and red end point markers to select different frames as the beginning and end frames. The Fade In and Fade Out settings allow you to adjust how long the frames fade in and out. You move the start point marker to the point where the bird opens its eyes.

2. **Drag the** Start point marker ⌷ **approximately to the 00:01.00 mark on the timebar**

   The video will start at this point. This looks good, so you preview the movie in slide show view.

3. **Click OK, click the** Slide Show button 🖵 **on the status bar, then press [Esc]**

   The video shows the bird's eyes open. You would like a picture of the bird turning to the side to be visible when the video is not playing, so you find a good image to select as the poster frame.

4. **Click the** Video Tools Format tab, **click the** Play button ▶ **on the playback controls, then click the** Pause button ❙❙ **when the video reaches approximately the 00:05.00 mark in the time code,**

   Now that you have selected a frame, you are ready to make it the poster frame.

5. **Click the** Poster Frame list arrow **in the Adjust group, then click** Current Frame

   The bar in the playback controls indicates that the poster frame is set, as shown in Figure N-15. To complete the video's appearance in the presentation, you add a style to it.

6. **Click the** More button ▾ **in the Video Styles group, point to the** Beveled Frame, Gradient effect **in the Subtle section (fourth column of the first row) of the Video Styles gallery, compare your screen to Figure N-16, then click the** thumbnail

   The video now has a gray frame around it. You want the video to play as soon as the slide is visible.

7. **Click the** Video Tools Playback tab, **click the** Start list arrow, **click** Automatically, **press [F5], watch the slide show, return to Normal view, then save your changes**

FIGURE N-14: Viewing the Trim Video dialog box

Trim Video button

Click to adjust how long the video fades in and out

Green start point marker

Red end point marker

Timebar

Length of video

FIGURE N-15: Setting a poster frame

Poster Frame button

Frame set as poster frame

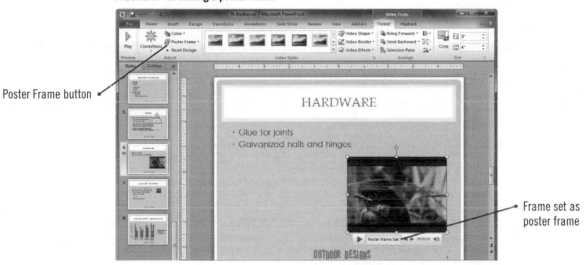

FIGURE N-16: Applying a video style to a video

In Step 6, click this style

Video style preview

Setting Slide Timing and Transitions

There may be times when you want to run a presentation automatically, without manually controlling the slide progression, such as when you want the presentation to run unattended at a kiosk or booth. You might also want to customize how slides appear in a slide show. To accomplish this, you can set slide timings and transitions in PowerPoint. A **timing** is the number of seconds a slide remains on the screen before advancing to the next one. A **transition** is a special effect that determines how a slide appears as it enters or leaves the screen. You can adjust settings for individual slides or apply one setting to multiple slides. 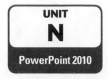 You want to make it easy for Jihong to concentrate on her message instead of running the slide show. You decide to set the timing for the presentation to eight seconds, add a consistent slide transition, and add an audio transition to the last slide.

STEPS

1. **Move to Slide 1, click the Transitions tab, then click the More button ⊡ in the Transition to This Slide group**

   You decide to add a transition to the first slide.

2. **Click the Cube transition in the second row of the Exciting section, as shown in Figure N-17**

   The Cube transition is applied to the slide. When a slide has media, animation, or a transition applied to it, such as the sound you added to Slide 2 and the video you inserted in Slide 6, a small star icon 🌠 appears beneath the slide number in the Slides pane. Now that you have selected a transition, you want to apply these settings to the entire presentation.

   > **QUICK TIP**
   > To adjust the timing or transition for an individual slide, select the slide, then adjust the settings as desired.

3. **Click the Apply To All button in the Timing group**

   The transition you applied to Slide 1 is now applied to all slides in the presentation. The star icon appears on every slide in the Slides pane. You now want to set the slide show to advance automatically after a set amount of time.

   > **QUICK TIP**
   > To remove a transition for the current slide, click the More button on the Transition to This Slide gallery, then click None.

4. **In the Timing group, click the On Mouse Click check box to deselect it, click the After check box to select it, click the up arrow until 00:08.00 appears in the After text box, then click the Apply To All button**

   Each slide will remain on the screen for eight seconds before automatically advancing to the next slide. During a presentation, you can manually override these settings by using any slide progression method: pressing [Spacebar], pressing [Enter], clicking the Next Slide button ➡ on the Slide Show toolbar, or clicking the left mouse button.

5. **Click the Slide Sorter button 🖽 on the status bar, then adjust the zoom as needed so that all slides are visible**

   The slide timing and animation icons are visible beneath each thumbnail.

6. **Move to Slide 8, click the Sound list arrow in the Timing group, click Drum Roll, compare your screen to Figure N-18, then click the Preview button in the Preview group**

   The Drum Roll sound plays during the transition to Slide 8. You can preview any special effects added to a slide in Slide Sorter view.

   > **TROUBLE**
   > Be aware that you can easily overwhelm or distract your audience if you apply several different slide transitions or insert too much media in a presentation.

7. **Press [F5], view the slide show, switch to Normal view, then save your changes**

   The slide transitions, timing, animation, and sounds play in the slide show.

FIGURE N-17: Selecting a slide transition

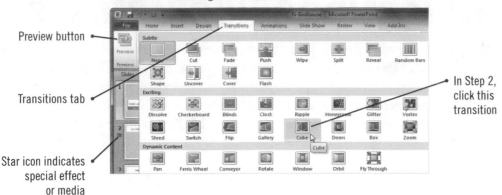

Preview button

Transitions tab

Star icon indicates special effect or media

In Step 2, click this transition

FIGURE N-18: Inserting a transition sound in a slide in Slide Sorter view

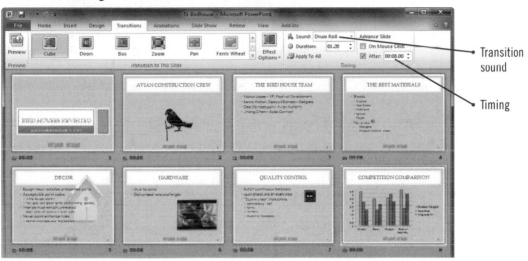

Transition sound

Timing

Compressing and optimizing media

Being able to include video and audio files in a presentation is great for your audience, but as the creator, you need to be aware of the file size of your presentation. A large file may be difficult to share with others or may exceed a user's e-mail storage. Large files can also be slow to load and play, which will cause users to move on before they see more than a slide or two. Ideally, your presentation should be as small as possible while maintaining visual and audio quality. Achieving that balance can be difficult. Fortunately, the Info tab in Backstage view contains features that optimize your presentation for your audience. The Compress Media button lets you see how much space the media files in your presentation currently take up. When you click the button, you can choose an option for sharing your presentation for other users (Presentation Quality), posting it to the Internet (Internet Quality), or attaching it to an e-mail (Low Quality). PowerPoint automatically displays the Optimize Compatibility button when it detects that you have inserted media whose format might be incompatible when other users try to play it. Click the button to optimize the video.

FIGURE N-19: Optimize Compatibility and Compress Media options on the Info tab

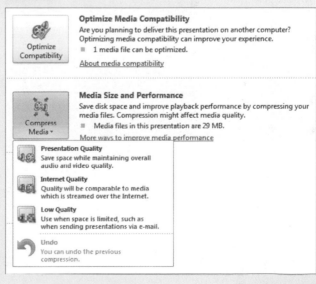

Animating Slide Objects

Just as transitions animate the way slides advance on-screen during a slide show, you can animate individual text objects and images in a slide, such as clip art, photos, illustrations, and charts. You select an animation from the Animations tab, and adjust how and when the animation effect plays. You can also apply multiple animations to an object. Once you have adjusted the animation settings perfectly, you can use the Animation Painter to apply those same settings to another object. 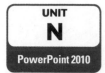 You decide to animate the bulleted text in Slide 6 and use the Animation Painter to copy the animation to the text in Slide 3.

STEPS

1. **Double-click Slide 6 to display it in Normal view**

2. **Click anywhere in the bulleted text, click the Animations tab, click the More button ▾ in the Animation group, then click the Bounce animation in the Entrance section of the Animation gallery, as shown in Figure N-20**

   The bullets bounce in. You want to adjust the entrance so that both items bounce in at the same time but have a slight delay before entering.

3. **Click the Effect Options button in the Animation group, then click All at Once**

   The two lines bounce in together. If you have multiple animations, you can adjust when they play in the Timing group. Click the Start list arrow, then click On Click to have them start when you click the mouse, With Previous for them to play simultaneously, and After Previous for them to play in a sequence.

QUICK TIP
You can modify other effect options and timing for an animation by clicking the Animation Pane button in the Advanced Animation group, clicking the effect arrow for the object, then clicking an option.

4. **Click the Animation Delay up arrow in the Timing group until 01.50 appears in the text box, click the Start list arrow, click With Previous, then click the Preview button in the Preview group**

   The video begins to play, and the bulleted items bounce in all at once after a short time, as shown in Figure N-21. You want to apply these settings to another object.

5. **Make sure the video has stopped playing in the preview, click anywhere in the bulleted list, then click the Animation Painter button in the Advanced Animation group**

   The Animation Painter transfers the animation and any custom settings to any other object in any open presentation.

QUICK TIP
The Animation Painter transfers animation attributes to objects just as the Format Painter transfers formatting to text and graphics.

6. **Move to Slide 3, then click the Animation Painter ⌖ anywhere in the slide, as shown in Figure N-22**

   The delayed bounced animation is transferred to the list of names.

7. **Press [F5], view the slide show from the beginning, return to Normal view, then save your changes**

   The animation plays with the settings you applied to them.

FIGURE N-20: Selecting an animation

In Step 2, click this animation option

Animations tab

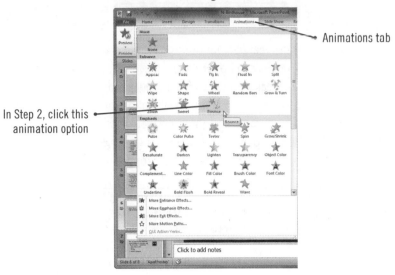

FIGURE N-21: Previewing animation applied to text

Selected animation

Delay setting

Animation playing during preview

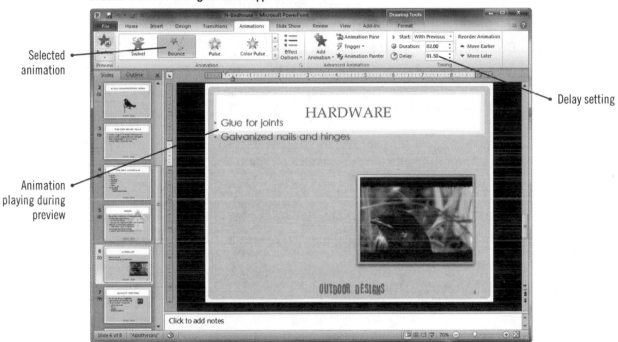

FIGURE N-22: Using the Animation Painter

Click the bulleted list to transfer the animation and settings

Polishing and Running a Presentation

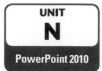
Creating Speaker Notes

Even experienced speakers can feel nervous or anxious giving a presentation. As a presenter, having speaker notes on hand that list key points can be very helpful, even if you just glance at them from time to time. For your audience, distributing speaker notes with handouts provides additional detail and background. You enter speaker notes in the Notes area in Normal view or in Notes Page view. When you print speaker notes, each slide is printed on its own page, and the notes you added—including graphics—appear beneath the slide on the page. ⬛⬛⬛⬛ Jihong has asked you to add some speaker notes to a couple of slides in the presentation to ensure she does not miss important information.

STEPS

> **QUICK TIP**
> You can add graphics to your notes in Notes Page view.

1. **Move to** Slide 1, **click the** Notes pane, **then type** Many companies make recycled plastic products – here's why wood kits are still supreme.

   The text appears in the Notes pane. Jihong has sent you notes to add on the team slide.

> **QUICK TIP**
> For longer sentences, the text wraps automatically, as when typing text in a Word document.

2. **Move to** Slide 3, **click the** Notes pane, **type** Marco: Won 1st place at the Fiery Food Show for Green Chili Enchiladas, **then type the following text, each on its own line**:

   Kecia: Won a local Emmy for a pet safety ad when she was 17

   Deepak: Has a first-edition collection of Octavia Butler novels

   Dee: Taught her parrot to say "I'm really a dinosaur"

   Jihong: Was first-chair clarinet in her college marching band

   The default space allotted to the Notes pane is not sufficient to view all of your notes. You can resize the Notes pane so that you can see all the text.

3. **Position the pointer over the** top border **of the Notes pane until the pointer changes to** ⬌, **then drag the border up until all the text is visible, as shown in Figure N-23**

   All of the text is visible in the Notes pane.

> **TROUBLE**
> The status bar does not contain a button for Notes Page view.

4. **Click the** View tab, **then click the** Notes Page button **in the Presentation Views group**

   The slide opens in Notes Page view, as shown in Figure N-24. You want to print only the pages that have notes.

5. **Click the** File tab, **click** Print, **click the** Full Page Slides list arrow, **then click** Notes Pages **in the Print Layout section at the top**

   The Preview pane changes to show the slide with notes.

> **QUICK TIP**
> To change the page orientation from default portrait to landscape, click the Portrait Orientation list arrow, then click Landscape.

6. **Click the** Slides text box **in the Settings section, type** 1,3, **then compare your screen to Figure N-25**

   Only pages 1 and 3 are selected to print.

7. **Save your changes, close the presentation, then exit PowerPoint**

FIGURE N-23: Resized Notes pane

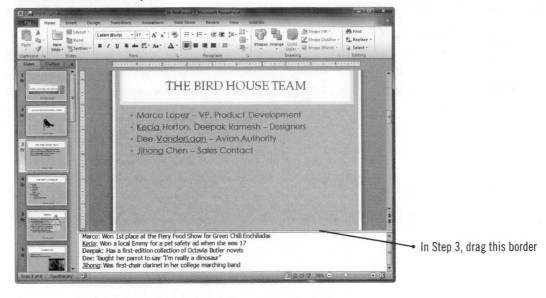

In Step 3, drag this border

FIGURE N-24: Viewing a slide and notes in Notes Page view

Notes Page button

Notes Page view

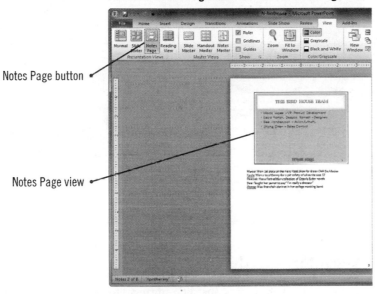

FIGURE N-25: Printing Notes Pages

Print button

Selected printer; your printer will differ

Only slides 1 and 3 are selected to print

Notes Pages selected to print

Notes Pages preview

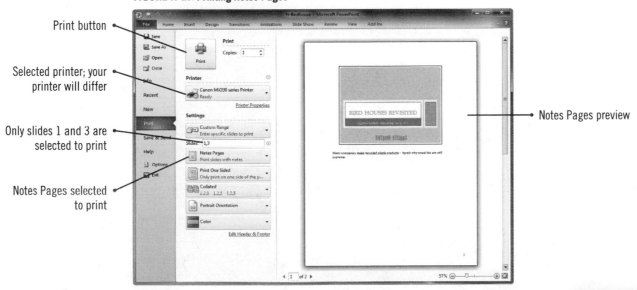

Polishing and Running a Presentation

Practice

Concepts Review

For current SAM information, including versions and content details, visit SAM Central (http://www.cengage.com/samcentral). If you have a SAM user profile, you may have access to hands-on instruction, practice, and assessment of the skills covered in this unit. Since various versions of SAM are supported throughout the life of this text, check with your instructor for the correct instructions and URL/Web site for accessing assignments.

Label the PowerPoint window elements shown in Figure N-26.

FIGURE N-26

Match each term with the statement that best describes it.

7. **Animation Painter**
8. **Transition**
9. **Trim**
10. **Remove Background**
11. **Transition sound**

a. Audio that plays as one slide advances to the next slide in a presentation
b. To edit the length of a sound or video
c. Transfers animation settings to another object
d. Deletes pixels in an image
e. A special effect that determines how a slide advances on the screen

Select the best answer from the list of choices.

12. Which of the following statements about animations is not correct?

  a. You can only apply them to clip art.

  b. You can apply multiple animations to an object.

  c. You can control the speed at which they play.

  d. You can easily edit them.

13. Which dialog box do you open to edit the start and end points of a video?

  a. Edit Video

  b. Fade

  c. Trim Video

  d. Play/Pause

14. Which of the following best describes a transition?

  a. Determines the amount of time a slide is visible

  b. Determines how long an animated object plays

  c. Determines whether media plays automatically or needs to be clicked

  d. Determines how a slide appears as it enters or leaves the screen

15. Which button deletes pixels from an image?

  a. Remove Opacity Color

  b. Remove Background

  c. Remove Opaqueness

  d. Remove Color

Skills Review

1. Add a shape.

  a. Start PowerPoint, open the file N-2.pptx from where you store your Data Files, then save it as **N-Natural Fiber Rug Sales**.

  b. Move to Slide 6.

  c. Make sure that the rulers are visible; if necessary, use a tool on the View tab to display them.

  d. Insert a Down Ribbon shape on the slide. Begin dragging at the 3" mark at the right on the horizontal ruler and the 2" mark at the top of the vertical ruler, then drag to the 2½" mark on the vertical ruler and the 4½" mark on the horizontal ruler. (*Hint*: This shape is located in the Stars and Banners section in the Shapes gallery.)

FIGURE N-27

  e. Open the Quick Styles gallery, then apply the Moderate Effect – Light Green, Accent 2 style to the shape.

  f. Select the shape if necessary, open the Shape Fill gallery, open the Texture gallery, then apply the Green marble texture to the shape.

  g. Type **Banner Year** in the shape, make the text bold, resize and position the shape if necessary, then compare your shape to Figure N-27.

  h. Save your changes.

2. Add clip art.

  a. Move to Slide 7, then insert a new Title and Content slide.

  b. Click the title placeholder, then type **To the Future....**

  c. Click the Clip Art icon in the content placeholder.

FIGURE N-28

  d. Make sure that only Illustrations is selected as the selected media file type, type **rug** in the Search for text box, click Go, then insert the clip art shown in Figure N-28.

  e. Open the Picture Styles gallery, then click the Rotated, White style. (*Hint*: The effect is in the third row.)

  f. Close the Clip Art task pane, then save your changes.

3. Work with pictures.

  a. Move to Slide 2, then use a command on the Insert tab to open the Insert Picture dialog box.

  b. Insert the file sisal.jpg from where you store your Data Files.

  c. Use a command in the Arrange group to send the object to the back of the slide.

   d. Click the Crop button in the Size group, then drag the top border down below the green bar.

   e. Click the Color button, then recolor the photo to Tan, Accent color 5 Light. (*Hint*: The effect is on the bottom row.)

   f. Save your changes.

4. Add sound and video.

   a. Move to Slide 1, then use a command on the Insert tab to insert audio from clip art.

   b. Search for **future**, then insert the sound **Bright Future**.

   c. On the Audio Tools Playback tab, select the check boxes to hide the sound during the show and to loop until stopped, click the Start list arrow, click Play across slides, then play the sound.

   d. Move to Slide 3, then use a command on the Insert tab to insert a video.

   e. Navigate to where you store your Data Files, insert the video **afghanrug.wmv**, then play it.

   f. Change the size of the video to 3" H by 4" W, then move the video to the bottom-right corner of the slide.

   g. View the slide show from the beginning, then save your changes.

5. Edit a video.

   a. Make sure the video is selected in Slide 3, then use a command on the Video Tools Playback tab to open the Trim Video dialog box.

   b. Play the video, then pause it at approximately the 00:04.013 mark.

   c. Drag the start point marker to that position on the timebar, then click OK to close the Trim Video dialog box.

   d. Play the video, then pause it at approximately the 00:01.90 mark.

   e. Use a command on the Video Tools Format tab to select the current frame as the poster frame. On the Video Tools Playback tab, click the Rewind after Playing check box. (*Hint*: Look in the Video Options group.)

   f. Open the Video Styles gallery on the Video Tools Format tab, then apply the Beveled Oval, Black style in the Moderate section.

   g. Switch to the Video Tools Playback tab, click the Start list arrow in the Video Options group, then click Automatically.

   h. Press [F5], watch the video, then save your changes.

6. Set slide timing and transitions.

   a. Open the Transitions gallery on the Transitions tab.

   b. Select the Cover transition, then apply it to all the slides. (*Hint*: The transition is in the second row of the Subtle section.)

   c. In the Timing group, deselect the On Mouse Click check box, click the After check box, set the time to three seconds, then apply the timing to all the slides.

   d. Change to Slide Sorter view.

   e. Move to Slide 8, then add the Push transition sound to the slide.

   f. View the slide show from the beginning, return to Slide Sorter view, then compare your screen to Figure N-29.

   g. Save your changes.

FIGURE N-29

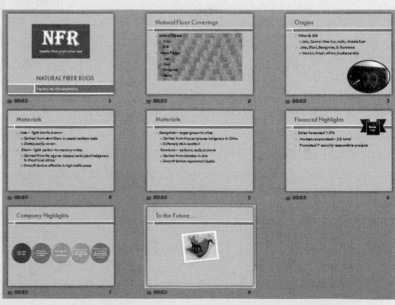

7. Animate slide objects.

   a. Switch to Normal view, move to Slide 6, then click the content text object.

   b. Apply the Wipe animation to the list. (*Hint*: This effect is located in the Entrance category.)

   c. Click the Effect Options button, then click From Top.

   d. Change the animation delay to 00.25 seconds.

   e. Click the Animation Painter button, move to Slide 8, then click the clip art.

   f. Preview the slide show, then save your changes.

Skills Review (continued)

8. Create speaker notes.

  a. Move to Slide 2, then type in the Notes pane: **Weaving started in Egypt at least 8,000 years ago**.

  b. Move to Slide 6, then type in the Notes pane: **Green building and government projects have been very successful**
     Working with international groups is very promising
     New podcasts bring in many visitors to the Web site

  c. Increase the size of the Notes pane to accommodate the notes text.

  d. View the slides in Notes Page view.

  e. Click Print on the File tab, then select Notes Pages as the print layout.

  f. Select Slides 2 and 6 to print as notes pages.

  g. Print the Notes Pages if your lab allows printing.

  h. Save your changes, close the presentation, then exit PowerPoint.

Independent Challenge 1

You work at A Fine Ruse—a local, independent weekly newspaper. To boost readership, you have decided to host an Annual Best of Ruse contest, honoring a host of different categories. Readers will send in their winning entries, and the paper will devote an issue to the contest. Your job is to come up with categories that are distinctive, interesting, and sure to elicit a response. You want to present your ideas to your colleagues for feedback and fine-tuning.

  a. Start PowerPoint, open the file N-3.pptx from where you store your Data Files, then save it as **N-Best of Ruse**.

  b. Insert a shape in Slide 1 and add text of your choosing to the shape. (*Hint*: Modify the shape fill, outline, and effects as desired.)

  c. Insert clip art in Slides 6, 7, and 8, choosing clips that pertain to each topic, and apply styles or effects as desired. (*Hint*: When searching, use keywords that are relevant to the slide title.)

  d. Insert photographs from the Clip Organizer in Slides 5 and 9, choosing photos that pertain to each topic. Apply styles or effects as desired.

  e. Insert clip art videos in Slides 3 and 4, choosing clips that pertain to each topic.

  f. Insert sounds in Slides 6 and 9, choosing sounds that pertain to each topic. Hide both sounds during the show. Trim sound clips as needed. (*Hint*: Open the Trim Audio dialog box using a button in the Editing group on the Audio Tools Playback tab; the Trim Audio feature operates the same as the Trim Video feature.)

  g. Apply the Checkerboard slide transition to the presentation, and set the timing to 3 seconds. (*Hint*: Look in the Exciting section.)

  h. Add the Hammer transition sound to Slide 2.

  i. Add the Complementary Color animation to the title that starts With Previous in Slide 2.

  j. Add the Pulse effect animation that starts After Previous to the SmartArt in Slide 2.

  k. Add the Teeter animation to the text beneath the title in Slide 1. Customize settings as desired, then use the Animation Painter to apply the animation to text in Slide 3.

  l. Add the following notes to Slide 2:
     Allow readers to submit their own categories and winners
     Include side pieces from local personalities listing their favorites

  m. Add your name to the footer, switch to Slide Sorter view, then compare your presentation to the sample shown in Figure N-30.

FIGURE N-30

Independent Challenge 1 (continued)

Advanced Challenge Exercise

- Add an additional animation to at least one object.
- Add an additional video to at least one of the other slides in the presentation.

n. Save your changes, print the Notes page for Slide 2, close the presentation, then exit PowerPoint.

Independent Challenge 2

Your graphics and Web design company, Grafik Traffic, just merged with another large graphics business, Pipeline Design. As you have begun to work on joint projects, you have realized that members of the Pipeline Design staff are not well-versed in copyright law. You create a PowerPoint presentation for in-house training on the basics of copyright law.

a. Start PowerPoint, open the file N-4.pptx from where you store your Data Files, then save it as **N-Copyright 101**.

b. Search for a clip art image using the keyword **constitution**, then insert it in Slide 3. Adjust the image as desired so that it complements the look of the slide.

c. Search for a clip art image using the keyword **unicorn**, then insert it in Slide 2. Adjust the image as desired so that it complements the look of the slide.

d. Navigate to where you store your Data Files, then insert the video fedgovt.wmv in Slide 1. Trim and adjust the video, and rearrange other elements as desired.

e. Insert a photograph in Slide 9, then apply styles and effects to it.

f. In Slide 9, search for "gavel" audio, then insert the sound in the slide to play automatically and be hidden during the show.

g. Animate and customize the bulleted text in a slide, then use the Animation Painter to copy the animation to at least five other slides.

h. Apply the Doors slide transition to all slides, then adjust the slide timing as desired.

i. Add the following notes to Slide 5:
The copyright holder (who may not be the creator) has rights over work: reproduce, prepare derivative works, distribute copies, perform, and display the work

j. Add your name and the slide number to the slide footer, view the slide show, then compare your Slide 9 to the sample shown in Figure N-31.

FIGURE N-31

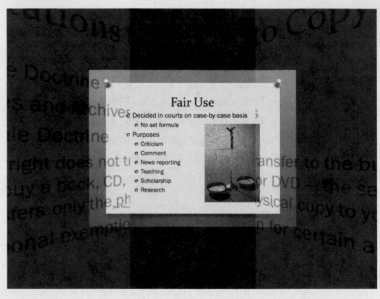

Advanced Challenge Exercise

- Add a video or photo from the Clip Art task pane of your choosing to a slide in the presentation, then apply two different animations to the object.

k. Save your changes, print Slide 5, close the presentation, then exit PowerPoint.

Independent Challenge 3

You are a business consultant specializing in customer relations. You have been hired to do a workshop for a small business that has a great product, but the company's internal processes need some improvement. You create a PowerPoint presentation that emphasizes customer relationships.

a. Start PowerPoint, open the file N-5.pptx from where you store your Data Files, then save it as **N-Customer Trust**.

b. On Slide 1, add the Wipe Entrance animation to the subtitle that starts With Previous.

c. Move to Slide 4, search for clip art with the keyword **R**, then insert the clip. Adjust the photo, then send it in back of the bulleted text. Resize as necessary. Refer to Figure N-32.

FIGURE N-32

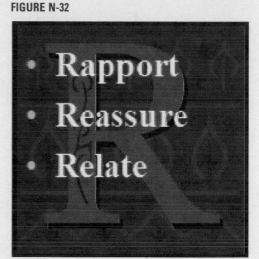

d. Move to Slide 5, insert the image file **sandcastle.jpg** from where you store your Data Files, move it behind the text, than apply the effects and styles of your choice.

e. Add one clip art image to Slide 7, and a photo, video, or clip art image to the slide of your choice. Add effects and styles as desired.

f. Add at least one sound or transition sound of your choice.

g. Add at least one shape to a slide of your choice. Modify the shape fill, outline, and effects as desired.

h. Add a slide transition choice, and adjust slide timing as desired.

i. Animate at least one text object or image on a slide.

j. Animate each slide title in Slides 2-7, then add an additional animation to a title in the presentation.

k. Add notes to at least two slides.

l. Add your name to the footer, then switch to Slide Sorter view.

m. Save your changes, close the presentation, then exit PowerPoint.

Real Life Independent Challenge

Take advantage of your new skills in PowerPoint to create a presentation for friends, family, or coworkers. Create a slide show about your favorite hobby or topic of interest, and intersperse the slides with related facts or stories.

a. Start PowerPoint, create a new file from an installed theme or template, then save the file as **N-My Personal Favorite** where you store your Data Files.

b. Insert photos of your topic, either from your computer or from the Clip Organizer. (*Hint*: Apply various Picture Styles to the photos.)

c. Create slides describing the item, person, or creature, or relating to something in the photos, then insert relevant clip art, video, and sounds in at least three slides.

d. Apply slide transitions, sounds, and slide timings to the presentation.

e. Add at least one shape to the presentation.

f. Add notes on at least two slides.

g. Animate objects as desired, and use the Animation Painter.

h. Add your name to the footer.

i. Save your changes, then print the Notes pages if your lab allows printing.

j. Close the presentation, then exit PowerPoint.

Visual Workshop

Create a slide that resembles Figure N-33. Save the presentation as **N-Networking Smarts** where you store your Data Files. Use default settings for each element. (*Hints*: Start with a blank presentation; after you apply the design theme, add a new Title and Content slide. For the photo, search on the keyword **keyboard keys**. For the animation, click the More button, click More Entrance Effects, then look in the Basic section of the Animation gallery.) Add your name to the slide footer, then print the slide. Save your changes, close the presentation, then exit PowerPoint.

FIGURE N-33

Integrating Office 2010 Programs

So far you have created many documents, worksheets, databases, and presentations using individual Office programs. You can also create documents that combine information from different Office programs, such as a newsletter you create with Word that also contains a chart created with Excel. You can also capture a screen or part of a screen in any open window as an image to paste into a document or save as an image file. 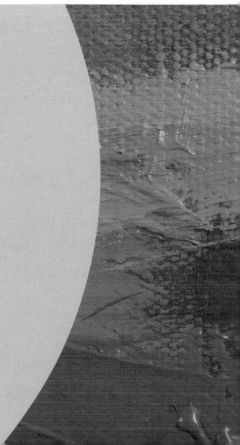 Jihong Chen, assistant sales manager for Outdoor Designs, needs you to insert an Excel chart into a presentation she created, create slides from a Word outline, and insert a screen capture into a slide. She also has a letter for the shareholders; she needs you to paste a linked chart into the letter, and then send it out as a mail merge form letter. You will use several Office applications to accomplish these tasks.

OBJECTIVES

Insert an Excel chart onto a PowerPoint slide

Insert PowerPoint slides from a Word document

Insert screen captures into a Word Document

Insert text from a Word file into an open document

Link an Excel chart to a Word document

Update a linked Excel chart in a Word document

Insert Access fields into a Word document

Perform a mail merge

Inserting an Excel Chart into a PowerPoint Slide

An Excel chart is an excellent tool for communicating numerical data visually. You can create an Excel chart in a PowerPoint slide to convey financial results or trends to your audience. When you create a chart in PowerPoint, you **embed** data that is editable in Excel into the presentation. Once the chart is created, you can update it when you open the spreadsheet in Excel or when you activate the Chart Tools tab in PowerPoint. ▓▓▓▓▓ Jihong has given you a presentation she created for the quarterly sales meeting and a hard copy of sales figures. You need to insert a chart comparing sales, so you decide to create the chart directly in PowerPoint.

STEPS

1. **Start PowerPoint, open the file O-1.pptx from where you store your Data Files, then save it as O-Sales and Projections.pptx**

QUICK TIP

You can also insert a chart by clicking the Insert Chart button in the Illustrations group on the Insert tab.

2. **Move to Slide 2, then click the Insert Chart icon 📊 in the content placeholder**

3. **In the Insert Chart dialog box, click the Clustered Cylinder style (first column, second row) as shown in Figure O-1, then click OK**

   Excel opens with sample data in a new spreadsheet, and the two program windows appear side by side on the screen, as shown in Figure O-2. In PowerPoint, a chart based on the sample data appears in the slide and the Chart Tools Design tab is active. You replace the sample data in Excel with figures from Jihong's report.

QUICK TIP

If you want to use only certain cells from the Excel worksheet in your PowerPoint chart, you do not need to delete the sample data in Excel; instead, you can drag the lower-right corner of the data range to the desired cell.

4. **Replace the data in the worksheet with the data in the following table:**

cell	data	cell	data	cell	data	cell	data
		B1	Q4 2012	C1	Q4 2013	D1	Projected Q4 2014
A2	Northeast	B2	525,000	C2	544,100	D2	579,000
A3	Midwest	B3	478,300	C3	491,000	D3	516,000
A4	Southeast	B4	389,600	C4	400,000	D4	419,200
A5	West	B5	415,700	C5	427,500	D5	453,000

   As you enter the data in Excel, the chart data in the slide updates automatically.

5. **Click the File tab in Excel, then click Exit**

   The PowerPoint window maximizes, and the updated chart slide fills the screen, as shown in Figure O-3. It is not necessary to save the spreadsheet in Excel; if you later edit the chart data from PowerPoint, the data opens in a new spreadsheet.

6. **Save your changes to the presentation**

FIGURE O-1: Choosing a chart style in the Insert Chart dialog box

Chart styles and templates

In Step 3, click this style

OK button

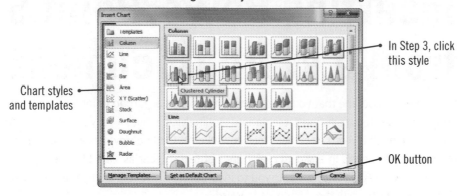

FIGURE O-2: Viewing PowerPoint and Excel split screen

Chart Tools Design tab

Click to open spreadsheet in Excel

Sample chart inserted onto PowerPoint slide

Sample data

Spreadsheet open in Excel

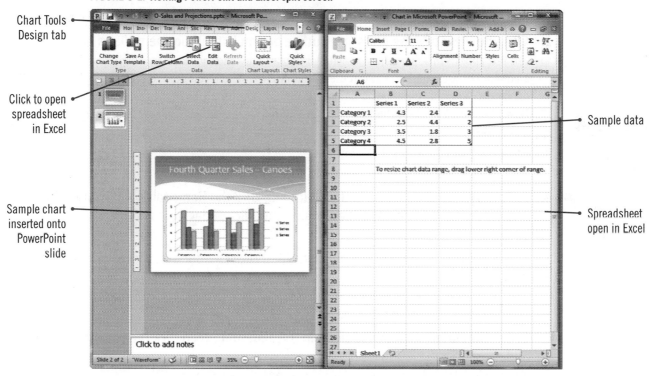

FIGURE O-3: Completed chart

Chart updated with data entered in Excel

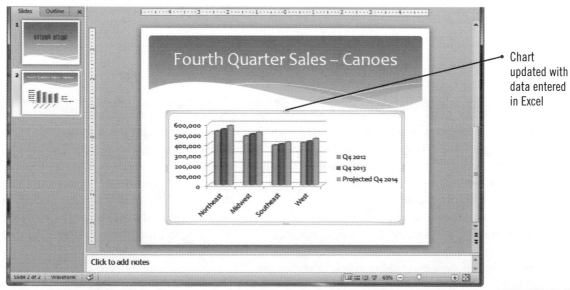

Inserting PowerPoint Slides from a Word Document

You can use an outline that you have created in Word as a starting point for a new PowerPoint presentation, or to add slides to an existing presentation. Outline view makes it easy to see how a document is organized. When you insert a Word document into PowerPoint, Outline view lets you easily see how the structure will translate to the levels in a slide. Level 1 lines of text appear as slide titles, and lower-level text appears as bulleted text. Jihong wants you to incorporate one of her outlines as new slides in the presentation. First, you want to view the document in Word.

STEPS

1. **Start Word, then open the file O-2.docx from where you store your Data Files**

2. **Click the View tab, then click the Outline button in the Document Views group**

   The text appears in a hierarchical structure using headings and subheadings, which structures it perfectly for a PowerPoint presentation. You can use Outline view any time you need to organize topics or restructure a document. You can adjust the outlining structure by clicking the Promote, Demote, and Move Up or Move Down buttons. You can change the view by clicking the Expand or Collapse buttons in the Outline Tools group, as shown in Figure O-4.

3. **Click the File tab, then click Exit**

   The Word document closes.

4. **In PowerPoint, click Slide 2 in the Slides tab, click the Home tab if necessary, click the New Slide list arrow in the Slides group, then click Slides from Outline**

   The Insert Outline dialog box opens.

5. **Navigate to where you store your Data Files, click O-2.docx, as shown in Figure O-5, then click Insert**

   Three new slides are inserted into the presentation, as shown in Figure O-6. The new slides are formatted in the theme font from the Word document.

6. **Select the three newly added slides in the Slides tab, then click the Reset button in the Slides group**

   The newly added slides are formatted in the theme of the presentation.

7. **Add your name to the slide footer, save your changes, then close the presentation**

> **QUICK TIP**
> To save a presentation's handouts as a Word document, click the File tab, click Save & Send, click Create Handouts at the bottom of the middle pane, click the Create Handouts button in the right pane, select a page layout, then click OK.

> **TROUBLE**
> You may also need to edit the Theme Colors or Theme Fonts of slides created from outlines.

Using outlines in Word and PowerPoint

If you want to create an outline in Word that you can use as the basis for a PowerPoint presentation, it is best to create or structure a document that is formatted for this purpose. Start a new document in Word, click the View tab, then click the Outline button in the Document Views group. As you type your outline text, use the Outline Level list arrow in the Outline Tools group to apply a heading level for each line. Use the Heading 1 style for slide titles, Heading 2 for the first level of indented text, and so on. It is important that you use the built-in heading styles in Word when you create your outline because the heading tags determine the structure of the outline when it is imported into PowerPoint. When the outline is complete, save and close the Word document.

You can also save a PowerPoint presentation in outline format and then open it in Word. To save a PowerPoint outline, click the File tab, click Save As, click the Save as type list arrow, then click Outline/RTF (*.rtf). Next, open the document in Word, then resize or reformat the text as desired.

Promote to
Heading 1
button

Promote
button

Move Up and
Move Down
buttons

Text in
outline
structure

Demote
button

Click to
return to
Print
Layout view

Demote to
Body Text
button

Collapse
and Expand
buttons

Integration 2010

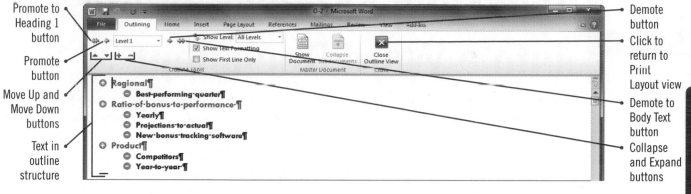

In Step 5, click
this file

Insert button

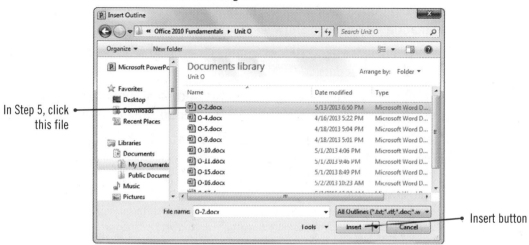

Slides added
from outline

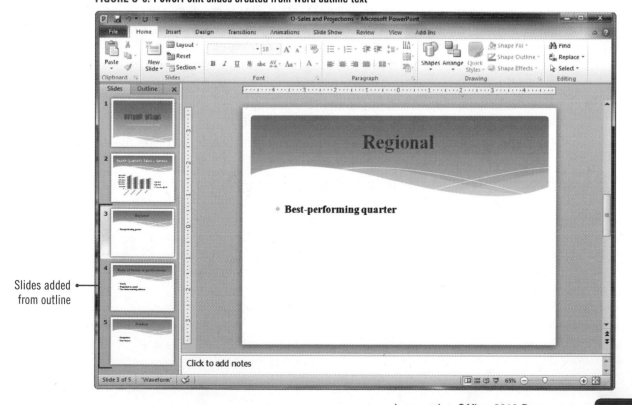

Integrating Office 2010 Programs

Inserting Screen Captures into a Word Document

The Screenshot feature is available in Word or PowerPoint, and allows you to capture an image from another non-minimized program window and instantly insert it into an open Word document or PowerPoint presentation. You can take a screenshot of an entire window or part of a window, which gives you a quick way to include graphics or data you could not otherwise insert.  Jihong wants to include a screenshot from a PowerPoint presentation as a logo in a letter to shareholders. You use the Screenshot tool to capture a clip of the slide as it plays in Slide Show view.

1. **In PowerPoint, open the file O-3.pptx from where you store your Data Files, then watch the animation play in Slide Show view**

2. **Start Word, open the file O-4.docx from where you store your Data Files, then save it as O-Shareholder letter.docx**

3. **Press [Ctrl][Home] to move to the top of the document, press [Enter] to insert a new line, press [▲] to move up a line, then click the Center button ≡ in the Paragraph group**

4. **Click the Insert tab, then click the Screenshot button in the Illustrations group**

   Thumbnails of open programs that are not minimized to the task bar appear in the list, as shown in Figure O-7. To insert a full screen, simply click a thumbnail in the Available Windows section. You decide to capture just part of the image in Slide Show view. When you use the Screen Clipping option, Word automatically switches to the previous window, which is the first thumbnail shown in the Available Windows section. If you have multiple programs open and maximized or in restore down mode, be sure that the window from which you want to capture a clip is the first thumbnail.

   > **TROUBLE**
   > You may need to wait a few moments for ╋ to appear before you can drag to select the screen clip.

5. **Click Screen Clipping, when the ╋ pointer appears, drag a selection box around the image starting at the upper-left corner, as shown in Figure O-8, then release the mouse button**

   The Screen Clipping feature switches to the PowerPoint Slide View screen, where you can select any area on the screen. When you release the mouse button, Word inserts the captured screen area as a bitmap image into the document. If you are inserting a screen or screen clip in PowerPoint, PowerPoint automatically centers the image on the slide. You can adjust color and apply artistic effects and styles to the captured image. The image of the ocean canoeist is a little large for the letter, so you resize it.

   > **QUICK TIP**
   > To save the screen clip as a new file, right-click the image, click Save as Picture from the menu, type a name, select a file type, then click Save.

6. **Click the Shape Height text box in the Size group, type 2, press [Enter], click a blank part of the window, then compare your letter to Figure O-9**

   The image is resized and centered on the page. You can adjust the image and apply styles and effects to it as you would any photograph.

   > **TROUBLE**
   > Remember when shooting a screen clip from the Internet that your assumption should always be that the content is protected by copyright.

7. **Save your changes to the document, close the presentation in PowerPoint, then exit PowerPoint**

FIGURE O-7: Options for the Screenshot button

Screenshot button; your size might differ

Previous window

Click to select a screen clip

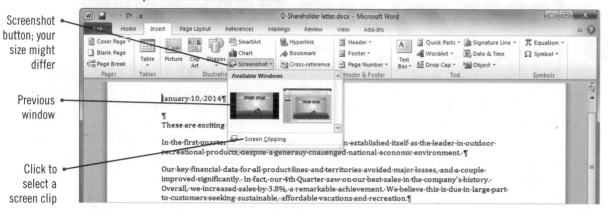

FIGURE O-8: Selecting a screen clip

Begin dragging here

Selected screen clip

Stop dragging here

Crosshair pointer

FIGURE O-9: Screen clip inserted into a Word document

Inserted and resized screen clip

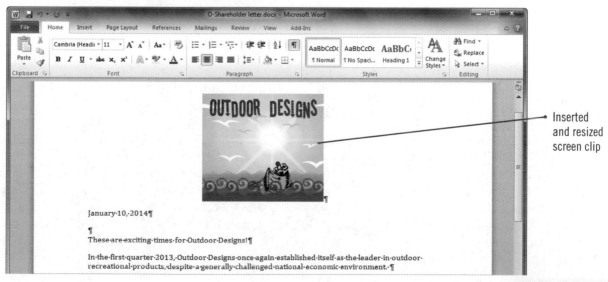

Inserting Text from a Word File into an Open Document

As you work, you might want to combine two files into one, or insert another document into the current one. Although you can easily copy and paste information between two or more open documents, it is sometimes easier to insert the contents from a file without having to open it first.  Jihong wants you to include sales highlights from a document she created in the letter to shareholders that you have been working on.

1. **In Word, scroll down if necessary, position the insertion point on the blank line immediately following the text Strategic highlights:, click the Insert tab, click the Insert Object list arrow in the Text group, then click Text from File**

   The Insert File dialog box opens.

2. **Navigate to where you store your Data Files, click O-5.docx as shown in Figure O-10, then click Insert**

   The contents of the file, consisting of five lines of text, are inserted at the bottom of the letter, as shown in Figure O-11.

3. **Select the five lines of text you just inserted, click the Home tab, click the Bullets list arrow ⊞ ▾ in the Paragraph Group, then point to the hollow bullet style, as shown in Figure O-12**

4. **Click the hollow bullet style**

   The sales highlights text is formatted in a bulleted list.

5. **Press [Ctrl][End], then press [Ctrl][Enter]**

   A new page is inserted at the end of the document.

6. **Save your changes to the document**

Placing an Access table in a Word document

In addition to inserting a Word file into a Word document, you can insert data from other applications, such as Access. You can insert an Access table into a Word document by various methods. You can copy the entire table or individual records and paste them into a Word document. You can also use the Export feature in Access to export objects, such as a table, query, report, or form. To export from Access, open the database, verify that it is free of errors, open the Navigation Pane, then select the object you want to export. Click the External Data tab, click the More button in the Export group, click Word, choose the desired options, then click OK. Note that Access always exports to a new Rich Text Format (RTF) file; you cannot export to an open Word document. The object in Word is a regular table; it does not link back to the Access database. Therefore, any modifications you make to an exported table in Word affect only the Word document. Depending on the number of fields, you may need to reformat the table in Word.

FIGURE O-10: Insert File dialog box

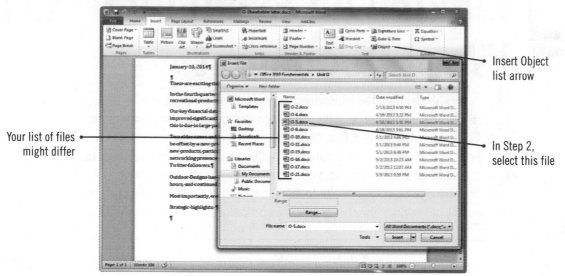

Your list of files might differ

Insert Object list arrow

In Step 2, select this file

FIGURE O-11: File inserted into letter

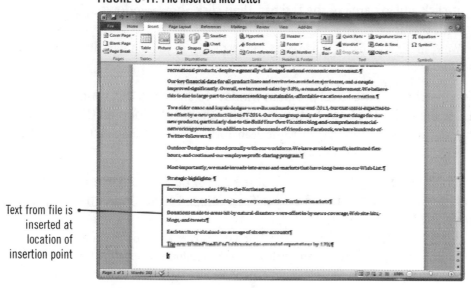

Text from file is inserted at location of insertion point

FIGURE O-12: Formatting bulleted text

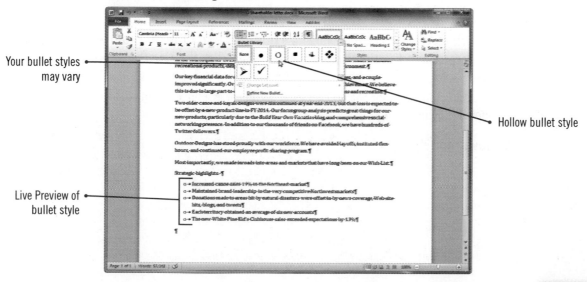

Your bullet styles may vary

Hollow bullet style

Live Preview of bullet style

Integrating Office 2010 Programs

Linking an Excel Chart to a Word Document

Linking data shares updated information between files and programs. A **link** displays information from a **source** file, which is the original file containing the data, and the **destination** file, the location to which that data is copied or moved. In a Word document, linked data looks just like inserted or embedded data. However, you can edit the linked data in its native program just by double-clicking it. ████ Jihong wants to add data from the focus group to the shareholder letter. She is not certain if she wants to include the data, the chart, or both. You decide to link the Excel spreadsheet to the shareholder letter so that if Jihong updates any of the data, the changes will be updated automatically in the letter.

1. **Start Excel, open the file O-6.xlsx from where you store your Data Files, then save it as O-Focus Group.xlsx**

   The worksheet contains data and a chart.

2. **Right-click a blank area of the taskbar, then click** Show windows side by side **in the shortcut menu**

   The Word and Excel program windows are tiled vertically, so you can switch between them while viewing both documents.

3. **Click anywhere in the Excel program window to switch to this window, select the** range A1:D6, **then click the** Copy button 📋 **in the Clipboard group on the Home tab**

   When windows are tiled, clicking anywhere in an inactive program window activates it so that you can work in the window. The cells are copied to the clipboard.

4. **Switch to Word, click the** blank line **at the top of page 2, click the** Paste list arrow **in the Clipboard group, point to the** Link & Keep Source Formatting button 📋, **as shown in Figure O-13, then click** 📋

   A Live Preview of the copied cells appears. Using the Link & Keep Source Formatting option automatically applies the current Excel style to the table and permits automatic updating from Word or Excel, which is useful if you want to paste the same data in multiple files and not have to worry about updating each file every time the data changes.

5. **Switch to Excel, press [Esc], click the** chart, **then click** 📋

   The chart object is copied to the clipboard.

6. **Switch to Word, click the** Maximize button 🔲 **on the program window title bar, press [Enter] twice, click the** Paste list arrow, **then click the** Use Destination Theme & Link Data button 📋

   The chart appears in the Shareholder letter document as a linked chart object in the current Word theme, as shown in Figure O-14.

7. **Save your changes**

FIGURE O-13: Selecting a paste option for copied Excel cells

In Step 4, click this option

Live Preview of linked Excel cells

Selected cells in Excel

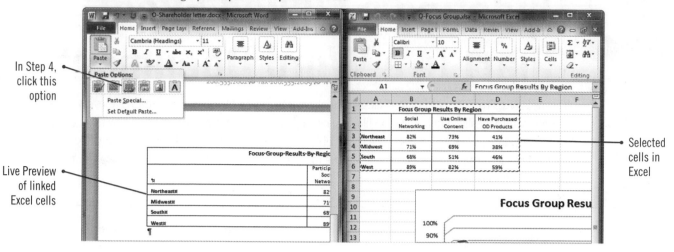

FIGURE O-14: Viewing Excel chart pasted as a link in Word

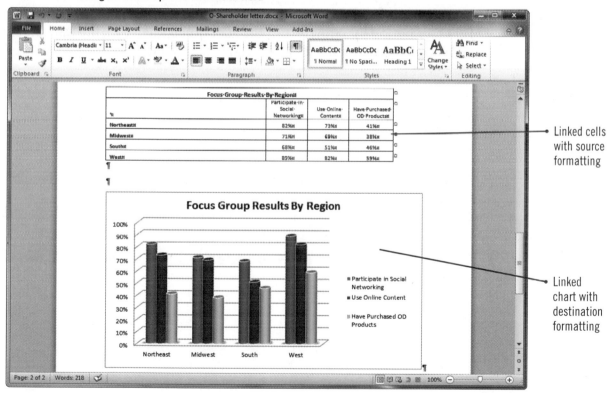

Linked cells with source formatting

Linked chart with destination formatting

Updating a Linked Excel Chart in a Word Document

The beauty of working with linked files is the ability to update the source file and have every linked object update automatically in its destination file. You can also update a linked object manually by right-clicking it and clicking Update Link or by selecting the linked object and pressing [F9]. The [F9] key updates links in any Office application. Jihong just received updates to the focus-group data for the South region.  You make the changes in Excel and view the updated results in the linked Word document.

STEPS

1. **Right-click a blank area of the taskbar, then click** Show windows side by side **in the shortcut menu**

2. **Switch to Excel, edit the data in the Focus Group workbook to match that in the following table, then click an empty cell in Excel:**

Cell	Data
B5	71
C5	54
D5	50

   The chart columns in Excel and in Word also change as you enter new figures, as shown in Figure O-15.

3. **Maximize the Excel program window, select the data in the workbook, click the Fill Color button list arrow** ⬛▾ **in the Font group, then click the** Dark Blue, Text 2, Lighter 80% color **(in the fourth column, second row)**

   The cells are shaded in blue.

   > **QUICK TIP**
   > When you open a Word document that contains linked data, Word prompts you to update links.

4. **Switch to Word, right-click the** table, **compare your screen to Figure O-16, then click** Update Link

   The table is updated to the format changes you made in Excel.

5. **Switch to Excel, save your changes, close the worksheet, then exit Excel**

6. **Click the** chart object, **click the** Chart Tools Design tab, **click the** More button ▾ **in the Chart Style group, then click** Style 34, **(second column, fifth row)**

   The chart design style is changed. Because you selected to paste the chart with destination style, any style changes you make in the future to the chart in Excel will not be reflected in the Word document.

7. **Click a blank area in the window, compare your screen to Figure O-17, then save your changes to the document**

FIGURE O-15: Viewing updated data from a linked file

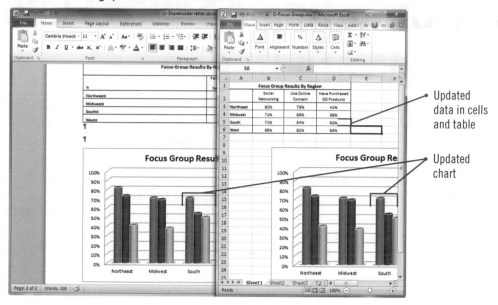

Updated data in cells and table

Updated chart

FIGURE O-16: Updating data in Word

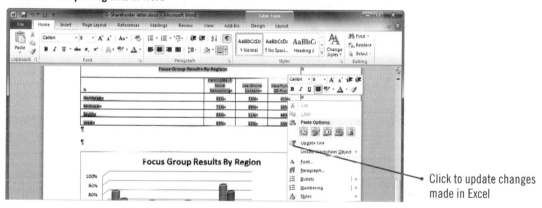

Click to update changes made in Excel

FIGURE O-17: Updated objects

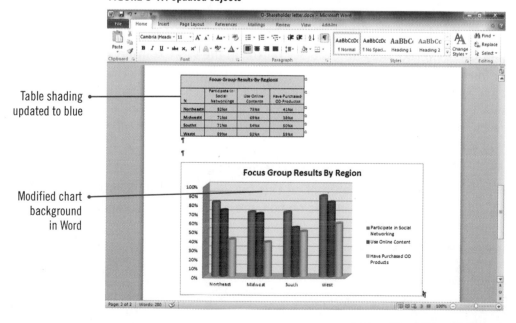

Table shading updated to blue

Modified chart background in Word

Integrating Office 2010 Programs

Inserting Access Fields into a Word Document

A **form letter** is a document that contains standard body text and a custom heading containing the name and address for one of many recipients. The letter, or **main document**, is usually created in Word; the data for the custom heading, also known as the **data source**, is usually compiled in a table, a worksheet, or a database such as Access. From these two files—the main document and the data source—you create a third file, a **merged document**, consisting of multiple personalized letters. This process is called **mail merge**. Before performing a mail merge, you add **merge fields** to the main document, which are placeholders to indicate where the custom information from the data source should appear.  Jihong asks you to send the shareholder letter to the company's four principal investors, and gives you a file containing their names and addresses. Before you merge the shareholder letter with the database file, you need to insert fields into the main document.

STEPS

1. **Switch to Word, press [Ctrl][Home] to move the top of the document, then click the blank line beneath the date**

2. **Click the Mailings tab, click the Start Mail Merge button in the Start Mail Merge group, compare your screen to Figure O-18, then click Letters**

   The document is now identified as a main document and is ready for you to add fields, such as names, addresses, and salutations, from the data source. You can also perform a mail merge for e-mail messages, address labels, envelopes, or a catalog or directory.

3. **Click the Select Recipients button in the Start Mail Merge group, then click Use Existing List**

   The Select Data Source dialog box opens. In addition to an Access database, you can select from a variety of data sources, such as an Outlook address book, data from an Excel spreadsheet, or a Word document or an HTML file that contains a single table.

4. **Navigate to where you store your Data Files, click O-7.accdb, then click Open**

   The Select Data Source dialog box closes. Although the Access database file is designated as the data source, Access does not need to be open in order to use the data.

5. **Click the Edit Recipient List button in the Start Mail Merge group**

   The Mail Merge Recipients dialog box opens, as shown in Figure O-19. Here you can view the records in the data source file and select, filter, and sort data so that you can send the mail merge letter to specific recipients. You want to include all the recipients in the database, so you do not need to make changes to this dialog box.

6. **Click OK, then click the Address Block button in the Write & Insert Fields group**

   The Insert Address Block dialog box opens, where you can select the format for the address block and preview it. The address block is created using the Title, First Name, Last Name, Address 1, Address 2, City, State, and Postal Code fields from the Access database file. Word automatically arranged the fields as shown in the Preview window because this is a common format for fields in a mail merge letter.

7. **Click OK**

   The block field, <<AddressBlock>>, appears in the document.

8. **Press [Enter] twice, click the Greeting Line button in the Write & Insert Fields group, click OK in the Insert Greeting Line dialog box, press [Enter], then compare your screen to Figure O-20**

   In the Insert Greeting Line dialog box, you can select the format for and preview the greeting line. The greeting will appear as "Dear <<Title>> <<Last_Name>>," for each recipient. The greeting line field <<GreetingLine>> is inserted into the document.

9. **Save your changes to the document**

Integrating Office 2010 Programs

FIGURE O-18: Selecting a Mail Merge option

Mailings tab

Start Mail Merge button

In Step 2, click this option

Insertion point should be on new blank line

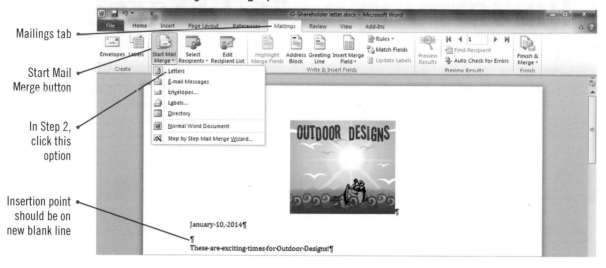

FIGURE O-19: Mail Merge Recipients dialog box

Clicking this check box adds or removes the recipient

Currently selected data source

Options to organize recipient list

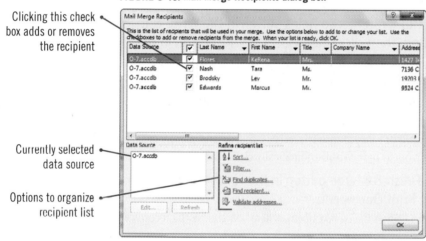

FIGURE O-20: Viewing inserted merge fields

Edit Recipient List button

Greeting Line button

Address Block button

Inserted fields

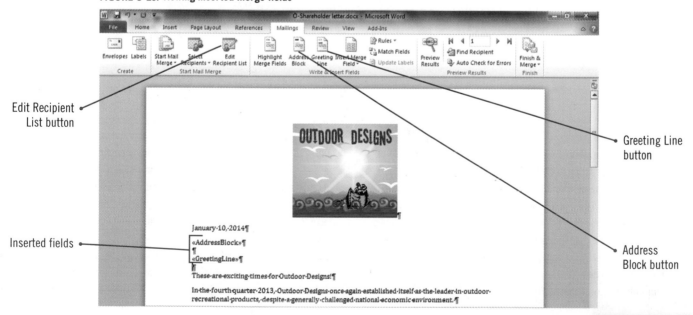

Performing a Mail Merge

After you set up a main document, specify a data source, and insert merge fields, you are ready to merge, or combine, the standard text with the custom information to create personalized documents. You can preview the mail merge to ensure that all the information displays properly in the final document. Now that the main document—the shareholder letter—has merge fields inserted, you are ready to preview and then merge it with the data source to create the final mail merge letters. You also want to print one of the merged letters for Jihong's review.

STEPS

QUICK TIP

You can also perform a mail merge using step-by-step instructions by clicking the Start Mail Merge list arrow in the Start Mail Merge group, then clicking Step by Step Mail Merge Wizard.

1. **Click the Highlight Merge Fields button in the Write & Insert Fields group, then compare your screen to Figure O-21**

   The merge fields <<AddressBlock>>, which includes all the necessary name and address fields from the data source, and <<GreetingLine>> are shaded in gray, making it easy to see where merged data will be inserted into the letter. Other commands in the Write & Insert Fields group include the Insert Merge Field button, which allows you to insert any field from the data source document; the Rules button, which allows you to select records that meet certain conditions; and the Match Fields button, which allows you to match or map fields in a data source.

2. **Click the Highlight Merge Fields button in the Write & Insert Fields group to turn off highlighting, then click the Preview Results button in the Preview Results group**

   The name, address, and salutation for the first recipient in the data source file replace the fields in the document. See Figure O-22.

3. **Click the Next Record button ▶ in the Preview Results group three times**

   The data from each record appears in its respective letter. You can use buttons in the Preview Results group to move backward or forward through records, find a particular record, and check for errors. You can click Auto Check for Errors to have Word automatically check each document for errors.

TROUBLE

To add custom text to individual letters, click Edit Individual Documents, move to the individual letters you want to customize, then type the desired text.

4. **Click the Finish & Merge button in the Finish group, compare your screen to Figure O-23, then click Print Documents**

   The Merge to Printer dialog box opens, where you choose the records you want to print.

5. **Click the Current record option button, then click OK if your lab allows printing**

   The Print dialog box opens. The fourth record in the merge letter is set to print.

6. **In the Print dialog box, click OK if your lab allows printing, or click Cancel**

7. **Save your changes, close the document, then exit Word**

Using mail merge to send personalized e-mail messages

While it is easy to send an e-mail message to several recipients at once using the carbon copy (CC) feature in Outlook, you are limited to sending the same message to everyone. Using mail merge to create the e-mail message enables you to personalize messages, ensuring that only the recipient's e-mail address appears in the To: text box in the e-mail message. The steps for creating an e-mail mail merge are basically the same as for a letter mail merge. The main document can be a Word document, and the data source file can be your Outlook contact list. When you click the Start Mail Merge button to begin the mail merge, click E-Mail Messages. Next, click the Select Recipients button, click Select from Outlook Contacts, then follow the prompts to choose the correct address book and import the contacts folder. When you are ready to merge the final document, click the Finish & Merge button in the Finish group, then click Send E-mail Messages. Note that you cannot add a recipient to the Cc (carbon copy) or Bcc (blind carbon copy) fields. If you want to receive a copy of the e-mail message, add your e-mail address to the Mail Merge Recipients list.

FIGURE O-21: Viewing highlighted merge fields

Highlight Merge Fields button

Insert Merge Field button

Highlighted merge fields

Rules button

Preview Results button

Match Fields button

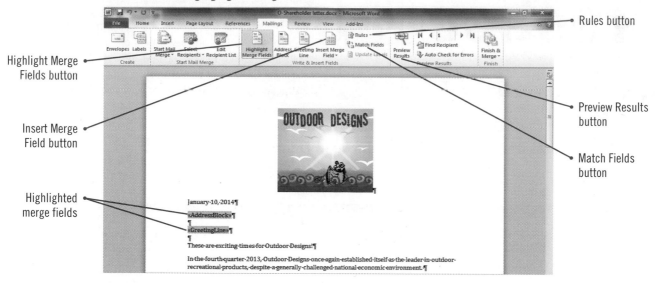

FIGURE O-22: Previewing merged file

First Record button

Previous Record button

First record from source data file

Last Record button

Next Record button

Currently displayed record

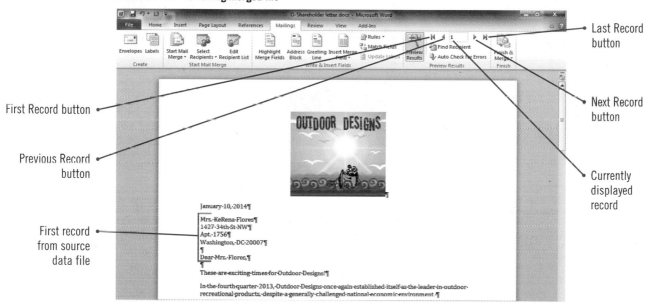

FIGURE O-23: Printing merged letters

Finish & Merge button

In Step 4, click this option

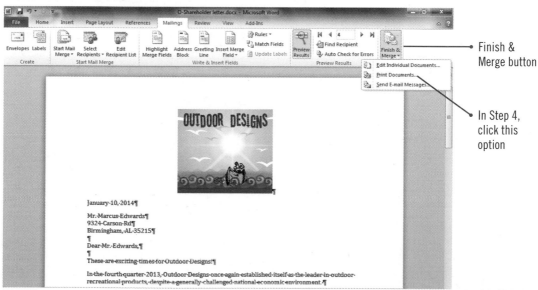

Practice

Concepts Review

For current SAM information, including versions and content details, visit SAM Central (http://www.cengage.com/samcentral). If you have a SAM user profile, you may have access to hands-on instruction, practice, and assessment of the skills covered in this unit. Since various versions of SAM are supported throughout the life of this text, check with your instructor for the correct instructions and URL/Web site for accessing assignments.

Label the elements of the Word window shown in Figure O-24.

FIGURE O-24

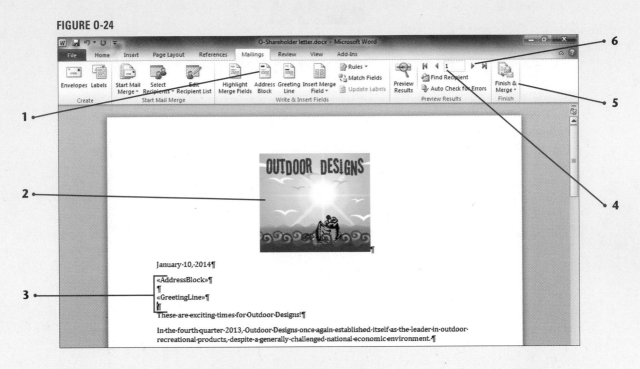

Match each term with the statement that best describes it.

7. **Linked object**
8. **Address block**
9. **Screenshot**
10. **Outline view**
11. **Mail merge**

a. Updates data automatically in a destination file when source file is updated
b. Presents text in a hierarchical structure in Word and automatically formats headings and subheadings
c. The process of combining a main document and a source data file to create custom documents
d. A feature that captures an image from another program
e. A combination of fields from a source file

Select the best answer from the list of choices.

12. Which of the following is *not* true about the Screen Clipping feature?

   a. You cannot use it in another document.

   b. You can apply an artistic effect to it.

   c. It is a bitmap image.

   d. You can use any open window.

13. Which of the following indicate a merge field?

   a. [[AddressBlock]]

   b. {{AddressBlock}}

   c. ++AddressBlock ++

   d. << AddressBlock>>

14. Receiving a prompt to update data in a document indicates that:

   a. The document has been published to the Web.

   b. The document has an embedded object.

   c. The document contains a linked object.

   d. The document is a mail merge document.

15. Which of the following cannot be captured by Screen Clipping?

   a. A program window minimized to the taskbar

   b. A Web browser window

   c. A maximized window

   d. A window in Restore Down view

Skills Review

1. Insert an Excel chart into a PowerPoint slide.

   a. Start PowerPoint, open the file O-8.pptx from where you store your Data Files, then save it as **O-Landscape Lightning Sales.pptx**. (*Hint*: Throughout this exercise, maximize windows as necessary.)

   b. Move to Slide 2, then use the content placeholder to insert a pie chart using the Exploded pie in 3-D style (fifth column).

   c. In Excel, enter the following data:

Cell	Data	Cell	Data
A2	Garden	B2	6.7
A3	Deck	B3	7.3
A4	Path	B4	8.4
A5	Water	B5	2.6
B1	Sales		

   d. Exit Excel without saving the worksheet.

2. Insert PowerPoint slides from a Word document.

   a. Start Word, then open the file O-9.docx from where you store your Data Files.

   b. View the document in Outline view.

   c. Close the document, then exit Word.

   d. In PowerPoint, insert the file O-9.docx using the Slides from Outline command.

   e. Use a button in the Slides group to reset the slides to the presentation themes.

   f. Add your name to the slide footer on every page, move to Slide 1, then save your changes.

3. Insert screen captures into a Word document slide.

   a. In PowerPoint, make sure Slide 1 is selected, then start Word.

   b. Open the file O-10.docx from where you store your Data Files, then save it as **O-Landscape Lightning Events.docx**.

   c. Position the insertion point at the top of the page, click the Insert tab, click Screenshot in the Illustrations group, then click Screen Clipping.

   d. In PowerPoint, select the lightning logo and text in Slide 1. (*Hint*: Include some extra space around the image and text.)

   e. Click the More button in the Picture Styles gallery, then apply the Soft Edge Rectangle to the clip.

   f. Change the Shape Height of the clip to 1.3 in the Size group, then save your changes and exit PowerPoint.

Skills Review (continued)

4. **Insert text from a Word file into an open document.**
   a. Switch to Word. Position the insertion point at the beginning of the line that starts **As marketing managers**, then insert the file O-11.docx as Text from File. (*Hint*: Click a button on the Insert tab.)
   b. Select the three lines of text you just inserted from the file, then format it as a bulleted list using a square black bullet style.
   c. Save your changes.

5. **Link an Excel chart to a Word document.**
   a. Start Excel, open the file O-12.xlsx, then save it as **O-Landscape Lightning Event Analysis.xlsx**.
   b. Show Word and Excel side by side.
   c. Switch to Excel, then select and copy the range A2:D4.
   d. Switch to Word, press [Ctrl][End], insert a blank line, click the Paste list arrow, then click the Link & Keep Source Formatting option.
   e. Switch to Excel, then copy the chart.
   f. Switch to Word, insert a blank line after the inserted cells, click the Paste list arrow, then click the Use Destination Theme & Link Data button.
   g. Click a cell in the table, then click the Distribute Rows button in the Cell Size group on the Table Tools Layout tab.
   h. Save your changes, then close the document.

6. **Update a linked Excel chart in a Word document.**
   a. In Excel, change cell B3 to **86** and cell B4 to **73**. (*Hint*: Maximize the window if necessary.)
   b. Switch to Word, open the O-Landscape Lightning Events document, then update the document with data from the linked file. (*Hint*: Right-click a cell in the table, then click Update Links, if necessary.)
   c. Switch to Excel, save and close the worksheet, then exit Excel.
   d. In Word, select the chart, click the Shape Outline button in the Shape Styles group on the Chart Tools Format tab, point to Weight, then click 4½ pt.
   e. Save your changes.

7. **Insert Access fields into a Word document.**
   a. Move to the top of the document, then insert two blank lines below the date.
   b. Start a letters mail merge.
   c. Use a command on the Mailings tab to open file O-13.accdb as the selected recipient list.
   d. Use a command on the Mailings tab to view the Mail Merge Recipients dialog box, then accept the defaults and close the dialog box.
   e. Use a command on the Mailings tab to insert an address block, then insert two blank lines in the document.
   f. Use a command on the Mailings tab to insert a greeting line that uses just the first name, then insert one line after this line. (*Hint*: In the Insert Greeting Line dialog box, click the Greeting line format name list arrow, then click "Joshua.")
   g. Save your changes.

8. **Perform a Mail Merge.**
   a. Use a command on the Mailings tab to highlight the merge fields, then turn off highlighting.
   b. Preview your results, reviewing each record in the mail merge.
   c. Finish the mail merge, then print the current record if your lab allows it.

Skills Review (continued)

d. Select the chart, drag a sizing handle inward until the chart fits on the first page, then compare your screen to Figure O-25.

e. Save your changes, close the document, then exit Word.

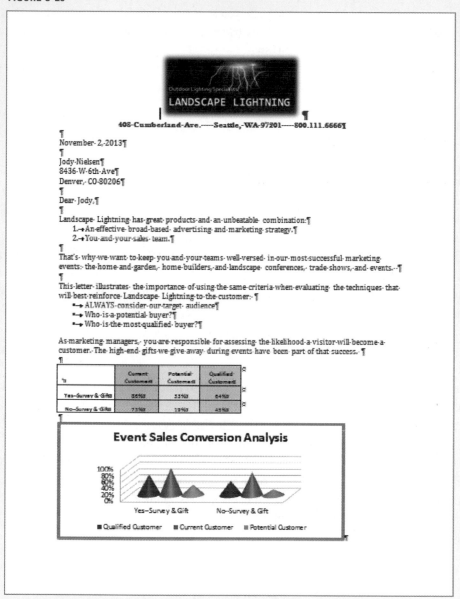

Independent Challenge 1

You are the new intern assigned to Nikkie Kaye, the manager of customer service at Luggage xPress. The company delivers lost luggage to airline customers staying at large hotels and also handles luggage pickup for travelers. Luggage xPress is beginning to franchise operations to other cities, and Nikkie needs your help in preparing a PowerPoint presentation. She also needs you to send out a personalized form letter to clients who had lost luggage.

a. Start PowerPoint, open the file O-14.pptx from where you store your Data Files, then save it as **O-Luggage xPress Franchise.pptx** where you store your Data Files. (*Hint*: Throughout this exercise, maximize windows as necessary.)

b. In Slide 2, insert a pie chart using the Pie in 3-D style.

c. In Excel, enter the following data and select only that data to display in the chart. (*Hint*: Drag the blue line up to cell B3.)

Cell	Data
B1	Stats
A2	3 Million Bags Lost
B2	3,000,000
A3	Over 1/2 Million Bags Lost Forever
B3	530,000

d. Following Slide 2, insert slides from an outline using the file **O-15.docx**.

e. Add your name to the footer of all slides except the title slide, then save your changes and exit PowerPoint.

f. Start Word, open the file O-16.docx from where you store your Data Files, then save it as **O-Luggage xPress Feedback Letter.docx**.

g. Go to the end of the page, insert a new page, open the file O-17.docx, then use the Screen Clipping feature to insert the image from the O-17.docx file at the top of the new page. Center the image.

h. Press [Enter] until the insertion point is below the inserted screen clip.

i. Start Excel, open the file O-18.xlsx from where you store your Data Files, then save it as **O-Luggage xPress Feedback Chart.xlsx**.

j. Copy the chart in Excel, switch to Word, then paste the chart so that it uses destination theme and link data.

k. Change the chart style to Style 48. (*Hint*: Select the Chart Tools Design tab; click the last style in the last row and column.)

l. Switch to Excel, change cell B3 to 66, save your changes to the workbook, then exit Excel.

m. Switch to Word, insert a blank footer in the document, then add your name, left-aligned.

n. Move to the top of the first page of the document, place the insertion point on the blank line beneath the date, then create a letters mail merge that uses file O-19.accdb as the data source file and includes the Address Block and Greeting Line fields. Use the default field formats, and insert blank lines as appropriate.

o. Preview your results, finish the merge file, then print the third record if your lab allows it.

p. Save and close the document.

q. Close any open files, then exit all open programs.

Independent Challenge 2

You and your business partner, chef Melanie Nakano, are planning to start a new restaurant in Ann Arbor, Michigan. You need to apply for a start-up loan to get the business going. Your first task is to write a cover letter that will accompany your loan package to several banks. You also want to prepare a PowerPoint presentation of a few menu items that potential lenders can view on your Web site.

a. Start Word, then write a letter that you can send to banks along with the loan package. You will add recipient information in a future step; for now, write the body of the letter, including the name and location of your new restaurant, why you are applying for the loan, why the business will be successful, and how much you would like to borrow.

b. Save the letter as **O-Restaurant loan letter.docx** where you store your Data Files. (*Hint*: Throughout this exercise, maximize windows as necessary.)

c. Start Excel, open the file O-20.xlsx from where you store your Data Files, then save it as **O-Restaurant sales comparison.xlsx**. This chart shows the success of similar restaurants in a comparable city.

d. Change the chart style, chart layout, or individual chart elements as desired, then copy the chart object.

e. In Word, insert the chart, keeping source formatting and link data.

f. Start a letters mail merge, then create a new recipient list with at least four entries. To create the list, click the Select Recipients button in the Start Mail Merge group, then click Type New List. Enter names and addresses in the New Address List dialog box, clicking New Entry as needed. When the list is complete, click OK, then save the file where you store your Data Files as **O-Restaurant bank loan list.accdb**.

g. At the top of the Word document, insert Address Block and Greeting Line fields. Insert blank lines between the fields as appropriate.

h. Insert a blank footer and add your name, left-aligned.

i. Preview the mail merge, print the first record if your lab allows it, then save and close the document.

j. Start PowerPoint, create a presentation that contains a title slide with the name of your restaurant and a slogan, plus four slides that highlight menu items, then save it as **O-Restaurant Menu.pptx** where you store your Data Files.

k. Apply a theme and transitions, insert clip art and photographs as desired, then add your name to the footer or header.

l. Create a new blank presentation, copy, paste, and arrange some of all of the clip art you previously inserted, then insert a screen clipping of that collage into the first slide of the restaurant menu presentation. Add styles or effects to the new image as desired. Do not save the new presentation. (*Hint*: The Screenshot button is in the Image group on the Insert tab.)

m. Save and close any open files, then exit any open programs.

Independent Challenge 3

The Sweet Lake Bass Fishing Challenge is organizing its annual Memorial Day weekend event, which features the region's largest bass-fishing contest and a fish-off that benefits local charities. The organization's president, Duane Roberts, has asked you to create a PowerPoint presentation that includes information about bass fishing and financial information for potential sponsors and participants, and to publish it to the Web.

a. Start PowerPoint, create a new, blank presentation using any theme you like, customize it for bass (or a different fish species if you prefer) and change the color scheme if you wish, then save it as **O-Fishing Event.pptx** where you store your Data Files. (*Hint*: Throughout this exercise, maximize windows as necessary.)

b. Create at least two slides, including a title slide, then add your name to the footer on all slides except the title slide.

c. Use the Slides from Outline command to insert content from the file O-21.docx into the presentation.

d. Adjust formatting as needed for the newly added slides. Insert clip art and photographs as desired.

e. At the end of the presentation, add a new slide titled **We Got Bass**, start Excel, then create a worksheet and a chart in the style of your choice that show the largest fish caught over each of the past five years. (*Hint*: Enter years in one row and bass weights in a second row. An acceptable weight range for this category is 5–12 pounds.)

f. Save the worksheet as **O-Fishing Record.xlsx** where you store your Data Files.

g. In PowerPoint, paste the chart you created in Excel linked with either source or destination formatting.

Advanced Challenge Exercise

- Start Word, then create an informal confirmation letter for the event. Type the following text in the first line of the document: **Sweet Lake Bass Fishing Challenge Confirmation Form**. Format this text so that it will stand out from the body of the letter. Include lines for first names, last names, street, city, state, zip code, phone number, entrance fee paid, and team name. Below the heading you typed, write at least two paragraphs for the letter body text, confirming that the recipient is registered for the event. Add your name to the footer.
- Capture all or part of a screen in another program.
- Save the file as **O-Fishing Confirmation ACE.docx** where you store your Data Files.
- Start a mail merge. Create a Mail Merge Recipients list that has at least four records and includes data in the following fields: First Name, Last Name, Address 1, City, State, and ZIP Code. Save the file as **O-Fishing Registration ACE.accdb** where you store your Data Files.
- Below the heading at the top of the document, insert address block and greeting line fields, finish the mail merge by merging to the printer, then print the second letter if your lab allows printing.

h. Close any open files, then exit all programs.

Real Life Independent Challenge

Creating a form letter is a great way to manage your correspondence with efficiency and style. You can use the mail merge features in Word to personalize thank-you notes, e-mail messages, and invitations. Think of an event for which you would like to use personalized form letters to save time yet still include a personal touch. It could be a thank-you note to recipients of a recent party or special event, a party invitation, or perhaps a change of address notice. Then create a personalized form letter you can send to at least four recipients.

a. Start Word, then save a new document as **O-My event.docx** where you store your Data Files. (*Hint*: Throughout this exercise, maximize windows as necessary.)

b. Write a brief letter containing the text of the thank-you, invitation, or other notice. Add clip art or photographs as desired.

c. Include two sentences: one asking the recipient to confirm his or her e-mail address; and the other, to confirm his or her home phone number.

d. Add your name as the signatory to the document.

e. Create a letter mail merge, then create a Mail Merge Recipients list that has at least four records and includes first name, last name, street, city, state, zip code, home phone, and e-mail address. Save the file as **O-My event list.accdb** where you store your Data Files.

f. At the top of the document, insert address block and greeting line fields. Insert blank lines as needed, and format the greeting line in an informal style.

g. After the sentence asking to confirm their e-mail address, insert the Email_Address field. (*Hint*: Use the Insert Merge Field button in the Write & Insert Fields group.)

h. After the sentence asking to confirm their home phone, insert the Home_Phone field. (*Hint*: Use the Insert Merge Field button in the Write & Insert Fields group.)

i. Complete the mail merge, then print the first record if your lab allows printing.

j. Save and close any open files, then exit Word.

Visual Workshop

Using the skills you learned in this unit, create the PowerPoint slide shown in Figure O-26. To get started, create a new blank presentation using the Grid theme, insert a Title and Content slide, then add your name to the footer to appear in all slides. Select a Clustered Bar chart. (*Hint*: Use the following regular fuel mileage values: 1908: 20; 1998: 23; Present & Beyond: 26.) Make any other changes or additions to the presentation to match Figure O-26. Save the presentation as **O-Fuel Economy.pptx**, then save the worksheet as **O-Fuel Economy.xlsx** where you store your Data Files. Print the slide if your lab allows printing. Save your changes, close any open files, then exit all programs.

FIGURE O-26

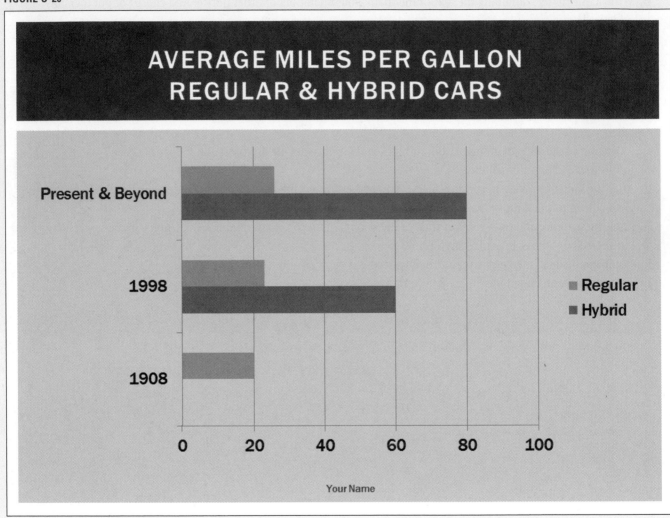

Working with Windows Live and Office Web Apps

If the computer you are using has an active Internet connection, you can go to the Microsoft Windows Live Web site and access a wide variety of services and Web applications. For example, you can check your e-mail through Windows Live, network with your friends and coworkers, and use SkyDrive to store and share files. From SkyDrive, you can also use Office Web Apps to create and edit Word, PowerPoint, Excel, and OneNote files, even when you are using a computer that does not have Office 2010 installed. You work in the Vancouver branch of Quest Specialty Travel. Your supervisor, Mary Lou Jacobs, asks you to explore Windows Live and learn how she can use SkyDrive and Office Web Apps to work with her files online.

(*Note*: SkyDrive and Office Web Apps are dynamic Web pages, and might change over time, including the way they are organized and how commands are performed. The steps and figures in this appendix were accurate at the time this book was published.)

OBJECTIVES

Explore how to work online from Windows Live

Obtain a Windows Live ID and sign in to Windows Live

Upload files to Windows Live

Work with the PowerPoint Web App

Create folders and organize files on SkyDrive

Add people to your network and share files

Work with the Excel Web App

Exploring How to Work Online from Windows Live

You can use your Web browser to upload your files to Windows Live from any computer connected to the Internet. You can work on the files right in your Web browser using Office Web Apps and share your files with people in your Windows Live network. ▰▰▰ You review the concepts and services related to working online from Windows Live.

- **What is Windows Live?**

  Windows Live is a collection of services and Web applications that you can use to help you be more productive both personally and professionally. For example, you can use Windows Live to send and receive e-mail, to chat with friends via instant messaging, to share photos, to create a blog, and to store and edit files using SkyDrive. Table WEB-1 describes the services available on Windows Live. Windows Live is a free service that you sign up for. When you sign up, you receive a Windows Live ID, which you use to sign in to Windows Live. When you work with files on Windows Live, you are cloud computing.

- **What is Cloud Computing?**

  The term **cloud computing** refers to the process of working with files online in a Web browser. When you save files to SkyDrive on Windows Live, you are saving your files to an online location. SkyDrive is like having a personal hard drive in the cloud.

- **What is SkyDrive?**

  SkyDrive is an online storage and file sharing service. With a Windows Live account, you receive access to your own SkyDrive, which is your personal storage area on the Internet. On your SkyDrive, you are given space to store up to 25 GB of data online. Each file can be a maximum size of 50 MB. You can also use SkyDrive to access Office Web Apps, which you use to create and edit files created in Word, OneNote, PowerPoint, and Excel online in your Web browser.

- **Why use Windows Live and SkyDrive?**

  On Windows Live, you use SkyDrive to access additional storage for your files. You don't have to worry about backing up your files to a memory stick or other storage device that could be lost or damaged. Another advantage of storing your files on SkyDrive is that you can access your files from any computer that has an active Internet connection. Figure WEB-1 shows the SkyDrive Web page that appears when accessed from a Windows Live account. From SkyDrive, you can also access Office Web Apps.

- **What are Office Web Apps?**

  Office Web Apps are versions of Microsoft Word, Excel, PowerPoint, and OneNote that you can access online from your SkyDrive. An Office Web App does not include all of the features and functions included with the full Office version of its associated application. However, you can use the Office Web App from any computer that is connected to the Internet, even if Microsoft Office 2010 is not installed on that computer.

- **How do SkyDrive and Office Web Apps work together?**

  You can create a file in Office 2010 using Word, Excel, PowerPoint, or OneNote and then upload the file to your SkyDrive. You can then open the Office file saved to SkyDrive and edit it using your Web browser and the corresponding Office Web App. Figure WEB-2 shows a PowerPoint presentation open in the PowerPoint Web App. You can also use an Office Web App to create a new file, which is saved automatically to SkyDrive while you work. In addition, you can download a file created with an Office Web App and continue to work with the file in the full version of the corresponding Office application: Word, Excel, PowerPoint, or OneNote. Finally, you can create a SkyDrive network that consists of the people you want to be able to view your folders and files on your SkyDrive. You can give people permission to view and edit your files using any computer with an active Internet connection and a Web browser.

FIGURE WEB-1: SkyDrive on Windows Live

Browser window

SkyDrive - Windows Live tab

By default, one folder is available on SkyDrive; you can create additional folders

The name of the person who signed into Windows Live and SkyDrive appears here

Monitors the amount of space still available on your SkyDrive

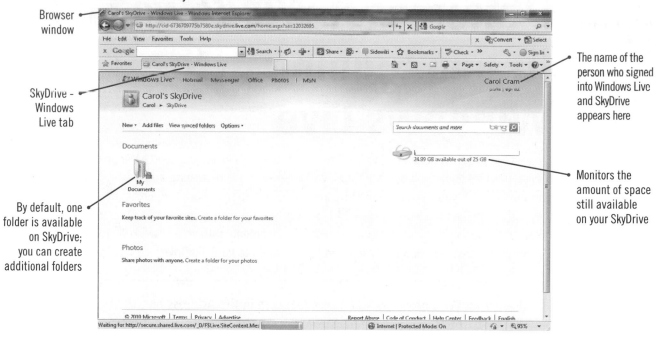

FIGURE WEB-2: PowerPoint presentation open in the PowerPoint Web App

Browser window

Ribbon available in PowerPoint Web App

The presentation in PowerPoint Web App maintains the same look and feel as the same presentation in the desktop version of PowerPoint

Name of PowerPoint presentation open in PowerPoint Web App

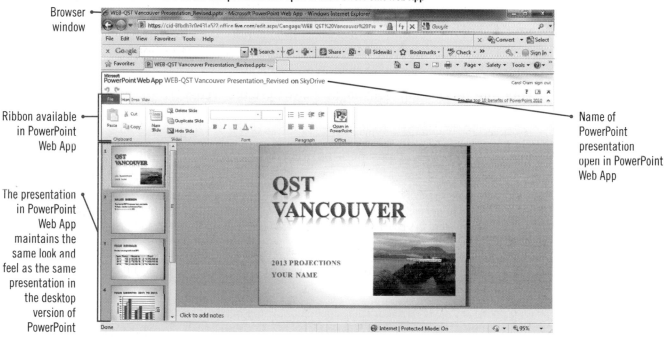

TABLE WEB-1: Services available via Windows Live

service	description
E-mail	Send and receive e-mail using a Hotmail account
Instant Messaging	Use Messenger to chat with friends, share photos, and play games
SkyDrive	Store files, work on files using Office Web Apps, and share files with people in your network
Photos	Upload and share photos with friends
People	Develop a network of friends and coworkers, then use the network to distribute information and stay in touch
Downloads	Access a variety of free programs available for download to a PC
Mobile Device	Access applications for a mobile device: text messaging, using Hotmail, networking, and sharing photos

Obtaining a Windows Live ID and Signing In to Windows Live

To work with your files online using SkyDrive and Office Web Apps, you need a Windows Live ID. You obtain a Windows Live ID by going to the Windows Live Web site and creating a new account. Once you have a Windows Live ID, you can access SkyDrive and then use it to store your files, create new files, and share your files with friends and coworkers. ▓▓▓▓ Mary Lou Jacobs, your supervisor at QST Vancouver, asks you to obtain a Windows Live ID so that you can work on documents with your coworkers. You go to the Windows Live Web site, create a Windows Live ID, and then sign in to your SkyDrive.

STEPS

QUICK TIP

If you already have a Windows Live ID, go to the next lesson and sign in as directed using your account.

1. **Open your Web browser, type home.live.com in the Address bar, then press [Enter]**

   The Windows Live home page opens. From this page, you can create a Windows Live account and receive your Windows Live ID.

2. **Click the Sign up button** *(Note: You may see a Sign up link instead of a button)*

   The Create your Windows Live ID page opens.

3. **Click the Or use your own e-mail address link under the Check availability button or if you are already using Hotmail, Messenger, or Xbox LIVE, click the Sign in now link in the Information statement near the top of the page**

4. **Enter the information required, as shown in Figure WEB-3**

   If you wish, you can sign up for a Windows Live e-mail address such as yourname@live.com so that you can also access the Windows Live e-mail services.

TROUBLE

The code can be difficult to read. If you receive an error message, enter the new code that appears.

5. **Enter the code shown at the bottom of your screen, then click the I accept button**

   The Windows Live home page opens. The name you entered when you signed up for your Windows Live ID appears in the top right corner of the window to indicate that you are signed in to Windows Live. From the Windows Live home page, you can access all the services and applications offered by Windows Live. See the Verifying your Windows Live ID box for information on finalizing your account set up.

6. **Point to Windows Live, as shown in Figure WEB-4**

   A list of options appears. SkyDrive is one of the options you can access directly from Windows Live.

TROUBLE

Click I accept if you are asked to review and accept the Windows Live Service Agreement and Privacy Statement.

7. **Click SkyDrive**

   The SkyDrive page opens. Your name appears in the top right corner, and the amount of space available is shown on the right side of the SkyDrive page. The amount of space available is monitored, as indicated by the gauge that fills with color as space is used. Using SkyDrive, you can add files to the existing folder and you can create new folders.

8. **Click sign out in the top right corner under your name, then exit the Web browser**

   You are signed out of your Windows Live account. You can sign in again directly from the Windows Live page in your browser or from within a file created with PowerPoint, Excel, Word, or OneNote.

FIGURE WEB-3: Creating a Windows Live ID

Click to sign in using a Hotmail, Messenger, or Xbox Live account

Once your registration is complete, you will be asked to verify your ID

A different code will appear on your screen

Type your e-mail address

You can choose to get a Windows Live e-mail address

Enter the information required

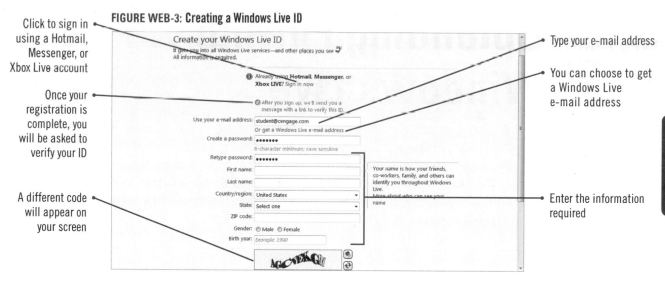

FIGURE WEB-4: Selecting SkyDrive

SkyDrive in the list of Windows Live options

Information about your Windows Live network

Your name appears here

Click to quickly add people to your network

An advertisement appropriate for your location appears here

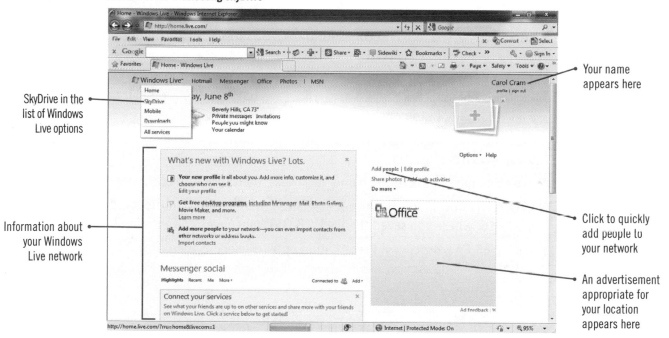

Verifying your Windows Live ID

As soon as you accept the Windows Live terms, an e-mail is sent to the e-mail address you supplied when you created your Windows Live ID. Open your e-mail program, and then open the e-mail from Microsoft with the Subject line: Confirm your e-mail address for Windows Live. Follow the simple, step-by-step instructions in the e-mail to confirm your Windows Live ID. When the confirmation is complete, you will be asked to sign in to Windows Live, using your e-mail address and password. Once signed in, you will see your Windows Live Account page.

Uploading Files to Windows Live

Once you have created your Windows Live ID, you can sign in to Windows Live directly from Word, PowerPoint, Excel, or OneNote and start saving and uploading files. You upload files to your SkyDrive so you can share the files with other people, access the files from another computer, or use SkyDrive's additional storage. ⬛⬛⬛⬛⬛ You open a PowerPoint presentation, access your Windows Live account from Backstage view, and save a file to SkyDrive on Windows Live. You also create a new folder called Cengage directly from Backstage view and add a file to it.

STEPS

1. **Start PowerPoint, open the file** WEB-1.pptx **from the drive and folder where you store your Data Files, then save the file as** WEB-QST Vancouver Presentation

2. **Click the** File tab, **then click** Save & Send

   The Save & Send options available in PowerPoint are listed in Backstage view, as shown in Figure WEB-5.

3. **Click** Save to Web

QUICK TIP

Skip this step if the computer you are using signs you in automatically.

4. **Click** Sign In, **type your e-mail address, press** [Tab], **type your** password, **then click** OK

   The My Documents folder on your SkyDrive appears in the Save to Windows Live SkyDrive information area.

5. **Click** Save As, **wait a few seconds for the Save As dialog box to appear, then click** Save

   The file is saved to the My Documents folder on the SkyDrive that is associated with your Windows Live account. You can also create a new folder and upload files directly to SkyDrive from your hard drive.

6. **Click the** File tab, **click** Save & Send, **click** Save to Web, **then sign in if the My Documents folder does not automatically appear in Backstage view**

7. **Click the** New Folder button **in the Save to Windows Live SkyDrive pane, then sign in to Windows Live if directed**

8. **Type** Cengage **as the folder name, click** Next, **then click** Add files

9. **Click** select documents from your computer, **then navigate to the location on your computer where you saved the file WEB-QST Vancouver Presentation in Step 1**

10. **Click** WEB-QST Vancouver Presentation.pptx **to select it, then click** Open

    You can continue to add more files; however, you have no more files to upload at this time.

11. **Click** Continue

    In a few moments, the PowerPoint presentation is uploaded to your SkyDrive, as shown in Figure WEB-6. You can simply store the file on SkyDrive or you can choose to work on the presentation using the PowerPoint Web App.

12. **Click the** PowerPoint icon 🄿 **on your taskbar to return to PowerPoint, then close the presentation and exit PowerPoint**

FIGURE WEB-5: Save & Send options in Backstage view

PowerPoint file

Save & Send area in Backstage view

Save to Web option

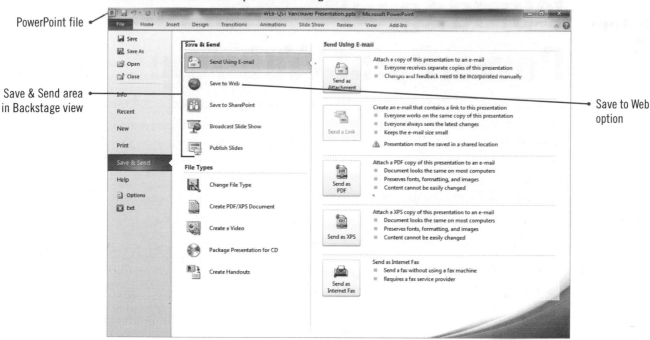

FIGURE WEB-6: File uploaded to the Cengage folder on Windows Live

Browser window

Path to file

Current folder menu bar

Uploaded file

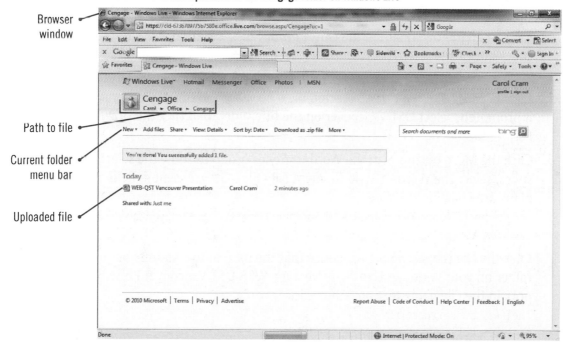

Working with the PowerPoint Web App

Once you have uploaded a file to SkyDrive on Windows Live, you can work on it using its corresponding Office Web App. **Office Web Apps** provide you with the tools you need to view documents online and to edit them right in your browser. You do not need to have Office programs installed on the computer you use to access SkyDrive and Office Web Apps. From SkyDrive, you can also open the document directly in the full Office application (for example, PowerPoint) if the application is installed on the computer you are using. ▄▄▄ You use the PowerPoint Web App to make some edits to the PowerPoint presentation. You then open the presentation in PowerPoint and use the full version to make additional edits.

STEPS

1. **Click the WEB-QST Vancouver Presentation file in the Cengage folder on SkyDrive**

   The presentation opens in your browser window. A menu is available, which includes the options you have for working with the file.

2. **Click Edit in Browser, then if a message appears related to installing the Sign-in Assistant, click the Close button ❌ to the far right of the message**

   In a few moments, the PowerPoint presentation opens in the PowerPoint Web App, as shown in Figure WEB-7. Table WEB-2 lists the commands you can perform using the PowerPoint Web App.

3. **Enter your name where indicated on Slide 1, click Slide 3 (New Tours) in the Slides pane, then click Delete Slide in the Slides group**

   The slide is removed from the presentation. You decide to open the file in the full version of PowerPoint on your computer so you can apply WordArt to the slide title. You work with the file in the full version of PowerPoint when you want to use functions, such as WordArt, that are not available on the PowerPoint Web App.

4. **Click Open in PowerPoint in the Office group, click OK in response to the message, then click Allow if requested**

   In a few moments, the revised version of the PowerPoint slide opens in PowerPoint on your computer.

5. **Click Enable Editing on the Protected View bar near the top of your presentation window if prompted, select QST Vancouver on the title slide, then click the Drawing Tools Format tab**

6. **Click the More button ⏷ in the WordArt Styles group to show the selection of WordArt styles, select the WordArt style Gradient Fill - Blue-Gray, Accent 4, Reflection, then click a blank area outside the slide**

   The presentation appears in PowerPoint as shown in Figure WEB-8. Next, you save the revised version of the file to SkyDrive.

7. **Click the File tab, click Save As, notice that the path in the Address bar is to the Cengage folder on your Windows Live SkyDrive, type WEB-QST Vancouver Presentation_Revised. pptx in the File name text box, then click Save**

   The file is saved to your SkyDrive.

8. **Click the browser icon on the taskbar to open your SkyDrive page, then click Office next to your name in the SkyDrive path, view a list of recent documents, then click Cengage in the list to the left of the recent documents list to open the Cengage folder**

   Two PowerPoint files now appear in the Cengage folder.

9. **Exit the Web browser and close all tabs if prompted, then exit PowerPoint**

FIGURE WEB-7: Presentation opened in the PowerPoint Web App from Windows Live

Browser window

Name of Web App

PowerPoint Web App Ribbon

URL is the file location

FIGURE WEB-8: Revised PowerPoint presentation

PowerPoint title bar

PowerPoint Ribbon

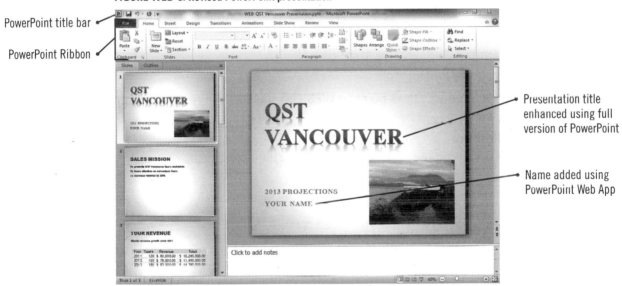

Presentation title enhanced using full version of PowerPoint

Name added using PowerPoint Web App

TABLE WEB-2: Commands on the PowerPoint Web App

tab	commands available
File	• Open in PowerPoint: select to open the file in PowerPoint on your computer • Where's the Save Button?: when you click this option, a message appears telling you that you do not need to save your presentation when you are working on it with PowerPoint Web App. The presentation is saved automatically as you work. • Print • Share • Properties • Give Feedback • Privacy • Terms of Use • Close
Home	• Clipboard group: Cut, Copy, Paste • Slides group: Add a New Slide, Delete a Slide, Duplicate a Slide, and Hide a Slide • Font group: Work with text: change the font, style, color, and size of selected text • Paragraph group: Work with paragraphs: add bullets and numbers, indent text, align text • Office group: Open the file in PowerPoint on your computer
Insert	• Insert a Picture • Insert a SmartArt diagram • Insert a link such as a link to another file on SkyDrive or to a Web page
View	• Editing view (the default) • Reading view • Slide Show view • Notes view

Web Apps

Creating Folders and Organizing Files on SkyDrive

As you have learned, you can sign in to SkyDrive directly from the Office applications PowerPoint, Excel, Word, and OneNote, or you can access SkyDrive directly through your Web browser. This option is useful when you are away from the computer on which you normally work or when you are using a computer that does not have Office applications installed. You can go to SkyDrive, create and organize folders, and then create or open files to work on with Office Web Apps. ![icon] You access SkyDrive from your Web browser, create a new folder called Illustrated, and delete one of the PowerPoint files from the My Documents folder.

STEPS

TROUBLE
Go to Step 3 if you are already signed in.

1. **Open your Web browser, type home.live.com in the Address bar, then press [Enter]**
   The Windows Live home page opens. From here, you can sign in to your Windows Live account and then access SkyDrive.

TROUBLE
Type your Windows Live ID (your e-mail) and password, then click Sign in if prompted to do so.

2. **Sign into Windows Live as directed**
   You are signed in to your Windows Live page. From this page, you can take advantage of the many applications available on Windows Live, including SkyDrive.

3. **Point to Windows Live, then click SkyDrive**
   SkyDrive opens.

4. **Click Cengage, then point to WEB-QST Vancouver Presentation.pptx**
   A menu of options for working with the file, including a Delete button to the far right, appears to the right of the filename.

5. **Click the Delete button ⊠, then click OK**
   The file is removed from the Cengage folder on your SkyDrive. You still have a copy of the file on your computer.

6. **Point to Windows Live, then click SkyDrive**
   Your SkyDrive screen with the current selection of folders available on your SkyDrive opens, as shown in Figure WEB-9.

7. **Click New, click Folder, type Illustrated, click Next, click Office in the path under Add documents to Illustrated at the top of the window, then click View all in the list under Personal**
   You are returned to your list of folders, where you see the new Illustrated folder.

8. **Click Cengage, point to WEB-QST Vancouver Presentation_Revised.pptx, click More, click Move, then click the Illustrated folder**

9. **Click Move this file into Illustrated, as shown in Figure WEB-10**
   The file is moved to the Illustrated folder.

FIGURE WEB-9: Folders on your SkyDrive

Current location

Folders currently available

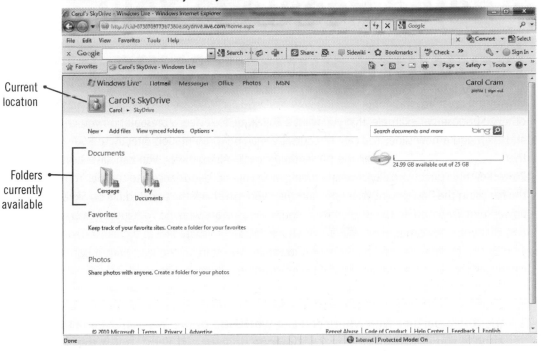

FIGURE WEB-10: Moving a file to the Illustrated folder

Click to move file to this location

Be sure to rename a file before moving it if you are moving it to a location where another copy of the same file exists

Name of file to be moved

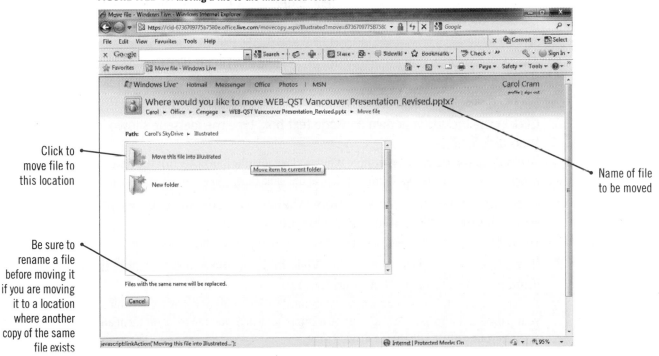

Adding People to Your Network and Sharing Files

One of the great advantages of working with SkyDrive on Windows Live is that you can share your files with others. Suppose, for example, that you want a colleague to review a presentation you created in PowerPoint and then add a new slide. You can, of course, e-mail the presentation directly to your colleague, who can then make changes and e-mail the presentation back. Alternatively, you can save time by uploading the PowerPoint file directly to SkyDrive and then giving your colleague access to the file. Your colleague can edit the file using the PowerPoint Web App, and then you can check the updated file on SkyDrive, also using the PowerPoint Web App. In this way, you and your colleague are working with just one version of the presentation that you both can update. You have decided to share files in the Illustrated folder that you created in the previous lesson with another individual. You start by working with a partner so that you can share files with your partner and your partner can share files with you.

STEPS

TROUBLE
If you cannot find a partner, read the steps so you understand how the process works.

1. **Identify a partner with whom you can work, and obtain his or her e-mail address; you can choose someone in your class or someone on your e-mail list, but it should be someone who will be completing these steps when you are**

2. **From the Illustrated folder, click Share**

3. **Click Edit permissions**

   The Edit permissions page opens. On this page, you can select the individual with whom you would like to share the contents of the Illustrated folder.

4. **Click in the Enter a name or an e-mail address text box, type the e-mail address of your partner, then press [Tab]**

   You can define the level of access that you want to give your partner.

5. **Click the Can view files list arrow shown in Figure WEB-11, click Can add, edit details, and delete files, then click Save**

   You can choose to send a notification to each individual when you grant permission to access your files.

TROUBLE
If you do not receive a message from Windows Live, your partner has not yet completed the steps to share the Illustrated folder.

6. **Click in the Include your own message text box, type the message shown in Figure WEB-12, then click Send**

   Your partner will receive a message from Windows Live advising him or her that you have shared your Illustrated folder. If your partner is completing the steps at the same time, you will receive an e-mail from your partner.

7. **Check your e-mail for a message from Windows Live advising you that your partner has shared his or her Illustrated folder with you**

   The subject of the e-mail message will be "[Name] has shared documents with you."

QUICK TIP
You will know you are on your partner's SkyDrive because you will see your partner's first name at the beginning of the SkyDrive path.

8. **If you have received the e-mail, click View folder in the e-mail message, then sign in to Windows Live if you are requested to do so**

   You are now able to access your partner's Illustrated folder on his or her SkyDrive. You can download files in your partner's Illustrated folder to your own computer where you can work on them and then upload them again to your partner's Illustrated shared folder.

9. **Exit the browser**

FIGURE WEB-11: Editing folder permissions

Folder permissions will be changed for the Illustrated folder

Click to select network permission options

Type email address to continue to add people

Person whose permission status will change

Click to select person from list of contacts

Click to select permission option

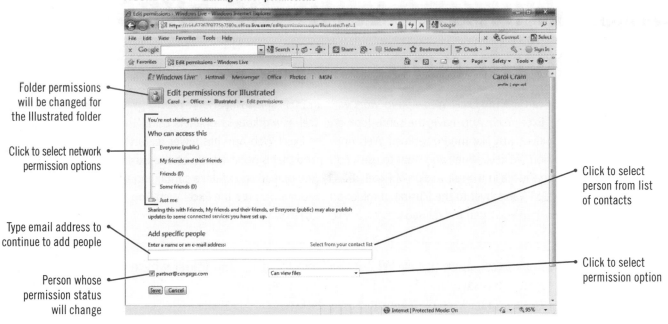

FIGURE WEB-12: Entering a message to notify a person that file sharing permission has been granted

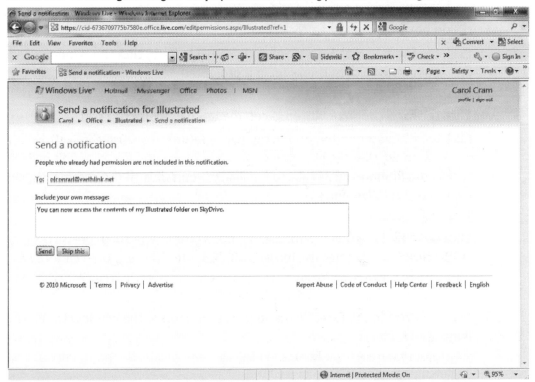

Sharing files on SkyDrive

When you share a folder with other people, the people with whom you share a folder can download the file to their computers and then make changes using the full version of the corresponding Office application.

Once these changes are made, each individual can then upload the file to SkyDrive and into a folder shared with you and others. In this way, you can create a network of people with whom you share your files.

Working with the Excel Web App

You can use the Excel Web App to work with an Excel spreadsheet on SkyDrive. Workbooks opened using the Excel Web App have the same look and feel as workbooks opened using the full version of Excel. However, just like the PowerPoint Web App, the Excel Web App has fewer features available than the full version of Excel. When you want to use a command that is not available on the Excel Web App, you need to open the file in the full version of Excel.  You upload an Excel file containing a list of the tours offered by QST Vancouver to the Illustrated folder on SkyDrive. You use the Excel Web App to make some changes, and then you open the revised version in Excel 2010 on your computer.

STEPS

1. **Start Excel, open the file WEB-2.xlsx from the drive and folder where you store your Data Files, then save the file as WEB-QST Vancouver Tours**

   The data in the Excel file is formatted using the Excel table function.

> **TROUBLE**
> If prompted, sign in to your Windows Live account as directed.

2. **Click the File tab, click Save & Send, then click Save to Web**

   In a few moments, you should see three folders to which you can save spreadsheets. My Documents and Cengage are personal folder that contains files that only you can access. Illustrated is a shared folder that contains files you can share with others in your network. The Illustrated folder is shared with your partner.

3. **Click the Illustrated folder, click the Save As button, wait a few seconds for the Save As dialog box to appear, then click Save**

> **QUICK TIP**
> Alternately, you can open your Web browser and go to Windows Live to sign in to SkyDrive.

4. **Click the File tab, click Save & Send, click Save to Web, click the Windows Live SkyDrive link above your folders, then sign in if prompted**

   Windows Live opens to your SkyDrive.

5. **Click the Excel program button 🗷 on the taskbar, then exit Excel**

6. **Click your browser button on the taskbar to return to SkyDrive if SkyDrive is not the active window, click the Illustrated folder, click the Excel file, click Edit in Browser, then review the Ribbon and its tabs to familiarize yourself with the commands you can access from the Excel Web App**

   Table WEB-3 summarizes the commands that are available.

7. **Click cell A12, type Gulf Islands Sailing, press [TAB], type 3000, press [TAB], type 10, press [TAB], click cell D3, enter the formula =B3*C3, press [Enter], then click cell A1**

   The formula is copied automatically to the remaining rows as shown in Figure WEB-13 because the data in the original Excel file was created and formatted as an Excel table.

8. **Click SkyDrive in the Excel Web App path at the top of the window to return to the Illustrated folder**

   The changes you made to the Excel spreadsheet are saved automatically on SkyDrive. You can download the file directly to your computer from SkyDrive.

9. **Point to the Excel file, click More, click Download, click Save, navigate to the location where you save the files for this book, name the file WEB-QST Vancouver Tours_Updated, click Save, then click Close in the Download complete dialog box**

   The updated version of the spreadsheet is saved on your computer and on SkyDrive.

10. **Exit the Web browser**

FIGURE WEB-13: Updated table in the Excel Web App

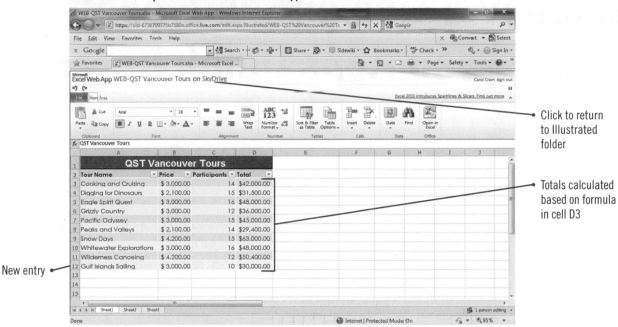

Click to return to Illustrated folder

Totals calculated based on formula in cell D3

New entry

TABLE WEB-3: Commands on the Excel Web App

tab	commands available
File	• Open in Excel: select to open the file in Excel on your computer • Where's the Save Button?: when you click this option, a message appears telling you that you do not need to save your spreadsheet when you are working in it with Excel Web App; the spreadsheet is saved automatically as you work • Save As • Share • Download a Snapshot: a snapshot contains only the values and the formatting; you cannot modify a snapshot • Download a Copy: the file can be opened and edited in the full version of Excel • Give Feedback • Privacy Statement • Terms of Use • Close
Home	• Clipboard group: Cut, Copy, Paste • Font group: change the font, style, color, and size of selected labels and values, as well as border styles and fill colors • Alignment group: change vertical and horizontal alignment and turn on the Wrap Text feature • Number group: change the number format and increase or decrease decimal places • Tables: sort and filter data in a table and modify Table Options • Cells: insert and delete cells • Data: refresh data and find labels or values • Office: open the file in Excel on your computer
Insert	• Insert a Table • Insert a Hyperlink to a Web page

Exploring other Office Web Apps

Two other Office Web Apps are Word and OneNote. You can share files on SkyDrive directly from Word or from OneNote using the same method you used to share files from PowerPoint and Excel. After you upload a Word or OneNote file to SkyDrive, you can work with it in its corresponding Office Web App. To familiarize yourself with the commands available in an Office Web App, open the file and then review the commands on each tab on the Ribbon. If you want to perform a task that is not available in the Office Web App, open the file in the full version of the application.

In addition to working with uploaded files, you can create files from new on SkyDrive. Simply sign in to SkyDrive and open a folder. With a folder open, click New and then select the Web App you want to use to create the new file.

Windows Live and Microsoft Office Web Apps Quick Reference

To Do This	Go Here
Access Windows Live	From the Web browser, type **home.live.com**, then click Sign In
Access SkyDrive on Windows Live	From the Windows Live home page, point to Windows Live, then click SkyDrive
Save to Windows Live from Word, PowerPoint, or Excel	File tab | Save & Send | Save to Web | Select a folder | Save As
Create a New Folder from Backstage view	File tab | Save & Send | Save to Web | New Folder button
Edit a File with a Web App	From SkyDrive, click the file, then click Edit in Browser
Open a File in a desktop version of the application from a Web App: Word, Excel, PowerPoint	Click Open in [Application] in the Office group in each Office Web App
Share files on Windows Live	From SkyDrive, click the folder containing the files to share, click Share on the menu bar, click Edit permissions, enter the e-mail address of the person to share files with, click the Can view files list arrow, click Can add, edit details, and delete files, then click Save

Glossary

Absolute cell reference In Excel, a cell reference that does not change when the formula is copied and pasted to a new location. For example, the formula "=$B$5*C5" in cell D5 does not change to "=$B$6*C6" when you copy the formula to cell D6. *See also* Relative cell reference.

Accessories Built-in programs that come with Windows 7.

Active cell In an Excel worksheet, the current location of the cell pointer.

Active window The window that you are currently using, if multiple windows are open, the window with the darker title bar.

Address A sequence of drive and folder names that describes a folder's or file's location in the file hierarchy; the highest hierarchy level is on the left, with lower hierarchy levels separated by the ▶ symbol to its right.

Address bar In a window, the white area just below the title bar that shows the file hierarchy, or address of the files that appear in the file list below it; the address appears as a series of links you can click to navigate to other locations on your computer.

Aero A Windows 7 viewing option that shows windows as translucent objects and features subtle animations; only available on a computer that has enough memory to support Aero and on which a Windows Aero theme has been selected.

Aero Flip 3D A Windows 7 feature that lets you preview all open folders and documents without using the taskbar and that displays open windows in a stack; only available if using a Windows Aero theme.

Aero Peek A Windows 7 feature that lets you point to a taskbar icon representing an open program and see a thumbnail (small version) of the open file; only visible if the computer uses a Windows Aero theme.

Alignment The horizontal or vertical position of numbers or text, relative to the page margins. Text can be right-, center-, left-, top-, or bottom-aligned, or justified between the margins. *See also* Justified text.

Alt text Alternate text in a Web page that describes a picture or other element that has not yet loaded; you can add alt text to an element so that a user can read it while the element loads or if it is missing.

Animation Painter A tool that copies animation settings from one object so that you can apply them to another.

Application program Software you can use to perform a task, such as creating a document, analyzing data, or creating a presentation. Also called a program.

Area chart A line chart in which each area is colored or patterned to emphasize the relationships between pieces of charted information.

Argument A value, cell reference, or text used in an Excel function. Commas or a colon separate arguments and parentheses enclose them; for example, AVERAGE(A1,10,5) or SUM(A1:A5).

Arial A popular sans serif font, often used for headlines.

Ascending order A way to sort records in a database table or data in a spreadsheet, in which fields are ordered numerically from 0–9 or alphabetically from A–Z.

AutoCorrect A feature that automatically corrects certain words as you type after you press [Spacebar].

AutoCorrect Options button A button that appears after Office makes an automatic text or formatting correction that contains a menu of options you can choose from.

AutoFit A feature that automatically resizes a table column to fit the longest entry when a column boundary is double-clicked.

AutoNumber data type In Access, a data type that assigns a unique sequential number to each record.

AVERAGE function Calculates the average value of the arguments.

Axis titles Labels in a chart that identify the values for each axis in the chart.

Backstage view Commands and tools to help you work with your files, which are available when you click the File tab in any Office application.

Backup A duplicate copy of a file that is stored in another location.

Bar chart A chart that displays worksheet data as a series of horizontal bars.

Bibliography A list of citations from works referenced in a document that is usually placed at the end of the document.

Bitmap A graphic that displays a picture image as a matrix of pixels on a grid.

Bold A font style that makes text appear in thicker type; used to emphasize text in a document, spreadsheet, database, or presentation.

Browser A program, such as Microsoft Internet Explorer, designed to access the Internet.

Bullet A small graphic, usually a dot, used to identify items in a list.

Calculated field A field that displays a value that is the result of a formula that contains field values and mathematical operators.

Canvas In the Paint accessory program, the area in the center of the program window that you use to create drawings.

Caption property In Access, a label that appears in a form, report, or in Datasheet view in place of the actual field name.

Case sensitive Describes a program's ability to differentiate between uppercase and lowercase letters; usually used to describe how an operating system evaluates passwords that users type to gain entry to user accounts.

Category axis *See* x-axis.

Cell The intersection of a row and a column in an Excel worksheet or a Word table.

Cell address In Excel, a row letter followed by a column number that specifies the location of a cell.

Cell pointer The dark border that surrounds the active cell in an Excel worksheet.

Cell range *See* Range.

Cell reference The address of a cell in an Excel worksheet that defines its location in the worksheet by column letter and row number (for example, A1), and that can be used in formulas and functions.

Center-aligned text Text that is placed evenly between the margins.

Chart A graphic representation of selected worksheet data.

Chart area A chart object that is the background behind the chart.

Chart layout In Excel, a predefined arrangement of chart elements that you can apply to any chart.

Chart objects Individual components of a chart, such as the chart background or legend, which you can move or resize independently.

Chart sheet A worksheet in an Excel workbook that contains a chart.

Chart style A predefined set of chart colors and fills that you can apply to any chart.

Check box A square box that you click to add a check mark (also known as selecting) or remove a checkmark (also known as deselecting) to turn an option on or off.

Click To press and release the left mouse button once. Also called single-clicking.

Clip A media file, such as a piece of art, an animation, video, or photograph, available through the Clip Art task pane.

Clip art Ready-to-use electronic artwork.

Clip Art task pane In Word, a window that opens on the right side of the document window that lets you search for clip art, animations, videos and photographs on your hard drive and on the Office Online Web site.

Clipboard A temporary storage space on your computer's hard disk containing information that has been cut or copied. *See also* Windows Clipboard, Office Clipboard.

Close button To quit a program or remove a window from the desktop. The Close button usually appears in the upper-right corner of a window.

Cloud computing The process of working with files online in a virtual environment.

Color scales In Excel, shading patterns that use two or three colors to show the relative values of a range of cells.

Column chart A chart that displays worksheet data as a series of vertical columns.

Column separator In Access in Datasheet view, the border between two field names that you can drag or double-click to adjust the width of the column.

Column sparkline A miniature column chart that fits in one cell that includes a bar for each cell in a selected range.

Command A directive that provides access to a program's features.

Command button In a dialog box, a button that carries out an action. A command button usually has a label that describes its action, such as Cancel or Help. If the label is followed by an ellipsis (…), clicking the button displays another dialog box.

Complex formula A formula in Excel that contains more than one mathematical operator (for example, +, –, *, or /).

Conditional formatting In Excel and Access, formatting that is applied to cells in a spreadsheet or fields in a form or report when specified criteria are met.

Context sensitive Help Onscreen guidance tools that appear in the form of text descriptions or instructions when the mouse points to a particular screen element, to describe the function of the element or provide instructions on how to perform a particular task.

Contextual tab A tab that only appears when a particular type of object is selected.

Control An object on an Access form or report that is composed of the field label and the field value text box and that displays data, performs calculations, or is used for decoration. Examples include fields, text boxes, and graphic images.

Copy A command that copies selected text in a document to the Windows and Office Clipboard; copied text is also left in its original location.

COUNT function Calculates the number of values in the argument list.

Criteria In Access, conditions or qualifications that determine whether a record is chosen for a filter or query. In Excel, specified conditions that that determine whether a row in a table is displayed.

Cut A command that removes selected text or objects from a document and places them on the Windows and Office Clipboard, usually to be pasted into another location.

Data bars In Excel, colored bars that make it easy to identify the large and small values in a selected range of cells and also highlight the relative value of cells to each other.

Data marker A bar, area, dot, slice, or other symbol in a chart that represents a single data point or value that originates from a worksheet cell.

Data series In a chart, a sequence of related numbers that show a trend, such as sales amounts of various months, quarters or years.

Data source The database file that stores the variable information for a form letter or other mail merge document.

Data table In Excel, a grid in a chart that contains the chart's underlying worksheet data, and which is usually placed below the x-axis.

Data type A specific category of data in a database field, such as text, dates, or numbers.

Database An organized collection of data related to a particular topic or purpose and stored electronically in a file.

Database management program A program used to store, organize, display, and retrieve information, such as names and addresses, product inventories, and employee data.

Database object In Access, one of seven program components that you can create and modify to store, retrieve and work with data. Tables, objects, queries, reports, macros, forms, pages, and modules are objects you can create in Access.

Datasheet view A view in Access that displays records in a grid format, making records easy to compare, sort, and edit.

Default setting A setting that is preset by the operating system or program, such as desktop color or font size.

Design view In Access, the view that shows the structure of a table, form, query, or report. Use this view to modify the design by editing or moving controls or to modify table structure by adding, deleting, or editing fields and field properties.

Desktop The screen that appears when you first start Windows 7, providing access to your computer's programs and files and to the Internet.

Desktop background The shaded area behind your desktop objects; can show colors, designs, or photographs, which you can customize.

Desktop publishing program A program that lets you create printed documents combining text and graphics.

Destination file When linking and embedding data between documents, the target file or program.

Detail section In Access, the section of a form or report that displays the field labels and data for each record.

Details pane A pane located at the bottom of a window that displays information about the selected disk, drive, folder, or file.

Device A hardware component that is part of your computer system, such as a disk drive or a pointing device.

Dialog box A window in which you enter information needed to carry out a command. Clicking most dialog box launchers and some buttons on the Ribbon opens a dialog box in which you must select options before the Office program can carry out the command.

Dialog box launcher *See* Launcher.

Document window An area within the Word program window that displays the current document.

Documents folder The folder on your hard drive used to store most of the files you create or receive from others' might contain subfolders to organize the files into smaller groups.

Double-click To press and release the left mouse button twice quickly.

Draft view In Word, a view that displays the text and some graphic elements in a document without showing exactly how all the elements in the document will print.

Drag To move an item to a new location using the mouse.

Drag and drop The action of moving or copying selected text in a document by dragging it with the mouse and placing it at a new location.

Drive A device that reads and saves files on a disk and is also used to store files; floppy drives read and save files on floppy disks, whereas hard drives read and save files on your computer's built-in hard disk.

Drive name A name for a drive that consists of a letter followed by a colon, such as C: for the hard disk drive.

Edit To modify the contents of an existing file.

Embed The process of inserting data from one program into another program and being able to edit the data in the program in which it was originally created.

Embedded object A separate copy of a file that is inserted in a file in a different program and that you can edit using the tools of the program in which it was created.

Encrypt Access security feature that compacts and scrambles a database file so that it is difficult for unauthorized users to decipher.

Endnote A note or citation that corresponds to a number or symbol in a document and appears at the end of the document. *See also* Footnote.

End-of-cell mark In Word, the mark in each cell in a table; all text entered in the cell is entered to the left of the end-of-cell mark.

End of row mark In Word, the clipmark at the end of each row in a table.

Expression In Access, a combination of fields, values, and mathematical operators (similar to a formula in Excel).

Field A specific category of information in a database such as name, address, or phone number. Usually organized in the smallest possible unit to facilitate organization, such as last name and first name.

Field description In a database table in Access, a descriptive comment that explains the purpose of a field, to help the person entering data into it.

Field list A list that contains all the fields in a database table; used to add fields to forms or reports.

Field name In an Access table, column headings in a table that indicate the type of information entered for each field value text box.

Field properties In Access, settings and characteristics that determine the way data is stored, displayed, or manipulated in a field, such as the length of a text field or the number of decimal places in a number field.

Field value In Access, the data entered in a field for a particular record.

File An electronic collection of data that has a unique name, distinguishing it from other files.

File extension Sequence at the end of a filename, after the period, which identifies the program that created the file.

File hierarchy A logical structure for folders and files that mimics how you would organize files and folders in a filing cabinet.

File list In Windows Explorer, the right section of the window; shows the contents of the folder selected in the Navigation pane on the left.

File management The process of organizing and keeping track of files and folders.

File properties Details that Windows stores about a file, such as the date it was created or modified.

File tab Tab on the Ribbon that contains commands and tools that let you work with the whole document. For instance, you use the File tab to open, save, print, and close documents. The File tab is present in all Office programs.

Filename A name given to a file that distinguishes it from other files.

Fill handle A small square that appears on the lower right corner of a selected worksheet cell that you can drag to the right or down to copy the cell's contents into adjacent cells.

Filter A command that displays only the data that you want to see in an Excel worksheet or an Access database table based on criteria you set.

Filter drop-down list In an Excel table, a menu that appears when you click the filter drop down arrow in a column heading that let you apply a filter or a sort order to the data in table.

First line indent In a document, when the first line of text in a paragraph is indented from the left margin by a specified amount of space.

Floating image An image that can be dragged to any location on a page, and to which text wrapping has been applied.

Folder An area on a disk that contains a collection of files and/or other folders that you use to help you organize your files.

Folder name A unique, descriptive name for a folder that helps to identify the folder's contents.

Font A set of characters in a particular design; for example, Arial or Times New Roman.

Font effects Special enhancements to fonts such as small caps, shadow and superscript that you can apply to selected text in a document, spreadsheet, database, or presentation.

Font size The size of a font, measured in points. One point measures $1/72$".

Font style Attribute that changes the appearance of text when applied; bold, italic, and underline are common font styles.

Footer Text that appears just above the bottom margin of every page in a document.

Footnote A note or citation that corresponds to a number or symbol in a document, and which is placed at the bottom of the document page. *See also* Endnote.

Foreign key In Access, where two tables that have a one-to-many relationship, the primary key in the second table that is shared by the first table.

Form A database object that is used to enter, edit, or display records in a database one at a time.

Form controls In Access, elements in a form that make it possible to enter data; such as text boxes, scroll bars, or check boxes. A common type of form control consists or a field label and a field value text box.

Form letter A merged document that contains standard body text and a custom header for each recipient.

Formatting To enhance the appearance of text in a document, spreadsheet, database, or presentation without changing the content. Also refers to the process of preparing a disk so it can store information.

Formula An equation that calculates a new value from existing values. Formulas can contain numbers, mathematical operators, cell references, and built-in equations called functions. *See also* Functions.

Formula AutoComplete In Excel, a feature that helps you enter a formula in a cell by suggesting a listing of functions as you type letters and providing syntax information to help you write the formula correctly.

Formula bar In Excel, the area below the Ribbon where you enter or edit a formula or data in the selected cell.

Full Screen Reading view In Word, view that displays the active document in a magnified view that is optimal for reading on screen

Function A prewritten formula you can use instead of typing a formula from scratch. Each function includes the function name, a set of parentheses, and function arguments separated by commas and enclosed in parentheses. *See also* Formula.

Gadget An optional program you can display on your desktop that presents helpful or entertaining information, such as a clock, current news headlines, a calendar, a picture album, or a weather report.

Graphic Interchange Format (GIF) File format for graphics that is often used for line art and clip art images.

Gridlines Horizontal and vertical lines connecting to the X-axis and Y-axis in a chart that make it easier to identify the value of each data series.

Group On a tab on the Ribbon, a set of related commands located together above a name.

Group footer The part of an Access report that contains the chosen group field name and appears at the end of each group of records.

Group header The part of an Access report that contains the Group field name; used when the information in a report is grouped by a chosen field or fields.

Grouping A way of organizing information in an Access report by a field or field values to make spotting trends or finding important information easier.

Handouts In PowerPoint, hard copies of a presentation that are printed for distribution to an audience.

Hanging indent A type of paragraph indent in a Word document in which the second and subsequent lines of text in a paragraph indent further than the first line by a set amount of space.

Hard disk A disk that is built into the computer (usually drive C) on which you store files and programs.

Hard page break A page break inserted manually in a Word document to cause the text following the page break to begin at the top of a subsequent page.

Header Text that appears just below the top margin of every page in a document.

Header row In Excel, the row at the top of a table that contains column headings.

Highlighting When an icon is shaded differently, indicating it is selected. *See also* Select.

Home tab The tab on the Ribbon that contains the most frequently used commands in the active Office 2010 program.

Homegroup A named group of Windows 7 computers that can share information, including libraries and printers.

Horizontal axis In an Excel chart, is the horizontal line at the base of a chart that shows categories. Also called the x- or category axis.

Icon Graphical representation of computer elements such as files and programs.

Inactive window Refers to a window or program that is open but not currently in use.

Indent A set amount of space between the edge of a paragraph and the right or left margin.

Inline graphic A graphic that is part of a line of text and moves with it when the text moves.

Insertion point In a Word document, a blinking vertical line indicating the point where text will be inserted when you type.

Italic A font style that makes text appear slanted; used to emphasize text in a document.

Joint Expert Photographic Experts Group (JPEG) File format that is often used for photographs because it uses and compresses color so well.

Justified text Text aligned equally between the right and left margins.

Keyboard shortcut A keyboard alternative for executing a menu command (for example, [Ctrl][X] for Cut).

Keywords Words that you type into a search engine text box or a task pane that relate to a particular topic, and which the program will use to search its database for related topics, images, sound files, or other items.

Label Descriptive text used to identify worksheet data in Excel, and titles or brief descriptions in Access.

Landscape Layout orientation for a document that specifies to print the page so it is wider than it is long.

Launch To start a program that was previously closed.

Launcher Small arrow located to the right of a group name on the Ribbon that when clicked opens a dialog box or task pane where you can enter additional information to complete a task. Also called a dialog box launcher.

Layout In PowerPoint, an arrangement of placeholders and formatting configured to support a particular type of content.

Layout view In Access, a view in which you can see data in a form or report, and also make simple formatting changes.

Left indent In Word, a set amount of space between the left margin and the left edge of an entire paragraph.

Legend Area in a chart that explains what the labels, colors, and patterns of the chart represent.

Library A window that shows files and folders stored in different storage locations; default libraries in Windows 7 include the Documents, Music, Pictures, and Videos libraries.

Line chart A graph of data mapped by a series of lines. Because line charts show changes in data or categories of data over time, they are often used to document trends.

Line sparkline A miniature line chart that fits in one cell and is ideal for showing a trend over a period of time.

Link To paste content from one file (the source file) into another (the destination file) and maintain a connection with the source file.

List box A box in a dialog box containing a list of items. To choose an item, you click the list arrow and then click the desired item.

Live Preview A feature that allows you to preview how a formatting option will look on the page before actually choosing that option.

Log in To select a user's account name when a computer starts up, giving access to that user's files.

Log off To close all windows, programs, and documents, then display the Welcome screen.

Mail merge The process of combining a Word form letter that contains field names with data from a data source to create a third document that contains multiple personalized letters or labels.

Main document A document that stores the standard body text for a form letter or other mail merge document.

Margin In a document, the amount of space between the edge of the page and the text in your document.

MAX function Calculates the largest value in the argument list.

Maximize button On the right side of a window's title bar, the center button of three buttons; use to expand a window so that it fills the entire screen. In a maximized screen, this button turns into a Restore button.

Maximized windows To enlarge a window so that it takes up the entire screen. The Maximize button is usually located in the upper-right corner of a window.

Menu A list of available commands.

Menu bar A bar near the top of the program window that provides access to most of a program's features through categories of related commands.

Merge To combine information from a data source, such as an Access database table, with standard text contained in a Word document to create personalized form letters or other mail merge documents. *See also* Mail merge.

Merge fields Field names from a specified data source that act as placeholders for variable information in a form letter or other mail merge document.

Merged document A file or printout that contains all the personalized letters in a mail merge document.

Microsoft Access Database management program created by Microsoft Corporation you can use to store, organize, retrieve, and display information, such as names, addresses, product inventories, and employee data.

Microsoft Excel Spreadsheet program created by Microsoft Corporation you can use to manipulate, analyze, and chart quantitative data.

Microsoft Office Web Apps A set of scaled-down versions of Microsoft Office applications that run over the Internet.

Microsoft OneNote A software program you can use to capture and store information such as Web site addresses, graphics, notes written by your or others, or text pulled from a report.

Microsoft Outlook An e-mail program and information manager created by Microsoft Corporation that comes with Microsoft Office that you use to send and receive email, schedule appointments, maintain to do lists, and store contact information.

Microsoft PowerPoint Presentation graphics program created by Microsoft Corporation you can use to develop materials for presentations, including electronic slide shows, computer-based presentations, speaker's notes, and audience handouts.

Microsoft Publisher A desktop publishing program created by Microsoft Corporation that comes with Microsoft Office 2010 Professional that lets you create printed documents combining text and graphics, such as newsletters, brochures, letterheads, business cards, and other publications.

Microsoft Windows 7 An operating system.

Microsoft Word A word processing program created by Microsoft Corporation you can use to create text-based documents such as letters, memos, and newsletters.

MIN function Calculates the smallest value in the argument range.

Mini toolbar In Word, a group of buttons that appears on screen when text is selected that contains commonly used buttons for formatting text.

Minimize button On the right side of a window's title bar, the left-most button of three buttons; use to reduce a window so that it only appears as an icon on the taskbar.

Mouse pointer *See* Pointer.

Move To remove a selection from its original location and place it in a new location that you specify.

Name box In Excel, displays the name or reference of the currently selected cell in the worksheet.

Navigate To move around in your computers' folder and file hierarchy.

Navigate downward To move to a lower level in your computers' folder and file hierarchy.

Navigate upward To move to a higher level in your computers' folder and file hierarchy.

Navigation bar Bar containing buttons at the bottom of the Access program window that let you move among records in a table.

Navigation Pane In Access, a pane to the left of the database window that displays all the objects in the database. In Word, a pane to the left of the document window that helps you to find specific text in a document and navigate a document.

Normal style In Word, a built-in style that is the default paragraph style for any new, blank Word document, and that is defined as 11-point Calibri.

Normal view In PowerPoint, a view that displays the presentation in three areas: a pane on the left that alternates between the Slides tab and Outline tab, and on the right, the Slide pane and below it, the Notes pane.

Notes pages Pages you can create in PowerPoint that contain a miniature version of each slide plus speaker notes added in the Notes pane.

Notes pane In PowerPoint in Normal view, the area below the Slide pane into which text can be typed to remind the presenter of key points to make to an audience.

Notification area An area on the right side of the Windows 7 taskbar that displays the current time as well as icons representing programs; displays pop-up messages when a program on your computer needs attention.

Number format A format applied to numbers in cells that represents different number types, such as currency, decimal, date, or percent.

Object A graphic or other item or set of items that can be moved and resized as a single unit. In Excel, the components of a chart are called objects. In Access, objects are a collection of principal program components that you can create and modify, including tables, queries, forms, reports, pages, macros, and modules. In PowerPoint, each graphic or text element is an object. In Word, any item that is embedded or linked to the document is called an object.

Office Clipboard A storage area for storing cut and copied items that can hold up to 24 items at once, and which is accessible from any Office program. *See also* Windows Clipboard.

One-to-many relationship In Access, the most common type of relationship that is defined for two tables, where the primary key field in one table is associated with multiple records in a second table.

Operating system A computer program that controls the basic operation of your computer and the programs you run on it. Windows 7 is an example of an operating system.

Option button A small circle in a dialog box that you click to select an option.

Order of operations The order in which Excel calculates a formula; the order of precedence is exponents, multiplication and division, addition and subtraction. Calculations in parentheses are evaluated first.

Outline tab The tab on the Outline/Slides pane in PowerPoint that displays the text contained on each slide in a presentation.

Outline view In Word, a view that shows only the headings in a document.

Page break The point at which text in a document flows to the top of a new page.

Page footer The part of an Access report that contains the current date and page number and appears at the bottom of each page.

Page header The part of an Access report that contains the field labels and appears at the top of every page of the report.

Page Layout tab In Word, the tab on the Ribbon that contains commands to lay out and format a document.

Paint A graphics program that comes with Windows 7.

Pane A section of a divided window.

Paragraph In Word, any text that ends with a hard return.

Paste A command in the Clipboard group on the Home tab that copies information from the Windows Clipboard or Office Clipboard into a document at the location of the insertion point.

Pie chart A circular chart that displays data in one data series as slices of a pie. A pie chart is useful for showing the relationship of parts to a whole.

Pixel A small square of color that comprises a digital image.

Play button In PowerPoint, the video control button that appears in Slide Show view; when clicked, the video for the current slide plays.

Plot area In a chart, the area behind the data markers.

Point A unit of measurement used to measure characters; a point equals $1/72$ of an inch; also to position the mouse pointer in a particular location on your screen.

Pointer The typically arrow-shaped object on the screen that follows the movement of the mouse. The shape of the mouse pointer changes depending on the program and the task being executed. Also called a mouse pointer.

Pointing device A device that lets you interact with your computer by controlling the movement of the mouse pointer on your computer screen; examples include a mouse, trackball, touchpad, pointing stick, on-screen touch pointer, or a tablet.

Pointing device action A movement you execute with your computer's pointing device to communicate with the computer. The five pointing device actions are point, click, double-click, drag, and right-click.

Portrait Layout orientation for a document that specifies to print the page so that it is longer than it is wide.

Poster frame An image on your computer or created from a video frame to serve as the video's cover or preview image on the slide.

Power button 1) The physical button on your computer that turns your computer on. 2) The Start menu button or button on the right side of the Welcome screen that lets you shut down or restart your computer. Click the button arrow to log off your user account, switch to another user, or hibernate the computer to put your computer to sleep so that your computer appears off and uses very little power.

Presentation graphics program Software designed for creating on-screen slide shows, 35mm slides, overhead transparencies, and other business presentation materials.

Preview pane A pane on the right side of a window that shows the actual contents of a selected file without opening a program; might not work for some types of files.

Primary key field In Access, a field that ensures that each record is unique in a table.

Print Layout view A view in Word that displays layout, graphics, and footnotes exactly as they will appear when printed.

Print Preview A view that shows exactly how a document will look when it is printed and contains options specific to previewing the printed document.

Program Software you can use to perform a task, such as create a document, analyze data, or create a presentation. Also called an application.

Program window The window that opens after you start a program, showing you the tools you need to use the program and any open program documents.

Properties Characteristics of a specific computer element (such as the mouse, keyboard, or desktop display) that you can customize; in Access, those characteristics of a specific field, section, object, or control that you can customize.

Query A database object that extracts data from one or more tables in a database according to set criteria.

Quick Access toolbar A group of buttons above the File tab that lets you perform the most common tasks such as undoing or redoing an action or saving a file and which is available to use no matter what tab is currently active.

Quick Style Built-in styles for text elements, such as titles, headings, and captions.

Quick Style set A group of professionally coordinated styles that look great together and can be applied to a document to instantly change its overall appearance.

Random access memory (RAM) The area in a computer's central processing unit that programs use to perform necessary tasks while the computer is on. When you turn the computer off, all information in RAM is lost.

Range A selected area of adjacent cells in an Excel worksheet. Also called a cell range.

Reading view A view in PowerPoint that displays the presentation full-screen, but also includes title and status bars.

Record A collection of related fields that contains all information for an entry in a database such as a customer, item, or business.

Record source In Access, the table or query from which a report gets its data.

Recycle Bin A storage area on your computer's hard disk for deleted files, which remain in the Recycle Bin until you empty it. An icon on the desktop provides quick access to the Recycle Bin.

reference mark The mark next to a word in a document that indicates a footnote or endnote is associated with the word, and that is linked to the footnote or endnote.

Relate The process of specifying a relationship between two tables in Access.

Relational database A database that contains multiple tables that are related to each other and can share information. Access is a relational database management program.

Relative cell reference In Excel, a cell reference that changes when copied to refer to cells relative to the new location. For example, the formula "=B5*C5" in cell D5 changes to "=B6*C6" when you copy the formula to cell D6. *See also* Absolute cell reference.

Removable storage Storage media that you can easily transfer from one computer to another, such as DVDs, CDs, or USB flash drives.

Repaginate In Word, the automatic process of renumbering pages in a document, which can occur if you change the margin settings or add or delete text.

Replace A command in the Clipboard group on the Home tab that lets you search for a word or format in a document, spreadsheet, presentation, or database and insert another word or format in its place.

Report A summary of database information designed specifically for printing.

Report footer Information or images that appear at the bottom of the last printed page of a report.

Report header Area of a report that contains the report name and appears only at the top of the first printed page of a report.

Report view In Access, the default view when you open a report from the Navigation Pane. Report view looks similar to Print Preview, except that it displays the report in a continuous flow, without page breaks. You cannot edit in Report view.

Report Wizard In Access, a series of dialog box that automatically creates a report based on settings you specify.

Restore Down button On the right side of a maximized window's title bar, the center of three buttons; use to reduce a window to its last non-maximized size.

Ribbon A band that stretches across the top of each Office 2010 application program window that contains multiple tabs from which you choose commands to complete tasks.

Right indent In Word, when text in a paragraph is indented from the right margin.

Right-click To press and release the right mouse button once.

Row selector In Access, the small box to the left of each record that when clicked selects the entire record.

Scatter chart A chart that shows the relationship between two kinds of related worksheet data.

ScreenTip A concise description of a button or other screen element that appears when you point to the item.

Scroll To adjust your view to see portions of the program window that are not currently in a window.

Scroll arrow A button at each end of a scroll bar for adjusting your view in a window in small increments in that direction.

Scroll bar A bar that appears at the bottom and/or right edge of a window whose contents are not entirely visible; you click the arrows or drag the box in the direction you want to move. *See also* Scroll box.

Scroll box A rectangle located in the vertical and horizontal scroll bars that indicates your relative position in a file and that you can drag to view other parts of the file or window. *See also* Scroll bar.

Search criteria Descriptive text that helps Windows identify the program, folder, file, or Web site you want to locate.

Section In PowerPoint, an organizational tool that allows you categorize and format groups of slides.

Select To click or highlight an item in order to perform some action on it. *See also* Highlighting.

Select pointer The mouse pointer shape that looks like a white arrow oriented toward the upper-left corner of the screen.

Select query A commonly used query in which records are collected and displayed in a datasheet and can be modified.

Selection bar In Word, the area to the left of the left margin. You can select entire lines of text in the selection bar using the pointer.

Selection box A dashed-line rectangle surrounding a selected placeholder in PowerPoint.

Serial value A number used in an Excel worksheet that represents a date or time used in calculations; a date that is formatted in General format will appear as a serial value.

Sheet tab In Excel, a tab at the bottom of the worksheet window that displays the name of a worksheet in a workbook.

Shortcut A link that you can place in any location that gives you quick access to a file, folder, or program located on your hard disk or network.

Shortcut menu A menu that appears when you right-click an item.

Shut down The action you perform when you have finished working with your computer; after you shut down it is safe to turn off your computer.

Simple database A database that contains just one table.

Single-click *See* Click.

SkyDrive A large storage space on the Internet that you and others can access from any location. To establish a SkyDrive, you must set up your own ID on Windows Live, which is a set of free online services from Microsoft.

Slide An on-screen page for use in a slide show.

Slide Master Contains the layouts, design elements and other formatting attributes for a presentation.

Slide pane In Normal view in PowerPoint, an area of the program window that displays the text and graphics of a presentation slide as it would appear in a slide show.

Slide Show view A view in PowerPoint that displays presentation slides in full-screen and also displays all slide transitions and animation effects.

Slide Sorter view A view in PowerPoint that shows thumbnails of every slide in a presentation at a reduced size so you can reorder slides easily.

Slider An item in a dialog box that you drag to set the degree to which an option is in effect.

Slides In PowerPoint, on-screen pages for use in a slide show.

Slides tab In Normal view in PowerPoint, the area to the left of the Slide pane that displays thumbnails of every slide in a presentation.

SmartArt Ready-made conceptual diagrams that you can insert in an Office document and customize to create striking visuals to illustrate a process, hierarchy or relationship.

Soft page break Page breaks that are automatically inserted by Word at the bottom of a page.

Sort A command that organizes records in an Access database or columns in an Excel spreadsheet or a Word table numerically or alphabetically, and in ascending or descending order.

Source file When linking or embedding data between two files, the original file.

Sparkline A miniature chart that fits in one cell and illustrates trends in a selected range, usually adjacent to the sparkline.

Speaker notes In PowerPoint, notes that accompany slides; used to help the speaker remember important information that should not appear on the slides themselves.

Spin box A box with two arrows and a text box; allows you to scroll in numerical increments or type a number.

Split form In Access, a form that displays the underlying datasheet at the bottom and the data entry form above it.

Spreadsheet Another word for a workbook or worksheet.

Spreadsheet program A computer-based data analysis tool that displays numerical data in a row and column grid format, and which can perform numeric calculations.

Standard colors A group of ten colors that appear below the Theme Colors in any Office color palette that contain basic hues such as red, orange, green, and blue.

Start button A button on the taskbar that you use to start programs, find and open files, access Windows Help and Support Center, and more.

Status bar Area at the bottom of an Office program window that displays information such as the current page or record number, and important messages, such as the status of the current print job.

Style A defined set of formatting characteristics for a character or paragraph; can include the font, font size, font style, paragraph alignment, spacing of the paragraph, tab settings, and anything else that defines the format of the paragraph.

Subfolder A folder within another folder for organizing sets of related files into smaller groups.

Suite A collection of programs (sometimes called applications) that share a common user interface and are distributed together. Microsoft Office 2010 is a software suite.

SUM function In Excel, the function used to calculate the total of the arguments.

Summary information In an Access report, displays statistics about one or more fields in a database including statistics on the sum, average, minimum, or maximum value in any numeric field.

Switch User To lock your user account and display the Welcome screen so another user can log on.

Tab (Ribbon) In an Office 2010 program, an area on the Ribbon that contains groups of related commands for completing a specific type of task. In a Word document, a set position where text following a tab character aligns.

Tab In Word, a set position where text following a tab character aligns.

Tab indicator An icon on the ruler used to align text differently, such as to the right or center of a tab stop.

Tab stop A location on the ruler where the insertion point moves to when the Tab key is pressed.

Table In Access, a collection of related records. In Word, information displayed in a grid containing rows and columns. In Excel, A range of cells containing fields and records that you can analyze, sort, and filter separately from other cells in a worksheet.

Table style A predefined set of formatting attributes such as shading, fonts, and border color, that specifies how a table looks.

Taskbar A bar at the bottom of the Windows desktop that contains the Start button, icons for all open programs and files, and the notification area.

Text box Text object that automatically wraps text and can be resized or moved.

Text placeholder A designated area on a PowerPoint slide for entering text, such as titles, subtitles, and body text.

Theme A predesigned set of formatting specifications for fonts and colors that you can apply to an Office 2010 file to achieve a coordinated overall look throughout the document, workbook, presentation, or database.

Themes gallery In PowerPoint, thumbnails of the themes installed on the computer.

Thumbnails Small representations of clip art images that appear in the Clip Art task pane during a search. In PowerPoint, small representations of presentation slides that appear on the Slides tab to the left of the slide window.

Times New Roman Type of serif font traditionally used in newspapers.

Timing The amount of time a slide is displayed during an on-screen presentation.

Title bar The horizontal bar at the top of a window that displays the program name and the name of the active file.

Title slide The first slide in a PowerPoint presentation.

Toolbar A customizable set of buttons that allows you to activate commands using one mouse click.

Total row In Excel, an extra row at the bottom of a table that can be used to display subtotals and other calculations.

Touch pointer A pointer on the screen for performing pointing operations with a finger if touch input is available on your computer.

Transition The way a slide first appears in a slide show and replaces the previous slide.

Translucency The transparency feature of Windows Aero that enables you to locate content by seeing through one window to the next window.

Trim To edit the start or end frames of a video to determine its length.

USB flash drive Also called a pen drive, flash drive, jump drive, keychain drive, or thumb drive. A removable storage device for folders and files that you plug into a USB port on your computer; makes it easy to transport folders and files to other computers.

User account A special area in a computer's operating system where users can store their own files.

User Interface The collection of buttons and tools you use to interact with a software program.

Value axis The vertical line that defines the left edge of a chart, and usually measures values. Also called the y-axis. *See also* vertical axis.

Vertical axis The vertical line that defines the left edge of a chart, and usually measures values. Also called the or value y-axis.

View A preset configuration that determines which elements of a file are visible on-screen in an Office program; does not affect the actual content of the document.

View buttons Buttons at the far right of the status bar that you use to change your view of the document.

Web Layout view A view that shows how a document will look if you save it as a Web page.

Welcome screen An initial startup screen that displays icons for each user account on the computer.

Win/Loss sparkline A miniature chart that shows either a bar (representing a gain) or a bar (representing a loss for a selected cells.

Window Rectangular-shaped work area on a screen that might contain icons, the contents of a file, or other usable data.

Windows Aero *See* Aero.

Windows Clipboard A temporary storage area in your computer's memory for cut and copied items. *See also* Office Clipboard.

Windows Explorer A program that you use to manage files, folders, and shortcuts.

Windows Metafile Format (WMF) File format that is used for graphics, including most of the Clip Art available in Microsoft Office.

Word processing program A program used to create and manipulate text-based documents, such as memos, newsletters, or term papers.

Word wrap In Word, a feature that automatically pushes text to the next line when the insertion point meets the right margin.

Workbook In Excel, a collection of related worksheets saved in a single Excel file.

Worksheet An Excel spreadsheet comprised of rows and columns of information that is used for performing numeric calculations, displaying business data, presenting information on the Web, and other purposes.

Wrap *See* Word wrap.

Wrapping style The settings for how text flows in relation to a graphic.

X-axis The horizontal line in a chart that contains a series of related values from the worksheet. Sometimes called the horizontal or category axis.

Y-axis The vertical line in a chart that contains a series of related values from the worksheet. Also called the vertical or value axis.

Zoom slider Located to the right of the View buttons, used to set the magnification level of your document.

Index